PRENTICE-HALL

Grammar and Composition

Level 5

Prentice-Hall

Grammar
and
Composition

Level 5

SERIES AUTHORS

Mary Beth Bauer, Language Arts Consultant, Houston, Texas

Lawrence Biener, Chairperson, Department of English, Locust Valley, New York

Linda Capo, Writer and English Teacher, Ithaca, New York

Gary Forlini, Writer and English Teacher, Pelham, New York

Karen L. Moore, English and Speech Teacher, Saratoga, California

Darla Shaw, Reading Coordinator, Ridgefield, Connecticut

Zenobia Verner, Professor of Curriculum and Instruction, Houston, Texas

425
GRA

PRENTICE-HALL, INC., Englewood Cliffs, New Jersey

SERIES TITLES

Prentice-Hall Grammar and Composition: Level 1
Prentice-Hall Grammar and Composition: Level 2
Prentice-Hall Grammar and Composition: Level 3
Prentice-Hall Grammar and Composition: Level 4
Prentice-Hall Grammar and Composition: Level 5
Prentice-Hall Grammar and Composition: Level 6

SUPPLEMENTARY MATERIALS

Annotated Teacher's Editions—Levels 1–6
Test Program—Levels 1–6

Acknowledgments: page 830

ISBN 0-13-696856-2

10 9 8 7 6 5 4 3 2 1

Prentice-Hall International, Inc., London
Prentice-Hall of Australia Pty. Ltd., Sydney
Prentice-Hall of Canada, Ltd., Toronto
Prentice-Hall of India Private Ltd., New Delhi
Prentice-Hall of Japan, Inc., Tokyo
Prentice-Hall of Southeast Asia Pte. Ltd., Singapore
Whitehall Books Limited, Wellington, New Zealand

Contents

Preface   14

Grammar   17

Chapter **1**   The Parts of Speech   18

1.1 Nouns and Pronouns   18
Nouns 18 ▪ Pronouns 22

1.2 Verbs   29
Action Verbs and Linking Verbs 29 ▪ Transitive and
Intransitive Verbs 32 ▪ Verb Phrases 33

1.3 Adjectives and Adverbs   34
Adjectives 35 ▪ Adverbs 39

**1.4 Prepositions, Conjunctions, and
Interjections**   43
Prepositions 43 ▪ Conjunctions 46 ▪ Interjections 50

Chapter **2**   Analyzing Parts of Speech   52

**2.1 Identifying Parts of Speech According
to Use**   52
Parts of Speech in Sentences ▪ 52

Chapter **3**   Basic Sentence Parts and Patterns   55

3.1 Subjects and Verbs   55
Complete Subjects and Complete Predicates 56
▪ Fragments 57 ▪ Simple Subjects and Simple
Predicates 58

3.2 Subjects in Different Kinds of Sentences   62
The Four Functions of Sentences 62 ▪ Hard-to-Find
Subjects 64

3.3 Complements   68
Direct Objects 69 ▪ Indirect Objects 70 ▪ Objective
Complements 72 ▪ Subject Complements 73

3.4 Reviewing Basic Sentence Patterns   75
Five Basic Patterns ▪ 75

3.5 Diagraming Basic Parts of Sentences   78
Subjects and Verbs, Adjectives and Adverbs 78
▪ Compound Sentence Parts 79 ▪ Sentences with
Hard-to-Find Subjects 80 ▪ Complements 82

Chapter **4**   Phrases and Clauses   85

4.1 Prepositional and Appositive Phrases   85
Prepositional Phrases 85 ▪ Appositives and Appositive
Phrases 88

4.2 Verbal Phrases   91
Participles and Participial Phrases 92 ▪ Gerunds and
Gerund Phrases 96 ▪ Infinitives and Infinitive
Phrases 98

4.3 Adjective, Adverb, and Noun Clauses   101
Adjective Clauses 102 ▪ Adverb Clauses 106 ▪ Noun
Clauses 108

4.4 Sentences Classified by Structure   111

**4.5 Diagraming Sentences with Phrases and
Clauses**   114
Prepositional Phrases 114 ▪ Appositive Phrases 116
▪ Verbal Phrases 116 ▪ Compound, Complex, and
Compound-Complex Sentences 120

Chapter **5**   Avoiding Sentence Faults   128

5.1 Fragments and Run-ons   128
Fragments 128 ▪ Run-on Sentences 131

5.2 Misplaced and Dangling Modifiers   134
Misplaced Modifiers 134 ▪ Dangling Modifiers 136

5.3 Faulty Parallelism   137
Correct Parallelism in Sentences 138 ▪ Faulty Parallel
Structures 139

5.4 Faulty Coordination   142
The Use of *And* in Compound Sentences 142
▪ Revising Sentences with Faulty
Coordination 144

Review Exercises: Grammar   147

Usage 151

Chapter **6**   Verb Usage   152

6.1 Verb Tenses   152
The Six Verb Tenses 153 ▪ The Four Principal
Parts 154 ▪ Regular and Irregular Verbs 156 ▪ Verb
Conjugation 164

6.2 Expressing Time Through Tense   168
Past, Present, and Future Time 168 ▪ Modifiers That
Indicate Time 175 ▪ Sequence of Tenses 175

6.3 The Subjunctive Mood   182
The Correct Use of the Subjunctive Mood 183
▪ Auxiliary Verbs That Help Express the Subjunctive
Mood 184

6.4 Voice   185
Active and Passive Voice 186 ▪ Using Active and
Passive Voice 188

Chapter **7**   Pronoun Usage   190

7.1 Case   190
The Cases of Personal Pronouns 191 ▪ The Nominative
Case 193 ▪ The Objective Case 195

7.2 Special Problems with Pronouns   198
Using *Who* and *Whoever* Correctly 198 ▪ Using
Pronouns Correctly in Elliptical Clauses 202

Chapter **8**   Agreement   205

8.1 Subject and Verb Agreement   205
The Number of Nouns, Pronouns, and Verbs 206
▪ Agreement with Singular and Plural Subjects 207
▪ Compound Subjects 211 ▪ Confusing Subjects 214

8.2 Pronoun and Antecedent Agreement   220
Agreement Between Personal Pronouns and
Antecedents 220 ▪ Personal Pronoun and Indefinite
Pronoun Agreement 224 ▪ Agreement Between
Reflexive Pronouns and Antecedents 227

**8.3 Special Problems with Pronoun
Agreement**   228
Avoiding Vague, Overly General Pronoun

8 *Contents*

References 228 ▪ Avoiding Ambiguous Pronoun
References 231 ▪ Avoiding Distant Pronoun
References 233

Chapter **9**   Adjective and Adverb Usage   236

9.1 Degrees of Comparison   236
Recognizing Degrees of Comparison 237 ▪ Regular
Forms 238 ▪ Irregular Forms 240 ▪ Double
Comparisons 242

9.2 Clear Comparisons   244
Using Comparative and Superlative Forms 244
▪ Balanced Comparisons 246 ▪ *Other* and *Else* in
Comparisons 247 ▪ Modifiers That Should Not Be
Used in Comparisons 248

Chapter **10**   Miscellaneous Usage Problems   250

10.1 Negative Sentences   250
Double Negatives 250 ▪ The Correct Use of Negative
Words 251 ▪ Understatement 253

10.2 Eighty Common Usage Problems   254

Chapter **11**   Levels of Language   278

11.1 The Varieties of English   279
Standard English 279 ▪ Nonstandard English 282

Review Exercises: Usage   286

Mechanics   293

Chapter **12**   Capitalization and Abbreviation   294

12.1 Capitalization   294
Capitals for First Words 295 ▪ Capitals for Proper
Nouns 297 ▪ Capitals for Proper Adjectives 305
▪ Titles of People and Things 307 ▪ Capitals for
Personal and Business Letters 311

12.2 Abbreviation   314
Abbreviating Names and Titles 315 ▪ Abbreviating
Time References and Geographical Locations 319
▪ Abbreviating Latin Phrases, Measurements, and
Numbers 324 ▪ Abbreviating the Names of Business
and Government Groups 328 ▪ Other Commonly Used
Abbreviations 330

Chapter **13**　Punctuation　333

13.1 End Marks　333
Using End Marks to Conclude Sentences and
Phrases 333 ▪ Periods and Question Marks in Other
Situations 336

13.2 Commas　338
Commas That Separate Independent Clauses 338
▪ Commas That Separate Items in a Series and
Certain Adjectives 340 ▪ Commas That Set Off
Introductory Material 343 ▪ Commas That Set Off
Parenthetical Expressions and Nonessential
Material 345 ▪ Commas in Other Situations 348

13.3 Semicolons and Colons　354
The Semicolon 354 ▪ The Colon 357

13.4 Quotation Marks and Underlining　361
Quotation Marks for Direct Quotations 361 ▪ Using
Other Punctuation Marks with Quotation
Marks 365 ▪ Using Quotation Marks in Special
Situations 367 ▪ Distinguishing Between the Uses of
Underlining and Quotation Marks 371

13.5 Dashes, Parentheses, and Brackets　376
Dashes 376 ▪ Parentheses 379 ▪ Brackets 381

13.6 Hyphens　383
Using Hyphens with Numbers, Word Parts, and
Words 383 ▪ Using Hyphens to Divide Words at the
End of a Line 386

13.7 Apostrophes　388
Forming Possessives of Nouns with Apostrophes 388
▪ Forming Possessives of Pronouns 391 ▪ Forming
Contractions with Apostrophes 392 ▪ Using
Apostrophes in Special Situations 394

Review Exercises: Mechanics　395

Vocabulary and Spelling　399

Chapter **14**　Vocabulary Building　400

14.1 Techniques for Building Vocabulary　400
Studying Words You Need to Know in School 401
▪ Expanding Your Vocabulary on Your Own 402

14.2 Using Context   404

Using Context Clues in Textbook Reading 406 ▪ Using Context Clues in General Reading 407 ▪ Using Context Clues in English Classes 409

14.3 Using Structure   411

Prefixes 411 ▪ Roots 414 ▪ Suffixes 416

Chapter **15**   Spelling Improvement   420

15.1 Techniques for Improving Spelling   420

Methods of Learning Words 420 ▪ Diagnosing Problem Areas 424

15.2 A Catalog of Spelling Rules   426

Using the *ie* and *ei* rule 426 ▪ Making Spelling Changes to Form Plurals 427 ▪ Adding Prefixes to Roots 428 ▪ Adding Suffixes to Roots 429 ▪ Working with Confusing Groups of Suffixes 431

Study Skills   435

Chapter **16**   Basic Study Skills   436

16.1 Studying, Listening, and Speaking   436

Evaluating Your Study Skills 436 ▪ Listening Skills 438 ▪ Speaking Skills 440

16.2 Note-Taking and Outlining   442

Two Basic Kinds of Outlines 443 ▪ Adding Columns and Summaries 446 ▪ Adding Annotations 449

Chapter **17**   Test-Taking Skills   452

17.1 Classroom and Standardized Tests   452

Classroom Tests 452 ▪ Standardized Tests 456

17.2 Vocabulary Questions   463

Taking Synonym Tests 464 ▪ Taking Antonym Tests 465 ▪ Taking Sentence Completion Tests 466 ▪ Taking Analogy Tests 468

17.3 Reading Comprehension Questions   471

Basic Reading Comprehension Questions 471 ▪ Cloze Reading Comprehension Questions 480

Chapter **18** Library and Reference Skills 483

18.1 The Library 483

Planning Your Research 484 ■ Using the Card Catalog 485 ■ Finding Books 494 ■ Coping with the "Missing Book" Problem 499

18.2 Reference Materials 500

General Reference Books 501 ■ Specialized Reference Books 505 ■ Periodicals and Related Material 513 ■ Choosing the Right Reference Materials 516

18.3 The Dictionary 518

Kinds of General Dictionaries ■ What Dictionaries for Students Contain 523

Composition 535

Chapter **19** Sentence Length and Structure 536

19.1 Improving Length and Structure 536

Different Sentence Lengths 537 ■ Different Sentence Openers and Sentence Structures 542

19.2 Exploring New Ideas for Structure 546

Experimenting with Different Kinds of Sentences 547 ■ Experimenting with Different Patterns 550 ■ Using Professional Models 553

Chapter **20** The Use of Words 556

20.1 Using Words Effectively 556

Developing a More Direct Style 557 ■ Choosing the Most Vivid Words 563 ■ Using an Appropriate Tone 568

20.2 Exploring Different Word Choices 574

Considering Different Shades of Meaning 574 ■ Using Comparisons to Make Your Ideas More Vivid 576 ■ Creating Different Moods 579 ■ Using Professional Models 581

Chapter **21** Clear Thinking in Writing 585

21.1 Making Clear Connections 585

Using Transitions 586 ■ Joining Ideas Through

Coordination and Subordination 589 ■ Establishing and Following Logical Orders 597

21.2 Exploring Other Issues of Logic 600
Avoiding Errors in Logic 600 ■ Using Professional Models 605

Chapter **22** Effective Paragraphs 608

22.1 Recognizing Key Features of Paragraphs 608
The Topic Sentence 608 ■ Supporting Information 611 ■ Unity 614 ■ Coherence 616 ■ Special Kinds of Paragraphs 623

22.2 Planning and Writing Paragraphs 626
Writing the Topic Sentence 626 ■ Developing Support for a Topic Sentence 630 ■ Organizing the Paragraph 635 ■ Writing the Paragraph 637

22.3 Revising and Rewriting Paragraphs 639
Revising Topic Sentences 640 ■ Revising Supporting Information 643 ■ Revising Paragraphs for Unity 647 ■ Revising for Coherence 649 ■ Revising for Style 654

Chapter **23** Kinds of Paragraphs 657

23.1 Expository and Persuasive Paragraphs 657
Writing Expository Paragraphs 658 ■ Writing Persuasive Paragraphs 662

23.2 Descriptive and Narrative Paragraphs 668
Writing Descriptive Paragraphs 668 ■ Writing Narrative Paragraphs 673

Chapter **24** Essays 679

24.1 The Importance of Form, Unity, and Coherence 679
The Key Features of an Essay 679 ■ Unity and Coherence 687

24.2 Planning, Writing, and Revising Essays 693
Planning an Essay 693 ■ Developing Support for a Thesis Statement 698 ■ Organizing Your Essay for Unity and Coherence 700 ■ Writing the Essay 703 ■ Revising the Essay 704

24.3 Writing Essays with Different Purposes 708
Writing Expository Essays 708 ■ Writing Persuasive Essays 714

Chapter **25** Library Papers 722

25.1 Special Characteristics of Library Papers 722
The Use and Citation of Sources 723 ▪ Structure and Features of a Library Paper 731

25.2 From Idea to Final Paper 736
Finding a Suitable Topic 736 ▪ Researching and Organizing the Library Paper 739 ▪ Writing and Revising the Paper 744

Chapter **26** Papers About Literature 751

26.1 The Literary Review 751
Key Features of a Literary Review 752 ▪ Structure of a Literary Review 758

26.2 Writing the Literary Review 762
Reacting to a Work of Literature 762 ▪ Developing Support for a Literary Review 766 ▪ Organizing a Literary Review 769 ▪ Writing the Review 770

Chapter **27** Letters and Précis 775

27.1 Writing Personal and Business Letters 775
Writing Personal Letters 775 ▪ Writing Business Letters 783

27.2 Writing Précis 791
The Key Features of a Précis 792 ▪ Planning, Writing, and Revising a Précis 796

Chapter **28** Essay Examinations 801

28.1 Writing Answers to Essay Exam Questions 801
Budgeting Your Time 801 ▪ Identifying What the Essay Question Is Asking 803 ▪ Preparing and Outlining an Answer 805 ▪ Writing and Checking Your Answer 808

Manuscript Preparation 813

Index 817

Acknowledgments 830

Preface

This book has a single purpose—to help you deal more effectively with the English language. The content, organization, and special features have all been designed to help you reach this goal.

Content

Unit One, Grammar, covers parts of speech and the parts of sentences, while giving you a number of useful methods for correcting basic sentence faults. Unit Two, Usage, zeroes in on problems that may arise in using verbs, pronouns, adjectives, and adverbs. It also includes a special section listing eighty common usage problems and a section on different levels of language. Unit Three, Mechanics, helps you decide when to capitalize, when to abbreviate, and when to use commas, quotation marks, and other forms of punctuation. Unit Four, Vocabulary and Spelling, provides strategies for building your knowledge of words and improving your spelling. Unit Five, Study Skills, offers numerous ideas for getting more out of the time you spend studying, listening to classroom lectures, taking notes, taking tests, and researching topics in the library. Unit Six, Composition, begins with ideas for making your sentences clearer and more interesting, moves on to steps for writing paragraphs, and ends with steps and other useful methods for writing essays, library papers, literary reviews, letters, précis, and answers to questions on essay examinations.

Organization

While your class may study any or all of the sections in the book in depth, you will find that the book has an equally important use as a reference work, not only in your English classes but also on any other occasions when you want to write or speak with particular effectiveness.

As a Textbook. All the units are divided into chapters, each of which is divided into sections. The sections themselves are then divided into subsections. A glance at the Table of Contents, which begins on page 5, and a brief survey of a few of the text chapters should show you how this works.

The sections are short and can usually be covered in a day or two. Before beginning each section, you will find it useful to preview the subsections. Which areas do you consider yourself strong in? Which areas are you weak in? As you work through the subsections, you will find one or more exercises at the end of each subsection. You can use these to preview or test your understanding of the topics covered. At the end of each section, you will find an Application which asks you to put all the skills you have reviewed or learned in the section to work in a practical exercise. This will give you a chance to check your overall understanding and ability to use the material in the section.

As a Reference Tool. In and out of school, you are likely to find situations in which knowing correct punctuation, correct spelling, and standard usage can make a difference. If you have questions on these matters, there are three places you can go in this book to find the answers. You can check the Table of Contents at the front of the book, you can check the Key of Major Concepts at the back of the book, or you can use the Index. Note that the Index uses bold numbers to show you where to find rules and definitions.

You might think up two or three questions right now and try the three methods of looking up the answer. See which one works best for you and practice using it.

Special Features

In addition to becoming familiar with the overall organization of the text, you may find it useful to explore some of the special features.

Clear Rules. All major rules and definitions are printed in bold type and written in easy-to-understand language. The bold numbers in the index indicate pages where rules and definitions can be found.

Numerous Examples. For most rules you will find a number of examples, each pointing out a different aspect of the rule. Whether you are studying a section or using it for quick reference, make sure you check all of the examples to be certain you understand all aspects of the rule.

Exercises for Each Subsection. Each subsection has one or more exercises. This will make it possible for you to tell what concepts you have mastered completely and what concepts you will need to review more thoroughly.

Applications for All Sections. The practical Application at the end of each section lets you put what you have been learning to work, generally in some writing exercise. At the same time, you will be checking your mastery of the ideas in the section.

Charts Covering Important Concepts. Throughout the book you will find important concepts highlighted in charts. This will make it possible for you quickly to identify and check your understanding and knowledge of essential ideas.

Charts Offering Useful Steps. Charts are also used to illustrate step by step processes: for identifying parts of speech, for taking good notes, for developing different materials in compositions, and for numerous other topics.

Checklists. One of the most important uses of charts is for revision checklists. What should you do when you have finished writing the first draft of a paragraph or essay? The checklists in the composition unit give some valuable suggestions.

Numerous Composition Models. One of the best ways to increase your own writing skill is to examine the works of professional writers and of other students. Throughout the composition unit you will find models by other writers with important elements clearly labeled.

A Special Unit on Study Skills. The study skills unit can help you review and develop a number of skills that will be immediately useful in a number of situations. You may want to look first at the suggestions in Section 16.1 for improving your studying, listening, and speaking skills.

A Special Section on Manuscript Preparation. This section at the end of the book can be immensely useful any time you need to prepare a written work that you want to be well received.

Three Reference Aids. The Table of Contents, the Index, and the Key of Major Concepts at the back of the book all can help you zero in on the rules and examples you need when you are using the book for quick reference.

Grammar

1

The Parts of Speech

2

Analyzing Parts of Speech

3

Basic Sentence Parts and Patterns

4

Phrases and Clauses

5

Avoiding Sentence Faults

Chapter 1

THE PARTS OF SPEECH

Every word in English, depending on its meaning and use in a sentence, can be identified as one of eight *parts of speech*.

THE PARTS OF SPEECH		
nouns	adjectives	prepositions
pronouns	adverbs	conjunctions
verbs		interjections

This chapter will provide a comprehensive look at all of these parts of speech. Nouns, pronouns, and verbs are considered first because they make such elementary sentences as *Music entertains her* possible. Adjectives and adverbs, which are treated next, are used to add description and detail to the first three parts of speech. Prepositions, conjunctions, and interjections, which are treated last, are the relaters, joiners, and attention-getters that make limitless varieties of sentences possible.

1.1 Nouns and Pronouns

Nouns and pronouns are an essential part of language. Together, these two important parts of speech make it possible for people to label and refer to everything around them.

■ Nouns

You probably recall this common definition of a noun.

A **noun** is the name of a person, place, or thing.

The kinds of words that are classified under the categories of *person* or *place* are self-evident.

PERSON: Bob, girl, swimmer, Mrs. Yang, Uncle Doug

PLACE: kitchen, St. James Street, canyon, Germany

The category *thing*, on the other hand, contains several subcategories: living things, nonliving things, ideas, actions, conditions, and qualities.

LIVING THINGS: duck, wasp, daffodil

NONLIVING THINGS: teapot, salt, clock

IDEAS: capitalism, recession, freedom

ACTIONS: competition, destruction, labor

CONDITIONS: joy, health, wealth

QUALITIES: compassion, intelligence, drive

Although you should generally rely on definitions to help you identify nouns, you may also be able to identify a word as a noun by its ending. Some common noun suffixes are *-dom*, *-ism*, *-ment*, *-ness*, *-ship*, and *-tion*.

EXAMPLES: kingdom   kindness

communism   seamanship

establishment   anticipation

Concrete and Abstract Nouns.   Nouns can be grouped not only as people, places, and things but also according to the characteristics of the things they name. A *concrete* noun names something that you can physically see, touch, taste, hear, or smell. An *abstract* noun names something that you cannot perceive through any of your five senses.

Concrete Nouns	Abstract Nouns
mother	hope
fabric	improvement
chocolate	evil
music	desperation
perfume	cooperation

Singular and Plural Nouns. A noun can also indicate *number*. *Singular* nouns name one person, place, or thing. *Plural* nouns name more than one. Most plural nouns are formed by adding either *-s* or *-es* to their singular forms. The plurals of some nouns, however, are formed in other ways and must be memorized.

Singular Nouns	Plural Nouns
meal	meals
bush	bushes
knife	knives
alumnus	alumni

Collective Nouns. *Collective* nouns name *groups* of persons or things. They can be either singular or plural depending on the meaning you wish to assign to them. (See Section 8.1 for more details about their use as singular or plural nouns.)

COLLECTIVE NOUNS	
army	company
cast	crew
choir	faculty
class	fleet

Compound Nouns. A noun that is made up of two or more words acting as a single unit is called a compound noun. Compound nouns may be written as separate words, hyphenated words, or combined words.

COMPOUND NOUNS	
Separate Words	life preserver, coffee table, bird dog
Hyphenated Words	jack-o'-lantern, aide-de-camp, daughter-in-law
Combined Words	scrollwork, dreamland, porthole

Since compound nouns usually begin as separate words and evolve into combined words, you may sometimes be confused about their spelling. Always check a dictionary. If the compound is not listed, you should then spell it as two or more separate words.

Common and Proper Nouns. Any noun may be categorized as either *common* or *proper*. A *common* noun names any one of a class of people, places, or things. A *proper* noun names a specific person, place, or thing. Notice in the following chart that proper nouns are capitalized while common nouns remain uncapitalized. (See Section 12.1 for specific rules of capitalization.)

Common Nouns	Proper Nouns
soldier	General Patton, Admiral Harding
valley	Death Valley, Valley of the Kings
holiday	Fourth of July, Halloween

A *noun of direct address*—that is, the name of a person you are talking to directly—is always proper, as is a family title before a personal name.

COMMON NOUN: I saw my *uncle* at the airport.

PROPER NOUN (direct address):   I will leave, *Mother*, as soon as they come.

PROPER NOUN (family title):   I received a postcard from *Cousin* Lee.

EXERCISE A: Identifying the Types of Nouns. Identify each of the following nouns according to whether it (1) names a *person, place,* or *thing,* (2) is *concrete* or *abstract,* (3) is *singular* or *plural,* (4) is *collective,* (5) is *compound,* and (6) is *common* or *proper.*

EXAMPLE: freedom of the press—(1) thing, (2) abstract, (3) singular, (4) not collective, (5) compound, (6) common

1. coat
2. editor-in-chief
3. Dallas
4. Julian Street
5. make-believe
6. joy
7. maintopsail
8. happiness
9. Ensign Alice Ross
10. velvet
11. wristwatches
12. wisdom
13. tablespoon
14. Lake Louise
15. flock
16. beauty
17. committee
18. walnuts
19. man-of-war
20. wisdom teeth

■ Pronouns

To avoid the awkward repetition of a noun, speakers and writers use another part of speech—*pronouns.*

A **pronoun** is a word used to take the place of a noun or group of words acting as a noun.

They, his, she, and *it* are pronouns in the following examples. The words the pronouns stand for are indicated by the arrows. Notice that the pronoun *it* takes the place of a group of words.

EXAMPLES: A crowd quickly gathered. Looking, up *they* saw a

man inch *his* way up the skyscraper.

Sailing along the Hudson was fun; Tina said *she* would

like to do *it* again.

The words the arrows point to are the pronouns' *antecedents.*

An **antecedent** is the noun (or group of words acting as a noun) for which a pronoun stands.

Most pronouns have specific antecedents but some do not. The rest of this section will describe the different kinds of pronouns found in English and explain whether or not they have antecedents.

Personal Pronouns.   Personal pronouns are the pronouns most commonly used to refer to particular people, places, and things.

Personal pronouns are pronouns that refer to (1) the person speaking, (2) the person spoken to, or (3) the person, place, or thing spoken about.

The following chart lists all of the personal pronouns. The first-person pronouns refer to the person speaking. The second-person pronouns refer to the person spoken to. The third-person pronouns refer to the person, place, or thing that is spoken about.

PERSONAL PRONOUNS		
	Singular	**Plural**
First Person	I, me, my, mine	we, us, our, ours
Second Person	you, your, yours	you, your, yours
Third Person	he, him, his she, her, hers it, its	they, them, their, theirs

In the following examples, notice that only the third-person pronouns have an antecedent that is expressly stated in the sentence. In the other two examples, the antecedents are implied.

FIRST PERSON: When *we* go, *we* will take *our* boat with *us*.

SECOND PERSON: *You* must bring *your* water skis with *you*.

THIRD PERSON: John said *he* saw the cow run through *his* corn fields.

Reflexive and Intensive Pronouns.   These pronouns end in *-self* or *-selves*. Though these two types of pronouns share the same form, they function differently in sentences.

A **reflexive pronoun** is a pronoun that adds information to a sentence by pointing back to a noun or pronoun near the beginning of the sentence.

An **intensive pronoun** is a pronoun that simply adds emphasis to a noun or pronoun in the same sentence.

The eight reflexive and intensive pronouns are formed from personal pronouns.

REFLEXIVE AND INTENSIVE PRONOUNS		
	Singular	**Plural**
First Person	myself	ourselves
Second Person	yourself	yourselves
Third Person	himself, herself, itself	themselves

As you can see in the following examples, the reflexive pronouns add necessary information, and the removal of the pronouns would change the meaning of the sentences. The intensive pronouns, on the other hand, are used only for emphasis. They could be removed from the sentences without altering the meaning of the sentences. Notice also that all the antecedents are clearly stated.

REFLEXIVE: Babies soon feed *themselves.*

We watched *ourselves* on the TV monitor.

INTENSIVE: The President *himself* admitted that he was wrong.

I sautéed the mushrooms *myself.*

Demonstrative Pronouns.   These pronouns are used to point out one or more nouns.

A **demonstrative pronoun** is a pronoun that directs attention to a specific person, place, or thing.

There are only four demonstrative pronouns.

DEMONSTRATIVE PRONOUNS	
Singular	**Plural**
this, that	these, those

Demonstrative pronouns may come either before or after their antecedents.

BEFORE: *That* is my first painting.

AFTER: The child held the propeller and a section of the wing. *These* were all that was left of the model airplane.

Relative Pronouns.   These pronouns are used to relate one idea in a sentence to another.

A **relative pronoun** is a pronoun that begins a subordinate clause and relates it to another idea in the sentence.

There are just five words that can act as relative pronouns.

, RELATIVE PRONOUNS				
that	which	who	whom	whose

In the following sentences, notice that the antecedents for the pronouns are found in the independent clauses. Thus, each pronoun relates, or links, the information in the subordinate clause to a word in the independent clause. (See Section 4.3 for more information about subordinate clauses.)

Independent Clause	Subordinate Clause
We will go to the store	*that* advertised a sale.
The poet addressed the committee	from *whom* she received the award.
We saw the person	*whose* catch had won the prize.

Interrogative Pronouns.   These pronouns are used to ask questions.

An **interrogative pronoun** is a pronoun used to begin a direct or indirect question.

There are five interrogative pronouns.

INTERROGATIVE PRONOUNS				
what	which	who	whom	whose

Notice in the first example that follows that the antecedent of an interrogative pronoun may not be known.

DIRECT QUESTION: *Who* knocked on the door?

INDIRECT QUESTION: The teacher read two papers. I asked *which* contained the better writing.

Indefinite Pronouns. Requiring no specific antecedents, these pronouns act very much like nouns.

Indefinite pronouns are pronouns that refer to people, places, or things, often without specifying which ones.

The following chart lists the most frequently used indefinite pronouns.

INDEFINITE PRONOUNS				
Singular			**Plural**	**Singular or Plural**
another	everyone	nothing	both	all
anybody	everything	one	few	any
anyone	little	other	many	more
anything	much	somebody	others	most
each	neither	someone	several	none
either	nobody	something		some
everybody	no one			

Although indefinite pronouns do not require specific antecedents, they often have them.

NO SPECIFIC ANTECEDENT: *Nothing* was achieved at the meeting.

Most turned right; *few* went left.

SPECIFIC ANTECEDENT: *One* of the drivers did not have insurance.

I made currant sherbet. You may have *some* if you wish.

EXERCISE B: Recognizing Antecedents. One or two pronouns have been underlined in each of the following sentences. Write each pronoun and its antecedent on your paper. For those antecedents that are indefinite or implied, write *indefinite* or *implied*.

1. As the boy bicycled down the road, <u>he</u> turned left at the first corner.
2. Danielle must get <u>herself</u> to the bus station if <u>she</u> wants to leave at that time.

3. My mother told <u>me</u> to give my brother <u>his</u> lunch when he got home.
4. It was my brother's birthday, but the family gave <u>him</u> a present <u>that</u> was meant for me.
5. You <u>yourselves</u> admitted to planning the prank.
6. Ray, <u>your</u> new car looks so clean next to <u>ours</u>.
7. The girls supplied <u>themselves</u> with plenty of food for <u>their</u> hike.
8. <u>Those</u> are the shoes I want, but Mother says <u>she</u> will not buy them for me.
9. <u>We</u> rode in a taxicab <u>whose</u> driver wove the vehicle expertly through the heavy traffic.
10. Grant connected <u>his</u> car stereo and then sat listening to <u>it</u> for several hours.

EXERCISE C: **Identifying the Different Types of Pronouns.** Read the following paragraph, noting the underlined pronouns. Decide what kind of pronoun each one is and write the answer on your paper: *personal, reflexive, intensive, demonstrative, relative, interrogative,* or *indefinite.*

When snow (1) <u>that</u> is held in place by friction is dislodged, (2) <u>it</u> can cause a serious avalanche. (3) <u>This</u> is a vast amount of snow cascading down a mountainside. The snow (4) <u>itself</u> can exert over 22,000 pounds of pressure per square inch and travel over 192 miles per hour. (5) <u>Few</u> caught in an avalanche are able to save (6) <u>themselves</u>, but St. Bernards have been trained to locate victims. They have rescued over 2,500 people during (7) <u>their</u> three hundred years of service. (8) <u>Many</u> believe that St. Bernards carry little barrels (9) <u>that</u> contain brandy to revive those they save. (10) <u>This</u>, however, is fiction. (11) <u>Which</u> of the dogs has the best rescue record? (12) <u>None</u> of the animals has a more impressive list than Barry, (13) <u>who</u> saved over forty avalanche victims. Though Barry performed (14) <u>his</u> heroics in the nineteenth century, St. Bernards are still on duty today so that you can entrust (15) <u>yourself</u> and your safety to these shaggy guardians of the snowy slopes.

EXERCISE D: **Using the Correct Pronouns.** The pronouns have been omitted from the following paragraph. Copy the paragraph onto your paper, inserting an appropriate form of the pronoun indicated in each blank.

The sun finally revealed (1) _____ as (2) _____ burst
reflexive personal

forth from behind the cloudy cloak (3) _____ hid it. The
relative

sun's rays soon warmed the campers, and (4) _____ awoke,

personal

rubbing the sleep from (5) _____ eyes. Since the children

personal

(6) _____ were responsible for preparing breakfast, the site

intensive

was quickly bustling with activity. (7) _____ did (8)_____

indefinite   *personal*

assigned duties, and before long, the aroma of coffee (9) _____

relative

had been freshly brewed filled the air. "(10) _____ wants

interrogative

breakfast?" shouted the cooks. "(11) _____ is (12)_____

demonstrative   *personal*

last call!" Whether it was the altitude, the strenuous activity,

or the good food, (13) _____ arrived at the table immedi-

indefinite

ately. (14) _____ was willing to take chances where food

indefinite

(15) _____ was concerned.

intensive

APPLICATION: Locating Nouns and Pronouns. The following
paragraph contains many nouns and pronouns. List all of the
nouns and pronouns contained in each sentence on your paper.
(Note that some of them may be used as adjectives.) Be prepared to identify each of the nouns and each of the pronouns
by name.

(1) The American alligator is a hardy creature. (2) It has
survived almost unchanged over a span of many centuries.
(3) At last count, almost half a million of these reptiles lived in
the state of Louisiana alone. (4) A female lays about sixty eggs;
these embryos are no bigger than the size of a chicken's egg.
(5) When the young are born, they measure eight to nine inches
in length. (6) As this oversized lizard grows, it eats insects, tad-
poles, and crayfish as its primary diet. (7) Scientists have made
an interesting discovery regarding the scales on the underside
of this unfriendly serpent. (8) Just as no two human fingerprints are identical, so the alligator's scales form unique patterns. (9) Because of their tenacity, these inhabitants of the
southern United States should continue to thrive within our
boundaries. (10) We, however, must make sure the encroach-
ments of civilization do not inflict irreparable damage on their
environment.

Verbs 1.2

Verbs can be used to help make a statement, ask a question, or deliver a command. Every complete sentence must have at least one verb, which may consist of as many as four words.

A verb is a word or group of words that expresses time while showing an action, a condition, or the fact that something exists.

ACTION: The tires *screeched*.

CONDITION: Our apricots *tasted* sweet.

EXISTENCE: The monkey *should be* in the next cage.

Verbs have a major effect on *syntax*—that is, on the way words are put together and are related to one another in sentences. Because of this effect, verbs are generally divided into two main categories: *action verbs* and *linking verbs*.

■ Action Verbs and Linking Verbs

Action verbs, as their name implies, express action. They are used to tell what someone or something does, did, or will do. Linking verbs, on the other hand, are used to express a condition or the fact that something exists.

Action Verbs.   The majority of verbs in English express action.

An action verb is a verb that tells what action someone or something is performing.

In the first example that follows, the verb tells what action the students are performing. Similarly, in the second example, the verb tells what the radio did.

ACTION VERBS: The art students *are learning* about perspective.

The radio *blared*.

The person or thing that performs the action is called the *subject* of the verb. In the preceding examples, *students* and *radio* are the subjects of *are learning* and *blared*.

Notice, also, in the examples that the action expressed by the verbs does not have to be visible. Words expressing mental activities, such as *learn*, *think*, or *decide*, are also considered action verbs.

Linking Verbs.   Linking verbs never express action. Instead, they link, or join, words in a sentence.

A **linking verb** is a verb that connects its subject with a word at or near the end of the sentence.

In the following examples, notice how the linking verbs act to connect words at the beginning and end of the sentences.

LINKING VERBS: Mr. McVeigh *is* our neighbor.

The cake batter *should be* smooth.

The verb *be* is the most common linking verb. If you do not already know all of the forms of this verb, study the following chart.

THE FORMS OF *BE*			
am	am being	can be	have been
are	are being	could be	has been
is	is being	may be	had been
was	was being	might be	could have been
were	were being	must be	may have been
		shall be	might have been
		should be	must have been
		will be	should have been
		would be	will have been
			would have been

Most often, the forms of *be* will function as linking verbs and express the condition of the subject. Occasionally, however, they may merely express existence, usually by showing, with other words, where the subject is located.

EXAMPLES: The catsup *is* in the refrigerator.

The keys *must be* here.

A few other verbs can also serve as linking verbs.

OTHER LINKING VERBS		
appear	look	sound
become	remain	stay
feel	seem	taste
grow	smell	turn

EXAMPLES: The sheets *smelled* fresh and clean.

The driver *stayed* alert.

The bridge *appeared* safe.

Some of these verbs may also act as action—not linking—verbs. To determine whether the word is functioning as an action verb or as a linking verb, insert *am, are,* or *is* in place of the verb. If the substitute makes sense while connecting two words, then the original verb is a linking verb.

LINKING VERB: The witness *sounded* nervous. (The witness *is* nervous.)

ACTION VERB: The witness *sounded* the alarm.

LINKING VERB: The runners *turned* pale with exhaustion. (The runners *are* pale.)

ACTION VERB: The runners *turned* the corner.

EXERCISE A: Identifying Action and Linking Verbs. Identify each underlined verb in the following sentences as either an action verb or a linking verb.

1. The puppy <u>raced</u> around the living room.
2. I <u>smelled</u> a gas leak.
3. Our dinner <u>should be</u> ready by now.
4. The accident victim <u>remained</u> unconscious.
5. Your behavior <u>might have been</u> less rude.
6. The hinges <u>sounded</u> rusty as I pulled the door open.
7. He <u>submitted</u> his latest poems for the contest.
8. The huge dog <u>was</u> ferocious.
9. Lisa <u>decided</u> to apply to West Point.
10. Our walnuts <u>tasted</u> bitter.

2

■ Transitive and Intransitive Verbs

All verbs can be described as either *transitive* or *intransitive* depending on whether they transfer action to another word in a sentence.

A verb is **transitive** if it directs action toward someone or something named in the same sentence. It is **intransitive** if it does not direct action toward someone or something named in the same sentence.

The word toward which a transitive verb directs its action is called the *object* of the verb. Intransitive verbs never have objects. You can determine whether a verb has an object by asking *What?* after the verb. (See Section 3.3 for more information about objects of verbs.)

TRANSITIVE: The outfielder *caught* the ball. (Caught *what?* The *ball.*)

We *ate* the entire cake. (Ate *what?* The *cake.*)

INTRANSITIVE: She *slept* in the hammock. no object

The child *coughed* loudly. no object

Notice in the examples that the action of the transitive verbs is done *to* something. The catching is done to the ball; the eating is done to the cake. The action of the intransitive verbs, however, is just done. Nothing receives the action of the sleeping or the coughing.

Since linking verbs do not express action, they are always intransitive. Most action verbs, however, can be either transitive or intransitive, depending on their use in a sentence. Some are either always transitive or always intransitive.

TRANSITIVE OR INTRANSITIVE: I already *sliced* the bread. Obj

This knife *slices* well.

ALWAYS TRANSITIVE: The judge *sentenced* the criminal. Obj

ALWAYS INTRANSITIVE: The guilty dog *slunk* away.

EXERCISE B: Identifying Transitive and Intransitive Verbs. Write the verbs from the following sentences on your paper and indicate whether they are *transitive* or *intransitive*.

1. The townspeople took a siesta each afternoon.
2. For a few extra dollars each week, she ironed clothes.
3. The mother smiled at the infant in her arms.
4. The eel slid along the floor of the ocean.
5. The crew ate lunch under an old oak tree.
6. We purchased tickets for the play *The Elephant Man*.
7. The pup tent collapsed from the high winds.
8. Our neighbors continually complain about the weather.
9. With reluctance, he swallowed the medicine.
10. Time stretched before us.

■ Verb Phrases

When a verb consists of more than one word, it is called a *verb phrase*.

Helping verbs are verbs that can be added to another verb to make a single **verb phrase.**

Helping verbs, often called *auxiliary verbs* or *auxiliaries,* add meaning to other verbs. As many as three helping verbs may precede the key verb in a verb phrase. Notice how helping verbs can change the meaning of the following sentence.

SINGLE VERB: I *wrote* a song today.

VERB PHRASES: I *will write* a song today.

I *should have written* a song today.

This song *might have been written* by me.

All of the forms of *be* listed on page 30 can be used with other verbs to form verb phrases. The verbs listed in the following chart can also be used as helping verbs.

HELPING VERBS OTHER THAN *BE*			
do	have	shall	can
does	has	should	could
did	had	will	may
		would	might
			must

A verb phrase is often interrupted by other words in a sentence. When looking for a verb in a sentence, first find the main verb; then check to see if it is preceded by helping verbs.

INTERRUPTED VERB PHRASES: I *will* definitely not *write* a song today.

Should I *have written* a song today?

EXERCISE C: Using Verb Phrases. Copy each of the following sentences onto your paper, filling in the blanks with an appropriate verb phrase.

1. The train _____ _____ _____ the station soon.
2. We _____ probably not _____ the wedding next week.
3. The car _____ _____ along the freeway.
4. _____ I _____ _____ a present for my sister?
5. The vacationers _____ _____ money from their bank.
6. The fields _____ _____ _____ _____ over a week ago.
7. I _____ _____ in a special performance.
8. Instead of doing this, I _____ definitely _____ _____ right now.
9. The house _____ _____ _____ before we can move in.
10. I _____ not _____ this book.

APPLICATION: Writing Sentences with Different Kinds of Verbs. Use each of the following verbs in a sentence of your own, supplying the form of the verb indicated in parentheses. Try to make your sentences interesting.

1. look (as an action verb)
2. look (as a linking verb)
3. rest (as a transitive verb)
4. rest (as an intransitive verb)
5. help (with two helping verbs)

1.3   Adjectives and Adverbs

Adjectives and adverbs are *modifiers*. In other words, they are the parts of speech that slightly change the meaning of other words by adding description or by making them more specific. Adjectives modify nouns and pronouns; adverbs modify verbs, adjectives, and other adverbs.

■ Adjectives

Without adjectives, much of the color in language would be lost. These words allow people to describe in more detail the nouns and pronouns about which they are speaking or writing.

> An **adjective** is a word used to describe a noun or pronoun or to give a noun or pronoun a more specific meaning.

Adjectives modify nouns and pronouns by providing information that answers any of the following questions about the noun or pronoun: *What kind? Which one? How many?* or *How much?*

EXAMPLES: *hot* onions (*What kind* of onions?)

that book (*Which* book?)

seventeen marbles (*How many* marbles?)

more exercise (*How much* exercise?)

These examples show the usual location of an adjective—preceding a noun. Sometimes, however, the adjective is located after the noun it modifies.

EXAMPLE: The bicycle looked *new.*

When an adjective modifies a pronoun, it is commonly found following the pronoun, but, on occasion, it can precede the pronoun.

AFTER: We were *sweaty* after our workout.

BEFORE: *Sweaty* after the workout, we took quick showers.

Finally, a single noun or pronoun may have more than one adjective modifying it.

EXAMPLE: The *tall agile* athlete easily made the basketball team.

Articles.   The three most common adjectives are the articles *a, an,* and *the. A* and *an* are the *indefinite* articles; they re-

fer to any one of a class of nouns. *The,* the *definite* article, refers
to a specific noun.

INDEFINITE: *a* contest, *an* opportunity

DEFINITE: *the* winner

Compound Adjectives.   Like nouns, adjectives can be compound—that is, they can be made up of more than one word.
Most compound adjectives are hyphenated; some are written
as combined words. Check a dictionary when you are in doubt.

HYPHENATED: *long-term* commitment, *crescent-shaped* moon

COMBINED: *coldblooded* animals, *lifelong* friendship

Proper Adjectives.   Also like nouns, some adjectives can be
proper. Proper adjectives are formed from proper nouns and
always begin with a capital letter.

PROPER NOUNS: Victoria   Spain

PROPER ADJECTIVES: *Victorian* literature   *Spanish* castles

Compound proper adjectives are usually written as two separate words.

EXAMPLE: *South American* birds

Nouns, Pronouns, and Verbs Used as Adjectives.   Occasionally, words that are usually nouns, pronouns, and verbs
will function as adjectives. When used as adjectives, these
parts of speech will answer any one of the four questions for
adjectives: *What kind? Which one? How many?* and *How much?*
  A noun used as an adjective will modify another noun and
answer the question *What kind?* or the question *Which one?*

NOUNS USED AS ADJECTIVES	
Common Nouns	
potato	*potato* soup
party	*party* hat

Proper Nouns	
Roosevelt	the *Roosevelt* era
Maine	a *Maine* lobster

Certain pronouns can also be used as adjectives modifying nouns, as the examples in the following chart illustrate. The seven personal pronouns that are listed at the beginning, known either as *possessive adjectives* or as *possessive pronouns* when they act as adjectives, do double duty: They are pronouns because they have antecedents; at the same time they are adjectives because they modify nouns by answering the question *Which one?*

PRONOUNS USED AS ADJECTIVES	
Possessive Adjectives	
my, your, his, her, its, our, their	Antecedent The man shaved off *his* beard. *Our* car finally broke down.
Demonstrative Adjectives	
this, that, these, those	*That* test took me three hours. *Those* roses wilted in the heat.
Interrogative Adjectives	
which, what, whose	*Which* job will you take? *Whose* money is on the table?
Indefinite Adjectives	
Used with singular nouns: another, each, either, little, much, neither, one	Give me *another* chance.
Used with plural nouns: both, few, many, several	*Few* people attended the musical.

Used with singular or plural nouns: all, any, more, most, other, some	Give me *some* water, please. We received *some* donations from them.

When verbs are used as adjectives, they usually end in *-ed* or in *-ing*. (See Section 4.2 for more about verbs that function as adjectives.)

VERBS USED AS ADJECTIVES

The *rippling* water felt refreshing to them.

The *washed* clothes were neatly folded.

Remember that nouns, pronouns, and verbs can be considered adjectives only when they modify other nouns or pronouns. Study the following examples to see how their function can change from one sentence to another.

Regular Function	As an Adjective
Noun The *blood* coursed through the veins.	The *blood* count was fine.
Pronoun *That* stood out from the crowd.	*That* pottery stood out from the crowd.
Verb The President *vetoed* the bill.	The *vetoed* bill was reintroduced in the next session of Congress.

EXERCISE A: Identifying Adjectives. The underlined words in the following paragraph are either nouns or pronouns. Copy each word onto your paper and then write all the adjectives, if any, that modify it. Be prepared to identify any nouns, pronouns, or verbs used as adjectives.

(1) <u>Insects</u> seem as indestructible as (2) <u>they</u> are innumerable. Most (3) <u>experts</u> say that one (4) <u>reason</u> for this is their (5)

ability to adapt to different (6) <u>environments</u>. Some (7) <u>insects</u> can live in icebound (8) <u>streams</u> while (9) <u>others</u> prefer hot (10) <u>springs</u> that may reach 50°C. Their small (11) <u>size</u> also accounts for their continued (12) <u>survival</u>. Some North American (13) <u>insects</u> measure one one-hundredth of an inch, and that size makes (14) <u>them</u> hard to see and even harder to exterminate. But their amazing (15) <u>power</u> to reproduce probably contributes most to their (16) <u>durability</u>. Generally, these prolific (17) <u>creatures</u> can reproduce several (18) <u>times</u> during one (19) <u>season</u>. (20) <u>Many</u> lay enormous (21) <u>numbers</u> of eggs. (22) <u>Few</u> can surpass a fertile queen (23) <u>termite</u>, which may lay as many as 30,000 (24) <u>eggs</u> in a single twenty-four-hour (25) <u>period</u>.

EXERCISE B: Using Adjectives in Your Own Writing. Choose one of the following nouns and imagine the object that the word represents in terms of color, shape, location, and condition. Then in five or six sentences, describe this object in detail, using as many different adjectives as you can. Do *not* start your description with such words as "It looks like . . ." or "It was . . ."

A key	A book
A house	A car
A body of water	An animal
A person	A fire
A dessert	A plant

■ Adverbs

Like adjectives, adverbs describe or make other words more specific.

An adverb is a word that modifies a verb, an adjective, or another adverb.

An adverb that modifies a verb answers any of four questions: *Where? When? In what manner? To what extent?* An adverb that modifies an adjective or another adverb answers *To what extent?* When an adverb functions in this second manner, it is often called an *intensifier* because it increases or decreases the intensity of the adjective or adverb it modifies.

The following chart shows adverbs modifying verbs, adjectives, and other adverbs. Notice particularly the positions of the adverbs. When an adverb modifies a verb, it may come before or after the verb, or may interrupt a verb phrase. When an adverb modifies an adjective or another adverb, it generally comes immediately before the adjective or other adverb.

Adverbs Modifying Verbs	
Where?	**When?**
The balloon floated *up*.	Your letter arrived *today*.
Your wallet is *here*.	*Now* I will go.
In what manner?	**To what extent?**
The evening *quickly* passed.	We have *just* finished eating.
The boy was *eagerly* awaiting the news.	She did *not* warn me.
Adverbs Modifying Adjectives	**Adverbs Modifying Adverbs**
To what extent?	**To what extent?**
I am *extremely* hungry.	He drives *rather* carefully.
The *overly* tired worker collapsed.	The glass was *not* completely empty.

Adverbs as Parts of Verbs.   Some adverbs are parts of verbs. As such, they no longer function as modifiers. Notice in the following examples that the adverbs do not answer any of the usual questions for adverbs. Instead they help make up the transitive verbs *close up* and *shut off*.

EXAMPLES: The family closed *up* the summer house.

Please shut *off* the sprinklers.

Nouns Used as Adverbs.   A few words that are usually nouns can function as adverbs that answer the questions *Where?* or *When?* Some of these words are *home, yesterday, to-day, tomorrow, mornings, afternoons, evenings, nights, week, month,* and *year*.

EXAMPLES: We raced *home*. (Raced *where?*)

I saw them last *month*. (Saw *when?*)

Adverb or Adjective?   Some adverbs and adjectives share the same form. You can distinguish between them by determining the part of speech of the word they modify: Adverbs modify verbs, adjectives, and adverbs; adjectives modify nouns and pronouns.

ADVERB: The train arrived *early*. (Arrived *when?*)

ADJECTIVE: She took the *early* train to work. (*Which* train?)

Most adverbs and adjectives, however, do not share the same form. Many adverbs are formed by adding *-ly* to an adjective.

ADJECTIVES: *slow* approval, *hasty* decision

ADVERBS: approved *slowly*, decided *hastily*

Some adjectives end in *-ly* too. Do not assume, therefore, that any word ending in *-ly* is an adverb.

ADJECTIVES: a *lonely* house, his *ghostly* smile

EXERCISE C: Identifying Adverbs. Each of the following sentences contains one to three adverbs. Copy the sentences onto your paper, underlining each adverb. Then draw an arrow from the adverb to the word it modifies.

1. The surf-casters bore their catch of fish triumphantly.
2. As they hiked along the trails, the child fell steadily behind.
3. Unexpectedly, the baseball sailed through the new window.
4. The instructions were completely accurate, and we arrived soon afterward.
5. Tomorrow we must leave extremely early.
6. The tourniquet was bound tightly and professionally.
7. You will find the office if you go straight and turn left at the very first intersection.
8. Eventually, they will totally restore this historical landmark.

9. The boys ran quite hastily toward the wrecked car.
10. They have partially tiled the roof and will finish it soon.

EXERCISE D: Adding Adverbs. Fill in each blank in the following paragraphs with an adverb. Write the adverb next to the appropriate number on your paper.

(1) _____ perched in the upper seats of the stadium, a family is (2) _____ watching a circus (3) _____. It may seem (4) _____ odd to see a high-wire act occurring ten floors (5) _____ . But that is what can happen when someone watches a show at the (6) _____ large Louisiana Superdome.

The Superdome can (7) _____ astound even the (8) _____ casual observer. A tour alone leads the visitor (9) _____ through a maze of twists and turns, (10) _____ covering over two miles. This (11) _____ massive structure reaches (12) _____ for (13) _____ twenty-seven stories; the roof stretches 680 feet in diameter. A television system is (14) _____ located, composed of six individual screens, each one the size of a (15) _____ large living-room floor. Created (16)_____ for the Superdome, the system cost (17) _____ 1.3 million dollars. For those (18) _____ wealthy and devoted sports fans, the Superdome designers (19) _____ provided sixty-four private suites. (20) _____ decorated with couches, wall-to-wall carpeting, a refreshment bar, and plush box seats—a suite at the Superdome can be yours for a mere $150,000 a year.

APPLICATION: Writing Sentences with Adjectives and Adverbs. The underlined word in each of the following sentences is either an adjective or an adverb. If the word is an adjective, write a sentence of your own in which you use it as an adverb. If the word is an adverb, use it in a sentence as an adjective.

1. The <u>deep</u> lake held some huge bass.
2. Frank talked <u>loud</u> so that his grandmother could hear him.
3. The rocket shot <u>high</u> into the air.
4. That razor does not give me a <u>close</u> shave.
5. Draw a <u>straight</u> line connecting points A and B.
6. I felt <u>better</u> after I had some breakfast.
7. The ice cream is still too <u>hard</u> to serve.
8. The paper clip held the papers <u>tight.</u>
9. She reads poetry <u>well.</u>
10. The bells rang <u>late</u> throughout the day.

Prepositions, Conjunctions, and Interjections

Two of the last three parts of speech—prepositions and conjunctions—work in sentences as connectors. *Prepositions* relate one word to another, while *conjunctions* join words, groups of words, or even whole ideas. *Interjections*, on the other hand, are emotionally expressive words that work as attention-getters.

■ Prepositions

Prepositions perform the important job of linking words within a sentence. They enable a speaker or writer to show relationships between separate things. The relationships may involve such things as location, direction, cause, or possession.

A **preposition** is a word that relates the noun or pronoun following it to another word in the sentence.

The best way to recognize prepositions is to familiarize yourself with the most common ones, which are shown in the following chart. Notice that some prepositions are composed of more than one word. These are sometimes called *compound prepositions*.

PREPOSITIONS			
aboard	below	in place of	over
about	beneath	in regard to	owing to
above	beside	inside	past
according to	besides	in spite of	prior to
across	between	instead of	regarding
after	beyond	into	round
against	but	in view of	since
ahead of	by	like	through
along	by means of	near	throughout
alongside	concerning	nearby	till
amid	considering	next to	to

among	despite	of	toward
apart from	down	off	under
around	during	on	underneath
as of	except	on account of	until
aside from	for	onto	unto
at	from	on top of	up
atop	in	opposite	upon
barring	in addition to	out	with
because of	in back of	out of	within
before	in front of	outside	without
behind			

In the following examples, notice how the prepositions relate the italicized words.

LOCATION: The tree *fell* behind the *house.*

DIRECTION: The tree *fell* toward the *shed.*

CAUSE: The tree *fell* on account of the *wind.*

POSSESSION: *Leaves* from the *tree* littered the lawn.

Prepositional Phrases.   Prepositions are always part of a group of words called a *prepositional phrase.* A prepositional phrase begins with a preposition and ends with a noun or pronoun known as the *object of the preposition.* Notice in the last of the following examples that a prepositional phrase may contain more than one object.

EXAMPLES: The ice *in the lemonade* cooled the drink.

I saw the movie *with her.*

Shawn checked *under the couch and chair.*

Although a prepositional phrase can consist of as few as two words, it is usually longer because of the addition of words to modify the object of the preposition.

EXAMPLES: behind her
behind the seat
behind the newly upholstered car seat

Preposition or Adverb? You may experience some difficulty in telling prepositions and adverbs apart. *Around, down, in, off, on, out, over,* and *up* are some of the words that can function either as a preposition or as an adverb. Just remember that for a word to be a preposition it must be followed by an object of the preposition.

PREPOSITION: The ball rolled *down the drain.*

ADVERB: The child fell *down.*

EXERCISE A: Identifying Prepositional Phrases. Write the prepositional phrases from each sentence in the following paragraph. After writing them in order on your paper, circle each preposition.

(1) The tails of birds and animals are not only a source of beauty but a useful appendage to their bodies. (2) Because of their tails, beavers can transmit a warning regarding impending danger. (3) With its rattle, a rattlesnake shakes a warning to those around that they should watch where they are stepping. (4) Apart from their protective uses, the tails also help animals with the more practical side of life. (5) Kangaroos and lizards would not move with such agility without their tails for balance. (6) With their very long tails, wagtails, a kind of bird, disturb insects in the grass and thus secure their food. (7) In addition to these uses, the tail also helps many animals communicate during courtship. (8) A coyote holding his tail high above him is expressing interest in his mate. (9) Similarly, by means of his tail feathers, a male peacock displays his interest in front of the hen. (10) The swordtail, a tropical fish often found in home aquariums, also uses his tail in a courtship dance.

EXERCISE B: Distinguishing Between Prepositions and Adverbs. Identify the underlined word in each of the following sentences as either a *preposition* or an *adverb*. If the word is a preposition, write its object on your paper.

1. You will find the shovel <u>outside</u> the door of the shed.
2. The captain sent the passengers <u>below</u> during the storm.
3. I saw that movie <u>over</u> and over.
4. The painter climbed <u>up</u> the ladder.
5. The paper airplane sailed erratically <u>around</u> and then crashed.
6. At noon, the doctor went <u>out.</u>
7. Because of the rain the track meet was held <u>inside</u> today.

8. The speed skater raced <u>around</u> the turn.
9. The flower pot fell <u>off</u> the sill.
10. The smoke drifted lazily <u>up</u> the chimney.

EXERCISE C: Using Prepositional Phrases. Prepositional phrases have been left out of the following paragraph. Copy the paragraph onto your paper, inserting appropriate and interesting prepositional phrases in the blanks.

The track meet was scheduled (1) _____, and we were told to meet (2) _____. As usual, I was "running" late. (Did you catch that pun?) I found my running shoes (3) _____; my track shorts were (4) _____. Finally, I was organized and dashed (5) _____, but the bus had already left (6) _____. I raced home and asked my mother (7) _____. She agreed and I got (8) _____. My mother is an extremely cautious driver, and we crawled (9) _____. When I breathlessly arrived, I had five minutes to prepare for my race. Since I had already had a good workout, I ran the race (10) _____.

■ Conjunctions

Unlike prepositions, which relate words, conjunctions connect words, phrases, and ideas.

A **conjunction** is a word used to connect other words or groups of words.

There are three main kinds of conjunctions in English: *coordinating*, *correlative*, and *subordinating* conjunctions. A special kind of adverb, called a *conjunctive adverb*, is often also considered a conjunction.

Coordinating Conjunctions. Coordinating conjunctions connect similar parts of speech, or they connect groups of words that are of equal grammatical weight.

COORDINATING CONJUNCTIONS			
and	for	or	yet
but	nor	so	

The following examples show these conjunctions connecting similar parts of speech and groups of words that are grammatically alike.

WITH NOUNS AND PRONOUNS: Her friends *and* she are planning a party.

WITH VERBS: The waves thundered *and* pounded the shore.

WITH ADJECTIVES: The dog's fur is soft, silky, *and* clean.

WITH ADVERBS: The carpenter works quickly *but* efficiently.

WITH PREPOSITIONAL PHRASES: Do not walk to the left *nor* to the right.

WITH DEPENDENT IDEAS: She felt that I could do it *but* that I wouldn't take the time.

WITH COMPLETE IDEAS: They didn't drink the coffee, *for* it was too strong.

Correlative Conjunctions.   Correlative conjunctions also join equal elements in sentences. These conjunctions, however, always work in pairs.

CORRELATIVE CONJUNCTIONS
both . . . and   either . . . or   neither . . . nor
not only . . . but also   whether . . . or

The following examples show some of the many ways these conjunctions may be used.

WITH NOUNS: *Neither* Lola *nor* Peter will perform in the play.

WITH NOUNS AND PRONOUNS: *Whether* Bob *or* I will attend has not been decided.

WITH ADJECTIVES: Yogurt is *not only* nutritious *but also* delicious.

WITH PREPOSITIONAL PHRASES: We saw jellyfish *both* near the pier *and* along the beach.

WITH COMPLETE IDEAS: *Either* you go to the store *or* you must do the laundry.

Subordinating Conjunctions.   Subordinating conjunctions join two complete ideas by making one of the ideas subordinate—that is, dependent on the other.

SUBORDINATING CONJUNCTIONS			
after	because	lest	till
although	before	now that	unless
as	even if	provided	until
as if	even though	since	when
as long as	how	so that	whenever
as much as	if	than	where
as soon as	inasmuch as	that	wherever
as though	in order that	though	while

Subordinating conjunctions always begin subordinate clauses, but they need not come between the ideas they connect, as the second of the following examples illustrates. (See Section 4.3 for more information about subordinate clauses.)

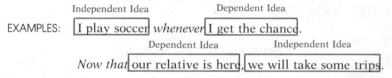

EXAMPLES:

Independent Idea
I play soccer *whenever* I get the chance.

Dependent Idea
Now that our relative is here, we will take some trips.

Sometimes identifying subordinating conjunctions is difficult since several of these conjunctions can also function as prepositions or adverbs. *After, before, since, till,* and *until* often begin prepositional phrases; *after, before, when,* and *where* can also work as adverbs.

SUBORDINATING CONJUNCTION: *Before* you buy the stereo, check other prices.

PREPOSITION: Come home *before* dark.

ADVERB: We had seen the museum *before.*

Conjunctive Adverbs.   A conjunctive adverb is an adverb that acts as a conjunction to connect complete ideas. Conjunctive adverbs are also known as *transitions* because they act as bridges between different ideas. They help, for example, in showing comparisons, contrasts, or results.

CONJUNCTIVE ADVERBS		
accordingly	for example	nevertheless
again	furthermore	on the other hand
also	however	otherwise
besides	in addition	then
consequently	indeed	therefore
finally	moreover	thus

Notice the punctuation before and after the conjunctive adverbs in the following examples. (See Sections 13.2 and 13.3 for more about the use of commas and semicolons with conjunctive adverbs.)

EXAMPLES: The berries were sweet; *nevertheless,* I added some sugar to them.

The circus starts at 8:00 P.M.; we should, *therefore,* leave soon.

The scholarship examination was difficult. It included, *for example,* poems we had never studied.

EXERCISE D: Identifying Conjunctions in Sentences. Each of the following sentences contains one conjunction. Write the conjunction on your paper, and then identify it as either *coordinating, correlative,* or *subordinating.*

1. Either we leave now or we don't go at all.
2. I want Rosa and you to play the leads in the play.
3. Before we have lunch, I want to swim some laps.
4. I will bake a cake so that we have enough for the bake sale.
5. We will stay until they hand out the awards.
6. White, blue, or beige upholstery would suit the color of the room.
7. Even though he has little experience, I plan to hire him.
8. Will you get the phone, for I have to leave right now?
9. Since we mowed the lawn, the whole house seems to look better.
10. It doesn't matter to me if you take Brian to the park.

EXERCISE E: Distinguishing Between Subordinating Conjunctions, Prepositions, and Adverbs. Identify each underlined word in the following sentences as a *subordinating conjunction, preposition,* or *adverb.*

1. They have been out fishing <u>since</u> dawn.
2. <u>When</u> does school begin?
3. You will have to wait <u>until</u> the competition is held again next year.
4. The results will not be published <u>till</u> June.
5. I will meet you <u>where</u> we met last week.
6. My knees began to shake <u>when</u> they called my name.
7. I had driven a motorcycle once <u>before.</u>
8. <u>After</u> the fifteenth, we can pick up our checks.
9. <u>Where</u> are the suitcases kept?
10. I had no idea job-hunting could be so exhausting <u>until</u> this week.

EXERCISE F: Using Conjunctive Adverbs. Connect the ideas in each of the following pairs of sentences by inserting an appropriate conjunctive adverb. Write the related sentences on your paper.

EXAMPLE: The ship's engine broke down. The Coast Guard had to tow it to port.

The ship's engine broke down. Consequently, the Coast Guard had to tow it to port.

1. I must turn the report in on time. My grade will be lowered.
2. Mandy could buy a condominium. She could rent for another year.
3. I do not want to cook. We have no food in the house.
4. She missed the ship. She had to fly to the next port to meet it.
5. I work at a department store. I write feature articles in my spare time.
6. The race took four hours. They won.
7. We have plenty of room in the car. If you follow us, you might get lost.
8. Voice training would improve his voice. He does not have the money for lessons.
9. The dam broke. No one was injured in the flood.
10. You must watch the road signs. You drove through a stop sign at the last corner.

■ Interjections

Though small in size, interjections can express strong emotions. Unlike other parts of speech, these words never have a grammatical connection to other words in a sentence.

2

An **interjection** is a word that expresses feeling or emotion and functions independently of a sentence.

Interjections can express a variety of feelings, such as joy, fear, anger, surprise, exhaustion, dismay, or sorrow.

SOME COMMON INTERJECTIONS				
ah	dear	help	oh	tsk tsk
aha	goodness	hey	ouch	well
alas	gracious	hurray	psst	whew

As the following examples demonstrate, interjections are set off from the rest of the sentence by either an exclamation mark or a comma.

EXAMPLES: *Whew!* That was a close call!

Hey, wait a minute!

EXERCISE G: Using Interjections. Write five sentences that contain examples of the type of interjection appropriate for the following emotions or feelings. Then underline the interjections in your sentences.

1. joy
2. pain
3. hesitation
4. surprise
5. impatience

APPLICATION: Using Prepositions and Conjunctions to Expand Sentences. Expand each of the following sentences by adding prepositions and conjunctions and any other words that are necessary. Write the new sentences on your paper, circling the prepositions and underlining the conjunctions that you add.

EXAMPLE: I prepared the dessert.

Jody <u>and</u> I <u>not only</u> prepared the dessert (for) Thanksgiving

dinner <u>but</u> <u>also</u> the turkey (with) chestnut dressing.

1. I played my new record album.
2. The campfire blazed.
3. The noise awoke the entire neighborhood.
4. A dozen red balloons floated upward.
5. The artist used green paint.

Chapter 2

Analyzing Parts of Speech

Looking through a dictionary, you may have noticed that many words can function as more than one part of speech. Many words change from one part of speech to another as their meaning and function in a sentence changes.

2.1 Identifying Parts of Speech

To function means "to serve in a particular capacity." In determining a part of speech, you must always be aware that the function of a word may change from sentence to sentence.

■ Parts of Speech in Sentences

Look, for example, at the many roles played by the word *well* in the following sentences.

AS A NOUN: Our *well* ran dry.

AS A VERB: After every scolding, tears *well* in the child's eyes.

AS AN ADJECTIVE: My sister feels quite *well*.

AS AN ADVERB: Ralph did *well* on the test.

A quick review of the definition of each part of speech is provided in the following charts. Look at the column in each of the charts entitled "Questions to Ask Yourself." It shows you what to ask to determine how a word is being used in a sentence.

Nouns, Pronouns, and Verbs. A noun names a person, place, or thing. A pronoun stands for a noun. A verb shows action, condition, or existence.

Part of Speech	Questions to Ask Yourself	Examples
Noun	Does the word name a person, place, or thing?	Our *visit* to the *Grand Canyon* delighted *Rosa*.
Pronoun	Does the word stand for a noun?	*I* gave *some* to *him*.
Verb	Does the word tell what someone or something did?	We *played* baseball.
	Does the word link the noun or pronoun before it with an adjective or noun that follows?	Mother *appeared* happy. The woman *was* a lawyer.
	Does the word merely indicate that something exists?	The family *is* here.

The Other Five Parts of Speech. An adjective modifies a noun or pronoun. An adverb modifies a verb, adjective, or another adverb. A preposition relates a noun or pronoun following it to another word. A conjunction connects words or groups of words. An interjection expresses feeling or emotion.

Part of Speech	Questions to Ask Yourself	Examples
Adjective	Does the word tell what kind, which one, how many, or how much?	*Those three* apples are an *unusual* color.
Adverb	Does the word tell where, when, in what manner, or to what extent?	Go *home*. Leave *now*. Drive *very slowly*. I am *thoroughly* tired.
Preposition	Is the word part of a phrase that ends with a noun or pronoun?	*Near* our house, the carnival was *in* full swing.

| Conjunction | Does the word connect other words in a sentence or between sentences? | *Both* you *and* I will go *because* they need more people. *Besides*, it will be fun. |
| Interjection | Does the word express feeling or emotion and function independently of the sentence? | *Hey*, give me that! *Ouch*, that hurt! |

EXERCISE A: Identifying Parts of Speech. Words have been underlined and numbered in the following paragraph. Identify the part of speech of each underlined word on your paper.

When and (1) <u>where</u> did fans first originate? (2) <u>According to</u> (3) <u>historians</u>, the Chinese used fans as early as 3000 B.C. It is (4) <u>also</u> well known that (5) <u>the</u> kings and queens of Egypt were (6) <u>efficiently</u> cooled by (7) <u>palm</u> fans waved by servants. Serving an important (8) <u>function</u> in early (9) <u>religious</u> ceremonies, fans (10) <u>brushed away</u> flies from sacred vessels. By 700 A.D., the (11) <u>Japanese</u> invented the (12) <u>folding</u> fan (13) <u>and</u> added the bright colors that are characteristic of the oriental fan. (14) <u>But</u> it (15) <u>is</u> the Portuguese (16) <u>whom</u> we can thank for introducing fans to Europe (17) <u>in</u> the 1500's. So popular did (18) <u>they</u> become that (19) <u>many</u> of the men (20) <u>during</u> the reign of Louis XV carried them. Artists of the 1800's found the fan a delightful canvas on which to paint, and the (21) <u>works</u> of great masters grace the folds of some fans. (22) <u>Alas</u>, this device is used (23) <u>today</u> primarily as a decorative (24) <u>wallhanging</u>, seldom as a part of (25) <u>our</u> attire.

EXERCISE B: Identifying Troublesome Parts of Speech. Two words have been underlined in each of the following sentences. Identify the part of speech of each word on your paper.

1. The <u>garden</u> hose should be near the rose <u>garden</u>.
2. We <u>run</u> the dogs once each day in the dog <u>run</u> out back.
3. I don't like <u>either</u>, but I must choose <u>either</u> one or the other.
4. <u>Help</u>, I am stuck and need <u>help</u>!
5. The chair fell <u>over</u> and then rolled <u>over</u> the rug.

APPLICATION: Using Words as Different Parts of Speech. Write ten sentences of your own using each of the following words in two ways.

blue   that   sneezes   up   well

Chapter 3

Basic Sentence Parts and Patterns

When babies first begin to communicate, they utter a single word to convey their needs. Later, children begin to use sentences that contain both a subject and an action word. By the age of four or five, most children have become familiar with the basic speech patterns and use many principles of grammar. With time, their sentences become more complex and sophisticated. In studying a language, it often helps to view it in the way a child learns it—looking first at the simplest sentence parts and then using that knowledge to examine more difficult sentence patterns. This chapter will focus on how words of different parts of speech are combined to form basic sentence patterns.

Subjects and Verbs 3.1

Language is the tool with which people shape their ideas and communicate them to others. For the communication to be meaningful, a speaker or writer must choose appropriate words and put them in an order that the listener or reader can follow and understand.

In any language, the basic unit of thought that expresses meaning is the sentence. It is generally ordered in some expected pattern. In English, every sentence has two essential parts, a *complete subject* and a *complete predicate*, which in turn are made up of other parts. Being aware of these parts and of how they are related to each other can help you avoid unintentionally letting the order of your words get in the way of your ideas.

■ Complete Subjects and Complete Predicates

A group of words in English is considered a sentence when it has two parts, either clearly stated or implied: a *complete subject* and a *complete predicate*.

> A **sentence** is a group of words with two main parts: a **complete subject** and a **complete predicate**. Together, these parts express a complete thought.

A *complete subject* is the noun, pronoun, or group of words acting as a noun, plus any modifiers, that tells *who* or *what* the sentence is about. The *complete predicate*, on the other hand, is the verb or verb phrase, plus any modifiers and complements, that tells what the complete subject does or is. (See Section 3.3 for a definition of complements.) As the examples in the following chart show, complete subjects and complete predicates can vary in length.

Complete Subject	Complete Predicate
Dogs	bark.
My favorite hideout	is in the old oak tree.
Jane and Paul	went scuba diving and sailing.
A little girl with pigtails	licked her ice cream cone happily.

Although the complete subject usually comes first, occasionally, part of a complete predicate will be found at the beginning of a sentence with the rest at the end. In the following example, the adverb *yesterday* modifies *visited*.

EXAMPLE: Yesterday | my family | visited my aunt.

EXERCISE A: Recognizing Complete Subjects and Complete Predicates. Copy the following sentences onto your paper, drawing a slash between the complete subject and the complete predicate. Some sentences may require more than one slash.

1. My grandmother knitted a sweater.
2. The ruler was only eight inches long.
3. The parachuters jumped from the plane.

4. Tomorrow I will clean out the cupboard.
5. Snails and aphids ruined my garden.
6. Lilting melodies filled the air around us.
7. I ate cookies, roast, and iced pineapple at the fair.
8. Yesterday her rash had almost disappeared.
9. The class dissected and studied the specimens.
10. A new brand of cereal came out on the market recently.

■ Fragments

If a group of words does not contain a complete subject and a complete predicate, it is not a sentence, but a *fragment*.

A **fragment** is a group of words that does not express a complete thought.

Because a fragment does not express a complete thought, it often causes a breakdown in communication. To become a sentence, a fragment must have the missing part added to it. Notice how the different kinds of fragments in the following chart have been corrected. In the first example, the fragment lacks a complete predicate; in the second, a complete subject. In the third example, the fragment is missing both a complete subject and part of a complete predicate.

Fragments	Complete Sentences
The gardener with the mustache.	The gardener with the mustache *trimmed the hedge*. (Complete predicate added.)
Rushed through the department store.	*The shoppers* rushed through the department store. (Complete subject added.)
On a cold, frosty morning.	*We drank hot chocolate* on a cold, frosty morning. (Complete subject and rest of complete predicate added.)

In conversations, fragments usually do not present a problem since repetition, tone of voice, gestures, and facial expression all help to complete the meaning. In writing, however, fragments should be avoided since the reader is alone with the words on the page and cannot go to the writer for clarification. An exception, of course, is in writing that represents speech, such as the dialogue in a play or short story. Even then, fragments must be used carefully so that the reader can follow the flow of ideas.

Another exception is the occasional use in writing of *elliptical sentences*, in which the missing word or words can easily be understood.

ELLIPTICAL SENTENCES: Good night. (= *I hope you have a* good night.)

Why so restless? (= Why *are you* so restless?)

(See Section 5.1 for more about fragments and how to correct them in your writing.)

EXERCISE B: Locating and Correcting Sentence Fragments. Each of the following items is either a sentence or a fragment. If the item is a fragment, rewrite it to make it a sentence. If the item is a sentence, write *complete* on your paper.

1. Sang a traditional melody.
2. A fierce wind tore at the trees.
3. Around the next bend.
4. A persistent burglar alarm.
5. Dodged the speeding ball.
6. Inhaled the fragrance of the abundant wild flowers.
7. An invasion from outer space was the movie's theme.
8. A safe speed limit down the steep hill and around the sharp turns.
9. Conscientious drivers always buckle their seat belts.
10. Handcuffs the suspect in an armed robbery.

■ Simple Subjects and Simple Predicates

Each complete subject and complete predicate contains a word or group of words that is essential to the sentence. Without these elements, known as the *simple subject* and *simple predicate*, a sentence is considered incomplete.

The **simple subject** is the essential noun, pronoun, or group of words acting as a noun that cannot be left out of the complete subject.

The **simple predicate** is the essential verb or verb phrase that cannot be left out of the complete predicate.

In the following chart, the simple subjects are underlined once, and the simple predicates are underlined twice. Notice the other words in the sentences: They either modify the simple subject and simple predicate or help the simple predicate complete the meaning of the sentence.

SIMPLE SUBJECTS AND SIMPLE PREDICATES	
Complete Subject	**Complete Predicate**
The popular and busy <u>restaurant</u>	<u>filled</u> quickly.
<u>Gerard Manley Hopkins</u>	<u>destroyed</u> nearly all of his early poetry in 1868.
The tiny <u>nation</u> of San Marino	<u>has</u> always <u>received</u> most of its income from the sale of postage stamps.

In the last example, notice that the simple subject is *nation*, not *San Marino*. The object of a preposition can never be a simple subject. Notice also that the simple predicate is a verb phrase, *has received*, that is interrupted by an adverb.

NOTE ABOUT TERMINOLOGY: From this point on in this book, the term *subject* will be used to refer to a simple subject, and the term *verb* will be used to refer to a simple predicate. Whenever subjects and verbs need to be indicated in examples, subjects will be underlined once and verbs twice.

Locating Subjects and Verbs.   Knowing a method for locating subjects and verbs in sentences will enable you to check your own writing and, in turn, help you avoid fragments. Some people find it easier to locate the subject first. If you use this method, first ask yourself, "What word tells what this sentence is about?" After determining this word to be the subject, ask, "What did the subject do?" This gives you the verb.

If, on the other hand, you can pick out verbs more easily, ask first, "What is the action verb or linking verb in this sentence?" After you have the answer, ask, "Who or what?" before the verb. The answer will be the subject of the verb.

Notice how these methods work with the following sentence.

EXAMPLE: The red lights signaled a warning.

To find the subject first ask, "What word tells what this sentence is about?"

ANSWER: lights   (*Lights* is the subject.)

Then to find the verb ask, "What did the *lights* do?"

ANSWER: signaled   (*Signaled* is the verb.)

To find the verb first, ask, "What is the action verb or linking verb in this sentence?"

ANSWER: signaled   (*Signaled* is the verb.)

Then to find the subject, ask, "Who or what *signaled*?"

ANSWER: lights   (*Lights* is the subject.)

If you are still having trouble locating subjects and verbs, simplify the sentence by eliminating some of the modifiers. Mentally cross out adjectives, adverbs, and prepositional phrases.

EXAMPLE: A pleasant breeze from the bay cooled the city efficiently.

With this simpler version of the sentence, you can now easily employ one of the sets of questions to determine the subject and verb.

More Than One Subject or Verb.   So far, the examples you have studied contained only one subject and one verb. Sometimes, however, a sentence may contain a *compound subject* or *compound verb*.

A **compound subject** is two or more subjects that have the same verb and are joined by a conjunction such as *and* or *or*.

In the following examples, the parts of the compound subjects are underlined once. Verbs are underlined twice.

EXAMPLES: The <u>salt</u> and <u>vinegar</u> <u>are</u> on the table.

<u>Ginnie</u> or <u>Howard</u> <u>will play</u> the piano.

Neither the <u>unions</u> nor the <u>management</u> <u>wanted</u> to see a strike.

Verbs also can be compound.

A **compound verb** is two or more verbs that have the same subject and are joined by a conjunction such as *and* or *or*.

EXAMPLES: She <u>sneezed</u> and <u>coughed</u> throughout the play.

You either <u>could walk</u> or <u>run</u> in this race.

<u>We</u> <u>walked</u> through the door and <u>stared</u> at the destruction.

Some sentence constructions may contain both compound subjects and compound verbs.

EXAMPLE: The <u>dog</u> and <u>cat</u> <u>eyed</u> each other, <u>circled</u> warily, and then <u>advanced</u> into combat.

EXERCISE C: Identifying Subjects and Verbs.

Copy each of the following sentences onto your paper, drawing a slash between the complete subject and the complete predicate. Then underline the subject once and the verb twice.

1. Our good friends breed turkeys on their ranch.
2. The heat spell left us tired and uncomfortable.
3. The majority of the students voted for a trip to the beach.
4. I contemplated the words of Thoreau.
5. Many people with red hair also have freckles.
6. The curtain did not rise at the scheduled time.
7. The spinning blades of the helicopter whipped the air around us.
8. I will arrange a dental appointment tomorrow.
9. My new car should arrive this week.
10. The clerks in the shoe department worked overtime during the sale.

EXERCISE D: Locating Compound Subjects and Compound Verbs.

Each of the following sentences contains either a compound subject, a compound verb, or both. Write the subject and verb for each sentence on your paper.

1. Either Clint or Helen will win first place.
2. In that race, the competitors first run, then swim, and finally bicycle.
3. The cream and sugar sat within easy reach.
4. I added water to the dry ingredients, mixed the batter, and poured it into the pan.
5. The flora and fauna of the Amazon forest have not yet been fully cataloged and studied by scientists.

APPLICATION: Developing Sentences from Subjects and Verbs. The first of the following two lists contains nouns that are suitable for subjects. The second contains verbs. The last five groups of words in each list are compound parts. Write ten sentences of your own using all of these subjects and verbs in any combination you wish.

Subjects	*Verbs*
1. airplane	provide
2. committee	were stampeding
3. cattle	depleted
4. erosion	battered
5. music	were set
6. vitamins, minerals	discussed, voted
7. wind, rain	banked, descended
8. diamonds, rubies	can soothe, can excite
9. onions, garlic	were displayed, were sold
10. stamps, coins	were chopped, were added

3.2 Subjects in Different Kinds of Sentences

Being able to find subjects and verbs in sentences is a useful skill. It can help you not only in understanding complicated sentences when you read but also in checking the clarity and logic of your thoughts when you write. In most English sentences, a subject comes before its verb. This usual pattern makes finding subjects and verbs easy. At times, however, this pattern is reversed. In these cases, other nouns and pronouns or other parts of speech may masquerade as the subject and make it more difficult to find the real subject.

This section will first explain the four functions of English sentences and then examine the positions subjects take in these sentences.

■ The Four Functions of Sentences

Though all sentences contain subjects and verbs, not all sentences function in the same way. Though their elements may be similar, their patterns differ in order to convey different purposes. All sentences can be classified according to one of four functions: *declarative*, *interrogative*, *imperative*, and *exclamatory*.

A *declarative* sentence is the most common sentence used in speaking and writing. It generally expresses facts and opinions.

A **declarative** sentence states an idea and ends with a period.

EXAMPLES: Dogs bite about twenty-eight mail carriers every day.

We should try to encourage school spirit.

An *interrogative* sentence is one that poses a question.

An **interrogative** sentence asks a question and ends with a question mark.

EXAMPLES: Where did you hide my socks?

Why should we vote for this proposition?

An *imperative* sentence is used to make a demand or request.

An **imperative** sentence gives an order or a direction and ends with a period or an exclamation mark.

If an imperative sentence also expresses force or emotion, as does the second example that follows, an exclamation mark should be used at the end rather than a period.

EXAMPLES: Bring me those scissors.

Do not touch that burner!

An *exclamatory* sentence, the last classification, shows strong emotion.

An **exclamatory** sentence conveys strong emotion and ends with an exclamation mark.

The first three examples that follow show sentences that would normally be considered declarative, interrogative, and imperative. They are considered exclamatory sentences here, however, because their intent is to express strong emotion. The third sentence might also be called imperative since an imperative sentence can end with an exclamation mark. The last sentence is purely exclamatory, with an understood subject and verb.

EXAMPLES: I won!

Do you believe that!

Come quickly!

Fire!

EXERCISE A: Identifying the Four Functions of Sentences. Identify the function of each of the following sentences as *declarative, interrogative, imperative,* or *exclamatory*. Then indicate on your paper the punctuation that you should use at the end of each sentence.

1. This area gets poor television reception
2. Do you want to leave Friday afternoon or Saturday morning
3. I don't need an operation after all
4. My friend does not care for diet drinks
5. When will the loan be ready
6. Fill the car with gas on your way home
7. I wonder where my turtle has gone
8. Ask Mindy to stop by after school
9. The sunset cast a rosy glow on the walls of the building
10. Stop reading my personal mail

EXERCISE B: Writing Sentences with Different Functions. Write a sentence for each of the following numbers, using the subject and function indicated. For example, the first sentence should be a *declarative* sentence about *wild animals*.

	Declarative	Interrogative	Imperative	Exclamatory
Wild Animals	1	2	3	4
Holidays	5	6	7	8
School Activities	9	10	11	12

■ Hard-to-Find Subjects

Most sentences have subjects that can easily be found; some, however, because of their function, contain subjects that are more elusive. Each of the four sentence functions deserves individual examination. In all of the following examples, subjects are underlined once, verbs twice.

Subjects in Declarative Sentences. In all but two kinds of declarative sentences, the subject comes in the normal position before the verb. The exceptions are sentences beginning with *there* or *here* and sentences that are inverted for emphasis.

When *there* or *here* is found at the beginning of a declarative sentence, it is often mistaken for the subject.

There or *here* is never the subject of a sentence.

The only exception to this rule occurs when *there* or *here* is referred to as a word, as in the rule itself. Otherwise, in normal use, these words are usually adverbs that modify the verb by pointing out *where*. Occasionally, *there* may be used merely to start the sentence and have no adverbial function at all. In this case, *there* is an *expletive*.

In the following examples, note the position of the subjects—after the verbs. If you have difficulty locating subjects in such sentences, try rearranging the sentence logically in your mind so that *there* or *here* comes after the verb. If *there* sounds awkward after the verb, it may be an expletive, as in the last two examples in the chart. Then simply drop *there* from the sentence before rearranging the words.

Sentences Beginning with *There* or *Here*	Sentences Rearranged with Subject Before Verb
There <u>are</u> the lost <u>keys</u>.	The lost <u>keys</u> <u>are</u> there.
Here <u>is</u> the <u>ticket</u> for your trip.	The <u>ticket</u> for your trip <u>is</u> here.
There <u>is</u> no <u>money</u> available.	No <u>money</u> <u>is</u> available.
There <u>may be</u> unknown <u>forces</u> at work.	Unknown <u>forces</u> <u>may be</u> at work.

The other kind of declarative sentence that varies from the usual subject-verb order is used to put special emphasis on the subject by deliberately placing it at the end.

In some declarative sentences, the subject follows the verb in order to receive greater emphasis.

Such inverted sentences usually begin with prepositional phrases. Starting in this way and shifting the words found at the beginning of the sentence to the middle or to the end often tends to make the subject more visible.

Sentences Inverted for Emphasis	Sentences Rephrased with Subject Before Verb
Beneath the pillows of the couch <u>smoldered</u> the <u>cigarette</u>.	The <u>cigarette</u> <u>smoldered</u> beneath the pillows of the couch.
Around the corner <u>careened</u> the speeding <u>car</u>.	The speeding <u>car</u> <u>careened</u> around the corner.

Subjects in Interrogative Sentences.   In some interrogative sentences, the subject comes before the verb in a normal sequence and, thus, is easily identified.

EXAMPLE: Which <u>car</u> <u>gets</u> the best mileage?

Often, however, the sequence is naturally inverted, making the subject in an interrogative sentence more difficult to locate.

In interrogative sentences, the subject often follows the verb.

An inverted interrogative sentence can begin with a verb, a helping verb, or one of the following words: *what, which, whose, who, when, why, where,* or *how.* To locate the subject in a question, mentally rephrase the sentence to make it declarative. Examine the following examples, which show how to shift the word order.

Questions	Rephrased as Statements
<u>Is</u> the <u>zoo</u> open in the morning?	The <u>zoo</u> <u>is</u> open in the morning.
<u>Do</u> <u>they</u> <u>own</u> that house?	<u>They</u> <u>do own</u> that house.
When <u>will</u> the <u>coffee</u> <u>be done</u>?	The <u>coffee</u> <u>will be done</u> when.

Subjects in Imperative Sentences.   The subject of an imperative sentence is usually implied rather than specifically stated.

In imperative sentences, the subject is understood to be *you*.

Notice in the following chart that the subjects of the imperative sentences on the left are not directly expressed. The examples on the right illustrate where the subjects are understood to occur in the sentences.

Imperative Sentences	With Understood *You* Added
First <u>draw</u> a horizontal line.	First (<u>you</u>) <u>draw</u> a horizontal line.
After the movie, <u>come</u> home right away.	After the movie, (<u>you</u>) <u>come</u> home right away.
Loretta, <u>show</u> me your new hat.	Loretta, (<u>you</u>) <u>show</u> me your new hat.

In the last example, notice that *Loretta,* the name of the person being addressed, is not the subject of the sentence. The subject is still understood to be *you.*

Subjects in Exclamatory Sentences.   Some exclamatory sentences follow the same word order as interrogative and imperative sentences do.

In an exclamatory sentence, the subject may come after the verb or may be understood to be *you*.

To find the subject in most exclamatory sentences, simply follow the same techniques that you would for finding subjects in interrogative or imperative sentences.

EXAMPLES: How <u>could</u> I <u>have known</u>! (I <u>could have known</u> how.)

Be still! ([<u>You</u>] <u>be</u> still.)

Some exclamatory sentences may be so elliptical that both their subject and verb may be understood. For such sentences you will have to use your common sense and determine the unstated subject (and verb) from context.

Exclamatory Sentences with Understood Subjects and Verbs	With Understood Parts Added
Snake!	(<u>You</u>) <u>watch out</u> for the snake!
More pay!	<u>We</u> <u>demand</u> more pay!

EXERCISE C: **Locating Hard-to-Find Subjects.** Each of the following sentences contains a subject that either follows its verb or is understood. Copy each sentence onto your paper, adding words or rephrasing it to make the subject appear before its verb. Then underline the subject once and the verb twice.

1. Finish your chores first.
2. Where did the customer go? ˙
3. Off to the left sat the expectant hunter.
4. Here is the screwdriver from the tool chest.
5. Avalanche!
6. Call the store before closing time.
7. At what time do the gates close?
8. Hooray, the last day of school!
9. Bring the dictionaries to this room.
10. There sits a grand old gentleman.

APPLICATION: **Writing Different Kinds of Sentences with Hard-to-Find Subjects.** Write a sentence following each of these directions. Underline your subjects once and your verbs twice.
Answers will vary; samples given for first two.
1. Write a declarative sentence beginning with *here*.
2. Write a declarative sentence beginning with *there*.
3. Write a declarative sentence that has its subject at the end.
4. Write an interrogative sentence beginning with a verb.
5. Write an interrogative sentence beginning with *will*.
6. Write an interrogative sentence beginning with *what*.
7. Write an imperative sentence with a caret (⌃) for *you*.
8. Write an imperative sentence naming the person addressed.
9. Write an exclamatory sentence beginning with *what*
10. Write an exclamatory sentence with a caret for *you*.

3.3 Complements

The word *complement* normally means "that which completes or brings to perfection." Many things in the world are complete in themselves; others need complements before they are considered complete or perfect. The same is true of sentences. In some, the meaning is complete when it contains no more than a subject and a verb with perhaps some modifiers, as in "I laughed" or "I laughed whole heartedly." In other sentences, however, the verb needs more than modifiers to complete the meaning of the sentence, as in "The storm definitely ruined ..." or "The marathon <u>runners</u> <u>are</u> ..." These sentences require a complement to finish the meaning of the verb: for example, "The <u>storm</u> definitely <u>ruined</u> the crop"; "The marathon <u>runners</u> <u>are</u> exhausted."

> A **complement** is a word or group of words that completes the meaning of the predicate of a sentence.

There are five different kinds of complements in English: *direct objects, indirect objects, objective complements, predicate nominatives,* and *predicate adjectives.* The last two are often grouped together as *subject complements.*

This section will explain how each complement works to complete the meaning of sentences. It will also show you how to recognize the different complements in sentences.

■ Direct Objects

Found only with transitive verbs, direct objects complete the verb by receiving action from it.

> A **direct object** is a noun, pronoun, or group of words acting as a noun that receives the action of a transitive verb.

EXAMPLES: <u>We</u> <u>baked</u> a c^{DO}ake.

         I <u>invited</u> her to the party.

To find a direct object in a sentence, ask *What?* or *Whom?* after an action verb. If you find no answer, the verb is intransitive and has no direct object. (See Section 1.2 for more about transitive and intransitive verbs.)

EXAMPLES: I <u>was reading</u> the book until midnight. (Was reading *what?* Answer: *book*)

        A <u>hornet</u> <u>stung</u> him on the back of his neck. (Stung *whom?* Answer: *him*)

        The <u>car</u> <u>crashed</u> into a tree. (Crashed *what?* Answer: none; the verb is intransitive.)

In the last example, *tree* is the object of the preposition *into.* It is not the direct object. Remember that an object of a preposition can never be a direct object.

Also remember that a verb may have more than one direct object, called a *compound direct object*. If a sentence contains a compound direct object, asking *What*? or *Whom*? after the action verb will give you two or more answers.

EXAMPLES: We <u>baked</u> a cake and two loaves of bread.
                    DO   DO

I <u>invited</u> both Donna and her to the party.

EXERCISE A: Recognizing Direct Objects. Some of the following sentences contain direct objects and some do not. For those sentences containing a direct object, write the verb and the direct object on your paper. For those sentences without a direct object, write only the verb. Some sentences have compound direct objects.

1. Many mystery authors develop memorable and lasting characters in their books.
2. For instance, Ellery Queen and Hercule Poirot have fought evil in novel after novel.
3. Sherlock Holmes helped Scotland Yard with many unsolved crimes.
4. In 1930, Agatha Christie's Miss Marple solved her first case.
5. Readers still love Perry Mason and Lieutenant Tragg.
6. With unbelievable consistency, Perry Mason uncovered the vital clues.
7. Dorothy Gilman introduced her heroine only a few years ago.
8. In Gilman's book, Mrs. Pollifax, a grandmother, applies for a job as a spy with the CIA.
9. Almost every young person has read the Nancy Drew and Hardy Boys mysteries.
10. Recently, the movie *Murder by Death* lampooned many of the most beloved fictional detectives.

■ Indirect Objects

Indirect objects are found in sentences already containing a direct object.

An **indirect object** is a noun or pronoun that comes after an action verb and before a direct object. Its purpose is to name the person or thing that something is given to or done for.

An indirect object is usually found after such verbs as *ask, bring, buy, give, lend, make, promise, show, teach, tell,* or *write*.

EXAMPLES:
> I <u>taught</u> Randy the alphabet.
> (IO: Randy, DO: alphabet)
>
> We <u>gave</u> the car a thorough cleaning.
> (IO: car, DO: cleaning)

To find the indirect object in a sentence, first make certain that the sentence contains a direct object. Then ask *To or for whom?* or *To or for what?* after the verb and direct object.

EXAMPLES:
> I <u>brought</u> her the slides. (Brought slides *to or for whom?* Answer: *her*)
>
> I <u>gave</u> the plant some water. (Gave water *to or for what?* Answer: *plant*)

Like direct objects, indirect objects may be compound.

EXAMPLE:
> I <u>lent</u> Richard and Tom my tent.
> (IO: Richard, IO: Tom, DO: tent)

To avoid confusing an indirect object with a direct object, remember to ask yourself the right questions. First ask *What?* or *Whom?* after the action verb to find a direct object. Then ask *To or for whom?* or *To or for what?* after the verb and direct object to find an indirect object.

EXAMPLE:
> Stephanie <u>will send</u> me a postcard from Egypt.
> (To whom? me — IO; What? postcard — DO)

In identifying indirect objects, it is also important to remember that an indirect object is never the object of the preposition *to* or *for* and that an indirect object never follows a direct object.

EXAMPLES:
> She <u>brought</u> the sweater for her sister.
> (DO: sweater, Obj of Prep: sister)
>
> She <u>brought</u> her sister a sweater.
> (IO: sister, DO: sweater)

Sister does not function as an indirect object in the first sentence. Only when the word is shifted to the position before the direct object and when the preposition *for* is dropped does *sister* become an indirect object.

EXERCISE B: **Recognizing Indirect Objects.** Two items in each of the following sentences are underlined. Write each item on your paper and identify it as a *direct object, indirect object,* or *object of a preposition.*

EXAMPLE: Frank gave his <u>friends</u> <u>vegetables</u> from his garden.

friends—indirect object
vegetables—direct object

1. The employee told her <u>boss</u> a blatant <u>lie</u>.
2. We sang the book's <u>praises</u> to our <u>friends</u>.
3. When will Lloyd buy his <u>sister</u> a birthday <u>present</u>?
4. The courier delivered the <u>package</u> to <u>him</u>.
5. They drove over the <u>hills</u> and into the <u>village</u>.
6. Terry taught <u>herself</u> <u>Spanish</u>.
7. We wrote <u>Aunt Emma</u> and <u>Uncle Alvin</u> a letter.
8. I ordered <u>soup</u> and <u>salad</u> with my dinner.
9. Show the department store <u>clerk</u> that faded <u>shirt</u>.
10. We cataloged the <u>books</u> for the <u>library</u>.

■ Objective Complements

Objective complements, like indirect objects, occur only in sentences that already contain a direct object. As its name suggests, an objective complement completes the meaning of the direct object in a sentence.

> An **objective complement** is an adjective, noun, or group of words acting as a noun that follows a direct object and describes or renames it.

Objective complements are found only after such verbs as *appoint, call, consider, elect, label, make, name,* or *think.*

EXAMPLES: We <u>appointed</u> Toby secretary.

They <u>named</u> the baby Dawn.

I <u>consider</u> her the most qualified candidate for the Senate seat.

As the examples illustrate, the sentences almost seem to have two direct objects; however, the objective complement renames or describes the real direct object.

To determine whether a word is an objective complement, say the verb and direct object, and then ask *What*?

EXAMPLE: The <u>professor</u> <u>called</u> the student brilliant. (Called the student *what*? Answer; *brilliant*)

DO

As with the other sentence parts, an objective complement can be compound.

EXAMPLE: The <u>professor</u> <u>called</u> the student brilliant and witty.

DO   OC   OC

EXERCISE C: Using Objective Complements. The following sentences are missing objective complements. Copy the sentences onto your paper, adding appropriate objective complements of the types indicated.

1. My grandfather thinks me <u>(adjective)</u>.
2. Yesterday, the committee appointed Harold <u>(noun)</u>.
3. The Board of Trustees named the new building <u>(noun)</u>.
4. The theater critics thought the stand-in <u>(adjective)</u> and <u>(adjective)</u>.
5. I consider my dog <u>(noun)</u>.
6. The community elected Mr. Whipple <u>(noun)</u>.
7. The buttermilk in the batter makes the cake <u>(adjective)</u> and <u>(adjective)</u>.
8. I hereby designate this spot <u>(noun)</u>.
9. I labeled the container <u>(noun)</u>.
10. Pat nominated herself <u>(noun)</u>.

■ Subject Complements

Direct objects, indirect objects, and objective complements follow action verbs. Linking verbs are followed by subject complements. (See Section 1.2 for more about linking verbs.)

A **subject complement** is a noun, pronoun, or adjective that follows a linking verb and tells something about the subject of the sentence.

There are two kinds of subject complements: *predicate nominatives* and *predicate adjectives*.

Predicate Nominatives.   The words *nominative*, *noun*, and *pronoun* all come from the same Latin word, *nomen*, meaning "name." Knowing this common derivation can help you remember what a predicate nominative is.

A **predicate nominative** is a noun or pronoun that follows a linking verb and renames, identifies, or explains the subject of the sentence.

In the following examples, notice that the subject and predicate nominative are merely different words for the same person, place, or thing. The linking verb acts as an equal sign between them.

EXAMPLES: Ms. Casey <u>became</u> an accou^{PN}ntant.

My <u>choice</u> for the job <u>is</u> ^{PN}he.

<u>Robert Penn Warren</u> <u>is</u> a well-known po^{PN}et, nov^{PN}elist, and

^{PN}essayist.

As the last example shows, a predicate nominative, like any other sentence part, can be compound.
   Predicate Adjectives.   As its name indicates, a predicate adjective is not a noun or pronoun, but an adjective.

A **predicate adjective** is an adjective that follows a linking verb and describes the subject of the sentence.

In the following examples, notice that the predicate adjectives refer to the subjects by describing them. Notice also that the predicate adjective in the second sentence is compound.

EXAMPLES: The sanded <u>plank</u> of wood still <u>feels</u> ^{PA}rough.

Today the <u>waves</u> <u>seemed</u> ^{PA}wild and ^{PA}angry.

EXERCISE D: Identifying Subject Complements. Each of the following sentences contains a subject complement. Some are compound. Write each complement on your paper and identify it as a *predicate nominative* or *predicate adjective*.

1. Despite the frost, the fruit trees remained healthy.
2. The student will become either an accountant or a banker.
3. The blister grew more painful.
4. The house looked a mess after the party.

5. Through the early morning mist, the fog horn sounded mournful and distant.
6. Cockroaches are pests in many households around the world.
7. The man seems a competent violinist.
8. The baking bread smelled delicious.
9. The numbers on the calculator appeared faint.
10. At the beginning of the race the competitors felt exuberant and confident.

APPLICATION: Using Complements in Your Own Writing. Recall a memorable incident in your life and write a paragraph or two describing it and explaining why it is meaningful to you. Make a conscious effort to use each of the five kinds of complements at least once. Be prepared to identify them in your sentences.

Reviewing Basic Sentence Patterns 3.4

The simplest sentence pattern has a subject and a verb. Subjects, verbs, and the different kinds of complements comprise five other basic sentence patterns. These kernel patterns are the foundation on which more complicated structures can be built. This section will review these basic patterns, which were introduced in the earlier sections of this chapter, to help you increase your awareness of the range of expression available to you in English.

■ Five Basic Patterns

Sentences with complements follow set patterns.

In the English language, subjects, verbs, and complements follow five **basic sentence patterns.**

Except when they act as predicate adjectives or objective complements, adjectives are never part of a sentence's basic pattern. Neither are adverbs, conjunctions, interjections, or prepositional phrases. As you study the examples in the following charts, mentally eliminate all of these additional words. The skeleton of the sentences will then become more visible to you.

The Pattern Without Complements.   As just mentioned, the simplest pattern for an English sentence is a subject followed by a verb. In this pattern, the verb will always be an intransitive verb.

| SENTENCE PATTERN WITHOUT COMPLEMENTS ||
Pattern	Examples
S-V	The <u>dog</u> <u>growled</u> at the stranger in the red dress. Our <u>guests</u> <u>are</u> here.

The Three Patterns with Transitive Verbs.   A transitive action verb is always followed by a direct object. As noted in Section 3.3, a sentence with a direct object may also contain an indirect object before the direct object or an objective complement after the direct object.

| SENTENCE PATTERNS WITH TRANSITIVE VERBS ||
Pattern	Examples
S-AV-DO	<u>Kelly</u> <u>read</u> the book quickly. (DO) <u>I</u> <u>hit</u> him on the jaw. (DO)
S-AV-IO-DO	Mr. <u>Melko</u> <u>brought</u> me the survey results. (IO, DO) <u>I</u> <u>gave</u> the room a new coat of paint. (IO, DO)
S-AV-DO-OC	The <u>newspaper</u> <u>called</u> the swimmer a champion. (DO, OC) The book's <u>ending</u> <u>made</u> him sad. (DO, OC)

The Two Patterns with Linking Verbs.   A linking verb is always followed by a subject complement—either a predicate nominative or a predicate adjective.

SENTENCE PATTERNS WITH LINKING VERBS	
Pattern	Examples
S-LV-PN	That <u>man</u> <u>is</u> the thief! [PN] <u>One</u> of the finalists <u>is</u> he. [PN]
S-LV-PA	The barbecue <u>coals</u> <u>are</u> hot. [PA] The <u>singer</u> <u>sounds</u> flat. [PA]

Patterns with Compound Parts. Any of these basic patterns can be expanded by making one or more of the sentence parts compound.

EXERCISE A: **Identifying Basic Sentence Patterns.** Copy the following sentences onto your paper, underlining the subjects once and the verbs twice, and circling the complements. Then, using the abbreviations introduced in the charts, identify the sentence patterns. Be alert for compounds.

1. The breakfast cook scrambled my eggs.
2. The men and women in the audience laughed appreciatively.
3. I named my new car Otto.
4. The toddler looked happy and well-fed.
5. The drizzle ended in the early afternoon.
6. Rabbits can be good pets for children.
7. We made the deserted house clean and habitable.
8. After hours of work, I promised myself a midday break.
9. Skunks smell offensive to most people.
10. Today we washed the windows and vacuumed the rugs.

APPLICATION: **Writing Sentences in a Variety of Patterns.**
Construct sentences with the following patterns. Underline your subjects once and your verbs twice and label your complements.

1. S-V
2. S-AV-DO
3. S-AV-IO-DO
4. S-AV-DO-OC
5. S-LV-PN
6. S-LV-PA
7. S-S-AV-DO-OC-DO-OC
8. S-AV-IO-IO-DO
9. S-LV-PA-LV-PA
10. S-S-AV-IO-DO-AV-DO-OC

3.5 Diagraming Basic Parts of Sentences

Diagrams of sentences are like blueprints. They can help you visualize the structure of sentences. This section will show you how to diagram basic sentences.

■ Subjects and Verbs, Adjectives and Adverbs

Learning to diagram sentences begins with learning to diagram the subject-verb sentence pattern and one-word modifiers.

Subjects and Verbs.   To diagram the most basic subject-verb sentence pattern, draw a horizontal line and place the subject on the left and the verb on the right. Separate the two with a vertical line.

EXAMPLE: Jerome Martin would have frowned.

| Jerome Martin | would have frowned |

Adjectives and Adverbs.   Adjectives and adverbs are placed on slanted lines below the words they modify.

EXAMPLE: The big fly landed there.

Always diagram articles (*a, an, the*), pronouns used as adjectives (*his, her, our,* and so on), and possessive nouns (such as *Karen's*) on a slanted line.

When an adverb modifies an adjective or another adverb, it is written below the word it modifies and is connected to the other word by a perpendicular line.

EXAMPLE: The very delicious dessert was prepared quite quickly.

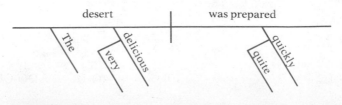

EXERCISE A: Diagraming Subjects and Verbs, Adjectives and Adverbs. Diagram each of the following sentences.

1. Harry skates well.
2. The tiny dancer fell down.
3. My brother draws quite professionally.
4. The huge dog always barks.
5. A very enthusiastic crowd will clap loudly.

■ Compound Sentence Parts

Compounds are usually joined by conjunctions. In a diagram, a conjunction is written on a dotted line.

Compound Subjects and Verbs. To indicate a compound subject or compound verb, divide the horizontal line into as many parts as needed. Indicate the conjunction with a vertical dotted line. Notice both the position of the correlative conjunction *neither . . . nor* and the position of the helping verb *were* in the following example.

EXAMPLE: Neither the forks nor the knives were washed, sorted, and put away.

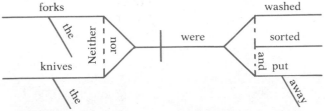

When placing modifiers in sentences containing compound subjects and verbs, be careful to position the modifier with the word it modifies. Notice in the following examples that *the* and *today*, which modify *both* of the compound elements, are each drawn on lines descending from the diagram's main line.

EXAMPLE: The frequent yawns and loud sighs could be heard clearly.

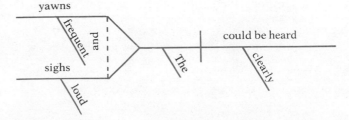

EXAMPLE: Today, we ran hard but rested often.

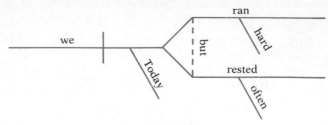

Compound Adjectives and Adverbs.   The following example illustrates how compound adjectives and adverbs are diagramed.

EXAMPLE: The daring and exciting acrobat fell suddenly but safely.

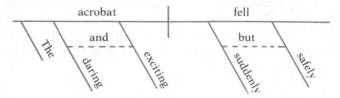

EXERCISE B: **Diagraming Compound Parts of Speech.** The following sentences contain compounds. Diagram each sentence.

1. My teacher and her husband live here.
2. The burglar entered quickly but silently.
3. The bright and witty entertainer will perform tonight.
4. The frightened squirrels ran away and hid.
5. The sick child was feverishly tossing and turning.

■ Sentences with Hard-to-Find Subjects

Some sentences vary from the usual subject-verb sentence pattern. Three of these include imperative sentences, interrogative sentences, and sentences that begin with *here* or *there*.

Imperative Sentences.   When *you* is understood to be the subject of an imperative sentence it is written in parentheses.

EXAMPLE: Go home.

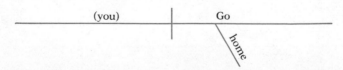

Interrogative Sentences.   In interrogative sentences, the subject often comes after the verb or between the parts of a verb phrase. In diagraming, however, the order reverts to the normal subject-verb pattern.

EXAMPLE: Will Steve play?

Steve	Will play

Sentences Beginning with *There* or *Here*.   When *there* or *here* functions as an adverb, put the word on a slanted line beneath the verb.

EXAMPLE: Here is your coat.

If *there* is an expletive used merely to begin the sentence, write it on a horizontal line over the subject.

EXAMPLE: There is a good restaurant nearby.

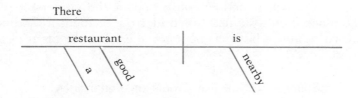

NOTE ABOUT EXPLETIVE STYLE: The placement of the expletive is also used for interjections and nouns of direct address.

EXAMPLE: Well, John, are you going?

Well	

John	

you	are going

EXERCISE C: Diagraming Sentences with Hard-to-Find Subjects. Diagram each of the following sentences on your paper.

1. There was an explosion nearby.
2. Allan, begin immediately.
3. Ouch, here is the painful splinter!
4. Will Lee and Tim exercise tomorrow?
5. Here comes Peter now.

■ Complements

Since complements complete verbs, they are placed on the predicate side of the diagram.

Direct Objects.   Place the direct object on the main horizontal line following the verb. Separate the direct object from the verb with a short vertical line.

EXAMPLE: I stapled the papers.

If a compound direct object occurs, diagram it as you would a compound subject or compound verb. In addition, remember, if a word modifies only one of the compound elements, place it on a slanted line under the element it modifies. If a word modifies both elements, place it on the stem of the diagram.

EXAMPLE: Stan counted the many coins and dollar bills.

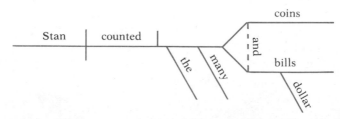

Indirect Objects.   Indirect objects are located directly under the verb on a short horizontal line extending from a slanted line.

EXAMPLE: He lent me a cassette tape.

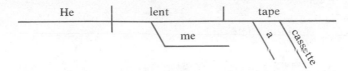

Diagram a compound indirect object according to the following example.

EXAMPLE: She gave Vic and Marilyn her business card.

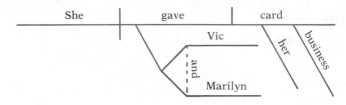

Objective Complements. Objective complements sit on the base line after the direct object. A short slanted line pointing toward the direct object separates them.

EXAMPLE: The club elected her president.

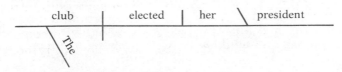

Diagram compound objective complements according to the following example.

EXAMPLE: We considered him kind but very foolish.

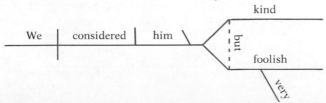

Subject Complements. Both subject complements—predicate nominatives and predicate adjectives—are diagramed in the same manner. Place them on the base line following the verb. Separate them from the verb with a line slanting toward the subject.

EXAMPLE: The puppy felt soft.

The format for diagraming compound subject complements is just like that for direct objects.

EXERCISE D: Diagraming Complements. Construct sentences with the following patterns. Include appropriate adjectives and adverbs. Then diagram the sentences you have written.

1. S-V-DO
2. S-V-IO-DO
3. S-S-V-IO-DO
4. S-V-DO-OC-OC
5. S-V-PA-PA

APPLICATION: Diagraming Different Kinds of Sentences. The following sentences use all of the different diagraming skills introduced in this section. Diagram each sentence on your paper.

1. Are Henry and Mike practicing their tournament speeches?
2. Poison oak and wildflowers were growing together.
3. Tomorrow, Kevin and I will sail, fish, and hike.
4. The granite mountain jutted majestically skyward.
5. Carlos, feed that hungry cat right now.
6. Alas, there is no time left.
7. My dear aunt left me several thousand dollars.
8. The old bridge appears both too narrow and too unsafe.
9. The delicate but colorful butterfly sat perfectly still.
10. My manager thinks me very efficient and quite reliable.

Phrases and Clauses

A skillful dancer can perform more than elementary footwork, and an accomplished musician can play more than simple scales and melodies. Similarly, a proficient writer knows how to venture beyond the comfortable haven of basic sentence patterns. This chapter will describe the various kinds of phrases and clauses that you can use to expand the basic patterns and to achieve greater precision and vigor in your writing style.

Prepositional and Appositive Phrases 4.1

One-word adjectives and adverbs can add detail and color to writing. Sometimes, however, they cannot convey all the ideas and relationships that a writer needs to express. In these cases, *phrases* can often help the writer overcome the inadequacies of the one-word modifiers.

> A **phrase** is a group of words, without a subject and verb, that functions in a sentence as one part of speech.

Two types of phrases frequently used to extend sentences are *prepositional phrases* and *appositive phrases*.

■ Prepositional Phrases

In Section 1.4, a prepositional phrase was described as a preposition followed by a noun or pronoun called the object of the preposition. The object may be compound and may have modifiers.

EXAMPLES:

Prep   Obj   Obj
near the table and chairs

Prep   Obj
after a cool, refreshing swim

This section will show how prepositional phrases function as either adjectives or adverbs within sentences.

Adjectival Phrases. A prepositional phrase that describes a noun or pronoun is adjectival.

> An **adjectival phrase** is a prepositional phrase that modifies a noun or pronoun by telling what kind or which one.

Since nouns and pronouns serve in sentences as subjects, direct objects, indirect objects, objective complements, predicate nominatives, or objects of prepositions, any of these sentence parts can be modified by adjectival phrases.

EXAMPLES:

The painting *in the corner* is my favorite. (*Which* one?)

We flew a plane *with twin engines*. (*What kind* of plane?)

I sent my cousin *in Detroit* some photographs of us. (*Which* cousin?)

The dictator declared himself president *for life*. (*What kind* of president?)

A narwhal is a whalelike mammal *with a long tusk* *on its forehead*. (*What kind* of mammal? *What kind* of tusk?)

Sometimes more than one adjectival phrase may modify the same word.

EXAMPLE:

The person *on the corner* *with his hand raised* is my brother.

Adverbial Phrases. A prepositional phrase that acts as an adverb is adverbial.

An **adverbial phrase** is a prepositional phrase that modifies a verb, adjective, or adverb by pointing out where, when, in what manner, or to what extent.

Notice in the following examples how adverbial phrases answer any one of the four questions for adverbs.

MODIFYING A VERB: We sat *on the park bench.* (Sat *where?*)

He should arrive *within the hour.* (Arrive *when?*)

Will you dance *with me?* (Dance *in what manner?*)

Except for the border, the quilt was finished. (Was finished *to what extent?*)

MODIFYING AN ADJECTIVE: I am frightened *of the dark.* (Frightened *in what manner?*)

MODIFYING AN ADVERB: He left early *in the morning.* (Early *when?*)

Sentences can contain more than one adverbial phrase, and all of them can modify the same word.

EXAMPLE: *During the cool morning hours,* we climbed *to the summit.* (Climbed *when?* Climbed *where?*)

EXERCISE A: Identifying Adjectival and Adverbial Phrases. The sentences in the following paragraphs include prepositional phrases. Next to the appropriate number on your paper, write the prepositional phrases contained in each sentence. After each phrase write *adjectival* or *adverbial.* Be prepared to identify the word each phrase modifies.

(1) Charles Darwin introduced the theory of the survival of the fittest. (2) He believed that either animals adapt to their environment or they perish because of it. (3) The anteater with its almost laughable appearance is one beast that appears to have adapted extremely well. (4) These animals, which live throughout Central and South America, exist almost solely on

ants and termites. (5) The anteater's snout can smell the insects from a distance of twenty feet. (6) Since the beasts suffer from nearsightedness, this highly developed sense of smell is important to their survival. (7) In addition, on their front feet, anteaters are equipped with sharp claws that may grow to four inches in length. (8) With these tools, anteaters dig up and expose the anthills or termite nests. (9) Finally, their sticky tongues can be extended over two feet. (10) This helps anteaters consume thirty thousand ants during a single day.

■ Appositives and Appositive Phrases

The word *appositive* comes from a Latin verb meaning "to put near or next to." Although they are not modifiers, appositives and appositive phrases are similar to adjectival phrases in that they add detail to nouns and pronouns.

Appositives.   Following its definition, an appositive is a word placed "near or next to" another word.

> An **appositive** is a noun or pronoun placed after another noun or pronoun to identify, rename, or explain it.

Notice in the following examples how the appositive represents the same person or thing as the word it follows. Its purpose, however, is to add additional information to the preceding idea.

EXAMPLES: I will win the race with my best stroke, *the butterfly*.

His favorite flowers, *snapdragons*, grew everywhere in the garden.

Be alert when punctuating appositives. If an appositive contains *nonessential* material (material that can be removed from the sentence without altering its meaning), set the appositive off from the rest of the sentence with commas or other appropriate punctuation, as in the preceding examples. If, on the other hand, the material is *essential* to the meaning of the sentence, no punctuation is necessary.

EXAMPLES: The short story *"Fire and Ice"* has a sad ending.

My brother *Howard* left for Europe today.

(See Section 13.2 for more about punctuating appositives.) Note also that the terms *restrictive* and *nonrestrictive* are sometimes used instead of *essential* and *nonessential*.)

Appositive Phrases. An *appositive phrase* is simply an appositive with one or more modifiers.

> An **appositive phrase** is a noun or pronoun with modifiers, placed next to a noun or pronoun to add information and details.

The modifiers in an appositive phrase can be adjectives, adjectival phrases, or other words that function as adjectives.

EXAMPLES: My cat, *a champion in all respects*, has a litter of kittens due soon.

That hat, *the navy blue one with white edging*, would match my ski jacket.

Appositives and appositive phrases can add information to almost any noun or pronoun in a sentence. The following examples show some of the ways appositive phrases can be used.

WITH A SUBJECT: Mrs. Ellingson, *an expert on career planning*, spoke to the entire assembly.

WITH A DIRECT OBJECT: I won the door prize, *a fifty dollar gift certificate*.

WITH AN INDIRECT OBJECT: I sold Dean, *my friend's older brother*, my old set of golf clubs.

WITH AN OBJECTIVE COMPLEMENT: We stained the paneling walnut—*my favorite wood grain*.

WITH A PREDICATE NOMINATIVE: Our new automobile is a green station wagon—*a family car*.

WITH AN OBJECT OF A PREPOSITION: I bought a stack of books, *all Gothic mysteries*, to read on vacation.

Both appositives and appositive phrases can begin with the word *not* in order to set up a dramatic contrast.

EXAMPLE: I thought you were my friends, *not my enemies!*

Like other sentence parts appositives and appositive phrases can also be compound.

EXAMPLES: The dry ingredients—*baking soda, salt, and flour*—were mixed first.

Paul, *an Eagle Scout and varsity athlete*, received the Outstanding Student award this year.

Be alert for opportunities to use appositives and appositive phrases to rid your writing of unnecessary words. Often, two sentences can be combined into one by condensing the information from one sentence into an appositive.

TWO SENTENCES: The professor is a world-renowned expert on medieval history.

He lectured today on the construction of castles during this period.

SENTENCE WITH APPOSITIVE PHRASE: The professor, *a world-renowned expert on medieval history*, lectured today on the construction of castles during this period.

EXERCISE B: Identifying Appositives and Appositive Phrases.

Write each appositive or appositive phrase from the following sentences on your paper.

1. That tent over there, the large one with orange trim, looks right for our family.
2. Several ports—St. Thomas, Grenada, and Caracas—provided good souvenir shopping.
3. The soup of the day is Manhattan clam chowder, a tomato-based soup.
4. The couple named the child Miley, an old family name.
5. The play *Morning's at Seven* kept us laughing continuously.
6. The children, not the teenagers, can get reduced air fares.
7. The road, really no more than a semi-paved trail, leads to the hunting lodge.
8. The clerk gave the two children, Dana and Connie, a piece of candy.

9. The young fruit trees were planted in special soil—a compost rich in nutrients.
10. I eat fresh fruit, my favorite breakfast food, every morning.

EXERCISE C: Using Appositives and Appositive Phrases in Sentences. Combine each of the following pairs of sentences by taking the information from one and turning it into an appositive or appositive phrase.

1. Mr. Kirk has been a mail carrier for twenty-five years. He will retire early next year.
2. Backpackers enjoy hiking into Desolation Valley. It is an uninhabited region filled with hundreds of lakes.
3. The tiny birds sat within two feet of the living room window. I think they were wrens.
4. We will visit several famous spots while staying in New York. They include the Empire State Building, Central Park, and the Statue of Liberty.
5. The king thoroughly enjoyed all seven courses of the royal banquet. He was a rotund little man with too many chins.

APPLICATION: Using Prepositional and Appositive Phrases in Sentences. Copy the following paragraph onto your paper, inserting the kind of phrase indicated in parentheses in each blank.

The circus began in a burst of song and color. Out came the clowns, (1) (appositive). They danced (2) (prepositional) and then played tricks (3) (prepositional). Next, the ringmaster, (4) (appositive), pointed (5) (prepositional). There, tightrope walkers balanced (6) (prepositional). They gave the audience, (7) (appositive), a wave from their lofty heights. Suddenly, two performers, (8) (appositive), lost their balance and fell (9) (prepositional). Luckily, they were not injured (10) (prepositional), for as the performers always say, the show must go on!

Verbal Phrases 4.2

The verb is a versatile part of speech. Besides its usual function in a sentence, it can also function as a noun, adjective, or adverb. When it functions as any of these parts of speech, it is called a verbal.

A **verbal** is a word derived from a verb but used as a noun, adjective, or adverb.

Verbals share two important characteristics with verbs: (1) Verbals may be modified by adverbs and adverbial phrases, and (2) they can have complements. When a verbal has a modifier or complement, it is known as a *verbal phrase*. This section will introduce the three kinds of verbals—participles, gerunds, and infinitives.

■ Participles and Participial Phrases

Many adjectives are actually verbals known as *participles*.

A **participle** is a form of a verb that acts as an adjective.

EXAMPLES: The *running* water caused a flood.

The *dreaded* fruit fly infiltrated the valley.

Forms of Participles.   There are three kinds of participles: *present participles*, *past participles*, and *perfect participles*. Study the following chart to see how each participle is formed. (See Section 6.1 for more about the forms of verbs and participles.)

Kind of Participle	Form	Examples
Present participle	Ends in *-ing*	It was a *taxing* day. The *smiling* child played in the mud.
Past participle	Usually ends in *-ed*, sometimes *-t*, *-en*, or another irregular ending	I drank *chilled* cider. Throw out that *broken* cup.
Perfect participle	Includes *having* or *having been* before a past participle	*Having rested*, I awoke refreshed. *Having been congratulated*, I felt proud.

As all of the examples in the preceding chart demonstrate, participles act like adjectives, answering the questions *Which one?* or *What kind?* about the noun or pronoun they modify. As the examples also show, most participles precede the word they describe.

Do not confuse a sentence's verb with a participle. Remember, always check the word's function in the sentence. If it expresses the action of the sentence, it is a verb; if it describes a noun or pronoun, it is a participle.

Functioning as a Verb	Functioning as a Participle
She *coveted* the ring.	The *coveted* ring was soon hers.
The accountant *swindles* his clients.	The *swindling* accountant was apprehended.

Participial Phrases.   When participles have complements or modifiers of their own, they become *participial phrases*.

A **participial phrase** is a participle that is modified by an adverb or adverbial phrase or that has a complement. The entire phrase acts as an adjective in a sentence.

The following examples illustrate some of the different kinds of modifiers and complements that a participial phrase may have. Notice that a participial phrase can either follow or precede the word it modifies.

WITH ADVERBS: The runner *sitting down over there* sprained his ankle.

WITH AN ADVERBIAL PHRASE: That bird *resting on the higher perch* has a thirty word vocabulary.

WITH A DIRECT OBJECT: *Tuning the radio*, I soon had a clear station.

In punctuating participial phrases, you must decide whether the information contained in the phrase is essential or nonessential material. A participial phrase that is nonessential to the basic meaning of a sentence is set off by commas, while one that is essential is not enclosed by punctuation.

Nonessential Participial Phrases	Essential Participial Phrases
Mark, *running with his scissors,* should be stopped.	The boy *running with those scissors* should be stopped.
Hello, Dolly!, written by Jerry Herman, was one of Broadway's most popular plays.	The musical *written by Jerry Herman* was one of Broadway's most popular plays.

See Section 13.2 for more information about punctuating participial phrases.

Nominative Absolutes. Participles contained in phrases grammatically separate from the rest of the sentence can show time, reason, or circumstance. These phrases are called *nominative absolutes.*

> A **nominative absolute** is a noun or pronoun followed by a participle or participial phrase that functions independently of the rest of the sentence.

As you examine the following examples, note the kind of information the nominative absolutes add to the sentences.

TIME: *One hour having elapsed,* we returned the call.

REASON: *The wizard's spell broken,* the people began the arduous task of rebuilding the village.

CIRCUMSTANCE: The boy could not reach the campsite, *his broken leg hurting him badly.*

Sometimes the participle *being* is understood rather than expressed in a nominative absolute. Each of the following sentences would normally be written without the word *being,* but the phrases would still be nominative absolutes.

EXAMPLES: *Our water (being) in short supply,* the grass in the lawn dried up.

The man sold us a new car, his profit (being) a tidy sum.

Be sure that you do not mistake a nominative absolute for the main subject and verb in a sentence. Since nominative absolutes are phrases, they cannot stand independently as complete sentences.

EXERCISE A: Recognizing Participles and Participial Phrases. Write the participle or participial phrase contained in each of the following sentences on your paper. Then indicate if it is *present*, *past*, or *perfect*.

1. Expecting good news, the student raced to the mailbox.
2. The slouching model soon found herself out of a job.
3. The witness protected by the two guards will be called to the stand soon.
4. I, having auditioned in the morning, waited anxiously for the results.
5. The soccer players, having grown faint from thirst, gratefully accepted the cold oranges.
6. We drink purified water in our home.
7. Famished from the exercises, the wrestler ate an entire pizza by himself.
8. The chef, having buttered the bread, warmed it in the oven.
9. Impeached by his dissatisfied constituents, the politician headed home in disgrace.
10. Hitting the shelf, I almost dislodged the jars of fruit.

EXERCISE B: Punctuating Participial Phrases. Copy the following sentences onto your paper, underlining each participial phrase. If the phrase is not essential to the meaning of the sentence, set it off with commas.

1. On the United States flag, the stars symbolizing the individual states currently total fifty.
2. The White House built on swamp land has sunk a quarter inch in thirty years.
3. A salami weighing 457 pounds was put on exhibit by the company.
4. After he was lost, a cat named Tiger traveled over 250 miles to reach his family.
5. Braille first introduced in 1825 provides a way for the blind to read.
6. A dance marathon lasting twenty-five weeks was finally stopped by the authorities.
7. Canada claimed by Cartier for France in 1534 is the second largest country in the world.

8. The Grand Old Opry featuring some of the best country singers attracts visitors from all over the United States.
9. Ships transporting grain and iron ore travel frequently along the Great Lakes.
10. The most intelligent person on record is a boy with an I.Q. measured at 210.

EXERCISE C: **Recognizing Nominative Absolutes.** Copy the following sentences onto your paper, underlining the subject once and the verb twice, and putting a box around the nominative absolute.

1. I collected on my roll of film, a week having gone by.
2. The day being too windy, we did not use our umbrellas.
3. I fixed dinner quickly, my stomach growling in anticipation.
4. The book being in great demand, a second printing was ordered.
5. The paint mixed, we dipped our brushes into it.

■ Gerunds and Gerund Phrases

When a verb ending in *-ing* functions as a noun, it is called a *gerund*.

A **gerund** is a form of a verb that acts as a noun.

EXAMPLES: *Swimming* is good exercise.

I admire her *singing*.

The Function of Gerunds in Sentences.   As nouns, gerunds can function in sentences in the same capacities as any other noun. The following chart illustrates some of these roles.

SOME USES OF GERUNDS IN SENTENCES	
As a Subject	*Painting* is a pleasant hobby.
As a Direct Object	I mastered *flying*.
As an Indirect Object	Mark Spitz gave *swimming* a new popularity.
As an Object of a Preposition	Pack carefully before *traveling*.

As a Predicate Nominative	The baby's newest skill is *crawling*.
As an Appositive	My new hobby, *golfing*, provides me with hours of relaxation.

Since verbs, participles, and gerunds all can end in *-ing*, distinguish between them by checking the word's use within the sentence.

AS PART OF A VERB PHRASE: The audience *is cheering*.

AS A PARTICIPLE: The singer enjoyed the *cheering* audience.

AS A GERUND (subject):   The *cheering* grew thunderously loud.

NOTE ABOUT GERUNDS AND POSSESSIVE PRONOUNS: Always use the possessive form of a personal pronoun before a gerund.

INCORRECT: We were annoyed by *them shouting*.

CORRECT: We were annoyed by *their shouting*.

Gerund Phrases.   Gerunds accompanied by modifiers or complements are called *gerund phrases*.

A **gerund phrase** is a gerund with modifiers or a complement, all acting together as a noun.

Examine the following gerund phrases to see some of the kinds of modifiers and complements they can contain.

GERUND PHRASES	
	Examples
Gerund with Adjectives	*His high-pitched, compulsive laughing* made me nervous.
Gerund with Adjectival Phrase	*Boasting about your successes* is not an endearing quality.
Gerund with Adverb	*Braking quickly* helped her avoid the collision.

Gerund with Adverbial Phrase	He made an art of *standing in place.*
Gerund with Direct Object	Mandy tried *erasing the computer's memory.*
Gerund with Indirect and Direct Objects	I suggested *lending her my dress.*

EXERCISE D: Identifying Gerunds and Gerund Phrases. Write the gerund or gerund phrase from each of the following sentences on your paper. Then identify its function as a *subject, direct object, indirect object, object of a preposition, predicate nominative,* or *appositive.*

1. Skating provides excellent exercise.
2. I just finished typing my term paper.
3. Sally wants a job in banking.
4. Compulsive gambling is a disease that is not easy to cure.
5. The artist has developed her natural gift, singing, exceptionally well.
6. One serious crime for hunters is poaching.
7. We finally stopped the bleeding from the cut in her leg.
8. Avoid mixing bleach with ammonia whenever you clean the house.
9. I became ill after eating the spoiled meat.
10. The clown's best trick was juggling.

■ Infinitives and Infinitive Phrases

A third type of verbal is the *infinitive.* Unlike participles and gerunds that act as only one part of speech, infinitives can function as three parts of speech.

An **infinitive** is a form of a verb that comes after the word *to* and acts as a noun, adjective, or adverb.

EXAMPLES: *To go* to Spain is my dream.

I ordered dinner *to go.*

She was happy *to go.*

Forms of Infinitives.   There are two kinds of infinitives: *present infinitives* and *perfect infinitives*. Study the following chart to see how each kind is formed. (See Section 6.1 for more information about the forms of verbs and infinitives.)

Kind of Infinitive	Form	Examples
Present infinitive	*To* plus the base form of a verb	I like *to laugh*. You need *to listen*.
Perfect infinitive	*To have* or *to have been* plus a past participle	I would have liked *to have succeeded*. She hoped *to have been elected*.

Do not confuse an infinitive with a prepositional phrase beginning with *to*. An infinitive will always be *to* plus a verb. A prepositional phrase beginning with *to* will end with a noun or pronoun.

INFINITIVES: to know, to spend

PREPOSITIONAL PHRASES: to me, to a resort

Sometimes, infinitives do not include the word *to*. After the verbs *dare*, *hear*, *help*, *let*, *make*, *please*, *see*, and *watch*, the *to* in an infinitive is usually understood rather than stated.

EXAMPLES: He didn't dare *move*.

She I have never heard her *sing*.

The Function of Infinitives in Sentences.   Since infinitives can function as nouns, adjectives, and adverbs, they can be used in almost any capacity in a sentence.

INFINITIVES USED AS NOUNS	
As a Subject	*To fly* scares many people.
As a Direct Object	With two weeks off, Nina planned *to relax*.
As a Predicate Nominative	This semester, all Joel wanted was *to pass*.

As an Object of a Preposition	The race was about *to start*.
As an Appositive	The suggestion, *to forfeit*, was not well received.

INFINITIVES USED AS MODIFIERS

As an Adjective	The whole team displayed an ardent desire *to participate.*
As an Adverb	The Golden Gate Bridge was a sight that was beautiful *to see.*

Infinitive Phrases.   Like other verbals, infinitives can be expanded into phrases.

An **infinitive phrase** is an infinitive with modifiers, a complement, or a subject, all acting together as a single part of speech.

The following examples show some of the ways infinitives can be expanded.

INFINITIVE PHRASES	
Infinitive with Adverb	Mr. Likins decided *to accept cheerfully.*
Infinitive with Adverbial Phrase	I like *to run in the morning.*
Infinitive with Direct Object	We decided *to phone the employment agency.*
Infinitive with Indirect and Direct Objects	Dr. Muench hurried *to buy her daughter a present.*
Infinitive with Subject and Complement	I wanted *the new student to be my friend.*

EXERCISE E: Identifying Infinitives and Infinitive Phrases. Write the infinitive or infinitive phrase from each of the following sentences on your paper. Then identify its part of speech as a *noun*, *adjective*, or *adverb*. If the infinitive or infinitive phrase is used as a noun, further identify its function as a *subject*, *direct object*, *predicate nominative*, *object of a preposition*, or *appositive*.

1. The bus to Houston is about to depart.
2. The doctor was known for her ability to perform complicated brain surgery.
3. The magician's greatest feat was to disappear in a puff of smoke.
4. The future is often unpleasant to contemplate.
5. I watched the soccer team play.
6. I dared not interrupt the judge.
7. The boxer was glad to have been given a rematch.
8. My friend bought a new coat to wear to the opera.
9. He was happy to have been the center of attention.
10. Let us go to the movies tonight.

APPLICATION: Writing Sentences Using Verbals. Use each of the following verbs in three sentences—first as a participle, then as a gerund, and finally as an infinitive. Underline the verbal in each of your sentences.

run   dance   live   grow   open

Adjective, Adverb, and Noun Clauses   4.3

While a phrase is a group of words without a subject and a verb, a *clause* does include a subject and a verb.

A clause is a group of words with its own subject and verb.

There are two basic kinds of clauses: *independent clauses* and *subordinate clauses*.

An independent clause can stand by itself as a complete sentence.

Every complete sentence must contain an independent clause—either standing by itself or connected to one or more other independent clauses or subordinate clauses.

ONE INDEPENDENT CLAUSE: *Gone with the Wind* has become a classic movie.

TWO INDEPENDENT CLAUSES: My back ached, but I went to school anyway.

INDEPENDENT + SUBORDINATE CLAUSE: The coastal communities were evacuated as the hurricane approached.

Examine the last example closely. *The coastal communities were evacuated* is an independent clause because it makes a complete statement and can stand alone as a declarative sentence. *As the hurricane approached*, however, is only part of a complete thought even though it has a subject (*hurricane*) and verb (*approached*). Clauses such as this one, which cannot stand independently, are known as subordinate clauses.

> A **subordinate clause,** although it has a subject and a verb, cannot stand by itself as a complete sentence; it can only be part of a sentence.

A subordinate clause becomes meaningful only when it is attached to an independent clause. Then it can add details and show relationships that are often not possible with single words or phrases. Like phrases, however, subordinate clauses function in sentences as single parts of speech: either as adjectives, adverbs, or nouns. This section will describe each of these three uses of subordinate clauses.

■ Adjective Clauses

One way to describe, limit, or qualify any noun or pronoun in a sentence is to use an adjective clause.

> An **adjective clause** is a subordinate clause that modifies a noun or pronoun by telling what kind or which one.

An adjective clause appears after the noun or pronoun it modifies and functions exactly as a single-word adjective would. An adjective clause is connected to the word it modifies usually by one of the relative pronouns (*who*, *whom*, *whose*, *which*, or *that*) but sometimes by a relative adverb (such as *when*, *where*, *why*, *before*, *after*, or *since*).

EXAMPLES: My car, *which has a dented fender*, will be repaired today.

Here is the message from the lawyer *who just called*.

My birthday is the day *after you leave*.

Essential and Nonessential Adjective Clauses. Like participial and appositive phrases, adjective clauses are set off by punctuation only when they are not essential to a sentence's meaning.

An adjective clause that is not essential to the basic meaning of a sentence is set off by commas. An essential clause is not set off.

The following chart contrasts nonessential and essential adjective clauses.

Nonessential Adjective Clauses	Essential Adjective Clauses
Nancy Marchand, *who plays Mrs. Pynchon on the television show* <u>Lou Grant</u>, has also starred on Broadway.	The woman *who plays Mrs. Pynchon on the television show* <u>Lou Grant</u> has also starred on Broadway.
I visited the home of Washington Irving, *who wrote* <u>The Legend of Sleepy Hollow</u>.	I visited the home of the gentleman *who wrote* <u>The Legend of Sleepy Hollow</u>.

The essential adjective clauses in the chart are not set off by commas because they cannot be omitted without changing the sentences' basic message. The adjective clauses on the left, however, merely provide additional information. (See Section 13.2 for more information about punctuating adjective clauses.)

Introductory Words in Adjective Clauses. Relative pronouns and relative adverbs not only introduce adjective clauses but also function within the subordinate clause.

A relative pronoun or relative adverb (1) connects the adjective clause to the modified word and (2) acts within the clause as a subject, direct object, or other sentence part.

To determine the role of a relative pronoun within a clause, first isolate the adjective clause from the rest of the sentence. Then find the subject and verb of the adjective clause. Since clauses are sometimes in inverted order, you may need to rearrange the words.

The following chart shows the various roles of relative pronouns in adjective clauses.

THE USES OF RELATIVE PRONOUNS WITHIN THE CLAUSE	
As a Subject	*Sentence:* The phone *that was just installed* does not work. *Clause:* that was just installed
As a Direct Object	*Sentence:* The swimmer *whom I coached last year* qualified for the Olympic trials. DO *Reworded clause:* I coached whom last year
As the Object of a Preposition	*Sentence:* That is the politician *on whom the investigators focused.* *Reworded clause:* the investigators focused on Obj of Prep whom
As an Adjective	*Sentence:* I saw a plant *whose blossoms open only at night.* Adj *Clause:* whose blossoms open only at night

NOTE ABOUT UNDERSTOOD RELATIVE PRONOUNS: Sometimes a relative pronoun is understood rather than expressed. It nevertheless still functions in the sentence.

EXAMPLES: The car *(that) Ted drove* won the race.

Two guests *(whom) we invited* never arrived.

Unlike relative pronouns, relative adverbs can act only as adverbs within the clause.

	THE USE OF RELATIVE ADVERBS WITHIN THE CLAUSE
As an Adverb	*Sentence:* I wanted to celebrate the day *after I quit.*
	Reworded clause: I <u>quit</u> after — Adv

EXERCISE A: Identifying Adjective Clauses. Each of the following sentences contains an adjective clause. Write each adjective clause on your paper. Then underline its subject once and verb twice. Finally, circle the relative pronoun or relative adverb and identify its function in the clause. (Watch for omitted but understood relative pronouns.) Be prepared to identify the noun or pronoun that each adjective clause modifies.

1. The white shark that was caught by two fishermen had to be released.
2. I prefer that radio station, which plays only classical music.
3. The columnist interviewed an author whose recent book had been on the bestseller list for fifty weeks.
4. The place where the meeting was scheduled was all the way across town.
5. The issue on which the argument centered seemed trivial.
6. Dr. Bower, whom the community implicitly trusts, has written several articles for medical journals.
7. I used the pen that still had plenty of ink.
8. You should know the reason why he scolded you.
9. My neighbor, the woman whose house is filled with valuable antiques, is planning to have a garage sale.
10. The ham I baked had a streak of gristle running through it.

EXERCISE B: Punctuating Essential and Nonessential Clauses. The following sentences contain adjective clauses, all without punctuation. Copy each sentence onto your paper, underlining the adjective clause and adding commas only where necessary.

1. Milk which is used in many recipes causes allergic reactions in some people.
2. The falcon that the boy had raised was returned to the wild.
3. Jerry Lewis who began his career as a child star now helps with the muscular dystrophy campaign.
4. The bed that was advertised at thirty percent off was out of stock.
5. I just cooked my dinner which took only twenty minutes in the microwave oven.

■ Adverb Clauses

Adverb clauses serve the same function in sentences as one-word adverbs and adverbial phrases do.

An **adverb clause** is a subordinate clause that modifies a verb, adjective, adverb, or verbal. It does this by pointing out where, when, in what manner, to what extent, under what condition, or why.

Each adverb clause contains a subject and verb, though not the main subject and verb in the sentence, and is introduced by a subordinating conjunction, such as *although, because, if, than, where,* or *while*. (For a more complete list, see page 48.)

As the examples in the following chart illustrate, an adverb clause can modify any word an adverb can.

ADVERB CLAUSES	
Modified Word	**Examples**
Verb	You will find your door key *where you left it.*
Adjective	The children were nervous *whenever the train entered a tunnel.*
Adverb	The concert lasted longer *than the audience's enthusiasm did.*
Participle	The engine, purring *after I adjusted it,* seemed as good as new.
Gerund	Walking *wherever I go* gives me good exercise.
Infinitive	The group wanted to rehearse again *after the afternoon performance ended.*

Some adverb clauses are *elliptical*, especially those beginning with *as* or *than*. In an elliptical adverb clause, the verb, or both the subject and verb, are understood but not actually stated. They nevertheless still function to make the clause express a complete idea.

VERB UNDERSTOOD: I am taller *than he (is)*.

SUBJECT AND VERB UNDERSTOOD: Robert Penn Warren has published almost as many novels *as (he has published) collections of poetry*.

(See Section 7.2 for information about using pronouns correctly in elliptical clauses.)

EXERCISE C: Identifying Adverb Clauses. Write the adverb clause from each of the following sentences on your paper. Then indicate whether it modifies a verb, adjective, adverb, or verbal.

1. The President waited until he had heard the reports of all his advisors.
2. After the mayor cut the ribbon, the store filled with customers.
3. The pine forest muffled all outside noises when I stood in its midst.
4. To discuss problems whenever they arise is a good policy for any marriage.
5. The turtle crawled slowly as though it were exhausted by the effort.
6. Eating before I exercise makes me sluggish during the workout.
7. The concert will be held as long as enough tickets are sold.
8. The man, straining as he lifted the dresser, dislocated his back.
9. I was glad that my mother agreed with my plan so emphatically.
10. To talk in a courtroom after you are told to stop is to risk a charge of contempt.

EXERCISE D: Recognizing Elliptical Clauses. Write the elliptical adverb clause from each of the following sentences on your paper, adding the understood words, in parentheses, where they belong.

1. The company pays Mr. Hilton considerably more than Mr. Gurney.
2. Polls show that students are not as knowledgeable about current events as adults.
3. You play card games better than Vic.
4. The nurse is not as qualified as the doctor on such matters.
5. The woodshop teacher helps Allison more than me.

■ Noun Clauses

The last of the three subordinate clauses is the *noun clause*.

A **noun clause** is a subordinate clause that acts as a noun.

Noun clauses can perform any function in a sentence that a single-word noun can.

The following chart shows these functions.

USES OF NOUN CLAUSES IN SENTENCES	
Function in Sentence	**Examples**
Subject	*Whoever works during the lunch break* gets to leave early.
Direct object	You will type *whatever she needs*.
Indirect object	She gave *whoever attended the demonstration* free samples.
Object of a preposition	I will shop at *whichever store you wish*.
Predicate nominative	A long rest is *what the doctor ordered*.
Appositive	The assembly debated the proposal *that taxes be reduced by ten percent*.

Noun clauses frequently begin with *who, whom, whose, which,* or *that,* the same words that can begin adjective clauses. Some other words that can begin noun clauses are *whoever, whomever, whichever, what, whatever, where, how, when, if,* and *whether.*

Besides serving to introduce a noun clause, these words sometimes function within the clause as adjectives, subjects, direct objects, or some other sentence part.

SOME USES OF INTRODUCTORY WORDS IN NOUN CLAUSES	
Function in Clause	**Examples**
Adjective	Elsa could not pick *which movie she wanted to see.*
Adverb	We want to know *how we should dress for the party.*
Subject	I want the recipe from *whoever made that delicious casserole.* (S)
Direct object	*Whomever you select for the job* will be approved. (DO)
Introductory word only	The doctor determined *that she had the measles.*

When *that* has no function in the noun clause, other than as an introductory word, it is often omitted.

EXAMPLE: I know *(that) you tried your best.*

Since some of the words that introduce noun clauses also introduce adjective and adverb clauses, do not let the introductory word be your only guide to determining the type of clause. Always check the function of the clause in the sentence. With noun clauses, you can also try substituting the words *it, you, fact,* or *thing* for the clause. If the sentence when read retains its smoothness, you probably have a noun clause.

NOUN CLAUSE: I knew *that this would happen.*

SUBSTITUTION: I knew *it.*

EXERCISE E: Identifying Noun Clauses. Write the noun clause from each of the following sentences on your paper. Then indicate whether it is functioning as a *subject, direct object, indirect object, object of a preposition, predicate nominative,* or *appositive.* Be prepared to identify the function of the introductory word within the noun clause.

1. The records on whatever stock remains unsold are in the safe.
2. You may sell whoever wants drinking glasses those blue ones for half price.
3. Where that dog is now is a mystery to me.
4. After the bake sale was over, we bought whatever they had left.
5. My goals are what I want them to be.
6. They determined how the leak had started.
7. I will give a special prize to whoever writes the best paper.
8. The politician gave whoever was in the auditorium campaign buttons to wear.
9. Our decision will be whatever the majority decides.
10. The problem, how the city will maintain its subway system, needs to be discussed now.

EXERCISE F: Identifying Subordinate Clauses. A clause is underlined in each of the following sentences. Identify the clause as *adjective*, *adverb*, or *noun* on your paper.

1. Take the layout to the printer <u>who gives the best price</u>.
2. <u>When the holiday season begins</u>, the stores are jammed with frantic shoppers.
3. <u>Whoever wants a ride to the store</u> had better go to the car immediately.
4. Frankenstein's monster, <u>which Mary Shelley first envisioned in a dream in 1816</u>, is often thought to symbolize the outcast in society.
5. Daydreaming <u>when I should be working</u> is often a problem.
6. Go to the store and buy <u>whatever is on my list</u>.
7. The flight <u>we were scheduled to take</u> was canceled.
8. Trish annoys Dale more <u>than me</u>.
9. My friends decided to go buy ice cream cones <u>after the dance was over</u>.
10. <u>Even though he paid his overdue bills</u>, the company canceled his credit card.

APPLICATION: Using Subordinate Clauses to Combine Sentences. Combine each of the following pairs of sentences into one sentence by turning one of the sentences into the type of clause indicated. Write the new sentence on your paper and underline the subordinate clause.

EXAMPLE: Combine using an adjective clause.
        a. We were having turkey for dinner.
        b. It smelled delicious.

        The turkey <u>we were having for dinner</u> smelled delicious.

1. Combine using an adjective clause.
   a. Charles Dickens wrote *A Christmas Carol*.
   b. He also wrote many other classics, such as *Oliver Twist* and *David Copperfield*.
2. Combine using an adverb clause.
   a. The farmer milked the cows.
   b. Next, she checked on the pigs.
3. Combine using a noun clause.
   a. Someone will get the scholarship.
   b. This will be determined by a faculty committee.
4. Combine using an adverb clause.
   a. The music went faster.
   b. I could not sing along that fast.
5. Combine using an adjective clause.
   a. I opened a new book.
   b. Its pages felt crisp and clean to my touch.
6. Combine using an adverb clause.
   a. The man kept running.
   b. He soon was out of breath.
7. Combine using a noun clause.
   a. My parents' problem needed to be resolved.
   b. What should they prepare for their dinner party?
8. Combine using an adjective clause.
   a. The camera still works perfectly.
   b. I received it as a birthday gift many years ago.
9. Combine using an adverb clause.
   a. We will go to the fair on the second day.
   b. Opening day will be extremely crowded.
10. Combine using a noun clause.
    a. The union leaders made two proposals.
    b. They wanted the employees to receive a cost of living increase and added dental benefits.

Sentences Classified by Structure   **4.4**

Sentences are often classified according to the kind and number of clauses they contain. Different combinations of independent and subordinate clauses form four basic sentence structures: *simple, compound, complex,* and *compound-complex.*

A **simple sentence** consists of a single independent clause.

A **compound sentence** consists of two or more independent clauses joined by a comma and a coordinating conjunction (and, but, for, nor, or, so, yet) or by a semicolon.

A **complex sentence** consists of one independent clause and one or more subordinate clauses.

A **compound-complex sentence** consists of two or more independent clauses and one or more subordinate clauses.

As you study the examples of each structure in the following chart, notice that simple sentences can contain compound subjects, compound verbs, or both.

FOUR STRUCTURES OF SENTENCES	
Simple Sentences	We worked long hours at the polling booth. Neither Rod nor Fran telephoned me last night. Amazed at my results, I checked and rechecked my experiment.
Compound Sentences	My brother bought some stamps yesterday, and today he mounted them. Brad and I gobbled the cold oranges; they tasted good on such a hot day.
Complex Sentences	Subordinate Clause / Main Clause When the Fourth of July arrives, I plan to attend all the celebrations. Main Clause / Subordinate Clause Our drill team, which won the National Championship, will perform after the game is over. (Subordinate Clause) Main Clause / Subordinate Clause I will do whatever you say.
Compound-Complex Sentences	Main Clause / Subordinate Clause We walked along the river to the spot where it divides, and then we turned back. (Main Clause)

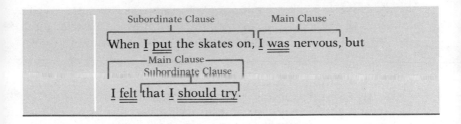

Notice in the examples that in complex and compound-complex sentences the independent clauses are called *main clauses* to distinguish them from subordinate clauses. The subject and verb of a main clause, in turn, are usually called *the subject of the sentence* and *the main verb* to distinguish them from the other subjects and verbs. You should also note that sometimes in a complex or compound-complex sentence a noun clause may be part of the main clause.

Being able to analyze the structure of sentences can help you understand long, involved sentences when you read. It can also help you check the logic and flow of your own ideas when you write.

EXERCISE A: **Identifying the Four Structures of Sentences.** Read the following sentences and determine their structure. Identify each as *simple, compound, complex,* or *compound-complex* on your paper.

1. As the dog raced away, the dog catcher chased it.
2. Picking up the phone, the child shouted into the mouthpiece.
3. During the war, families hung black curtains on their windows to prevent light from escaping at night.
4. My tooth ached; therefore, I made an appointment with the dentist.
5. Not wishing to receive a shot, the cow skittered away from the veterinarian.
6. The housekeeper set the table, and the family, feeling very hungry, sat down quickly.
7. That the day would be tiring was soon apparent, for I had three reports to type.
8. During the housecleaning, I changed the burned-out bulb in the lamp.
9. As I looked out the window, I noticed a nest, and nestled in its depths sat four tiny occupants.
10. Mr. Farnam arranged for his neighbor to pick up his newspaper and for me to water his plants during his stay in the hospital.

APPLICATION: Writing Sentences with Different Structures. Write sentences of your own according to the following instructions. Then underline each independent clause, including those in the simple sentences.

1. Write a simple sentence.
2. Write a simple sentence with a compound verb.
3. Write a simple sentence containing a verbal phrase.
4. Write a compound sentence in which the clauses are joined with a conjunction.
5. Write a compound sentence in which the clauses are joined by a semicolon.
6. Write a complex sentence with an adverb clause.
7. Write a complex sentence with an adjective clause and an adverb clause.
8. Write a complex sentence with a noun clause.
9. Write a compound-complex sentence with an adverb clause.
10. Write a compound-complex sentence with two subordinate clauses.

4.5 Diagraming Sentences with Phrases and Clauses

Each kind of phrase and clause is diagramed in a slightly different way so that it is visibly easy to differentiate them. In this section, besides diagraming phrases and clauses, you will learn to diagram compound, complex, and compound-complex sentences.

■ Prepositional Phrases

A prepositional phrase is diagramed directly beneath the word it modifies. The preposition goes on a slanted line and the object sits on a horizontal line. Place any modifiers of the object of the preposition on slanted lines below the horizontal line. If the object of the preposition is compound, diagram it in the same way other compound parts of a sentence are diagramed.

EXAMPLE: The cup of black coffee is sitting on the counter or the stove.

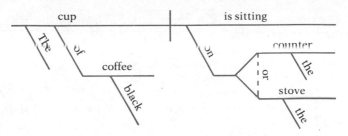

If a prepositional phrase modifies another prepositional phrase, diagram it below the other phrase.

EXAMPLE: She wore a blouse with ruffles of lace.

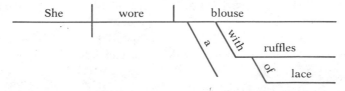

When a prepositional phrase modifies an adverb or adjective, an extra line is added.

EXAMPLE: He left early in the morning.

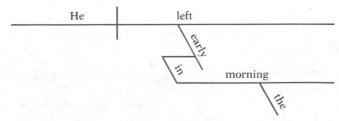

When two or more prepositional phrases modify the same word, place them side by side under the word they modify.

EXAMPLE: Go down the hall and to the left.

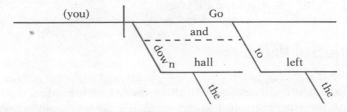

EXERCISE A: Diagraming Prepositional Phrases. Diagram the following sentences.

1. The magazine on that chair has an interesting article on birds and reptiles.
2. I sent my favorite coat to the cleaners today.
3. I ran quickly at the start of the race.
4. The police officer descended into the basement and disappeared into the great darkness.
5. My mother mixed the blueberry muffins and put them into the oven.

■ Appositive Phrases

Place an appositive in parentheses beside the noun or pronoun it follows. Position any modifiers of the appositive beneath it.

EXAMPLE: My friend, the one with the suitcase, is leaving for Greece.

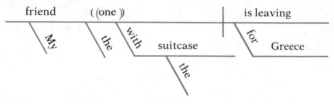

EXERCISE B: Diagraming Appositive Phrases. Diagram the following sentences.

1. Our dessert, strawberry crepes with whipped cream, pleased our guests immensely.
2. She received some placemats, orange ones, with yellow borders, from one guest at her party.
3. Later, we, all six of us, played charades.
4. The couple gave the babysitter, a neighborhood girl, a bonus for her excellent work.
5. With great delight, the audience watched the movie, a farce about airplane disasters.

■ Verbal Phrases

Diagrams for verbal phrases—built around participles, gerunds, and infinitives—are slightly more complicated than diagrams for prepositional and appositive phrases. As you study the following explanations and examples, remember that verbals are never diagramed on straight lines and that any verbal can have a complement.

Participles and Participial Phrases. Since a participle functions as an adjective, it is placed directly beneath the noun or pronoun it modifies. Unlike an adjective, however, a participle is written partly on a slanted line and partly on a horizontal line. Any modifiers are diagramed beneath it.

EXAMPLE: The cars honking loudly near my window disrupted my sleep.

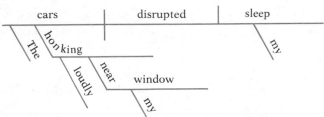

When a participle has a complement, such as a direct object, it is diagramed after the participle on the horizontal line. The usual line separates the complement from the participle.

EXAMPLE: Having received a big bonus, Mr. Jackson bought a new television.

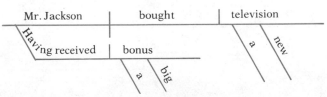

A nominative absolute, formed from a noun and participle that are grammatically separate from the rest of the sentence, is positioned above the rest of the sentence.

EXAMPLE: His work finished for the day, he headed home.

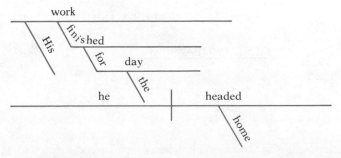

Gerunds and Gerund Phrases. Since gerunds function as nouns, they are found in diagrams wherever nouns can be located. Gerunds used as subjects, direct objects, or predicate nominatives are placed on a stepped line atop a pedestal. Any modifiers or complements are diagramed in the usual manner. The following model and example shows a gerund phrase used as a subject.

EXAMPLE: Catching a big fish from the surf was a great thrill.

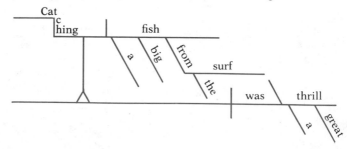

When a gerund or gerund phrase functions as an indirect object or as the object of a preposition, the stepped line extends from a slanted line.

EXAMPLE: We helped by carrying the packages from the car.

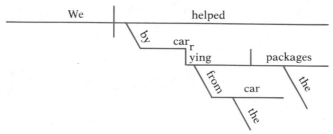

A gerund used as an appositive is placed on a pedestal, in parentheses, next to the noun or pronoun it accompanies.

EXAMPLE: My work, filing correspondence, is tedious.

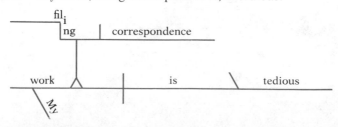

Infinitives and Infinitive Phrases. Because infinitives can act as nouns, adverbs, or adjectives, they are diagramed in several different ways. Like a gerund, an infinitive used as a noun is diagramed on a pedestal, but the line on which the infinitive sits is simpler. Any modifiers and complements that expand the infinitive into a phrase are diagramed in the usual manner. The following example shows an infinitive phrase used as a direct object.

EXAMPLE: Howard wanted to get Debbie a record album.

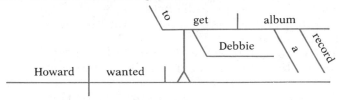

When an infinitive acts as an adjective or as an adverb, its diagram is similar to that of a prepositional phrase. Once again, any modifiers or complements are placed in their usual positions.

EXAMPLE: Today is the day to begin our work.

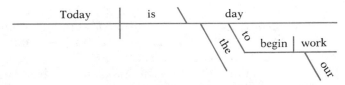

If an infinitive has an understood *to*, add it to the diagram but place it in parentheses. In addition, when an infinitive has a subject, place it on a horizontal line stretching out from the left side of the infinitive.

EXAMPLE: We saw Bob run into the grocery store.

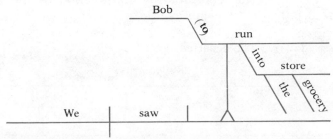

EXERCISE C: Diagraming Verbal Phrases. Diagram the following sentences.

1. Seeing the Picasso exhibit was an overwhelming experience for most people.
2. Leaping from the underbrush, a frightened doe began to cross in front of us.
3. Tatum wished to buy a horse for riding in shows.
4. We tricked them into revealing the winners.
5. To watch the sun rise, the campers awoke before dawn.
6. The consequences of the long strike, melons rotting on the vines, could be seen in the fields.
7. Providing free bus service for senior citizens will be an issue on our ballot.
8. My goal, to climb Mount Everest, will take careful planning.
9. Our club wants Annabelle to seek the nomination for treasurer.
10. The detectives were intent on trailing their suspect without his knowing.

■ Compound, Complex, and Compound-Complex Sentences

Up to this point, the diagraming rules that have been introduced pertained only to the diagraming of simple sentences. Diagrams for the other three sentence structures—compound, complex, and compound-complex sentences—follow the same basic rules. The major difference in diagraming these structures is that an additional horizontal baseline must be drawn for each clause in the sentence.

Compound Sentences. Compound sentences are composed of at least two independent clauses. Diagram each independent clause as you would a separate sentence. Then, join the verbs of the clauses with a dotted step line. On the step line, write either the coordinating conjunction or the semicolon that joins the two clauses.

EXAMPLE: I arrived; he departed.

Complex Sentences. To diagram complex sentences, you need to know how to diagram the three kinds of subordinate clauses—adjective, adverb, and noun clauses—and how to connect them to the independent clause.

Diagram an *adjective clause* below the main clause as if it were a separate sentence. Then join the adjective clause to the word it modifies with a slanted dotted line stretching from the relative pronoun or relative adverb. In the following example, the relative pronoun is a direct object in the subordinate clause, which modifies the subject of the main clause.

EXAMPLE: The man whom I telephoned is here.

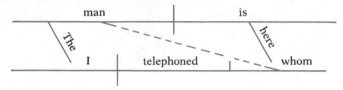

Remember, a relative pronoun can serve different functions in an adjective clause and must be placed in the diagram according to its use.

DIFFERENT FUNCTIONS OF THE RELATIVE PRONOUN IN ADJECTIVE CLAUSES	
Function of Relative Pronoun	**Examples**
Subject	I know the man *who was injured in the fire.*
Direct object	The waitress *whom you dislike* dropped another tray.

Object of a preposition	The woman *to whom you wrote* has replied.
Adjective	The artist *whose work is being exhibited* is my mother.
Understood pronoun (direct object)	The turkey *I am stuffing* weighs twenty pounds.

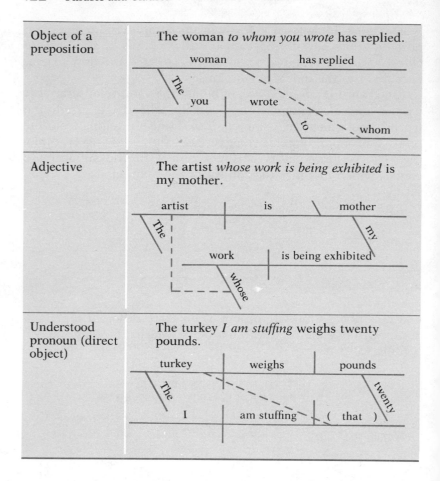

A relative adverb that introduces an adjective clause always modifies the verb in the subordinate clause.

EXAMPLE: I remember the last time when I visited Frankfurt.

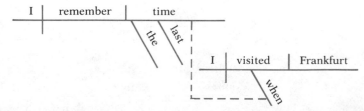

Diagram an *adverb clause* as you would an adjective clause; however, write the subordinating conjunction on the dotted line connecting the two clauses. This dotted line should extend from the verb in the adverb clause to the modified verb, adjective, adverb, or verbal in the main clause.

EXAMPLE: Since she left, I have had more time.

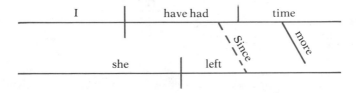

The following chart shows how to connect adverb clauses to verbs, adjectives, adverbs, and verbals. Notice especially the second example, in which the word left out of an elliptical clause is shown in the diagram in parentheses.

ADVERB CLAUSES	
Modified Word	**Examples**
Verb	I cleaned the house *before Jack arrived*.
Adjective	Marge is taller *than I*.
Adverb	I accidentally broke it yesterday *after you called*.

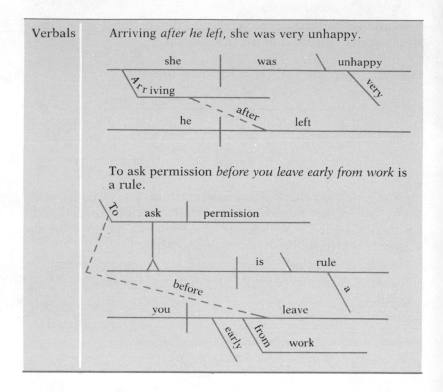

Verbals   Arriving *after he left*, she was very unhappy.

To ask permission *before you leave early from work* is a rule.

To diagram a *noun clause*, place the entire clause on a pedestal in the place the noun clause occupies within the main clause. In the following example the noun clause functions as the subject of the main clause.

EXAMPLE: Who will win remains a question.

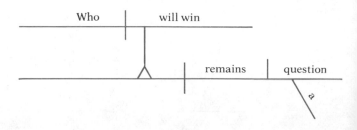

Remember that a noun clause can function in any role that a noun can: as a subject, direct object, indirect object, object of a preposition, and so on. Moreover, like a relative pronoun, a noun clause's introductory word can have different functions within the clause.

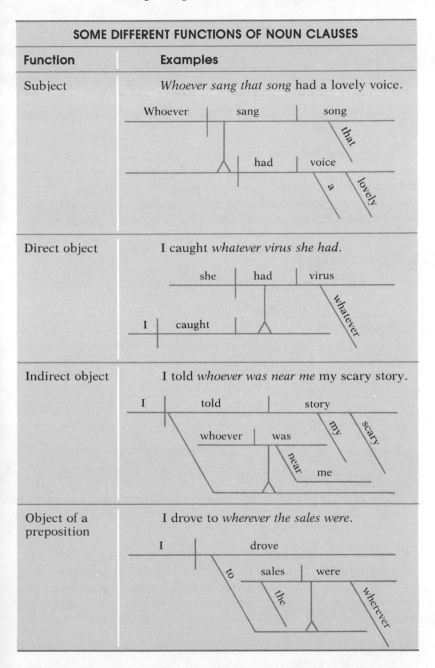

SOME DIFFERENT FUNCTIONS OF NOUN CLAUSES	
Function	**Examples**
Subject	*Whoever sang that song* had a lovely voice.
Direct object	I caught *whatever virus she had*.
Indirect object	I told *whoever was near me* my scary story.
Object of a preposition	I drove to *wherever the sales were*.

When a noun clause's introductory word has no other function than to introduce the clause, it is diagramed on the pedestal.

EXAMPLE: I heard that you were ill.

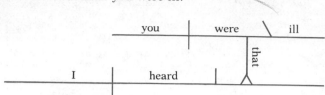

Compound-Complex Sentences.   Since you now know how to diagram both compound and complex sentences, compound-complex sentences should pose few problems. First, locate the independent clauses. Then diagram and connect each subordinate clause as you would if you were diagraming a complex sentence.

EXAMPLE: When I arrived at work, I had many disrupting telephone calls, but I still finished everything that I had to do.

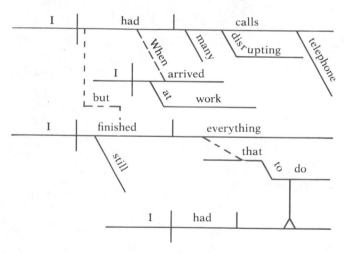

EXERCISE D: Diagraming Compound, Complex, and Compound-Complex Sentences.
Diagram the following sentences on your paper. The first three sentences are compound, the next four are complex, and the last three are compound-complex.

1. My arms ached from the exercise, but I continued to swim more laps.
2. The storm blew away the smog, yet by the next day, it had returned.
3. Did Helen attend the concert, or did she get a refund for her unused ticket?

4. Ursula LeGuin, who writes fantasy stories, will speak at the local college tonight.
5. I must get whatever is required to repair this lock.
6. Because the light is poor, the reading that I do tires my eyes.
7. When you buy a house, ask about any railroad tracks in the vicinity that might run too close to the house.
8. While I watched with interest, the carpet layers measured the carpet, but they miscalculated on the amount needed by several feet.
9. The girl looked forward to her upcoming marriage, but as the day grew close, she began to get cold feet.
10. To be granted an interview with the President was an honor, and the reporter worked diligently because she wanted to be equal to the honor.

APPLICATION: **Diagraming All Types of Sentences.** All kinds of diagraming rules apply to the following sentences. Diagram each one, and, if necessary, refer to the rules in this section and Section 3.5.

1. Will you go to the Orient on that extended vacation within the next month?
2. With his scissors flying, the hair stylist quickly trimmed the woman's locks, and then he used the blow dryer to finish her hair.
3. Early in the morning, I made the sour cream dip for my party planned for that night.
4. Alas, the dress that I had planned to wear has an ink mark on the front.
5. We had hoped to hear the news soon, but weeks have passed without a word.
6. You can find me near wherever the food is located.
7. Dragging his feet, the tired soldier marched along the parade route.
8. Do not worry because I will take whichever one you do not choose.
9. Typing letters is easier than writing them and allows you to say more.
10. To find time to relax has been nearly impossible with my recent schedule.

Chapter 5

Avoiding Sentence Faults

An inferior product is more often the result of slipshod work than of ignorance. If you, as a writer, have been told that your work is filled with grammatical errors, you have probably developed careless writing habits, one of which is not proofreading your final products. In this chapter, you will review or be introduced to ways of correcting the most common sentence errors that you may encounter when you proofread your work.

5.1 Fragments and Run-ons

Since people can think much faster than they can write, they often omit necessary words, punctuate awkwardly, or write unfinished thoughts. These mistakes lead to two of the most common sentence errors: fragments and run-on sentences.

■ Fragments

As you probably know, a fragment is a group of words masquerading as a sentence. Because it does not express a complete thought, a fragment can stymie a reader. Though used in some modern fiction and poetry, often with good artistic effect, fragments are generally considered an error in other kinds of writing, especially when the writer uses them unintentionally. Most fragments in writing are phrases, subordinate clauses, or words in a series.

Do not capitalize and punctuate phrases, subordinate clauses, or words in a series as if they were complete sentences.

If you find you are having a problem with fragments in your writing, read your work aloud to yourself. Listen to the natural pauses and stops. You should be able to hear where your sentences actually begin and end and to identify those passages that need to be revised.

Most fragments can be corrected simply by linking them up to words that come before or after them. For example, a noun and its modifiers (a noun phrase) that should be a subject may unintentionally be separated from its verb. Similarly other phrases or subordinate clauses may be detached from the words they should modify.

NOUN FRAGMENT: *A hawk perching in the treetop.* Was watching me with wary eyes.

CORRECT: A hawk perching in the treetop was watching me with wary eyes.

CLAUSE FRAGMENT: As I looked out over the field, suddenly I saw the deer. *Which again had come out of the woods.*

CORRECT: As I looked out over the field, suddenly I saw the deer, which again had come out of the woods.

In some situations you may need to rework a fragment phrase or clause more thoroughly. Sometimes, this revision will involve rearranging or omitting words and adding other punctuation. Study the following chart, which shows various phrase and clause fragments along with some examples of different ways to remedy the problem. The fragments in the second column are italicized.

PHRASE FRAGMENTS		
Type	**Example**	**Correction**
Prepositional phrase	The rooster crowed. *In the early morning hours.*	The rooster crowed *in the early morning hours.*
Participial phrase with pronoun	I bought a new reading chair. *One stuffed with down.*	I bought a new reading chair *stuffed with down.*
Gerund phrase	*Preparing the sauce.* It must be done soon.	*Preparing the sauce* must be done soon.

| Infinitive phrase | *To address the envelopes.* That was a tedious job. | *To address the envelopes* was a tedious job. |
| Appositive phrase | Sally hung her poster. *A print from the Dresden exhibit.* | Sally hung her poster, *a print from the Dresden exhibit.* |

CLAUSE FRAGMENTS

Adjective clause	He recited a quotation. *That I had never heard before.*	He recited a quotation *I had never heard before.*
Adverb clause	I felt lonely. *When I stared at the desolate land.*	*When I stared at the desolate land,* I felt lonely.
Noun clause	*Whatever the doctor says.* I will do it.	I will do *whatever the doctor says.*

Sometimes a series of words may be so long that it deludes you into believing that it is a complete sentence. Always check to see that the series has both a subject and a verb.

SERIES FRAGMENTS	
Fragment	**Sentence**
A large gold starfish measuring ten inches in diameter, a <u>barnacle</u> firmly attached to the piling of the rotting pier, and an empty shell lying in the sand.	A large gold <u>starfish</u> measuring ten inches in diameter, a <u>barnacle</u> firmly attached to the piling of the rotting pier, and an empty conch <u>shell</u> lying in the sand <u>fascinated</u> us.

EXERCISE A: Identifying and Correcting Fragments. Each of the following items contains one or more sentences, a fragment, or both a complete sentence and a fragment. If the words form one or more complete sentences, write *complete* on your paper. If the item contains a fragment, rewrite it to make it a complete sentence.

1. I found the book I was searching for. A collection of quotations from famous contemporary politicians.
2. The television news special ran for three consecutive nights.
3. Sipped at the steaming cup of coffee.
4. Failing to identify himself at the front gate. That is what brought the security guards running.
5. The window had been smashed with a crowbar. At the rear of the car.
6. The apartment manager gave the tenants their notice. They had thirty days to vacate.
7. Who the pickpocket was. That did not matter to us as much as getting back what was taken.
8. The willow trees with their branches bending gracefully low to sweep the green expanse of grass below.
9. The footsteps echoing down the long, deserted corridor.
10. I needed another quarter for the washing machine.

■ Run-on Sentences

A *run-on sentence*, often simply called a *run-on*, is two or more complete sentences that are unintentionally capitalized and punctuated as if they were one.

Use punctuation, conjunctions, or other means to join or separate the parts of a run-on sentence.

One kind of run-on, sometimes called a *fused sentence*, consists of two or more sentences that are not separated or joined by any punctuation at all. The other kind of run-on is sometimes called a *comma splice*. It consists of two or more sentences separated only by commas instead of by commas and conjunctions.

FUSED SENTENCE: The waves lashed the shore the beach houses were washed away.

COMMA SPLICE: In the morning the house was cold, however the sun soon warmed it up.

Like fragments, run-ons are usually the result of carelessness and haste. To avoid them, reread your work, aloud if necessary, listening for the natural stops that tell you where one sentence ends and another begins. If you find run-ons in your writing, correct them either by adding punctuation and conjunctions or by rewriting.

Study the examples in the following chart to learn both to recognize run-ons and to correct them in various ways.

FOUR WAYS TO CORRECT RUN-ONS	
With End Marks and Capitals	
Run-on	**Sentence**
Linda turned at the sudden noise a bird had crashed into the picture window.	Linda turned at the sudden noise. A bird had crashed into the picture window.
With Commas and Conjunctions	
Run-on	**Sentence**
I baked the cake this morning, I did not frost it until this afternoon.	I baked the cake this morning, but I did not frost it until this afternoon.
With Semicolons	
Run-on	**Sentence**
The stallion kept trying to jump the fence, however he failed each time.	The stallion kept trying to jump the fence; however, he failed each time.
By Rewriting	
Run-on	**Sentence**
My aunt stayed with us for the holidays, my cousins came too.	My aunt and cousins stayed with us for the holidays. (simple sentence with compound subject)
	When my aunt stayed with us for the holidays, my cousins came too. (complex sentence beginning with subordinate clause)

EXERCISE B: Identifying and Correcting Run-on Sentences. Some of the following sentences are correct; others are run-ons. If the sentence is correct as written, write *complete* on your paper. If it is a run-on, rewrite it to make it correct. Use each of the four methods of correcting run-ons at least once.

1. I play the piano for many musicals moreover I give lessons to twenty students.
2. The electricity went out I looked everywhere for the candles.
3. Dwight lost the first game of backgammon, but he won the second.
4. As a boy, my dad could go to the movies for seventy-five cents, it cost thirty-five cents for the movie and forty cents for popcorn and a drink.
5. The roads were crowded with families leaving for the three-day weekend.
6. What time is the party, will you pick me up?
7. The first raindrops fell we then raced for cover.
8. Adult education classes will be taught this semester, they will not offer a class in Chinese cooking.
9. I caught him however he had already mailed the letter that I wanted back.
10. We earned money washing cars, therefore, we could afford to go to the concert.

APPLICATION: **Locating and Correcting Fragments and Run-ons.** The following selection contains some fragments and run-ons. If the numbered item contains no errors, write *correct* on your paper. If it does contain an error, rewrite it to make it correct.

(1) Stand up and be counted! The cry of the Census Bureau once every ten years. (2) Each decade, every man, woman, and child is counted, tabulated, and translated into statistics, they tell us the average income of Americans, the percentage of female graduates, the typical life span, and many other vital pieces of information. (3) Important decisions result from these census profiles. Apportionment for the federal legislature, as well as distribution of sought-after federal funds. (4) Some advertising companies even develop marketing strategies after studying the trends. Those graphed predictions for the next ten-year span.

(5) Who does all this counting? The Census Bureau with over two thousand professionals and 275,000 temporary census takers. (6) When the work is done, over three years will have elapsed over 300,000 pages of reports will have been produced. (7) The census will have cost the taxpayers well over $1 billion dollars, an amount that would be reduceable if more Americans sent their forms in on time.

(8) Where do these statistics go who reads them? (9) The important ones will fill many pages in the yearly almanacs and the others will be placed on computer tapes. (10) The American public will eventually have access through public libraries and government depositories to all the information obtained. These facts and figures that numerically catalog the life and times of the American people.

5.2 Misplaced and Dangling Modifiers

As a general rule, a modifier should be placed as close as possible to the word it modifies. If a modifier is misplaced or left dangling in a sentence, it will seem to modify the wrong word or no word at all. This section will examine both of these sentence errors and show you how to correct them.

■ Misplaced Modifiers

When a modifier is placed too far from the word it should modify, the meaning of a sentence can become confused.

> A **misplaced modifier** seems to modify the wrong word in the sentence.

Any phrase or clause that acts as an adjective or adverb can unintentionally be misplaced in a sentence.

MISPLACED MODIFIERS: Our instructor told us how to cut the wood *through written directions.*

I saw a great blue heron trimming its feathers yesterday *while driving past the reservoir.*

In the first example, the misplaced prepositional phrase seems to modify *cut* rather than *told*. In the second example, the misplaced elliptical clause seems to modify *trimming* rather than *saw*.

To correct such sentence errors, simply move the phrase or clause so that it is closer to the word that it should logically modify. Occasionally, some additional rewording may be necessary.

CORRECTED SENTENCES: *Through written directions*, our instructor told us how to cut the wood.

While driving past the reservoir yesterday, I saw a great blue heron trimming its feathers.

Sometimes a modifier may be misplaced in such a way that it seems to modify two words at the same time. These "squinting" modifiers, as they are sometimes called, are easily corrected by moving them closer to the word that should be modified and farther away from the word that should not be modified.

In the following example, notice that *after the game* seems to modify both *were told* and *to assemble*.

SQUINTING MODIFIER: The team members were told *after the game* to assemble in the locker room.

CORRECTED SENTENCES: *After the game* the team members were told to assemble in the locker room.

The team members were told to *assemble* in the locker room *after the game*.

EXERCISE A: Identifying and Correcting Misplaced Modifiers.

Each of the following sentences contains a misplaced modifier. Find the modifier and rewrite the sentence correctly on your paper.

1. The pianist played a new composition sitting on the piano bench.
2. Having turned sour, I threw out the milk.
3. We boarded the train in Boston heading toward our winter home in Florida.
4. We heard the bus had crashed on the radio.
5. My friend explained after school she was going to the dentist.
6. Cranky and tired, I put the baby down for a nap.
7. The seals looked hopefully at us desiring more sardines.
8. Growling with hunger, I filled my empty stomach with food.
9. We heard that a forest fire had started nearby while preparing to go on a vacation.
10. Barking loudly, I told the dog to be quiet.

■ Dangling Modifiers

A sentence's meaning can become confused when the word that a phrase or clause logically modifies is missing from the sentence. Such modifiers are said to dangle.

A **dangling modifier** seems to modify the wrong word or no word at all because the word it should modify has been omitted from the sentence.

Dangling modifiers, which are usually verbal phrases or elliptical adverb clauses, can usually be corrected in either of two ways: Either add the missing word to the main clause or rephrase the modifier to include the missing word.

DANGLING PARTICIPIAL PHRASE: *Playing football all afternoon,* my homework remained unfinished.

CORRECTED SENTENCES: *Playing football all afternoon,* I left my homework unfinished.

Because I was playing football all afternoon, my homework remained unfinished.

DANGLING INFINITIVE PHRASE: *To compete in the race,* the application must be completed today.

CORRECTED SENTENCES: *To compete in the race,* you must complete your application today.

Before you can compete in the race, you must complete your application today.

DANGLING ELLIPTICAL CLAUSE: Shoes must be worn *while shopping in the store.*

CORRECTED SENTENCES: Customers must wear shoes *while they are shopping in the store.*

While shopping in the store, customers must wear shoes.

EXERCISE B: Identifying and Correcting Dangling Modifiers.
Some of the following sentences contain dangling modifiers; others do not. If the sentence is correct, write *correct* on your

paper. If the sentence contains a dangling modifier, correct it using one of the techniques described in this section.

1. Enveloped in my warm blanket, the cold air was no problem.
2. To knit a sweater, all the yarn must be purchased at the same time.
3. Having underestimated the problem, very little could now be done.
4. To qualify for GI benefits, my service record needed verification.
5. While taking the inventory, the store continued to do business.
6. Trevor's brother bit him on the arm when seven years of age.
7. After examining all the evidence, the defendant was found guilty.
8. When the cat scratched at the door, we let her in.
9. Cutting out all the wordiness, the essay improved remarkably.
10. When ceasing to talk, the room suddenly became deathly quiet.

APPLICATION: Avoiding Misplaced and Dangling Modifiers.
Each of the following items is incomplete. Make each item into a complete sentence, using the construction in parentheses to fill in the blank. Make sure that you do not use any misplaced or dangling modifiers.

1. After working hard all day, (independent clause).
2. (infinitive phrase), I needed a large down payment.
3. Having finished the work, (independent clause).
4. (participial phrase), Roger caught sight of a large fish.
5. (adverb clause), Warren's brother made a toast.
6. We watched the survivors rescued (prepositional phrase).
7. Failing to bring our travelers' checks, (independent clause).
8. After (gerund phrase), I could not stop choking.
9. To make overseas telephone calls, (independent clause).
10. Hobbling across the street, (independent clause).

Faulty Parallelism 5.3

Unless the rails on which a train rides are parallel, the train will derail. In similar fashion, a series of ideas in a sentence will flow smoothly only when the grammatical structures are parallel. If one structure is different from the others, the entire meaning of the sentence can sometimes be "derailed." This section will explain the different kinds of parallelism that can be used in sentences and show you some methods for correcting faulty parallelism in your writing.

■ Correct Parallelism in Sentences

When a writer wishes to express a comparison or a series of ideas of equal importance, the ideas should be expressed in parallel grammatical structures.

Parallelism is the placement of equal ideas in words, phrases, or clauses of similar types.

Parallel grammatical structures can be two or more words of the same part of speech, two or more phrases of the same type, or two or more clauses of the same type. Sometimes, for emphasis, two or more sentences will follow the same pattern.

PARALLEL WORDS: I felt *feverish, achy,* and *nauseated.*

PARALLEL PHRASES: My goals this year include *making the soccer team, earning good grades,* and *getting a part-time job.*

PARALLEL CLAUSES: *That we were disorganized, that we were rushed* quickly became apparent.

PARALLEL SENTENCES: *I came. I saw. I conquered.* —Julius Caesar

Now examine the following excerpt from a speech that Winston Churchill delivered in the House of Commons during World War II. Notice how the echoing of the parallel structures builds to the concluding statement of determination.

EFFECTIVE USE OF PARALLELISM:

We shall not flag or fail. We shall go on to the end. We shall fight in France, we shall fight on the seas and oceans, we shall fight with growing confidence and growing strength in the air, we shall defend our island, whatever the cost may be, we shall fight on the beaches, we shall fight on the landing grounds, we shall fight in the fields and in the streets, we shall fight in the hills; we shall never surrender. —Winston Churchill

Notice also in the excerpt that parallel structures may be written with an understood word that is omitted after the first item in the series. Churchill, for example, did not repeat *with* in the series *with growing confidence and growing strength in the air.*

EXERCISE A: **Recognizing Parallel Structures.** Find the parallel structures in each of the following sentences and write them on your paper. Then identify what each is composed of: words, phrases, clauses, or whole sentences.

1. In our garden, we planted tomatoes, squash, and lettuce.
2. My evenings are spent grading papers, watching television, or crocheting an afghan.
3. We looked at slides that showed us opening presents, caught us blowing out candles, and pictured us celebrating Thanksgiving.
4. One half of Seabastian detested his mother's friends; the other half was allured by their glitter. —Vita Sackville-West
5. The puppies hopped, jumped, and ran until they were tired out.

■ Faulty Parallel Structures

Faulty parallelism occurs when a writer fails to use equal grammatical structures to express related ideas.

> Correct a sentence containing faulty parallelism by rewriting it so that each parallel idea is expressed in the same grammatical structure.

Faulty parallelism can involve words, phrases, and clauses in series as well as in comparisons.

Nonparallel Words, Phrases, and Clauses in Series. Check every series of ideas you write for parallelism. If, for example, you are describing something with a series of one-word adjectives, make sure you do not slip in a prepositional phrase when another one-word adjective is available and more suitable.

As you study the examples in the following charts, note how the nonparallel structures not only jar the natural flow of the sentences but also cloud meaning in many instances.

CORRECTING FAULTY PARALLELISM IN SERIES

Nonparallel Structures	Corrected Sentences
Noun · Noun *Strength, agility,* and Gerund Phrase *carefully concentrating* are the attributes of a successful wrestler.	Noun · Noun *Strength, agility,* and careful Noun *concentration* are the attributes of a successful wrestler.
Prep Phrase The mouse ran *across the* Prep Phrase *floor, under the table,* and *its* Clause *hole was the last stop.*	Prep Phrase The mouse ran *across the* Prep Phrase · Prep *floor, under the table,* and *into* Phrase *its hole.*
Gerund I was angry after *shoveling out* Phrase · Gerund Phrase *the car, driving through the* *snowstorm to school,* and then Infinitive Phrase *to find it closed.*	Gerund I was angry after *shoveling out* Phrase · Gerund Phrase *the car, driving through the* *snowstorm to school,* and then Gerund Phrase *finding it closed.*
My voice teacher says *that I* Noun Clause · Independent *have a strong voice,* but *I sing* Clause *off key.*	My voice teacher says *that I* Noun Clause · Noun *have a strong voice* but *that I* Clause *sing off key.*

As you can see in the examples, coordinating conjunctions such as *and, but, nor,* and *or* often connect items in a series. When you proofread your work, use them as a signal that alerts you to check the items they connect for parallelism.

Correlative conjunctions pose a special problem. Though such conjunctions as *both . . . and* and *not only . . . but also* connect just two items, take care to place each part of the conjunction so that only equal structures are connected. A common mistake is to include more words than are necessary under the umbrella of the first part of the conjunction.

NONPARALLEL: She not only *wanted to climb the pyramids* but also *to sail up the Nile.*

CORRECTED: She wanted not only *to climb the pyramids* but also *to sail up the Nile.*

Nonparallel Words, Phrases, and Clauses in Comparisons. Do not word a comparison in such a way that a phrase is unnecessarily linked with a clause or another type of phrase or another structure altogether. In the last example on the left in the following chart, note that although the phrases are similar their functions within the clauses make the comparison nonparallel.

CORRECTING FAULTY PARALLELISM IN COMPARISONS	
Nonparallel Structures	**Corrected Sentences**
Noun I prefer *concertos* to Gerund Phrase *listening to jazz.*	Noun I prefer *concertos* to Noun *jazz.*
Prep I bought the dress *because of* Phrase *its low price* rather than *that it* Clause *fits well.*	Prep I bought the dress *because of* Phrase Prep *its low price* rather than *for its* Phrase *fit.*
Gerund Phrase as DO I like *giving speeches* as much Gerund Phrase as S as *writing a story* thrills my sister.	Gerund Phrase as DO I like *giving speeches* as much as my sister likes Gerund Phrase as DO *writing stories.*

EXERCISE B: Correcting Faulty Parallelism. Each of the following sentences contains faulty parallelism. Write the sentences on your paper, putting each in proper parallel form.

1. I enjoy my job because of the opportunities it offers, the fringe benefits I receive, and I earn a good salary.
2. We have things to do, people to see, and places that should be visited.
3. We should invite people with whom you work and your friends from the swim club.
4. I have poor handwriting more because I am careless than that I have never been taught.
5. If I have all the ingredients and time becomes available, I will make some homemade bread.

6. The couple did not like the house since it had poor plumbing, and they would need to landscape the yard.
7. The comedian proved versatile, inventive, and kept us laughing.
8. I had steak, Tanya ate prime rib, but a hamburger is all that Vanessa ordered.
9. I voted for the sale of state bonds, for an increase in the number of state parks, and to have the state cut property tax.
10. My father both prepared the main course and the plum pie for dessert.

APPLICATION: **Writing Sentences Containing Parallel Structures.** Construct sentences using the following instructions. Each sentence *must* contain a parallel construction.

1. Write a sentence containing a series of three adjectives.
2. Compare two ideas using *more . . . than . . . .*
3. Use *and* to join two gerund phrases.
4. Construct a sentence with a series of three prepositional phrases.
5. Use *either . . . or* to join two infinitive phrases.
6. Use *not only . . . but also* to connect two subordinate clauses.
7. Combine two parallel sentences using *but.*
8. Use three parallel verb forms in a sentence.
9. Compare two ideas using *as much as.*
10. Write a sentence containing two parallel noun clauses.

5.4 Faulty Coordination

When two or more independent clauses of unequal importance are joined by *and*, the result is *faulty coordination*. This section will help you recognize faulty coordination and show you some methods that you can use to correct it.

■ The Use of *And* in Compound Sentences

To coordinate means "to place side by side in equal rank." Two independent clauses joined by the coordinating conjunction *and* to form a compound sentence should have equal rank. One idea should not be less important than the other.

Use *and* or other coordinating conjunctions only to connect ideas of equal importance.

In the following examples, the independent clauses on each side of the coordinating conjunction have equal value.

CORRECT COORDINATION: I will go, *and* Mickey will stay.

I made a casserole for the picnic, *and* Helen brought a salad.

Sometimes, however, writers carelessly use *and* to join independent clauses that either should not be joined or should be joined in another way so that the real relationship between the clauses will be clear. Then the faulty coordination puts all the ideas on the same level of importance whether or not they logically deserve to be. The precise relationship between the ideas is left haphazard and vague. (See Section 21.1 for more information about connecting your ideas logically.)

FAULTY COORDINATION: Catherine had an appointment for a job interview at eight o'clock, *and* with fifteen minutes remaining, she was hopelessly caught in rush-hour traffic.

We were best friends as children, *and* I have not seen her since we were graduated from elementary school.

The best film at the festival was shown last, *and* it was a documentary about an archaeological dig in China.

Occasionally, writers will carelessly string together many ideas with *and*. The sentence that results almost always plods along gracelessly.

STRINGY SENTENCE: The proctor called the roll *and* told us we would be on our honor *and* then he wrote the examination question on the board *and* he left the room *and* he did not come back until it was time to collect our papers.

EXERCISE A: Identifying Correct and Faulty Coordination. Each of the following sentences contains a coordinating conjunction. For the five sentences in which coordination is used correctly, write *correct* on your paper. For the others, write *faulty*.

1. The dry ingredients have been mixed, and they must now be added to the egg mixture.
2. The storm came up quickly, and most people are becoming soaked by the rain.
3. Samuel Clemens is a famous American writer, and he used the pen name Mark Twain.
4. I will slim down for the swim meet, and I will then swim much faster.
5. The artist finished the layouts, and the leaflets were taken to the printers.
6. My tires needed realigning, and the brakes needed adjusting.
7. The construction company finished the building and the supplies arrived and we stocked the shelves but our clerks were not trained and that will take several more weeks.
8. It was the grand opening of the restaurant, and we were the first customers they had.
9. At the nearby shopping center is a small restaurant, and it boasts that it has the best homemade pies in town.
10. The actor's newest movie was just released, but it is a science fiction picture.

■ Revising Sentences with Faulty Coordination

Faulty coordination can be corrected in several ways.

Revise sentences with faulty coordination by (1) putting unrelated ideas into separate sentences, (2) putting a less important or dependent idea into a subordinate clause, or (3) reducing an unimportant idea into a phrase.

Using the examples of faulty coordination given in the first part of this section, examine each of these methods for revision.

First, if the independent clauses joined by *and* are not closely related, separate them and drop the coordinating conjunction.

FAULTY COORDINATION: Catherine had an appointment for a job interview at eight o'clock, *and* with fifteen minutes remaining, she was hopelessly caught in rush-hour traffic.

CORRECTED SENTENCES: Catherine had an appointment for a job interview at eight o'clock. With fifteen minutes remaining, she was hopelessly caught in rush-hour traffic.

The second method of correcting faulty coordination takes a bit more thought. You will have to examine each independent clause and determine if one is less important or dependent on the other. If so, turn it into a subordinate clause.

FAULTY COORDINATION: We were best friends as children, *and* I have not seen her since we were graduated from elementary school.

CORRECTED SENTENCE: Although we were best friends as children, I have not seen her since we were graduated from elementary school.

The third method involves reducing an unimportant idea to a phrase—that is, changing the compound sentence into a simple sentence. An independent clause that can be reduced to a phrase will often begin with a pronoun and a linking verb, such as *he is* or *it was*. In the following example, notice that the second clause has been turned into an appositive phrase and made part of the first clause.

FAULTY COORDINATION: The best film at the festival was shown last, *and* it was a documentary about an archaeological dig in China.

CORRECTED SENTENCE: The best film at the festival, a documentary about an archaeological dig in China, was shown last.

Stringy sentences should be broken up and revised using any of the three methods just described. Often there will be several ways to regroup the ideas logically. Experiment with a few possibilities before making a choice. Here is one way that the stringy sentence on page 143 can be revised.

REVISION OF STRINGY SENTENCE: After the proctor called the roll, he told us we would be on our honor. Then, having written the examination question on the board, he left the room. He did not come back until it was time to collect our papers.

EXERCISE B: Correcting Faulty Coordination. Each of the following sentences contains faulty coordination. Write the sentences on your paper, correcting the error. Use each of the three methods of correction at least twice.

1. Clark Gable was one of America's finest actors, and he starred in *Gone with the Wind*.
2. The movie stars jogged to the park for exercise, and crowds filled the lawns and walkways.
3. The lava flows stretch many miles in Hawaii, and they cut a swath through the otherwise dense vegetation.
4. Someone built a miniature replica of the White House, and it has lights and a television that actually work.
5. The last of the suitcases was packed, and the family set off on vacation.
6. The alarm woke me up this morning, and it was still pitch black outside.
7. The sign read "Help Wanted," and Jill put in her application.
8. The salesclerk rang up my purchase, but she did it incorrectly and I asked her to re-total it and she obliged but she made another mistake and the manager finally had to come over to fix it.
9. *Star Wars* was Tom's favorite movie, and he saw it eighteen times.
10. The plane took off fifteen minutes behind schedule, and it arrived at its next stop on time.

APPLICATION: Avoiding Faulty Coordination in Sentence Writing. Combine each of the following pairs of sentences by using either coordination or subordination. Check each of your combined sentences for faulty coordination.

1. My eyelids felt heavy from lack of sleep. I lay down for a rest on the couch.
2. The clock chimed out nine bells. Stacy realized she had overslept.
3. Zip and Zoe, our dachshunds, play outside during the day. They sleep inside at night.
4. The mountain climber was stranded by an unexpected blizzard. He had to be rescued by helicopter.
5. Paul Zindel came to speak to a group of librarians. He wrote *The Pigman*.
6. Get the extra table leaf. It is in the hall closet.
7. I studied the children sitting beside me. They were watching in awe as the parade floats went by.
8. Devon played football in high school. He played soccer in college.
9. My brother received a painting from a friend. It shows an old farmhouse sitting near a thick copse.
10. The freeway needs immediate repair. All the lanes have huge, dangerous potholes.

Review Exercises: Grammar

REVIEW EXERCISE 1: Identifying the Parts of Speech

The following paragraph contains underlined words. Identify what part of speech each word is—*noun, pronoun, verb, adjective, adverb, preposition, conjunction,* or *interjection.* Write the correct answer next to the appropriate number on your paper.

(1) <u>Icebergs</u> are (2) <u>huge</u> masses of ice that (3) <u>break off</u> from the ends of glaciers and float (4) <u>into</u> the sea. The tall ones can extend over four hundred feet (5) <u>above</u> the surface of the ocean. (6) <u>Amazingly</u>, (7) <u>this</u> (8) <u>constitutes</u> only one tenth of an iceberg's mass. The rest sits (9) <u>below</u> the surface, a menace to ships in these cold (10) <u>water</u> regions. The biggest iceberg that has (11) <u>ever</u> been charted had a diameter of (12) <u>sixty</u> miles and a (13) <u>length</u> of well over two hundred miles. The (14) <u>North American</u> iceberg (15) <u>usually</u> originates in Greenland, (16) <u>but</u> icebergs (17) <u>can move</u> many miles from their area of birth. (18) <u>Today</u>, the International Ice Patrol reports the position of icebergs and charts (19) <u>their</u> migration. (20) <u>Alas</u>, the Ice Patrol, which came into (21) <u>existence</u> in 1914, arrived (22) <u>too</u> late to help the (23) <u>Titanic</u>, (24) <u>but</u> (25) <u>they</u> do prevent many accidents from occurring with today's vessels.

REVIEW EXERCISE 2: Using Basic Sentence Patterns

Construct sentences with the following patterns. Then diagram each of the sentences you have written.

1. Subject-Subject-Verb-Direct Object-Direct Object
2. Subject-Linking Verb-Predicate Adjective-Predicate Adjective
3. Subject-Verb-Indirect Object-Indirect Object-Direct Object
4. Linking Verb-Subject-Predicate Nominative
5. Helping Verb-Subject-Verb-Direct-Object-Objective Complement

REVIEW EXERCISE 3: Identifying Phrases

Identify each underlined item in the following sentences as a *prepositional phrase,* an *appositive phrase,* or a *verbal phrase.*

1. <u>Calling the dogs off the hunt</u> proved almost impossible <u>for the police officer.</u>

2. The newspaper article, <u>the one on alcoholism</u>, had some excellent advice on coping <u>with the problem</u>.
3. The train <u>scheduled at 5:10 P.M.</u> never arrived <u>at my stop</u>.
4. I gave the gift, <u>a book containing rhymes and poems</u>, to her <u>on her last birthday</u>.
5. <u>Yelling with pain</u>, the child produced a finger <u>swollen by a bee sting</u>.
6. <u>Until today</u> I thought you were playing <u>according to the rules</u>.
7. I will go <u>to the hills</u> <u>to fly my kite</u>.
8. My frog, <u>a winner with those legs</u>, will compete <u>in the frog jumping contest</u>.
9. Naturally, <u>being called lazy</u> is not a complimentary statement <u>about your personality</u>.
10. Three cities—<u>New York, Chicago, and Miami</u>—tried <u>to lure the convention to their areas</u>.

REVIEW EXERCISE 4: Expanding Sentences with Clauses

Combine each of the following pairs of sentences into one sentence, using the type of clause indicated.

1. Use an adjective clause: My grandfather gave me the toaster. It always burns the toast.
2. Use a noun clause: Someone will get a prize. It will be the one who answers the question correctly.
3. Use an adverb clause: The plane landed. Some islanders then welcomed us with leis.
4. Use an adjective clause: My friend was hired as an artist at Disney World. He draws caricatures of people.
5. Use an adverb clause: You must eat this liver. You need more iron.
6. Use an adjective clause: My cat is nearly five years old. She is expecting a litter of kittens.
7. Use an adverb clause: I survived the first cut of the football season. I may still be placed on waivers.
8. Use an adjective clause: Some people's bikes have lights. These people are safer at night.
9. Use an adverb clause: Danny was gone for seven days. An important letter from the college arrived.
10. Use an adjective clause: Our cruise will be on that ship. It says Sun Princess on the bow.

REVIEW EXERCISE 5: Diagraming Expanded Sentences

Indicate whether each of the following sentences is *compound*, *complex*, or *compound-complex*. Then diagram the sentence.

1. While we slept in the tent, raccoons wandered through our camp and stole some food.
2. We all knew that she was capable of directing the choir, but Deedee did not want the responsibility.
3. The water level threatened to spill over the top of the dam, yet the spillway prevented any flooding from occurring.
4. While standing on the edge of the Grand Canyon, I beheld its breathtaking beauty.
5. Our friends wanted to help us move, but we managed by ourselves.

REVIEW EXERCISE 6: Recognizing Sentence Errors

Each of the following sentences contains a sentence error. Indicate what kind of error it is—*fragment, run-on, misplaced* or *dangling modifier, faulty parallelism*, or *faulty coordination*. Then rewrite the sentence correctly on your paper.

1. I ordered the program guide, and I listen to the radio quite often.
2. The flea market had many booths full of items, however I did not find anything I wanted.
3. The garbage truck picks up the bin, dumps the trash into the back, and grinding it up.
4. While taking a shower, the phone rang.
5. Margaret told us before school she had seen a bike accident.
6. The peaches were ripe but we didn't pick them and they rotted and soon spoiled peaches lined the driveway.
7. The oak tree stood across the lake that was fifty feet tall.
8. I want a spouse who works hard, enjoys life, and with lots of money.
9. The meat sizzling hot on the grill.
10. The crew put fresh asphalt on the road, no potholes remained when they were done.

REVIEW EXERCISE 7: Writing Your Own Sentences

Write sentences of your own, using each of the following instructions.

Function	Structure	Additions
1. Imperative	Simple	Include an adverb.
2. Declarative	Complex	Use a participle.
3. Interrogative	Complex	Use an adjective clause.
4. Exclamatory	Simple	Include an interjection.

5. Imperative	Compound	Put in an adjective.
6. Declarative	Compound-complex	Include an adverb clause.
7. Interrogative	Simple	Use an appositive.
8. Declarative	Compound	Use a correlative conjunction.
9. Declarative	Complex	Put in a noun clause.
10. Interrogative	Compound	Use the conjunction *or*.

UNIT

Usage

6
Verb Usage

7
Pronoun Usage

8
Agreement

9
Adjective and Adverb Usage

10
Miscellaneous Usage Problems

11
Levels of Language

Chapter 6

Verb Usage

When you consider the numerous forms and uses of verbs, the many words that can act as verbs, and the likelihood that a sentence will contain more than one verb, the chances for misusing verbs are very great. Only a highly sophisticated computer would be able to calculate the odds against perfect verb usage. To avoid most errors, therefore, it is important to know the rules that govern verb usage.

This chapter will show how verbs are formed and the different ways in which verbs indicate time. It will also explain how verbs help express facts, commands, and wishes or possibilities, and how verbs can show whether subjects perform or receive action.

6.1 Verb Tenses

In addition to expressing actions or conditions, verbs have different *tenses* to show when the action or condition occurred.

A **tense** is a form of a verb that shows time of action or state of being.

Notice in the following examples how different forms of the same verb indicate changes in time.

EXAMPLES: We *spend* our summers in Maine.

They *spent* over one thousand dollars for gasoline during their cross-country trip.

I *will spend* tomorrow working in the library.

I *have spent* most of today revising my work.

She *had spent* all of her money before she returned home.

We *will have spent* five thousand dollars before the renovations are complete.

■ The Six Verb Tenses

Verbs have six tenses that indicate when an action or condition is, was, or will be in effect. Within these tenses are three forms: *basic, progressive,* and *emphatic.* Basic verb forms are what you use most frequently. Progressive verb forms indicate a continuing action or state of being. Emphatic verb forms are used for emphasis, for questions, and for negative sentences. Notice in the following chart that emphatic forms are limited to the present and past tenses.

BASIC, PROGRESSIVE, AND EMPHATIC FORMS OF THE SIX TENSES			
Tense	Basic Form	Progressive Form	Emphatic Form
Present	run	am (*or* are, is) running	do run
Past	ran	was (*or* were) running	did run
Future	will run	will be running	
Present Perfect	have (*or* has) run	have (*or* has) been running	
Past Perfect	had run	had been running	
Future Perfect	will have run	will have been running	

The name assigned to a verb is a combination of its tense and its form. Thus, *do run* is called the present emphatic of the verb *run,* and *will have been running* is called the future perfect progressive of the verb *run.* The basic forms, however, are described by their tense names alone. For example, *will run* is simply called the future of the verb *run,* and *had run* is called the past perfect.

EXERCISE A: Recognizing Tenses. Write the verb forms in Column A on your paper. Then, next to each one, write the corresponding verb from Column B.

Column A	*Column B*
1. Present	a. do deliver
2. Past	b. will be entertaining
3. Future	c. fell
4. Present Perfect	d. are listening

5. Past Perfect
6. Future Perfect
7. Present Progressive
8. Past Progressive
9. Future Progressive
10. Present Perfect
    Progressive
11. Past Perfect Progressive
12. Future Perfect
    Progressive
13. Present Emphatic
14. Past Emphatic

e. has arrived
f. had been deceiving
g. understand
h. has been raining
i. did win
j. had begun
k. was sleeping
l. will have gone
m. will have been waiting
n. will decide

■ The Four Principal Parts

Every verb in the English language has four principal parts. It is from these four principal parts that all of the tenses are formed.

A verb has four principal parts: the **present** (base form), the **present participle,** the **past,** and the **past participle.**

Here, for example, are the four principal parts of the verb *run.*

PRINCIPAL PARTS OF *RUN*			
Present	**Present Participle**	**Past**	**Past Participle**
run	running	ran	run

The following chart shows which basic, progressive, and emphatic forms are derived from each of the four principal parts.

THE VERB FORMS OF *RUN* DEVELOPED FROM PRINCIPAL PARTS
The First Principal Part: *run*
Present: I *run* Future: I *will run* Present Emphatic: I *do run* Past Emphatic: I *did run*

The Second Principal Part: *running*
Present Progressive: I *am running*
Past Progressive: I *was running*
Future Progressive: I *will be running*
Present Perfect Progressive: I *have been running*
Past Perfect Progressive: I *had been running*
Future Perfect Progressive: I *will have been running*

The Third Principal Part: *ran*
Past: I *ran*

The Fourth Principal Part: *run*
Present Perfect: I *have run*
Past Perfect: I *had run*
Future Perfect: I *will have run*

Notice that helping verbs must be added to express some verb forms. For example, for the future tense you must add *will*, for the present perfect you must add *have*, for the past perfect you must add *had*, and for the future perfect you must add *will have*. The progressive forms require the addition of either a form of *be* or forms of both *have* and *be*, and the emphatic forms require either the present or past of *do*.

EXERCISE B: Identifying Principal Parts. Divide your paper into three columns and label them *Verb, Form,* and *Principal Part.* Then write the verb from each of the following sentences, its form, and the principal part from which it was derived in the appropriate columns.

EXAMPLE: Susan does work too hard.

Verb	Form	Principal Part
does work	present emphatic	present

1. The team always plans a strategy for the game.
2. I am preparing the soil for an organic garden.
3. You will never survive without adequate shelter.
4. They will have gone by then.
5. A careless painter was splattering the wallpaper.

6. Jack did fail the chemistry examination.
7. We will have been studying a long time.
8. It seemed an impossible task.
9. She had seldom seen such rejoicing in the city.
10. They have invited everyone in the class to the party.

■ Regular and Irregular Verbs

The changes that occur in the past and past participle of a verb's principal parts determine whether it is classified as *regular* or *irregular*.

Regular Verbs.   Most verbs are regular. This means that their past and past participles are formed according to a predictable pattern.

The past and past participle of a **regular verb** are formed by adding *-ed* or *-d* to the present form.

The following chart shows that the past and past participle of regular verbs are formed in the same manner. In the past participle, the helping verb *have* has been added in parentheses. Though the helping verb is not part of the past participle, it is included as a reminder that *have* (or *has*) is needed to form any of the perfect tenses.

PRINCIPAL PARTS OF REGULAR VERBS			
Present	**Present Participle**	**Past**	**Past Participle**
laugh	laughing	laughed	(have) laughed
wave	waving	waved	(have) waved
lift	lifting	lifted	(have) lifted
pretend	pretending	pretended	(have) pretended

Irregular Verbs.   Despite the fact that most verbs are regular, many verbs that you use every day are irregular. Their past and past participles are not formed according to a predictable pattern.

The past and past participle of an **irregular verb** are not formed by adding *-ed* or *-d*.

As you study the following charts, try to determine which of the irregular verbs give you trouble. Pay particular attention to changes in spelling. Notice, for example, that the final consonant of some of the present participles is doubled before the addition of *-ing* and that the final consonant of some of the past participles is doubled before the addition of *-en*. (Similar changes take place in some regular verbs.)

IRREGULAR VERBS WITH THE SAME PAST AND PAST PARTICIPLE			
Present	**Present Participle**	**Past**	**Past Participle**
bind	binding	bound	(have) bound
bring	bringing	brought	(have) brought
build	building	built	(have) built
buy	buying	bought	(have) bought
catch	catching	caught	(have) caught
creep	creeping	crept	(have) crept
fight	fighting	fought	(have) fought
find	finding	found	(have) found
fling	flinging	flung	(have) flung
forget	forgetting	forgot	(have) forgotten *or* (have) forgot
get	getting	got	(have) got *or* (have) gotten
grind	grinding	ground	(have) ground
hang	hanging	hung	(have) hung
hold	holding	held	(have) held
keep	keeping	kept	(have) kept
lay	laying	laid	(have) laid
lead	leading	led	(have) led
leave	leaving	left	(have) left
lend	lending	lent	(have) lent
lose	losing	lost	(have) lost
pay	paying	paid	(have) paid
say	saying	said	(have) said
seek	seeking	sought	(have) sought
send	sending	sent	(have) sent
shine	shining	shone *or* shined	(have) shone *or* (have) shined
show	showing	showed	(have) shown *or* (have) showed
sit	sitting	sat	(have) sat
sleep	sleeping	slept	(have) slept

spend	spending	spent	(have) spent
spin	spinning	spun	(have) spun
stand	standing	stood	(have) stood
stick	sticking	stuck	(have) stuck
sting	stinging	stung	(have) stung
strike	striking	struck	(have) struck
swing	swinging	swung	(have) swung
teach	teaching	taught	(have) taught
win	winning	won	(have) won
wind	winding	wound	(have) wound
wring	wringing	wrung	(have) wrung

IRREGULAR VERBS WITH THE SAME PRESENT, PAST, AND PAST PARTICIPLE

Present	Present Participle	Past	Past Participle
bid	bidding	bid	(have) bid
burst	bursting	burst	(have) burst
cost	costing	cost	(have) cost
cut	cutting	cut	(have) cut
hit	hitting	hit	(have) hit
hurt	hurting	hurt	(have) hurt
let	letting	let	(have) let
put	putting	put	(have) put
set	setting	set	(have) set
shut	shutting	shut	(have) shut
split	splitting	split	(have) split
spread	spreading	spread	(have) spread
thrust	thrusting	thrust	(have) thrust

IRREGULAR VERBS THAT CHANGE IN OTHER WAYS

Present	Present Participle	Past	Past Participle
arise	arising	arose	(have) arisen
be (am, is, are)	being	was (were)	(have) been
bear	bearing	bore	(have) borne

beat	beating	beat	(have) beaten *or* (have) beat
become	becoming	became	(have) become
begin	beginning	began	(have) begun
bite	biting	bit	(have) bitten
blow	blowing	blew	(have) blown
break	breaking	broke	(have) broken
come	coming	came	(have) come
do	doing	did	(have) done
draw	drawing	drew	(have) drawn
drink	drinking	drank	(have) drunk
drive	driving	drove	(have) driven
eat	eating	ate	(have) eaten
fall	falling	fell	(have) fallen
fly	flying	flew	(have) flown
freeze	freezing	froze	(have) frozen
give	giving	gave	(have) given
go	going	went	(have) gone
grow	growing	grew	(have) grown
know	knowing	knew	(have) known
lie	lying	lay	(have) lain
ride	riding	rode	(have) ridden
ring	ringing	rang	(have) rung
rise	rising	rose	(have) risen
run	running	ran	(have) run
see	seeing	saw	(have) seen
shake	shaking	shook	(have) shaken
shrink	shrinking	shrank	(have) shrunk
sing	singing	sang	(have) sung
slay	slaying	slew	(have) slain
speak	speaking	spoke	(have) spoken
spring	springing	sprang	(have) sprung
steal	stealing	stole	(have) stolen
stride	striding	strode	(have) stridden
strive	striving	strove	(have) striven
swear	swearing	swore	(have) sworn
swim	swimming	swam	(have) swum
take	taking	took	(have) taken
tear	tearing	tore	(have) torn
throw	throwing	threw	(have) thrown

wear	wearing	wore	(have) worn
weave	weaving	wove	(have) woven *or* (have) wove
write	writing	wrote	(have) written

If you run into a problem choosing the correct form of an irregular verb, you can either refer to one of these charts or consult a reliable dictionary, which will list irregular verb parts.

EXERCISE C: Completing the Principal Parts of Regular and Irregular Verbs. Number your paper from 1 to 25. At the top of your paper, write the names of the principal parts as heads for four columns. Then, without referring to your book, complete the columns on your paper by filling in the missing principal parts.

Present	Present Participle	Past	Past Participle
1. _____	_____	_____	laid
2. lose	_____	_____	_____
3. _____	smiling	_____	_____
4. _____	_____	built	_____
5. _____	_____	_____	lain
6. seek	_____	_____	_____
7. _____	_____	raised	_____
8. _____	_____	_____	led
9. _____	cooking	_____	_____
10. _____	_____	_____	burst
11. be	_____	_____	_____
12. _____	showing	_____	_____
13. wear	_____	_____	_____
14. _____	_____	_____	risen
15. put	_____	_____	_____
16. _____	_____	_____	blown
17. _____	_____	set	_____
18. _____	spending	_____	_____
19. drift	_____	_____	_____
20. _____	_____	scrubbed	_____
21. _____	_____	wrote	_____
22. _____	sitting	_____	_____
23. drink	_____	_____	_____
24. _____	_____	_____	broken
25. prepare	_____	_____	_____

EXERCISE D: Choosing the Correct Forms of Irregular Verbs.
Choose the correct verb from the choices in parentheses for each of the following sentences.

1. This professor has never (teached, taught) on a college level before.
2. Anyone would have (ran, run) away in that situation.
3. After each success Barney (grew, growed) surer of himself.
4. The fearless knight drew his sword and (slayed, slew) the dragon.
5. In her fury she (flinged, flung) a bowl of chili at her departing guests.
6. Our hockey team (strived, strove) to win back the trophy it had lost last year.
7. Blake had carefully (shaken, shook) pepper all over his meat and potatoes.
8. Mom and I (catched, caught) several beautiful trout in this stream.
9. He said he (saw, seen) some very imaginative drawings done by preschool children.
10. Mike (drawed, drew) a sketch of the history teacher.
11. The thief silently (creeped, crept) up the stairs toward the master bedroom.
12. Swarms of insects had (stung, stinged) the campers' faces while they slept.
13. Rhythmically he (swang, swung) the scythe through the row of wheat.
14. The sheriff (seeked, sought) to discover Bonnie and Clyde's hideout.
15. We had (flew, flown) many miles over the desert before we spotted an oasis.
16. You should have (gone, went) to the store before it closed.
17. Mary's friend (showed, shown) her how to crochet.
18. She has (lain, lay) in a coma for nearly a month.
19. In the movie a hideous monster (leaded, led) the girl to a lost civilization.
20. He was (binded, bound) by his oath not to speak to his captors.
21. I should have (known, knowed) he couldn't be relied on.
22. He (losed, lost) everything he owned when the stock market crashed.
23. Another climber had already (sticked, stuck) a flag on top of the mountain.
24. Bill has (teared, torn) his pants on a nail protruding from the fence.
25. The storm had (began, begun) as soon as we arrived at the picnic area.

26. Mickey (winded, wound) the rope around his wrist to keep his pet safe.
27. I (did, done) my best on this art project, but it won't win an award.
28. Her suitor (strided, strode) across the courtyard and demanded that she come to the window.
29. The frightened girl told the king she had (spinned, spun) straw into gold.
30. The Indians (grinded, ground) corn on this large, flat rock.
31. The villagers (drank, drunk) contaminated water, and many are sick.
32. Vanessa (striked, struck) out on her first turn at bat.
33. My mother had (risen, rose) before daybreak just to finish sewing my dress.
34. The sleeping sentry (sprang, sprung) to attention when the captain shouted his name.
35. Jessica (blew, blowed) a sour note on her trumpet.
36. She (wringed, wrung) the soapy water from the clothes.
37. Mr. Field had (hanged, hung) his diploma in the living room for all to see.
38. I regretted that I had (broke, broken) the irreplaceable antique.
39. Maude has (bore, borne) her guilt in silence for too long.
40. They had (fallen, fell) from a high position of authority.
41. They (winned, won) the jackpot with one lucky guess.
42. After the spell had been cast, the princess (sleeped, slept) for a hundred years.
43. My family and I had (driven, drove) past the city limits before we found a motel.
44. His coat (burst, busted) open as he finished the last of the pie.
45. Mrs. Clemens' harsh words (hurt, hurted) her son more than she realized.
46. This isn't the first time Ellen has (stole, stolen) items from my locker.
47. The child (shrank, shrunk) from touching the cold reptile's skin.
48. Lillian might have (swam, swum) to safety, but she chose to rescue her drowning brother.
49. I'd like to read the book she had (written, wrote) just before her death.
50. We (split, splitted) the bill between us.

EXERCISE E: Writing the Correct Forms of Irregular Verbs. For each of the following sentences give the appropriate past or past participle form of the verbs in parentheses.

1. I (bring) the beverage for the party, but I have not (get) the paper cups yet.
2. The rabid dog had (bite) someone, and no one could relax until it had been (catch).
3. If I had (lend) him the money, he wouldn't have (steal) it.
4. He has always (speak) the truth because he has (grow) up in an atmosphere of trust.
5. Its owner had (hit) the dog repeatedly so it (shrink) from everyone.
6. Tom had (know) in advance that he would be (throw) a curve ball.
7. She (fight) for her ideals and (spend) a week in prison before being vindicated.
8. The woman had (weave) a golden thread in the tapestry that (hang) from her wall.
9. This trio has (sing) all over Europe, and one member of the group has (write) all of the lyrics to their songs.
10. I (find) that I had (buy) a cheap reproduction but had paid the price of an original.
11. His face had (freeze) with horror just before the warrior (slay) him.
12. Every morning the cook (arise) before the others and soon (ring) the bell to announce breakfast.
13. Jed's father had a pair of leather boots that he had been (give) when he (ride) in the rodeo.
14. We (see) that he had (beat) his opponent with one hand tied behind his back.
15. The luxurious mink coat that Claire (wear) last winter she (give) away to a stranger.
16. After he had (drive) half way across the United States, Carl (take) stock of his dwindling funds.
17. She (swim) to shore and (wring) the water from her hair.
18. I should have (go) to the auction and (bid) for one of those grandfather clocks.
19. Their pet monkey (swing) from the chandelier and then (shake) its fist at us.
20. The penitent boy (swear) that he would make reparations for the window he had (break).
21. The guests had (drink) and (eat) until they were satisfied.
22. The small girl gleefully (thrust) a pin into the balloon but cried miserably when it (burst).
23. Jake had (build) two platforms that we could (put) the speakers on.
24. The young actor's name (shine) on the marquee and he silently thanked those who had (teach) him to persist.
25. They (pay) a high price for the misdeeds they had (do).

■ Verb Conjugation

One way to learn the different forms of a verb is through conjugation.

A **conjugation** is a list of the singular and plural forms of a verb in a particular tense.

To conjugate a verb—for example, the verb *run*—first review its principal parts.

PRINCIPAL PARTS OF *RUN*			
Present	**Present Participle**	**Past**	**Past Participle**
run	running	ran	run

The next step is to match the singular personal pronouns (*I*, *you*, *he*, *she*, *it*) and the plural personal pronouns (*we*, *you*, *they*) with the correct verb forms for each of the different tenses.

The basic verb forms use three of the principal parts: the present to form the present and future tenses, the past to form the past tense, and the past participle to form the three perfect tenses.

CONJUGATION OF THE BASIC FORMS OF *RUN*		
Present	Singular	Plural
First Person	I run	we run
Second Person	you run	you run
Third Person	he, she, it runs	they run
Past		
First Person	I ran	we ran
Second Person	you ran	you ran
Third Person	he, she, it ran	they ran
Future		
First Person	I will run	we will run
Second Person	you will run	you will run
Third Person	he, she, it will run	they will run

Present Perfect		
First Person	I have run	we have run
Second Person	you have run	you have run
Third Person	he, she, it has run	they have run

Past Perfect		
First Person	I had run	we had run
Second Person	you had run	you had run
Third Person	he, she, it had run	they had run

Future Perfect		
First Person	I will have run	we will have run
Second Person	you will have run	you will have run
Third Person	he, she, it will have run	they will have run

A complete conjugation of the basic forms includes the two infinitives: The *present infinitive* consists of *to* before the present; the *perfect infinitive* consists of *to have* before the past participle.

INFINITIVE FORMS OF *RUN*	
Present Infinitive	to run
Perfect Infinitive	to have run

The six progressive forms use only one principal part: the present participle.

CONJUGATION OF THE PROGRESSIVE FORMS OF *RUN*		
Present Progressive	**Singular**	**Plural**
First Person	I am running	we are running
Second Person	you are running	you are running
Third Person	he, she, it is running	they are running
Past Progressive		
First Person	I was running	we were running

Second Person	you were running	you were running
Third Person	he, she, it was running	they were running
Future Progressive		
First Person	I will be running	we will be running
Second Person	you will be running	you will be running
Third Person	he, she, it will be running	they will be running
Present Perfect Progressive		
First Person	I have been running	we have been running
Second Person	you have been running	you have been running
Third Person	he, she, it has been running	they have been running
Past Perfect Progressive		
First Person	I had been running	we had been running
Second Person	you had been running	you had been running
Third Person	he, she, it had been running	they had been running
Future Perfect Progressive		
First Person	I will have been running	we will have been running
Second Person	you will have been running	you will have been running
Third Person	he, she, it will have been running	they will have been running

Notice in the preceding chart that when you conjugate the progressive forms of a verb, you are actually conjugating the basic forms of *be* (I *am*, I *was*, I *will be*, and so on) followed by a present participle.

The emphatic forms use only one principal part—the present—which is preceded by either *do* or *did*.

CONJUGATION OF THE EMPHATIC FORMS OF *RUN*		
Present Emphatic	**Singular**	**Plural**
First Person	I do run	we do run
Second Person	you do run	you do run
Third Person	he, she, it does run	they do run
Past Emphatic		
First Person	I did run	we did run
Second Person	you did run	you did run
Third Person	he, she, it did run	they did run

EXERCISE F: Conjugating Verbs. After studying the preceding charts for the conjugation of *run*, conjugate the following verbs in their basic, progressive, and emphatic forms.

1. listen   2. grow

APPLICATION: Writing Sentences Using Basic, Progressive, and Emphatic Verb Forms. Write a sentence of your own for each of the following verbs, using the form indicated.

1. Future perfect of *leave*
2. Present emphatic of *declare*
3. Past progressive of *let*
4. Future perfect progressive of *find*
5. Present of *ring*
6. Present of *provoke*
7. Past perfect of *swim*
8. Past perfect progressive of *sing*
9. Future progressive of *cook*
10. Present of *maintain*
11. Past of *sit*
12. Present perfect of *feed*
13. Present progressive of *awake*
14. Present emphatic of *entertain*
15. Past emphatic of *delight*
16. Present perfect progressive of *strike*
17. Perfect infinitive of *steal*
18. Future perfect progressive of *praise*
19. Future of *murmur*
20. Future perfect of *grow*

6.2 Expressing Time Through Tense

The basic, progressive, and emphatic forms of the six tenses show time within three general categories: present, past, and future. The seven past verb forms show time occurring before the present. The four future forms show time occurring after the present.

THREE CATEGORIES OF TIME		
Past ◄--------------------	**Present** **(now)** ----------------►	**Future**
Past Past Emphatic Present Perfect Past Perfect	Present Present Emphatic	Future Future Perfect
Past Progressive Present Perfect Progressive Past Perfect Progressive	Present Progressive	Future Progressive Future Perfect Progressive

As you will see in this section, each verb form has a particular use that makes it different from the other forms.

■ Present, Past, and Future Time

A clear understanding of the way verbs are used within the three categories of time is important for good usage.

Uses of Tense in Present Time.   There are three forms that indicate present time: the present *(I look)*, the present emphatic *(I do look)*, and the present progressive *(I am looking)*.

> The three forms of the present can be used to show present actions or conditions as well as various continuous actions or conditions.

The following chart shows the three most common uses of the basic form of the present.

USES OF THE PRESENT

Present action: The children *play.*

Present condition: Barbara *is* very upset.

Regularly occurring action: Birds *fly* south in the fall.

Regularly occurring condition: I *am* usually punctual.

Constant action: The earth *rotates* on its axis.

Constant condition: People *are* not infallible.

The present may also be used to relate historical events. Called the *historical present,* this use of the present is sometimes used in narration to bring to life past actions or conditions.

THE HISTORICAL PRESENT

Past action expressed in historical present: A haggard Lincoln *presents* the Gettysburg Address.

Past condition expressed in historical present: For the advancing German troops, the Russian winter *is* disastrous.

Another use of the present is called the *critical present.* It is frequently used in discussions of deceased authors and their literary works.

THE CRITICAL PRESENT

Action expressed in critical present: Ernest Hemingway *shows* his genius in *For Whom the Bell Tolls.*

Condition expressed in critical present: Robert Frost *is* a famous New England poet.

The present emphatic is used in four ways: for emphasis, for denying contrary assertions, for asking questions, and for negative sentences.

USES OF THE PRESENT EMPHATIC

For emphasis: The course *does require* a term paper.

For denying a contrary assertion: No matter what you say, the car *does need* new tires.

For a question: *Do* you *know* the answer?

For a negative sentence: That city *does* not *add* fluoride to its water.

Like all progressive forms, the present progressive is used to show a continuing action or condition.

USES OF THE PRESENT PROGRESSIVE

Continuing action: We *are planning* our vacation.
Continuing condition: The weather *is being* very unpredictable.

Uses of Tenses in Past Time. Past time includes seven verb forms: the past *(I looked)*, the past emphatic *(I did look)*, the present perfect *(I have looked)*, the past perfect *(I had looked)*, the past progressive *(I was looking)*, the present perfect progressive *(I have been looking)*, and the past perfect progressive *(I had been looking)*. Each of these forms has a different use.

The seven forms of the past can be used to show a variety of actions and conditions that began in the past.

In the first of the following charts, notice that adding such words as *yesterday* or *last year* changes the time expressed by the basic form of the past from indefinite to definite. Notice also that the actions and conditions both began *and ended* at some time in the past.

USES OF THE PAST

Completed action (indefinite time): The art exhibit *opened.*
Completed condition (indefinite time): There *was* a drought in
California.
Completed action (definite time): The art exhibit *opened* yesterday.
Completed condition (definite time): There *was* a drought last year
in California.

The past emphatic has the same uses as the present emphatic: for emphasis, for denying a contrary assertion, for asking questions, and for negative sentences.

USES OF THE PAST EMPHATIC

For emphasis: Rebecca *did apologize* for her rudeness.
For denying a contrary assertion: But I *did send* you a birthday
card!
For a question: *Did* Mrs. O'Leary's cow *kick* over the lantern?
For a negative sentence: I *did* not *hear* the announcement.

The next chart shows the uses of the present perfect. When used to express actions that began and ended at some indefinite time in the past, the present perfect is often interchangeable with the past. However, the present perfect differs from the past in two ways: (1) The time expressed by the present perfect is always indefinite; it cannot be made definite by adding such words as *yesterday* or *last year;* (2) the present perfect is able to show actions and conditions continuing from the past to the present.

USES OF THE PRESENT PERFECT

Completed action (indefinite time): I have *seen* an improvement.

Completed condition (indefinite time): I have *been* happier lately.

Action continuing to present: The baby *has slept* all afternoon.

Condition continuing to present: You *have been* lucky this week.

The past perfect is used to show that one past action or condition took place before another.

USES OF THE PAST PERFECT

Action completed before another past action: James Herriot *had worked* as a veterinarian before he began his book.

Condition completed before another past condition: She *had been* an accomplished acrobat until she injured her back.

The three progressive forms in past time are used to show different kinds of continuous actions or conditions, beginning and sometimes ending in the past.

USES OF THE PAST PROGRESSIVE

Continuous action completed in the past: We *were practicing* hard.

Continuous condition completed in the past: You *were* not *being* helpful when you left the room in a huff.

USE OF THE PRESENT PERFECT PROGRESSIVE

Past action continuing to present: The Petersons *have been seeding* their lawn.

USE OF THE PAST PERFECT PROGRESSIVE

Past action continuing from indefinite to definite time: I *had been repairing* the chair that you just sat on.

Notice in the preceding chart that only the past progressive can express continuous *conditions* in past time. The forms that would be needed to show a condition in the present perfect progressive *(has been being)* or the past perfect progressive *(had been being)* are not considered standard English. Instead, the present perfect *(has been)* or past perfect *(had been)* is used.

Uses of Tenses in Future Time.   There are four forms in the future: the basic form of the future *(I will look)*, the future perfect *(I will have looked)*, the future progressive *(I will be looking)*, and the future perfect progressive *(I will have been looking)*.

The four forms of the future can be used to show various actions or conditions that will occur in the future.

The next chart shows two of the ways to express future time.

USES OF THE FUTURE
Future action: The seismograph *will determine* the severity of the earthquake.
Future condition: Eventually this cheaper carpeting *will become* faded.

USES OF THE FUTURE PERFECT
Future action completed before another: Before winter comes I *will have painted* the house.
Future condition completed before another: The survivors *will have been* without food for many days by the time help arrives.

In the following chart, notice that the future progressive and the future perfect progressive are not used to express conditions since the forms *will be being* and *will have been being* do not exist in standard English. Instead, the future *(will be)* and future perfect *(will have been)* are used.

USE OF THE FUTURE PROGRESSIVE
Continuous action in the future: John *will be growing* tomatoes in the garden this summer.

USE OF THE FUTURE PERFECT PROGRESSIVE
Continuous future action completed before another: Janet *will have been driving* for eight hours by the time she reaches Chicago.

NOTE ABOUT THE FUTURE AND FUTURE PROGRESSIVE: The basic form of the present and the present progressive are often used with other words to express future time. In these cases they take the place of the future and the future progressive forms.

PRESENT SUGGESTING FUTURE: The former Congresswoman *announces* her candidacy for the Senate tomorrow.

PRESENT PROGRESSIVE SUGGESTING FUTURE: She *is leaving* for London next Thursday.

EXERCISE A: Recognizing the Uses of the Present. All of the verbs in the following sentences are in the present. Read each sentence and decide which use of the present is intended.

    A. Present action or condition
    B. Regularly occurring action or condition
    C. Constant action or condition
    D. Historical or critical present
    E. Emphatic use
    F. Continuing action or condition

1. This bus *departs* daily from the station at 9:15 A.M.
2. The bakers *are doing* their pre-dawn work.
3. Charles Dickens *writes* with the intention of educating his readers.
4. The children *are munching* on popcorn during the movie.
5. These advertisements *are promoting* inferior products.
6. A cuckoo *appears* every hour to announce the time.
7. The voyagers on the supposedly unsinkable ship *Titanic feel* secure.
8. Your dinner *is* ready now.
9. Authors *are* hardly ever the best critics of their own writing.
10. A dab of this cologne *does seem* sufficient.

EXERCISE B: Using the Past, the Past Emphatic, the Present Perfect, and the Past Perfect Forms. Use a verb in the form indicated in parentheses to complete each of the following sentences. Be prepared to explain why the indicated verb form is appropriate.

1. I (action—past perfect) my speech several days before it was due.
2. For no apparent reason, Belinda (condition—present perfect) argumentative and disagreeable.
3. The doorbell (action—past) me from a sound sleep.

4. For several hours we (action—present perfect) for a solution to the problem.
5. You (condition—past) unusually quiet last night.
6. This old wicker furniture (action—present perfect) apart.
7. Bill (condition—past perfect) afraid of heights until he became a paratrooper.
8. Yesterday Susan (past emphatic) in the swimming meet.
9. The exterior of the house (condition—past) shabby.
10. My dog Clancy (condition—present perfect) listless.

EXERCISE C: **Using the Progressive Forms in the Past.** Write five sentences of your own using each of the following verbs in the progressive form indicated. Be prepared to explain why the forms are appropriate for your sentences.

1. live—present perfect progressive
2. read—past progressive
3. clean—past perfect progressive
4. hope—present perfect progressive
5. talk—past progressive

EXERCISE D: **Using the Future Tenses.** Choose the correct future form from the choices in parentheses for each of the following sentences. Be prepared to identify the form and explain what kind of action it indicates.

1. If the river rises, the flood (will damage, will have damaged) the paintings.
2. Our friends (will have been staying, will be staying) in the beach house next week.
3. By the time she arrives home, the guests (will have gathered, will gather) for the party.
4. If the weather is good tomorrow, Blake and I (will picnic, will have been picnicking) in the park.
5. She (will be visiting, will have visited) four European cities before she returns home next month.
6. When she returns, she (will be influenced, will have been influenced) by the cultures of the nations she toured.
7. He (will be, will have been) happy if you send him a postcard from Kenya.
8. Next year they (will be living, will have been living) in Brazil for most of the summer.
9. By tonight, I (will have redecorated, will have been redecorating) the entire house.
10. Before the end of the winter, the ice on the pond (will have melted, will have been melting).

■ Modifiers That Indicate Time

Adverbs such as *often* or *sometimes* and phrases such as *once in a while* or *within a week* are often used to help clarify the time expressed by a verb.

Use modifiers to help clarify the time expressed by a verb.

EXAMPLES: *Occasionally* I enjoy complete solitude.

Marion *always* tried to see both sides of every issue.

By next year Bob will have finished his internship.

Used with the simple present or the present progressive, modifiers can help place the action in future time. In the first of the following sentences, *leave* is present, but the intent is future. In the second sentence, *am leaving* is present progressive, but the intent is future progressive.

EXAMPLES: *Tomorrow* I leave for Japan.

One week from today I am leaving for Europe.

EXERCISE E: Using Modifiers to Clarify Time. Rewrite each of the following sentences by adding a modifier that indicates time. Be prepared to explain the difference your addition has made.

1. The flowers and trees come to life.
2. Our neighbors rake their leaf piles into our yard.
3. A break from routine will help you gain a new perspective.
4. Fred and his friends are going cross-country skiing.
5. Herds of buffalo roamed across the plains.

■ Sequence of Tenses

When a sentence is complex or compound-complex, the tense of the verb in the main clause often determines the tense of the verb in the subordinate clause. The form of a participle or infinitive is also often dependent on the tense of the main verb in the sentence.

Verbs in Subordinate Clauses. It is often necessary to check the tense of the main verb in a sentence before deciding the tense for the verb in a subordinate clause.

The tense of a verb in a subordinate clause should follow logically from the tense of the main verb.

Study the combinations of tenses in the following charts.
Notice how the choice of tenses affects the logical relationship
between the events that are being described. Certain combinations show that the events are *simultaneous*—that they happened at the same time. Other combinations show that the
events are *sequential*—that one event preceded or followed another. By checking the sequence of tenses in your own writing,
you can make sure you express your meaning clearly and
logically.

SEQUENCE OF TENSES		
Main Verb in Present		
Main Verb	**Subordinate Verb**	**Meaning**
I *know* . . .	*Present* that you *work* hard. *Present Emph* that you *do work* hard. *Present Prog* that you *are working* hard.	Simultaneous events: All events take place in present time.
I *know* . . .	*Past* that you *worked* hard. *Past Emph* that you *did work* hard. *Present Perf* that you *have worked* hard. *Past Prog* that you *were working* hard. *Present Perf Prog* that you *have been working* hard.	Sequential events: The working comes before the knowing.
I *know* . . .	*Past Perf* that you *had worked* *Past* hard and *succeeded.* *Past Perf Prog* that you *had been working* *Past* hard and *succeeded.*	Sequential events: The working comes before the success, both of which come before the knowing.

| I *know* . . . | Future
that you *will work* hard.

that you *will be working* hard. | Sequential events:
The knowing comes before the working. |
| I *know* . . . | Future Perf
that you *will have worked* hard
Present
before I ever *see* any of the results.
Future Perf Prog
that you *will have been working* hard before I ever
see any of the results. | Sequential events:
The knowing comes before the working, both of which come before the seeing. |

Main Verb in Past

| I *knew* . . . | Past
that you *worked* hard.
Past Emph
that you *did work* hard.
Past Prog
that you *were working* hard. | Simultaneous events:
All events take place in past time. (Notice that the present, the present perfect, and their progressive and emphatic forms cannot be used with a main verb in the past.) |
| I *knew* . . . | Past Perf
that you *had worked* hard
Past
when I *saw* the results.
Past Perf Prog
that you *had been working* hard
Past
when I *saw* the results. | Sequential and simultaneous events:
The working comes before the knowing and the seeing—two simultaneous events in past time. |

Main Verb in Future

| I *will know* . . . | Present
if you *work* hard.
Present Emph
if you *do work* hard.
Present Prog
if you *are working* hard. | Simultaneous events:
All events take place in future time. |

| I *will* know . . . | Past
that you *worked* hard.
Past Emph
that you *did work* hard.
Present Perf
that you *have worked* hard.
Present Perf Prog
that you *have been working* hard. | Sequential events:
The working comes
before the knowing. |

When a main verb is in one of the perfect or progressive forms, the verb in a subordinate clause will usually be in either the present or past, depending on sense.

If the Main Verb Is . . .	Then the Subordinate Verb Should Usually Be . . .
Present Progressive Present Perfect Progressive Future Perfect Future Progressive Future Perfect Progressive	Present
Present Perfect Past Progressive Past Perfect Past Perfect Progressive	Past

EXAMPLES:

Present Prog   Present

He *is practicing* until he *gets* it right.

Present Perf Prog   Present

She *has been studying* Arabic because she *plans* to visit Egypt next fall.

Future Perf   Present

The bus *will have departed* by the time we *arrive* at the terminal.

Future Prog   Present

I *will be working* at a garage after I *finish* school.

Future Perf Prog
They *will have been waiting* a year when their new house
Present
is finally ready.

Present Perf   Past
She *has forgotten* how he *suffered.*

Past Prog   Past
We *were swimming* when the rain *started.*

Past Perf   Past
I *had been* a member of the club long before you *were.*

Past Perf Prog   Past
The tree *had been dying* until we *discovered* the cause.

When checking the sequence of tenses in your sentences, rely on logic rather than on hard-and-fast rules. If you first sort out in your own mind whether the events you are describing are simultaneous, sequential, or combinations of both, then you should have few problems making verbs express the precise meaning you intend.

NOTE ABOUT *WOULD HAVE:*   Do not repeat the helping verbs *would have* in a subordinate clause beginning with *if* when the main verb also contains *would have.* Instead, make the subordinate verb past perfect.

INCORRECT: If you *would have* arrived sooner, you *would have* met my friend.

CORRECT: If you *had arrived* sooner, you *would have* met my friend.

Time Sequence with Participles and Infinitives.   The form of a participle or infinitive often determines whether the event it describes is simultaneous with or sequential to another event. Remember that participles can be present *(hearing),* past *(heard),* or perfect *(having heard).* Infinitives can be either present *(to hear)* or perfect *(to have heard).*

The form of a participle or infinitive should set up a logical time sequence in relation to a verb in the same clause or sentence.

The relation between a verb and a present or past form of a verbal is seldom a usage problem when the events they express are simultaneous.

SIMULTANEOUS EVENTS	
In Present Time	*Present* *Present* *Hearing* the alarm, we *run* for safety. I *want to know* the answer.
In Past Time	*Present* *Past* *Hearing* the alarm, we *ran* for safety. *Past* *Heard* hundreds of miles away, the eruption *sounded* like thunder. *Past* *Present* I *wanted to know* the answer.
In Future Time	*Present* *Future* *Hearing* the alarm, we *will run* for safety. *Future* *Present* I *will want to know* the answer.

Sequential action is expressed by the relation of a perfect participle or perfect infinitive to a verb. The event expressed by such a verbal should always logically precede the event expressed by the verb.

SEQUENTIAL EVENTS	
In Present Time	*Perfect* *Present Prog* *Having heard* the alarm, we *are running* for safety. (The hearing comes before the running.) *Present* *Perfect* I *am* glad *to have met* you. (The meeting comes before the being glad.)
In Past Time	*Perfect* *Past* *Having heard* the alarm, we *ran* for safety. (The hearing comes before the running.) *Past* *Perfect* *Past* He *was* glad *to have met* you before you *left*. (The meeting comes before the being glad and the leaving.)

Spanning Past and Future Time	Perfect Future *Having heard* this news, we *will stay* home. (The hearing—a past event—affects the staying, a future event.) Future Perfect Many years from now she *will be* glad *to have met* you. (The meeting comes before the being glad.)

EXERCISE F: Recognizing the Correct Forms of Verbs in Subordinate Clauses and of Participles and Infinitives. Number your paper from 1 to 10. Notice that the main verb has been underlined in each of the following sentences. Rewrite each sentence to include the construction indicated in parentheses. The underlined verb should determine the form of a verb in a subordinate clause, the form of a participle, or the form of an infinitive. Study the example that follows before you start rewriting the sentences.

EXAMPLE: I <u>was</u> sorry I spoke so harshly. (Change *spoke* to a perfect infinitive.)

                I was sorry to have spoken so harshly.

1. I <u>understand</u>. (Add a subordinate clause containing the present perfect of *be*.)
2. Sally <u>tried</u> growing herbs in the rocky soil. (Change *growing* to a present infinitive.)
3. Jeff <u>will be studying</u> hard. (Add a subordinate clause containing the present of *learn*.)
4. The campers <u>claimed</u> they saw a grizzly bear. (Change *saw* to a perfect infinitive.)
5. They <u>will find</u> the answer. (Add a subordinate clause containing the present perfect of *see*.)
6. He <u>waited</u> for their reaction. (Add a phrase containing the perfect participle of *describe*.)
7. We finally <u>reached</u> our destination. (Add a subordinate clause containing the past perfect of *travel*.)
8. The director <u>will be making</u> suggestions. (Add a subordinate clause containing the present of *follow*.)
9. She <u>remembers</u> only too well. (Add a subordinate clause containing the past of *betray*.)
10. The puppy <u>asked</u> for shelter by scratching at the door. (Add a phrase containing the past participle of *frighten*.)

APPLICATION: Correcting Errors in Tense. The following paragraph contains many errors in tense. Rewrite the paragraph, making the necessary corrections. Circle the verbs that you have corrected.

(1) *The Little Prince,* a wonderful book by Antoine de Saint-Exupéry, is a story that everyone should be reading at least once. (2) It has been narrated by a pilot who must repair his airplane or else have perished on the Sahara Desert. (3) While the pilot had been thus isolated, a little prince from a tiny planet becomes his friend. (4) As the prince will talk about his experiences, the pilot discovered truths for his own life. (5) He will have learned that friendship creates responsibility. (6) He also began to understand that the real essentials are things that are invisible: The most accurate source of vision was the heart. (7) In the end the little prince had returned to his planet, and the pilot's life can never be the same. (8) For him, the stars may sometimes sound like millions of bells. (9) At other times, the bells became tears. (10) But to understand this, you must first read the book.

6.3 The Subjunctive Mood

In modern English there are three *moods,* or ways in which a verb can express an action or condition: indicative, imperative, and subjunctive. The first two are familiar moods found in most of the sentences that you write or speak. The *indicative mood,* the most often used of the three, is used to make factual statements and to ask questions. The *imperative mood* is used to give orders or directions.

INDICATIVE: She *is* concerned for others.

IMPERATIVE: *Be* concerned for others.

The third mood, however, often poses problems, even for the well educated.

Verbs in the *subjunctive mood* differ from verbs in the indicative mood in only two significant ways: (1) In the present tense, a third-person singular verb in the subjunctive mood does not have the usual *-s* or *-es* ending. (2) In the present tense, the subjunctive mood of *be* is *be,* and in the past tense, it is *were,* regardless of which personal pronoun or noun the verb follows.

Indicative Mood	Subjunctive Mood
Make sure that he *stays* here.	I prefer that he *stay* here.
The employees *are* not always punctual.	The company requires that all employees *be* punctual.
I *was* sad.	If I *were* sad, I would tell you.

The uses of the subjunctive mood are limited in modern English; nevertheless, it is important to know when the subjunctive should be used and to use the subjunctive verb forms correctly.

■ The Correct Use of the Subjunctive Mood

The subjunctive mood in modern English has two general uses.

Use the **subjunctive mood** (1) in clauses beginning with *if* or *that* to express an idea that is contrary to fact or (2) in clauses beginning with *that* to express a request, a demand, or a proposal.

By remembering the two ways in which subjunctive verbs differ from indicative verbs and by checking your *if* and *that* clauses, you can learn to use the subjunctive mood correctly.

Expressing Ideas Contrary to Fact.   Ideas that are contrary to fact are usually expressed as wishes or conditions. The subjunctive mood helps indicate that what is being expressed is not now and may never be true.

EXAMPLES: She wishes that she *were* a stronger person. (She is not now and may never be strong.)

We would very much like that your friend *stay* for dinner. (The friend is not now staying.)

If he *weren't* tired, he'd go to the dance tonight. (However, he is tired.)

Expressing Requests, Demands, and Proposals.   Although this second use of the subjunctive mood also indicates that the ideas being expressed are not now true, it implies that they could or should be true soon. A verb that expresses a request, a demand, or a proposal is often followed by a *that* clause, which will generally call for a verb in the subjunctive mood.

**VERBS USUALLY FOLLOWED BY *THAT*
CLAUSES AND SUBJUNCTIVE VERBS**

request	demand	propose
ask	insist	suggest
prefer	order	move
	determine	
	require	

REQUEST: We ask that everyone *be* silent during the demonstration.

DEMAND: The professor insists that every student *attend* all classes.

PROPOSAL: I move that the minutes of the last meeting *be* read.

EXERCISE A: Using the Subjunctive Mood. Each of the following sentences contains a verb in the indicative mood that should be subjunctive. Rewrite each sentence to correct the verb.

1. If there was a concert tonight, we would go.
2. I wish that I was free to choose.
3. The teacher prefers that he sits in the front row.
4. The law in this state requires that you are sixteen before you apply for a driver's license.
5. Her grandparents proposed that she stays with them while her parents are away.
6. I wish that I was more imaginative.
7. She spoke to him as if he was a child who understands nothing.
8. The judge ordered that the defendant stands trial as charged.
9. The boy shrieked as if the shadow he saw was a monster.
10. He would prefer that his son goes to a military school.

■ Auxiliary Verbs That Help Express the Subjunctive Mood

Since certain helping verbs suggest conditions contrary to fact, they can often be used in place of the usual subjunctive forms.

Could, would, or *should* can be used to help a verb express the subjunctive mood.

In the following chart, the sentences on the left contain the usual past subjunctive form of the verb *be*: *were*. The sentences on the right have been reworded with *could*, *would*, and *should*.

THE SUBJUNCTIVE MOOD EXPRESSED THROUGH AUXILIARY VERBS	
If Joshua *were* here, he'd know what to do.	If Joshua *could be* here, he'd know what to do.
If I *were* to leave now, the job would never get finished.	If I *would leave* now, the job would never get finished.
If you *were* to go to Rome, what would you want to see first?	If you *should go* to Rome, what would you want to see first?

EXERCISE B: Using Auxiliary Verbs to Express the Subjunctive Mood. Each of the following sentences contains a subjunctive verb used correctly. Rewrite each sentence, using an auxiliary verb to help express the subjunctive mood.

1. If Paul were more cheerful, we'd all have a better time.
2. If you were to meet him after all these years, you would be surprised at how little he has changed.
3. The room would be neater if you were to clear away the newspapers.
4. I would prepare a gourmet meal if you were to stay for dinner.
5. If Mary were to come to the party, I would have to leave.

APPLICATION: Writing Sentences Using the Subjunctive Mood. Use each of the following phrases in a sentence of your own that contains the subjunctive mood. Underline the subjunctive verbs in your sentences.

1. suggest that
2. were to see
3. that you be
4. if I were
5. could be more friendly

Voice   6.4

Previous sections have shown how verbs change form depending on tense and mood. This section will discuss how most verbs can also change form to show whether or not the subject performs the action or has the action performed on it. This quality of verbs is known as *voice*.

Voice is the form of a verb that show whether or not the subject is performing the action.

Linking verbs cannot indicate voice; action verbs can. In English there are two voices: *active* and *passive*.

■ Active and Passive Voice

A verb is active when the subject performs the action and passive when the subject receives the action.

Active Voice.   Any action verb, regardless of whether it is transitive or intransitive (that is, with or without a direct object), can be in the active voice.

A transitive or intransitive verb is **active** when its subject performs the action.

In the following examples, the subjects perform the action. The first example contains a transitive verb and, therefore, has a direct object, which receives the action of the verb. The second example has no direct object; its verb is intransitive.

ACTIVE VERBS: Mike *introduced* the new manager.

    They *believe* halfheartedly.

Passive Voice.   Most action verbs can also be used in the passive voice.

A verb is **passive** when its action is performed upon the subject. A passive verb almost never has a direct object and is always a verb phrase made from a form of *be* plus the past participle of a transitive verb.

In the following examples, the subjects receive the action— that is, they have the action performed upon them. The first example names the performer, *Mike*, but Mike is now the object of the preposition *by* instead of the subject. In the second example, the performer of the action is not mentioned. Notice that neither example has a direct object.

PASSIVE VERBS:

S   V   Obj of Prep

The new manager *was introduced* by Mike.

S   V

They *were believed* because of their integrity.

The tense of the helping verb *be* determines the tense of a passive verb. For example, when *be* is in the present tense, the passive verb is also in the present tense. The past participle does not change. Following is a short conjugation of the verb *choose* in the passive voice. Notice that there are only two progressive forms in the passive voice and no emphatic forms.

SHORT CONJUGATION OF *CHOOSE* IN THE PASSIVE VOICE	
Tense	**Passive Form**
Present	she is chosen
Past	she was chosen
Future	she will be chosen
Present Perfect	she has been chosen
Past Perfect	she had been chosen
Future Perfect	she will have been chosen
Present Progressive	she is being chosen
Past Progressive	she was being chosen

EXERCISE A: Distinguishing Between Active and Passive Voice. Label the verb from each of the following sentences *active* or *passive*.

1. His bizarre behavior was ridiculed by his peers.
2. This wildlife sanctuary protects endangered species.
3. The senior class will collect money for a trip to Washington.
4. This new film is praised by the critics for its honesty.
5. A suicide prevention organization operates twenty-four hours a day.
6. By this time tomorrow the letter will have been read by the admissions committee.
7. Two astronauts, anchored to the craft by nylon ropes, floated in outer space.
8. As a responsible citizen, Bill is being called for jury duty.
9. Newspaper reporters swarmed around the scene of the crime.
10. At the entrance to the mansion, a haughty butler asked us to come to the back door.

11. The story about Big Foot is being investigated by a team of naturalists.
12. A Republican has not been elected from this district for several years.
13. The announcements pertaining to school cancellations will be made on a local radio station.
14. You must groom your dog carefully before the contest.
15. A pathway from the house to the garage was being shoveled by my older brother.
16. Susan will have returned from her vacation by now.
17. A trophy had been awarded to the winner of the archery contest.
18. Two rows of poplars had been planted as a windbreak by the previous owners of the house.
19. A Brazilian architect designed this plaza.
20. My friends and I have been wondering about the existence of the unidentified flying objects.

EXERCISE B: Conjugating Verbs in the Passive Voice. Conjugate each of the following four verbs in the passive voice using only the personal pronoun indicated in parentheses. Use the chart on page 187 as your model.

1. elect (with *I*)
2. prepare (with *you*)
3. show (with *she*)
4. give (with *we*)

■ Using Active and Passive Voice

Once you are able to distinguish between active and passive voice, you can apply this knowledge to your own writing. The active voice is generally stronger than the passive voice.

Use the active voice whenever possible.

Often either voice may be used to express the same information. The active voice, however, is more direct and economical. Unless you have a specific reason for using the passive voice, use the active voice. Notice in the following pair of sentences, for example, that the first sentence sounds better because it is shorter and more direct.

ACTIVE VOICE: Mr. and Mrs. Simon *celebrated* their anniversary.

PASSIVE VOICE: The anniversary *was celebrated* by Mr. and Mrs. Simon.

The passive voice has two important uses in English.

Use the passive voice (1) to emphasize the receiver rather than the performer of an action or (2) to point out the receiver when the performer is unknown or unimportant.

RECEIVER EMPHASIZED: Karen *was shocked* by her friend's remark.

PERFORMER UNKNOWN: A car *was abandoned* near the hospital.

PERFORMER UNIMPORTANT: The townspeople *will be evacuated* before the volcano erupts.

EXERCISE C: Using the Active Voice. Ten sentences in Exercise A contain verbs in the passive voice. Rewrite each of these sentences in the active voice, changing or adding words as necessary. Be prepared to explain whether the active or passive voice is better.

EXERCISE D: Correcting Unnecessary Use of the Passive Voice. Most of the underlined verbs in the following paragraph are in the passive voice. Rewrite the paragraph changing passive verbs into active ones when you think active verbs will improve the paragraph. It is not necessary to change every passive verb.

Her mother (1) had been buried three days. Now, standing in her mother's kitchen, Emma (2) was made uneasy by the heavy silence of the house. What already dulled memory of sound (3) was being forgotten? Then she (4) remembered. A black cloth (5) hung over the cage, where it (6) had been placed many evenings ago. Inside, shrouded in darkness, (7) would be the canary, a birthday present that (8) had been gleefully given by the grandchildren. Death (9) was so unfair. But the bird still (10) lived. As the cloth (11) slid to the floor, the canary's head (12) was untucked from beneath its wing. Its slight body (13) was shaken with a weak but persistent song of life.

APPLICATION: Using Voice Correctly in Writing. Describe an incident in which you experienced something that illustrated the positive value of life. Include two appropriate uses of the passive voice: one that emphasizes the receiver rather than the performer of an action and another in which the performer is not named. Make sure that all of the other verbs in your description are in the active voice.

7

Pronoun Usage

At one time, nouns and pronouns in the English language always changed form according to their use in a sentence. For example, the form a noun would have as a subject was different from its form as a direct object. Though today English relies more on syntax (the order of words in a sentence) than on changes in form to indicate a word's use, this old characteristic of English has not entirely disappeared. Nouns still change form when they are used to show possession: An apostrophe and an *s* (the *flower's* stem) or just an apostrophe (the *teams'* mascot) is added to the usual form of the noun. This change, however, is a minor one when contrasted with the changes that take place in some pronouns. *He*, for example, which is used for subjects (*He* is angry), becomes *him* for objects (I told *him* the news) and *his* for possession (I understand *his* objections).

The relationship between the form of a noun or a pronoun and its use in a sentence is known as *case*. This chapter will explain the various cases and show you how to use them correctly.

7.1 Case

Case is a characteristic of only two parts of speech: nouns and pronouns.

Case is the form of a noun or pronoun that indicates how it is used in a sentence.

In English there are three cases: *nominative, objective,* and *possessive.* The following chart lists the various uses of the three cases.

Case	Use in a Sentence
Nominative	subject of a verb predicate nominative nominative absolute
Objective	direct object indirect object object of a verbal object of a preposition subject of an infinitive
Possessive	to show ownership

Nouns usually present no problem since their form is changed only to show possession: An *'s* is added for most singular nouns; an apostrophe is added for most plural nouns. In the first of the following sentences, *tree* is nominative because it is a subject. In the second example, *tree* is objective because it is the object of a preposition. The form, however, is the same. The third example shows the forms that change, the singular and plural possessive forms of *tree*.

NOMINATIVE: The *tree* lost a limb in the storm.

OBJECTIVE: A bird built its nest in the *tree*.

POSSESSIVE: The small *tree's* growth was stunted by several larger *trees'* heavy branches.

Unlike nouns, personal pronouns have many different forms to show whether they are in the nominative case, the objective case, or the possessive case. Because personal pronouns have many different forms, you must be careful to use the correct one. First, consider the various forms in which personal pronouns may appear.

■ The Cases of Personal Pronouns

The following chart groups personal pronouns according to the three cases. Because the forms of *you* and *it* are the same for both the nominative and the objective case, they rarely cause a usage problem.

	Nominative	Objective	Possessive
Singular	I you he, she, it	me you him, her, it	my, mine your, yours his, her, hers, its
Plural	we you they	us you them	our, ours your, yours their, theirs

Study the pronouns in the chart above and learn to identify each of them by case. Remembering the personal pronouns as well as each case and its uses will help you avoid errors in usage.

EXERCISE A: Identifying Case. Number your paper from 1 to 20. For each of the following sentences, write the case of the indicated pronoun.

1. *Her* staunch support has not gone unnoticed.
2. The exam should cause *him* no difficulty.
3. It seems that we and *they* have much in common.
4. Before you use the computer, ask *them* for a demonstration.
5. My friends and I appreciate their leaving *their* cabin for us to use.
6. Sally made this dragon kite for you and *me*.
7. Before reading Shakespeare's comedies, *we* studied the Elizabethan Age.
8. This plaster cast was made to resemble *her*.
9. The audience stirred restlessly, *he* having spoken for nearly two hours.
10. Hiding *them* made him an accessory to the crime.
11. After Jean whispered the password, the guard admitted *her*.
12. The fields were prepared for planting by two oxen, a plow, and *him*.
13. Let *me* decide which path to take.
14. The ushers at the wedding will be he and *I*.
15. Apologetically, the waitress served *us* the cold soup.
16. The responsibility for this negligence is *ours* alone.
17. *We* tilled the fields and planted his crops without any assistance.
18. The swimming team captain will be either Monica or *she*.
19. A full moon cast *its* soft light on the ground below.
20. In our opinion the best women's fashion designer is *she*.

■ The Nominative Case

The nominative case is used when a personal pronoun acts in one of three ways.

Use the **nominative case** for the subject of a verb, for a predicate nominative, and for the pronoun in a nominative absolute construction.

NOMINATIVE PRONOUNS	
As a Subject	*They* plan the menu, and *we* do the cooking.
As a Predicate Nominative	The only person left in the auditorium was *she*.
In a Nominative Absolute	*He* having finished his lecture, the students strode briskly from the room.

Informal Use of the Predicate Nominative. Although formal usage requires a nominative pronoun after a linking verb, people frequently use the objective case in informal situations. For essays, term papers, and other school or business work, however, you should make it a point to use only nominative pronouns for predicate nominatives.

FORMAL: It was *I* who answered the telephone.

INFORMAL: It was *me* who answered the telephone.

Nominative Pronouns in Compounds. When you use a pronoun as part of a compound subject or compound predicate nominative, make sure that the pronoun is in the nominative case.

COMPOUND SUBJECT: Joanne and *I* will make a great team. (*Not* "Joanne and me . . .")

Maria and *he* cannot keep any secrets from each other. (*Not* "Maria and him . . .")

COMPOUND PREDICATE NOMINATIVE: The most frequently absent members of this class are Sylvia and *she*. (*Not* " . . . Sylvia and her.")

The remaining contestants were Fran and *they*. (*Not* " . . . Fran and them.")

You can easily check whether the pronoun is correct in a compound construction by skipping the noun and using the pronoun separately in the sentence. You should then be able to hear if the pronoun you have chosen is correct.

Nominative Pronouns with Appositives. Sometimes a pronoun used as a subject or as a predicate nominative will be followed by a noun in apposition. The pronoun should be in the nominative case as though it were by itself.

EXAMPLES: *We* Bostonians are proud of our city's history. (*Not* "Us . . . are proud . . .")

The ones to decide the best candidate for office are *we* the American people. (*Not* "The ones . . . are us . . .")

EXERCISE B: Using Pronouns in the Nominative Case. Complete each of the following sentences by supplying an appropriate nominative pronoun. Write the pronoun on your paper and indicate whether it is a *subject, predicate nominative,* or *nominative absolute.*

1. _____ and Paula will present their report first.
2. The ones to establish correct procedure are _____, the committee.
3. Without any doubt Charlene and _____ deserve credit for their fund raising efforts.
4. _____ having gently lifted the soufflé from the oven, the meal was ready.
5. _____ and Amy collaborated to write a book.
6. Joaquín and _____ were sent to help the refugees.
7. _____ and I are learning that colors affect our emotions.
8. No one today could find Judge Crater, _____ having vanished decades ago.
9. The best sailors on this lake are _____ boys.
10. Marc and _____ are both good at pantomime.
11. It is _____ myself who should be held accountable.
12. Two representatives at the convention will be _____ and he.
13. Mr. Levitt's new receptionist will be _____.
14. You and _____ cannot lift that package by yourselves.
15. Esther and _____ were always my favorite aunts.
16. The Baxters and _____ plan to visit the Pyramids.
17. Near the horizon Karl and _____ could see the top of the castle tower.

18. _____ having disregarded all warnings, the family boarded the leaky boat.
19. One of the best auctioneers is _____.
20. "The culprit is _____!" cried the excited witness.

■ The Objective Case

Objective pronouns are used for any kind of object in a sentence as well as for subjects of infinitives.

Use the **objective case** for the object of any verb, verbal, or preposition, or for the subject of an infinitive.

OBJECTIVE PRONOUNS	
As a Direct Object	The experienced hikers left *them* far behind.
As an Indirect Object	The blaring music gave *her* a headache.
As an Object of a Participle	The problem bothering *him* remained a secret.
As an Object of a Gerund	Finding *me* will not be easy for you.
As an Object of an Infinitive	They want to show *us* their new sailboat.
As an Object of a Preposition	There is not one good choice among *them*.
As a Subject of an Infinitive	They want Paulo and *me* to take their place.

Objective Pronouns in Compounds.   As with the nominative case, most usage problems in the objective case occur with pronouns in compounds. To avoid errors use the pronoun in question by itself. In the following examples, the objective case pronouns are correct.

COMPOUND DIRECT OBJECT: The helicopter rescued (Bill and) *me*. (*Not* " . . . rescued . . . I.")

COMPOUND INDIRECT OBJECT: Al sent (Carol and) *her* tickets to the play. (*Not* " . . . sent . . . she tickets to the play.")

Again, by skipping the noun you should be able to hear if the pronoun you have chosen is correct.

Objective Pronouns with Appositives.   When a pronoun used as an object or as the subject of an infinitive has an appositive, use the objective case just as you would if the pronoun were by itself.

EXAMPLES: The coach encouraged *us* athletes. (*Not* ". . . encouraged we . . ."){DO, Appos}

A state map showed *us* confused passengers the route taken by the bus. (*Not* " . . . showed we . . .") {IO, Appos}

The hostel provided rest for *us* travel-weary cyclists. (*Not* " . . . for we . . .") {Obj of Prep, Appos}

The guide urged *us* stragglers to hurry up. (*Not* " . . . we . . . to hurry up.") {S of Infin, Appos}

NOTE ABOUT THE POSSESSIVE CASE: Although errors are less often made in the possessive case than they are in the other two cases, mistakes are frequently made when pronouns are used before gerunds. In the following examples, *"him* objecting," *"you* maintaining," and *"me* sitting" may sound correct, but they are not. A pronoun before a gerund should be in the possessive case.

EXAMPLES: *His* objecting to the rules caused an uproar.

I respect *your* maintaining an optimistic outlook.

Tad's dog resents *my* sitting on her favorite chair.

Another error to watch for is using an apostrophe with a possessive pronoun. Possessive forms such as *yours, hers, ours,* and *theirs* already indicate ownership. Remember also that *its* and *their* are possessive pronouns, whereas *it's* and *they're* are contractions meaning "it is" and "they are."

PRONOUNS: That cat is *ours*. (*Not* "our's")

Her face had lost *its* youthfulness.

Their flight may be delayed.

CONTRACTIONS: *It's* not too late to change your mind.

They're planning to stay in Houston a week.

EXERCISE C: **Using Pronouns in the Objective Case.** Complete each of the following sentences by supplying an appropriate objective pronoun. Write only the pronoun on your paper.

1. This replica of a Mississippi steamboat was made by Lee and _____.
2. The old clothes made Charles and _____ look like a Victorian couple.
3. Bentley sent _____ to inspect the summer cottage.
4. A lifeguard tried to warn Philip and _____.
5. Jackie sent _____ the picture she had taken of my sister and me.
6. That chimpanzee just grinned at my brother and _____.
7. Since there was only one empty seat on the bus, the old gentleman sat next to _____.
8. Give _____ students a chance before you reject the idea.
9. I would like to recommend Michelle and _____.
10. As a goodwill ambassador, he left _____ feeling reassured.
11. This flamboyant hat with trailing feathers was designed especially with _____ in mind.
12. Leaving _____ behind by themselves may be a mistake.
13. Their overly indulgent parents bought _____ everything they could possibly want.
14. When can we expect _____ to arrive?
15. We often think about Uncle Wilbur and _____.
16. Inform _____ of her right to an attorney.
17. My lazy friend asked me to provide _____ and Sean with the correct list.
18. The aroma of baked goods lured _____ hungry workers into the bakery.
19. Doesn't this tranquil scene give _____ girls a sense of peace?
20. Between you and _____ there are only differences of opinion.

APPLICATION: **Writing Sentences with Nominative, Objective, and Possessive Pronouns.** Write ten sentences of your own using the following pronouns as indicated. Then label each pronoun *nominative, objective,* or *possessive.*

1. Use *she and I* as the subject of a verb.
2. Use *our* before a gerund.
3. Use *them* as a direct object.

4. Use *me and you* as the object of a preposition.
5. Use *he* as part of a nominative absolute construction.
6. Use *we* followed by an appositive as the subject of a verb.
7. Use *theirs* after a linking verb.
8. Use *us* as an indirect object followed by an appositive.
9. Use *me* as the subject of an infinitive.
10. Use *he and they* as a compound predicate nominative.

7.2 Special Problems with Pronouns

As discussed in the previous section, the incorrect case form of a pronoun may sometimes sound correct. "The broken ladder left Jim and *we* boys stranded on the roof" may not seem wrong, but a nominative pronoun has been used where an objective pronoun belongs. Thus, the sentence is incorrect. This section will focus on other specific problems involving choices between the case forms of pronouns.

■ Using *Who* and *Whoever* Correctly

Deciding which form of *who* and *whoever* to use can easily be a problem. The pronoun *who* and its different forms are used in questions or in subordinate clauses. *Whoever* usually begins a subordinate clause.

Learn to recognize the various cases of *who* and *whoever* and to use them correctly in sentences.

By learning the uses of the various forms of *who* and *whoever*, you can avoid most of the confusion over making the correct choice.

The Cases of *Who* and *Whoever*. The following chart lists the forms for each of the three cases of *who* and *whoever* along with their uses.

THE FORM AND USES OF *WHO* AND *WHOEVER*		
Case	Pronoun	Use
Nominative	who, whoever	subject of a verb predicate nominative

Objective	whom, whomever	direct object object of a preposition
Possessive	whose, whosever	to show possession

The nominative pronouns *who* and *whoever* frequently act as interrogative pronouns in questions, filling the role of subject within the sentence. Both *who* and *whoever* can also act as predicate nominatives, but for *whoever* to do so is rare.

AS A SUBJECT: *Who* wrote the Bill of Rights?

   Whoever would commit such a heinous act?

AS A PREDICATE NOMINATIVE: The news commentator was *who*?

Problems often occur not when *who* and *whoever* are used in questions, but when they are used in complex sentences to begin a subordinate clause. In these cases it is important to remember that the pronoun's role within the subordinate clause determines its case.

EXAMPLE: Assign this unpleasant task to *whoever* is willing to accept it.

In this example the pronoun seems to be the object of the preposition *to*, in which position the pronoun should be *whomever*. However, within the subordinate clause, the pronoun acts as the subject of the verb *is*. Therefore, *whoever*, the nominative form, is correct. What then is the object of the preposition *to*? The entire subordinate clause is, not the pronoun.

To decide whether the case of a pronoun in a complex sentence is correct, first isolate the subordinate clause. If the clause is inverted, rearrange the words in subject-verb order. Then determine the pronoun's use.

EXAMPLE: Assign this unpleasant task to *whoever* is willing to accept it.

   Subordinate clause: whoever is willing to accept it

   Use of pronoun: subject of verb *is*

   Case for subject: nominative

The objective pronouns *whom* and *whomever* are also used in questions, as either direct objects or objects of prepositions.

If you are in doubt about the use of the pronoun in a question, reword the question as a statement and check to see what function the pronoun has in the sentence.

DO

AS A DIRECT OBJECT: *Whom* did you consult? (You did consult *whom*.)

AS THE OBJECT OF A PREPOSITION: For *whom* did the band perform?

Again, in complex sentences it is important to examine the pronoun's role within the subordinate clause before deciding whether a nominative or objective pronoun is called for. Follow the same steps you did previously: Isolate the clause, reword it if necessary (a clause correctly beginning with *whom* or *whomever* will always be inverted), and then determine the use of the pronoun.

EXAMPLE: This waiter is an unpleasant fellow *whom* I dislike.

   Subordinate clause: whom I dislike

   Reworded clause: I dislike whom

   Use of pronoun: direct object of *dislike*

   Case for direct object: objective

EXAMPLE: John charmed *whomever* he spoke with.

   Subordinate clause: whomever he spoke with

   Reworded clause: he spoke with whomever

   Use of pronoun: object of preposition *with*

   Case for object of a preposition: objective

Few people have any difficulty using the possessive pronoun *whose* unless they confuse the pronoun with the contraction *who's*, meaning "who is."

PRONOUN: *Whose* fingerprints were on the glass?

CONTRACTION: *Who's* the lucky winner?

The other possessive form, *whosever*, also causes few problems because it is so seldom used in modern English.

Determining Case in Subordinate Clauses with Parenthetical Expressions.   Sometimes parenthetical expressions such as *they say*, *I suppose*, or *experts predict* interrupt a subordinate clause. Simply ignore these expressions when choosing the case of *who* or *whoever* since they do not affect the rest of the clause. In the following examples, the parenthetical expressions are set off by commas.

EXAMPLES: Benedict Arnold was the traitor *who*, I think, most deserved punishment.

          Benedict Arnold was the traitor *whom*, I think, the patriots hated most.

NOTE ABOUT *WHOM* AND *WHOMEVER* IN SPOKEN ENGLISH: The use of *whom* and *whomever* is decreasing rapidly in spoken English. *Who* and *whoever* are used informally in all situations except when the objective forms sound better. In the following example, *who* sounds correct because it is separated from its preposition *for*.

INFORMAL: *Who* did you buy this gift for?

When the pronoun directly follows its preposition, people still generally use the objective form *whom*.

FORMAL AND INFORMAL: For *whom* did you buy this gift?

EXERCISE A: Using the Forms of *Who* and *Whoever*. Complete the following sentences with the correct formal form of *who* or *whoever*. Then identify the pronoun's use in the sentence.

EXAMPLE: Give the tickets to _____ wants them.

      whoever   subject of <u>wants</u>

1. The participants were _____ ?
2. Feel free to interview _____ you wish.
3. Troubadors were minstrels _____ spread folk songs all over southern France.
4. _____ did Ed ask for a ride?
5. _____ would support such a cause?
6. Jack talked about those _____ choose to bury their heads in the sand.
7. The clerk is courteous to _____ she helps.
8. Someone, _____ was the last to leave, should have turned off the lights.
9. Wendy is looking forward to meeting you, _____ she has heard so much about.
10. _____ sequined jacket is this?
11. Mr. Perkins is the teacher _____ we believe the students prefer as yearbook advisor.

12. I will vote for _____ promises to reduce inflation.
13. Save your ridiculous jokes for _____ you hope will listen.
14. Joanne is a person _____ character will not allow her to be deceptive.
15. _____ will be successful in balancing the budget?
16. Ask _____ you believe would like to attend the lecture.
17. We didn't know _____ left the cryptic message.
18. Come in, _____ you are.
19. The boys thanked _____ they had received the tip from.
20. William Faulkner is the author _____ I think wrote *The Sound and the Fury*.

EXERCISE B: Writing Sentences with Forms of *Who* and *Whoever*. For each of the following items, write a sentence using the form of the pronoun indicated in parentheses.

EXAMPLE: *Whomever* (as a direct object)

The first love sonnets were written for <u>whomever</u> the poet admired.

1. *Who* (as a predicate nominative)
2. *Whoever* (as the subject of a subordinate clause)
3. *Whom* (as a direct object)
4. *Whomever* (in a question)
5. *Who* (as a subject)
6. *Whom* (in a question beginning "With whom...")
7. *Whomever* (as a direct object)
8. *Who* (as the subject of a subordinate clause)
9. *Whom* (as the object of a preposition)
10. *Whom* (as a direct object in a subordinate clause)

■ Using Pronouns Correctly in Elliptical Clauses

Another problem with pronoun usage occurs in complex sentences containing an elliptical clause—that is, a clause in which some words are understood rather than stated. Such clauses are usually used in making comparisons. When the subject, verb, or both have been omitted from the second part of the comparison, errors may occur.

In elliptical clauses beginning with *than* or *as*, use the form of the pronoun that you would use if the clause were fully stated.

The following two models show the structure of complex sentences containing elliptical clauses. Notice in the boxes on the right that the position of the pronoun in relation to the omitted words determines whether the pronoun should be nominative or objective.

Words Left Out After Pronoun

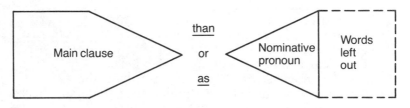

Words Left Out Before Pronoun

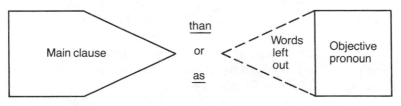

The following examples illustrate the models; the understood words have been included in parentheses.

WORDS LEFT OUT AFTER PRONOUN: Amanda is as strong as *he* (is strong).

WORDS LEFT OUT BEFORE PRONOUN: My friend Betty sent Karen more postcards than (she sent) *me.*

When you choose a pronoun for an elliptical clause, mentally complete the clause. If the understood words would normally come after the pronoun, use a nominative pronoun (*I, we, he, she, they*). If the understood words would normally come before the pronoun, use an objective pronoun (*me, us, him, her, them*).

In some situations the case of the pronoun completely changes the meaning of the sentence, as in the following examples.

NOMINATIVE PRONOUN: I liked his brother more than *he* (did).

OBJECTIVE PRONOUN: I liked his brother more than (I liked) *him.*

EXERCISE C: Choosing the Correct Pronoun in Elliptical Clauses. Copy each of the following sentences onto your paper and complete the elliptical clause. Then cross out the incorrect pronoun from the choices in parentheses.

EXAMPLE: He was as delighted as (I, me).

He was as delighted as (I, ~~me~~) was delighted.

1. This flutist has a better tone than (he, him).
2. You are more perceptive than (she, her).
3. Old memories mean more to me than (he, him).
4. Nancy earns more money than (she, her).
5. A horror movie scares Barbara more than (she, her).
6. Sharon will do more for the junior class than (she, her).
7. My brother plays chess as well as (she, her).
8. Do these children look as healthy as (they, them)?
9. He can speak more authoritatively on that than (I, me).
10. These flowers are less delicate than (they, them).

APPLICATION 1: Writing Sentences with Elliptical Clauses. Use each of the following items in sentences of your own containing elliptical clauses. Check to see that you have used pronouns correctly by completing the elliptical clauses in parentheses.

EXAMPLE: friendlier than they

Our new neighbors are friendlier than they (are friendly).

1. as quick as I
2. less than me
3. neater than he
4. more than us
5. as witty as he
6. as belligerent as they
7. craftier than she
8. as welcome as her
9. sadder than me
10. as stubborn as we

APPLICATION 2: Correcting Errors in Pronoun Usage. Rewrite each of the following sentences to eliminate the error.

1. I don't trust Samantha, whom I think was the guilty one.
2. Whose assuming that we caused this incredible confusion?
3. Mike is a better judge of character than me.
4. He is as insulting as her.
5. They wonder who the senator will entrust with the job.
6. We saw the actor who we had formed a fan club for.
7. Whom should I say is calling?
8. Whomever should receive the reward will be the person to whom I give the money.
9. The hostess asked who's pocketbook had been left behind.
10. They photographed whomever would pose.

Agreement

If you have ever labored over an intricate jigsaw puzzle, you know that you must take time if you are to complete it successfully. Each piece must be placed exactly as it should be or you will not be able to complete the picture. You cannot force a puzzle piece to fit where it does not belong.

The pieces of a sentence are somewhat similar to the pieces of a jigsaw puzzle. The pieces of a sentence can be forced into places where they do not belong, but the result will be no more acceptable than it would be in a jigsaw puzzle with its pieces forced to fit where they do not belong. In order to write effectively, you need to be sure that all of the parts of each sentence fit together flawlessly. To do this, you have to be certain that subjects and verbs agree in number and that pronouns agree with their antecedents both grammatically and logically.

Subject and Verb Agreement 8.1

Making a subject agree with its verb involves three steps, which you usually perform automatically. First, you find the subject of the sentence. Next, you determine whether that subject is singular or plural. Finally, you distinguish between the singular and plural forms of a verb and match your choice with the subject. Sometimes, however, the nature of the subject or the pattern of the sentence can play tricks on the mind. In these cases you should consciously slow down the process and carefully check the steps.

By now you should easily be able to find the subject of a sentence. If you cannot, review Sections 3.1 and 3.2. Otherwise, you can begin your study of agreement by learning about the *number* of nouns, pronouns, and verbs.

■ The Number of Nouns, Pronouns, and Verbs

In the English language only three parts of speech have number: nouns, pronouns, and verbs.

Number refers to the two forms of a word: singular and plural. Singular words indicate one; plural words indicate more than one.

Recognizing the difference between singular and plural nouns and pronouns should not be a problem for you at this time. The plurals of most nouns are formed simply by the addition of -*s* or -*es* to the singular form. There are also some plurals such as *children* that are formed irregularly. The singular and plural forms for personal pronouns are the ones used for the three cases discussed in Section 7.1.

SINGULAR NOUNS: The yellow *bus* stopped while the *child* crossed the *road*.

PLURAL NOUNS: Several *buses* waited for the *children* to disperse along the *roads*.

SINGULAR PRONOUNS: *I* left *my* goldfish with *him*.

PLURAL PRONOUNS: *We* left *our* goldfish with *them*.

The number of verbs is something you probably automatically use correctly most of the time. However, there are two areas where problems can occur: (1) when you use verbs in the present tense and (2) when you use verbs in tenses using the helping verb *be*.

The first of these areas is covered in the following chart. Notice that the only change in form is in the third-person singular column, where an -*s* or -*es* is added to the base form of the verb.

SINGULAR AND PLURAL VERBS IN THE SIMPLE PRESENT TENSE		
Singular		**Plural**
First and Second Person	**Third Person**	**First, Second, and Third Person**
(I, you) spend	(he, she, it) spends	(we, you, they) spend
(I, you) go	(he, she, it) goes	(we, you, they) go

Confusion can be avoided if you remember that nouns take -*s* and -*es* in their plural form and verbs take -*s* and -*es* in their singular form.

The second problem area involves the helping verb *be* when it is used to indicate whether a verb phrase is singular or plural. The following chart shows only those forms of *be* that change between singular and plural. All the other forms of *be* rarely cause agreement problems.

THE HELPING VERB *BE*	
Singular	**Plural**
(I) am	(we) are
(he, she, it) is	(they) are
(I, he, she, it) was	(we, they) were
(he, she, it) has been	(they) have been

Once you can distinguish between the singular and plural forms of nouns, pronouns, and verbs, you can learn how to eliminate specific errors in agreement.

EXERCISE A: Determining the Number of Nouns, Pronouns, and Verbs. For each of the following items, indicate whether the noun or pronoun is singular or plural. Then choose the verb in parentheses that agrees with the noun or pronoun.

EXAMPLE: flags (waves, wave)

  plural   wave

1. centimeter (is, are)
2. they (was, were)
3. grease (splatters, splatter)
4. grapes (ferments, ferment)
5. mystery (appeals, appeal)
6. wings (flutters, flutter)
7. crows (caws, caw)
8. lights (is flashing, are flashing)
9. mice (trembles, tremble)
10. water (drips, drip)

■ Agreement with Singular and Plural Subjects

There are two basic rules of agreement.

A singular subject must have a singular verb.

A plural subject must have a plural verb.

In the following examples, the subjects are underlined once, the verbs twice.

SINGULAR SUBJECT AND VERB: <u>Alice</u> <u>tries</u> to excel in academics.

This white <u>mouse</u> <u>is</u> a pet.

<u>He</u> <u>has been appearing</u> on television.

PLURAL SUBJECT AND VERB: The <u>girls</u> <u>try</u> to excel in academics.

These white <u>mice</u> <u>are</u> pets.

<u>They</u> <u>have been appearing</u> on television.

Intervening Phrases and Clauses.   Unlike the preceding examples, some sentences contain a phrase or clause between a subject and its verb. In these sentences simply ignore that phrase or clause when checking for agreement.

A phrase or clause that comes between a subject and its verb does not affect the subject-verb agreement.

In the first of the following examples, the prepositional phrase separating the subject and its verb does not affect the agreement between the singular subject and its verb. In the second, the intervening clause does not affect the agreement between the plural subject and its verb.

EXAMPLES: The <u>clown</u> with the large, sad eyes <u>looks</u> pathetic.

The <u>people</u> who have been waiting in the downpour <u>look</u> drenched.

In checking agreement pay particular attention to parenthetical expressions that come between a subject and its verb. These expressions are set off by commas or other punctuation and usually begin with such words as *along with*, *as well as*, *including*, and so on. They do not affect subject-verb agreement.

EXAMPLES: Your <u>theory</u>, as well as the theories of your colleagues, <u>lacks</u> adequate support.

These silver <u>coins</u>, along with this gold one, <u>were</u> a gift from my grandparents.

Relative Pronouns as Subjects.   When *who*, *which*, or *that* acts as a subject within a subordinate clause, its verb will be singular or plural depending upon the number of the pronoun's antecedent.

The antecedent of a relative pronoun affects the pronoun's number and determines its agreement with a verb.

In the first of the following examples, the antecedent for *who* is *person*; therefore, the verb, *has applied*, is singular because *person* is singular. In the second example, the antecedent of *who* is *trainees*; the verb, *have applied*, is plural because *trainees* is plural. In both sentences the relative pronoun *who* acts as the subject of a subordinate clause.

EXAMPLES: Carla is the only person out of many trainees who has applied for the position of manager.

Carla is the only qualified person out of the many trainees who have applied for this position.

EXERCISE B: Making Singular and Plural Subjects Agree with Their Verbs. In each of the following sentences, identify the subject and then choose the correct verb from the choices in parentheses. After the subject and verb, write *S* if the subject is singular and *P* if it is plural.

1. Overhead fans (was circulating, were circulating) the warm air in the emporium.
2. My turtle (lives, live) exclusively on chunks of hamburger and flies.
3. An artesian well (provides, provide) all the water they could ever use.
4. I (objects, object) to doing manual labor.
5. The stainless steel pans (lasts, last) for a lifetime.
6. A wood stove (is, are) their only source of heat.
7. Some people (prefers, prefer) to spend their weekends at home.
8. Thick wool (is sheared, are sheared) from the sheep.
9. We (jogs, jog) daily along the paths in the park.
10. The roses (was, were) a soft yellow.

EXERCISE C: Making Subjects and Verbs Separated by Phrases and Clauses Agree. In each of the following sentences, identify the subject and then choose the correct verb from the choices in parentheses. Write both subject and verb on your paper.

1. Peter, together with his brothers Marvin and Donald, (goes, go) ice skating every day.
2. The speakers, connected to the stereo by two thin wires, (rests, rest) on the bookshelf.
3. A falconer, a person who works with hawks, (is, are) now an uncommon sight.
4. This painting, just like that one, (costs, cost) far less.
5. Rocks that are formed from molten magma (is, are) igneous.
6. My little sister, accompanied by my mother, (has bought, have bought) her first pair of designer jeans.
7. Tomorrow the first customer, whoever that may be, (is going, are going) to receive a gift certificate.
8. The traffic light, which was supposedly repaired by the workers, still (changes, change) from red to amber.
9. The leader of the troops (oversees, oversee) maneuvers.
10. A child who is ignored by family members (expects, expect) little from others.
11. Another version, to be revealed in the next two issues, already (has been written, have been written).
12. I who have always liked math, unlike my sisters, (am planning, are planning) on taking the trigonometry course.
13. Your composition, as well as mine, (is, are) about the Incas.
14. The bright red lipstick on the models (makes, make) them look ghoulish.
15. The price, including state tax and shipping costs, (amounts, amount) to more than I can afford.
16. Your paper, which I read last night with the others, (has been, have been) posted on the bulletin board.
17. These shoes, not those, (was, were) the ones I meant to throw out.
18. A bedraggled basset hound with three puppies (was lying, were lying) in the mud.
19. Those people who came without folding chairs (was forced, were forced) to stand throughout the ceremony.
20. The country roads, covered by a thin layer of ice, (deceives, deceive) the motorist into thinking they are safe.

EXERCISE D: Making Relative Pronouns Agree with Their Verbs. Divide your paper into four columns and label them *Relative Pronoun*, *Antecedent*, *Number*, and *Verb*. Then fill in the information from each sentence, choosing the correct verb from the choices in parentheses.

EXAMPLE: The first person on the two teams who (scores, score) three points will win a special award.

Relative Pronoun	Antecedent	Number	Verb
who	person	singular	scores

1. Kathleen is popular with those classmates who (enjoys, enjoy) her vitality and exuberance.
2. Some snakes, which (is, are) a kind of reptile, are milked for their venom.
3. Every book on these shelves that (appears, appear) on your list should be read before you write your paper.
4. State health regulations apply to all employees in this establishment who (handles, handle) food.
5. I am one of the many people who (lives, live) for tomorrow.
6. Only those puppies from the litter that (exhibits, exhibit) aggressive behavior will be trained as guard dogs.
7. A lady slipper is a showy kind of orchid that (grows, grow) in acid soil in the northern United States.
8. Bob is the one person in a thousand who (has, have) this disease.
9. Alaric was the leader of the Visigoths who (was, were) buried in a riverbed so that his body might never be found by the Romans.
10. Lyle is a hard worker with many relatives who (counts, count) on him for financial support.

■ Compound Subjects

When *or*, *nor*, or *and* is used to connect two or more subjects, several different rules of agreement apply.

Singular Subjects Joined by *Or* or *Nor*.   The conjunctions *or* and *nor* call for a singular verb when each part of a compound subject is singular.

Two or more singular subjects joined by *or* or *nor* must have a singular verb.

In the following example, the conjunction *or* connects two singular subjects and indicates a singular compound subject.

EXAMPLE: Flagstone or brick makes a good patio.

Plural Subjects Joined by *Or* or *Nor*.   A plural counterpart to the preceding rule is obviously needed.

Two or more plural subjects joined by *or* or *nor* must have a plural verb.

EXAMPLE: Chopped <u>apples</u> or sprinkled <u>raisins</u> <u>make</u> a good topping.

Subjects of Mixed Number Joined by *Or* or *Nor*.   When the subjects joined by *or* or *nor* are mixed in number, problems often arise.

If one or more subjects are singular and the others are plural and they are joined by *or* or *nor*, the subject closest to the verb determines the agreement.

In the first of the following examples, the subject closer to the verb, *pins*, is plural and therefore requires a plural verb: *were holding*. In the second example, the situation is reversed. The singular subject *tape* is now closer to the verb; therefore, a singular verb, *was holding*, is needed.

EXAMPLES: Neither <u>tape</u> nor <u>pins</u> <u>were holding</u> the pieces of felt together.

Neither <u>pins</u> nor <u>tape</u> <u>was holding</u> the pieces of felt together.

Compound Subjects Joined by *And*.   When *and* joins two or more subjects, one rule covers most situations.

A compound subject joined by *and* is generally plural and must have a plural verb.

The conjunction *and* acts as a plus sign. Regardless of whether the compound parts are all singular, all plural, or mixed in number, they add up to a plural compound subject.

EXAMPLES: <u>Glue</u> and <u>tape</u> <u>were holding</u> the pieces of felt together.

<u>Pins</u> and <u>tacks</u> <u>were holding</u> the pieces of felt together.

<u>Pins</u> and a <u>tack</u> <u>were holding</u> the pieces of felt together.

Exceptions to this rule occur when the parts of the compound subject equal one thing and when the word *each* or *every* is used before a compound subject. Each of these situations requires a singular verb.

SINGULAR COMPOUND SUBJECTS: <u>Macaroni</u> and <u>cheese</u> <u>is</u> an easy dish to make.

Each <u>man</u> and <u>woman</u> <u>was waving</u> a flag.

EXERCISE E: Making Compound Subjects Agree with Their Verbs. Find the compound subject in each of the following sentences and write it on your paper. After writing the compound subject, choose the correct verb from the choices in parentheses and write it on your paper. Be prepared to explain which rule applies.

1. A tent and a sleeping bag (is, are) all the equipment you need.
2. Each bird and mammal in the sanctuary (wears, wear) an identification tag.
3. Neither a television program nor a movie (excites, excite) the imagination as well as a book.
4. A squirrel and several mice (resides, reside) in the attic of our house.
5. Rayon and nylon (is, are) synthetic, whereas cotton and linen are not.
6. A few children or one adult (raises, raise) the flag every morning.
7. Eddie or Maria (demonstrates, demonstrate) how this machinery functions.
8. Their sons or daughters often (helps, help) with the household tasks.
9. At this restaurant fish and chips (is, are) a Friday night special.
10. Sometimes a parrot or turtle (carries, carry) diseases to which people are vulnerable.
11. Either the class members or their representatives (attends, attend) each meeting.
12. Lemon peels or lime peels (flavors, flavor) this refreshing summer drink.
13. Your wheedling and begging for extra privileges (moves, move) me not in the slightest.
14. The twins or Alex (is going, are going) to prepare this evening's meal.
15. Every watercolor and oil painting (has, have) the artist's signature in the lower right corner.
16. Neither the stewardesses nor the pilots (knows, know) how to calm the terrified passengers.
17. When we went camping, pork and beans (was, were) what we lived on.
18. Whining or complaints (exhausts, exhaust) my mother's patience.
19. Their hostility and odd behavior (keeps, keep) them from being liked.
20. Neither a hotel nor a motel (provides, provide) the comforts of home.

■ Confusing Subjects

For various reasons the number of some subjects or their position within a sentence presents problems in subject-verb agreement. Following are explanations of the confusing situations you should watch for in checking agreement in your sentences.

Subjects in Inverted Sentences.   When the usual subject-verb order in a sentence is inverted, there may be problems in making the subject and verb agree.

A verb that comes before its subject must still agree with it in number.

For a variety of reasons, sentences are sometimes inverted. In the first of the following examples, the singular subject *rink* agrees with the singular verb *is*. The prepositional phrase at the beginning of the sentence does not affect agreement. In the second and third examples, *here* and *there* signal an inverted subject-verb pattern.

EXAMPLES: Beyond those buildings <u>is</u> a skating <u>rink</u>.

Here <u>is</u> <u>Jenny</u>.

There <u>are</u> quite a few <u>speakers</u> <u>scheduled</u> to talk.

One exception to this rule occurs when the expletive *it* is used to begin a sentence. In this situation the verb is always singular, regardless of the subject's number.

EXAMPLES: It <u>was</u> <u>she</u> whom I met.

It <u>was</u> <u>Anita</u> and <u>Clara</u> whom I met.

NOTE ABOUT *THERE'S* AND *HERE'S*:   *There's* and *here's*, contractions for *there is* and *here is*, are often misused. Remember that the singular verbs they contain cannot agree with plural subjects.

INCORRECT: There<u>'s</u> only a few <u>restrictions</u> to his freedom.

CORRECT: There <u>are</u> only a few <u>restrictions</u> to his freedom.

Subjects of Linking Verbs.   Another problem with agreement involves linking verbs and predicate nominatives.

A linking verb must always agree with its subject, regardless of the number of its predicate nominative.

When the subject is singular and the predicate nominative is plural, or the other way around, deciding upon the correct number for the verb can be difficult. Just remember that it is the subject and not the predicate nominative that determines the number of the verb. In the first of the following examples, the subject *blossoms* agrees with the plural verb *are* in spite of the singular predicate nominative *sign*. In the second example, the nouns are reversed. The subject *sign* agrees with the singular verb *is*, and *blossoms* is the predicate nominative.

EXAMPLES:
     Dogwood <u>blossoms</u> <u>are</u> one sign of spring.

     One <u>sign</u> of spring <u>is</u> dogwood blossoms.

Collective Nouns.   Collective nouns, such as *audience, family*, and *team*, name groups of persons or things and may be either singular or plural, depending on use.

A collective noun is singular and agrees with a singular verb when the group it names is considered to be a **single unit.**

A collective noun is plural and agrees with a plural verb when the group it names is considered to be **individuals** with different feelings or points of views.

SINGULAR: The <u>club</u> <u>has voted</u> unanimously to raise the dues.

            The <u>audience</u> <u>rises</u> as the judge enters the courtroom.

PLURAL: This <u>trio</u> <u>play</u> a harmonica, a steel guitar, and a banjo.

            The <u>herd</u> of wildebeests <u>scatter</u> as the lion approaches.

Singular Nouns with Plural Forms.   Other confusing subjects are nouns that look plural but are singular in meaning.

Nouns that are plural in form but singular in meaning agree with singular verbs.

Some of these nouns name branches of knowledge, such as *acoustics, civics, economics, ethics, mathematics, physics, politics,* and *social studies.* Others have singular meanings because, like collective nouns, they name single units: *confetti* (one mass of bits of paper), *measles* or *mumps* (one disease), and so on.

SINGULAR: <u>Physics</u> <u>is</u> a challenging subject.

<u>Mumps</u> <u>has been controlled</u> with a vaccine.

Some of these words can be difficult to use correctly. When words such as *acoustics* and *ethics* do not name branches of knowledge but rather indicate characteristics or qualities, their meanings are plural. Similarly, words such as *data, eyeglasses, media, pliers,* and *scissors,* although they name single items or collective ideas, generally take plural verbs. Whenever you have a question about these special nouns, check a dictionary.

PLURAL: The <u>acoustics</u> in the ancient outdoor theater at Epidauros <u>are</u> excellent.

The <u>data</u> <u>have been analyzed</u> by a computer.

The <u>pliers</u> <u>are</u> in the tool box.

Indefinite Pronouns.   The use of indefinite pronouns can also be confusing.

Depending on its form and meaning, an indefinite pronoun can agree with either a singular or a plural verb.

Refer to the list of indefinite pronouns on page 26. You will notice that some of the pronouns are always singular. These include those ending in *-one (anyone, everyone, someone),* those ending in *-body (anybody, everybody, somebody),* and those that imply one *(each, either).* Others are always plural: *both, few, many, others, several.* Some can be either singular or plural: *all, any, more, most, none, some.* Read through the list several times so that you will be able to recognize the number of indefinite pronouns.

The following are examples from each category.

ALWAYS SINGULAR: <u>Anyone</u> <u>draws</u> as well as that.

<u>Somebody</u> <u>has taken</u> your luggage by mistake.

<u>Each</u> of these problems <u>is</u> insoluble.

ALWAYS PLURAL: <u>Few</u> <u>have prepared</u> sufficiently.

<u>Others</u> <u>are planning</u> on bringing a beverage.

<u>Several</u> of these cuts <u>require</u> stitches.

EITHER SINGULAR OR PLURAL: <u>None</u> of the fruit <u>is</u> ripe.

<u>None</u> of the puzzle pieces <u>are</u> lost.

If the indefinite pronoun is one that can be either singular or plural, the antecedent of the pronoun determines the pronoun's number. In the first of the preceding examples, the antecedent of *none* is *fruit*, a singular noun; therefore, in this example, *none* is singular. In the second example, the antecedent of *none* is *pieces*, a plural noun; therefore, in this example, *none* is plural.

NOTE ABOUT *MANY A, NONE,* AND *ANY*:   *Many a* always precedes a singular subject, which therefore agrees with a singular verb.

EXAMPLE: Many a <u>person</u> <u>feels</u> faint from the intense heat.

None and *any* can sometimes be singular even when their antecedents are plural. In these cases, *none* means "not one" and *any* means "any one."

EXAMPLES: <u>None</u> of the glasses <u>is</u> clean.

Has <u>any</u> of the eggs <u>hatched</u> yet?

Titles.   The titles of books or other works of art may be misleading if they sound plural or consist of many words.

A title is singular and must have a singular verb.

The titles in the following examples look and sound plural, but they are singular and require singular verbs.

EXAMPLES: *Pictures at an Exhibition* by Moussorgsky <u>is</u> a marvelous piano suite.

Miró's *The Run of the Bulls* <u>is</u> one of this Spanish artist's many masterpieces.

Amounts and Measurements.   Most amounts and measurements, although they appear to be plural, express single units or ideas.

A noun expressing an amount or measurement is usually singular and must usually have a singular verb.

In the first three of the following examples, the subjects agree with singular verbs. *Twelve dollars* equals one sum of money; *three cups* equals one measurement; and *two thirds* equals one part of a whole. However, notice in the last example that the subject *half* refers to many individual items and is therefore plural.

EXAMPLES: <u>Twelve dollars</u> <u>covers</u> the cost.

<u>Three cups</u> of flour <u>is required</u>.

<u>Two thirds</u> of the produce <u>has spoiled</u>.

<u>Half</u> of the invitations <u>were dropped</u> in the mud.

EXERCISE F: Making Confusing Subjects Agree with Their Verbs.

Divide your paper into three columns and label them *Subject, Singular or Plural,* and *Verb.* For each of the following sentences, find the subject and write it in the first column. Then decide whether its meaning is singular or plural and write your answer in the second column. Finally, choose the correct verb from the choices in parentheses and write it in the third column.

1. A good combination of virtues (is, are) integrity and diligence.
2. As the vault was opened, everybody in the bank (was stunned, were stunned) by its emptiness.
3. *The Four Seasons,* by Vivaldi, (is, are) in my record collection.
4. Marauding ants (was, were) one reason for moving the picnic to another location.
5. Above our heads (is, are) a skylight.
6. Before Columbus landed there (was, were) no buying or selling of land.
7. Six feet (is, are) the amount of barbed wire needed to repair the fence.
8. None of the captives (was allowed, were allowed) to communicate with their families.
9. The news media (is beginning, are beginning) to mention the threat of chemical warfare again.
10. More of the waterfowl (is being killed, are being killed) by pollution from oil spills.
11. The squadron (was flying, were flying) in perfect formation.
12. Two spoonfuls of medicine (was, were) the prescribed dosage on the label.
13. The new virus (defies, defy) all efforts to control it.
14. All of the chocolate pudding for tonight's dinner (has been devoured, have been devoured) by a glutton.
15. Many a lawsuit (is settled, are settled) out of court.
16. Here (comes, come) Benjamin and Louise.
17. Now that I study three hours a night, physics (is, are) no longer difficult for me.

18. Robert Penn Warren's *All the King's Men* (concerns, concern) the ruthlessness of a politician.
19. In the apple tree, a flock of birds (perches, perch) on the branches.
20. The faculty (is going, are going) to prepare a new set of school rules.
21. Some glass ornaments hang from the ceiling, and others (rests, rest) on shelves.
22. Any of the group of candidates (has, have) a chance of winning the election.
23. A faulty alarm clock and a missed school bus (is, are) his usual excuse for tardiness.
24. Linguistics (was, were) a course that sent my average plummeting.
25. Over half of the animals (perishes, perish) in a forest fire of this magnitude.

APPLICATION: Applying the Rules of Subject and Verb Agreement. Complete each of the following sentences with an appropriate present-tense form of a verb. Be prepared to cite which rule of subject-verb agreement you used.

1. Claudio usually _____ the meal.
2. The audience _____ to applaud the stirring speaker.
3. Peaches and cream, my grandfather's quick but amazingly good specialty, _____ everyone.
4. Filberts or almonds _____ delicious roasted.
5. The captain of the ship's crew _____ the orders.
6. There _____ quite a few yodelers at this unusual competition.
7. Two pennies _____ more than your thoughts are worth.
8. The jury that has been deliberating for hours _____ about to give a verdict.
9. *The Brothers Karamazov* _____ a tortured work of art by the Russian author Dostoevsky.
10. Neither harsh detergents nor a chlorine bleach _____ on this delicate fabric.
11. Discarded bottles and torn paper _____ the appearance of this state park.
12. Either Raoul or his brother _____ Mrs. Holden to the bus stop.
13. Every blade of grass _____ as the harsh wind blows.
14. Your suggestion, as well as ours, _____ worth considering.
15. More of the story _____ in tomorrow's melodramatic sequel.

16. A measuring tape or yardstick ＿＿＿＿＿＿ all that you need for the job.
17. The news media in our city ＿＿＿＿＿＿ not very accurate in reporting national news.
18. Books, small appliances, and a child's rocker ＿＿＿＿＿＿ at the white elephant sale.
19. High on the mountain slopes ＿＿＿＿＿＿ bluebells.
20. Amy is the most likely choice for class president out of those who ＿＿＿＿＿＿ the position.

8.2 Pronoun and Antecedent Agreement

As discussed in previous sections, a pronoun's antecedent is the noun, or group of words acting as a noun, for which the pronoun stands. This section will show that just as a subject and a verb must agree, so must a pronoun and its antecedent.

■ Agreement Between Personal Pronouns and Antecedents

One rule of pronoun and antecedent agreement governs almost all of the others.

A personal pronoun must agree with its antecedent in number, person, and gender.

Previous sections explained that *number* is either singular or plural and that *person* indicates first, second, or third person—that is, the person speaking; the person spoken to; or the person, place, or thing spoken about.

Gender, a term not introduced previously, is a word used in reference to nouns and pronouns, which may be *masculine, feminine,* or *neuter.* In English, masculine words refer to males, feminine words refer to females, and neuter words refer to neither males nor females.

Notice in the following chart that the only personal pronouns that indicate gender are third person and singular. The other personal pronouns—*I, we, you, they,* and *them*—do not indicate gender.

GENDER OF NOUNS AND PERSONAL PRONOUNS					
Masculine		**Feminine**		**Neuter**	
Noun	Pronoun	Noun	Pronoun	Noun	Pronoun
brother	he	aunt	she	chair	it
son	him	niece	her	hunger	its
actor	his	actress	hers	Alabama	

In the following example, notice how the pronoun and antecedent agree in the three areas of number, person, and gender. The antecedent *Claire* is singular in number, is in the third person, and is feminine in gender. *Her* agrees with the antecedent since it too is singular, in the third person, and feminine.

EXAMPLE: *Claire* expressed *her* doubts about the plan.

Making Personal Pronouns Agree in Number with Compound Antecedents.   Just as compound subjects present difficulties in subject and verb agreement, compound antecedents can cause problems in pronoun and antecedent agreement. Keep the following three rules in mind when determining the number of compound antecedents.

Use a plural personal pronoun with two or more antecedents joined by *and.*

PLURAL: *Sharon* and *Stanley* have made *their* choice.

Use a singular personal pronoun with two or more singular antecedents joined by *or* **or** *nor.*

SINGULAR: Neither *Tom* nor *Hans* wants to spend *his* money to repair the old car.

An exception to these rules involves instances when it is necessary to distinguish between individual and joint ownership. A singular pronoun is used to refer to a compound antecedent when individual ownership is intended. A plural pronoun is used to indicate joint ownership.

SINGULAR (individual ownership):   My *mother* and *father* discovered that *his* old desk is a valuable antique. (Father owns the desk.)

PLURAL (joint ownership): My *mother* and *father* discovered that *their* old desk is a valuable antique. (Both parents own the desk.)

SINGULAR (individual ownership): Neither *Linda* nor *Monica* would let me ride *her* horse. (Linda and Monica each own a horse.)

PLURAL (joint ownership): Neither *Linda* nor *Monica* would let me ride *their* horse. (Linda and Monica own the same horse.)

The third rule applies to compound antecedents whose parts are mixed in number.

Use a plural personal pronoun if any part of a compound antecedent joined by *or* or *nor* is plural.

PLURAL: If my *sisters* or *Carol* arrives while I am out, tell *them* to wait for me.

Avoiding Shifts in Person and Gender.   Other errors in agreement with personal pronouns occur when there is an unnecessary shift in person or gender.

Do not shift person or gender between a pronoun and its antecedent.

A lack of consistency in person is usually the result of carelessness. Such an error can easily be corrected by replacing the incorrect pronoun with one that agrees. In the first of the following examples, the second-person pronoun *you* does not agree with its antecedent, *Kris*, which is third-person.

SHIFT IN PERSON: *Kris* is going to Bread Loaf, where *you* can meet famous poets and fiction writers.

CORRECT: *Kris* is going to Bread Loaf, where *he* can meet famous poets and fiction writers.

Another common error is a shift in gender. In the first of the following examples, the antecedent *ship* can agree in gender with either the feminine *her* or the neuter *it*, but the use of both pronouns is awkward. The corrected version maintains consistency by replacing *her* with *its*.

SHIFT IN GENDER: The *ship* came loose from *her* moorings, and *it* gently drifted out to sea.

CORRECT: The *ship* came loose from *its* moorings, and *it* gently drifted out to sea.

Dealing with Generic Masculine Pronouns.   Traditionally, a masculine pronoun has been used in reference to a singular antecedent whose gender is unknown. Such use of the masculine pronoun is said to be *generic,* meaning the pronoun covers both masculine and feminine genders in general.

Use a masculine pronoun (*he, him,* or *his*) with a singular antecedent whose gender may be either masculine or feminine.

In the following example, the gender of *officer* is not specified.

EXAMPLE: Each *officer* of the club must pay *his* dues in advance.

Although use of the generic masculine pronoun is still widespread, many of today's writers avoid it by rephrasing their sentences.

EXAMPLES: Each *officer* of the club must pay dues in advance.

All *officers* of the club must pay *their* dues in advance.

EXERCISE A: Making Personal Pronouns Agree with Their Antecedents. Complete each of the following sentences with an appropriate personal pronoun. Be sure that your pronoun agrees with an antecedent in the sentence.

1. The navigator lost _____ bearings in the turbulent weather.
2. Did rain, snow, or sleet stop the paper girl from making _____ deliveries?
3. Every nation has a right to _____ own self-determination.
4. A medical student should take _____ education seriously.
5. She should remember that _____ was the first to object.
6. Neither my sisters nor Susan brought _____ lists of references to the library.
7. When Frank fell asleep on the grass, _____ didn't wake up until dusk.

8. Laura and Alyssa are carefully planning _____ trip to Honolulu.
9. Mr. Graymore and _____ associate will represent us.
10. Frank and Cate searched the house for hours but couldn't find _____ mother.

EXERCISE B: Correcting Shifts in Person and Gender. Choose the correct pronoun from the choices in parentheses in each of the following sentences. Be sure that the pronoun agrees in person and gender with its antecedent.

1. If a person is amoral, society will attempt to impose restrictions on (your, his) actions.
2. Since that nation has not clearly defined its foreign policy, (she, it) has created distress abroad.
3. We have come to the conclusion that we must have some knowledge of current events if (we, you) are to get ahead in the world.
4. Let's not fill ourselves on the first course of this elaborate meal since (you, we) will be served four additional courses.
5. Many women are finding out that (she, you, they) can compete successfully with men in sports.
6. Belle is studying math, a course (she, you) must pass before graduating.
7. After a person has worked long and hard, (we, they, he) deserves some relaxation.
8. We should realize that (you, they, we) can't achieve success without some effort.
9. Please remember to express some gratitude since (you, we) should not take such favors for granted.
10. Typical of my friends and me is (our, their) delight in a good time.

EXERCISE C: Revising Sentences with Generic Masculine Pronouns. Two sentences in Exercise A use a generic masculine pronoun. Rewrite them to eliminate the generic pronoun.

■ Personal Pronoun and Indefinite Pronoun Agreement

When an indefinite pronoun such as *each*, *all*, or *most* is the antecedent of a personal pronoun, errors in agreement sometimes result. (See page 26 for a complete list of indefinite pronouns.)

Use a singular personal pronoun when the antecedent is a singular indefinite pronoun.

An intervening phrase or clause does not affect the agreement between a personal pronoun and its antecedent. In the first of the following examples, the antecedent is *each*, not *mobiles*, which is the object of a prepositional phrase.

In the next two examples, notice that although the *gender* of the personal pronouns (*his, her*) is determined by other words in the sentences (*boys, girls'*), the *number* of the personal pronouns is determined by the singular antecedents (*one, somebody*).

EXAMPLE: *Each* of these mobiles can be hung from *its* wire. (*Not* " . . . their wire.")

EXAMPLES: Only *one* of the boys wore *his* uniform. (*Not* " . . . their uniform.")

    Somebody in the girls' gym left *her* locker open. (*Not* ". . . their locker")

In some situations strict grammatical agreement may not sound logical. When a personal pronoun's antecedent is a singular indefinite pronoun but the content of the sentence makes singular agreement seem foolish, let the meaning of the sentence determine the number of the personal pronoun. In the following example, *each* is the singular antecedent but for the sake of logic the personal pronoun should be plural.

ILLOGICAL: When *each* of the telephones rang simultaneously, I answered *it* as quickly as possible.

CORRECT: When *each* of the telephones rang simultaneously, I answered *them* as quickly as possible.

NOTE ABOUT AGREEMENT WITH SINGULAR INDEFINITE PRONOUNS: In speaking and in informal writing, it is becoming increasingly acceptable to use the plural personal pronoun *their* to refer to singular indefinite pronouns such as *everybody, everyone, nobody,* and *no one*. In formal writing, however, the traditional *his,* or a rephrasing of the sentence, is still preferred by most.

INFORMAL: *Everybody* looks forward to *their* vacations.

FORMAL: *Everybody* looks forward to *his* vacation.

FORMAL AND INFORMAL: *Everybody* looks forward to a vacation.

EXERCISE D: Making Personal Pronouns Agree with Indefinite Pronouns. Number your paper from 1 to 20. Choose the correct pronoun from the choices in parentheses in each of the following sentences and write it on your paper. Be prepared to explain the reason for your choice.

1. Anybody who brought marshmallows to the Camp Fire Girls' barbecue also had to bring (her, their) whittled sticks.
2. Each of the candles shed (its, their) light into the gloom of the dusty attic.
3. While all of the musicians played in different keys, the conductor tried desperately to direct (him, them).
4. With no one to hear (her, their) discordance, every one of the girls practiced a different melody.
5. Everyone in the crowd screamed for (his, their) right to a full performance.
6. Before somebody can join this sorority, (she, he, they) must have an outstanding academic record.
7. Before it began to rain, most of the bathers had gathered (his, their) belongings and left the beach.
8. Someone on this train frightened its occupants with (his, their) intention of robbery.
9. None of the passengers offered (his, their) seat to the old man.
10. Each of my nieces revealed (her, their) greed.
11. Since every one of our customers suffered from acute indigestion, we refunded (his, their) money.
12. Any one of the representatives can voice (his, their) disapproval of a bill.
13. Either of these mules will carry (its, their) load without protesting.
14. No one would dare express (her, their) thoughts on this controversial issue.
15. Each one of the delicate flowers closes (its, their) petals when touched.
16. If any one of the guests arrives late, take (him, them) to one of the extra tables.
17. Somebody with cleats on (his, their) shoes has been standing under this window.
18. Everybody in the house of mirrors laughed at (his, their) funny reflection.
19. Either of the designers can give (her, their) personal touch to this drab room.
20. Any of the uneaten leftovers should be placed in (its, their) own serving dish.

■ Agreement Between Reflexive Pronouns and Antecedents

Reflexive pronouns end in *-self* or *-selves* and are used correctly only when they refer to a word occurring earlier in the sentence, as in *Frank made dinner for himself.*

A reflexive pronoun must agree with an antecedent that is clearly stated.

Avoid using a reflexive pronoun whenever it can logically be replaced by a personal pronoun. In the following example, the antecedent of *myself* is not clearly stated. The personal pronoun *me* should be used instead.

POOR: Our parents always trust my sister and *myself.*

CORRECT: Our parents always trust my sister and *me.*

EXERCISE E: Using Reflexive Pronouns Correctly. Two of the following sentences are correct; the others contain agreement problems involving reflexive pronouns. For each correct sentence, write the reflexive pronoun and its antecedent on your paper. Rewrite each of the faulty sentences to correct the usage errors.

1. Rachel and myself are the only ones taking the exam.
2. We painted the house and refurnished it ourselves.
3. The student with the most talent for public speaking is himself.
4. Who but yourself would have remembered my birthday?
5. You should give yourself a rest.

APPLICATION: Demonstrating the Rules of Pronoun and Antecedent Agreement. Use each of the following antecedents in a sentence of your own with a meaningful pronoun. Make sure that the pronoun and its antecedent agree in person, number, and gender.

1. flight attendant
2. Robert nor Douglas
3. actor
4. diamond
5. each
6. everyone
7. daughter
8. any
9. Karen or her sister
10. some

8.3 Special Problems with Pronoun Agreement

Once you are familiar with the basic rules for pronoun-antecedent agreement, you can refine your skills in this area. This section will show you how to avoid some common errors that can obscure the meaning of your sentences.

■ Avoiding Vague, Overly General Pronoun References

As in other areas of pronoun usage, one basic rule governs the other, more specific rules.

A pronoun's antecedent should always be stated or clearly understood.

When a pronoun is used in a vague or overly general way, confusion arises.

Antecedents for *Which, This, That,* and *These*. The pronouns *which, this, that,* and *these* are often used incorrectly to refer to a vague or overly general idea.

The pronouns *which, this, that,* and *these* should not be used to refer to a vague or overly general idea.

In the following sentence, for example, it is impossible to point out exactly what *these* stands for since *these* refers to a group of words.

OVERLY GENERAL REFERENCE: Jay was carsick, the dog was restless, and the air conditioner was not working. *These* made our trip through the desert extremely uncomfortable.

There are two possible ways to correct errors of this sort: (1) Turn the pronoun into an adjective that modifies a specific noun, or (2) revise the sentence to eliminate *which, this, that,* or *these*.

CORRECT: Jay was carsick, the dog was restless, and the air conditioner was not working. *These misfortunes* made our trip through the desert extremely uncomfortable.

CORRECT: Jay's carsickness, the dog's restlessness, and the air conditioner's refusal to work made our trip through the desert extremely uncomfortable.

Antecedents for *It, They,* and *You*.   The personal pronouns *it, they,* and *you* are used incorrectly when they have no antecedents or when their antecedents are vague and overly general.

The personal pronouns *it, they,* and *you* should not be used with implied or vague antecedents.

Again, there are two possible methods of correction to choose from: (1) Replace the personal pronoun with a specific noun, or (2) revise the sentence and replace the personal pronoun with one that clearly agrees with an antecedent.

In the first of the following examples, *it* has only a vague antecedent. In the second example, *they* has no antecedent at all.

OVERLY GENERAL REFERENCE: Marge wants to visit that museum. *It* should be a worthwhile experience.

CORRECT: Marge wants to visit that museum. The *experience* should be worthwhile.

OVERLY GENERAL REFERENCE: I enjoyed reading *The Turn of the Screw,* but *they* never explained who was guilty.

CORRECT: I enjoyed reading *The Turn of the Screw,* but the *author* never explained who was guilty.

CORRECT: I enjoyed reading *The Turn of the Screw* by Henry James, but *he* never explained who was guilty.

The personal pronoun *you* is commonly misused in a slightly different way. *You* should be used only when the reference is truly to the reader or listener. In the first of the following examples, *you* is overly general and should be replaced with a precise pronoun, such as *we* or *they*. In the second example, *you* is meaningless unless the reader or listener attended the same school as the speaker's great-aunt. The pronoun should be replaced with a specific noun.

OVERLY GENERAL REFERENCE: *You* couldn't understand a word Jim said.

CORRECT: *We* couldn't understand a word Jim said.

OVERLY GENERAL REFERENCE: In the school my great-aunt attended, *you* were expected to keep silent in the hallways.

CORRECT: In the school my great-aunt attended, *students* were expected to keep silent in the hallways.

NOTE ABOUT *IT*:   In many idiomatic expressions, *it* has no specific antecedent. In statements such as *"It* is late," *"It* is raining," and *"It* is true," the idiomatic use of *it* is accepted as standard English.

EXERCISE A: Correcting Vague, Overly General Pronouns.

Rewrite each of the following sentences to correct the faulty pronoun agreement.

1. The jugglers used four apples, two pears, and a hard-boiled egg in their act. That wasn't easy.
2. In Mexico you must be a citizen to own oceanside property.
3. A small child can easily choke on hard candy, which parents must be careful to prevent.
4. The state has determined that auto emissions must be reduced. A new law will ensure it.
5. Jason frequently exaggerates the truth, and this causes me to be skeptical of his stories.
6. When the star emerged from the auditorium, they kept the crowds behind barriers.
7. The Johnsons serve escargots at their banquets, which not everyone likes.
8. Since many twentieth-century poets use obscure symbols, it often confuses readers.
9. Katy thinks she is incapable of being hurt. This leads her to take risks.
10. From where my cousin lives in Athens, you can see the Acropolis.
11. One of my friends is an excellent chess player, which is a challenging game.
12. On last night's news, it talked about our military strength in the Pacific.
13. Rob is arrogant, inconsiderate, and rude. These are not appreciated by the customers.
14. Nat is too shy and compromising, which have always been his major faults.

15. When my family gathers for a holiday, it always leads to a good time.
16. We raked the leaves, turned over the soil, and planted the seedlings. This took all afternoon.
17. In the arena they try to attract the bull's attention with a red blanket.
18. To stalk elephants, you must be downwind of them.
19. An infant needs to know that you will provide nourishment and comfort.
20. We were disappointed with the performance of the play because they forgot many of their lines.

■ Avoiding Ambiguous Pronoun References

A pronoun is said to be *ambiguous* when it can refer to more than one antecedent.

A pronoun should never refer to more than one antecedent.

When a pronoun has more than one possible antecedent, the sentence is unclear and difficult to understand. What follows is an explanation of how to avoid two situations involving ambiguous pronoun references.

Personal Pronouns with Two or More Antecedents.   Careful writers always make sure that a personal pronoun's antecedent is unmistakable.

A personal pronoun should always be tied to a single, obvious antecedent.

In the following sentence, for example, *she* is confusing because it can refer to either *Jean* or *Sandra.*

AMBIGUOUS REFERENCE: Jean asked Sandra if *she* could leave work early.

The best way to correct this kind of error is by rewriting the sentence.

CORRECT: Jean asked Sandra for permission to leave work early.

CORRECT: Jean asked Sandra whether or not Sandra could leave work early.

Ambiguous Repetition of Personal Pronouns.   Careless repetition of a personal pronoun in a sentence can unintentionally obscure meaning.

Do not repeat a personal pronoun in a sentence if it can refer each time to a different antecedent.

AMBIGUOUS REPETITION: When Jon asked his father if *he* could borrow the car, *he* said *he* needed it to go to work.

To whom do the second and third *he's* refer? To eliminate the confusion, one of the repeated pronouns should be replaced.

CORRECT: When Jon asked his father if *he* could borrow the car, *Jon* said *he* needed it to go to work.

CORRECT: When Jon asked his father if *he* could borrow the car, his *father* said *he* needed it himself to go to work.

In the second corrected sentence, notice that the intensive pronoun *himself* helps clarify the meaning.

EXERCISE B: Correcting Ambiguous Pronoun References. Rewrite each of the following sentences to correct the ambiguous pronoun references.

1. We looked everywhere for the article in the magazine, but we couldn't find it.
2. Andrea told Mimi that she was being given a promotion.
3. When my uncle takes my little brother to the park, he is very happy.
4. The Fillmores were supposed to send us some rock samples when they returned from their trip, but they haven't arrived yet.
5. The child carried a rabbit costume with a big, fluffy tail, and the elevator door slammed shut on it.
6. The gypsy took out her crystal ball and placed it on the table. When she looked into it for a picture of the future, it seemed hazy.
7. The process for solving this problem is complicated. It requires concentration, so let's go through it again.
8. When Mark told Michael that he was moving to Iowa, he said he would miss his best friend.
9. Although the air and the water in the pool are chilly, it will become warmer as the day progresses.
10. When I gave Sean my answer it disappointed him, but it seems he is all right now.

11. We carefully studied her face for a sign of assent, but it never changed. It seemed hopeless, so we turned away.
12. Mr. Hays told Scott that his days as an employee for the firm were numbered because he would soon be replaced with a computer.
13. Ann was wearing a dress with horizontal stripes and a wide-brimmed hat. It made her look short and squat.
14. I searched for the dirt road where the old house had been, but it had disappeared.
15. If Rick would just listen to Mel's explanation, he would understand that he hasn't been behaving normally.
16. Our aunt and uncle brought our nieces and nephews with them, and while they relaxed on the porch we played volleyball.
17. Hugh will tell Sid that he has a letter from his cousin in Canada.
18. Hansel and Gretel were created by Jacob and Wilhelm Grimm, and they have entertained youngsters for generations.
19. Even though the ground is still wet from last night's shower and rain is predicted for this afternoon, it may still be dry enough for tomorrow's game to proceed as planned.
20. Iago plotted to destroy Cassio because he was jealous of his appointment as lieutenant.

■ Avoiding Distant Pronoun References

Another rule for pronoun references involves those situations in which the pronoun is so far from its antecedent that confusion develops.

A personal pronoun should always be close enough to its antecedent to prevent confusion.

A distant pronoun reference can be corrected in either of two ways: (1) Move the pronoun closer to its antecedent, or (2) eliminate the pronoun by changing it to a noun.

In the following example, *it* is too far from the antecedent *leg*. The first corrected version moves *it* closer to *leg*. The second corrected version eliminates *it* through rewriting.

DISTANT REFERENCE: Margaret carefully shifted her weight from her injured leg. Two days ago she had fallen, cutting herself badly on the broken glass that littered the street. Now *it* was swathed in bandages.

CORRECT: Margaret carefully shifted her weight from her injured leg. Now *it* was swathed in bandages. Two days ago she had fallen, cutting herself badly on the broken glass that littered the street.

CORRECT: Margaret carefully shifted her weight from her injured leg. Two days ago she had fallen, cutting herself badly on the broken glass that littered the street. Now *her leg* was swathed in bandages.

EXERCISE C: Correcting Distant Pronoun References.

Each of the following groups of sentences has at least one pronoun located too far from its antecedent. Rewrite each group to correct the distant reference.

1. Several crumbling steps led down to the cellar where no one had been for years. Once the walls had been lined with the delicate wines from his father's vineyard. Arturo wondered whether they could support him.
2. At the helm stood the captain, gazing into the distance as waves lapped softly at the ship's sides. Stealthily the pirate crept abroad. A shout to alert the slumbering crew gurgled in his throat.
3. Pieces of bleached driftwood lay undisturbed by the few people who sometimes came to wander on the sandy beach. They were twisted into fantastic shapes.
4. Hank plodded slowly along behind the plow, muttering to himself about the newfangled machinery his neighbor had purchased. Well, he thought, it had done the job for him and his family in the past and would do so now.
5. Mary sat enshrouded in plastic. Like a porcupine prepared to defend itself, the beautician's mouth was spiked with bobbypins with which she mercilessly jabbed the scalp. Inexperienced fingers rapidly twisted the wet strands of hair tightly around metallic spools. Gritting her teeth, she repressed a sudden urge to slap her assailant.

APPLICATION: Correcting Special Problems with Pronoun Agreement.

Rewrite each of the following sentences to correct the errors in pronoun agreement. Be prepared to cite the rule that applies to each of your corrections.

1. The curriculum includes electives. This gives everyone something to look forward to.
2. They explained the humor of the situation to me, but it never made any sense.
3. Arnold took his date to the party, which everyone thought was a waste of time.

4. Linda insisted on entertaining us by singing an aria while she moved about on roller skates. This baffled all of us.
5. The novice performer stuck her head into the young lion's mouth—something you should not try unless you have had years of training.
6. The movie was excellent, but they didn't make it clear whether the heroine lived or died.
7. Paul insulted Roger by telling him that he didn't want him to tag along with him.
8. It doesn't seem likely that Connie will be here tonight. It is too far from Cincinnati for it to be feasible.
9. I forgot to ask him to water the flowers. But it is too late for it to make any difference.
10. Scattered throughout the park were many benches that were always occupied. On one sat an old man who came daily to feed the pigeons. On another, a young girl read a book of poetry. It was a refuge for the homeless and the lonely.
11. Sandy wore unusual shirts that bore strange messages. They often made him the center of attention.
12. Jim was a foreign correspondent in Nicaragua, and that was difficult.
13. Wooden ponies with heads held proudly whirled around. The striped canopy, its colors blurred, made Ellen dizzy. They gripped the bits in their teeth and seemed to snort.
14. At camp the older boys agreed to teach archery to the younger boys, who in turn agreed to stop their practical jokes. They never doubted they had the better half of the arrangement.
15. Saber-toothed tigers and other fierce animals stalked early hunters, and you had to develop weapons for self-defense.
16. An ambitious student asked his teacher if he could present a lecture on Einstein's Theory of Relativity.
17. Karen established her own catering services for parties and banquets, which were very successful.
18. If Nan is friends with her, it is because it is part of her nature to be kind to everyone.
19. Lena won her brown belt in karate, and it gave her a sense of accomplishment.
20. The old woman touched the strings, and the harp came to life. Encouraged by the sweetness of sound, she closed her eyes, ignoring the exquisite pain in her fingers, and remembered the day it had been given to her.

9

Adjective and Adverb Usage

Effective use of adjectives and adverbs can make the difference between a dull sentence and an interesting one. Skilled writers use these two parts of speech much as an artist uses color—for contrast, for emphasis, and for shades of meaning.

Another use of modifiers is to make comparisons. In "The air is *fresher* and the grass *greener* after a rainfall" present conditions are compared with past conditions. A slight change in *fresh* and *green* in "The air is *freshest* and the grass *greenest* after the first spring rainfall" leads to a comparison of one condition with all other conditions. The forms of these adjectives are determined by whether the words are used to compare two or more than two things.

The first section in this chapter will show you how to form different adjectives and adverbs to make comparisons. The second section will explain ways of avoiding some common usage problems involving comparisons. If you have difficulty identifying adjectives and adverbs in sentences, begin by reviewing Section 1.3.

9.1 Degrees of Comparison

In addition to simply describing something, modifiers are often used to make comparisons. In English special *degrees*, or forms, of adjectives and adverbs are used for this purpose.

Adjectives and adverbs have different forms to show **degrees of comparison.**

The three degrees are called *positive*, *comparative*, and *superlative*.

THE THREE DEGREES OF COMPARISON
1. The *positive* degree is the form of an adjective or adverb when it is not being used in a comparison. This is the basic form of the adjective or adverb that you will find listed in a dictionary.
2. The *comparative* degree is the form used to compare *two* things.
3. The *superlative* degree is the form used to compare *three or more* things.

■ Recognizing Degrees of Comparison

The following chart lists several adjectives and adverbs in each of the three degrees. Notice the three different ways that the words change form to indicate the comparative and superlative degrees: (1) with *-er* and *-est*, (2) with *more* and *most*, and (3) with entirely different words.

Positive	Comparative	Superlative
Adjectives		
quick	quicker	quickest
pleasant	more pleasant	most pleasant
bad	worse	worst
Adverbs		
quickly	more quickly	most quickly
pleasantly	more pleasantly	most pleasantly
badly	worse	worst

EXERCISE A: Recognizing Positive, Comparative, and Superlative Degrees. Each of the following sentences contains an adjective or adverb in the positive, comparative, or superlative degree. Write each modifier on your paper and identify its part of speech and degree.

1. Their taste in furniture is more ornate than mine.
2. Ursula is the most artistic person in her family.
3. I work worse under pressure.
4. She responded to the treatment more quickly than the doctors anticipated.

5. The wisest policy is to wait until Tom approaches us with his problem.
6. His philosophy is difficult to understand.
7. Jamie's talent for persuasion is irresistible.
8. She is the candidate's most eager supporter.
9. Your foot will feel more numb unless you walk on it.
10. The new student did badly on the aptitude test.

■ Regular Forms

Adjectives and adverbs can be either regular or irregular, depending on how their comparative and superlative degrees are formed. Fortunately, the comparative and superlative degrees of most adjectives and adverbs are formed regularly. Two rules govern the formation of regular modifiers. The first concerns modifiers of one or two syllables; the second concerns modifiers of three or more syllables.

> Use *-er* or *more* to form the comparative degree and *-est* or *most* to form the superlative degree of most one- and two-syllable modifiers.

The most frequently used method for forming the comparative and superlative degrees of one- and two-syllable modifiers is with *-er* and *-est* rather than with *more* and *most*. Even though English is a flexible language and generally allows the use of either method, *more* and *most* should be avoided whenever the construction sounds awkward, as in "Phil is *more smart* than you think," or "Kim was the *most fast* runner on the team."

The following examples show one- and two-syllable modifiers developed in the customary manner with *-er* and *-est*.

EXAMPLES:	bright	brighter	brightest
	late	later	latest
	crafty	craftier	craftiest
	subtle	subtler	subtlest

Notice, however, that all adverbs ending in *-ly*, regardless of the number of syllables, always form their comparative and superlative degrees with *more* and *most*.

EXAMPLES: freely   more freely   most freely

happily   more happily   most happily

More and *most* are also used with a number of one- and two-syllable adjectives when *-er* or *-est* would sound awkward. If you rely on your ear to determine which words sound awkward with *-er* or *-est,* you should make the right choice of form.

EXAMPLES: just   more just   most just

pleasing   more pleasing   most pleasing

vicious   more vicious   most vicious

friendless   more friendless   most friendless

When a modifier consists of three or more syllables, the comparative and superlative degrees are easily formed.

Use *more* and *most* to form the comparative and superlative degrees of all modifiers of three or more syllables.

EXAMPLES: delicate   more delicate   most delicate

governable   more governable   most governable

representative more representative   most representative

NOTE ABOUT COMPARISONS WITH *LESS* AND *LEAST*:   *Less* and *least* mean the opposite of *more* and *most* and can be used to form the comparative and superlative degrees of most modifiers.

EXAMPLES: smooth   less smooth   least smooth

acceptable   less acceptable   least acceptable

explicitly   less explicitly   least explicitly

EXERCISE B: **Forming the Comparative and Superlative Degress of Regular Modifiers.** Each of the following sentences contains the positive degree of a regular modifier. For each sentence write two sentences of your own—one using the comparative degree of the modifier and the other using the superlative degree. Underline the comparative and superlative forms in your sentences.

EXAMPLE: Cottage cheese and fruit make a *light* meal.

The <u>lighter</u> shade of green is my choice.

The <u>lightest</u> of touches was made by the butterfly wings.

1. He moved *quickly* to pull the child from danger.
2. Do not breathe those *irritating* fumes.
3. Building this rock wall is an *arduous* task.
4. She *virtuously* promised never to steal again.
5. The response of the audience was *thunderous*.
6. We will *soon* have to leave for the movie.
7. Jake *tersely* commented on my new car.
8. A *lively* interpretation of this waltz is what we need.
9. Miss Elkin's judgment is always fair.
10. Edward Albee's *Seascape* is an *inspirational* play.

■ Irregular Forms

The comparative and superlative degrees of a few adjectives and adverbs are formed in such unpredictable ways that they must be memorized.

The irregular comparative and superlative forms of certain adjectives and adverbs must be memorized.

Study the following chart and make a mental note of the irregular modifiers that you are likely to misuse. Then memorize them.

IRREGULAR FORMS OF MODIFIERS		
Positive	Comparative	Superlative
bad	worse	worst
badly	worse	worst
far	farther	farthest
far	further	furthest
good	better	best
ill	worse	worst
late	later	last *or* latest
little (amount)	less	least
many	more	most
much	more	most
well	better	best

Two pairs of these irregular modifiers deserve special attention because their positive forms are often confused. The two pairs are *bad* and *badly*, and *good* and *well*. To avoid misusing these words in sentences, it is important first to remember each one's part of speech: *Bad* and *good* are adjectives; *badly* is an adverb; *well* can be either an adjective or an adverb. Next it is important to remember (1) that linking verbs (*am, feel, look, smell, sound, taste,* and so on) are usually followed by predicate adjectives that modify the subject and (2) that action verbs (*do, play, run, swim,* and so on) are often followed by adverbs that modify the verb. The following two patterns illustrate these facts. (See Section 1.2 for more information about action and linking verbs.)

BASIC PATTERNS:　Subject—Linking Verb—Adjective

Subject—Action Verb—Adverb

An error in usage occurs when a linking verb is followed by an adverb, such as *badly,* or when an action verb is followed by an adjective, such as *bad* or *good.* These sentence patterns are incorrect because they force one part of speech to do the job of another.

INCORRECT (linking verb plus adverb):　S　LV　Adv　This soup tastes *badly*.

CORRECT:　This soup tastes *bad*.

INCORRECT (action verbs plus adjectives):　S　AV　Adj　Nelson did *good* on the chemistry exam.
S　AV　Adj
We played *bad* in yesterday's game.

CORRECT:　Nelson did *well* on the chemistry exam.

We played *badly* in yesterday's game.

NOTE ABOUT *GOOD* AND *WELL*:　As adjectives, *good* and *well* differ slightly in meaning. *Good* usually refers to quality or appearance.

EXAMPLES:　His grades are *good*.
I look *good* in red clothes.

Well usually refers to satisfactory conditions or to a person's health.

EXAMPLES: Everything is *well* between us.

I'm not feeling *well* today.

EXERCISE C: **Forming the Comparative and Superlative Degrees of Irregular Modifiers.** This exercise is similar to Exercise B on page 239 except that in this exercise the modifiers are irregular. Follow the same directions.

1. *My Ántonia* is a *good* book about immigrant settlers in the Middle West.
2. He has *little* patience with himself when he makes silly mistakes.
3. He arrived *late* for his appointment.
4. *Many* chickens died in the hundred-degree heat.
5. Too many rides on the roller coaster made him *ill*.
6. Melanie had a *bad* reaction to sulfa drugs.
7. *Much* water spilled from the bucket.
8. The molten silver burned Johnny's hand *badly*.
9. The miners went *far* below the earth's surface.
10. You did *well* to admit your mistake.

EXERCISE D: **Distinguishing Between** *Bad, Badly, Good, and Well.* Complete each of the following sentences with *bad, badly, good,* or *well*.

1. To my regret I always do _____ in anything requiring manual dexterity.
2. After a year of strenuous training, the boxer still performed _____ in the ring.
3. The house smells _____ in this humid weather.
4. A child should be _____ without being bribed.
5. He lives _____ on his inheritance.
6. After having severe respiratory problems, the tenor sang _____ on opening night.
7. Marty looks _____ in both tweeds and tailored suits.
8. She is very _____ about offering to help in an emergency.
9. Velma did not look _____ after her unfortunate experience.
10. A cold shower feels _____ when the temperature is in the nineties.

■ Double Comparisons

Double comparisons are problems that may arise with either regular or irregular modifiers.

Do not add both -*er* and *more* (or *less*) or both -*est* and *most* (or *least*) to a regular modifier. Furthermore, never add these endings or words to any irregular comparative or superlative form.

The problem with double comparisons is that they are unnecessarily repetitive. Read the following contrasting examples. The incorrect forms should sound wrong.

INCORRECT: Your suitcase is *more heavier* than mine.

CORRECT: Your suitcase is *heavier* than mine.

INCORRECT: This puppy is the *least saddest* of all.

CORRECT: This puppy is the *least sad* of all.

INCORRECT: His migraine headache is *worser* than ever.

CORRECT: His migraine headache is *worse* than ever.

INCORRECT: Our house is the *most farthest* one from town.

CORRECT: Our house is the *farthest* one from town.

EXERCISE E: Correcting Errors with Modifiers. Fifteen of the following sentences contain double comparisons. Five are correct. If the sentence is correct, write *correct* on your paper. If the sentence contains a double comparison, rewrite the sentence correctly.

1. Without proper medication, the condition will only become more worse.
2. Such a thought couldn't be more further from my mind.
3. Tad was the oldest boy in the family.
4. This spring water is the coldest and most freshest of any in this part of the country.
5. Jack is the least likeliest choice for representative.
6. Her coffee is the worstest I have ever tasted.
7. *Star Wars* is the most spectacular movie I have seen.
8. Going through the attic on a rainy day is more pleasanter than just sitting doing nothing.
9. If you pretend she is joking, her unpleasant criticism will be less worse.
10. I get up more earlier in the morning now that it is so late in the season.
11. His sprinting to victory was the greatest accomplishment for the school.

12. This homemade fudge is more better than what you buy in the store.
13. My parents clean the house more thoroughly and more oftener than is necessary.
14. At this high altitude, headaches are more commoner than at sea level.
15. Jane's comment on the party was the least offensive of them all.
16. Seals provide one of the most softest skins, but I object to their being slaughtered.
17. Sean was the more courageous of the two.
18. Your answer to this question is more worse than I thought it would be.
19. *Ben Hur* is one of the most excitingest stories set in Biblical times.
20. Foods with preservatives are worser for a person than natural foods.

APPLICATION: **Using the Degrees of Comparison in Sentences.**
Write sentences of your own using each of the following words in the degree indicated.

1. private—comparative
2. little—superlative
3. humble—positive
4. sudden—comparative
5. slowly—superlative
6. likely—superlative
7. much—comparative
8. badly—positive
9. bad—comparative
10. good—positive

9.2 Clear Comparisons

Once you have mastered the forms of regular and irregular adjectives and adverbs in the three degrees, you can learn how to use these forms to avoid problems in comparisons. Common problems include (1) using the wrong degree, (2) mistakenly comparing unrelated things, (3) illogically comparing related things, and (4) using modifiers illogically.

■ Using Comparative and Superlative Forms

One basic rule covers the correct use of comparative and superlative forms.

Use the comparative degree to compare two persons, places, things, or ideas. Use the superlative degree to compare three or more persons, places, things, or ideas.

No mention of specific numbers is necessary when you are making a comparison. The context of the sentence should indicate whether two or more items are being compared.

COMPARATIVE: Beth is *more dependable* than Florence.

My car gives a *smoother* ride than his.

This food is *more nourishing* than that.

He requires *less* to make him happy than she does.

SUPERLATIVE: Beth is the *most dependable* girl I know.

My car gives the *smoothest* ride of any I have ever driven.

This food is the *most nourishing* you could have.

He requires the *least* possible number of material things to make him happy.

NOTE ABOUT THE SUPERLATIVE DEGREE FOR EMPHASIS: Sometimes the superlative degree is used just for emphasis, without any specific comparison.

EXAMPLES: He is the *greatest!*

She was *most treacherously* betrayed.

EXERCISE A: Using the Comparative and Superlative Degrees Correctly. For each of the following sentences, choose the correct comparative or superlative form from the choices in parentheses.

1. Damage done by this tornado was far (worse, worst) than that done by the last one.
2. Kenny is the (more, most) interesting person at this party.
3. His caricatures of politicians are (funnier, funniest) than usual when he is angry.
4. She is the (younger, youngest) person ever to win an Olympic gold medal.
5. Which major city in Maine is the (farther, farthest) from the coast?
6. The book is (less, least) suspenseful now that I know the ending.

7. Without doubt, Mia is (better, best) at acting than her sister.
8. I was (more, most) humiliated by my social blunder.
9. Were you the (weaker, weakest) member of the team?
10. Put your (better, best) car model on display and hide these others at home.

■ Balanced Comparisons

When you write a comparison, you need to be certain that the two or more things being compared are properly balanced. Otherwise, the comparison may be illogical and even ridiculous.

Make sure that your sentences compare only items of a similar kind.

An unbalanced comparison is confusing because it lacks sense. In the following unbalanced examples, the sentences illogically compare dissimilar things.

UNBALANCED: *John's thesis* is more carefully researched than *Dave*.

CORRECT: *John's thesis* is more carefully researched than *Dave's*.

UNBALANCED: The *milk of a goat* is richer than a *cow*.

CORRECT: The *milk of a goat* is richer than the *milk of a cow*.

UNBALANCED: The *damage* from yesterday's flood is less than the *one* last year.

CORRECT: The *damage* from yesterday's flood is less than *that* from last year's.

As you can see, *thesis* cannot be compared to *Dave*; a goat's *milk* cannot be compared to a whole *cow*; *damage* from a flood cannot be compared to a flood. In the last set of examples, note also the use of pronouns. In the unbalanced sentence, *one* is incorrect because it refers to *flood* rather than to *damage*. In the corrected sentence, however, *that* clearly refers to *damage*.

EXERCISE B: Making Balanced Comparisons. Rewrite each of the following sentences to correct the poorly balanced comparison.

1. The bill of a duck is broader and flatter than a chicken.
2. Aunt Mary's homemade blackberry jam is sweeter than Aunt Helen.
3. The mileage we get on this car is better than that car.
4. A stroll through the park is less invigorating than the beach.
5. The speakers on Tim's new stereo are better than Jeff's stereo.
6. The horn of a rhino is more valuable to poachers than an elephant.
7. Replacing the roof with slate tiles will be more expensive than shingles.
8. Today's weather is warmer than yesterday.
9. The dog was sidetracked because the scent of the deer was stronger than the rabbit.
10. These directions for assembling a radio are less complicated than a tricycle.

■ *Other* and *Else* in Comparisons

Another illogical comparison, which is similar to an unbalanced comparison, results when something is inadvertently compared with itself.

When comparing one of a group with the rest of the group, make sure that your sentence contains the word *other* or the word *else.*

Adding the words *other* or *else* in such situations will make the comparison clear.

ILLOGICAL: I think John was *more inspired than any* player on the team.

CORRECT: I think John was *more inspired than any other* player on the team.

ILLOGICAL: Ruth worked *harder than anyone* in the office.

CORRECT: Ruth worked *harder than anyone else* in the office.

In the first set of examples, *John,* who is one of the players on the team, cannot logically be compared to all of the players on the team. The addition of *other* excludes John from the remaining group of players. In the second set of examples, *Ruth* cannot be compared to all of the workers in the office since she herself is one of those workers. The addition of *else* excludes her from the rest of the group.

EXERCISE C: Using *Other* and *Else* in Comparisons. Rewrite each of the following sentences to correct the illogical comparison.

1. This cereal is more nutritious than any brand.
2. Your explanation of photosynthesis is simpler than anyone's.
3. Our neighbor Mr. Baxter is a better carpenter than anyone in town.
4. She reads more mystery stories than anyone I know.
5. Seneca Lake is deeper than any of the Finger Lakes.
6. Sheila's talent for writing is greater than anyone's in the class.
7. He attracts more notice than anyone in his family.
8. This eight-week-old beagle is harder to train than any puppy.
9. The landscaping in this yard is more lovely than any on this street.
10. Rich eats a heartier meal here than anyone who comes to this diner.

■ Modifiers That Should Not Be Used in Comparisons

Some modifiers cannot logically be used to make comparisons because their meanings are *absolute*—that is, their meanings are entirely contained in the positive degree. For example, if one line is *vertical,* another line cannot be *more vertical.* Either a line is vertical or it is not; there are no degrees of verticalness in between.

Avoid using absolute modifiers illogically in comparisons.

Some common absolute modifiers are *dead, entirely, fatal, final, identical, opposite, perfect,* and *unique.*

ILLOGICAL: Of all the plants with the blight, this one is the *least dead.*

BETTER: Of all the plants with the blight, this one is the *least damaged.*

Many common expressions, however, use absolute modifiers in comparisons, and their meanings are quite clear.

EXAMPLES: What could be *more perfect* than a vacation in Spain!

The first line you drew was *straighter* than this one.

Although such exceptions to the rule are acceptable, with a little effort you should be able to find a more suitable word that will express your meaning exactly.

EXERCISE D: Avoiding Illogical Modifiers in Comparisons. Each of the following sentences contains an absolute modifier used in a comparison. Rewrite any sentence in which the absolute modifier is used illogically. Write *correct* for any sentence in which you think the modifier is used idiomatically and clearly. Be prepared to explain the reason for your decisions.

1. This coin is the most unique one in my collection.
2. The tarantula's bite was less fatal than we thought it would be.
3. After the hike he was more entirely exhausted than she was.
4. My second try at making an omelet was more nearly perfect than my first.
5. The wall and ceiling are more perpendicular at one end of the room than they are at the other end.
6. I wish my hair were straighter than it is.
7. Of the five puppies in the litter, that one is most identical to the sire.
8. This will be our most final chance to win the championship.
9. That poet's style could not be more opposite from mine.
10. By revising my essay, I made it more perfect.

APPLICATION: Writing Clear Comparisons. For each of the following items, write an effective comparison in one sentence.

EXAMPLE: Compare two animals of the same species.

Brown bears are smaller than grizzly bears.

1. Compare your own taste in clothing with a friend's.
2. Compare one country's form of government with another country's form of government.
3. Compare the difference in height between brothers.
4. Compare three of your favorite movies.
5. Compare the achievements of two athletes in a specific sport.

10

Miscellaneous Usage Problems

Many usage problems that can spoil the clarity of your writing do not fall into any of the broad categories of usage that were covered in preceding chapters. Some of these problems arise when there is a conflict between standard and non-standard usage. Others have to do with differences between acceptable and less preferred usage. Some words can cause problems merely because they have similar meanings or spellings. The next two sections are intended to help you refine your skills in these areas and to increase your understanding and appreciation of the English language, which continues to grow and change.

10.1 Negative Sentences

In modern English, a sentence needs only one negative word to express a negative idea. More than one negative word can make the sentence confusing.

■ Double Negatives

A sentence that contains two negative words when only one is needed is said to have *double negatives*.

Do not write sentences with **double negatives**.

In the following sets of examples, notice that double negatives can easily be corrected. Simply eliminate one negative word or the other.

DOUBLE NEGATIVES: Carol *couldn't* do *no* work.

CORRECT: Carol *couldn't* do any work.

Carol could do *no* work.

DOUBLE NEGATIVES: They *never* go *nowhere*.

CORRECT: They *never* go anywhere.

They go *nowhere*.

DOUBLE NEGATIVES: *Nobody* did *nothing* to help.

CORRECT: *Nobody* did anything to help.

Each person did *nothing* to help.

Many sentences can correctly contain more than one negative word, as the following example shows. Notice, however, that each clause in the sentence contains only one negative word.

EXAMPLE: We *couldn't* tow the car because we *didn't* have a cable.

EXERCISE A: Avoiding Double Negatives. Rewrite each of the following sentences to eliminate the double negatives.

1. He didn't listen to none of my explanation before he accused me.
2. Never ask nobody for money.
3. Martin wasn't nowhere near the vase when it fell.
4. We couldn't go to the movies because we hadn't no more than three dollars.
5. Without a passport no one can't cross the border into Italy.
6. My best friend didn't give me no birthday present.
7. The children were so excited that they couldn't listen to no one.
8. The detective dusted for fingerprints but there weren't none.
9. You had better not go nowhere in this weather.
10. Frozen meat shouldn't never be refrozen.

■ The Correct Use of Negative Words

The English language offers three ways for making sentences negative. The rule for avoiding double negatives applies regardless of which method you use.

Using Single Negative Words.   A common method for writing negative sentences is to use one negative word, such as *never, no, nobody, nothing, nowhere, not,* or the contraction *-n't.* (Notice that each of these words begins with the letter *n.*)

DOUBLE NEGATIVES: I *didn't* like *none* of the new fashions.

CORRECT: I *didn't* like any of the new fashions.
I liked *none* of the new fashions.

Using *But* Negatively.   The word *but* can also be used in a negative sense. When it is used in this way, it should not be accompanied by another negative word.

DOUBLE NEGATIVES: She *hadn't but* one request.

CORRECT: She had *but* one request.
She had *only* one request.

Other Negative Words.   Other words that can have negative meanings are *barely, hardly,* and *scarcely.* Do not use these words with other negative words.

DOUBLE NEGATIVES: They *weren't barely* out to sea when the storm hit.

CORRECT: They were *barely* out to sea when the storm hit.

They *weren't* far out to sea when the storm hit.

DOUBLE NEGATIVES: He *couldn't hardly* see without his glasses.

CORRECT: He could *hardly* see without his glasses.

He almost *couldn't* see without his glasses.

DOUBLE NEGATIVES: We *hadn't scarcely* finished our meal.

CORRECT: We had *scarcely* finished our meal.
We *hadn't* quite finished our meal.

EXERCISE B: Correcting Double Negatives. The following phrases contain double negatives. Eliminate the error and expand each phrase into a sentence.

1. wasn't but a single apple
2. isn't scarcely listening
3. weren't nothing special
4. nobody never wanted
5. not barely recognizable
6. haven't taken no aspirin
7. shouldn't buy none
8. never travel nowhere
9. couldn't hardly remember
10. don't let no one

■ Understatement

Sometimes a writer wishes to express an idea indirectly. The technique used for such roundabout expressions is called *understatement*. Reasons for using understatement are to minimize the importance of an idea or to draw the reader's attention to the idea. Understatement is often achieved by writing a sentence in which a word with a negative prefix, such as *in-*, *un-*, or *non-*, is used with a negative word.

EXAMPLES: Sleepless nights with a small infant are *hardly infrequent.*

His sudden resignation was *not unexpected.*

EXERCISE C: Writing Understatements. Rewrite each of the following sentences using understatement. Underline the negative word and the negative prefix in each of your sentences.

1. The teacher was pleased with the students' oral book reports.
2. Taking out the trash now is possible.
3. The king was impressed with the prophet's prediction of victory in battle.
4. Stan's violent behavior was defensible.
5. She was enchanted with the tropical paradise.
6. I am satisfied with this luxurious hotel room.
7. David's insulting remark was excusable.
8. Remembering to take the keys out of the car was important.
9. Barbara jogging in the early morning was a common sight.
10. To wear a raincoat and boots in this miserable weather is advisable.

APPLICATION: Writing Negative Sentences. None of the following sentences contains a negative word. Rewrite each sentence to express a negative idea.

1. It was easy for the scholar to read the faded ink on the ancient manuscript.
2. Their elaborate party was planned weeks in advance, and everybody came.
3. All summer she sat on the porch and wished that she could go somewhere.
4. Everything we said gave him some feeling of consolation.
5. There was enough stew to feed the hungry family.
6. Sudden thaws in the spring always flood the basement.
7. Some of these old coins are worth a fortune.
8. Ben was finishing the last question when the exam officially ended.

9. A computer can crack this coded message.
10. All that the thieves had left in the tomb was the stone sarcophagus.

10.2 Eighty Common Usage Problems

To gain the greatest benefit from this collection of eighty usage problems, you should first read all of the entries, making note of the specific problems that you may need to study. Then complete the exercises at the end to check your knowledge. This miscellany can also be of help to you throughout the year, as you prepare formal written or spoken material for any subject area.

When using this miscellany, keep in mind that the entries are listed in alphabetical order. When an entry includes two or more items, they usually will be in alphabetical order too. If you cannot locate a particular item here, refer to the index at the back of the book.

(1) *A* and *An*. The article *a* is used before consonant sounds; *an*, before vowel sounds. When using *a* and *an* before words beginning with *h*, *o*, or *u*, check to make sure that you have chosen the correct article. Sometimes these three letters have consonant sounds; at other times they have vowel sounds.

CONSONANT SOUNDS: a *h*eavy burden (*h*-sound)

a *o*ne-sided conversation (*w*-sound)

a *u*niform code (*y*-sound)

VOWEL SOUNDS: an *h*onorable mention (no *h*-sound)

an *o*dious task (*o*-sound)

an *u*nderlying theme (*u*-sound)

(2) *Accept* and *Except*. *Accept*, a verb, means "to receive." *Except*, a preposition, means "leaving out" or "other than."

VERB: She *accepted* the honor with reluctance.

PREPOSITION: *Except* for Sue, no one was prepared.

(3) *Accuse* and *Allege*. Notice the distinction in the meanings of these two verbs. *Accuse* means "to blame" or "to bring a charge against." *Allege* means "to claim something that has not been proved."

EXAMPLES: He was *accused* of vandalism.

The clerk *alleged* that a masked woman threatened her at gunpoint.

(4) *Adapt* and *Adopt*. *Adapt*, a verb, means "to change." *Adopt*, also a verb, means "to take as one's own."

EXAMPLES: She *adapted* her schedule to meet the job's requirements.

Many children wait to be *adopted*.

(5) *Advice* and *Advise*. Notice the difference in meaning between these related words. *Advice* is a noun, meaning "an opinion." *Advise* is a verb, meaning "to give an opinion to."

NOUN: Your *advice* is unsolicited.

VERB: I *advise* you to seek professional help.

(6) *Affect* and *Effect*. *Affect* is almost always a verb meaning "to influence" or "to bring about a change in." *Effect*, usually a noun, means "result." Occasionally, *effect* is a verb; then it means "to bring about" or "to cause."

VERB: Exposure to good literature *affected* his interest in reading.

NOUN: One *effect* of chemotherapy is nausea.

VERB: The transition to solar power was *effected* last winter.

(7) *Aggravate*. *Aggravate* means "to make worse." Avoid using this word to mean "to annoy."

PREFERRED: Rubbing your eye will just *aggravate* the redness.

LESS ACCEPTABLE: Don't *aggravate* me with your questions.

(8) *Ain't*. *Ain't*, originally a contraction of *am not*, is not considered acceptable standard English. Avoid using it in all writing.

NONSTANDARD: We *ain't* seen any results yet.

CORRECT: We *haven't* seen any results yet.

(9) *All Ready* and *Already.* *All ready*, two separate words, is an expression meaning "ready." The expression functions as an adjective. *Already* is an adverb meaning "by or before this time" or "even now."

ADJECTIVE: Is everyone *all ready* to leave?

ADVERB: Expenses have *already* been deducted.

(10) *All Right* and *Alright.* *Alright*, though it is seen more and more frequently in print, is not considered a correct spelling. Always use the two-word form in your writing.

PREFERRED: It is *all right* to use a pencil.

LESS ACCEPTABLE: He is going to be *alright*.

(11) *All Together* and *Altogether.* These two adverbs have different meanings. *All together* means "all at once." *Altogether* means "completely" or "in all."

EXAMPLES: Let's shout *all together*.

It was *altogether* commendable to act as he did.

(12) *A Lot, Alot,* and *Allot.* *A lot* is an informal expression meaning "a great many" or "a great amount." Avoid using it in formal writing. *Alot* is nonstandard and should never be used. *Allot*, a verb, means "to divide in parts" or "to give out in shares."

NONSTANDARD: There are *alot* of winter sports.

CORRECT: There are *a lot* of winter sports.

BETTER: There are *many* winter sports.

VERB: Appropriate punishments were *allotted* to the offenders.

(13) *Among* and *Between.* *Among* and *between* are both prepositions. *Among* always implies three or more. *Between* is usually properly used with just two things.

EXAMPLES: The colorful fish swimming *among* the rocks were easily spotted.

The differences *between* Cindy and Helen were too great.

(14) *Anxious.* *Anxious* means "worried," "uneasy," or "fearful." Do not use it as a substitute for *eager.*

AMBIGUOUS: They were *anxious* to see their new grandchild.

CLEAR: They were *eager* to see their new grandchild.

CLEAR: They were *anxious* about their new grandchild's health.

(15) *Anyone, Everyone, Any One,* and *Every One.* *Anyone* and *everyone* mean respectively "any person" and "every person." *Any one* means "any single person (or thing)," and *every one* means "every single person (or thing)."

EXAMPLES: *Anyone* with decorating talent could improve this room.

Everyone disliked the new wallpaper.

Any one of those patterns would have been better.

Every one of the rose bushes had been pulled up.

(16) *Anyway, Anywhere, Everywhere, Nowhere,* and *Somewhere.* These adverbs should never end in *s.*

NONSTANDARD: I know you are in a hurry, but you must step to the back of the line *anyways.*

CORRECT: I know you are in a hurry, but you must step to the back of the line *anyway.*

(17) *As.* Do not use the conjunction *as* to mean "because" or "since."

PREFERRED: I can sleep late tomorrow *since* there is no school.

LESS ACCEPTABLE: I can sleep late tomorrow *as* there is no school.

(18) *As To.* *As to* is considered awkward. Replace it with a single preposition, such as *about, for,* or *of.*

NONSTANDARD: We expressed some doubts *as to* his competence.

CORRECT: We expressed some doubts *about* his competence.

(19) *At.* Do not use *at* after *where.* Simply eliminate it.

NONSTANDARD: Where are my gardening tools *at?*

CORRECT: Where are my gardening tools?

(20) *At About.* Avoid using *at* with *about.* Simply eliminate either *at* or *about.*

PREFERRED: The interview ended *at* noon.

The interview ended *about* noon.

LESS ACCEPTABLE: The interview ended *at about* noon.

(21) *Awful* and *Awfully.* *Awful* is used informally to mean "extremely bad." *Awfully* is used informally to mean "very." Both modifiers are overused and should be replaced with more descriptive words. In formal writing use *awful* only to mean "inspiring fear."

INFORMAL: My latest painting is *awful.*

BETTER: My latest painting is *amateurish.*

INFORMAL: He is *awfully* irritable.

BETTER: He is *irascible.*

FORMAL: They knew that some *awful* being dwelt in the mountains.

(22) *A While* and *Awhile.* *A while* is an article and a noun and is usually used after the preposition *for.* *Awhile* is an adverb, which in itself means "for a while."

NOUN: For *a while* she walked aimlessly in the rain.

ADVERB: Remain here *awhile* where you are safe.

(23) *Beat* and *Win.* *Beat* means "to overcome (an opponent)." *Win* means "to achieve victory in." Do not use *win* in place of *beat.*

INCORRECT: The Rangers *won* the Islanders at Madison Square Garden.

CORRECT: The Rangers *beat* the Islanders at Madison Square Garden.

(24) *Because.* Do not use *because* after *the reason.* Rephrase the sentence using one or the other.

NONSTANDARD: The *reason* I took this course was *because* the subject interested me.

CORRECT: I took this course *because* the subject interested me.

CORRECT: The *reason* I took this course was that the subject interested me.

(25) *Being That* and *Being As*. Avoid using either expression. Use *since* or *because* instead.

NONSTANDARD: *Being that* (or *as*) you collect pottery, I bought this
bowl for you.

CORRECT: *Since* (or *Because*) you collect pottery, I bought this bowl
for you.

(26) *Beside* and *Besides*. As prepositions, these two words
have different meanings and cannot be interchanged. *Beside*
means "at the side of" or "close to." *Besides* means "in addition to."

EXAMPLES: *Beside* him was his dog King.

Besides Rick, Patty and Nick were at the gathering.

(27) *Bring* and *Take*. *Bring* means "to carry from a distant
place to a nearer one." *Take* means the opposite: "to carry from
a near place to a more distant place."

EXAMPLES: *Bring* us a souvenir from England.

Take this letter to the post office.

(28) *Burst, Bust,* and *Busted*. *Burst* is the standard present,
past, and past participle of the verb *burst*. *Bust* and *busted* are
nonstandard forms.

NONSTANDARD: You can *bust* the balloon with a pin.

They *busted* into laughter.

CORRECT: You can *burst* the balloon with a pin.

They *burst* into laughter.

(29) *Can* and *May*. Use *can* to mean "to have the ability to."
Use *may* to mean "to have permission to" or "to be possible or
likely to."

ABILITY: A cheetah *can* outrun most other animals.

PERMISSION: Of course you *may* ask questions.

POSSIBILITY: You *may* be served with a subpoena.

(30) *Can't Help But.* This is a nonstandard expression. Use *can't help* plus a gerund instead.

NONSTANDARD: We *can't help but* admire your perseverance.

CORRECT: We *can't help admiring* your perseverance.

(31) *Clipped Words.* Avoid using clipped or shortened words, such as *gym*, *phone*, and *photo*, in formal writing.

FORMAL: Please enclose a *photograph* of yourself.

INFORMAL: Please enclose a *photo* of yourself.

(32) *Different From* and *Different Than.* Though the distinction is beginning to disappear, careful writers prefer *different from* to *different than*.

PREFERRED: Their southern climate is *different from* ours.

LESS ACCEPTABLE: Their southern climate is *different than* ours.

(33) *Doesn't* and *Don't.* Do not use *don't* with third-person singular pronouns and nouns. Use *doesn't* instead.

NONSTANDARD: She *don't* believe in corporal punishment.

   The machine *don't* take long to complete its cycle.

CORRECT: She *doesn't* believe in corporal punishment.

   The machine *doesn't* take long to complete its cycle.

(34) *Done.* *Done* is the past participle of the verb *do*. It should always follow a helping verb.

NONSTANDARD: Her mother *done* all of the baking for their large family.

CORRECT: Her mother *had done* all of the baking for their large family.

(35) *Due To.* *Due to* means "caused by." It should only be used to begin a phrase that clearly and logically modifies a noun. When in doubt try replacing *due to* with another expression, such as *because of*.

NONSTANDARD: I am burned *due to* overexposure at the beach.

CORRECT: My burn is *due to* overexposure at the beach.

(36) ***Due To The Fact That.*** All these words are unnecessary. Use *since* or *because* instead.

PREFERRED: There will be no electricity this morning *because* the power lines are down.

LESS ACCEPTABLE: There will be no electricity this morning *due to the fact that* the power lines are down.

(37) ***Each Other*** **and** ***One Another.*** *Each other* and *one another* are usually interchangeable. At times, however, *each other* is more logically used in reference to only two; *one another*, in reference to more than two.

EXAMPLES: We should learn to listen to *each other* (or *one another*).

Both parents always supported *each other's* decision.

As members of a small community, we respect *one another's* property.

(38) ***Emigrate*** **and** ***Immigrate.*** Notice the difference in the meanings of these two verbs. *Emigrate* means "to leave a country for a new residency." *Immigrate* means "to enter a country to establish a residency."

EXAMPLES: My Swedish mother *immigrated* to this country when she was a young girl.

My mother *emigrated* from Sweden.

(39) ***Enthusiastic*** **and** ***Enthused.*** *Enthusiastic* is the standard form. Avoid using *enthused*.

NONSTANDARD: No one was more *enthused* about the rodeo than I.

CORRECT: No one was more *enthusiastic* about the rodeo than I.

(40) ***Etc.*** *Etc.* is an abbreviation of the Latin phrase *et cetera*, meaning "and so on." Thus, it is wrong to write *and etc.* In formal writing it is best to avoid using this abbreviation altogether.

INCORRECT: The baby's layette included diapers, shirts, gowns, *and etc.*

CORRECT: The baby's layette included diapers, shirts, gowns, *etc.*

FORMAL: The baby's layette included diapers, shirts, gowns, and other necessary items.

(41) *Farther* and *Further*. *Farther* refers to distance. *Further* means "additional" or "to a greater degree or extent."

EXAMPLES: Which is *farther* from the city, the ocean or the mountains?

Further details will be discussed later.

(42) *Fewer* and *Less*. Use *fewer* with things that can be counted. Use *less* with qualities and quantities that cannot be counted.

EXAMPLES: *fewer* calories, *fewer* strengths, *fewer* dependents

less gravel, *less* misery, *less* light

(43) *Former* and *Latter*. *Former* refers to the first of two previously mentioned items. *Latter* refers to the second of the two.

EXAMPLE: Uncle Bert brought me a silver bracelet and a stuffed iguana from Mexico. The *former* I wore gladly; the *latter* was consigned to the attic.

(44) *Get*, *Got*, and *Gotten*. All forms of the verb *get* are acceptable in standard usage, but it is best to avoid using *get*, *got*, and *gotten* in formal writing.

INFORMAL: Please *get* out.

FORMAL: Please *leave*.

Whenever possible, try to use a more specific word in place of *get*.

ACCEPTABLE: *get* permission, *got* stronger, have *gotten* a degree

BETTER: *obtain* permission, *became* stronger, have *earned* a degree

(45) *Good*, *Lovely*, and *Nice*. These three adjectives are weak and overused. Whenever possible, substitute a more specific adjective.

WEAK: *good* attitude, *lovely* home, *nice* evening

BETTER: *positive* attitude, *stately* home, *relaxing* evening

(46) *Healthy* and *Healthful*. People are *healthy;* things are *healthful*.

PREFERRED: A *healthful* diet includes fruits and vegetables.

LESS ACCEPTABLE: A *healthy* diet includes fruits and vegetables.

(47) *In* and *Into*. *In* refers to position. *Into* suggests motion.

POSITION: He left all of the advertisements *in* the mailbox.

MOTION: He put the advertisements *into* (not *in*) the mailbox.

(48) *Irregardless*. Avoid using this word. Use *regardless* instead.

NONSTANDARD: You are expected to get to school on time, *irregardless* of the weather.

CORRECT: You are expected to get to school on time, *regardless* of the weather.

(49) *Its* and *It's*. *Its* is a possessive personal pronoun; *it's* is a contraction for *it is*.

EXAMPLES: He held the cup of steaming coffee and savored *its* warmth.

He *It's* too soon to make a prediction.

(50) *Kind Of* and *Sort Of*. Do not use *kind of* and *sort of* to mean "rather" or "somewhat."

NONSTANDARD: I felt *kind of* disappointed.

CORRECT: I felt *rather* disappointed.

(51) *Learn* and *Teach*. *Learn* means "to acquire knowledge." *Teach* means "to give knowledge to."

EXAMPLES: We *learned* how to express our anger clearly.

Our parents *taught* (not *learned*) us how to do so.

(52) *Leave* and *Let*. *Leave* means "to allow to remain." *Let* means "to permit." Do not reverse the meanings.

NONSTANDARD: *Let* me alone!

CORRECT: *Leave* me alone!

NONSTANDARD: *Leave* me be the judge of my own actions.

CORRECT: *Let* me be the judge of my own actions.

(53) *Lie* and *Lay*. Notice the difference in the meanings and uses of these two verbs. *Lie* means "to recline." Its principal parts are *lie, lying, lay, lain*. As an intransitive verb, it does not take an object. *Lay* means "to put or set down." Its principal parts are *lay, laying, laid, laid*. As a transitive verb, it usually does take an object.

LIE: *Lie* on the grass and look at the clouds.

   After mowing the lawn, he *lay* in the hammock.

   These wet towels have *lain* on the floor since yesterday.

LAY: *Lay* the blankets on the shelf.

   He *laid* the logs on the grate.

   We have *laid* a runner the length of the aisle.

(54) *Like*, *As*, and *As If*. *Like* is a preposition meaning "similar to." *As* and *as if* are conjunctions. *As* means "in the same way that." *As if* means "that" or "as it (or someone) would if."

NONSTANDARD: This tastes *like* fresh apple juice should taste.

CORRECT: This tastes *as* fresh apple juice should taste.

CORRECT: This tastes *like* fresh apple juice.

NONSTANDARD: It looks *like* it will rain.

CORRECT: It looks *as if* it will rain.

(55) *Lose* and *Loose*. *Lose* is always a verb, generally meaning "to miss from one's possession." *Loose* is usually an adjective or part of such idioms as *cut loose, turn loose,* or *break loose*.

EXAMPLES: Don't *lose* my new address.

   Tim's front tooth was *loose*.

   Turn *loose* the captives.

(56) *May Be* and *Maybe*. *May be* is a helping verb and verb. *Maybe* is an adverb meaning "perhaps."

VERB: There *may be* some truth to his accusation.

ADVERB: *Maybe* we will arrive at the same conclusion.

(57) Of. Do not write *of* after a helping verb such as *should, would, could,* or *must.* Use *have* instead. Moreover, do not use *of* after *outside, inside, off,* and *atop.* Simply eliminate it.

NONSTANDARD: She *could of* postponed our meeting indefinitely.

CORRECT: She *could have* postponed our meeting indefinitely.

PREFERRED: They placed a flag *atop* the mountain.

LESS ACCEPTABLE: They placed a flag *atop of* the mountain.

(58) OK, O.K., and Okay. In informal writing *OK, O.K.,* and *okay* are acceptably used to mean "all right." Do not use either the abbreviations or *okay* in formal writing, however.

FORMAL: Your proposal seems all right.

INFORMAL: Your proposal seems *okay.*

(59) Ought. Never use *ought* with *have* or *had.* Simply eliminate *have* or *had.*

NONSTANDARD: Even without instructions I *had ought* to be able to assemble this toy.

CORRECT: Even without instructions I *ought* to be able to assemble this toy.

(60) Outside Of. Do not use this expression to mean "besides" or "except."

NONSTANDARD: *Outside of* the custodians and Melanie, hardly anyone helped clean the gymnasium.

CORRECT: *Except* for the custodians and Melanie, hardly anyone helped clean the gymnasium.

(61) Plenty. *Plenty* is a noun that is usually correctly followed by *of,* as in *plenty of room.* It does not mean "very."

NONSTANDARD: We were *plenty* worried about your being alone.

CORRECT: We were *very* worried about your being alone.

(62) Plurals That Do Not End In -s. The plurals of certain nouns from Greek and Latin are formed as they were in their original language. Words such as *criteria, media,* and *phenomena* are plural and should not be treated as if they were singular (*criterion, medium, phenomenon*).

INCORRECT: That *criteria* prevents many manuscripts from being selected.

CORRECT: Those *criteria* prevent many manuscripts from being selected.

INCORRECT: The news *media is* sure to give us good coverage of election returns.

CORRECT: The news *media are* sure to give us good coverage of election returns.

(63) Precede and Proceed. *Precede* means "to go before." *Proceed* means "to move or go forward."

EXAMPLES: *Precede* the detailed instructions with a brief explanation.

You may *proceed* to give us your report.

(64) Principal and Principle. As an adjective, *principal* means "most important" or "chief." As a noun, it means "a person who has controlling authority." *Principle*, always a noun, means "a fundamental law."

ADJECTIVE: Our *principal* means of transportation is the subway.

NOUN: The school's *principal* is always eager to see students.

NOUN: We discussed the *principles* of the Knights of the Round Table.

(65) Raise and Rise. *Raise*, a transitive verb that generally takes an object, means "to lift," "to increase," or "to grow." *Rise*, an intransitive verb that does not take an object, means "to move upward" or "to be increased."

EXAMPLES: *Raise* your hand as a signal.

The hill gradually *rises*.

(66) Real. *Real* means "authentic." The use of *real* to mean "very" or "really" should be avoided in formal writing.

FORMAL: The Rembrandt on the wall is *real*.

INFORMAL: She is *real* happy.

BETTER: She is *very* happy.

(67) Says. *Says* should not be used as a substitute for *said*.

NONSTANDARD: Next he *says* to her, "Move over!"

CORRECT: Next he *said* to her, "Move over!"

(68) Set and Sit. *Set*, a transitive verb that generally takes an object, means "to put (something) in a certain place." *Sit*, an intransitive verb that does not take an object, means "to be seated."

EXAMPLES: *Set* the cushion next to the table.

Let's *sit* on a cushion in front of the fire.

(69) Shall and Will. These helping verbs are interchangeable in most instances. Except in questions asking for permission or agreement, however, *will* is the more commonly used form.

EXAMPLES: *Shall* I wait for you?

I *will* wait for you.

(70) Slow and Slowly. Although *slow* can now be used as either an adjective or an adverb, careful writers still use it only as an adjective. *Slowly* is preferred as the adverb.

CORRECT: Her progress has been *slow*.

PREFERRED: Drive *slowly* along this road.

LESS ACCEPTABLE: Drive *slow* along this road.

(71) So. *So* is acceptable as a conjunction. It should not be used, however, to begin a sentence.

STANDARD: Stop the car *so* I can get out.

NONSTANDARD: We could barely hear him. *So* we listened closely.

CORRECT: We could barely hear him. Therefore, we listened closely.

(72) Than and Then. *Than* is used in comparisons. Do not confuse it with the adverb *then*, which usually refers to time.

EXAMPLES: The second exercise is more difficult *than* the first.

Let the dough rise and *then* knead it.

(73) That, Which, and Who. Be sure to use these relative pronouns correctly. *That* refers to people or things; *which* refers only to things; *who* refers only to people.

PEOPLE: He is a man *that* (or *whom*) we can rely on.

THINGS: This is the satellite *that* (or *which*) orbited the earth.

(74) Their, There, and They're. Do not confuse the spellings of these three words. *Their*, a possessive pronoun, always modifies a noun. *There* can be used either as an expletive at the beginning of a sentence or as an adverb. *They're* is a contraction for *they are*.

PRONOUN: *Their* prognosis is very optimistic.

EXPLETIVE: *There* is little we can do.

ADVERB: *There* is the culprit!

CONTRACTION: *They're* suburbanites.

(75) Them, Them There, These Here, This Here, and That There. *Them* is always a personal pronoun, never an adjective. When a sentence calls for an adjective, use *those* in place of either *them* or *them there*. To correct a sentence containing *these here*, *this here*, and *that there*, simply leave out *here* and *there*.

NONSTANDARD: *Them* letters have no return address.

CORRECT: *Those* letters have no return address.

NONSTANDARD: *These here* African violets are easy to grow.

CORRECT: *These* African violets are easy to grow.

(76) To, Too, and Two. Do not confuse the spellings of these three words. *To*, a preposition, begins a prepositional phrase or an infinitive. *Too*, an adverb, modifies adjectives and other adverbs. Do not forget the second *o*. *Two* is a number.

PREPOSITION: *to* the park, *to* a party

INFINITIVE: *to* sleep, *to* give

ADVERB: *too* dismal, *too* blatantly

NUMBER.   *two* lilies, *two* opportunities

(77) Unique. *Unique* means "one of a kind." It should not be used to mean "odd," "interesting," or "unusual." Since the word means "one of a kind," such expressions as *most unique*, *very unique*, and *extremely unique* are illogical and should not be used.

NONSTANDARD: Yours is an *extremely unique* architectural plan.

CORRECT: Yours is a *unique* architectural plan.

(78) Ways. *Ways* is plural. Do not use it after the article *a*. Use instead the singular form *way*.

NONSTANDARD: We are *a* long *ways* from our destination.

CORRECT: We are *a* long *way* from our destination.

(79) When and Where. Do not use *when* or *where* directly after a linking verb.

NONSTANDARD: The weekends *are when* we enjoy family-oriented activities.

That shop is *where* you can buy rare shells.

CORRECT: On the weekends we enjoy family-oriented activities.

You can buy rare shells at that shop.

In addition, do not use *where* as a substitute for *that*.

NONSTANDARD: I heard on the radio *where* people are trading professional services.

CORRECT: I heard on the radio *that* people are trading professional services.

(80) -wise. Avoid using this suffix to create new words for a particular situation.

PREFERRED: This is a good, tax-sheltered investment.

LESS ACCEPTABLE: This is a good investment, *taxwise*.

EXERCISE A: Avoiding Usage Problems (1–10). For each of the following sentences, choose the correct expression from the choices in parentheses. Try to complete the exercise without looking back in the book.

1. (Advice, Advise) me as you think best.
2. The patient (accuses, alleges) malpractice by the surgeon.
3. Is it (all right, alright) to dress informally?
4. Carol was adversely (affected, effected) by the new regulation.
5. He refuses to (accept, except) his limitations.
6. I (ain't, am not) prepared to reveal the source of this information.
7. A reptile can gradually (adapt, adopt) to changes in temperatures.
8. Stop that (aggravating, annoying) chatter.
9. (Accept, Except) for you, no one showed interest in planning a party.
10. The (affect, effect) of having been a hostage for so long was to make him withdrawn.
11. Dinner is (all ready, already) to be served.
12. We felt awed when the professor described (a, an) universe beyond our comprehension.
13. False rumors only served to (aggravate, annoy) an already tense situation.
14. From a distance everything seemed (all right, alright).
15. The unsuspecting student was (accused, alleged) of stealing a grape from the market.
16. (All ready, Already) winter is approaching.
17. Their (advice, advise) never failed to anger us.
18. A change in personnel was (affected, effected) by the new administration.
19. We spent (a, an) uneventful day at home.
20. Let's (adapt, adopt) her suggestion as one of our company's policies.

EXERCISE B: Avoiding Usage Problems (11–20). Follow the directions for Exercise A.

1. (A lot, Alot) of us felt that we had been robbed of our rights.
2. (Every one, Everyone) of the pigeons expected to be fed by the people seated on benches.
3. Does anyone know where the fuse box (is, is at)?
4. An enormous sign of welcome was strung (among, between) the two posts.
5. Your tuxedo is (all together, altogether) inappropriate.

6. Aunt Mary dotes on Bill (as, since) he is her only nephew.
7. (Regarding, As to) her honesty, there can be no question.
8. All of us shouted a greeting (at, at about) the same time.
9. Fiery sparks rained down (everywhere, everywheres) on the streets below.
10. Each of the children was (allotted, aloted) a small piece of chocolate.
11. On the first day of vacation, Ginny is usually (anxious, eager) to see all of her old friends.
12. We searched diligently to find where the keys (were, were at).
13. Jim glossed over his own error (as, since) he yearned to be praised rather than criticized.
14. The clerk praised the merchandise (as to, for) its durability.
15. The new manager hired (every one, everyone) on a part-time basis.
16. We began singing (all together, altogether).
17. The mail usually arrives (about, at about) ten o'clock in the morning.
18. I lost the gold necklace (somewhere, somewheres) in the house.
19. I (anxiously, eagerly) waited to see if my excuse would be deemed plausible.
20. Black stripes were woven (among, between) the green, red, and blue stripes to form an interesting plaid.

EXERCISE C: Avoiding Usage Problems (21–30). Follow the directions for Exercise A.

1. I was (awfully, very) sorry to learn of his illness.
2. (Beside, Besides) swollen glands, he also had a sore throat.
3. We selected a latex paint (being as, since) it is easy to clean.
4. The reason Al is so knowledgeable about other countries is (because, that) his Dad always took him everywhere.
5. I jogged (a while, awhile) before dusk.
6. The visiting Canadian team (beat, won) our less experienced hockey team.
7. (Because, Being that) she is an experienced jeweler, I asked her to appraise my diamond.
8. (The main reason these evergreens are brown is, These evergreens are brown) because there is little acid in the soil.
9. Marilyn looked (awful, pale) in the bright light of day.
10. The koala remained motionless on a branch for (a while, awhile).
11. The proud father posed with his daughter (beside, besides) him.

12. I was hoping that our team would (beat, win) the championship.
13. Everyone (burst, busted) into the room and enthusiastically began talking.
14. You (can, may) dribble the ball three times before shooting.
15. I (can't help asking, can't help but ask) how much you paid for that emerald.
16. Remember to (bring, take) these boots to be repaired.
17. She (couldn't help but like, couldn't help liking) his congenial manner.
18. I (can, may) envision a city rising from this wasteland.
19. Soon the sun will (bust, burst) through the clouds.
20. Be here early and (bring, take) a warm jacket since our car's heater isn't working properly.

EXERCISE D: Avoiding Usage Problems (31–40). Follow the directions for Exercise A.

1. I have submitted an outline of the (exam, examination) as you requested.
2. Thousands of Cubans (emigrated, immigrated) to Florida's shores.
3. This white bread tastes good, but it (doesn't, don't) have much nutritional value.
4. As the three boys stepped into the haunted house, they strengthened (each other's, one another's) determination with encouraging words.
5. Please report to Ms. Edwards in our (ad, advertising) department.
6. We (done, have done) everything possible to make them feel welcome.
7. The counterplot was successful (because, due to the fact that) our agents performed so cleverly.
8. (Because of, Due to) technical difficulties, the movie will be interrupted.
9. Our family (emigrated, immigrated) from Italy in the nineteenth century.
10. We explained that driving in Britain was (different from, different than) driving in the United States.
11. Make a copy of this letter (due to the fact that, since) you may need it for your records.
12. All of Sandra's friends have their own cars, but she (doesn't, don't).
13. My absence was (because of, due to) an illness in the family.
14. I was so (enthusiastic, enthused) about the possibility of winning the contest that I forgot to mail the entry form.

15. Since everyone told a different version of the accident, we undermined (each other's, one another's) credibility.
16. Crepes are (different from, different than) pancakes.
17. I (done, had done) unexpectedly well on the physics examination.
18. Laurel's trousseau includes many woolen blankets, imported linens, brocade curtains, (and other household items, and etc.).
19. His severe case of anemia is (due to, because he has) malnutrition.
20. "I (done, have done) nothing illegal," said the defendant to the judge.

EXERCISE E: Avoiding Usage Problems (41–50). Follow the directions for Exercise A.

1. He can add no (farther, further) information to this report.
2. They took their children to see *Fantasia* and *Cinderella*. The (former, latter) was more delightful to the children because they love fairy tales.
3. (Colorful, Lovely) wildflowers grew in profusion over the hillside.
4. This car uses (fewer, less) gasoline than any other car of comparable size.
5. You can (climb, get) to the treehouse by using this rope.
6. Doctor Lawrence had a (nice, soothing) bedside manner.
7. My two favorite holidays are Thanksgiving and New Year's. I think the (former, latter) is a good time to remember all that I have.
8. There are (fewer, less) complaints about service now that the company has increased the number of repairmen.
9. This is the remarkable story of a German shepherd who walked (farther, further) than would seem possible to find his owner.
10. Take a (close, good) look at this drawing.
11. We (got, secured) a loan for a major home improvement.
12. Push the wagon (in, into) the barn.
13. (Irregardless, Regardless) of your excuse, you must take the test today.
14. (Its, It's) feathers glowing irridescently, the peacock strutted across the lawn.
15. Ruth prepared (healthful, healthy) meals for her children.
16. Being without transportation was (rather, sort of) inconvenient.
17. (Its, It's) never too late to improve.
18. I don't want to see that movie, (irregardless, regardless) of the critics' raves.

19. I feel strong and (healthful, healthy) after weeks of rest and exercise.
20. Mindy was (kind of, somewhat) disappointed to find her lobster traps empty.

EXERCISE F: Avoiding Usage Problems (51–60). Follow the directions for Exercise A.

1. She (learned, taught) the seal how to clap its flippers.
2. (May be, Maybe) Bill can open the window if he tries hard.
3. Rabbit tastes (as, like) chicken.
4. These dirty dishes have (laid, lain) in the sink for two days.
5. Nothing remained in the drawer (except, outside of) a black and white photograph.
6. Will you please (leave, let) him alone while he is studying.
7. (Inside, Inside of) the cavern was a deep pool.
8. He prefers a shirt with a (loose, lose) collar.
9. Obsidian chips easily (as, like) glass does.
10. Scurrying noises indicate that a family of mice (may be, maybe) living in the closet.
11. (Leave, Let) me go by myself.
12. Anyone who (looses, loses) the invitation will still be admitted to the banquet.
13. We must inform the public that this fire-retardant chemical is not (okay, safe).
14. This large silo (had ought, ought) to hold our surplus grain.
15. The chimpanzee (learned, taught) how to communicate using sign language.
16. A solution of salt and water (had ought, ought) to kill these persistent weeds.
17. (Except for, Outside of) Amy and Carol, no one came to the barbecue.
18. (Lay, Lie) the injured cat on this blanket.
19. She sounds (as if, like) she has a cold.
20. The wisteria (should have, should of) been pruned to limit its rapid growth.

EXERCISE G: Avoiding Usage Problems (61–70). Follow the directions for Exercise A.

1. The nurse could feel a pulse beating (slow, slowly) in the patient's wrist.
2. Mike was (plenty, very) angry when he realized that he had been duped.
3. Snow was a strange (phenomena, phenomenon) in New Orleans.

4. An unshod horse will have (plenty, very) sore hooves after walking on this road.
5. The print media (carry, carries) much more advertising than television does.
6. When the fire alarm sounds we will (precede, proceed) down the corridor.
7. Then, before I could explain, he (said, says) that I was fired.
8. Their (principal, principle) export is soybeans.
9. (Set, Sit) this tape recorder anywhere, and it will record the least audible sound.
10. The elementary school (principal, principle) has resigned.
11. Our grandparents were (real, very) proud to show their grandchildren their prize heifers.
12. (Shall, Will) we plan on your joining us?
13. Her voice was (raised, rose) in supplication.
14. The (preceding, proceeding) diagram illustrates this concept.
15. After a long discussion, the broker (said, says) that I should sell the stocks now.
16. Gladys has always longed for a window seat that she could (set, sit) in.
17. They (raised, rose) the flag before the game began.
18. He objects to your methods because they violate his (principals, principles).
19. Matt was (real, really) astonished by the sudden materialization of his dream.
20. The Tennessee walking horse moved (slow, slowly) around the arena.

EXERCISE H: Avoiding Usage Problems (71–80). Follow the directions for Exercise A.

1. Bison are animals (that, who) once roamed freely on the Great Plains.
2. (I, So I) asked for a drink of water.
3. A third-degree burn is worse (than, then) a first-degree burn.
4. The monks rose early to pray and (than, then) worked in the monastery's garden until it was time for them to have breakfast.
5. (So then, Then) he carefully unfolded the napkin and placed it on his lap.
6. Virginia Woolf was a woman (which, who) suffered severely from depression.
7. If (to, two) answers are possible, select the better one.
8. (Their, They're) delight in good literature was evidenced by numerous large bookcases lining the walls.

9. Ask (those, them there) hefty fellows to help us lift the wagon from the ditch.
10. The magician asked someone in the audience (to, too) help her with her next trick.
11. Milan is a considerable (way, ways) from Rome.
12. We should not mail these figurines because (there, they're) very fragile.
13. Summers are (a season when, when) we feel a greater sense of freedom.
14. (Businesswise, In business matters), Stella had much to learn.
15. Put (these, these here) plants where the sunlight is strongest.
16. Jackie had to run a long (way, ways) before the mail carrier heard her.
17. (Their, There) must not be another delay in the shipment of supplies needed by the earthquake victims.
18. An acrobat must never be (to, too) daring.
19. Every snowflake has a (unique, very unique) shape.
20. A sandy ocean bottom is (the place where, where) a sand dollar may be found.

EXERCISE I: Correcting Usage Problems. Twenty of the following twenty-five sentences contain an error in usage. If the sentence is correct, write *correct* on your paper. Rewrite all of the others to correct the mistakes.

1. Your persistent demands do nothing but aggravate me.
2. You may ride anyone of the horses in the stable.
3. Bring a good book with you since the flight to Athens takes eight hours.
4. I have no idea where we are at.
5. He don't know how to behave in public.
6. Due to an early frost, the crop is less than what had been estimated.
7. If we work all together, we will finish soon.
8. You should of seen the expression on her face when we shouted, "Surprise!"
9. A sonnet usually got fourteen lines.
10. A capybara is different than a rat in that it sometimes grows over four feet in length.
11. Jeff looks like he is sick.
12. Human beings have adapted to almost every climate on earth.
13. Walk slow so that I can keep up with you.
14. No one from the class is going to the concert outside of you and me.
15. Your sweater maybe in the hall closet.

16. Overcooked, boiled vegetables are less healthy for you than crisp, steamed vegetables.
17. Think more and ask less unnecessary questions.
18. We live in the farther house, the one beside the big maple tree.
19. Your own principals chould help you solve ethical problems.
20. The students were anxious about the debate even though they had thoroughly prepared their arguments.
21. My parents said that I can borrow the car tonight if I promise to wash and wax it this weekend.
22. The dolls are made so that one fits inside of another.
23. The new drug effected an immediate recovery.
24. If you let that oriental rug lay in direct sunlight, the colors will fade.
25. The cat has been setting for hours under the bird feeder.

APPLICATION: Using Expressions Correctly. Write a sentence of your own for each of the following words or expressions.

1. principle
2. former . . . latter
3. further
4. ought
5. done
6. emigrate
7. have lain
8. adapt
9. as
10. less
11. between
12. can
13. maybe
14. aggravate
15. except
16. slow
17. healthful
18. advise
19. awful
20. media
21. any one
22. affect
23. besides
24. different from
25. due to

11

Levels of Language

There are two main categories of English usage: standard and nonstandard. Standard English is the preferred method of speaking and writing for the majority of Americans. It encompasses the most widely accepted uses of grammar, pronunciation, and the meanings of words. Nonstandard English, in contrast, is not commonly used by the majority of Americans. It includes variations in grammar, pronunciation, and meanings that are restricted to smaller groups by such factors as geography or profession.

Within these two broad categories are various levels of language. Standard English, for example, includes formal and informal language. On the other hand, dialect, slang, and overly technical language are usually considered nonstandard.

LEVELS OF LANGUAGE	
Standard	**Nonstandard**
Formal	Dialect
Informal	Slang
	Overly technical language

None of these levels of language is always right or always wrong. Such factors as time, place, and occasion contribute to determining which level is appropriate. For example, if you were addressing a large audience that had come to hear you speak on prison conditions, your choice of words and even your bearing would be different from what they would be if you were discussing the same subject while trout fishing with a friend. Similarly, the technical language used at a symposium of nuclear physicists is not appropriate at a town meeting where residents may discuss the pros and cons of a proposed nuclear power plant.

As a student of English, you should have a solid command of standard usage because this usage is what will establish you as a person with education. You will also need to be familiar with this usage for higher levels of education, for particular careers, and in many other situations throughout your life.

The Varieties of English 11.1

It has been estimated that English is the native language of over 350 million people around the world, second only to Chinese. If non-native speakers of English are included, the number nearly doubles. With such vast numbers of people speaking English, it seems obvious that the English spoken by an Australian will be different in many ways from the English spoken by an American. Even within one nation English may vary from one region to another. Though there are many varieties of English, it is reassuring to know that the differences are not so great that they make communication impossible between speakers of English from diverse parts of the globe.

As a student of English, you should be aware not only of the level of English you are expected to use in school but also of the variations you may have learned in earlier years, at home, from friends, or from living in a different part of the world. This section will help you sharpen that awareness by explaining the characteristics of several levels of English.

■ Standard English

Standard English, the language used by most educated people, is spoken and written somewhat differently in formal and informal situations. Both formal and informal English are considered acceptable. There is, however, a marked difference between the style and tone of each. The distinction may be as simple as whether you invite a respected but unfamiliar person into your home with "Won't you please come in?" or whether you shout "Come on in!" to a close relative.

Formal English.   Formal English is the language considered appropriate for any serious writing. It need not be pompous, difficult, or excessively complicated. Nevertheless, it requires much practice before it can be used with absolute clarity and precision.

Formal English is English that adheres to traditional standards of correctness. It is characterized by an extensive vocabulary, complete grammatical constructions, and elaborate sentence structures. It avoids unnecessary contractions, casual expressions, and colloquialisms.

The following excerpt illustrates formal English. Notice that it contains no contractions, casual expressions, or colloquialisms.

EXAMPLE:

The last government in the Western world to possess all the attributes of aristocracy in working condition took office in England in June of 1895. Great Britain was at the zenith of empire when the Conservatives won the General Election of that year, and the Cabinet they formed was her superb and resplendent image. Its members represented the greater landowners of the country who had been accustomed to govern for generations. As its superior citizens they felt they owed a duty to the State to guard its interests and manage its affairs. They governed from duty, heritage and habit—and, as they saw it, from right.
—Barbara W. Tuchman

Informal English. Although you need to be able to express your ideas formally, you should also feel comfortable with informal English in casual situations.

Informal English is English that is colloquial or conversational. Its vocabulary is somewhat less extensive than that of formal English; it permits looser grammatical constructions and uses shorter sentence structures.

Remember that informal English is still considered standard English. It is the language most educated people use every day—in newspapers, on television, in letters, in advertisements, and in casual conversation. Although it may include contractions, casual expressions, and colloquialisms, it usually does not contain slang or improper grammar.

The following excerpt is from a humorous article in which the author contemplates the many things in life that people refer to as "nice." Notice the contractions, the casual expressions such as "rotten" and "right away," and the simplicity of the sentences and words.

EXAMPLE:

> I guess what got me thinking along these lines was the day. It was a nice day. Not one of the great days, to be sure, but not really rotten either. It was the kind of day when it doesn't really rain, but the sun doesn't really make much show either; the kind of day when you feel stiff all over and 10 years older than you really are, but not like you might have to go into the hospital right away. In short, a nice day. —Russell Baker

If you compare this quotation with the quotation on page 280, you should notice a definite contrast between the two.

EXERCISE A: Identifying Formal and Informal English. Read each of the following quotations carefully. If the quotation is an example of formal English, write *formal*. If it is an example of informal English, write *informal*.

1. And while it's nice to dabble around town in, you will never discover its true delights until you take it out in the open, where the road unreels like a balloon with a hole punched in it. —Larry Griffin
2. I have received a letter this morning that has astonished me exceedingly. As it principally concerns yourself, you ought to know its contents. I did not know before, that I had *two* daughters on the brink of matrimony. —Jane Austen
3. On November 7, 1974, in New York City, I was privileged to stand by the side of a very brave man as he met the press for the first time after reaching American soil—and freedom. Simas Kudirka, a slight, forty-five-year-old Lithuanian seaman, had risked everything and endured more than most men are capable of in his struggle to escape the tyranny of the Soviet State. —James L. Buckley
4. Hardin paints under her Indian name, "Tsa-sah-wee-eh," which means Little Standing Spruce in the Tewa language of the Santa Clara pueblo, and always adds the symbol of a small spruce tree to her signature. Although she was not brought up in the Indian traditions of the pueblo after the age of six, she has seriously studied the designs and art of her heritage. —Louann Faris Culley
5. The mood of next spring's fashion is one of gilt-edged innocence. Decadence has had its day. No more tie-dyed T-shirts and faded blue jeans, no more studied sloppiness, no more aching by the newly rich to look like the "nouveau pauvre." —William Safire

6. Within the serious sensualist and true aesthete, outrage seethes. How sweet it would be to expose and annihilate every source of culinary insult and nutritional malpractice. But there is a Great American Appetite for garbage—for junk food, for selective sadism and snobbery, for food that is stale, crisply petrified, demoisturized, sappy-sweet, and waterlogged. —Gael Greene
7. The problem of a giant aircraft carrier is how to keep 4,000 men busy and happy although they are constantly in each other's hair twenty-four hours a day. —Art Buchwald
8. Does your mom try to stuff a hot dinner down you when you've just had three hamburgers and a double malted after school? —Erma Bombeck and Bill Keene
9. "Recreation" in the present-day Western sense has always seemed to me to be an unhealthy regression to childishness. I have therefore despised it, and I believe I have been right. —Arnold Toynbee
10. As we drove through the fertile English countryside, the grass was thick and green despite the January cold. A light frost added gemlike sparkle. Tiny homes, many with thatched roofs, stood as sentinels over small parcels of farmland while a solitary stone castle surveyed them, the remnants of former wealth and glory. Struck by the simple beauty of this panorama I thought, "This is England." — Paula James Kaplan

■ Nonstandard English

The line that divides nonstandard English from informal standard English is a thin one. It is not, however, impossible to tell the difference in most situations. Three categories of nonstandard English that are reasonably easy to distinguish from informal English are *dialect, slang,* and *overly technical language.*

Dialect.   Dialect is language whose use is restricted to a specific geographical location or to a specific social or ethnic group. It is considered nonstandard because its use is not widespread.

> **Dialect** is a nonstandard form of English that is confined to a particular geographical area or social group. It is characterized by words, expressions, pronunciations, and grammatical constructions that are not commonly found in standard English.

The following is an excerpt from Scott's *The Heart of the Mid-Lothian*. Read it aloud. Even though many of the words may be unfamiliar, you should still be able to understand the meaning of most if not all of the words.

EXAMPLE:

> Dear Mr. Butler, keep a good heart, for we are in the hands of Ane that kens better what is gude for us than we ken what is for oursells. I hae nae doubt to do that for which I am come—. I canna doubt it—I winna think to doubt it—because, if I haena full assurance, how shall I bear myself with earnest entreaties in the great folk's presence? But to ken that ane's purpose is right, and to make their heart strong, is the way to get through the warst day's darg. —Sir Walter Scott

Slang.　Slang includes words such as "gross" and phrases such as "hang in there" that achieve a widespread but generally temporary popularity. Most slang does not continue to be used long enough for it to be established as standard. These expressions usually die quickly and are replaced by new ones.

Slang is a nonstandard form of English that is generally colorful and expressive but short-lived.

The following is an excerpt from *Babbitt*, a novel published by Sinclair Lewis in 1922. Many of the slang expressions are so dated that they may be unfamiliar to you. Notice that the language is extremely conversational and that the general level of the passage is nonstandard.

EXAMPLE:

> And then most folks are so darned crooked themselves that they expect a fellow to do a little lying, so if I was fool enough to never whoop the ante I'd get the credit for lying anyway! In self-defense I got to toot my own horn, like a lawyer defending a client—his bounden duty, ain't it, to bring out the poor dub's good points? —Sinclair Lewis

Overly Technical Language.　Overly technical language, often called *jargon*, has an essential function for people who are knowledgeable in a particular area, such as science or technology. However, it includes terminology that an ordinary person cannot easily understand. It is considered nonstandard simply because it is used by a limited number of people.

Overly technical language is a nonstandard .form of English because it is limited in its proper use to specific areas of knowledge.

The following excerpt is an example of overly technical language from the teaching profession. Unless you have studied education, this passage will probably overwhelm you with words you do not understand.

EXAMPLE:

> Verbal coding requires not only the naming of the lexical stimulus but also identifying it semantically. If poor readers are slower at verbal coding, they will take longer to identify the concept the name represents. They may not retrieve all facets of the concept or may retrieve it incompletely or less specifically than the task demands. The facets of a concept are really its schema, a network of names reflecting a breadth and depth of information about it. To understand a name requires accessing its schema. Deeper processing would even entail retrieving sub-schemata represented in the original schema. —Renee Weisberg

EXERCISE B: Identifying Dialect, Slang, and Overly Technical Language.

Read each of the following quotations carefully. Label each one *dialect*, *slang*, or *overly technical language*. Be prepared to explain the reasons for your decisions.

1. "That's ridic'lous!" Ella says. "When a girl says she can't make up her mind, it shows they's nothing to make up." —Ring Lardner
2. Yes, you always knew that for you and all the other little people in the world, there ain't no Easy Street in life, and that all you can do is try to earn your living. But I don't want to sound like I was kicking or complaining. —James T. Farrell
3. The inertial systems have virtually no divergence and the Omega system no tendency toward lane slip.
4. Born here, maybe, Miss Meggie darlin', but wit' a name like O'Neill now, he's as Irish as Paddy's pigs, not meanin' any disrespect to yer sainted father, Miss Meggie, may he rest in peace and sing wit' the angels. —Colleen McCullough
5. "Been a fine day," said the candy man, hollowly. "First time in a month I've felt first-class. Hit it up down old Madison, hollering out like I useter. Think it'll rain tomorrow?" —O. Henry
6. We'd feel pretty glum if we got stuck in some Main Street burg and tried to wise up the old codgers to the kind of life we're use to here. —Sinclair Lewis
7. Aw'd rayther, by th'haulf, hev 'em swearing i' my lugs

frough morn tuh neeght, nur hearken yah, hahsiver!
—Emily Brontë

8. Throughout the instructional sequence, the teacher has acted as a facilitator to help students to generate ideas. — Susan Gary

9. There are two complications with latent heat-of-fusion energy storage using eutectic salts: the salts' low thermal conductivity and the volume change that accompanies fusion. —Richard Stepler

10. "Here this fellow that calls himself The Misfit is aloose from the Federal Pen and headed toward Florida and you read here what it says he did to these people. Just you read it. I wouldn't take my children in any direction with a criminal like that aloose in it. I couldn't answer to my conscience if I did. —Flannery O'Connor

APPLICATION: **Identifying Different Levels of Usage.** Identify each of the following passages as *standard* or *nonstandard* English. If the passage is standard, further identify it as *formal* or *informal.* If the passage is nonstandard, identify it as *dialect, slang,* or *overly technical language.*

1. Sometimes I get so darn sick and tired of all this routine and the accounting at the office and expenses at home and fussing and stewing and fretting and wearing myself out worrying over a lot of junk that doesn't really mean a doggone thing . . . —Sinclair Lewis

2. Whet, whoiever knew yah wur coming? Yah sud ha' send word! They's nowt norther dry—nor mensful abaht t'place: nowt is n't! —Emily Brontë

3. The best Mother's Day present I ever got was a mole—a satiny, sleek little animal—all done up in a shoe box full of grass. —Pat B. Goodwin

4. Shut your eyes, reader. Do you hear the thundering of wheels? Those are the stolypin cars rolling on and on. Those are the red cows rolling . . . they are arresting someone all the time, cramming him in somewhere, moving him about. —Alexander Solzhenitsyn

5. And too besides I give you bellyache like you never see bellyache. Perhaps you lie a long time with the bellyache I give you. Perhaps you don't get up again with the bellyache I give you. So keep yourself quiet and decent. You hear me? —Jean Rhys

6. What makes me feel so bad dis time 'uz bekase I hear sumpn over yonder on de bank like a whack, er a slam, while ago, en it mine me er de time I treat my little 'Lizabeth so ornery. —Mark Twain

7. A stewardess hands me a program. Good. Maybe I can kill the month by hanging around Grandmother's airport reading it, then turn up at the old dear's house on turkey day, after all. —Russell Baker

8. Close attention was of course paid to all engine-tuning variables, like the Rajay turbocharger (set at only 4 psi, since all-out power wasn't part of the program), the K-Jetronic fuel-injection system, and the Lambda-sond emissions system.

9. Schools can be humane and still educate well. They can be genuinely concerned with gaiety and joy and individual growth and fulfillment without sacrificing concern for intellectual discipline and development. —Charles E. Siberman

10. "Poor child!" said Rachel, wiping her eyes; "but thee mustn't feel so. The Lord hath ordered it so that never hath a fugitive been stolen from our village. I trust thine will not be the first." —Harriet Beecher Stowe

Review Exercises: Usage

REVIEW EXERCISE 1: A Review of Terms

In this unit many terms and definitions were introduced. How many do you remember? Answer each question as completely as possible.

1. Which are the six basic tenses?
2. What are the four principal parts of a verb?
3. How are the progressive forms of the six tenses created?
4. To what tenses are the emphatic forms limited?
5. What is the difference between the way regular and irregular verbs form their past and past participles?
6. What is a conjugation?
7. What are the three main categories of time?
8. What is the use of the historical present? Of the critical present?
9. How can modifiers help a verb indicate time?
10. What determines the correct form of a verb in a subordinate clause? Of a participle or infinitive?
11. What are the uses of the indicative mood? Of the imperative mood? Of the subjunctive mood?
12. What auxiliary verbs can be used to help a verb express the subjunctive mood?

13. When is a verb active? How is the passive voice formed?
14. What are the uses of the passive voice?
15. When is the nominative case used? The objective case? The possessive case?
16. What is an elliptical clause?
17. What problem arises when using pronouns in elliptical clauses?
18. What is meant by the term "agreement"?
19. How must a subject and a verb agree?
20. Why might there be confusion over the endings of third-person singular verbs in the present tense and plural nouns?
21. What is an antecedent?
22. How must a pronoun agree with its antecedent?
23. What is the use of the positive degree of adjectives and adverbs? Of the comparative degree? Of the superlative degree?
24. How are the comparative and superlative degrees of regular adjectives and adverbs formed?
25. In comparisons involving adjectives and adverbs, what is meant by "irregular forms"?
26. When is a comparison "balanced"?
27. What is meant by the term "double negatives"?
28. What is the difference between standard and nonstandard English?
29. List two examples of situations when only formal English should be used. List two examples of situations when informal English should be used.
30. Why are dialect, slang, and overly technical language considered nonstandard English?

REVIEW EXERCISE 2: The Principal Parts of Verbs

Divide your paper into four columns and label the first *Present*, the second *Past Participle*, the third *Past*, and the fourth *Past Participle*. Then list the principal parts of each of the following verbs.

1. do		11. drive	
2. swim		12. close	
3. be		13. take	
4. set		14. know	
5. steal		15. write	
6. drink		16. shrink	
7. lose		17. burst	
8. examine		18. tear	
9. go		19. bring	
10. ring		20. hit	

REVIEW EXERCISE 3: Conjugation

Conjugate the following verbs as indicated. Notice that one column calls for the basic forms, one for the progressive forms, and one for the emphatic forms.

Basic Forms	*Progressive Forms*	*Emphatic Forms*
1. build (with *you*)	6. pay (with *she*)	11. listen (with *he*)
2. find (with *he*)	7. wear (with *they*)	12. begin (with *I*)
3. cost (with *it*)	8. run (with *you*)	
4. lead (with *she*)	9. show (with *it*)	
5. ride (with *they*)	10. ride (with *I*)	

REVIEW EXERCISE 4: Tenses

Write a sentence of your own for each of the following verbs, using the tense indicated in parentheses. Underline the verb in each sentence.

1. give (historical present)
2. walk (present emphatic)
3. make (past)
4. sit (future perfect progressive)
5. choose (past perfect)
6. throw (future progressive)
7. raise (past perfect progressive)
8. write (critical present)
9. sleep (past perfect)
10. blow (future perfect)
11. teach (present progressive)
12. beat (past progressive)
13. strike (present)
14. grow (past emphatic)
15. be (critical present)
16. lie (present perfect progressive)
17. come (present progressive)
18. order (present perfect)
19. put (future)
20. freeze (past progressive)

REVIEW EXERCISE 5: Tense Sequence

Write sentences of your own that include each of the following verbs or verbals. Be sure that the form of the verb in the subordinate clause or the form of the verbal is logically related to the main verb in each sentence. Underline the main verbs.

Verb in Subordinate Clause	*Participle*	*Infinitive*
1. rose	5. watching	8. to belong
2. cook	6. smiling	9. to have agreed
3. will have given	7. having begun	10. to have seen
4. had gone		

REVIEW EXERCISE 6: Mood

Identify the mood of each underlined verb in the following sentences as *indicative, imperative,* or *subjunctive.*

1. <u>Will</u> his stoutness <u>hinder</u> him in jumping this hurdle?
2. If I <u>were</u> a paratrooper, I would surely have baled out of the airplane.
3. If Randy <u>should leave</u>, I would regret it.
4. <u>Close</u> the shutters before you leave the cabin.
5. The director demands that each performer <u>come</u> to rehearsal prepared to work.
6. He <u>had</u> a rudimentary knowledge of science.
7. Slowly <u>release</u> the clutch and press down on the accelerator.
8. Would that I <u>were</u> living during the reign of Richard the Lion-Hearted.
9. Please <u>take</u> good care of yourself.
10. They <u>did</u> not <u>reach</u> the summit of the peak.

REVIEW EXERCISE 7: Voice

Identify the voice in each of the following sentences as *active* or *passive.* Then rewrite each of the sentences you have identified as passive in the active voice.

1. The interpretation of dreams was used by Sigmund Freud.
2. A glass cage contained two tarantulas.
3. This sundial was placed here a century ago by the previous owners of this house.
4. Horizontal lines on the television screen ruined the picture.
5. Cars with standard transmissions are still preferred by many drivers.
6. The mural was ruined by graffiti.
7. Should Jane have accepted his request?
8. Our finite minds cannot comprehend eternity.
9. A grand tour of the city was given to us by our host.
10. These glasses change color according to the intensity of the sun.

REVIEW EXERCISE 8: Case

Choose the correct pronoun in each of the following sentences from the choices in parentheses. Then indicate whether the pronoun is in the *nominative, objective,* or *possessive* case.

1. (Whoever, Whomever) would agree to such a proposal?
2. (We, Us) voters should read the newspapers carefully during an election year.
3. He is nearly as tall as (she, her).

4. (Who's, Whose) signature is that?
5. Give these letters to (whoever, whomever) is sitting at the desk.
6. It was (they, them) who patented this invention.
7. For (who, whom) did the boy leave these flowers?
8. (He, Him, His) lying once will only lead to more lies.
9. Betty is more friendly than (he, him).
10. Louis and (he, him) planned the surprise party.
11. Sidney flattered (whoever, whomever) he thought would help him.
12. The person selected for vice president was (who, whom)?
13. (Your's, Yours) is the worst explanation I have ever heard.
14. This man is a sharp-tongued cynic (who, whom) I dislike.
15. The most aggressive advertising is done by (they, them).
16. Is Jackie as clever as (she, her)?
17. We asked (who, whom) the man in the silk suit was.
18. (Them, Their) haggling over prices gives them a sense of accomplishment.
19. (Who, Whom) do you think gave you the authority?
20. Travel expenses will have to be shared between you and (I, me).

REVIEW EXERCISE 9: Pronoun References

Rewrite each of the following sentences to correct the pronoun reference.

1. Madge swims like an otter. That makes her a good swimming instructor.
2. The story made me cry, which everyone thought was funny.
3. I liked the movie, but they certainly didn't follow the plot of the book.
4. It is unlikely that they will destroy the building. It is a historical landmark, and it would be an unfortunate loss.
5. Romeo and Juliet chose death. Their love was ill-fated because of circumstances beyond their control. They thought it was their only choice.

REVIEW EXERCISE 10: Agreement

Read each of the following sentences carefully. In fifteen of the sentences, the subject and verb or pronoun and antecedent do not agree. Rewrite these sentences to correct the agreement error. Then identify the sentences that are correct and label them *correct*.

1. The teacher, followed by his students, are now leaving the auditorium.

2. Neither Kate nor Jane has answered the telephone.
3. Our cat gave birth to her kittens this morning, and it has hidden them somewhere.
4. The cream and especially the sugar adds too many calories to these strawberries.
5. Art and myself decided to get short haircuts for the summer.
6. Elizabeth is the only one of the girls who have won a scholarship.
7. *Tanglewood Tales* are a collection of stories by Nathaniel Hawthorne.
8. Anybody who wants free tennis lessons may sign his name to this list.
9. Most of the design have been blurred by water.
10. That statue without any arms or legs looks incomplete.
11. The data have been gathered from numerous sources.
12. Neither sprigs of parsley nor bunches of grapes seems right on this plate.
13. Ten cents buy nothing of any value.
14. Some eclairs and one pie was all that remained in the bakery window.
15. One symptom of this disease are raised red spots.
16. Balloons, lanterns, or a cardboard clown looks decorative at a child's birthday party.
17. Your necktie, as well as mine, are hopelessly out of style.
18. Each boy in the club wants to use their beach privileges.
19. There is several reasons for the conflict between Lance and his father.
20. Spaghetti and meatballs are his favorite dish.

REVIEW EXERCISE 11: Degrees of Comparison

Each of the following sentences contains a comparative or superlative form used correctly. Label each *comparative* or *superlative* and then rewrite the sentence using the other form. You may have to change some words.

EXAMPLE: He is more grateful than she is.

Comparative

He is the most grateful of all.

1. Theirs is the best pasta in town.
2. He is less suited for this type of work than his sister is.
3. This shrimp is fresher than the lobster.
4. He did the most talking of any candidate.
5. Mr. Kenyon is the least permissive teacher in the school.
6. She has more talent as a painter than the rest of us.

7. Look no further than me for someone to believe you.
8. Oscar was the most tenacious bulldog you could ever imagine.
9. Miranda had access to the highest circles of the elite.
10. Lynn is more threatened by domineering people than I am.

REVIEW EXERCISE 12: Clear Comparisons

Each of the following sentences contains an error in comparison. Find the error in each and rewrite the sentence correctly.

1. This food is the worse I have ever tasted.
2. Hester is the most dependable of the two.
3. The Dead Sea is saltier than any enclosed body of water.
4. Last week's news was better than this week.
5. The invitation to her party was more unexpected than to her summer house.
6. A stainless steel pan will last longer than aluminum.
7. Your dress is more better suited to the occasion than mine.
8. John's feet are bigger than Tom.
9. Susan needs praise more than anyone in her class.
10. His car is faster than Dave.

REVIEW EXERCISE 13: Special Problems of Usage

Answer each of the following questions.

1. Why shouldn't you write *hadn't but* in a sentence?
2. Of *beside* and *besides*, which means "in addition to"?
3. Why isn't it correct to write *most unique*?
4. When should you use the word *fewer*?
5. How can you improve a sentence that has *as to* in it?
6. What is the difference between *farther* and *further*?
7. In what situations is *so* used as a conjunction?
8. What is the difference between *in* and *into*?
9. When should you avoid using forms of *get*?
10. What should you write in place of *alright*?
11. What is the difference between *precede* and *proceed*?
12. How can *effect* be used as a verb?
13. What part of speech is the word *advise*?
14. How should *that, which*, and *who* be used?
15. Why are other words often preferred to *good, lovely*, and *nice*?
16. What is the difference between *accept* and *except*?
17. What is wrong with the expression *and etc.*?
18. In what situations is standard English necessary?
19. What are some differences between dialect and slang?
20. When is technical language appropriate?

UNIT

Mechanics

12
Capitalization and Abbreviation

13
Punctuation

Chapter 12

Capitalization and Abbreviation

Early Roman scribes used thick-pointed pens to produce lettering, first on papyrus and later on parchment. With this thick writing instrument, it was much easier to write bold capital letters, each one separated from the next. Because this process was time-consuming, scribes soon began to shorten or abbreviate certain longer words so that the use of capital letters and abbreviations developed hand in hand.

As lettering pens improved, a system using capital and small letters slowly evolved. This system developed over the centuries into the systems of printing and cursive writing that are used today.

Although both capital and small letters were available in early English, most nouns still began with capital letters. Today, only certain nouns and other special words are capitalized, all following specific rules. Specific rules also developed over the years for abbreviation. This chapter discusses the basic rules for capitalization and abbreviation, grouping them into categories for easy study and reference.

12.1 Capitalization

As road signs help guide people to their destinations, so capital letters in writing help readers understand what they are reading. Capitalization signals the start of a new sentence or points out certain words within a sentence. Readers can follow and understand a written passage more easily with the visual clues that capitalization provides.

To **capitalize** means to begin a word with a capital letter.

■ Capitals for First Words

You should always signal the start of new ideas by capitalizing the first word in sentences, quotations, and certain phrases.

Capitalize the first words in declarative, interrogative, imperative, and exclamatory sentences.

DECLARATIVE: The report indicated that the work had been done satisfactorily.

INTERROGATIVE: Where did you put the reference book?

IMPERATIVE: Choose your college with great care.

EXCLAMATORY: What an astounding turn of events!

Quotations also begin with a capital if the quotation is a complete sentence.

Capitalize the first word in a quotation if the quotation is a complete sentence.

Study the following examples carefully. The first contains a quotation that is a single sentence. The second contains a quotation with two separate sentences, both of which are capitalized. The third contains a quotation that is one sentence divided by a "he said/she said" phrase. Only the first word of this quotation is capitalized. The last example contains a portion of a quotation that is not a complete sentence but is included in a longer sentence. Because the portion of the quotation does not start a complete sentence, no capital is used.

EXAMPLES: Joe exclaimed, "This sunset is spectacular!"

"Many people read detective stories," said Carolyn Sue. "They enjoy trying to figure out who the guilty person is."

"He is an excellent student," noted Randolph Smith, "but rather shy."

Marcia Gibson feels the speech was "the most inspiring speech given this year at Hunter High."

A sentence following a colon is also capitalized. However, a list of words or phrases following a colon is not.

Capitalize the first word after a colon if the word begins a complete sentence.

SENTENCE FOLLOWING A COLON: He repeated his contention with great conviction: He was not at the scene of the accident.

LIST FOLLOWING A COLON: She provided the class with a selected list of fabrics: cotton, wool, rayon, linen, silk, and polyester.

Certain phrases, such as interjections and question fragments, also require capitalization.

Capitalize the first word in interjections and question fragments.

INTERJECTIONS: Oh, no!   Wonderful!

QUESTION FRAGMENTS: What?   How many?

In most poetry the first word in each line is capitalized even when it does not start a new sentence.

Capitalize the first word in each line of most poetry.

EXAMPLE: I think that I shall never see
A poem lovely as a tree. —Joyce Kilmer

NOTE ABOUT *I* AND *O*:   Capitalize *I* and *O* no matter where they appear in a sentence. Do not, however, capitalize *oh* unless it appears at the beginning of a sentence.

EXAMPLES: Dorothy and I are going to play tennis after school.

"So strong you thump, O terrible drums—so loud you bugles blow." —Walt Whitman

EXERCISE A: Capitalizing First Words. Copy the following sentences and phrases onto your paper, adding capitals where necessary.

1. nonsense! what did Dr. Reston really expect?
2. "i who cannot see find hundreds of things to interest me," said Helen Keller.

3. i know exactly what he wanted: he wanted us to turn over all of our records to him.
4. edward Bulwer Lytton once wrote, "the easiest person to deceive is one's own self."
5. we wonder whether you would explain your theory once again.
6. the committee couldn't believe the terms of the contract.
7. drive carefully! the life you save may be your own.
8. she reported about three kinds of ships: schooners, steamboats, and clipper ships.
9. tell me where you got that photo.
10. "nature has given us two ears," said Henrietta Temple, "but only one mouth."
11. "we all live in a state of ambitious poverty," wrote Juvenal, a writer who lived in the first century.
12. perhaps i made a mistake.
13. i know i am but summer to your heart,
    and not the full four seasons of the year. —Edna St. Vincent Millay
14. the poet Alfred Lord Tennyson wrote, "o, hark, o, hear!"
15. "this homework assignment is very difficult," sighed Maria. "it will probably take me three hours to finish it."
16. did you buy this record yesterday? where?
17. abraham Lincoln said that the United States was "conceived in liberty."
18. sit down, please.
19. "perhaps," she whispered, "the movie will have a surprise ending."
20. where did you go after school?

■ Capitals for Proper Nouns

Nouns, as you probably remember, are either common or proper. Common nouns identify classes of persons, places, or things.

EXAMPLES: infant, daughter, principal

  street, kitchen, city

  picture, ship, magazine

Proper nouns, on the other hand, name specific examples of each class and should be capitalized.

Capitalize all proper nouns.

EXAMPLES: Jennifer, Coach Wilkens, Governor Percy

Main Street, Halloran House, Chicago

Portrait of Sylvette, Mayflower, Sports Illustrated

The capitalization of names, which is rather straightforward, will be treated first. The capitalization of other proper nouns is not as simple. The charts that accompany the treatment of these other proper nouns are designed to help you in two ways: (1) to teach specific rules of capitalization, and (2) to provide a quick reference for checking a specific item. Familiarize yourself with both the categories and the examples in each chart.

Names.   Each part of a person's full name—the given name, the middle name, and the surname—should be capitalized.

Capitalize each part of a person's full name.

EXAMPLES: Jean Grogan, R. R. Brightway, Ernesto Sanchez

Some surnames consist of several parts. If a surname begins with *Mc, O',* or *St.,* the letter immediately following this beginning part is also capitalized.

EXAMPLES: McCormack, O'Hara, St. Nicholas

On the other hand, there are no specific rules for capitalizing surnames beginning with *de, D', la, le, Mac, van,* or *von.* You should always ask for the correct spelling of these names to insure accuracy.

EXAMPLES: La Croix or Lacroix, Von Jahn or von Jahn

You should also capitalize the proper names that are given to animals.

EXAMPLES: Kermit, Chauntecleer, Rin Tin Tin

Geographical and Place Names.   Although there is a wide variety of categories of geographical and place names, a single general rule for capitalization applies.

Capitalize geographical and place names.

Examples of different kinds of geographical and place names are listed in the following chart. Each item should serve as a model for others that are similar in form.

GEOGRAPHICAL AND PLACE NAMES	
Streets:	Madison Avenue, First Street, Chicken Valley Road
Boroughs, Towns, and Cities:	Brooklyn, Oakdale, Michigan City
Counties, States, and Provinces:	Champlain County, New Mexico, Quebec
Nations and Continents:	Austria, the Congo Republic, the United States of America, Africa, South America
Mountains:	the Adirondacks, Mount Washington
Valleys and Deserts:	the San Fernando Valley, the Mojave Desert, the Gobi Desert
Islands and Peninsulas:	Aruba, the Faroe Islands, Cape York Peninsula
Sections of a Country:	the Northeast, the Ukraine, the Great Plains
Scenic Spots:	the Sphinx, the Leaning Tower of Pisa, Stonehenge, Gateway National Park
Rivers and Falls:	the Danube River, Victoria Falls
Lakes and Bays:	Lake Cayuga, Green Bay, the Bay of Biscayne
Seas and Oceans:	the Red Sea, the Indian Ocean
Celestial Bodies:	the Milky Way, Mars, the Big Dipper
Monuments and Memorials:	the Tomb of the Unknown Soldier, Kennedy Memorial Library, the Soldiers and Sailors Monument
Buildings:	Madison Square Garden, the Cleveland Museum of Art, the Astrodome
School and Meeting Rooms:	Room 6, Laboratory 3B, the Red Room, Conference Room C

NOTE ABOUT CAPITALIZING DIRECTIONS: Words indicating direction can be used in two ways: (1) to name a section of a larger geographical area, or (2) simply to give or indicate direction. These words are capitalized only when they refer to a section of a larger geographical area.

EXAMPLES: There is a rapid population growth in the *Southwest.*

The railroad terminal is about half a mile to the *east.*

NOTE ABOUT CAPITALIZING NAMES OF CELESTIAL BODIES: Two celestial bodies whose names you should *not* capitalize are *moon* and *sun*. They are exceptions to the rule. In addition, *earth* should be capitalized only when it is referred to as one of the planets. Do not capitalize *earth* when it is preceded by the article *the*.

EXAMPLE: When the *moon* passes between the *sun* and the *earth*, a solar eclipse occurs.

NOTE ABOUT CAPITALIZING *THEATER, HOTEL, UNIVERSITY,* AND SIMILAR WORDS: Do not capitalize words such as *theater, hotel, university, park*, and so forth unless the word is used as part of a proper name.

EXAMPLES: The game at *Candlestick Park* starts at eight.

I will meet you at the *park*.

Events and Times.   References to historical events, periods, and documents should be capitalized, along with dates and holidays.

Capitalize the names of specific events and periods of time.

SPECIFIC EVENTS AND TIMES	
Historical Events:	the Siege of Troy, the Black Plague, the Battle of Saratoga, World War I, Strategic Arms Limitation Talks (SALT)
Historical Periods:	the Manchu Dynasty, the Age of Napoleon, the Reformation, the Romantic Age
Documents:	the Bill of Rights, the Gettysburg Address, the Constitution of the United States
Days and Months:	Monday, September 22, the second week in May
Holidays:	Labor Day, Veterans Day, Martin Luther King Day
Religious Days:	Rosh Hashana, Christmas
Special Events:	the Riverhead High School Clambake, the World Series, Lakeside Art Show, Tanglewood Music Festival

Most college dictionaries and general encyclopedias include extensive listings of historical events and periods that can be consulted if you are unsure about capitalization.

NOTE ABOUT CAPITALIZING NAMES OF SEASONS: Although days and months are capitalized, you should not capitalize references to the seasons.

EXAMPLE: I love *fall* with its crisp air and colorful trees.

Various Groups. Particular care should be taken in using capitals correctly when referring to groups of all kinds. Included in this broad category are organizations, government bodies, political parties, races, nationalities, the languages spoken by different nationalities, and the religions of various groups.

Capitalize the names of various organizations, government bodies, political parties, races, nationalities, and the languages spoken by different groups as well as references to the religions of various groups.

VARIOUS GROUPS	
Clubs:	Rotary, Knights of Columbus, San Francisco Athletic Club
Organizations:	the Red Cross, American Association of University Women, the Urban League
Institutions:	the Metropolitan Museum of Art, the Chicago Symphony, the Mayo Clinic
Schools:	John F. Kennedy High School, Exeter Academy, Michigan State University, Colby College
Businesses:	General Motors, R. J. Whipple and Sons, Prentice-Hall, Inc.
Government Bodies:	Bureau of Motor Vehicles, Federal Trade Commission, House of Representatives, Parliament, North Atlantic Treaty Organization
Political Parties:	Republicans, the Democratic Party
Races:	Negro, Caucasian, Mongoloid
Nationalities:	American, Mexican, Chinese, Israeli, Canadian, Swiss

Languages:	English, Italian, Polish, Swahili
Religious References:	*Christianity:* God, the Lord, the Father, the Holy Spirit, the Bible, the New Testament, the Holy Father *Judaism:* God, the Lord, the Prophets, the Torah, the Talmud *Islam:* Allah, the Prophets, the Koran, Mohammed, Muslims *Hinduism:* Brahma, the Bhagavad Gita, the Vedas *Buddhism:* the Buddha, Mahayana, Hinayana

NOTE ABOUT CAPITALIZING PRONOUN REFERENCES: Pronouns referring to the Judeo-Christian deity are always capitalized.

EXAMPLE: I prayed for *His* help.

NOTE ABOUT CAPITALIZING REFERENCES TO MYTHOLOGICAL GODS: When referring to ancient mythology, you should *not* capitalize the word *god*.

EXAMPLES: the *gods* of Olympus

the Greek *goddess* Athena

Other Proper Nouns. There remain only a few other categories of proper nouns to be considered.

Capitalize the names of awards, the names of specific types of air, sea, space, and land craft, and brand names.

OTHER IMPORTANT PROPER NOUNS	
Awards:	the Pulitzer Prize, Phi Beta Kappa, the National Book Award in History
Specific Air, Sea, Space, and Land Craft:	the Boeing 747, the *Queen Elizabeth 2*, *Apollo V*, Ford Mustang
Brand Names:	Nabisco Wheat Thins, Alka-Seltzer

EXERCISE B: Capitalizing Proper Nouns. In the following sentences, most of the proper nouns have not been capitalized.

Read each sentence carefully, decide which nouns need capitalization, and write the sentences on your paper with correct capitalization.

1. Manila, on the island of luzon, is the largest city in the philippines.
2. In europe the first outbreak of the black plague occurred in 1346.
3. The four daughters of the greek god zeus were athena, hebe, artemis, and aphrodite.
4. They, together with eight other olympians, lived on mount olympus.
5. The republican party and the democratic party plan to hold separate rallies at the capitol building in washington, d.c.
6. Approximately 90,000 troops from the north and the south were engaged in the battle of antietam on september 17, 1862.
7. Of the faculty members, only professor watkins could speak fluently in five languages: english, french, german, polish, and russian.
8. In our bible class, we compared the old testament with the new testament.
9. A special exhibit of historic autos was held at the bergen county mall on riverfront road.
10. Mary o'hara wrote to the university of maryland and to georgetown university for college bulletins.
11. I finally located the headquarters of seaboard world airlines in new york.
12. Professor david b. davis received a pulitzer prize for his book on slavery.
13. Sacred to islam are allah, the prophets, the koran, and, of course, mohammed.
14. Our family hopes to vacation on waikiki beach at either christmas or easter.
15. I can always spot the moon, but I have trouble with the milky way and the big dipper.
16. My father wants to see the john f. kennedy center for the performing arts and the smithsonian institution.
17. Some of the activities of the 1980 winter olympics were held at whiteface mountain in lake placid, new york.
18. Reverend h. h. russell founded the anti-saloon league in oberlin, ohio, on may 24, 1893.
19. The ithaca high school thespians will perform on april 18 and 19.
20. Until recently, I had not visited most cities in asia, africa, and south america.

EXERCISE C: More Work with Proper Nouns. Some of the following sentences contain proper nouns that should be capitalized. Copy the sentences onto your paper, adding capitals where necessary. If a sentence requires no further capitalization, write *correct* on your paper.

1. I wrote to peter medawar, the 1960 winner of the nobel prize for medicine.
2. Our teacher asked for a description of the rivers, mountains, and deserts in that area of the country.
3. Denmark, located on the jutland peninsula, is particularly proud of copenhagen, a beautiful, cosmopolitan city.
4. The middle ages lasted almost a thousand years, from 476 to 1450.
5. The beautiful sternwheel steamboat the delta queen still cruises regularly on the mississippi river.
6. Which representatives will attend the international trade conference next month?
7. In the battle of britain in world war II, winston churchill rallied the british.
8. The papers of w. h. auden, the british poet, are housed at the new york public library.
9. On July 10, 1919, the treaty of versailles, which included a provision for the establishment of the league of nations, was submitted to the senate.
10. The three religions we are studying are christianity, judaism, and islam.

EXERCISE D: Using Proper Nouns in Sentences. Follow the directions for each of the following items. Be sure to capitalize all of the proper nouns in each of your sentences.

1. Write a sentence about the Bill of Rights as part of the United States Constitution.
2. Write a sentence in which you name and describe the purpose of two clubs or organizations.
3. Describe a visit to a city or a vacation resort.
4. Write a sentence in which you mention a day of the week, a month, and a year.
5. Write a sentence in which you refer to two schools by name.
6. Write a sentence about a famous battle.
7. Write a sentence in which you mention a theater, museum, or other cultural center by name.
8. Write a sentence about a person who speaks at least three languages and name the languages.
9. Describe a famous monument or memorial you have seen.
10. Mention two rivers by name in a sentence.

■ Capitals for Proper Adjectives

A proper adjective is either an adjective formed from a proper noun or a proper noun used as an adjective. Most proper adjectives should be capitalized.

Capitalize most proper adjectives.

PROPER ADJECTIVES FORMED FROM PROPER NOUNS:

Japanese, Shakespearean, Biblical, Congressional

PROPER NOUNS USED AS ADJECTIVES:

a United States delegation, the Stevenson speeches, a Shakespeare festival, a Bible seminar

Care must be taken in a number of cases to use proper adjectives correctly. One problem deals with proper adjectives that are no longer capitalized.

Do not capitalize certain frequently used proper adjectives.

EXAMPLES: herculean, french fries, pasteurized, quixotic, venetian blinds

Brand names, which are often used as proper adjectives, may also create a problem.

Capitalize a brand name used as an adjective, but do not capitalize the common noun it modifies.

EXAMPLES: Seiko watches, Charlie perfume

A problem may also arise when two proper adjectives are used with one common noun.

Do not capitalize a common noun used with two proper adjectives.

Compare the adjectives and the nouns in the following chart. In the first column, the adjectives and nouns work together to form proper nouns. In the second column, the fact that there are two separate proper adjectives makes it impossible to form a single proper noun. Thus the common nouns at the end remain uncapitalized.

One Proper Adjective	Two Proper Adjectives
Republican Party	Republican and Democratic parties
Washington Street	Washington and Madison streets
Suez Canal	Suez and Panama canals

Prefixes used with proper adjectives should always be treated with care.

Do not capitalize prefixes attached to proper adjectives unless the prefix refers to a nationality.

The prefixes in the first two of the following examples do not require capitalization. The second two, because they refer to nationalities, are capitalized.

EXAMPLES: pro-Arab

all-American

Sino-Japanese

Anglo-American

Occasionally, you may come across a proper adjective hyphenated in another way.

In a hyphenated adjective, capitalize only the proper adjective.

EXAMPLE: Chinese-speaking American

EXERCISE E: Identifying Proper Nouns and Proper Adjectives. Copy each of the following items onto your paper and identify it as a *common noun*, a *proper noun*, a *proper adjective*, or *one or more proper adjectives used with a common noun*.

1. Elizabethan
2. boulevard
3. Grand Central Terminal
4. Biblical
5. *Titanic*
6. herculean
7. United Nations
8. British
9. quotations
10. Hilton and Sheraton hotels
11. Lake Drive
12. concourse
13. Charles Dickens
14. Boulder Dam
15. nephew
16. Pakistan
17. American flag
18. Anglo-French
19. Hollywood Boulevard
20. exhibition

EXERCISE F: Capitalizing Proper Nouns and Proper Adjectives.
Each of the following items is partially or completely incorrect. Copy each item onto your paper, making the necessary corrections.

1. Shore Front parkway
2. Pro-Hispanic demonstrators
3. a boeing 747
4. French-Speaking tourists
5. a congressional investigation
6. Venetian blinds
7. an All-American program
8. the oman peninsula
9. macbeth and lady macbeth
10. his massachusetts campaign
11. Joseph Conrad's Novels
12. a swedish stamp collection
13. a brazilian festival
14. an Amtrak Train
15. charlotte and emily brontë
16. Democratic party
17. platte and missouri rivers
18. a rachmaninoff piano concerto
19. king george V
20. the liberal and conservative parties

EXERCISE G: Using Proper Nouns and Adjectives in Sentences.
List five proper nouns of your own, and use each one in a sentence. Then list five proper adjectives, and use each in a sentence.

■ Titles of People and Things

A number of important rules for capitalization apply both to people and to things.

Capitalize titles of people and titles of works.

Titles of People. The following rule deals with several different types of titles that may be given to people. Study the rule to learn how to capitalize all of these titles correctly.

Capitalize a person's title when it is followed by the person's name or when it is used in direct address.

PRECEDING PROPER NAME: Professor Dickstein visited our social studies class.

IN DIRECT ADDRESS: Sir, I wonder whether you'd give us an interview.

IN A GENERAL REFERENCE: Did you have an appointment with the doctor?

The following chart illustrates the correct form for a variety of titles. Study the chart carefully, paying particular attention to compound titles and titles with prefixes or suffixes.

SOCIAL, BUSINESS, RELIGIOUS, MILITARY, AND GOVERNMENT TITLES	
Commonly Used Titles:	Sir, Madam, Professor, Doctor, Reverend, Bishop, Sister, Father, Rabbi, Corporal, Major, Admiral, Mayor, Governor, Ambassador
Abbreviated Titles:	*Before names:* Mr., Mrs., Dr., Hon. *After names:* Jr., Sr., Ph.D., M.D., D.D.S., Esq.
Compound Titles:	Vice President, Secretary of State, Lieutenant Governor, Commander in Chief
Titles with Prefixes or Suffixes:	ex-Congressman Randolph Governor-elect Loughman

Some titles for high-ranking officials are *always* capitalized. These titles include those of the President, Vice President, Chief Justice, and the Queen of England.

Capitalize the titles of certain high government officials even when the titles are not followed by a proper name or used in direct address.

EXAMPLE: The Senate approved the *President's* choice for *Chief Justice.*

Occasionally, the titles of other government officials may be capitalized as a sign of respect when referring to a specific person whose name is not given.

EXAMPLE: The *Senator* gave a rousing speech.

Relatives are often referred to by titles. These references should be capitalized.

Capitalize titles showing family relationships when the title is used with the person's name or in direct address. The title may also be capitalized when it refers to a specific person, except when the title comes after a possessive noun or pronoun.

WITH THE PERSON'S NAME.   In the summer Uncle Ted spends a lot of time gardening.

IN DIRECT ADDRESS: I'll get it for you, Grandmother.

REFERRING TO A SPECIFIC PERSON: Is Auntie coming for dinner?

WITH A POSSESSIVE NOUN: Sue's cousin Laura is on a business trip to Mexico.

WITH A POSSESSIVE PRONOUN: Their uncle Al made chili for dinner.

Titles of Things.   The titles of various works must also be capitalized.

Capitalize the first word and all other important words in the titles of books, periodicals, poems, stories, plays, paintings, and other works of art.

The following chart lists examples to guide you in capitalizing titles and subtitles of various works. Note that none of the articles (*a, an,* and *the*) is capitalized unless it is the first word of a title. Conjunctions and prepositions, which also are considered unimportant words, are not capitalized unless they are the first word in the title or contain more than four letters.

TITLES OF WORKS	
Books:	*Up the Down Staircase* *High Peaks and Clear Roads: A Guide for Safe and Easy Outdoor Skills*
Periodicals:	*International Wildlife* *The Saturday Review of Literature*
Poems:	"My Last Duchess" "When Lilacs Last in the Dooryard Bloom'd"
Stories:	"Everyday Use" "The Ship Who Sang"
Plays:	*The Devil's Disciple* *Guys and Dolls*

Paintings:	*The Green Violinist* *Portrait of the Artist Surrounded by Masks*
Music:	*Surprise Symphony* "Scarborough Fair"

Titles of courses of study sometimes require capitalization as well.

Capitalize titles of courses when the courses are language courses or when the courses are followed by a number.

WITH CAPITALS: Latin, Biology 2, English III

WITHOUT CAPITALS: geology, psychology, woodworking

EXERCISE H: Capitalizing Titles of People and Things. Each of the following sentences requires additional capitalization. Copy each sentence onto your paper, adding capitals when necessary.

1. Barbara w. tuchman's highly regarded best seller is entitled *a distant mirror: the calamitous 14th century.*
2. The speaker, ex-senator morton, entertained the audience with his anecdotes.
3. We will invite grandmother, grandfather, aunt lucy, uncle jim, and mr. and mrs. mcdowell to the party.
4. At the seminar professor charles speculated on the place former secretary of state kissinger will occupy in history.
5. I gave my cousins subscriptions to *seventeen* and *sports illustrated.*
6. I repeat, commissioner grant, you have not answered my question.
7. William o. douglas, the late supreme court justice, was a great defender of civil liberties.
8. At the meeting we explained our concerns to governor-elect o'hara.
9. One of edna st. vincent millay's best sonnets is "on hearing a symphony of beethoven."
10. Did admiral halsey and commander in chief roosevelt both sing "the star-spangled banner"?

EXERCISE I: Using Titles of People in Sentences. Use each of the following titles exactly as written in a sentence of your own.

1. Mr. Frank Gordon, our former congressman
2. Secretary of the Treasury Roberts
3. Robert S. Stanton, Ph.D.
4. Sister Grace and Father Kelly
5. Senator-elect Bullock
6. ex-Congressman L. Joseph
7. the lieutenant governor
8. Dr. and Mrs. John Greene
9. The Honorable George Denes, judge of the civil court
10. Ambassador Sir Andrew Nevins of Great Britain

■ Capitals for Personal and Business Letters

Both personal and business letters require capitals in certain places.

Capitalize the first word and all nouns in letter salutations and the first word in letter closings.

The following chart gives examples for the salutations and closings of both personal and business letters, along with examples of capitals found in other parts of such letters.

Personal Letters	
Heading:	420 Pine Top Road Locust Valley, New York 11560 September 18, 19 _____
Salutation:	Dear Judy, Dear Uncle Frank,
Closing:	Your best friend, Your nephew,
Business Letters	
Heading:	46 Ventura Boulevard Encino, California 91316 January 4, 19 _____
Inside Address:	Films Incorporated 1144 Wilmette Avenue Wilmette, Illinois 60091

| Salutation: | Madame:
Dear Sir:
Dear Ms. Reiss: |
| Closing: | Yours truly,
Sincerely yours,
Very truly yours, |

EXERCISE J: Capitalizing Parts of a Letter. All of the capital letters have been left out of the following letter. Copy the letter onto your paper, adding the necessary capitals.

461 carol drive
joliet, illinois 60435
april 4, 19 ____

ms. rhoda h. karpatkin
executive director
<u>consumer</u> <u>reports</u>
256 washington street
mount vernon, new york 10550

dear ms. karpatkin:

i was very pleased to read your article "are americans over-regulated?" in the january, 1980, issue of <u>consumer</u> <u>reports</u>.

i find it difficult to understand why members of congress have tried to prevent the federal trade commission from investigating certain kinds of consumer frauds. why shouldn't the federal trade commission require used-car dealers to disclose the condition of a car to a prospective purchaser? why should anyone be against requiring a thirty-day trial period after the purchase of a hearing aid?

you mention that consumers want more government regulation. the survey by the market science institution of the harvard business school in which only 27 percent of the public asked for less government regulation certainly shows how most consumers feel. this feeling is reinforced by the sampling of the opinion research corporation in which 54 percent of the public felt that "too little government action

was being taken" in looking out for the interests of the
consumer.

thank you and your magazine for alerting consumers.
following your lead, i just wrote to my representative, urging
her to support the efforts of the federal trade commission.

sincerely yours,

_____

(sign your name)

APPLICATION 1: Using All of the Rules of Capitalization. Copy
each of the following sentences onto your paper, inserting capitals where necessary.

1. all of the delegates will assemble in conference room 12 at
the holiday inn.
2. the art institute in chicago featured an exhibition of italian
sculpture in july and august.
3. i want to see stonehenge and stratford-on-avon when i visit
england this summer.
4. one of ogden nash's most delightful poems is "portrait of
the artist as a prematurely old man."
5. senator-elect martin plans to vote for the environmental
improvement act after the senate session begins.
6. "a horse! a horse! my kingdom for a horse!" comes from
shakespeare's play *richard III.*
7. the hastings railroad station is more than a mile to the
north.
8. former secretary of transportation george taylor is the
principal speaker.
9. why don't you consult *a dictionary of literary terms* by j. a.
cuddon?
10. the republic of chad, formerly a part of french equatorial
africa, was proclaimed on november 28, 1958.
11. the polaroid, which was invented by edwin land, was the
first instant picture camera.
12. during world war II, japanese-americans from california
were interned by the thousands.
13. falstaff, malvolio, and sir toby belch are three of shakespeare's most effective humorous characters.
14. the new testament contains descriptions of the life of jesus
of nazareth.
15. gordon grant's *black baller passing the battery* is one of his
best marine paintings.

16. the new york athletic association will be pleased to send you a membership brochure.
17. my sister graduated with honors and was elected to phi beta kappa.
18. the high priest of lamaism, a sect of buddhism practiced in tibet, is called the dalai lama.
19. our friends are going to the imperial theater on labor day.
20. in 1797 charles c. pinckney, minister to the french republic, proclaimed, "millions for defense, but not one cent for tribute."

APPLICATION 2: Using Capitals in Your Own Writing. Write a paragraph describing a book you have read or a movie or television drama you have seen recently. Include in your paragraph eight of the following items, correctly capitalized.

1. The title of the book, movie, or television drama
2. The name(s) of the place(s) where the story takes place
3. The names of two of the main characters
4. The nationalities of the characters
5. The language(s) spoken by the characters
6. The name of a business where one of the characters works
7. The names of any organizations the characters belong to
8. The names of any buildings, monuments, parks, or scenic spots mentioned
9. The date(s) or time period in which the story takes place
10. The brand name of an object associated with one of the main characters
11. The titles of the main characters
12. A memorable statement made by one of the main characters

12.2 Abbreviation

The use of abbreviations, or shortened words, can be traced back almost to the beginning of written language. Thousands of years ago, at a time when each character was laboriously chiseled into stone or lettered on parchment, scribes and other artisans sought ways to lessen their labors by abbreviating.

To **abbreviate** means to shorten an existing word or phrase.

Over the years elaborate systems of abbreviation developed in almost every language. It is not uncommon, for example, for some modern unabridged English dictionaries to list more than 3,000 different abbreviations.

In your high school career, you have probably been warned by more than one teacher to avoid the excessive use of abbreviations. There are times when abbreviations are appropriate and times when they are not. This section will review some familiar abbreviations, introduce some new ones, and provide guidelines for the use of abbreviations.

■ Abbreviating Names and Titles

The rules for abbreviating names and titles are somewhat complicated. Make certain that you understand each rule, and study the examples carefully. The first rule deals with abbreviating people's names.

Names of People.   Always use a person's full name the first time you use it in formal writing. In addresses or lists, you may use initials in place of the given name.

> Use a person's full given name in formal writing, unless the person uses initials as part of his or her formal name.

IN FORMAL WRITING: William Brooks, the noted artist, arrived for his lecture.

IN ADDRESSES OR LISTS: William Brooks or W. Brooks

When the same person is mentioned more than once in formal writing, he or she may sometimes be referred to by last name or by last name with a title in later references.

IN LATER REFERENCES: Mr. Brooks greeted the audience.

Brooks discussed the Impressionists at length.

Titles of People.   The social titles by which we refer to people are among the most frequently abbreviated words.

> Abbreviations of social titles before a proper name begin with a capital letter and end with a period. They can be used in any type of writing.

SOCIAL TITLES: Mr., Messrs. (plural of Mr.), Mrs., Mme. (Madame or Madam), Mmes. (plural of Mme. or Mrs.)

With the exception of *Miss*, which has no abbreviation, social titles are usually abbreviated. Social titles should, however, always be followed by a proper name.

USED INCORRECTLY: The Mr. answered the door.

USED CORRECTLY: Mr. Jordan and Miss Clark represented the faculty.

Messrs. Brown and Kelly are our top sales representatives.

NOTE ABOUT *MS.*:   *Ms.* is not an abbreviation of a word, although it starts with a capital and ends with a period. It may be used before a proper name to refer to either a single or a married woman.

In addition to social titles, there are more formal titles of a professional, religious, political, and military nature that are used frequently.

Abbreviations of other titles used before proper names also begin with a capital letter and end with a period. They are used less often in formal writing.

The following chart lists some common titles of position and rank, along with their abbreviations.

ABBREVIATIONS OF COMMON TITLES			
Professional		**Religious**	
Dr.	Doctor	Rev.	Reverend
Atty.	Attorney	Fr.	Father
Prof.	Professor	Sr.	Sister
Hon.	Honorable	Br.	Brother
Political		**Military**	
Pres.	President	Cpl.	Corporal
Supt.	Superintendent	Sgt.	Sergeant
Rep.	Representative	Lt.	Lieutenant
Sen.	Senator	Capt.	Captain
Gov.	Governor	Maj.	Major
Treas.	Treasurer	Col.	Colonel
Sec.	Secretary	Brig. Gen.	Brigadier General
Amb.	Ambassador	Cmdr.	Commander
Com.	Commissioner	Vice Adm.	Vice Admiral

Other abbreviations of titles of position and rank can be found in the dictionary. Abbreviations of all of these titles should be used only when a person's full name is used. Do not abbreviate these titles when you use them only with a person's last name.

EXAMPLES: Rear Adm. Arthur Wilson chatted with the visitors.

Rear Admiral Wilson chatted with the visitors.

Prof. Elaine Lytle has written another book.

Professor Lytle has written another book.

The only major exception to this rule is the abbreviation *Dr.* This abbreviation often appears in front of only a last name.

EXAMPLE: We received an encouraging report from Dr. Slovak.

Some titles appear after people's names.

Abbreviations of titles after a name start with a capital letter and end with a period. They are set off with commas from the rest of the sentence and can be used in any type of writing.

Abbreviations of academic degrees are often used when it is necessary to establish the educational credentials of a person.

ABBREVIATIONS OF ACADEMIC DEGREES			
B.A. (or A.B.)	Bachelor of Arts	Ph.D.	Doctor of Philosophy
B.S. (or S.B.)	Bachelor of Science	R.N.	Registered Nurse
M.A. (or A.M.)	Master of Arts	M.D.	Doctor of Medicine
M.S. (or S.M.)	Master of Science	D.D.S.	Doctor of Dental Surgery
M.B.A.	Master of Business Administration	Esq.	Esquire (lawyer)
M.F.A.	Master of Fine Arts	LL.D.	Doctor of Laws
Ed.D.	Doctor of Education	D.D.	Doctor of Divinity

EXAMPLES: Elliot Cotton, Ed.D., was appointed headmaster.

I reviewed the application of Phyllis Sloan, D.D.S.

Two other titles, *Jr.* and *Sr.*, are also placed after the full name of a person and set off by commas.

EXAMPLES: Arthur Schlesinger, Jr., is a well-known historian.

Oscar B. Jones, Sr., is still chairman of the board.

Although abbreviations for titles after a name can be used in any kind of writing, you should never use both a title before a name and an academic degree with the same meaning after the name.

INCORRECT: Dr. Marilyn B. Katt, M.D., testified for the defense.

CORRECT: Dr. Marilyn B. Katt testified for the defense.

Marilyn B. Katt, M.D., testified for the defense.

EXERCISE A: Using Titles Correctly in Sentences. Rewrite each of the following formal sentences, correcting the error in the abbreviated title.

1. John R. Wilkens Sr bequeathed his coin collection to his son.
2. I finally contacted Prof. Ted Ross, Ph.D., at his office.
3. Miss. Wilson chose three cheerleaders.
4. Do you agree with Lt. Gen. Williamson?
5. Messrs. James Wax arrived late to school.
6. Robert Lester, our Sen., introduced another bill.
7. Amb. O'Keefe left for Great Britain this morning.
8. Shirley Henderson, d.d.s., discussed proper care of the gums.
9. Nurse Betty Lopez, R.N., took a sample of blood.
10. Rev. Louis and Fr. Golan appeared together at the meeting.
11. Arnold Weber, Sir, is highly regarded in Parliament.
12. Can you convince Capt. Simms to attend our graduation ceremony?
13. I would like to recommend Dr. Max Weinstein, M.D.
14. Mr George Denes and Mrs Tracy Artandi were elected to the Parents' Council.
15. Mmes. Gloria Todd volunteered to lead the drive.
16. Are you familiar with M.D. Franz R. Beckenhaus?
17. Laura Ames, ed.d., is the principal.
18. Can you believe Gov. Swan's amazing statement?

19. Sanford Peters Jr. has decided to study geology.
20. Robert Riggins M.A. has decided to write a book.

EXERCISE B: **Using Abbreviated Titles in Sentences.** Write original sentences using each of the following abbreviated titles.

1. Jr.	6. Capt.
2. LL.D.	7. Lt. Gen.
3. Scn.	8. Esq.
4. Prof.	9. B.A.
5. R.N.	10. Mme.

■ Abbreviating Time References and Geographical Locations

Abbreviations are often used in referring to time and geographical locations. Certain conventions govern the use of each
type of abbreviation.

Time References.   Time references include time spans, the
abbreviations A.M. and P.M., and the abbreviations B.C. and
A.D. In formal writing you should never use abbreviations for
time spans.

> Abbreviations for clocked time begin with a small letter and
> end with a period. Abbreviations for days of the week or
> months of the year begin with a capital letter and end with a
> period. These abbreviations are not used in formal writing.

CLOCKED TIME:	sec. second(s)	hr. hour(s)
	min. minute(s)	yr. year(s)

DAYS OF THE WEEK:	Mon. Monday	Fri. Friday
	Tues. Tuesday	Sat. Saturday
	Wed. Wednesday	Sun. Sunday
	Thurs. Thursday	

MONTHS OF THE YEAR:	Jan. January	July July
	Feb. February	Aug. August
	Mar. March	Sept. September
	Apr. April	Oct. October
	May May	Nov. November
	June June	Dec. December

Although the preceding abbreviations should not be used in formal writing, you may use the abbreviations A.M. and P.M. in both formal and informal writing.

For abbreviations of time before noon and after noon, either capital letters followed by periods or small letters followed by periods are acceptable. They can be used in any type of writing.

EXAMPLES: A.M. or a.m. (ante meridiem, before noon)

P.M. or p.m. (post meridiem, after noon)

These abbreviations should be used only with numerals. If you use words to refer to the time of day, do not use the abbreviations.

EXAMPLES: At 5:15 a.m. a convoy of trucks crossed the border.

There will be a performance at six tonight.

You should also avoid using redundant expressions such as *this morning* or *this evening* with these abbreviations.

REDUNDANT EXPRESSIONS: He arrived home at 6:30 p.m. this evening.

This morning at 10:07 a.m. the electricity went off.

The abbreviations B.C. and A.D. can also be used in any type of writing. They must always, however, be used with historical dates.

Abbreviations for historical dates before and after the birth of Christ require capital letters followed by periods. They can be used in any type of writing.

The abbreviation B.C. means "before Christ." A.D., an abbreviation for the Latin phrase *anno Domini,* means "in the year of the Lord." These abbreviations are most common when you use numerals to refer to dates. B.C. should follow the numerals; A.D. may either follow or precede the numerals.

EXAMPLES: The event occurred in 37 B.C.

The group traveled to the city in A.D. 350.

The group traveled to the city in 350 A.D.

When a writer does not use either B.C. or A.D., it is assumed that A.D. is intended. In the following example, the writer is referring to the third century of the Christian calendar.

EXAMPLE: A series of natural calamities occurred in the third century.

If you wish to use A.D. with the word *century*, always place A.D. after *century*.

EXAMPLE: A series of natural disasters occurred in the third century A.D.

Geographical Locations. There are many abbreviations for locations, and almost all of them should be used with caution.

Abbreviations for geographical terms before or after a proper noun begin with a capital letter and end with a period. They are seldom used in formal writing.

The following chart lists some common abbreviations of geographic locations.

COMMON GEOGRAPHICAL ABBREVIATIONS					
Apt.	Apartment	Dr.	Drive	Prov.	Province
Ave.	Avenue	Ft.	Fort	Pt.	Point
Bldg.	Building	Is.	Island	Rd.	Road
Blk.	Block	Mt.	Mountain	Rte.	Route
Blvd.	Boulevard	Natl.	National	Sq.	Square
Co.	County	Pen.	Peninsula	St.	Street
Dist.	District	Pk.	Park, Peak	Terr.	Territory

These abbreviations may be used in addresses, lists, note-taking, and other similar kinds of informal writing. They should generally not be used in formal writing, however.

Two sets of abbreviations for states exist. The traditional abbreviations are shortened forms of the state names, beginning with a capital and ending with a period. There are no traditional abbreviations for Alaska, Hawaii, Iowa, and Utah.

The second set of abbreviations are those instituted by the United States Postal Service. Each abbreviation consists of two capital letters, without any period. The Postal Service encourages their use on envelopes, along with the use of postal ZIP codes.

> Traditional abbreviations for states begin with a capital letter and end with a period. They are seldom used in formal writing. The official Postal Service abbreviations for states require capital letters with no periods. They are seldom used in formal writing.

Since many merchants, publishers, and other advertisers in newspapers and magazines have adopted the Postal Service abbreviations, it is probable that they will grow in popularity, especially since they are in many cases shorter than the older forms and do not require punctuation.

Following is a chart listing both types of state abbreviations.

STATE ABBREVIATIONS					
State	Traditional	Postal Service	State	Traditional	Postal Service
Alabama	Ala.	AL	Montana	Mont.	MT
Alaska	Alaska	AK	Nebraska	Nebr.	NB
Arizona	Ariz.	AZ	Nevada	Nev.	NV
Arkansas	Ark.	AR	New Hampshire	N.H.	NH
California	Calif.	CA	New Jersey	N.J.	NJ
Colorado	Colo.	CO	New Mexico	N. Mex.	NM
Connecticut	Conn.	CT	New York	N.Y.	NY
Delaware	Del.	DE	North Carolina	N.C.	NC
Florida	Fla.	FL	North Dakota	N. Dak.	ND
Georgia	Ga.	GA	Ohio	O.	OH
Hawaii	Hawaii	HI	Oklahoma	Okla.	OK
Idaho	Ida.	ID	Oregon	Ore.	OR
Illinois	Ill.	IL	Pennsylvania	Pa.	PA
Indiana	Ind.	IN	Rhode Island	R.I.	RI
Iowa	Iowa	IA	South Carolina	S.C.	SC
Kansas	Kans.	KS	South Dakota	S. Dak.	SD
Kentucky	Ky.	KY	Tennessee	Tenn.	TN
Louisiana	La.	LA	Texas	Tex.	TX
Maine	Me.	ME	Utah	Utah	UT
Maryland	Md.	MD	Vermont	Vt.	VT

Massachusetts	Mass.	MA	Virginia	Va.	VA
Michigan	Mich.	MI	Washington	Wash.	WA
Minnesota	Minn.	MN	West Virginia	W. Va.	WV
Mississippi	Miss.	MS	Wisconsin	Wis.	WI
Missouri	Mo.	MO	Wyoming	Wyo.	WY

NOTE ABOUT D.C.: The traditional abbreviation for the District of Columbia is D.C.; the Postal Service abbreviation is DC. Use the traditional abbreviation in formal writing whenever it follows the word *Washington.*

EXAMPLE: My cousin lives in Washington, D.C.

EXERCISE C: Identifying Time and Geographical Abbreviations. Copy each of the following abbreviations onto your paper, and write its meaning next to it.

1. MO
2. Co.
3. B.C.
4. Blk.
5. Pen.
6. hr.
7. ME
8. Rte.
9. TN
10. a.m.

EXERCISE D: Understanding Geographical Abbreviations. Follow the directions in each of the following items. Write your answers in complete sentences.

1. Why should "this morning" not be used with the abbreviation *a.m.?*
2. Where should the abbreviation *B.C.* be placed in reference to the year?
3. What is the meaning of *anno Domini?*
4. Why are there now two sets of abbreviations for states?
5. What are two advantages of the official United States Postal Service abbreviations for states?
6. What can the reader assume if neither *B.C.* nor *A.D.* is mentioned in a date?
7. When should you use the abbreviations for time spans, such as *sec., min., hr.,* or *yr.?*
8. Where should the abbreviation *A.D.* be placed in reference to the year?
9. When should you use such geographic abbreviations as *Bldg., Terr.,* and *Natl.?*
10. What are the Postal Service abbreviations for the two newest states, Alaska and Hawaii?

■ Abbreviating Latin Phrases, Measurements, and Numbers

Sometimes you may want to use abbreviations for Latin phrases, measurements, and numbers in your writing.

Latin Phrases. In the upper grades and in college, you will probably encounter an increasing number of abbreviations of Latin phrases. These abbreviations are frequently used in note-taking, footnotes, and bibliographies.

Use small letters and periods for most abbreviations of Latin expressions. These abbreviations are not used in formal writing.

The following chart lists many of the Latin abbreviations you are likely to come across in your reading. Note that *i.e.* is an exception in that it is often used in formal writing.

ABBREVIATIONS FROM LATIN		
Abbreviation	**Latin Phrase**	**Meaning**
ad inf.	ad infinitum	to infinity
c., ca., *or* circ.	circa	about (used with dates)
e.g.	exempli gratia	for example
et al.	et alii	and others
etc.	et cetera	and so forth
ex lib.	ex libris	from the books (of)
ex off.	ex officio	officially; by the virtue of one's office
f.		and the following (page or line)
ff.		and the following (pages or lines)
ib. *or* ibid.	ibidem	in the same place
i.e.	id est	that is
in loc. cit.	in loco citato	in the place cited
n.b. *or* N.B.	nota bene	note well; take notice
non seq.	non sequitur	it does not follow
per an.	per annum	by the year
pro tem.	pro tempore	for the time; temporarily
viz.	videlicet	to wit; namely
vs.	versus	against

Many of the most frequently used Latin abbreviations are set off by commas because the English words they replace would be set off by commas.

EXAMPLES: He wants to continue his studies, i.e., to get a degree in fine arts.

She listed several of her interests, e.g., boating, law, classical music, and traveling.

Measurements. In homemaking, industrial arts, mathematics, and science, it is important to know the abbreviations for frequently used measurements.

With traditional measurements use small letters and periods to form the abbreviations. With metric measurements use small letters and no periods to form the abbreviations. These abbreviations are not used in formal writing except with numerals.

The following chart lists some common traditional measurements.

ABBREVIATIONS OF TRADITIONAL MEASUREMENTS					
in.	inch(es)	tsp.	teaspoon(s)	pt.	pint(s)
ft.	foot, feet	tbsp.	tablespoon(s)	qt.	quart(s)
yd.	yard(s)	oz.	ounce(s)	gal.	gallon(s)
mi.	mile(s)	lb.	pound(s)	F.	Fahrenheit

Note that the abbreviation for Fahrenheit is capitalized, an exception to the rule.

Metric measurements, unlike traditional measurements, are used worldwide. Thus, it is helpful to know these abbreviations as well as the traditional ones. Complete listings of metric measurements and their abbreviations are available in dictionaries and other reference sources.

ABBREVIATIONS OF METRIC MEASUREMENTS			
mm	millimeter(s)	g	gram(s)
cm	centimeter(s)	kg	kilogram(s)
m	meter(s)	L	liter(s)
km	kilometer(s)	C	Celsius

Note the use of capitals for the abbreviations of liter and Celsius.

Numbers.   There are several rules to help you decide whether to spell out numbers or use numerals.

In formal writing spell out most numbers or amounts less than one hundred and any other numbers that can be written in two words or less.

EXAMPLES: The twenty-two soccer players were exhausted when the game was over.

The school has 835 students.

Occasionally, a number that should be written in numerals will appear at the beginning of a sentence. Try to rewrite the sentence, placing the number in another position. If this is not possible, use the following rule.

Spell out all numbers found at the beginning of the sentence.

ACCEPTABLE: Four hundred and sixty paintings were exhibited at the museum.

BETTER: The exhibit at the museum contained 460 paintings.

Certain types of numbers, on the other hand, are almost always written in numerals.

Use numerals when referring to fractions, decimals, and percentages, as well as for dates and addresses.

Remember to place these figures within sentences to avoid having to spell them out.

FRACTION: The bookcase is 39½ inches wide.

DECIMAL: The flood waters measured 48.7 inches.

PERCENTAGE: The concert was attended by 78 percent of the students from our schools.

DATE: The party will be on April 16.

ADDRESS: He lives at 22 Woods Drive.

EXERCISE E: Identifying Abbreviations of Latin Phrases. Copy each of the following abbreviations onto your paper, and write its English meaning next to it.

1. et al.
2. non seq.
3. ex off.
4. ibid.
5. pro tem.

6. per an.
7. viz,
8. ex lib.
9. N.B.
10. in loc. cit.

EXERCISE F: Checking for Correct Use of Abbreviations of Latin Phrases, Measurements, and Numbers. Each of the following items contains one or more abbreviations of a Latin phrase, measurement, or number. Consider any item not labeled otherwise to be formal writing. If an item is incorrect, rewrite it correctly on your paper. If it is correct, write *correct* on your paper.

1. Road sign: Fort Wayne 52 km
2. The bout pits Long John Maxey vs. Killer Kane.
3. Leslie spoke to her parents, her counselor, her teacher, etc.
4. N.B.: Abbreviations should not be used in many formal situations.
5. Once again I spoke to my boss circ. getting a raise.
6. 623 campers hiked to the top of the mountain last summer.
7. Recipe: 2 tsps. lemon juice
            3 tbsps. vegetable oil
8. You need six in. of ribbon for the collar.
9. Active ingredients: honey, lemon oil, 2.5 g ammonium chloride, 3.5 g ascorbic acid, and menthol in a sugar base.
10. I am prepared to take whatever action is necessary, viz., going to the district attorney.
11. Footnote: Ibid.
12. The oz. weight on the scale is not accurate.
13. Are you able to convert F. readings to C?
14. The tbsps. in my sterling silver set tarnish too rapidly.
15. The professor offered some help, i.e., he told me which reference book to consult.
16. Use two qts. of milk with one pt. of water.
17. The abbreviation *ibid.* is often used in footnotes to indicate that something can be found in the same place as the preceding citation.
18. The latest temperature reading is 33°C.
19. The doctor asked e.g. what I had eaten in the last 3 days.
20. Footnote: c. A.D. 150.

EXERCISE G: Understanding Abbreviations of Latin Phrases, Measurements, and Numbers. Follow the directions in each of the following items. Write your answers in complete sentences.

1. How are most abbreviations of Latin phrases formed?
2. How is an abbreviation such as *e.g.* or *i.e.* punctuated in a sentence?
3. Name two Latin abbreviations that are often used in footnotes.
4. Why is it incorrect to say *and etc.?*
5. What should precede the abbreviations of measurements?
6. How do the abbreviations for *inch, yard,* and *pound* form their plurals?
7. Why is the abbreviation for Fahreheit (F.) an exception to the general rule?
8. How are abbreviations of plural metric measurements formed?
9. What types of numbers are almost always written in numerals?
10. Why is it better to place numerical references within rather than at the beginning of sentences?

■ Abbreviating the Names of Business and Government Groups

Many businesses abbreviate the final word in their titles.

An abbreviated word in a business name begins with a capital letter and ends with a period. Most of these abbreviations are not used in formal writing.

BUSINESS ABBREVIATIONS: Co. (Company); Inc. (Incorporated)

Bros. (Brothers); Ltd. (Limited)

Limit your use of these abbreviations in formal writing to *Inc.* and *Ltd.*

You will also find that many businesses, labor unions, and other groups are referred to by abbreviations formed from the first letter of each word in the organization's name.

Use all capital letters and no periods to abbreviate the names of familiar organizations, large business firms, labor unions, government agencies, and other things whose abbreviated names are pronounced letter by letter as if they were words. These abbreviations are often used in formal writing.

The following chart lists examples of organizations that use this type of abbreviation.

ABBREVIATIONS FOR ORGANIZATIONS		
Business Firms:	ABC	American Broadcasting Company
	TWA	Trans-World Airlines
	GM	General Motors
Labor Unions:	UAW	United Auto Workers
	AFM	American Federation of Musicians
	ILA	International Longshoremen's Association
Government Agencies:	FCC	Federal Communications Commission
	FDIC	Federal Deposit Insurance Corp.
	CIA	Central Intelligence Agency
Others:	GOP	Republican Party (Grand Old Party)
	TB	tuberculosis
	EKG	electrocardiogram

It is acceptable to use these abbreviations in all types of writing. Common practice is to write out the name of an unfamiliar item the first time it is mentioned. The abbreviation is usually enclosed in parentheses immediately following the name. After that, the abbreviation can be used alone.

EXAMPLE: The Federal Deposit Insurance Corporation (FDIC) announced a new policy today. The FDIC is the organization that insures savings deposits in banks across the country.

Acronyms are also used to abbreviate the names of some organizations. An acronym is formed from the first letter or letters of a group of words and is pronounced as a word.

Use all capital letters and no periods for acronyms that form the names of organizations. These acronyms are often used in formal writing.

FAMILIAR ACRONYMS:	UNESCO	United Nations Educational, Social, and Cultural Organization
	CARE	Cooperative for American Relief Everywhere, Inc.
	ALCOA	Aluminum Company of America
	NATO	North Atlantic Treaty Organization

Again, common practice is to write out the name of the organization the first time it is mentioned, followed by the acronym in parentheses. Some acronyms, such as NATO and CARE, are so well known, however, that they are generally used without further identification.

EXERCISE H: Checking Abbreviations of the Names of Business and Government Groups. Copy each of the following sentences onto your paper, correcting any abbreviation errors. If a sentence is already correct, write *correct* on your paper.

1. I read an interesting article about Nato.
2. Our social studies class watched an interesting film about the Un. Auto Wkers.
3. Our school sent a contribution to C.A.R.E.
4. My uncle has recovered from TB.
5. I wonder whether the Fed. Communications C. will send us the information.
6. The CIA probably has information about that problem.
7. The patient was given an E.K.G. to see if her heart was functioning properly.
8. They bought tickets to fly on Trans-World Airlines.
9. Do you work at Aluminum Co. of Am.?
10. She bought the coat from Brooks Bros.

■ Other Commonly Used Abbreviations

Some of you will probably soon be entering the business world. Abbreviations are used extensively there in writing orders, preparing invoices, and keeping records. The following chart of abbreviations will be particularly helpful to you. Read it several times until you are familiar with the abbreviations.

Many of these abbreviations are also seen frequently in newspapers and other periodicals. A knowledge of these abbreviations will improve your comprehension significantly.

OTHER COMMONLY USED ABBREVIATIONS

anon.	anonymous	L.	left
approx.	approximately	mdse.	merchandise
assoc. or assn.	associate or association	meas.	measure
aux. or auxil.	auxiliary	mfg.	manufacture
bibliog.	bibliography	mgr.	manager
bkt.	basket	misc.	miscellaneous
bu.	bushel	mkt.	market
bull.	bulletin	M.O.	money order
bx(s).	box(es)	m.p.h.	miles per hour
cap.	capital letter	No.	number
C.O.D.	cash on delivery	paren.	parenthesis
dept.	department	Pat. Off.	Patent Office
disc.	discount	pc(s).	piece(s)
doz.	dozen(s)	pg.	page
ea.	each	pp.	pages
ed.	edition, editor	pkg.	package
equiv.	equivalent	poet.	poetical, poetry
est.	established	prop.	proprietor
fict.	fiction	pr(s).	pair(s)
gov. or govt.	government	pseud.	pseudonym
G.P.O.	General Post Office	pub.	published, publisher
Gr.	Greek, Grecian	pvt.	private
grad.	graduate, graduated	recd.	received
grat.	gratis (free of charge)	ref.	reference, referee
hdqrs.	headquarters	rhet.	rhetorical, rhetoric
hosp.	hospital	r.p.m.	revolutions per minute
ht.	height	R.	right
ill. or illus.	illustrated	sc.	scene
incl.	including, inclusive	sp.	spelling, species
intro.	introductory, introduction	spec.	special, specific
ital.	italics	treas.	treasury, treasurer
k. or kt.	karat or carat	vol.	volume
		wkly.	weekly
		wt.	weight

EXERCISE I: Identifying Common Abbreviations. Copy each of the following abbreviations onto your paper, and write its English meaning next to it.

1. govt.
2. dept.
3. r.p.m.
4. anon.
5. mgr.

6. ref.
7. No.
8. ed.
9. pg.
10. wkly.

APPLICATION: Using All of the Abbreviation Rules. Write ten sentences of your own, using abbreviations of each of the following items.

1. a social title
2. a political or military title
3. an academic degree
4. a time before noon
5. a year after the birth of Christ
6. a mailing address
7. a measurement of an ingredient in a recipe
8. a fraction
9. a government agency
10. an acronym

Chapter 13

Punctuation

Punctuation is more than a haphazard sprinkling of commas, periods, and question marks throughout a paragraph. To punctuate correctly requires a knowledge of the parts of a sentence and their relationships to each other. It also requires an understanding of different types of sentences and the punctuation marks used either to separate or to join them.

An effort to master thoroughly the rules in this chapter will help you greatly in your writing. Study the rules carefully and refer to this chapter whenever you are uncertain about a particular problem in punctuation.

End Marks 13.1

The three end marks are the period (.), the question mark (?), and the exclamation mark (!). End marks are used mainly to conclude sentences.

■ Using End Marks to Conclude Sentences and Phrases

Different end marks are used to conclude different types of sentences and phrases.

The Period.   The period is the most common of the end marks.

> Use a period to end a declarative sentence, a mild imperative, and an indirect question.

A declarative sentence, as you know, is a statement of fact or opinion.

STATEMENT OF FACT: The flood destroyed a number of farm crops.

STATEMENT OF OPINION: We expect economic conditions to improve.

An imperative sentence gives a direction or a command. Often the first word of an imperative sentence is a verb.

DIRECTION: Read the first three chapters and summarize the contents.

COMMAND: Stand at attention, soldier.

Some declarative sentences include an indirect question.

INDIRECT QUESTION: My father wondered why my brother didn't agree.

The Question Mark.   A direct question requires a reply and a question mark.

Use a question mark to end an interrogative sentence, an incomplete question, or a statement intended as a question.

Often the word order as well as the punctuation of an interrogative sentence is different from that of a declarative sentence.

EXAMPLES: Why don't you agree?

Have you ever wanted to meet the principal?

A question mark is also used with one or more interrogative words when a complete sentence is not necessary.

EXAMPLES: Periods are used with most abbreviations. Why?

Please tell me the price. How much?

Occasionally, a question mark is used at the end of a statement that asks a question.

EXAMPLES: My qualifications are not satisfactory?

This car has fuel injection?

Use care, however, in ending statements with question marks. In many cases it is better to rephrase the statement as a direct question.

STATEMENT WITH A QUESTION MARK: My proposal wasn't accepted?

REVISED INTO A DIRECT QUESTION: Wasn't my proposal accepted?

The Exclamation Mark.   An exclamation mark calls attention to an exclamatory sentence, an imperative sentence, or an interjection. Because it is a dramatic punctuation mark and indicates strong emotion, it should be used sparingly.

Use an exclamation mark to end an exclamatory sentence, a forceful imperative sentence, or an interjection expressing strong emotion.

EXCLAMATORY SENTENCES: This discovery has worldwide implications!

You must have misunderstood her!

IMPERATIVE SENTENCES: Please tell the truth!

Never swim alone again!

Depending on emphasis, an exclamation mark or a comma can be used with an interjection. The exclamation mark, of course, shows greater emphasis.

WITH AN EXCLAMATION MARK: Oh! What a terrible accident!

WITH A COMMA: Oh, he does that all of the time.

EXERCISE A: Using End Marks to Conclude Sentences and Phrases. The end marks have been left out of the following sentences. Copy each sentence onto your paper and punctuate it properly.

1. To whom did you give the award for citizenship
2. Incredible I can't believe our basketball team won ten straight
3. Watch out This road is dangerous
4. Lisa asked when the next performance is scheduled
5. How can we tell which pair of sneakers is better
6. You divided your report into three sections Why
7. How wonderful Did you expect to win
8. The fish has tiny bones in it Chew it carefully
9. What makes the Marx Brothers still so funny
10. The Narragansett Indians were clustered in what is now Washington County, Rhode Island

■ Periods and Question Marks in Other Situations

Many abbreviations require the use of periods. A small number do not. If you are in doubt about whether to use periods with abbreviations, consult Section 12.2.

Use a period to end most abbreviations.

Following are a few examples of abbreviations with periods and abbreviations without periods.

ABBREVIATIONS WITH PERIODS: a.m.   Dr.   Jan.   Conn.

oz.   i.e. $4.35   Bros.

ABBREVIATIONS WITHOUT PERIODS: TV   SST   NAACP   cm

When an abbreviation ending with a period comes at the end of a sentence, do not add another period as an end mark.

INCORRECT: The patient was treated in the emergency room by Beth Fields, M.D..

CORRECT: The patient was treated in the emergency room by Beth Fields, M.D.

If a sentence requires an end mark other than a period, however, add the end mark.

EXAMPLE: Was the patient treated in the emergency room by Beth Fields, M.D.?

Periods are also used after numbers and letters in outlines.

Use a period after numbers and letters in outlines.

EXAMPLE: I. Using end marks
            A. The period
                1. Use at the end of declarative sentences
                2. Use at the end of mild imperatives
                3. Use at the end of indirect questions

The one special use of question marks is to show uncertainty.

Use a question mark in parentheses (?) after a fact or statistic to show its uncertainty.

EXAMPLE: Cleopatra was born in 69 (?) B.C.

Never use the question mark in parentheses if you can verify a fact or statistic. Use it only when the information cannot be verified.

EXERCISE B: Using Periods and Question Marks in Other Situations. Copy the following items onto your paper, adding periods where necessary. Indicate uncertainty about any years that appear in the items as well. If an item does not require any change, write *correct* on your paper.

1. I. Fly fishing
        A. Tackle
            1. Rod
            2. Reel
            3. Lures
2. The recipe listed the following: 2 oz. of melted cheese and 2 tsp. of vegetable oil.
3. Must you always watch TV after dinner?
4. The roar of the SST is deafening.
5. Dr. Johnson's office hours begin at 2:00 P.M.
6. The envelope was addressed to Ms J N Sanford, 23 Rayburn Ave, San Antonio, Tex
7. A civilization with well-planned cities existed in the Indus Valley in Pakistan as long ago as 3000 B.C.
8. The bill showed a charge for 18 gal of gas.
9. Enterprises Ltd , was the name of her company.
10. The ticket stub showed the following date: Feb 14.

APPLICATION: Understanding the Use of End Marks. Answer each of the following questions, using complete sentences.

1. When is it appropriate to use an exclamation mark in your writing?
2. What is the difference between a direct and an indirect question?
3. How are most abbreviations punctuated?
4. What is a declarative sentence? An imperative sentence? How should both be punctuated?
5. What is an interjection? What are two ways to punctuate an interjection?

13.2   Commas

The comma is used to separate a number of basic elements and to set off many different kinds of added elements within sentences. As you learn the rules for the correct use of the comma, you will at the same time reinforce your understanding of sentence structure. Learn the rules thoroughly, making certain you fully understand each relationship described in the different rules.

■ Commas That Separate Independent Clauses

A single independent clause expresses a complete thought and often stands alone as a simple sentence. Two independent clauses, correctly joined and punctuated, form a compound sentence. Conjunctions used to connect independent clauses are called coordinating conjunctions. The seven coordinating conjunctions are *and, but, for, nor, or, so,* and *yet.*

Use a comma before the conjunction to separate two independent clauses in a compound sentence.

EXAMPLES: I had several meetings with my guidance counselor, and then I decided to apply to five carefully chosen colleges.

My mother loves to visit foreign countries, but my father prefers to explore the United States.

She may begin work on her term paper in history tonight, or she may postpone her research until the weekend.

As you can see from the preceding examples, the ideas in the independent clauses in a compound sentence are clearly related to each other. Compound sentences should not be formed unless there exists some type of relationship between the independent clauses.

Although a comma and a coordinating conjunction are used to separate two independent clauses in a compound sentence, a comma is not used to separate a compound verb in a simple sentence. Compare the following two examples.

COMPOUND SENTENCE: Leslie visited the shopping mall this morning, and she purchased a one-piece, yellow bathing suit.

SIMPLE SENTENCE: Leslie visited the shopping mall this morning and purchased a one-piece, yellow bathing suit.

The second sentence has only one subject, *Leslie*. A comma is not used to separate the compound verb *visited* and *purchased*. Before placing a comma before a conjunction, you should always make sure that you have a complete sentence on both sides of the conjunction, not just a compound verb.

EXERCISE A: Using Commas to Separate Independent Clauses. Copy each of the following sentences onto your paper, adding punctuation as needed.

1. The poor tarantula could not move fast for it had only seven instead of eight legs.
2. Ted wants to play basketball this morning but he plans to study for his Spanish test first.
3. Can you reach a decision now or will you require more testimony?
4. We plan to visit Greece and Turkey and then we hope to explore Israel and Egypt.
5. I love to bake cakes and pastries but my specialty is cream-filled doughnuts.
6. The poet William Blake was born in 1757 and like many other Londoners of that time he never attended school.
7. My brother is a student of the Bible so he is familiar with both the Old Testament and the New Testament.
8. My sister listens only to jazz but the rest of my family prefers rock music.
9. I don't care for most of the recent war movies nor did I care for some of the earlier ones.
10. My uncle will either fly in for the wedding or he will take the train.

EXERCISE B: Punctuating Simple Sentences and Compound Sentences. Some of the following sentences are simple sentences containing a compound verb that does not require a comma. Others are compound sentences that require a comma between the two independent clauses. Copy each sentence onto your paper, adding punctuation as needed. If a sentence requires no commas, write *correct*.

1. My sister plans to take several business courses and then open her own record shop.
2. The high school baseball season ends in early June and football practice begins in late July.

3. *The New York Times* is published here and abroad but *The Herald Tribune* has only a European edition.
4. Aspirin can occasionally cause intestinal bleeding but other drugs can also have dangerous side effects.
5. Most new fuel-efficient cars have four-cyclinder engines and offer a choice of manual or automatic transmission.
6. A home safe is useful but irreplaceable papers should be kept in a bank vault.
7. The car swerved sharply to the right and crashed into the picket fence.
8. Gold was discovered in California in January, 1848 but the first news of the discovery was not published until March.
9. I've always loved outdoor sports and often play tennis and softball.
10. We can get the information we need for our report from the library or we can visit the museum exhibit next week.

■ Commas That Separate Items in a Series and Certain Adjectives

Like independent clauses, items in a series and certain kinds of adjectives should be separated from each other by commas.

Series.   A series consists of three or more words, phrases, or subordinate clauses of a similar kind. A series can occur in any part of a sentence.

Use commas to separate three or more words, phrases, or clauses in a series.

WORDS: The report was clear, pertinent, and well written.

Apples, oranges, peaches, grapes, and cherries are ideal for a fruit salad.

PHRASES: We reached the Incan ruins by bus, by mule, and by foot.

We lifted the ancient chest from the water, onto the boat, and into the cabin.

CLAUSES: The survey revealed that many refugees had lost members of their families, that they had no money, and that they suffered severely from malnutrition and other diseases.

Notice in the preceding examples that the number of commas used in a series is one fewer than the number of items. If there are three items in the series, two commas are used.

As you may know, a variant style for series exists in which the last comma before the conjunction is dropped. If you choose to use this style, make sure that you use it consistently except in those cases where the last comma is needed to prevent confusion. Many writers prefer the full comma style because it allows them to be consistent in all cases.

CORRECT: The rugged mountains, the wild animals and the aroma of the pine trees made the trip memorable.

CONFUSING: The rugged mountains, the aroma of the pine trees and the wild animals made the trip memorable.

When using commas to separate items in a series, make sure that the earlier items in the series are not already connected by conjunctions such as *and* and *or*. When conjunctions are used to separate all of the items in a series, no commas are needed.

EXAMPLE: We wanted to play softball and to eat hot dogs and then to see the fireworks.

Commas should also not be used between items that are paired so often that they are thought of as one item. In the following example, *paper and pencil* are considered a single item.

EXAMPLE: The director asked us to bring our lunches, paper and pencil, and our books.

Adjectives.   When two or more adjectives precede a noun, the adjectives will often need to be separated by commas.

Use commas to separate adjectives of equal rank.

Adjectives are equal in rank if you can insert the word *and* between them without changing the meaning of the sentence. Another way to determine whether adjectives are of equal rank is to reverse the order in which they appear. If the sentence still sounds correct, the adjectives are of equal rank. Adjectives of equal rank are called *coordinate adjectives*.

EXAMPLES: A tall, dignified woman rose to speak.

The impatient, excited puppy yelped loudly.

If you cannot place the word *and* between the adjectives or reverse their order without changing the meaning of the sentence, do not use commas between them. Adjectives that must remain in a specific order are called *cumulative adjectives*.

> Do not use commas to separate adjectives that must stay in a specific order.

EXAMPLES: The red plaid jacket fit her perfectly.

Most serious accidents could be prevented.

EXERCISE C: Using Commas to Separate Items in a Series. Copy each of the following sentences onto your paper, inserting commas to separate items as needed.

1. We will not proceed until we raise sufficient funds until we get at least twenty volunteers and until we get complete government support.
2. The tall dark-haired and exotic-looking young star captured the hearts of the audience.
3. I particularly enjoy science history French and English.
4. Dad opened the door stared at the person standing there and reacted with obvious delight.
5. Here are the items of clothing you will need: shirts pants underwear socks a raincoat and a warm jacket.
6. Our company expects employees always to be well groomed neatly dressed and ready to work.
7. Smith reached his destination in twenty-two hours traveling by air by train and by taxi.
8. The candidate was told that his support had dwindled that campaign contributions were low and that his chances of election were poor.
9. Your idea is clever original and practical.
10. At the museum she saw paintings by Utrillo Cézanne Matisse Picasso and Manet.

EXERCISE D: Distinguishing Between Coordinate and Cumulative Adjectives. Some of the following sentences require commas to separate adjectives. Other sentences do not require commas. Copy the sentences onto your paper, inserting commas where necessary. For sentences that do not require commas, write *cumulative*.

1. It has been a cold rainy spring.
2. The limping exhausted runner barely finished the marathon.
3. The theater was filled with noisy excited children.

4. I gave my parents twelve red roses for their anniversary.
5. Soak your swollen sprained ankle in cold water.
6. A huge black cloud loomed overhead.
7. Because the boys were late, their worried angry parents could not sleep.
8. They could not swim in the churning pounding surf.
9. She pedaled off on the little red tricycle.
10. In a few short hours, we will be finished with our chores.

■ Commas That Set Off Introductory Material

Most introductory material is set off from the rest of a sentence with a comma.

Use a comma after an introductory word, phrase, or clause.

Study the following examples to see what types of introductory material should be set off with commas.

INTRODUCTORY WORDS:	Well, I find it difficult to make up my mind.
	Yes, Charles agrees with our choice.
	Oh, did she really say that?
NOUNS OF DIRECT ADDRESS:	Maria, who won the game?
COMMON EXPRESSIONS:	Of course, I'll do it for you.
INTRODUCTORY ADVERBS:	Certainly, you may borrow the book.
	Frantically, they searched for the missing coin.
PREPOSITIONAL PHRASES (of four or more words):	At the very top, my father paused to enjoy the view.
	In the back pocket of my jeans, you will find the keys.
PARTICIPIAL PHRASES:	Walking slowly, she reached the valley in about two hours.
	Written carefully, the speech was a masterpiece.
INFINITIVE PHRASES:	To get to the store before it closed, she ran all the way.
	To pass the test, they studied every night for a week.

ADVERBIAL CLAUSES: When the team got off the plane, hundreds of on-lookers began to cheer.

If you intend to travel abroad this summer, you should make your plans now.

The style for prepositional phrases varies from one writer to another. Although even single words may be set off with commas, most writers today do not use a comma with an introductory prepositional phrase of fewer than four words unless it is necessary to clarify the meaning of the sentence.

CLEAR: At the game we met our friends.

CONFUSING: Inside the house walls began to crumble.

CLEAR: Inside the house, walls began to crumble.

EXERCISE E: Using Commas After Introductory Material. Copy the following sentences onto your paper, inserting commas after introductory material where necessary. If a sentence does not require any commas, write *correct*.

1. Oh do you really believe that?
2. In front of the long column of troops on the field the general introduced his successor.
3. If you were to offer her another opportunity do you think she would accept your invitation?
4. Since you are interested in muckrakers I suggest you read Lincoln Steffens' *The Shame of the Cities*.
5. Chosen by secret ballot Professor Watkins immediately took charge of the committee.
6. Walking slowly and breathing heavily the campers finally straggled into town.
7. Without much hope the detectives searched the entire building.
8. While traveling in Europe Lord Byron began a long poem called *Childe Harold's Pilgrimage*.
9. Carefully the doctor prescribed the proper antibiotics.
10. After years of no regulation of business the Fair Labor Standards Act of 1938 set minimum ages for employment.
11. Concerned about the rash she asked about the incubation period of chicken pox.
12. To find the missing child the police scoured the entire neighborhood.
13. In time the animals adjusted to the change in their environment.

14. Although we understand your unwillingness to serve we wonder whether you might reconsider.
15. To open the package quickly she ripped the paper off.
16. Cheering wildly we watched our team win the finals.
17. When the sprinters neared the finish line everyone rose in excitement and anticipation.
18. Declining requests for autographs the rock singer pushed his way through the crowd.
19. Martin are you going to play tennis this afternoon?
20. Deserted after the storm the beach was strewn with rubble and debris.

■ Commas That Set Off Parenthetical Expressions and Nonessential Material

Commas are also used to set off two types of expressions that often fall in the middle or at the end of sentences.

Parenthetical Expressions. These are expressions of one or more words that, in a sense, interrupt the flow of a sentence. These parenthetical expressions are set off by one or more commas regardless of where they occur in a sentence.

Use commas to set off parenthetical expressions.

The following examples illustrate some common types of parenthetical expressions that should be set off with commas. Notice that a parenthetical expression may fall in the middle or at the end of a sentence. Notice also that each sentence is complete with or without the parenthetical expression.

NOUNS OF DIRECT ADDRESS:	Do you think, Ben, that you could help me?
	I'll set the table right away, Mother.
CERTAIN ADVERBS:	The tennis match, therefore, was called off.
	They did their best, however.
COMMON EXPRESSIONS:	I am explaining his theory, I believe, as clearly as I can.
	You know, of course, that she is unreliable.
CONTRASTING EXPRESSIONS:	I wore the red coat, not the blue one.
	English, not mathematics, is my favorite subject.

Nonessential Material. Depending on their importance in a sentence, appositives, participial phrases, and adjective clauses can be either essential or nonessential. (The terms *restrictive* and *nonrestrictive* may also be used.) It is important to understand the difference between the two types of material. An essential phrase or clause is necessary to the meaning of the sentence. It helps describe or identify the person or object the sentence is about.

ESSENTIAL APPOSITIVE: The part was played by the famous actor *Henry Fonda*.

ESSENTIAL PARTICIPIAL PHRASE: The man *wearing the white cap* is my uncle.

ESSENTIAL ADJECTIVE CLAUSE: The paragraph *that we propose to add* changes the entire focus of the bill.

The preceding examples illustrate three kinds of essential elements. In the first the appositive *Henry Fonda* identifies a specific actor. In the next example, the participial phrase *wearing the white cap* identifies a specific man. In the last example, the adjective clause *that we propose to add* identifies a specific paragraph. The items are all essential because they limit or restrict identification to the person or thing described in the appositive, phrase, or clause. Because they cannot be removed without changing the meaning of the sentence, they require no commas.

Compare these essential elements with nonessential appositives, phrases, and clauses. Nonessential elements also provide information, but that information is not necessary to the meaning of the rest of the sentence. Because nonessential elements do not alter the meaning of sentences, they *do* require commas.

Use commas to set off nonessential expressions.

NONESSENTIAL APPOSITIVE: The part was played by Henry Fonda, *the famous actor*.

NONESSENTIAL PARTICIPIAL PHRASE: Our first church, *erected at the turn of the century*, had a coal-burning furnace.

NONESSENTIAL ADJECTIVE CLAUSE: The original stamp, *which is now worth $75,000*, is kept in a bank vault.

Nonessential appositives, phrases, and clauses provide additional, but not essential, information. In the first example, Henry Fonda is clearly identified. The appositive *the famous actor* is not needed to identify a particular person. The same thing is true of the other examples. Although the nonessential material may be interesting, the sentences can be read without them and still make sense.

EXERCISE F: Using Commas to Set Off Parenthetical Expressions. Copy the following sentences onto your paper, inserting commas to set off parenthetical expressions.

1. His record I suppose should be a factor in the case.
2. I absolutely do not agree you know with your argument.
3. Another consideration should be her years of experience however.
4. Who is your favorite actor Bill?
5. She tried in fact to contact the owner several times.
6. The hostility of the group she believes will soon be overcome.
7. Do you want both the name and the address of each student Ms. James?
8. We played racquetball not tennis.
9. You must therefore arrive on time.
10. I must however admit that I was surprised.

EXERCISE G: Using Commas to Set Off Nonessential Material. Copy each of the following sentences onto your paper, inserting commas as needed. Do not insert commas in sentences with essential material. If a sentence does not require any commas, write *correct.*

1. State Highway 101 expanded to two lanes in 1953 needs to be widened to at least four lanes now.
2. This is Ms. Charney who is in charge of our research department.
3. The salesman who phoned yesterday morning is at the door.
4. The bus traveling more than ten miles above the speed limit was stopped by the police.
5. The farm described in the brochure has already been sold.
6. William Butler Yeats who was born on June 13, 1865 spent his early years at Sandymount which is not far from Dublin.
7. The girl driving the white sports car is the captain of the cheering squad.

8. *Macbeth* was written by William Shakespeare the most famous Elizabethan playwright.
9. The magazine formed by recent college graduates has become a huge success.
10. *The Nordic Prince* which is chartered by Royal Caribbean Cruises sails regularly to Caracas and Martinique.
11. *Plagues and Peoples* which was written by William H. McNeill describes the effects of pestilence and disease on world populations.
12. All of the buildings that were destroyed in the fire have been rebuilt.
13. I would like to introduce Dr. Ruth Pringle who will speak to us about nutrition this afternoon.
14. The train carrying vacationers to the resort was delayed two hours due to engine problems.
15. Maria Gonzalez my best friend was named to the National Honor Society.
16. This camera which has many automatic features is guaranteed for two full years.
17. Her note scribbled in pencil on a piece of yellow note paper was used as evidence in the case.
18. He is a reporter who has spent many years in Africa and Asia.
19. The tennis star John McEnroe accepted the award graciously.
20. President Lincoln smiling at his neighbors stood in the rear car as the train pulled out of Springfield.

■ Commas in Other Situations

Many other situations also require the use of commas.

Dates.   Commas help prevent confusion in dates made up of several parts, such as month, day, and year.

When a date is made up of two or more parts, use a comma after each item except in the case of a month followed by a day.

EXAMPLES: Thursday, September 26, is my birthday.

I saw the play on October 6, 1980.

On April 8, 1979, my brother was born.

If dates contain only months and years, commas are optional.

EXAMPLES: In August, 1980, they visited Sweden.

In August 1980 they visited Sweden.

Geographical Names.   Like dates, geographical names are often made up of several parts.

When a geographical name is made up of two or more parts, use a comma after each item.

EXAMPLES: My uncle in Des Moines, Iowa, is a lawyer.

We traveled to St. Albert, Ontario, Canada, by car.

Titles After a Name.   A title added after the name of a person or business also requires commas.

When a name is followed by one or more titles, use a comma after the name and after each title.

EXAMPLES: Theresa Kelly, M.D., is my doctor.

Arnold Simpson, Sr., Ph.D., lectured on Greek drama.

Did Prentice-Hall, Inc., publish this book?

Addresses.   Next consider the use of commas in addresses.

Use a comma after each item in an address made up of two or more parts.

EXAMPLE: We sent the package to S. C. Chung, 14 State Street, Sacramento, California   95827.

Notice in the preceding example that commas are placed after the name, street, and city. It is customary to leave extra space between the state and the ZIP code instead of inserting a comma.

In an address in a letter or on an envelope, most commas would be unnecessary. You would still need a comma, however, between the city and the state.

EXAMPLE: S. C. Chung
14 State Street
Sacramento, California   95827

Salutations and Closings.   Another comma rule also concerns letters.

Use a comma after the salutation in a personal letter and after the closing in all letters.

SALUTATIONS: Dear Jimmy,   Dear Aunt Harriet,   My dear friend,

CLOSINGS: Your friend,   Sincerely,   Yours truly,

Large Numbers.   Commas are also used to make large numbers easier to read.

With numbers of more than three digits, use a comma after every third digit counting from the right.

EXAMPLES: 186,000 miles per second

2,527 people

3,625,353 peanuts

Do not, however, use commas in ZIP codes, in telephone numbers, with page numbers, or with serial numbers.

ZIP CODE: 07624

TELEPHONE NUMBER: 207-555-2455

PAGE NUMBER: Page 1127

SERIAL NUMBER: 081 32 5334

Elliptical Sentences.   In an elliptical sentence, words are left out but are understood to function in the sentence. Inserting a comma in an elliptical sentence makes it easier to read.

Use a comma to indicate the words left out of an elliptical sentence.

EXAMPLE: David read the newspaper quickly; Rachel, more slowly.

Even though the words *read the newspaper* have been omitted from the second clause in the elliptical sentence, the meaning is not lost. The comma inserted in the place of the missing words helps to make the meaning clear.

Direct Quotations.   Commas are also used to set off direct quotations.

Use commas to set off a direct quotation from the rest of a sentence.

EXAMPLES: "I finished my book report," Linda stated happily.

Kevin sighed, "I wish mine were done."

"Perhaps," Linda replied, "yours will be better than mine because you've spent more time on it."

For Clarity.   You may also need to use the comma to prevent readers from misunderstanding a sentence.

Use a comma to prevent a sentence from being misunderstood.

UNCLEAR: After the storm clouds disappeared.

CLEAR: After the storm, clouds disappeared.

NOTE ABOUT THE CARELESS USE OF COMMAS: There are many rules to learn about the use of commas. Learn the rules and apply them in your writing. Do not, however, use commas where none are required. Because the comma is one of the most frequently used punctuation marks, some people sprinkle commas throughout their writing. Make certain that you know why you are inserting a particular comma in a sentence. In this way you will not overuse this important punctuation mark.

The following examples illustrate some of the ways in which commas are often misused. Study these examples and avoid these problems in your own writing.

MISUSED WITH ADJECTIVE AND NOUN: Yesterday, I saw a fluffy, aristocratic-looking, poodle.

CORRECT: Yesterday, I saw a fluffy, aristocratic-looking poodle.

MISUSED WITH COMPOUND SUBJECTS: Never did I think that the pile of books, and the stack of paper, would fall off the desk.

CORRECT: Never did I think that the pile of books and the stack of paper would fall off the desk.

MISUSED WITH COMPOUND VERBS: I thought about it for a while, and then asked her to leave.

CORRECT: I thought about it for a while and then asked her to leave.

MISUSED WITH COMPOUND OBJECTS: I fell in love with the ivied walls, and the beautiful lake.

CORRECT: I fell in love with the ivied walls and the beautiful lake.

MISUSED WITH PHRASES: The lilies were floating in the water, and drifting with the wind.

CORRECT: The lilies were floating in the water and drifting with the wind.

MISUSED WITH CLAUSES: She asked what you wanted, and where you were going.

CORRECT: She asked what you wanted and where you were going.

EXERCISE H: Using Commas with Dates, Geographical Names, and Titles.

Copy the following sentences onto your paper, inserting commas where necessary.

1. Rudyard Kipling was born in Bombay India on December 30 1865.
2. Paul Santini Jr. is in my Spanish class.
3. Lisa Sullivan D.D.S. has an office in Houston Texas.
4. The party on Friday February 6 was a huge success.
5. On June 12 1981 they will graduate.
6. Have you ever lived in Seattle Washington?
7. He is going to study in Paris France next year.
8. They camped in Calgary Alberta Province Canada last summer.
9. Smith Construction Company Inc. built the auditorium.
10. Early in June 1980 he began working as a landscaper.

EXERCISE I: Using Commas in Other Situations.

Copy the following letter onto your paper, inserting commas where necessary.

2304 South Street
Fort Lauderdale Florida 33316
December 18 1980

Dear Nat

I can tell from your last letter that your summer plans are all wrapped up. Your summer sounds terrific; mine questionable.

With high hopes I wrote to a number of summer travel camps to apply for a job as counselor. All but one have turned me down and I'm still waiting to hear from that one. I worry that maybe I got the address wrong. Maybe I wrote 182 Greenwood Lane Lawrenceville Vermont instead of 128 Greenwood Lane Lawrenceville Vermont. Maybe I got the ZIP code wrong and wrote 10663 instead of 01663. At least I've now memorized the page in the catalog (page 1423) where the address is found.

My parents are fond of telling me "Keep your chin up" but I'm still getting a bit nervous.

Your friend
Jody

APPLICATION 1: Using Commas Correctly. Copy each of the following sentences, inserting commas where necessary.

1. When I asked my father for advice he told me I was old enough to make my own decisions.
2. The five explorers traveling through the jungle in intense heat reached the bank of the river on Thursday June 5.
3. Reaching the platform Congressman Brooks the featured speaker waved to the crowd.
4. A monthly newsletter is published by the American Civil Liberties Union 22 East 40th Street New York NY 10016.
5. Alice will you please list the magazines newspapers and books you used in your bibliography.
6. Nancy London who is the best actress in the school intends to try for a professional career.
7. W. H. Auden the noted poet was born in York England on February 21 1907.
8. *Sports Illustrated* is my favorite magazine but I also like to read *Time* and *People.*
9. In New York we plan to visit the Statue of Liberty the United Nations the Museum of Modern Art and Yankee Stadium.
10. Well in spite of the large number of items I can consider your suggestions by the end of the week.
11. Barbara W. Tuchman the author of *A Distant Mirror* spoke to our history class.
12. In recent years the U.S. Postal Service has honored such women as Eleanor Roosevelt Frances Perkins and Dolly Madison.
13. Your plan lacks the support of most of our committee and must therefore be turned down.
14. Sailing into the harbor the *Dolphin* had to wait three hours to dock.
15. The unemployment rate much to the surprise of the experts declined steadily for five months.
16. One suit one jacket two shirts and a few other sundries are all you will need for the weekend.
17. If you see my mother the woman who usually sits at the receptionist's desk please tell her that I will be home late.

18. My uncle lives at 606 West Gouin Boulevard Montreal Canada.
19. Yes I was asked to memorize selections from Act I Act II and Act III.
20. For once Lucy you are absolutely right in choosing not to participate.
21. While we were waiting at the station Mr. Wexler our English teacher entertained us with some of his anecdotes.
22. Some of the earlier pioneers of the cinema are Varley Friese-Greene Edison Donisthorpe and Skladanowsky.
23. My favorite modern President is Harry Truman a man who said exactly what he meant.
24. In the back room under the trunk near the window Billy found the missing photo.
25. My sister's reasoning in fact was quite sound.

APPLICATION 2: Using Commas in Your Own Writing. Choose ten of the comma rules in this section and list them on your paper. Then write a friendly letter similar to the one in Exercise I, making sure that you use all of the rules at least once. When you have finished the letter, review the section to make sure that you have not misused any commas.

13.3 Semicolons and Colons

The semicolon (;) and the colon (:) are similar-looking punctuation marks with very different uses. A semicolon can be used to establish a relationship between two or more independent clauses and also to prevent confusion in sentences containing other internal punctuation marks. A colon can be used as an introductory device to point ahead to additional information as well as in other special situations.

■ The Semicolon

Semicolons are used to connect two independent clauses containing similar or contrasting ideas. Often, the independent clauses connected by a semicolon are similar to one another in structure as well as in meaning.

> Use a semicolon to join independent clauses that are not already joined by the conjunction *and, or, nor, for, but, so,* or *yet.*

A semicolon to separate independent clauses is not the most common way to separate independent clauses. In most cases they are separated with a comma and coordinating conjunction.

EXAMPLE: Our goal was to cover twenty miles the first day, but we only covered half that distance.

When you write a sentence containing two or more independent clauses and no coordinating conjunction, however, use a semicolon instead of a comma to join them.

The semicolon is a stronger punctuation mark than a comma. It replaces both the comma and the conjunction. Do not capitalize the word following the semicolon unless the word is a proper noun or a proper adjective.

EXAMPLES: They were noble souls; they not only possessed loving hearts, but brave ones. —Frederick Douglass

Lee would enjoy turnips at every meal; we would not enjoy any meal at which they were served.

Sometimes the first word of a second independent clause is a conjunctive adverb or a transitional expression.

Use a semicolon to join independent clauses separated by either a conjunctive adverb or a transitional expression.

Conjunctive adverbs are adverbs used as conjunctions to connect independent clauses. Common conjunctive adverbs are *also, furthermore, accordingly, besides, consequently, however, instead, namely, nevertheless, otherwise, similarly, therefore, indeed,* and *thus.* Transitional expressions are expressions that connect one independent clause with another. Transitional expressions include *as a result, first, second, at this time, for instance, in fact, on the other hand,* and *that is.*

CONJUNCTIVE ADVERBS: Our goal was to cover twenty miles the first day; instead, we covered half that distance.

I hope to complete my term paper this weekend; however, I may run into difficulties with my research.

TRANSITIONAL EXPRESSIONS: She won the race easily; in fact, she set a new state record for the event.

This year has been exceptionally dry; as a result, the farmers may harvest less grain.

Notice that in all of the preceding examples a comma separates the conjunctive adverb or transitional expression from the rest of the second independent clause because it serves as an introductory expression in the second independent clause.

Another use of the semicolon is with independent clauses or series that already contain a number of commas. The use of a semicolon can help prevent confusion in these sentences.

Consider the use of a semicolon to avoid confusion when independent clauses or items in a series already contain commas.

INDEPENDENT CLAUSES: Bess, who was suffering from laryngitis, was unable to make the speech; but Alan delivered it for her.

ITEMS IN A SERIES: In front of us were a column of refugees, many carrying heavy bundles of their belongings; a few old carts, battered and hardly able to roll; and several troop carriers, filled with soldiers in complete battle fatigues.

In the preceding example, semicolons are used to separate the three major parts of the series. Commas are used within each of the major parts to set off the modifying participial phrases. When items in a series contain appositives or adjective phrases, semicolons should also be used to separate the major parts of the series.

EXERCISE A: Understanding the Use of the Semicolon. Copy
each of the following sentences, inserting semicolons where necessary. Some of the sentences may require only a comma to separate independent clauses.

1. I expected an important package this morning therefore, I waited several hours for the mail.
2. Collins, who lives near the library, has been assigned to gather the information and Brooks will organize the final report.
3. Prince Edward Island is in Canada's Eastern Maritimes British Columbia is on the West Coast.
4. My friends intended to go shopping but they were unable to get someone to drive them.
5. "Perhaps the most valuable result of all education is the ability to make yourself do the thing you have to do, when it ought to be done, whether you like it or not it is the first lesson that ought to be learned." —Thomas Huxley

6. Our hope was to coordinate our efforts accordingly, we waited several hours for instructions.
7. On April 24, 1800, an act of Congress established the Library of Congress two provisions of the act were for "the purchase of such books as may be necessary for the use of Congress" and for "fitting up a suitable apartment" to house the new volumes.
8. My sister plans to attend college next year in fact, she has already been accepted at one.
9. After the hurricane we surveyed the shoreline, which bore the brunt of the storm inland bungalows, sheered of roofs and often a heap of rubble and local roads, strewn with debris and fallen trees.
10. My grandparents arrived early and my parents were somewhat embarrassed by the condition of our house.

■ The Colon

The colon (:) is a distinctive punctuation mark with a number of important uses. One important use of the colon is to introduce a list following an independent clause.

Use a colon before a list of items following an independent clause.

EXAMPLES: Be sure to bring the following: pen, paper, and dictionary.

As you know, the government of the United States has three important branches: the executive, the legislative, and the judiciary.

This summer we plan to visit a number of European countries: Austria, Belgium, Denmark, France, Spain, and West Germany.

It is possible, of course, to list details without using a colon. Compare the following examples with the preceding examples. Notice that such general words as *branches* and *countries* have been eliminated.

ALSO CORRECT: The government of the United States consists of the executive, the legislative, and the judiciary.

This summer we plan to visit Austria, Belgium, Denmark, France, Spain, and West Germany.

In each of the examples immediately preceding, the list is *not* preceded by an independent clause, so no colon is used.

You always should make sure that an independent clause precedes the list before you insert a colon. The independent clause before a list often ends in a phrase such as *the following* or *the following items.* These phrases may alert you to the need for a colon.

Colons are also used with some quotations.

Use a colon to introduce a quotation that is formal or lengthy or a quotation that does not contain a "he said/she said" phrase.

EXAMPLES: Who can forget Edward VIII's abdication statement: "I have found it impossible to carry the heavy burden of responsibility and to discharge my duties as King as I would wish to do without the help and support of the woman I love."

Pierre Van Paassen wrote: "Half of our misery and weakness derives from the fact that we have broken with the soil and that we have allowed the roots that bound us to the earth to rot."

A casual quoted remark or dialogue should be introduced by a comma even if it is lengthy. Reserve use of the colon for more formal situations and for quotations that do not contain "he said/she said" phrases.

Another use of the colon is to serve as an introductory device for a sentence that either amplifies or summarizes the preceding sentence.

Use a colon to introduce a sentence that summarizes or explains the sentence before it.

EXAMPLES: In 1750 Christopher Sower developed the first American-made printing press in Germantown, Pennsylvania: Only then was it possible to obtain a press that was not imported from Europe.

Bacteria have a cellular structure enclosed within a rigid cell wall: This structure makes it possible to divide them into three major groups.

Notice in the preceding examples that the first word of a sentence following a colon is capitalized.

Colons are also used to point to formal appositives that follow independent clauses.

Use a colon to introduce a formal appositive that follows an independent clause.

Because a colon is a stronger punctuation mark than a comma, using a colon gives more emphasis to an appositive it introduces.

EXAMPLE: I was surprised when I saw his new pet: a three-foot-long boa constrictor.

The colon has a number of other uses as well.

Use a colon in a number of special writing situations.

SPECIAL SITUATIONS REQUIRING COLONS	
Time Expressed in Numerals:	7:10 P.M. 12:01 A.M.
References to Periodicals (Volume Number Page Number):	*Psychology Today* 24: 189 *Science* 169: 611-612
Biblical References (Chapter Number Verse Number):	Deuteronomy 4:11
Subtitles of Books and Magazines:	*The Causes of World War I: A Chronology of Events*
Salutations in Business Letters:	Gentlemen: Dear Ms. Wilson:
Labels Used to Signal Important Ideas:	Warning: Trespassers will be prosecuted.
References to Publishers in One Style of Bibliography:	New York: Oxford University Press

EXERCISE B: **Understanding the Use of the Colon.** Copy each of the following items onto your paper, inserting colons where necessary.

1. My aunt arrived at the airport at 10 17.
2. Danger This water is polluted.
3. Dear Senator Robinson
4. I want to repeat my point of view clearly We cannot permit a change in policy at this time.

5. New York W.W. Norton and Company appeared in the bibliographical listing.
6. Sue Ellen intends to study several major composers Bach, Haydn, Mozart, Beethoven, Brahms, and Wagner.
7. A visit by the Queen of Sheba is described in First Kings 10 8.
8. The process is somewhat involved It requires three separate stages, each a month apart.
9. F. Scott Fitzgerald wrote "The test of a first-rate intelligence is the ability to hold two opposed ideas in the mind at the same time, and still retain the ability to function."
10. He excelled in one sport soccer.

APPLICATION 1: Using Semicolons and Colons Correctly. Copy each of the following items, adding semicolons and colons where necessary. Remember to capitalize the first word in a complete sentence following a colon.

1. Danger no lifeguard is on duty.
2. The professor specializes in one area of history the Civil War.
3. The first, unsuccessful landing was attempted at dawn a second at 3 00 A.M. surprised the defenders, overwhelming them within minutes.
4. She has done watercolors of many flowers phlox, cosmos, heliotrope, dahlia, and cleome.
5. Perched high on the hill was an old town the valley was dotted with a number of small hamlets.
6. A visit to Sandringham includes many delights the house and grounds, the nature trail, Sandringham Church, and the annual flower show held on July 30.
7. I never forgot Ruskin's line "Borrowers are nearly always ill-spenders, and it is with lent money that all evil is mainly done, and all unjust war protracted."
8. On May 22, 1819, the steamship *Savannah* sailed for Liverpool it was the first steam-propelled ship to cross the Atlantic.
9. Although Jim climbed as far up the tree as he could, he still did not feel safe from the bull in the pasture below and he shouted desperately for help.
10. The chairman consulted at least three other officials consequently, he made the decision to abandon the project.

APPLICATION 2: Writing Original Sentences Using Semicolons and Colons. Write ten sentences of your own following these instructions.

1. Write a sentence about animals using a semicolon to join two independent clauses with a close relationship.
2. Write a sentence about your best friend using a semicolon to join independent clauses separated by a conjunctive adverb.
3. Write a sentence about a career you are interested in using a semicolon to join independent clauses separated by a transitional expression.
4. Write a sentence about your school using semicolons to separate a series of items that contain internal punctuation.
5. Write a sentence about a sports event using a semicolon to join two independent clauses—each with its own internal punctuation.
6. Write a sentence describing a recipe and use a colon to introduce a list of items.
7. Use a colon to introduce a quotation of yours that you would like others to remember. Do not include a "he said/ she said" phrase.
8. Write a sentence about the school subject you like best using a colon to introduce a summary or explanation.
9. Write a sentence about one of your favorite people using a colon to introduce a formal appositive.
10. Write a sentence about the weather using time.

Quotation Marks and Underlining 13.4

Direct quotations from other people can support the ideas or arguments of a writer. Direct quotations also enliven short stories, novels, and other works of fiction. When the characters themselves speak, the writing becomes more exciting and meaningful.

The rules for punctuating direct quotations are many, and they are somewhat complicated. To master them, study the rules and examples in this section carefully. This section will also discuss the use of underlining as well as quotation marks to indicate different types of titles, names, and words.

■ Quotation Marks for Direct Quotations

Before the many types of direct quotations can be discussed, it is important to distinguish between direct and indirect quotations.

A **direct quotation** represents a person's exact speech or thoughts and is enclosed in quotation marks (" "). An **indirect quotation** reports the general meaning of what a person said or thought and does not require quotation marks.

DIRECT QUOTATION: The President said, "I will ask the next session of Congress to appropriate funds to help blighted urban communities."

INDIRECT QUOTATION: The President said that he would try to help blighted urban communities.

An indirect quotation rephrases someone else's words. They are not the exact words of the speaker. In a direct quotation, the words of the speaker are quoted exactly.

Both types of quotations are acceptable and are used frequently. Sometimes the exact words of the speaker will not be available, and the only way to express the speaker's sentiments will be to rephrase them in an indirect quotation. If the actual words of the speaker are available, however, they should usually be used to achieve dynamic, strong writing.

The easiest rule for using quotation marks involves uninterrupted quotations.

Use quotation marks before and after an uninterrupted direct quotation.

EXAMPLE: "I know of no way of judging of the future but by the past." —Patrick Henry

Notice that the preceding quotation begins with a capital letter. Each sentence of quoted material should always begin with a capital letter.

Many direct quotations contain two parts: the actual words of the speaker (the direct quotation) and a group of words identifying the speaker. The words identifying the speaker are called conversational tags or "he said/she said" phrases. They include such expressions as *she said, he replied, Mary asked, the professor explained,* and *the doctor asked.* The possibilities for conversational tags are almost endless, but they all have one feature in common: Conversational tags are *not* enclosed in quotation marks.

There are three ways of using a conversational tag in a sentence: as an introductory expression, as a concluding expression, or as an interrupting expression.

When an introductory expression precedes a direct quotation, place a comma or colon after the introductory expression and write the quotation as a full sentence.

EXAMPLE: My father explained, "I want you to know all of the traffic rules before you begin driving."

In the preceding example, the conversational tag comes first and is set off from the direct quotation with a comma. If the introductory expression is more formal in tone or if it contains no conversational tag, use a colon instead of a comma.

EXAMPLE: She stood proudly and gazed at the assembled crowd: "I would like to thank you for the honor you have awarded me."

Sometimes a direct quotation comes before a conversational tag.

When a concluding expression follows a direct quotation, write the quotation as a full sentence ending with a comma, question mark, or exclamation mark inside the quotation mark, and then write the concluding expression.

EXAMPLE: "I want you to know all of the traffic rules before you begin driving," my father explained.

In the preceding example, a comma follows the direct quotation and a period is used after the conversational tag since it ends the sentence. Notice also that the comma comes *before* the quotation mark.

There is a third way of using a conversational tag with a quotation: The conversational tag can interrupt the direct quotation.

When a direct quotation of one sentence is interrupted, end the first part of the direct quotation with a comma and a quotation mark, place a comma after the interrupting expression, and then proceed with a new quotation mark and the rest of the quotation.

EXAMPLE: "I want you to know all of the traffic rules," my father explained, "before you begin driving."

In this example the quotation itself is the same as before, but it has been interrupted by a conversational tag. Quotation marks now enclose both parts of the statement, and there are commas before and after the conversational tag. Once again, the commas come *before* the quotation marks.

The three methods of setting up a direct quotation with a conversational tag shown in the preceding examples are all commonly used. Writers generally use one type and then change to another to achieve variety in sentence structure.

Another rule must be followed when a conversational tag interrupts a quotation that is several sentences in length.

> When two sentences in a direct quotation are separated by an interrupting expression, end the first quoted sentence with a comma, question mark, or exclamation mark and a quotation mark; place a period after the interrupter; and then write the second quoted sentence as a full quotation.

EXAMPLE: "I want to have time to look for my children and see how many of them I can find. Maybe I shall find them among the dead," said Chief Joseph of the Nez Percé tribe of Native Americans. "Hear me, my chiefs, I am tired. My heart is sick and sad. From where the sun now stands I will fight no more forever."

Sometimes a writer chooses to quote only a phrase or a portion of a sentence. In this case, quotation marks are still placed around the quoted words, but no comma is needed between the quote and the rest of the sentence.

> When a quoted fragment is included in a sentence, enclose the quoted fragment in quotation marks, but do not use commas to set the fragment off from the rest of the sentence. Capitalize the first word of the fragment only when it falls at the beginning of the sentence or when it is a proper noun or a proper adjective.

EXAMPLE: In *Memories of Christmas*, Dylan Thomas mentions that one Christmas "was so much like another."

A phrase or portion of a sentence used at the beginning of a sentence should, of course, be capitalized.

EXAMPLE: "The bullfight is not a sport in the Anglo-Saxon sense of the word" is the way Hemingway begins his essay "Bullfighting."

EXERCISE A: Using Quotation Marks for Direct Quotations. Copy each of the following sentences onto your paper, adding punctuation as needed. Some of the sentences contain indirect quotations and do not require quotation marks. The quoted fragment has been underlined so that you can tell where it begins and ends. If no quotation marks are needed, write *correct*

1. Please don't do anything rash my mother begged.
2. If you have trouble understanding the chapter said Miss Knopf read it over a second time.
3. The theater manager insisted You must have a ticket before we can allow you to enter.
4. I can't believe the show is sold out she cried after I waited in line for two hours.
5. The policeman said that both lanes of the highway were temporarily closed.
6. Robert Frost wrote a poem about someone who stopped to watch some <u>woods fill up with snow.</u>
7. When I try to memorize a long speech I said I go through endless agony.
8. No, I'd prefer to visit Austria and Denmark this summer Jim replied. That is why I am saving all of the money I can this winter.
9. The senator explained that he could not possibly support the highway construction bill.
10. About two miles down the road, you will see a cluster of three or four restaurants explained the travel guide.

■ Using Other Punctuation Marks with Quotation Marks

Quotation marks are used in conjunction with many other punctuation marks. Unfortunately, the location of the quotation marks in relation to the other punctuation marks is not always the same. It varies depending on the other punctuation mark and, in some cases, on the meaning of the sentence.

The rule for commas and periods is always the same.

Always place a comma or a period inside the final quotation mark.

EXAMPLES: Fred said, "I'm ready if you are."

"Tell them to wait," Sally called.

The rule is the reverse when quotation marks are used with semicolons and colons.

Always place a semicolon or colon outside the final quotation mark.

EXAMPLES: I fully understand what she means by a "call for drastic action"; the situation becomes more pressing each day.

We emphatically deny his "nasty accusations": They are ill-founded and not based on fact.

The rules for the use of quotation marks with question marks and exclamation marks are more complicated.

Place a question mark or exclamation mark inside the final quotation mark if the end mark is part of the quotation and outside the final quotation mark if the end mark is not part of the quotation.

The question mark in the first of the following examples is placed inside the quotation marks because it belongs to the question itself. The same is true of the exclamation mark in the second example. It belongs inside the quotation mark because it is part of the statement itself.

EXAMPLES: Marie asked, "Have they phoned yet?"

The spokesman exclaimed, "We demand our rights!"

Notice the difference when you compare the preceding examples with the following ones. In the first example, the question mark belongs to the entire sentence. In the second the exclamation mark dramatizes both the sentence and the quote it contains.

EXAMPLES: Did the application ask, "What previous experience do you have"?

He denied having committed the crime, but his eyes flashed, "I am guilty"!

EXERCISE B: Using Other Punctuation Marks with Quotation Marks. Copy each of the following sentences onto your paper, adding quotation marks and any other punctuation marks that are needed. The quoted fragment in the third sentence is underscored.

1. Ask not what your country can do for you. Ask what you can do for your country.—John F. Kennedy
2. I'll be here next Thursday she cried, springing to the saddle. Good-bye. Quick, Ellen!—Emily Brontë
3. In the first sentence of George Orwell's *1984*, the clocks are striking thirteen.
4. The commander asked Have the troops taken their positions
5. I know what he expects she sighed If only I can reach those lofty goals.
6. Don't fire until you see the whites of their eyes
7. Rose, my love! cried Mrs. Maylie, rising hastily, and bending over her. What is this? In tears! My dear child, what distresses you?—Charles Dickens
8. I accept his "pledge of support" we need every volunteer we can get.
9. Did she ask, How can I help
10. Listen, I said to Raymond. You may be right.

■ Using Quotation Marks in Special Situations

You also need to know how to use quotation marks in dialogues and in quotations of more than one paragraph. In addition, there may be occasions when you want to include only a portion of a person's words in a quotation or to include one quotation within another. The following rules will guide you in these special situations.

Dialogue and Long Quotations. In many short stories and novels, the use of dialogue, or direct conversation between two or more people, plays an important role. Much of what is happening is indicated to the reader through the words of the characters. The writer combines, in dozens of different ways, paragraphs of description and dialogue to move the story forward.

There are no set rules in writing dialogue. Each writer develops his or her own style. The writer must follow the conventions for writing quotations, however, so that the reader will be able to understand who is speaking.

When writing dialogue, begin a new paragraph with each change of speaker. Use quotation marks at the beginning and at the end of each speaker's words.

Now examine the work of one writer to see how she develops her dialogue. In Harper Lee's *To Kill a Mockingbird*, Scout finds two sticks of chewing gum in a tree. After examining them for a while, she jams them into her mouth.

EXAMPLE:

When Jem came home he asked me where I got such a wad. I told him I found it.

"Don't eat things you find, Scout."

"This wasn't on the ground. It was in a tree."

Jem growled.

"Well it was," I said. "It was sticking in that tree yonder, the one comin' from school."

"Spit it out right now!"

I spat it out. The tang was fading anyway. "I've been chewing it all afternoon and I ain't dead yet, not even sick."

Jem stamped his foot. "Don't you know you're not supposed to even touch the trees over there? You'll get killed if you do!"

"You touched the house once!"

"That was different! You go gargle—right now, you hear me?"

"Ain't neither, it'll take the taste outa my mouth."

—Harper Lee

After reading the passage, analyze it line by line. Notice how the lines of description and and the lines of dialogue combine to move the story along. Some of the lines have conversational tags. Many do not because it is quite easy to follow the dialogue between Scout and Jem without them.

The next time you come across a passage of dialogue in your reading, analyze it in the same way. You should find many different patterns.

Another type of quotation consists of several paragraphs in a row. For this type of quotation, quotation marks are placed at the beginning of each paragraph and at the end of the final paragraph.

For quotations longer than a paragraph, put quotation marks at the beginning of each paragraph and at the end of the final paragraph.

EXAMPLE:

"When messages are misunderstood, it is easy to blame the speaker. The listener, however, must share the responsibility for effective communication. It takes a lot of concentration and effort to be a good listener. Statistics show, in fact, that most people are poor listeners. The average person misses about 75 percent of what he or she hears.

"The encouraging fact is that no one has to remain a poor listener. Listening, like speaking, reading, or writing, is a skill that can be learned. Learning to listen does, however, take a lot of self-motivation and practice." —J. Regis O'Connor

When you are quoting several paragraphs, make certain that you remember to include the final quotation mark.

Ellipsis Marks and Single Quotation Marks. In addition to dialogues and quotations of more than one paragraph, there are two other special problems involving the use of quotation marks that require close study. The first concerns the use of ellipsis marks (...) in a shortened quotation. Frequently, a writer wishes to include only a portion of a direct quotation in a piece of writing. Ellipsis marks are used to indicate that the writer is quoting only a part of someone else's words and that some words have been omitted.

Use three ellipsis marks in a quotation to indicate that words have been omitted.

Ellipsis marks can be used at the beginning, in the middle, or at the end of a quotation.

AN ENTIRE QUOTATION: "Whenever I prepare for a journey I prepare as though for death. Should I never return, all is in order. This is what life has taught me." —Katherine Mansfield

ELLIPSES AT THE BEGINNING: Katherine Mansfield speaks of preparing for a trip ". . . as though for death."

ELLIPSES IN THE MIDDLE: Katherine Mansfield once wrote, "This . . . life has taught me."

ELLIPSES IN THE MIDDLE: Katherine Mansfield once wrote: "Whenever I prepare for a journey I prepare as though for death. . . . This is what life has taught me."

ELLIPSES AT THE END: Katherine Mansfield once wrote, "Whenever I prepare for a journey I prepare as though for death. . . ."

Notice that when a period is part of the quotation, as in the last two examples, it is added to the ellipsis marks to conclude the sentence.

The second special problem involving quotation marks concerns a quotation within a quotation. A quotation within a quotation is set off with single quotation marks (' ') instead of the regular double marks (" "). The larger quotation is still set off with double quotation marks.

Use single quotation marks for a quotation within a quotation.

EXAMPLES: I can still hear our English teacher reciting the line from Poe: "Quoth the Raven, 'Nevermore.' "

"Then father thundered, 'I will not go!' and walked from the room."

Notice in the first of the preceding examples that the single quotation mark goes outside the period in the same way a double quotation mark does.

If setting up a quotation within a quotation causes confusion, you can rephrase the material to eliminate the quotation within a quotation.

EXERCISE C: Writing Original Dialogue. Write approximately a page of original dialogue. Use two or three different characters and include a few lines of description. Enclose the lines of dialogue in quotation marks. Include enough conversational tags so that there will be no confusion about who is speaking.

EXERCISE D: Using Ellipsis Marks and Single Quotation Marks. Copy each of the following sentences onto your paper, inserting double quotation marks (" ") and single quotation marks (' ') as needed.

1. "In a low voice, my sister whispered, Yes, and broke into a smile."
2. Wasn't it Richard Grafton who wrote, Thirty days hath September . . . , the poem that all children recite?
3. I remember the first line of my paper: "In *The Adventure of the Speckled Band*, the lady in black greets the great detective with, It is fear, Mr. Holmes. It is terror, and thus begins another adventure."
4. I love the Wordsworth poem that begins, I wandered lonely as a cloud. . . .
5. Part of the quote is . . . for happiness is the gift of friendship.
6. "Again and again I asked, Please, please come; but in the end he refused."
7. The lyric from *Showboat* ends with . . . then perhaps I might fall back on you.
8. "Then I told Mother, Stone walls do not a prison make . . . , and I thought she would hit the roof."
9. Patrick Henry's speech of March 23, 1775, ended with . . . but as for me, give me liberty or give me death!

10. "I wrote Shelley's famous line,'O Wind, if Winter comes, can Spring be far behind?'in my notebook."

■ Distinguishing Between the Uses of Underlining and Quotation Marks

There are a number of different ways of indicating titles in writing. In books, periodicals, and other printed publications, *italics*, a slanted type face, are used to indicate many types of titles. In handwritten or typed material, the writer underlines items that in print would be in italics. Other types of titles require the use of quotation marks.

PRINTED: In *The Saturday Review* there is an interesting article by Gwyn Jones called "A History of the Vikings."

TYPED: In The Saturday Review there is an interesting article by Gwyn Jones called "A History of the Vikings."

The following rules will enable you to use underlining and quotation marks correctly in titles as well as in other conventional situations.

Underlining. The titles of long works are generally indicated by underlining.

Underline the titles of long written works, the titles of publications that are published as a single work, the titles of shows, and the titles of works of art.

BOOKS: I want to read Carl N. Degler's At Odds, a book about women and the family in America.

I have just finished reading The Great Republic.

MAGAZINES: Both Time and Newsweek cover art and music.

The Atlantic Monthly is an outstanding magazine.

MUSICAL: Some critics called Oklahoma a work of genius.

OTHER: My mother had a subscription to the London Times.

The Future of Solar Energy is a pamphlet well worth reading.

NOTE ABOUT NEWSPAPER TITLES: The portion of the title that should be underlined will vary from newspaper to newspaper.

<u>The New York Times</u> should always be fully capitalized and underlined. Other papers, however, can usually be treated in one of two ways: the <u>Los Angeles Times</u> or the Los Angeles <u>Times</u>. Unless you know the true name of a paper, choose one of these two forms and use it consistently.

Several other types of items that would also be printed in italics should be underlined in handwritten or typed material.

Underline the names of individual air, sea, space, and land craft.

EXAMPLE: The President sent <u>Air Force I</u> to bring the visitor to Washington.

Underline foreign words or phrases not yet accepted into English.

EXAMPLES: She signed the letter <u>con amore</u>, "with love."

The French expression <u>mère de famille</u> means "mother of a family."

The composer's note read <u>con spirito</u>, "with spirit."

Some foreign words and phrases retain their foreign pronunciation but are no longer underlined or italicized because they are now considered part of our language.

NOT UNDERLINED: amour, caveat emptor, cliché, blitzkrieg, gourmet, milieu, siesta, staccato, chauffeur, pizza, dilettante

Individual words, letters, and numbers used as names for themselves are underlined or italicized to make them stand out.

Underline words, letters, or numbers used as names for themselves.

EXAMPLES: She repeatedly uses <u>nevertheless</u> to connect her ideas.

He has a strange way of writing his <u>f</u>'s and <u>t</u>'s.

Is that a <u>3</u> or an <u>8</u>?

Underlining or italics may also be used to emphasize a particular word or phrase.

Underline words that you wish to stress.

EXAMPLE: Be sure to study the rules <u>carefully</u>.

Do not overuse underlining to emphasize your meaning. It is usually better to rely on a precise choice and arrangement of words to convey your meaning.

Quotation Marks.   Like underlining, quotation marks are used to indicate certain titles.

Use quotation marks around the titles of short written works, episodes in a series, songs, parts of a long musical composition, or a work that is mentioned as part of a collection.

EXAMPLES: I admire Whitman's poem "I Hear America Singing."

"The Cask of Amontillado" is one of my favorite suspense stories.

His favorite song by the Beatles is "Something."

Read Chapter 1, "Dynamic Democracy," in <u>Freedom's Ferment</u>.

Titles Without Underlining or Quotation Marks.   Two types of titles should not be underlined or enclosed in quotation marks. The first type is made up of religious works.

Do not underline or place in quotation marks mentions of the Bible, its books, divisions, or versions, or other holy scriptures, such as the Koran.

EXAMPLE: Will you read from Genesis in the Old Testament?

The second type of title that should not be underlined or enclosed in quotation marks is made up of government documents.

Do not underline or place in quotation marks the titles of government charters, alliances, treaties, acts, statutes, or reports.

EXAMPLES: The Taft-Hartley Labor Act was passed by Congress in 1947.

We memorized the Preamble to the Constitution of the United States.

EXERCISE E: Recognizing the Many Uses of Underlining. Copy each of the following sentences onto your paper, underlining where necessary.

1. For many years the Queen Mary and the Queen Elizabeth ruled the seas.
2. In this paper I will use the book The Stranger to analyze the style of Albert Camus.
3. For some reason he never crossed his t's or dotted his i's.
4. Next season the plays Richard III, All's Well That Ends Well, and Henry V will be performed by the repertory theater.
5. Picasso's Guernica, now at the Museum of Modern Art, will eventually be returned to the artist's native country.
6. Some French restaurants use the expression carte du jour instead of menu.
7. The writer was identified by the way he wrote the numbers 2, 6, and 7.
8. Avoid using don't in the third-person singular.
9. The expression chacun pour soi means everyone for himself.
10. The magazine American Cinematographer regularly reviews the latest equipment used in the film industry.

EXERCISE F: Using Underlining and Quotation Marks for Titles. Copy each of the following sentences onto your paper, adding quotation marks or underlining as needed. If neither is required, write *correct.*

1. Two of Edwin Arlington Robinson's best poems are Richard Cory and Miniver Cheevy.
2. One of the newspapers we are discussing in journalism class is the St. Louis Post-Dispatch.
3. The pamphlet Historic Sites in Pennsylvania will be useful in your survey.
4. My favorite song from Brigadoon is The Heather on the Hill.
5. For suspense I always recommend Richard Connell's short story The Most Dangerous Game.
6. They memorized the Twenty-Third Psalm.
7. Read Chapter 1, The Jefferson Image, in Jefferson and Civil Liberties.
8. Don't you enjoy hearing the Gettysburg Address?
9. My brother received a subscription to Sports Illustrated for Christmas.
10. I was very impressed with the book The Sea Around Us by Rachel Carson.

APPLICATION 1: Using Quotation Marks and Underlining. Copy each of the following sentences onto your paper, adding quotation marks and underlining as needed.

1. I enjoyed Raisin in the Sun, a play by Lorraine Hansberry.
2. I wonder, she mused, whether the building will ever be completed.
3. I own a print of Paul Cézanne's painting The Cardplayers.
4. The 1959 National Book Award for Fiction read: The fiction prize has been awarded to Bernard Malamud for The Magic Barrel, a work radiant with personal vision. Compassionate and profound in its wry humor, it captures the poetry of human relationships at a point where reality and imagination meet.
5. Leonard Bernstein wrote the music for the shows West Side Story, Candide, and On the Town.
6. Will Rogers summed up Hoover's defeat by Roosevelt by stating, The little fellow felt that he never had a chance. . . .
7. Barron's Profiles of American Colleges is published in regional editions.
8. "Then my grandfather said, Forget him, and he never mentioned his name again."
9. I want to buy Sit Down and Talk to Me, the new Lou Rawls album.
10. The treaty will not be signed until all troops are removed, said the majority leader.
11. Yes, she answered. We have agreed to meet with their representative tomorrow.
12. I used the book The Life and Times of Chaucer by John Gardner for most of my research.
13. My aunt asked, How do you plan to go from Seattle to San Francisco?
14. Chapter 8, The Logic of Revolution, concludes with the War for Independence.
15. The full title of Richard Barber's book is The Arthurian Legends: An Illustrated Anthology.
16. I considered what you said, announced the principal, and decided to approve the plan.
17. Consider the German expression Borgen macht Sorgen, which means borrowing makes sorrowing.
18. I demand my rights! she exclaimed.
19. Try not to use ain't in your speech and never use it in your writing.
20. I bought a recording of Beethoven's Pastoral Symphony conducted by Neville Mariner.
21. The Tin Drum and The Marriage of Maria Braun are two outstanding German films.
22. No, my grandmother replied. I cannot wait for you.
23. Where will you live? the professor asked.
24. The mysteries of astronomy are explained in the book Man and the Stars by Hanbury Brown.
25. Do not print your t's and your p's.

APPLICATION 2: Writing an Imaginary Dialogue. Write an imaginary dialogue between two characters from different books or short stories. Have the characters argue about why people should read the book or story in which each appears. Be sure that your dialogue contains at least ten sentences and mentions the names of the characters and the title of the work in which each appears.

13.5 Dashes, Parentheses, and Brackets

This section will present some of the less frequently used punctuation marks: dashes (—), parentheses (( )), and brackets ([ ]). These punctuation marks should not be used indiscriminately. There are specific rules for the use of each. Even though you may not be called upon to use them often, it is important to learn the rules that govern their use.

■ Dashes

The dash, a much stronger mark than a comma, signals a sudden break in the structure or thought of a sentence.

A simple, dramatic punctuation mark, the dash should not be used haphazardly in place of the comma and other separators. Overuse of the dash reduces the dramatic effect it can have and indicates a lazy writer, one who has not mastered the other rules of punctuation.

There are several rules governing use of the dash, the first of which is the broadest.

Use dashes to indicate an abrupt change of thought.

A single dash should be used when a new thought occurs abruptly after other material in a sentence.

EXAMPLE: The article doesn't provide enough information—by the way, did you find it in the school library?

Dashes can also be used to set off ideas that briefly interrupt other ideas.

Use dashes to set off interrupting ideas in a dramatic fashion.

Notice in the second example that when the interrupting idea is a question the question mark is included. The same is true of an exclamation mark.

EXAMPLES: The sailboat was built—you may find this hard to believe—in less than a month.

The sailboat was built—where did they get the money?—in less than a month.

Sometimes you may also want to use a dash to pull together or summarize a group of items in a series.

Use a dash to set off a summary statement.

EXAMPLES: A good scholastic record, a pleasing personality, and good political connections—if you have all of these, you may be able to get a job in a congressional office.

Appositives may also be presented with dashes.

Use dashes to set off a nonessential appositive in the middle of a sentence (1) when the appositive is long; (2) when it is already punctuated; (3) when it is introduced by words such as *for example* or *that is;* and (4) when you want to be especially dramatic.

EXAMPLES: Two battles—the battle at Saratoga and the battle at Yorktown Heights—were the subject of his research.

Yesterday, I met three old neighbors from Chicago—Ed Wisloc, his sister Linda, and their friend Ann Stanley—whom I haven't seen in years.

Some students—for example, Tod, Fran, and Kevin—always do well on tests.

Nonessential modifiers that contain their own internal punctuation or that you wish to emphasize strongly may also be punctuated with dashes.

Use dashes to set off nonessential modifiers (1) when the modifier is already punctuated and (2) when you want to be especially dramatic.

WITH INTERNAL PUNCTUATION: The football player—who, despite a sprained ankle, managed to score the winning touchdown—was carried to the locker room on his teammates' shoulders.

FOR EMPHASIS: Her expertise on the clarinet—which she had mastered so well that many professionals could benefit from listening to her play—was responsible for her winning a music scholarship.

Finally, dashes may be used to set off one other special type of sentence interrupter—the parenthetical expression.

Uses dashes to set off a parenthetical expression (1) when the expression is long; (2) when it is already punctuated; and (3) when you want to be especially dramatic.

EXAMPLES: The searing heat—it was ninety all last week, and on Monday and Tuesday of this week it was over one hundred—has made our lawn turn brown.

The clown—have you ever seen such an elaborate costume?—gave each of the children a balloon.

EXERCISE A: Understanding the Use of the Dash. The following sentences, all written by professional writers, contain dashes properly used. Read each sentence carefully and then list the rule illustrated by the sentence.

1. Banks, utilities, insurance companies, and government bureaus have eagerly made room for yards of new equipment—so much faster is the computer than the old-fashioned bookkeeper and clerk. As a result, office work no longer is the growth industry it was—at least in terms of jobs. —Ben B. Seligman
2. Possibly only a dreamy child can fully grasp—or wants to—the difference between a family storeroom, an attic, and the public secondhand shop, and perhaps the difference is important only to herself. But all old junk, even when it has belonged to strangers, must vibrate in the imagination of sensitive observers with many exquisite overtones. —Winifred Welles
3. Here grow the noblest conifers in the world, averaging about two hundred feet in height, and from five to twenty feet in diameter—the majestic Douglas spruce. . . . The sequoia belt extends from the well-known Calaveras groves on the north to the head of Deer Creek on the south—a distance of nearly two hundred miles. —John Muir
4. As the cool stream gushed over one hand, she spelled into the other the word *water,* first slowly, then rapidly. I stood still, my whole attention fixed upon the motions of her fingers. Suddenly I felt a misty consciousness as of something forgotten—a thrill of returning thought; and somehow the

mystery of language was revealed to me. I knew then that "w-a-t-e-r" meant the wonderful cool something that was flowing over my hand. That living word awakened my soul, gave it light, hope, joy, set it free! —Helen Keller

5. Wages fell—even when profits were booming—until whole families labored at the machines for three or four dollars a week per worker; a twelve hour day was average, and a fourteen hour day was not unusual. Stop for a moment and reflect upon what it would be like to work a fourteen hour day—say from five o'clock in the morning till eight at night, with half an hour off for breakfast and half an hour for dinner—six days a week, in an ill-lighted, ill-ventilated factory. —Frederick Lewis Allen

■ Parentheses

Parentheses are used to enclose material in a sentence or a paragraph. Although commas are generally used for this purpose, parentheses are preferred in certain cases. Caution is needed, however. Parentheses are the strongest separators a writer can use. Because of their strength, they should be used infrequently.

Basic Uses of Parentheses.   Perhaps the most important use of parentheses is to set off asides or explanatory information. Even here caution must be used.

> Use parentheses to set off asides and explanations only when the material is not essential to the meaning of the sentence or when the aside or explanation consists of one or more sentences.

EXAMPLES: In 1945 Gabriela Mistral (her real name was Lucila Godoy) became the first Latin American to win the Nobel Prize for Literature.

Keats did not inherit his love of mythology. (His grandfather, in fact, owned a stable, and his father was a groom.)

Another use of parentheses is to set off numerical information.

> Use parentheses to set off the dates of a person's birth and death or other explanations involving numerals.

EXAMPLES: Emma Lazarus (1849–1887) wrote the poem inscribed on the pedestal of the Statue of Liberty.

The committee can be reached at (607) 555-3001.

The last rule for using parentheses involves items in a series.

Use parentheses around numbers and letters marking items in a series.

EXAMPLES: My history teacher ranks our great presidents this way: (1) Lincoln, (2) Washington, (3) Theodore Roosevelt, (4) Jefferson, and (5) Franklin D. Roosevelt.

Her report on energy will deal with the use of (a) wood, (b) coal, (c) oil, and (d) solar power.

Other Punctuation Marks Used with Parentheses.   Sometimes parentheses and other punctuation marks are used together. Several rules govern the use of parentheses used with other marks of punctuation.

When a parenthetical phrase or declarative sentence interrupts another sentence, do not capitalize the initial word or use any end mark inside the parentheses.

EXAMPLE: Sarah (she had always loved animals) took in the stray kitten and fed it.

Another rule governs the use of a question or exclamatory sentence in parentheses when it interrupts another sentence.

When a parenthetical question or exclamatory sentence interrupts another sentence, use both an initial capital and an end mark inside the parentheses.

EXAMPLES: The car (Do you think we could be out of gas?) won't start.

On Saturday (What a beautiful day it was!) we climbed to the top of Overlook Mountain and had a picnic.

When a sentence in parentheses falls between two other sentences, use the following rule concerning punctuation.

When a parenthetical sentence falls between two complete sentences, use both an initial capital and an end mark inside the parentheses.

EXAMPLE: I started working Saturday for a florist. (It was difficult to get up so early.) My duties include arranging flowers and delivering them all over town.

The final rule governing other punctuation used with parentheses involves phrases.

In a sentence with a parenthetical phrase, place any punctuation belonging to the main sentence after the second parenthesis.

EXAMPLES: When I got home (about four o'clock), she was waiting for me.

The artist had finally accepted the invitation to exhibit his works (after having been invited twice before); therefore, he spent the summer preparing the material for display.

EXERCISE B: Using Parentheses. Copy the following items onto your paper, adding parentheses, any other punctuation marks, and capitals where necessary.

1. The shorter route (it passes through the city and along a badly paved road) will get you there in two hours.
2. The book *Washington Square* the film is called *The Heiress* describes Catherine Sloper's romance with Morris Townsend.
3. Marie collects stamps in these special categories: a animals and birds, b flowers, c famous leaders, and d space travel.
4. The telephone number he left was 201 555-6701.
5. General Winfield Scott 1786–1866 was noted for his love of elaborate uniforms and military parades.
6. My brother do you think he will ever learn got into trouble again.
7. The actor came to town we were so excited and gave us his autograph.
8. As she walked down the street using crutches not very gracefully and she wished she had been more careful climbing the tree.
9. My alarm clock didn't go off perhaps we had had a power failure and I was late for school.
10. He returned he spent a year in Europe and joined his family's business.

■ Brackets

Brackets have one major use: to enclose a word or words inserted in a quotation by a writer who is quoting someone else.

> Use brackets to enclose a word or words inserted in a quotation by a writer who is quoting someone else.

EXAMPLE: Edmund Morris describes an attempt by Theodore Roosevelt to feed his hungry regiment during the Spanish-American War. "On the morning of June 26 [1898] Roosevelt got wind of a stockpile of beans on the beach [in Cuba] and marched a squad of men hastily down to investigate."

Brackets are sometimes also used with the Latin expression *sic* (meaning *thus*) in a quotation to show that the original writer misspelled a word or phrase. The expression *sic* calls attention to the original form used by the author.

EXAMPLE: As a recommendation he wrote, "He don't [sic] lie."

EXERCISE C: Using Brackets. Copy the following items onto your paper, adding brackets where necessary.

1. Her letter stated, "I recieved sic the order only yesterday."
2. Abraham Lincoln said: "We have come to dedicate a portion of that field the Gettysburg battlefield as a final resting place for those who here gave their lives that that nation might live."
3. Martin Luther King, Jr., stated his philosophy: "Let us not seek to satisfy our thirst for freedom by drinking from the cup of bitterness and hatred. He was speaking in Washington, D.C., in 1963. We must forever conduct our struggle on the high plane of dignity and discipline."
4. My little sister always says," Me sic want to go with you."
5. General Douglas MacArthur in a speech to the cadets at West Point said: "He the American soldier belongs to posterity as the instructor of future generations in the principles of liberty and freedom."

APPLICATION: Using Dashes, Parentheses, and Brackets in Your Own Writing. Follow the directions for each of the following.

1. Write an original sentence using dashes to indicate an abrupt change of thought.
2. Write an original sentence using a dash to present a dramatic summary statement.
3. Set off a nonessential appositive in the middle of an original sentence with dashes.
4. Use dashes in an original sentence to set off a nonessential modifier that contains punctuation.

5. Use a parenthetical sentence within another original sentence.
6. Use a parenthetical question within an original sentence.
7. Use parentheses to set off explanatory information involving numerals in an original sentence.
8. Use parentheses around numbers marking items in a series in an original sentence.
9. Use an original parenthetical sentence between two other original sentences.
10. Use brackets correctly in an original sentence.

Hyphens 13.6

Hyphens are used to join certain numbers and parts of words, to join some compound words, and to divide words at the ends of lines. Although it resembles the dash, the hyphen is distinctly shorter. In handwritten material be sure to make your hyphens half as long as your dashes. In typewritten material use one hyphen mark for a hyphen (-), and two hyphen marks for a dash (–).

■ Using Hyphens with Numbers, Word Parts, and Words

Hyphens are used with numbers, word parts, and words.

Numbers. Hyphens help to make the meaning of compound numbers clear.

Use a hyphen when writing out the numbers *twenty-one* through *ninety-nine*.

EXAMPLES: thirty-three inches

forty-seven acres

Hyphens are also used with some fractions.

Use a hyphen when writing fractions that are used as adjectives.

EXAMPLES: two-and-a-half inches

two-thirds majority

If a fraction is used as a noun instead of an adjective, the hyphen is not used.

EXAMPLE: Nine tenths of the report is completed.

Word Parts.   Certain word parts are also joined by hyphens.

Use a hyphen after a prefix that is followed by a proper noun or adjective.

EXAMPLES: pro-British

all-American

mid-October

Certain prefixes are often found before proper nouns and proper adjectives. They include the following: *ante-, anti-, mid-, post-, pre-, pro-,* and *un-.*
Three other prefixes and one suffix are always used with a hyphen.

Use a hyphen in words with the prefixes *all-, ex-, self-* and words with the suffix *-elect.*

EXAMPLES: all-powerful

ex-football player

self-adjusting brakes

president-elect

Compound Words.   Hyphens are also used to join some compound words.

Use a hyphen to connect two or more words that are used as one word, unless the dictionary gives a contrary spelling.

Some compound words are written as one word, others are written as separate words, and still others are joined by a hyphen. If you are uncertain as to how a compound word should be spelled, consult your dictionary.

EXAMPLES: brother-in-law

two-year-olds

jack-of-all-trades

secretary-treasurer

Compound modifiers, as well as compound nouns, sometimes require hyphens.

Use a hyphen to connect most compound modifiers that come before nouns. Do not use a hyphen when the modifier includes a word ending in *-ly* or in a compound proper adjective or a compound proper noun acting as an adjective.

EXAMPLES WITH HYPHENS: a strong-willed aunt

an up-to-date design

a well-deserved award

EXAMPLES WITHOUT HYPHENS: a highly unlikely suspect

the North American continent

the Sierra Nevada Mountains

Although compound adjectives in front of a noun are usually hyphenated, a hyphen is often not needed when compound adjectives follow a noun.

EXAMPLE: My aunt is strong willed.

If your dictionary spells a word with hyphens, however, that word always should be hyphenated.

EXAMPLE: That design is up-to-date.

For Clarity.   Another use of hyphens is to prevent the misreading of a word or group of words.

Use a hyphen within a word when a combination of letters might otherwise be confusing.

EXAMPLES: a bell-like sound

an S-curve

a semi-invalid

Confusion may also result if a reader combines certain words incorrectly. Use a hyphen to prevent this confusion.

Use a hyphen between words to keep the reader from combining them erroneously.

Note the differences in meaning in the following pairs of sentences.

EXAMPLES: The tennis player had to re-serve the ball.
Did you reserve this book?

The new-car owner drove very carefully.
The new car owner drove very carefully.

EXERCISE A: Using Hyphens to Combine Words. Copy each of the following items onto your paper, adding hyphens where necessary. If an item does not require a hyphen, write *correct* on your paper.

1. well educated person
2. greatly admired
3. twenty three years
4. un American
5. self satisfied
6. South American custom
7. well made chair
8. all American athlete
9. treasurer elect
10. father in law
11. anti war
12. semi independent
13. T shirt
14. bright eyed
15. ex lieutenant
16. pre Revolutionary War
17. old fashioned dress
18. L shaped building
19. one hundredth part
20. multi colored fabric

■ Using Hyphens to Divide Words at the End of a Line

Although you should try not to divide words at the end of a line, sometimes you may have to. Certain rules can help you divide words correctly when you must divide them.

The most important rule involves dividing words between syllables.

If a word must be divided, always divide it between syllables.

This rule indicates that you should never divide a one-syllable word. When you divide a word of more than one syllable, place the hyphen at the end of the first line as shown in the following example. Also take care never to use such a hyphen in the last line of a page.

EXAMPLE: Did you finish the difficult American history assignment that was due today?

If you are unsure of how to divide a word into syllables, consult a dictionary. Do not divide one-syllable words just because they are long.

Even if a word has more than one syllable, it should never be divided so that one letter stands alone.

Do not divide a word so that a single letter stands alone.

INCORRECT: hast-y   a-round   i-dentity

CORRECT: hasty   around   iden-tity

A special rule governs the division of proper nouns and proper adjectives

Do not divide proper nouns or proper adjectives.

INCORRECT: Jeff-rey   Euro-pean

CORRECT: Jeffrey   European

The final rule governing the division of words at the end of a line involves words that are already hyphenated.

Divide a hyphenated word only after the hyphen.

INCORRECT: I would like to introduce you to my new sis-
         ter-in-law.

CORRECT: I would like to introduce you to my new sister-
         in-law.

EXERCISE B: Using Hyphens to Divide Words at the End of a Line. The following words have been divided by hyphens as if they were at the end of a line. If the word has been divided properly, write *correct* on your paper. If it has been divided incorrectly, write the word as it should appear.

1. Anglo-Amer-ican
2. a-lone
3. thro-ugh
4. Pe-ter
5. Syl-via

6. si-xteen
7. i-dea
8. guilt-y
9. Span-iard
10. dre-am

APPLICATION: Using Hyphens in Your Own Writing. Write ten sentences of your own, each sentence illustrating a different rule about hyphens that you studied in this section.

13.7   Apostrophes

The following rules for using apostrophes are not difficult to remember. What is required, however, is careful attention to the meaning of each rule and to the examples illustrating their use. Read each rule carefully and then study the examples.

■ Forming Possessives of Nouns with Apostrophes

An apostrophe is used to show possession or ownership. The location of the apostrophe depends upon the characteristics of the noun.

Singular Nouns.   The first rule involves the use of the apostrophe with singular nouns.

> Add an apostrophe and *-s* to show the possessive case of most singular nouns.

EXAMPLES: the photograph of the girl   the girl's photograph

the leaf of the shrub   the shrub's leaf

the crib of the baby   the baby's crib

the shore of the lake   the lake's shore

the check of the waitress   the waitress's check

Notice that with a singular noun ending in *-s*, you may still usually use an *'s* to form the possessive. The only exception is when the addition of *'s* would make the resulting word difficult to pronounce. In these cases add only an apostrophe.

AWKWARD: Samuel Clemens's pen name was Mark Twain.

BETTER: Samuel Clemens' pen name was Mark Twain.

Plural Nouns.   Two rules are necessary to form the possessive case of plural nouns. First, there is a rule for forming the possessive case of plural nouns ending in *-s* or *-es*.

> Add an apostrophe to show the possessive case of plural nouns ending in *-s* or *-es*.

EXAMPLES: The T-shirts of the boys   the boys' T-shirts

the figures of the charts   the charts' figures

the uniforms of the sailors   the sailors' uniforms

There is also a rule for plurals that do not end in an *-s* or
-es.

**Add an apostrophe and *-s* to show the possessive case of plu-
ral nouns that do not end in *-s* or *-es*.**

EXAMPLES: the suits of the men   the men's suits

the playthings of the children   the children's playthings

Compound Nouns.   A compound noun contains two or
more words. To form the possessive of a compound noun, use
the following rule.

**Add an apostrophe and an *-s* (or just an apostrophe if the word
is a plural ending in *-s*) to the last word of a compound noun to
form the possessive.**

The following examples illustrate some of the different
kinds of compound nouns commonly used to form possessives.

NAMES OF BUSINESS AND ORGANIZATIONS: Johnson and Johnson's baby
powder

Red Cross's volunteers

University of Connecticut's
campus

TITLES OF RULERS AND LEADERS: King George III's army

editor-in-chief's decision

HYPHENATED COMPOUND NOUNS: my father-in-law's ranch

the secretary-treasurer's report

Expressions Involving Time, Amounts, and the Word *Sake*.
Possessive expressions involving time, amounts, and the word
sake also require the use of apostrophes.

**To form possessives involving time, amounts, or the word *sake*,
use an apostrophe and *-s* or just an apostrophe, depending
on whether the possessive is singular or plural.**

TIME: a week's vacation   three days' work

AMOUNT: a dime's worth   three dollars' worth

SAKE: for Heaven's sake   for goodness' sake

The final *-s* is often dropped in expressions involving *sake*, as in the last example.

Individual and Joint Ownership.   Sometimes people share ownership, and sometimes several people claim individual ownership. Notice how the difference affects the use of the apostrophe.

> To show **individual ownership,** add an apostrophe and *-s* at the end of each noun in a series. To show **joint ownership,** add an apostrophe and *-s* to the last noun in a series.

INDIVIDUAL POSSESSION: Susan's, Marie's, and Alice's papers were graded by the teacher.

JOINT POSSESSION: Wilson and Martin's dog is a bulldog.

Avoiding Problems with Possessive Nouns.   You can avoid problems in placing apostrophes to form possessive nouns if you check each time to make sure that the owner's complete name appears to the left of the apostrophe.

INCORRECT SINGULAR: Jame's book

CORRECT SINGULAR: James's book

INCORRECT PLURAL: two boy's coats

CORRECT PLURAL: two boys' coats

EXERCISE A: Using Apostrophes Correctly to Form Possessive Nouns. Copy each of the following sentences onto your paper, choosing the correct possessive form from the choices in parentheses.

1. My (mother's-in-law, mother-in-law's) baked scampi won a prize in a local contest.
2. He loaded all of the (women's, womens') luggage into the bus.
3. (Robert Burns's, Robert Burnses) poetry is written in dialect.
4. Is this really the (Joneses', Jone's) house?

5. The (boy's, boys') track team came in second in the state tournament.
6. (Margie and Trish's, Margie's and Trish's) projects received outstanding grades.
7. All of the reporters were asked to read the (editor's-in-chief, editor-in-chief's) style sheet.
8. (Brook's and Atkinson's, Brooks and Atkinson's) Department Store features a large variety of linens.
9. I've always been interested in (children's, childrens') art work.
10. An (electrician's, electricians') helper often serves as an apprentice on the job.

■ Forming Possessives of Pronouns

Two additional rules are needed to show possession with indefinite pronouns and personal pronouns. Indefinite pronouns require the use of an *'s* to show possession.

Use an apostrophe and -s with indefinite pronouns to show possession.

EXAMPLES: nobody's turn

one's homework

everybody's friend

somebody's house key

each other's handkerchiefs

one another's bathing caps

Notice in the last two examples that an apostrophe and *-s* are added only to the last word of a two-word indefinite pronoun.

A different rule applies when the possessives of personal pronouns are formed.

Do not use an apostrophe with the possessive forms of personal pronouns.

The possessive forms of personal pronouns (*his, hers, its, ours, yours, theirs,* and so on) already show possession. They do not need apostrophes because they already show ownership.

CORRECT: his old car   that house of ours

             that hobby of hers   that paper of yours

             its tail   that responsibility of theirs

Do not confuse the contractions *who's, it's,* and *they're* with possessive pronouns. *Who's, it's,* and *they're* are contractions for *who is, it is,* and *they are.* Remember that *whose, its,* and *their* show possession.

PRONOUNS: Whose book is this?

                Its door wouldn't close.

CONTRACTIONS: Who's coming to the party?

                  It's cold out today.

EXERCISE B: Using Apostrophes Correctly with Pronouns. Copy each of the following sentences onto your paper, choosing the correct form from the choices in parentheses.

1. This chemistry notebook obviously belongs to (her's, her).
2. (Someone else's, Someone elses') car was involved in the accident, not mine.
3. (Whose, Who's) briefcase is on the table?
4. Susan just found (someones', someone's) social security card.
5. Our pet Siamese cat always eats (it's, its) meals under the kitchen table.
6. My father decided that he would like (somebody else's, somebody elses') opinion.
7. I understand that our new neighbor's pool is larger than (their's, theirs).
8. I wonder what happened to (he's, his) report card.
9. I originally wanted to use (they're, their) lawn mower.
10. (Everybody's, Everybodys') attendance is requested.

■ Forming Contractions with Apostrophes

Apostrophes are often used to indicate contractions as well as possession. A contraction is formed by removing a letter or letters from an expression and replacing the missing letters with an apostrophe.

Use an apostrophe in a contraction to indicate the position of the missing letter or letters.

Contractions with Verbs. The most common type of contraction involves verbs.

VERB AND *NOT*:	should not	shouldn't
	cannot	can't
	will not	won't
	were not	weren't
	is not	isn't

PRONOUN AND THE VERB *WILL*:	she will	she'll

PRONOUN OR NOUN AND THE VERB *WOULD*:	he would	he'd
	they would	they'd

PRONOUN AND THE VERB *HAVE*:	they have	they've
	we have	we've

PRONOUN OR NOUN AND A *BE* VERB:	you are	you're
	she is	she's
	I am	I'm
	Michael is	Michael's
	where is	where's

Notice that one contraction in the preceding examples involves a change in letters as well as a replacing of letters with an apostrophe. *Will not* becomes *won't* in contracted form.

Contractions should be used sparingly in formal writing. Reserve them for those times when they are necessary for the flavor of dialogue. In other cases write out the whole word.

Contractions with Numbers and Poetry. Another type of contraction often used in informal writing is a contraction for the name of a year.

EXAMPLES:	the class of '83
	the blizzard of '88

Still another type of contraction is occasionally found in poetry.

EXAMPLES:	e'en (for *even*)
	o'er (for *over*)

Contractions with o', d', and l'. These letters followed by the apostrophe are often used to make up the abbreviated form of the longer phrase *of the* as it is spelled in several different languages.

EXAMPLES: o'clock   O'Sullivan   d'Martino   l'Abbé

As you can see, these contractions are used most often with surnames.

Contractions in Dialogues.   When writing dialogue, you will usually want to keep the flavor of the speaker's individual speaking style. Therefore, you should use any contractions the speaker might use. You may also want to include a regional dialect or a foreign accent. Since these often include unusual pronunciations involving omitted letters, you may have to insert apostrophes to indicate omitted letters.

EXAMPLES: 'Tis a long way you'll have to be goin'.

Don' you be afoolin' me.

As with most forms of punctuation, overuse of the apostrophe reduces its effectiveness and impact. Thus, you should not overuse the apostrophe—even in dialogues.

EXERCISE C: Using Apostrophes in Contractions. Write the contraction for each of the following items on your paper.

1. we have
2. who is
3. would not
4. the class of 1981
5. it is
6. they are
7. will not
8. is not
9. I am
10. he would

■ Using Apostrophes in Special Situations

In addition to using apostrophes to form possessives and contractions, you should use them in four other special situations.

Use an apostrophe and *-s* to write the plurals of numbers, symbols, letters, and words used to name themselves.

EXAMPLES: during the *1970's*   cross your *t's* and dot your *i's*

your *7's* and *1's*   similar *U's* and *V's*

two *!'s*   no *and's* and *but's*

EXERCISE D: Using Apostrophes in Special Situations. Write the plural form of each of the following items on your paper.

1. 1980
2. *and*
3. *C*
4. 1930
5. *6*
6. *but*
7. *!*
8. *i*
9. *2*
10. *?*

APPLICATION: Using Apostrophes in Your Own Writing. Write a sentence of your own for each of the following items.

1. Use the possessive case to show joint ownership of a horse.
2. Use the possessive case to indicate a book owned by Charles.
3. Use the possessive case to indicate a house owned by a family named Jones.
4. Use the possessive case to show individual ownership of shoes belonging to Maria and Louise.
5. Use the possessive case to indicate a baseball bat owned by Arthur.
6. Use the possessive case to indicate a lawn mower owned by your brother-in-law.
7. Use the possessive form of a personal pronoun to show ownership of a notebook.
8. Use the possessive form of an indefinite pronoun to show ownership of a pen.
9. Use the contraction of *who is*.
10. Use the plural of the word *however*.

Review Exercises: Mechanics

REVIEW EXERCISE 1: Reviewing Terms

This unit has introduced many new terms and their definitions. Answer each of the following questions as completely as possible.

1. How have the rules of capitalization changed over the centuries?
2. When would words such as *north* and *south* be capitalized? When would they not be capitalized?
3. Which words are not usually capitalized in a title unless they appear at the beginning?

4. In an address in either a business or a personal letter, which words would you capitalize?
5. What is an abbreviation? Why are abbreviations used? Which reference book would you consult to check the spelling of an abbreviation?
6. What do the abbreviations A.D. and B.C. stand for? How should they be used?
7. There are two ways to abbreviate the names of states. What are they? What is the official Postal Service abbreviation for your state?
8. Why are abbreviations of Latin expressions often used? List two examples.
9. What is unusual about abbreviations such as FTC, EKG, and UAW?
10. What is an acronym? List one.
11. What does the abbreviation *ital.* mean?
12. What are the common end punctuation marks?
13. What is the difference between a direct question and an indirect question? Give one example of each.
14. What is a declarative sentence? An interrogative sentence? An imperative sentence? An exclamatory sentence?
15. List three uses of the semicolon. List three uses of the colon.
16. What are the seven coordinating conjunctions? How would you punctuate a compound sentence with two independent clauses connected by one of these coordinating conjunctions?
17. How would you punctuate a complex sentence that begins with an introductory adverbial clause?
18. What is a series? How would you use commas to punctuate a series?
19. What is a noun of direct address? How would you use punctuation with a noun of direct address that occurs at the beginning of a sentence?
20. What is a parenthetical expression? What are two ways of using punctuation with a parenthetical expression?
21. What is an essential clause? How should punctuation be used with an essential clause in a complex sentence?
22. What is a nonessential clause? How should punctuation be used with a nonessential clause in a complex sentence?
23. What is a direct quotation? An indirect quotation?
24. What are ellipsis marks? When should they be used?
25. What kinds of titles should be underlined? What kinds of titles should be enclosed in quotation marks?
26. What are brackets? Give examples showing two uses of brackets in a sentence.
27. When is it proper to use a dash? Why should excessive use of the dash be avoided?

28. What is a hyphen? List three uses of the hyphen.
29. What is an apostrophe? How would you use an apostrophe to show possession with a singular noun? With a plural noun?
30. In addition to showing possession, what are two other uses of the apostrophe?

REVIEW EXERCISE 2: Using Capitalization and Abbreviation

Choose the correct version of each of the following items, and use it in a sentence of your own.

1. FBI *or* F.B.I.
2. Secretary of state Haig *or* Secretary of State Haig
3. Hudson River *or* Hudson river
4. Anglo-American *or* anglo-American
5. Amb. Roland Stevenson *or* Ambass. Roland Stevenson
6. Leaning Tower Of Pisa *or* Leaning Tower of Pisa
7. Dr. Arthur Brown, M.D. *or* Arthur Brown, M.D.
8. the Greek god Zeus *or* the Greek God Zeus
9. the Boston symphony *or* the Boston Symphony
10. Mister Weston *or* Mr. Weston
11. am *or* a.m.
12. Commander In Chief *or* Commander in Chief
13. Boulv. *or* Blvd.
14. Governor-elect Wilson *or* Governor-Elect Wilson
15. Calif. *or* Californ.
16. Dear sir, *or* Dear Sir:
17. Km *or* km
18. Lincoln Valley High School *or* Lincoln Valley high school
19. the sphinx *or* the Sphinx
20. the constitution of the United States *or* the Constitution of the United States
21. Spanish-speaking Americans *or* Spanish-Speaking Americans
22. Texs. *or* TX
23. tbsp. *or* tablsp.
24. Republican and Democratic Parties *or* Republican and Democratic parties
25. Misters *or* Messrs.

REVIEW EXERCISE 3: Using Punctuation Marks Correctly

Write sentences of your own using each of the following items.

1. The title of a book
2. A series of three verbs in a sentence

3. A noun of direct address used at the beginning of a sentence
4. Parentheses to enclose a number
5. A colon in front of a list of three items
6. A comma and   coordinating conjunction separating two independent clauses
7. An exclamation mark
8. A direct quotation followed by a conversational tag
9. *oh*, *well*, or *why* used at the beginning of a sentence
10. A nonessential clause in a complex sentence
11. A dash used to indicate a sudden change of thought
12. An introductory adverbial clause beginning with *although*, *since*, or *if*
13. A contraction of a subject and verb
14. An essential clause in a complex sentence
15. A present participial phrase used at the beginning of a sentence
16. A semicolon used to punctuate two independent clauses
17. An indirect question
18. "My father's car . . ." used at the beginning of a sentence
19. A compound sentence in which the second independent clause begins with the word *however*
20. A compound verb in a simple sentence

Vocabulary and Spelling

14
Vocabulary Building

15
Spelling Improvement

14

Vocabulary Building

If you were to compare the reading skills you now have with those you had in sixth or seventh grade, you would see a significant change. The amount of reading you do has undoubtedly increased, and you probably read more widely. One of the most important elements in this change is the increased size of your vocabulary. Actually, what is called your *reading* vocabulary will almost always be larger than your *speaking* vocabulary. Most people, in their reading, can understand many words that they never use in everyday conversation. A large reading vocabulary is a great advantage in your school work as well as in the reading you do for pleasure. A large speaking vocabulary is a great help in expressing your thoughts accurately as you communicate with others.

In this chapter you will find techniques for increasing both your reading and speaking vocabulary. The first section focuses on a variety of methods you can use to learn words you must know for your courses as well as methods you can use to expand your general knowledge of words. The second and third sections are devoted to practicing the skills you will need in order to use *two* of these methods—the first involving the context in which a word is used, the second involving the structural makeup of a word.

14.1 Techniques for Building Vocabulary

Whether you are learning words for a test in school or to expand your general knowledge, the best place to start is with a dictionary and a notebook. However, just looking up new words and recording them in a notebook does little to develop vocabulary. Real vocabulary development depends on an active desire to learn new words, the use of a number of helpful techniques, and continuous review.

■ Studying Words You Need to Know in School

A number of different techniques can be used to learn the words you need to understand the material in your different courses in school.

Set aside a special section in each of your course notebooks where you can enter new words and their definitions. Then use one or more of the following techniques to study and review the words.

Using a Three-Column Format.   Using a three-column format, either in your special notebook sections or on separate pieces of paper you use during review sessions, can be very helpful. In the first column, you should list the words you need to learn. In the third column, you should list the definitions of the words. In the second column you can enter temporary hints, or bridge words, that can help you in your initial review sessions. By folding the paper into three columns, you can cover up either the definitions or the words themselves and practice adding the missing parts.

The partial example that follows shows how this method works. Notice the bridge words in the second column that act as hints about the definitions of the words.

	Word	Bridge	Definition
	quandary	question	a state of uncertainty
○	euphoria	Wow!	a feeling of high spirits

Using Flash Cards.   Instead of using a three-column format, you can list the same information on the front and back of index cards. Place the word and the temporary bridge word on the front and the definition on the back. Then flip through the cards one by one trying to supply the information on the reverse side. After the first few review sessions with each group of cards, you can erase the bridge words and try supplying the definitions without any hints.

Using a Tape Recorder.   If you have access to a tape recorder, you may find that verbal practice works as well or better than written practice. You can read each word you want to learn onto the tape, pause for approximately ten seconds, and then add a definition followed by another new word. When you play back the tape, try to add each word's definition in the ten-second pause. Replay the tape until you can supply all of the definitions automatically.

EXERCISE A: **Listing and Studying Words.** Identify at least five words you will need to learn in each of the courses you are studying now and enter them, with their definitions, in each of your course notebooks. Study the words for a week using one or more of the methods listed here. Then test yourself by listing all of the words on paper and using each word in two different sentences that show your knowledge of the word's meaning.

■ Expanding Your Vocabulary on Your Own

There is always room for improvement in your vocabulary, improvement that can help you in school and later in your career. An increased knowledge of words can also be very useful when taking many different kinds of standardized tests.

Consider one or more of the following methods of expanding your vocabulary on your own.

Setting Daily or Weekly Goals.   Trying to memorize a long list of words all at once can be difficult. Learning one or two new words a day, however, is relatively simple. If practiced regularly, it can also lead to a very impressive knowledge of words.

The best way to begin is to buy a small notebook. Each day you should enter a new word and its definition, either a word you have come across in your reading or a word you have found in the dictionary. Then you should look for ways to use the new word either in your conversation or in your writing. Each time you use the word you should place a check in the notebook. Only by actually using the words will you make them a part of your vocabulary.

A similar method can be used on a weekly basis. Start each week with a list of three to five words. Then see how many of the words you can make your own by the end of the week.

Using Special Resource Materials.   A number of books and magazines can be used to expand your knowledge of words in a systematic way. In the self-help section of most bookstores, you will find many inexpensive paperbacks that offer special programs for learning new words. Popular magazines such as *Reader's Digest* also carry regular or occasional columns devoted to learning new words.

One of the most interesting ways of learning new words is through the use of books devoted to *etymology*: the study of the origins of words. These books, which are found in the 420 section of most libraries, often contain fascinating histories of words that make them easy to remember. Words such as *protean* and *Augean* can come alive once you know their histories.

Using Context and Structure in Daily Reading.   Although you must always check a dictionary if you want to be certain of the meaning of a new word, two special methods of learning new words can help you make excellent guesses about the meaning of new words you come across in your daily reading. When reading for pleasure, many people simply skip words they do not recognize because consulting a dictionary would be too much of an interruption. Instead of simply skipping the words, however, you can make intelligent guesses using context or structure.

The context of a word consists of its surrounding words. If you check the sentence in which a word is found you can often substitute a word that will work just as well in that position in the sentence. In many cases this substitution will be an approximate definition of the original word. In the following example, you can see that the word *handwritten* can very logically be substituted for the word *holographic*. If you check a dictionary, you will see that it is in fact a very good definition for the word.

EXAMPLE: Because the document was *holographic*, the beauty of his penmanship was apparent to all.

    Because the document was *handwritten*, the beauty of his penmanship was apparent to all.

Structure is simply a term for the various parts that make up a word. If you know the meaning of a number of prefixes (such as *re-* and *non-*), roots (such as *-ten-* and *-graph-*), and suffixes (such as *-tion* and *-ic*), you can generally make very good guesses about the meanings of words that contain these parts.

EXAMPLE: retention = re- (back) + -ten- (hold) + -tion (the action of)

     = the action of holding back

As with context, when you eventually check a dictionary you will usually find that your guess has been a good one. *Retention*, for example, actually does mean "the action of holding something back."

In the next two sections, you will find more details that will help you use context and structure in your reading.

EXERCISE B: **Adding New Words to Your Vocabulary.** Use one of the three methods suggested here to add at least ten new words to your vocabulary. After a week, test yourself on these words using the method suggested in Exercise A. Specify which of the methods you have used on your paper.

APPLICATION: **Putting New Words to Use.** Choose three of the words you learned in Exercise A and three of the words you learned in Exercise B and find some way of using all six words in a letter to a real or fictitious friend. If you think the friend is unlikely to know the meaning of the words, use them in a context that helps define them.

14.2   Using Context

This section will give you a chance to practice using context clues to determine the meaning of words you encounter in your reading, both in and out of school.

Use context clues in all of your reading to improve both your vocabulary and your general reading comprehension.

As mentioned in Section 14.1, the information in the sentence in which an unfamiliar word is used will often give you a clue to the meaning of the unfamiliar word. A context clue may occur in a sentence simply by chance, as a result of the way a writer expresses a thought. However, many writers add such clues deliberately to help their readers understand the ideas they are presenting.

The following chart gives examples of several different types of context clues. Study the chart so that you can later recognize the ways in which a writer may intentionally or unintentionally be giving you clues to the meaning of new or difficult words.

TYPES OF CONTEXT CLUES		
Clue	**Example**	**Method**
Formal definition	Because the patient was suffering, the doctor prescribed an *anodyne*, a medication to relieve pain.	Gives the reader the actual meaning of the word.
Familiar words	When she finally appeared, Theda was *bedecked* with as many ornaments as a well-decorated Christmas tree.	Uses familiar words to give the reader a clue. *Bedecked* means "adorned."
Comparison	Only one who had lived through a hurricane could appreciate the violence of the *typhoon*.	Compares *typhoon*, a violent tropical cyclone, with the more familiar *hurricane*.
Contrast	No longer popular or respected, the former leader has become the local *pariah*.	Couples the words *former leader* with *no longer popular or respected* to suggest that the leader is one who is avoided or shunned. *Pariah* means "social outcast."
Synonyms	The judge's remarks were *ambiguous*, vague, and inexact.	Uses the familiar words *vague* and *inexact* as synonyms for *ambiguous*.
Antonyms	The man spoke in *stentorian* tones, but his wife spoke softly.	Uses the familiar word *soft* as an antonym for *stentorian*.

Once you know the kinds of clues you may be given, you should also develop a strategy for putting the clues to work. The following chart gives an example of a sentence with a difficult word, along with three steps that can be used to guess the meaning of the word. You may find it helpful.

USING CONTEXT CLUES

Example: Because the patient was so *debilitated* from the medication, the long months in bed, and the illness itself, the doctors recommended a program of physical therapy and gradually increasing activity to build him back up.

Step 1:   Find other words in the sentence that give clues to the meaning of the unknown word.
The familiar words *medication, months in bed,* and *illness* suggest a weakened physical condition.
Other familiar terms and phrases such as *physical therapy, gradually increasing activity,* and *build . . . up* confirm this idea.

Step 2:   Test your definition in place of the unfamiliar word:
Because the patient was so *weak* from the medication, . . .

Step 3:   Confirm your guess by checking it in a dictionary:
debilitate means "make feeble; weaken."

Although, as the chart suggests, the only way to be sure of a meaning is to check it in a dictionary, you may sometimes find it easier simply to jot down the word and your guess and then check it later.

■ Using Context Clues in Textbook Reading

You can begin practicing your context skills on the following paragraph, which represents the type of textual material you might encounter in a social studies textbook. Read it completely to get the overall meaning. Then, use the steps in the preceding chart to help you determine the meaning of each underlined word.

EXAMPLE:

After George Washington publicly <u>implored</u> the American people to accept the new Constitution in a letter that expressed his full support, patriotic leaders began a campaign to ensure ratification. On foot, on horseback, and by coach, these <u>indomitable</u> men journeyed to farms, <u>hamlets</u>, and cities to explain the <u>gist</u> of the Constitution. They spread their important message with enthusiasm and <u>fervor</u>. They published letters and pamphlets demanding that the citizens set aside their <u>inconsequential</u> differences and stop making <u>derogatory</u> comments about the <u>ostensible</u> results if the document gained approval. The patriots' <u>striking</u> efforts to <u>cultivate</u> popular support were successful. Approval was assured by July of 1778, and the Constitutional Congress convened to select the officials to lead the new nation.

EXERCISE A: Choosing Meanings. Use your guesses from the preceding paragraph to complete the following questions. For each word, choose the definition that most closely matches the meaning of the word as it was used in the paragraph. Then write the letter of the correct definition next to the appropriate number on your paper.

1. hamlet
   (a) small ham
   (b) city
   (c) youth
   (d) small village

2. indomitable
   (a) unyielding
   (b) leader
   (c) to control
   (d) submissive

3. derogatory
   (a) questionable
   (b) belittling
   (c) unconquerable
   (d) praising

4. gist
   (a) of no consequence
   (b) ardor
   (c) main idea
   (d) grain

5. inconsequential
   (a) important
   (b) unimportant
   (c) disparaging
   (d) praising

6. cultivate
   (a) polite
   (b) discourage
   (c) develop
   (d) courteous

7. ostensible
   (a) extended
   (b) pretentious
   (c) intense
   (d) apparent

8. implore
   (a) regret
   (b) belittle
   (c) beg
   (d) examine

9. striking
   (a) claiming
   (b) impressive
   (c) hitting
   (d) subdued

10. fervor
    (a) zeal
    (b) temperature
    (c) calm
    (d) eloquent

■ Using Context Clues in General Reading

The following paragraphs about Alaska include words that you might find in an article in *National Geographic* or some other natural science magazine. As you read the passage, use your context skills to guess the meanings of the underlined words. Jot down your guesses on a sheet of paper.

EXAMPLE:

Alaska, the largest state in the Union, is a land of <u>peerless</u> beauty and endless variety. The <u>topography</u> includes towering mountain peaks, broad plains, and deep fertile valleys. The long coastline is indented with glacier-made <u>fiords</u> and <u>sounds</u> of great depth. <u>Cataracts</u> of unpolluted water rush down steep <u>crags</u> to form swiftly flowing rivers, which could be harnessed to provide hydroelectric power for the growing population.

Prospectors discovered the first <u>bonanza</u> of underground wealth when they panned for gold along the Yukon River. The discovery of rich veins of gold was just a <u>harbinger</u> of more wealth, for sixty years later, in 1957, geologists discovered vast pools of oil on the Kenai Peninsula.

One of the <u>paradoxes</u> of this fascinating state is that, despite Alaska's short growing season, farmers harvest quantities of fruits and vegetables of unusual size and beauty. The reason is that, during the summer, the sun shines twenty hours a day. This brief review of facts about Alaska should <u>dispel</u> any belief that it is a frozen wasteland of little value.

EXERCISE B: Choosing Meanings. Use your guesses to complete the following questions. For each word, choose the definition that most closely matches the meaning of the word as it was used in the passage about Alaska. Then write the letter of the correct definition next to the appropriate number on your paper.

1. fiord
   (a) gentle slope
   (b) waterfall
   (c) narrow inlet
   (d) automobile

2. crag
   (a) rugged rock
   (b) disperse
   (c) rough
   (d) uneven

3. harbinger
   (a) dispel
   (b) herald
   (c) wide channel
   (d) surface map

4. bonanza
   (a) ponderosa
   (b) rugged rock
   (c) without equal
   (d) rich vein of ore

5. paradox
   (a) surface feature
   (b) disperse
   (c) contradiction
   (d) without equal

6. dispel
   (a) large waterfall
   (b) rich vein of ore
   (c) narrow inlet
   (d) drive away

7. sound
   (a) pond
   (b) waterfall
   (c) hear
   (d) channel

8. cataract
   (a) long inlet
   (b) large waterfall
   (c) narrow inlet
   (d) lake

9. topography (a) rugged rock   (b) handwriting
               (c) map of surface   (d) forecasters
                   features
10. peerless   (a) invisible   (b) unrivaled
               (c) rich vein of   (d) disperse
                   gold or silver

■ Using Context Clues in English Classes

The following paragraphs are similar to material you might find in a grammar book, composition book, or any textbook that gives general directions for producing different kinds of writing. The underlined words, however, are not restricted to use in the English classroom but frequently appear in magazine articles or in the daily newspaper.

Read the paragraphs and try to determine from the context what the underlined words mean. Jot down your guesses on a sheet of paper.

EXAMPLE:

Within the range of written underline discourse there are several identifiable kinds of writing. One type of writing is called underline expository because it explains ideas in logical sequence. Another kind, called a underline critique, analyzes the strengths and weaknesses of a specific work. A review of a play, book, or film is a critique.

One of the most useful and necessary forms of writing, particularly for the job-seeking student, is the underline résumé. The résumé must include a detailed account of the applicant's previous employment and educational background. underline Peripheral information should not be included. The résumé must not be underline ambiguous since exactness and underline verisimilitude are required. The writer should avoid underline hyperbole when describing his or her qualifications. The résumé should be typed if possible. If the résumé is handwritten, legible underline cursive writing in blue or black ink is acceptable. The applicant must include enough necessary information and details to interest the personnel director. Remember, the reader of the résumé is not underline omniscient.

EXERCISE C: Choosing Meanings. Use your guesses to complete the following questions. The new words you have learned are listed in the first column. Choose the meaning that does *not* apply to the word. Write the letter of the incorrect definition next to the appropriate number on your paper.

1. peripheral   (a) central   (b) incidental
                (c) nonessential   (d) unimportant

2. cursive
(a) flowing
(b) disconnected
(c) joined letters
(d) not discon-
nected

3. expository
(a) creative
(b) like exposi-
tion
(c) explanatory
(d) containing an
explanation

4. verisimilitude
(a) truth
(b) lie
(c) fact
(d) appearance of
reality

5. hyperbole
(a) exaggeration
(b) overstatement
(c) not meant
literally
(d) understatement

6. omniscient
(a) having lim-
ited wisdom
(b) wise
(d) all-knowing
(c) having infi-
nite knowl-
edge

7. critique
(a) act of
criticism
(b) art of criticism
(d) analysis
(c) reviewer

8. résumé
(a) expanded
fiction
(b) summary
(d) statement of
qualification
(c) summing up

9. ambiguous
(a) vague
(b) precise
(c) not clear
(d) indefinite

10. discourse
(a) lecture
(b) formal treatment
of a subject
(c) disconnected
(d) written treat-
ment of a subject

APPLICATION 1: Using Words Learned from Context Clues. In the preceding passages you have increased your vocabulary through the study of thirty new words. Using twelve of these words, write a review of a film or TV show you have seen or of a book you have read.

APPLICATION 2: Using More Words Learned from Context. Exchange papers from Application 1 with another student. Read the paper you now have and write a letter to the reviewer. You may agree or disagree with the review. In your letter try to use at least five of the new vocabulary words.

Using Structure 14.3

Learning vocabulary through context involves a guess based on common sense. Learning vocabulary through structure involves a guess based on a knowledge of word parts. Since the meanings of many of these parts come from Greek and Latin, they must be memorized to be useful.

There are three types of word parts that may be combined to form new words. A *root* (or root word) such as *-duct-* in *production* or *friend* in *unfriendly* is the main part of a word and the part that carries the basic meaning. A *prefix* such as *pro-* in *production* or *un-* in *unfriendly* is a word part at the beginning of a word that adds to or changes the meaning of the root. A *suffix* such as *-tion* in *production* or *-ly* in *unfriendly* is a word part at the end of a word that changes the meaning or part of speech of the root.

Learn the meanings of common prefixes, roots, and suffixes in order to improve both your vocabulary and your general reading comprehension.

There are hundreds of prefixes, roots, and suffixes that can be combined to make words. However, knowing just a few key members of each group will enable you to analyze the structure and, then, determine the meaning of hundreds of words that you would not have known otherwise.

■ Prefixes

While the following chart lists only twenty-five prefixes in the first column, the examples in the third column show you the basic way in which hundreds of words can be formed from just a few prefixes. Note also that a knowledge of the prefixes can help you guess the meaning of the words. If a prefix can be spelled in various ways, these spellings are listed in parentheses next to the prefix. The abbreviations L., Gr., and O.E. stand for Latin, Greek, and Old English, the languages from which the prefixes have come.

As you study the words, try to jot down at least one additional example of a word that uses each prefix.

TWENTY-FIVE COMMON PREFIXES

Prefix	Meaning	Examples
ab- (a-, abs-) [L.]	away, from	abolish, avert, abstract
ad- (ac-, af-, al-, ap-, as-, at-) [L.]	to, toward	adjoin, acknowledge, affix, allure, appoint, assure, attribute
anti- [Gr.]	against	antiaircraft
circum- [L.]	around, about, surrounding, on all sides	circumstance
com- (co-, col-, con-, cor-) [L.]	with, together	compress, cooperate, collaborate, contribute, correspond
de- [L.]	away from, off, down	decontrol, debase
dis- (di-, dif-) [L.]	away, apart, cause to be opposite of	disbelief, disconnect, divert, diffuse
epi- [Gr.]	upon, over, on the outside	epidermis
ex- (e-, ec-, ef-) [L.]	forth, from, out	express, emigrate, eccentric, effluent
in- (il-, im-, ir-) [L.]	not, "un-"	inhuman, illegal, impossible, irregular
in- (il-, im-, ir-) [L.]	in, into, within, on, toward	indent, illuminate, immigrate, irrigate
inter- [L.]	between	international
mis- [O.E.]	wrong	misplace
mono- [Gr.]	alone, one	monopoly
non- [L.]	not	nonsense
ob- (o-, oc-, of-, op-) [L.]	toward, against	object, omit, occasion, offer
over- [O.E.]	above, in excess	overflow
post- [L.]	after	postgraduate
pre- [L.]	before	prefix
pro- [L.]	forward, forth, favoring, in place of	produce, protract

re- [L.]	back, again	renew
semi- [L.]	half, partly	semicircle
sub- (suc-, suf-, sup-) [L.]	beneath, under, below	submarine, success, sufficient, suppress
trans- [L.]	across	transport
un- [O.E.]	not	unknown

EXERCISE A: Defining Words with Prefixes. For each of the following words, choose the definition that most closely matches the meaning of the word. You may refer to the chart for the meanings of the prefixes. Write the letter of the correct definition next to the appropriate number on your paper. Then check your guesses in a dictionary.

1. dissect   (a) shrink   (b) divert   (c) diminish   (d) cut apart

2. propitious   (a) favorable   (b) prayer   (c) suspicious   (d) favor

3. abrupt   (a) broken   (b) turned down   (c) interrupt   (d) sudden

4. epigraph   (a) a motto at the beginning of a book   (b) something delayed for a long time   (c) a mistake made in writing   (d) a means of sending messages

5. prerequisite   (a) something needed after something else   (b) something needed before something else   (c) something not needed at all   (d) something desired but not essential

6. effluent   (a) coming together   (b) growing within   (c) wealthy   (d) flowing from

7. circumnavigate   (a) swim around   (b) sail toward   (c) sail around   (d) sail away

8. monoplane   (a) a tool for sanding   (b) an aircraft with one pair of wings

	(c) a field with a single figure in the distance	(d) a dull tone of voice
9. interpose	(a) withdraw (c) insert	(b) suppose (d) repose
10. antidisestab- lishmentarian	(a) a person against changing an established institution (c) a book written against a new idea	(b) a person in favor of changing an established institution (d) a book written in favor of establishing something new

■ Roots

Since roots carry the basic meaning of the word, they are the foundation of vocabulary development. To know the meaning of one root is to know the central, shared meaning of all the words built on that root. If, for example, you know that the root -*ten*-, with its different spellings shown in the following chart, means "to hold" or "to contain," you can be sure that all the words built on that root share that meaning. You can probably think of quite a list—*continent, detain, continue, tenure, entertain*—without trying very hard.

Like many roots, -*ten*- needs a prefix or a suffix to complete its meaning. Other roots, such as *act, form,* and *line,* can stand alone as a word or can be joined to prefixes (*inter*act, *re*form) or suffixes (act*ion,* line*age*) or both (*re*act*ionary, de*line*ation*).

Most of the twenty-five roots you will be working with here are derived from Latin. Most of them, like the root -*ten*-, need a prefix or suffix in order to work as a word. Such a root is called a *bound root*. Roots that can stand alone are called *free roots*.

As you study the roots in the following chart, try once again to think of at least one additional example for each item. When you are trying to memorize word parts, the best examples are generally those you provide yourself.

TWENTY-FIVE COMMON ROOTS

Root	Meaning	Examples
-cap- (-capt-, -cept-, -ceipt-, -ceive-, -cip-) [L.]	to take, seize	capable, captivate, accept, receipt, receive, recipient
-ced- (-ceed-, -cess-) [L.]	to go, yield	procedure, proceed, success
-dic- (-dict-) [L.]	to say, point out in words	indicate, edict
-duc- (-duce-, -duct-) [L.]	to lead	produce, reduce, conduct
-fac- (-fact-, -fec-, -fect-, -fic-) [L.]	to do, make	facsimile, manufacture, infection, defect, fiction
-fer- [L.]	to bring, carry	transfer, inference
-graph- [Gr.]	to write	autograph
-ject- [L.]	to throw	reject
-leg- (-log-) [Gr.]	to say, speak	legal, logic
-mit- (-mis-) [L.]	to send	admit, transmission
-mov- (-mot-) [L.]	to move	movement, motion
-plic- (-pli-, -ploy-, -ply-) [L.]	to fold	duplicate, pliable, employ, reply
-pon- (-pos-) [L.]	to put, place	postpone, depose
-puls- (-pel-) [L.]	to drive	pulsate, propel
-quir- (-ques-, -quis-) [L.]	to ask, say	inquire, question, inquisitive
-scrib- (-script-) [L.]	to write	describe, prescription
-sist- [L.]	to stand	insist
-spec- (-spect-) [L.]	to see	specimen, inspect
-string- (-strict-) [L.]	to bind, tighten	stringent, constrict
-ten- (-tain-, -tin-) [L.]	to hold, contain	tenure, detain, continent
-tend- (-tens-, -tent-) [L.]	to stretch	distend, extension, extent
-vad- (-vas-) [L.]	to go	invade, evasive
-ven- (-vent-) [L.]	to come	convene, inventor
-vert- (-vers-) [L.]	to turn	divert, subversive
-vid- (-vis-) [L.]	to see	evident, vision

EXERCISE B: Using Roots to Define Words. Copy the following words in the first column onto your paper, and underline the root in each. Then match each word with its meaning in the second column. Write the letter of the correct definition next to the appropriate number on your paper. Then check your guesses in a dictionary.

1. proficient	a. to give, grant, bestow
2. recessive	b. tending to or leading to
3. prologue	c. highly competent
4. captivate	d. tending to move back
5. confer	e. the act of holding forth a claim to something
6. conducive	
7. deploy	f. to move something to a different place
8. requisite	g. to capture the attention or affection of
9. pretension	h. an introduction to a speech or written work
10. transpose	
	i. to spread out
	j. something essential or demanded again and again
	k. tending to move in circles
	l. a conclusion to a speech or written work
	m. to hire for a job

■ Suffixes

As you know, a suffix is a syllable or group of syllables joined to the end of a word to form a new word. Some such word endings indicate simple grammatical changes in words without changing the part of speech. The endings *-s* and *-es*, for example, are used to form noun plurals (*window, windows, church, churches*). The endings *-er* and *-est* indicate degrees of comparison in modifiers (*tall, taller, tallest*). The endings *-ed* and *-ing* show a change in verb form (*walk, walked, walking*). However, the word endings you will study here have a somewhat different function. They change the meaning and, usually, the part of speech of the words to which they are added.

The following chart lists twenty common suffixes, which, like the prefixes studied earlier in the section, come from Latin, Greek, and Old English. In the third column, note the part of speech formed by each ending and again try to supply additional examples of your own.

TWENTY COMMON SUFFIXES

Suffix	Meaning and Examples	Part of Speech
-able (-ible) [L.]	capable of being; tending to: reliable, edible	adjective
-ac (-ic) [Gr.]	characteristic of; relating to: maniac, scenic	noun or adjective
-ance (-ence) [L.]	the act of; the quality or state of being: clearance, confidence	noun
-ant (-ent) [L.]	that shows, has, or does; a person or thing that shows, has, or does: defiant, servant, dependent	adjective or noun
-ate [L.]	making, applying, or operating on: decorate, activate	verb
-ful [O.E.]	full of; characterized by; having the ability or tendency to: scornful	noun or adjective
-fy [L.]	to make; to cause to become; to cause to have: clarify	verb
-ish [O.E.]	of or belonging to; rather; tending to: foolish	adjective
-ism [Gr.]	the act, practice, or result of; characteristic of the theory of: terrorism, communism	noun
-ist [Gr.]	a person who does or makes; a person skilled in; a believer in: violinist	noun
-ity [L.]	state of being; character; condition of: intensity	noun
-ive [L.]	tending to; a person: selective, objective, detective	adjective or noun
-ize (-ise) [Gr.]	to make: idolize, improvise	verb
-less [O.E.]	without; lacking: careless, ageless	adjective
-ly [O.E.]	in a certain way; at a certain time or place: harshly, hourly	adverb or adjective

-ment [L.]	result or product of: improvement, amazement	noun
-ness [O.E.]	state of being; quality: laziness	noun
-or [L.]	a person or thing that; a quality or condition that: spectator	noun
-ous (-ious) [L.]	marked by; given to: pompous, mysterious	adjective
-tion (ion, -sion, -ation, -ition) [L.]	the action of; the state of being: action, mission	noun

EXERCISE C: **Adding Suffixes.** To each of the following words, add a suffix to form a word that matches the part of speech listed in the third column. If you are uncertain of any spelling changes, consult your dictionary.

Word	Present Part of Speech	New Part of Speech to be Created
1. defect	noun	adjective
2. attend	verb	noun
3. induce	verb	noun
4. defense	noun	adjective
5. perfection	noun	noun
6. postpone	verb	noun
7. limit	noun	adjective
8. intense	adjective	adverb
9. material	noun	verb
10. confide	verb	adjective

APPLICATION: **Using Structure to Form New Words.** Professor James I. Brown at the University of Minnesota has found that the twenty prefixes and fourteen roots found in the following fourteen words can be combined to make over fourteen thousand relatively common English words. All of the prefixes and roots are among those you have studied in this section. Combine the prefixes and roots in the chart to make at least twenty new words, adding whatever suffixes you wish. Then write a short definition of each word you write, using the meaning of each part to arrive at the meaning of the new word. Check your meanings in the dictionary and then compare your list with those of your classmates to see how many words you came up with altogether.

Words	*Prefixes*	*Roots*
1. precept	pre-	-cap-
2. detain	de-	-ten-
3. intermittent	inter-	-mit-
4. offer	ob-	-fer-
5. insist	in-	-sist-
6. monograph	mono-	-graph-
7. epilogue	epi-	-leg-
8. aspect	ad-	-spec-
9. uncomplicated	un- com-	-plic-
10. nonextended	non- ex-	-tend-
11. reproduction	re- pro-	-duc-
12. indisposed	in- dis-	-pon-
13. oversufficient	over- sub-	-fac-
14. mistranscribe	mis- trans-	-scrib-

Chapter 15

Spelling Improvement

Ever since you started school, you have studied many spelling rules and have tried to memorize the spelling of thousands of words. Like most people, however, you probably still misspell some words when you write. The purpose of the first section in this chapter is to give you the editing and study skills you need to reduce the number of carelessly misspelled words in your written work. The purpose of the second section is to give you the materials needed to review basic rules. Linguists have discovered that the spelling is regular for eighty-five percent of the words in the English language. That means that these words follow definite patterns in the way they are spelled. By focusing on the rules that govern these patterns, you will be able to master the spelling of thousands of words.

15.1 Techniques for Improving Spelling

Perhaps the best way to improve your spelling is to proofread your own written work regularly, using a dictionary to correct any misspelled words. As you begin your proofreading, you will probably find that you are consistently misspelling the same words. This section will provide you with methods of learning those words. It will also give you a short diagnostic test that will allow you to check your basic understanding of the spelling rules presented in the next section.

■ Methods of Learning Words

Once you have identified a misspelled word and entered it in a special spelling section of your notebook, your next step is to learn to spell the word correctly.

Set aside a special section of your notebook for listing words that you find difficult to spell. Then use one or more of the following techniques to study and review the words.

Using a Dictionary to Gain Greater Understanding. A dictionary can be a great asset not only for the spelling of the words you are studying, but also for other information that may help you remember the words. The pronunciation of a word, for example, may show you that you have overlooked a syllable or a sound through carelessness or that you have added a syllable that does not belong. The origin of a word may reveal that you have neglected to double a letter because you did not realize that the word consisted of a prefix and root—*misstate* = *mis-* + *-state*, for example.

The meaning of a word may also offer a clue to your spelling error. There are many words in English that sound similar and that are easily confused. Checking the meaning may reveal that you mistook one word in such a pair for another.

Conducting Regular Review Sessions. Regular review sessions, conducted in a systematic way, can help you master a number of words. When studying the list of problem words in your notebook, you may find the steps in the following chart helpful.

STEPS FOR REVIEWING PROBLEM WORDS

1. *Look* at each word carefully. Observe the arrangement and pattern of letters in the word. For example, look at the word *moccasin*. Notice that there are two *c*'s and only one *s* in the word. Try to *see* the word in your mind.

2. *Pronounce* the word to yourself, making sure you pronounce each syllable. For example, pronounce *athletic*. Notice that there are only three syllables: *ath•let•ic*.

3. *Write* each word and then *check* to see that you have spelled it correctly.

4. *Review* your list of problem words until you can write each one correctly.

Using Memory Aids. A number of tricks can be used to help you remember the spelling of particularly difficult problem words, especially those that do not seem to follow any rules at all. One trick is to look for a familiar word within the problem word.

EXAMPLES: arctic   There is an *arc* in the *arc*tic.

criticize   If you *critic*ize, you're a *critic*.

principal   Can a princi*pal* be a *pal*?

twelfth   Look for the *elf* in tw*elf*th.

Another way to memorize the spelling of problem words is to associate the letters in one word with the letters in a related word.

EXAMPLES: capitol   A d*o*me is often part of a capit*o*l building. (Both words have an *o*.)

calendar   You look up d*a*tes on a calen*da*r. (Both words are spelled with *da*.)

Checking Spelling Demons. Spelling demons are words that cause problems for most or all people who use the English language. Some of these words are spelled according to rules. Others follow no special rules.

As you look over the following list, check to see how many of the words you can spell correctly using the Look, Pronounce, Write, and Review method described on page 421. Any words you are not sure of can be added to the list in your notebook. You are likely to find that the list of common problems will help you identify many of your own problem areas.

COMMON SPELLING DEMONS

abbreviate	congratulate	financial	prairie
absence	conscience	foreign	precede
accidentally	conscientious	grammar	preferable
accommodate	conscious	guarantee	preparation
accumulate	contemporary	handkerchief	privilege
achieve	continuous	hygiene	probably
acquaintance	controversial	immigrant	procedure
adjective	convenience	incorrigible	proceed
admittance	coolly	independence	prompt
adolescence	cordially	indigestion	pronunciation
advertisement	correspondence	inflammable	protein
aerial	counterfeit	initial	psychology
aerosol	courageous	inoculate	really
aggressive	courtesy	interfere	recede

aisle	criticism	irrelevant	receipt
allowance	criticize	journal	recommend
all right	curiosity	judicial	reference
amateur	curious	knowledge	rehearse
ambassador	deceive	laboratory	repetition
analysis	defendant	lawyer	restaurant
analyze	deficient	legitimate	rhythm
anecdote	delinquent	library	ridiculous
anniversary	desert	license	scissors
anonymous	despair	lieutenant	secretary
anxiety	desperate	lightning	separate
appearance	dessert	loneliness	sergeant
apprentice	development	maintenance	similar
argument	dining	mathematics	sincerely
assassinate	disappear	meanness	sophomore
athletic	disappoint	mediocre	souvenir
attendance	disastrous	merchandise	spaghetti
awkward	discern	meteor	straight
banquet	disciple	mileage	substitute
barrel	dissatisfied	millionaire	succeed
behavior	distinction	misspell	superintendent
believe	distinguish	mortgage	supersede
beneficial	doubt	naturally	surprise
benefited	earnest	necessary	suspicious
bicycle	economical	neighbor	syllable
bookkeeper	efficient	ninety	technique
bulletin	eighth	nuclear	technology
bureau	eligible	nuisance	temperament
business	embarrass	occasion	temperature
calendar	emergency	occasionally	temporary
cancel	equipped	occur	tenant
capital	enemy	occurred	thorough
capitol	envelope	omitted	tomatoes
captain	environment	opinion	tomorrow
career	equivalent	pamphlet	tragedy
carriage	exaggerate	parallel	truly
category	exceed	paralyze	twelfth
cemetery	exercise	particularly	unanimous
census	exhaust	permanent	unforgettable

changcable	exhibit	permissible	unnecessary
chauffeur	exhilarate	personally	vaccine
clothes	existence	perspiration	vacuum
colonel	explanation	physician	vegetable
column	extension	pigeon	villain
committee	extraordinary	pneumonia	vitamin
comparative	familiar	pollution	Wednesday
competitor	fantasy	possess	weird
concede	fascinate	possession	whether
condemn	February		

EXERCISE A: Spelling Problem Words Correctly. Write the following words on your paper, filling in the missing letters. Then check each word in the dictionary and enter any words you have misspelled in your notebook.

1. cen __ us
2. compar __ tive
3. exhil __ rate
4. mor __ gage
5. desp __ rate

6. econom __ cal
7. congra __ ulate
8. merchandi __ e
9. for __ __ gn
10. en __ my

■ Diagnosing Problem Areas

Many of the words in Exercise A are troublesome words that must simply be memorized. The words found in the following diagnostic test, however, are all examples of specific rules that you can learn to help overcome spelling problems. By taking the test and correcting it, you will be able to pinpoint specific areas where your spelling skills are weak. An analysis of these areas will indicate which of the basic spelling rules in Section 15.2 you will need to concentrate on.

Recognize areas in which your knowledge of basic spelling rules is weak and make a special effort to master the rules involved.

To take the following diagnostic test, read each sentence and then write the word that will correctly complete the sentence. Exercise B will show you how to analyze any errors you make, using the keyed items to the right of each sentence.

1. The accident _____ in front of the library. [Basic Rules for Suffixes]
   (a) occurred   (b) occured   (c) ocurred

2. I have difficulty _____ for Mr. Blank's exams. [Basic Rules for Suffixes]
   (a) studying   (b) studiing   (c) studing

3. How many _____ did you buy? [Basic Rules for Plurals]
   (a) tomatos   (b) tomatoes   (c) tomattos

4. The student was _____ about completing the assignment. [Special Rules for Confusing Suffixes]
   (a) conscientious   (b) conscienteous   (c) consientious

5. Kim couldn't _____ me with that big smile. [ie/ei Rule]
   (a) deceive   (b) decieve   (c) deseave

6. The story of the sudden cure was almost _____ . [Basic Rules for Suffixes and ie/ei Rule]
   (a) unbelieveable   (b) unbelievable   (c) unbeleivable

7. They had fond _____ of their graduation day. [Basic Rules for Plurals]
   (a) memories   (b) memorys   (c) memorries

8. Do you have a good _____ ? [Special Rules for Confusing Suffixes]
   (a) vocabulery   (b) vocabulary   (c) vocabullary

9. The moon is _____ tonight. [Basic Rules for Suffixes]
   (a) shining   (b) shinning   (c) shineing

10. How many words have you _____ ? [Basic Rules for Prefixes]
    (a) mispelled   (b) mispeled   (c) misspelled

EXERCISE B: Analyzing Your Spelling Errors. Correct your test by referring to the keyed items. Look up that particular rule in Section 15.2. Then analyze your errors in terms of the rules involved, and decide which of the rules in Section 15.2 you need to spend the most time with.

APPLICATION: Using Problem Words. Pick one of the rules you will need to review as a result of the analysis you conducted in Exercise B. Make a list of words that follow this rule and add any other words in your spelling notebook that follow the same rule. Then write a short paragraph about your favorite school activity using as many of the words as possible.

15.2 A Catalog of Spelling Rules

Learning the rules in this section will not only improve your spelling but will also save you time. Once you have mastered all of these rules, you will seldom have to stop to think about when to use *ei* or *ie*, how to form the plural of *waltz*, how to add the prefix *mis-* to the word *spell*, or when to change *y* to *i* before a suffix. Although you can profit from a thorough study of all of the rules, you may wish to concentrate on those that you diagnosed as your problem areas in the previous section.

■ Using the *ie* and *ei* Rule

Many people, when confronted with the need to spell words such as *receive* or *conceited*, probably think of the following well-known rule.

> Write *i* before *e*
> Except after *c*,
> Or when sounded like *a*
> As in *neighbor* and *weigh*.

While this rule applies to many words, there are a few exceptions that should be learned. For example, the following list contains some words in which you must write *e* before *i* even though the words do not have a *c* or the long *a* sound.

EXCEPTIONS:

counterfeit	height	seize
either	weird	their
foreign	neither	leisure

There are also a few words that follow a different rule.

When *c* is pronounced *sh*, the *i* comes before the *e*.

EXAMPLES: ancient efficient

conscience sufficient

EXERCISE A: Spelling *ie* and *ei* Words. Complete each of the *ie* and *ei* words in the following paragraph by inserting the missing letters in the correct order. To be sure of your spelling, check each word in the dictionary.

Even at the (1) h ____ ght of (2) th ____ r (3) ach ____ vements, the (4) ____ ght athletes (5) consc ____ ntiously practiced every day. Each of them (6) bel ____ ved (7) th ____ r (8) r ____ gn as champions would be (9) br ____ f if they were (10) conc ____ ted enough to think they could stay on top without hard work.

■ Making Spelling Changes to Form Plurals

One simple rule covers most noun plurals.

The plurals of most nouns can be formed by adding *-s* or *-es*.

The following chart summarizes the major types of choices and changes that must be made to form regular plurals.

CHOICES AND SPELLING CHANGES WHEN FORMING PLURALS			
Noun Ending	**Rule**	**Examples**	**Exceptions**
s, x, z, sh, ch	Add *-es*.	dresses, taxes, waltzes, wishes, benches	
o preceded by a consonant	Add *-es*.	toma*to*es	Musical terms: solos, banjos
o preceded by a vowel	Just add *-s*.	rode*o*s	
y preceded by a consonant	Change *y* to *i* and add *-es*.	canar*i*es, sk*i*es	
y preceded by a vowel	Just add *-s*.	ke*y*s, buo*y*s	

Some nouns that end in *-f* or *-fe*, such as *chief*, form plurals by adding *-s (chiefs)*, while others, such as *leaf*, change the *-f* to *-v* and add *-es (leaves)*. Still others have two correct forms *(hoofs, hooves)*. In addition, there are nouns that form the plural in irregular ways. Some of these are *ox, oxen; crisis, crises; medium, media*. Finally, a few nouns such as *deer* and *trout* do not change at all from singular to plural. If you are unsure of how to form a plural, always check a dictionary. If no plural form is given in the dictionary, simply add *-s* or *-es* to the singular form.

NOTE ABOUT OTHER SPECIAL PLURALS: When you are forming the plural of a compound word that is written as two or more separate or hyphenated words, pluralize the word that is being modified.

EXAMPLES: rule of thumb   rules of thumb

editor-in-chief   editors-in-chief

Note also that an apostrophe is used to form the plurals of letters, numbers, symbols, and words used as words, as explained in Section 13.7.

EXERCISE B: Forming Plurals. Make each of the following words plural. If you are unsure of the spelling of a word, check a dictionary.

1. radio
2. soprano
3. wife
4. fox
5. supply

6. lynx
7. chief
8. attorney-at-law
9. crisis
10. X-ray

■ Adding Prefixes to Roots

As you may recall, adding a prefix does not affect the spelling of the root.

When a prefix is added to a word, the spelling of the root word remains the same.

EXAMPLES: mis + spell = misspell

un + necessary =unnecessary

re + form = reform

For more examples of roots with prefixes added, you can refer to the chart on pages 412 and 413 in Section 14.3. Notice also the way in which certain prefixes in the chart change their spelling when they are joined to certain roots. The spelling of the prefix may change but the root remains the same.

EXAMPLES: *com-* becomes *cor-* before *respond: correspond*

in- becomes *im-* before *mortal: immortal*

EXERCISE C: Spelling Words with Prefixes. Form new words by combining the following seven prefixes with the ten roots. Remember that you may have to change the form of the prefix. Notice also that some of the roots can be used with more than one of the prefixes.

ad-, circum-, com-, in-, mis-, per-, pro-

1. -legal
2. -plex
3. -prove
4. -file
5. -operate

6. -pact
7. -mise
8. -reverent
9. -chief
10. -stance

■ Adding Suffixes to Roots

Suffixes are somewhat more difficult to add than prefixes because the letters in the root must occasionally be changed.

Become familiar with spelling changes that sometimes occur before a suffix is added.

The spelling of a word to which a suffix has been added is influenced by two things: (1) the ending of the word before the suffix and (2) the beginning letter of the suffix. The following chart summarizes the major situations in which the spelling of a root is changed before the addition of a suffix.

SPELLING CHANGES BEFORE SUFFIXES

Word Ending	Suffix Added	Rule	Exceptions
consonant +y (ply, happy)	most suffixes (able, ly)	Change y to i. pliable, happily	Most suffixes beginning with i: ply becomes plying hobby becomes hobbyist
vowel+y (annoy, play)	most suffixes (ance, ful)	Make no change. annoyance, playful	A few short words: day becomes daily gay becomes gaiety
any word ending in e (move, drive)	suffix beginning with a vowel (able, ing)	Drop the final e. movable, driving	1. Words ending in *ce* or *ge* with suffixes beginning in *a* or *o*: trace becomes traceable courage becomes courageous 2. Words ending in *ee* or *oe*: agree becomes agreeing toe becomes toeing 3. A few special words: dye becomes dyeing be becomes being
any word ending in e (peace, brave)	suffix beginning with a consonant (ful, ly)	Make no change. peaceful, bravely	A few special words: true becomes truly awe becomes awful argue becomes argument judge becomes judgment
consonant + vowel + consonant in a stressed syllable (mud', submit')	suffix beginning with a vowel (y, ed)	Double the final consonant. mud'dy, submit'ted	1. Words ending in *x* or *w*: row' becomes row'ing mix' becomes mix'ing 2. Words in which the stress changes after the suffix is added: refer' + ing becomes refer'ring BUT refer' + ence becomes ref'erence
consonant + vowel + consonant in an unstressed syllable (an'gel, fi'nal)	suffix beginning with a vowel (ic, ist)	Make no change. angel'ic, fi'nalist	No major exceptions

EXERCISE D: Spelling Words with Suffixes. Write the correct spelling for each of the following words on your paper.

1. retire + -ment
2. loyal + -ist
3. confer + -ence
4. hurry + -ing
5. rebel + -ion

6. comply + -ance
7. appear + -ance
8. convey + -or
9. abbreviate + -ion
10. imagine + -ary

■ Working with Confusing Groups of Suffixes

In some cases, recognizing the need for a spelling change before a suffix solves only part of the problem. There are a few groups of suffixes that sound very similar but are spelled differently. The paragraphs that follow will help you to distinguish between such confusing suffixes and to identify common words in which each occurs.

Learn to distinguish between confusing groups of suffixes.

-able, -ible. One particularly confusing pair of endings is made up of the suffixes *-able* and *-ible*. There are rules governing the use of these endings, but the rules depend on a knowledge of Latin verbs. To learn the spelling of some of the most common words using these endings, you can study the following lists. If you have any doubt about the proper ending, you should check a dictionary.

Common Words Ending In *-able*		Common Words Ending In *-ible*	
acceptable	imaginable	accessible	irresistible
advisable	inflammable	convertible	permissible
available	irritable	digestible	possible
believable	memorable	edible	responsible
capable	peaceable	eligible	reversible
comfortable	predictable	flexible	sensible
considerable	probable	horrible	terrible
dependable	reasonable	incredible	
desirable	reliable		
durable	taxable		

-ance (-ant) and -ence (-ent). These suffixes travel in pairs. If a noun has the *a* spelling (*elegance*), you can be quite sure that the corresponding adjective will as well (*elegant*). The same applies for nouns and adjectives with the *e* spelling (*adherence* and *adherent*).

The basic problem is knowing which spelling to use after which roots. The most helpful thing to remember is that words containing a "hard" *c* or *g* sound usually end with the *a* spelling: *arrogance*, *litigant*. Those with a "soft" *c* or *g* sound will usually have the *e* spelling: *emergence*, *deficient*. There are many -*ance* and -*ence* words, however, that do not contain soft or hard *c* or *g* sounds. To learn the spelling of some of these words, study the following lists.

Common Words Ending In -*ance*		Common Words Ending In -*ence*	
abundance	defiance	absence	excellence
acquaintance	importance	convenience	independence
appearance	radiance	correspondence	patience
brilliance	tolerance	difference	presence

-ary, -ery. Any problems you may have in deciding whether to spell a word with the ending -*ary* or -*ery* can generally be solved quite easily. As you can see from the following list, there are not many words that end in -*ery*.

COMMON WORDS ENDING IN -*ery*	
cemetery	nursery
distillery	scenery
millinery	stationery (note paper)
monastery	winery

If you learn the common -*ery* words, you will know that most other words with an ending that sounds similar will have the -*ary* spelling. If you have any doubt about whether a word ends in -*ary* or -*ery*, you can check the spelling in the dictionary.

-cy and -sy. Only a handful of English words end with -*sy*. If you learn those in the following chart, you can be reasonably safe in using *-cy* for the others. When in doubt, however, be sure to consult a dictionary.

COMMON WORDS ENDING IN *-sy*	
autopsy	epilepsy
biopsy	fantasy
courtesy	heresy
curtsy	hypocrisy
ecstasy	idiosyncrasy
embassy	pleurisy

-eous, -ious, -uous. Confusion sometimes arises over the spelling of words ending in *-eous*, *-ious*, and *-uous*. Some of this confusion can be resolved by paying strict attention to the pronunciation of the word. The words ending in *-uous*, for example, can be easily distinguished from the others if they are pronounced carefully. The following are the most common of these words.

COMMON WORDS ENDING IN *-uous*	
ambiguous	ingenuous
conspicuous	strenuous
continuous	sumptuous
fatuous	

Deciding whether to use *-eous* or *-ious* is more difficult, since pronunciation does not help you. In this case, it may be more helpful to memorize the spelling of some of the most common words in these two groups.

Common Words Ending in *-eous*		Common Words Ending in *-ious*	
advantageous	gorgeous	anxious	ingenious
beauteous	miscellaneous	cautious	laborious
courageous	outrageous	conscientious	precious
courteous	righteous	conscious	rebellious
erroneous	simultaneous	contagious	religious
		delicious	superstitious

-ify and -efy. As with many of the other pairs you have seen, one of these is much more common than the other. In this case, *-efy* is rarely used except for the four words in the following chart.

COMMON WORDS ENDING IN *-efy*	
liquefy	rarefy
putrefy	stupefy

EXERCISE E: Writing Words with Confusing Endings. Write each of the following words on your paper, filling in the blank(s) with the correct letter(s).

1. court __ __ __ s
2. caut __ __ __ s
3. convert __ ble
4. bound __ ry
5. liqu __ fy

6. irresist __ ble
7. hypocri __ y
8. correspond __ nce
9. stren __ __ __ s
10. gorg __ __ __ s

APPLICATION: Using Spelling Rules in Writing Sentences. Write as many sentences of your own as you need in order to include each of the following items. Use at least one plural noun in each sentence.

1. Three words spelled with *ei* or *ie*
2. Three words with prefixes
3. Six words with suffixes—one following each rule in the chart on page 430

UNIT

STUDY SKILLS

16
Basic Study Skills

17
Test-Taking Skills

18
Library and Reference Skills

16

Basic Study Skills

One of your main goals as a student should be to learn to study effectively. Good study habits often lead to a higher quality of work, better grades, greater self-confidence, and more free time. In addition, employers and college admissions directors are particularly interested in students who know how to use their time efficiently.

Some of the study skills that you can profit from practicing and developing are listening comprehension, oral participation, note-taking, and outlining. This chapter will discuss how to determine what your current study skills are and how to acquire new skills that will enable you to learn more quickly and easily.

16.1 Studying, Listening, and Speaking

When you work to improve your study skills, you should think both about the ones you already have that work well for you and about the ones you would like to acquire. You should discover the way you learn best and consider the amount of time you have to devote to studying. You should also try to develop a systematic approach to studying.

This section provides suggestions for self-evaluation, for gaining more from listening, and for learning to participate more effectively in class.

■ Evaluating Your Study Skills

Study skills are methods of taking in information, organizing time and ideas, approaching and carrying out assignments and tests, and improving your understanding and retention of information. Study skills can help you learn. Throughout your years in school, you have probably already developed a number of study skills. Evaluating your skills from time to time will tell you which skills you still need to develop or improve.

Evaluate your current study skills to determine which skills you have and which skills you still need to develop.

The following checklist can be used in evaluating your study habits.

CHECKLIST FOR STUDY SKILLS
1. Do you record all of your assignments and keep track of those which you have completed?
2. Do you plan your study time for each day and each week to enable you to balance your schoolwork with other commitments?
3. Do you maintain an organized notebook so that you can easily find notes from all your classes?
4. Do you take neat, clear, useful notes, labeled with the date and the topic?
5. Do you review your notes several times a week, particularly before tests?
6. Do you mentally (or in writing) summarize what you are trying to learn from your reading?
7. Do you try to predict questions that will be on exams based on material covered in class and readings, and do you study by trying to answer these questions?

If more than half of these practices are part of your regular approach to studying, you have already internalized some valuable study habits. If you do not follow many of these practices, however, you should work on them a few at a time. For example, you might begin to maintain an assignment book or set aside a few minutes several times a week to review notes from your different classes. With time and hard work, you can turn these basic skills into habits and concentrate on more complex study skills.

EXERCISE A: Developing Study Skills. Choose three skills listed in the preceding chart to practice. Plan to spend a week developing each skill. For each skill you select, briefly describe *how* and *when* you plan to work on the skill. For example, you might decide to work on summarizing your reading. After reading a section or chapter in a textbook, you might list the main ideas in a few sentences. At the end of the week you would have summaries to remind you of the important points in your reading assignments.

■ Listening Skills

Listening is probably the least practiced study skill. It requires concentration, which can be aided by summarizing the speaker's ideas, predicting the speaker's next point, questioning the speaker's ideas, and note-taking. If you fail to use these four related skills, you may be just hearing rather than listening.

> Listen actively by summarizing information in your mind, predicting what the speaker will say, questioning what the speaker is saying, and taking notes.

Since you will often be tested on material presented in class, listening skills are important. As a means of gaining information, listening may seem easier than reading, but listening actually requires concentration and effort. Because you can take in ideas almost three times as fast as most people can speak, your thoughts may wander. If your concentration fades, you may begin to daydream. For this reason, you should learn ways to focus on the speaker's message.

Whenever you listen you should organize the information in your mind. The ability to distinguish main ideas, major details, minor details, and extra information can help you. A main idea is a point that the speaker emphasizes and supports with additional information. Major details illustrate, explain, or develop main ideas. Minor details illustrate, explain, or develop major details. Summarizing, predicting, questioning, and note-taking can all help you to concentrate on these important ideas.

By summarizing while you listen, you can train yourself to listen for the key points. To summarize you should concentrate on main ideas. Learn to select the most important information from all of the ideas the speaker mentions. Mentally sort out the important from the less important information. In your mind review these main ideas in a running summary.

A second way to improve your listening ability is to practice predicting what the speaker will say next, based on information he or she has already given. Trying to predict forces you to pay close attention to the speaker's ideas and gives you no time for your mind to wander.

Another way to encourage active listening is to ask or jot down questions or relevant points that occur to you as you are listening. By asking a question, you are helping to clarify information for yourself as well as for the entire class. You are more likely to listen carefully and to retain information if you prepare yourself to talk about the topic or to pose a relevant question about it.

A fourth way to become an active listener is to take notes. Note-taking is probably the best way to train yourself to listen. As you attempt to capture the important parts of the message, you will be forcing yourself to listen for main ideas and major details. Section 16.2 explains ways to adapt your note-taking according to the information to which you are listening.

In addition to these four methods for becoming an active listener, you can also try the suggestions in the following chart.

SUGGESTIONS FOR BECOMING A GOOD LISTENER

1. Tune out distractions by focusing on the speaker as soon as he or she begins talking.
2. Concentrate on the speaker's words and not on his or her appearance or mannerisms.
3. Do not overact to emotional words; reserve judgment until the end of the presentation.
4. Try to connect the speaker's main ideas and major details in your mind in some sort of a pattern, perhaps using the image of a ladder or a wheel with spokes to group the ideas.
5. Listen for transitional words and phrases that signal the speaker's emphasis of an idea, introduction of a new step or topic, or conclusion: *most important, in addition,* and *finally,* for example.

EXERCISE B: Developing Listening Skills. Listen to a speech or editorial on radio or television on a topic such as sports, politics, international affairs, or community issues. The speech should be at least three minutes long. While you listen, mentally summarize the speaker's main ideas and try to predict the ideas the speaker will cover next. When the speech or editorial is finished, jot down a summary of what you heard. List any questions you would ask the speaker if you could. Also, list any comments or observations you would make to the speaker if you could.

EXERCISE C: Practicing Listening Skills in Class. Choose one listening skill that you particularly want to practice, such as mentally summarizing the speaker's main ideas, linking the speaker's main ideas and major details in a pattern in your mind, or jotting down questions you want to ask in response to a lecture. Then choose one class in which to work on this skill. After a week of practice, briefly describe your progress in developing the listening skill you chose.

■ Speaking Skills

Oral participation in class is an important part of learning. Once you have made a statement or expressed an opinion, you are actively involved. Participation also helps reinforce your understanding of the material, enabling you to recall the information later during tests.

Become a more involved learner by asking and answering questions and contributing to class discussions.

Most teachers base a fair portion of your total report card grade on your class participation. They feel that students who actively speak out in class show interest in the subject, prepare more for class, and gain a better understanding of the material than students who are silent.

Speaking in class discussions makes use of and reinforces at least four important skills. It involves the ability *to answer questions* asked by the teacher or by another student. It involves the ability *to ask questions* when the information is not clear or when you need additional information. It also involves the ability *to form and offer opinions* on the subject under discussion. Finally, it involves the ability *to add relevant information* that might further the discussion and increase other students' understanding.

Few of these skills are easily learned. Many people fear giving an incorrect response and appearing foolish in front of classmates. However, teachers usually appreciate students who make the effort to contribute ideas and get involved. Moreover, the more practice you have in participating, the easier it will be for you to raise your hand to ask or answer a question.

As you work on increasing your participation in class, try some of the suggestions in the following chart.

SUGGESTIONS FOR IMPROVING YOUR PARTICIPATION IN CLASS
1. Set goals for yourself; try to participate at least once in each class discussion.
2. List questions or comments that come to mind as the teacher lectures.
3. Make statements in complete sentences whenever possible.
4. Pose questions that ask not only for an explanation of information but for additional information as well.
5. Complete additional readings so that you will be able to make significant contributions to the discussion.
6. Listen carefully to what other people are saying so that you will not repeat what they say.
7. Base opinions that you give on specific information or examples.
8. Try to keep your comments as brief and to the point as possible.

Participating in class is a skill that you will need not only in school, but also in many areas of your adult life. It will prepare you to speak up at career-related meetings, political functions, and recreational activities. It will also make your day-to-day communication with people easier as well as give you greater confidence.

EXERCISE D: Determining the Importance of Oral Participation in Your School. Conduct a survey by consulting at least ten teachers in your school. Ask them to approximate what percentage of a student's grade is based on oral participation in class. Prepare a chart showing the findings of your survey.

EXERCISE E: Setting Goals for Oral Participation. Make a chart similar to the following one that shows your classes and the days of the week. Then decide upon a goal: for example, to make five to ten significant contributions in each class during the week. After each class, mark your chart under the class and the day. Write *A* if you answered a question, *Q* if you asked a question, *O* if you expressed an opinion, and *I* if you added information to the discussion. At the end of the week, examine your chart to see whether you have achieved your goal.

	Mon.	Tues.	Wed.	Thurs.	Fri.
English	1A	1O 1I			
Science	2Q				
Math	2A				
History	2O				
French	1A				

APPLICATION: Examining Your Basic Study, Listening, and Speaking Skills. At the end of each of the next three weeks, use the following questions to help you examine your progress in developing the study skills presented in this section.

1. What basic study skill or skills mentioned in the checklist on page 437 have you acquired or strengthened in the last week?
2. What study skill or skills do you think still need work?
3. Which of the methods for becoming an active listener have you found especially effective in the last week?
4. Which method do you think you should practice?
5. Have you made at least two or three verbal contributions in each of your classes in the last week?
6. What suggestions in the chart on page 441 could you give more attention to in the next week?
7. How would you rate your progress in developing study skills?

16.2 Note-Taking and Outlining

Every school day you take in information from a variety of sources: lectures and discussions in class, textbooks, and occasional outside readings. A well-kept notebook can be a valuable aid to remembering the information you take in. However, a notebook will be a valuable resource only if it is well organized, easy to follow, and up to date.

Your notebook is generally the best place to record the information you take in. In a notebook, you can separate essential information from incidental information and express important ideas in your own words. Since your notebook is for your own use, you can use a style that is easy for *you*. However, your note-taking should follow some basic rules.

GENERAL RULES FOR NOTE-TAKING

1. Write the date and the subject at the top of each page.
2. Keep your notes as brief as possible without leaving out *important* information.
3. Use outlining or columns to organize information.
4. Make sure that headings stand out from the details so that you can review the headings quickly.
5. Leave space between major topics so that you can fill in additional information later.
6. Abbreviate and use personal shorthand whenever possible, but be sure you do not abbreviate so much that you cannot read what you have written.
7. Rewrite original notes in a more organized fashion as a form of review.

■ Two Basic Kinds of Outlines

Outlining is a method of organizing information under major headings that represent main ideas. Outlines can be used for taking notes from lectures or readings as well as for organizing information for papers and speeches. Unless your teacher states otherwise, you will probably use the first of the following forms, the modified outline, for most of your notes. The second form, the formal outline, is also useful for notes and invaluable for written and oral assignments.

The Modified Outline. In a modified outline, main ideas are used as headings and important details are listed under each heading. Underlining is generally used to make each heading stand out. The details are then numbered, lettered, or marked with dashes and indented to separate them from the headings and make them easy to locate.

Use a modified outline for organizing ideas and details found in lectures and readings.

After the following paragraph there is a modified outline that sums up the information given in the paragraph.

LECTURE OR READING:

Miracle silicon chips are engraved with hundreds of electronic circuits. These chips are small enough to pass through the eye of a needle, yet they can store 64,000 pieces of information. They are already at work in the digital watch, the pocket calculator, and the microwave oven.

MODIFIED OUTLINE:
<u>Silicon Chips</u>
1. Are engraved with hundreds of electronic circuits
2. Are extremely small
3. Store 64,000 pieces of information
4. Are used in digital watches, calculators, and microwave ovens

The Formal Outline.   A formal outline is somewhat like a modified outline, but the details in a formal outline are broken down into smaller and smaller subsections. This type of outline is extremely useful for taking lengthy notes from textbooks or reference books. You can also use a formal outline to revise your first set of notes and to outline papers and speeches.

Use a formal outline for taking detailed notes from readings and for organizing your own thoughts.

The format for this kind of outline is very specific. The following example shows where the main ideas and the different levels of details should be placed.

FORMAL OUTLINE FORMAT:

I. First main idea
  A.⎫
  B.⎬Major details explaining I.
  C.⎭
    1.⎫
      ⎬Minor details explaining C.
    2.⎭
      a.⎫
        ⎬Sub-details about 2.
      b.⎭
        (1)⎫
            ⎬Additional sub-details about b.
        (2)⎭
II. Second main idea (and so on)

A number of features in the preceding skeleton outline should be noted. Most important are the use of indentation and the alternation of numbers and letters. Notice also the progression from Roman numerals to Arabic numerals to Arabic numerals in parentheses and the progression from capital letters to lower-case letters. These differing symbols signal the relative importance of the information.

An example of a formal outline is given after the following selection. This example, which relies on words and phrases, is called a *topic outline*. A formal outline that makes use of complete sentences for each item is called a *sentence outline*.

RESEARCH READING:

> Graphology is the study of handwriting to gain information about the writer's health, character, and personality. Each individual's handwriting is unique, and changes in an individual's life—for example, changes in career, changes in health, and aging—*do* cause changes in his or her handwriting.
>
> A graphologist looks first at the pressure and slant of a person's writing. Fine lines often indicate shyness, while heavy, thick lines may suggest a strong, powerful personality. An upward slant suggests an ambitious person, and a downward slant shows pride. Graphologists also carefully examine the formation of each letter.
>
> Many people feel that graphology is more like fortune telling than like science. Perhaps it should not be taken too seriously, but it can be fun to see how close it comes to revealing a person's character.

FORMAL OUTLINE:

I. Definition of graphology
   A. Study of handwriting
   B. Source of information about people
      1. Health
      2. Character
      3. Personality
   C. Based on natural occurrences
      1. Uniqueness of each person's handwriting
      2. Changes in life affect handwriting
         a. Changes in career
         b. Changes in health
         c. Aging
II. Items studied by graphologists
   A. Pressure
      1. Fine lines = shyness
      2. Heavy lines = strength and power
   B. Slant
      1. Upward slant = ambition
      2. Downward slant = pride
   C. Formation of individual letters
III. Value of graphology
   A. Similar to fortune telling
   B. Can be fun

A final characteristic of this type of outline can be seen in the minor details listed under I.C. Notice that only the second detail is subdivided. In a topic outline, you should subdivide an item only if there are at least two sub-entries. The first item in I.C. has not been divided because no sub-entries are mentioned in the reading.

EXERCISE A: Making a Modified Outline. Read the following short selection. Then outline the information using a modified outline with one or more heads, similar to the one on page 444.

Allergies are reactions caused by foreign substances, usually found in plant and animal tissues. Such substances may be neutral or even beneficial to many people, but they can be very harmful to people who are sensitive to them.

Two of the major difficulties in dealing with allergens—substances that cause an allergic reaction—are that they are found in so many commonplace substances and that they can enter the system in such a variety of ordinary ways. Such basic foods as milk, eggs, and wheat are allergens to many people and create particular problems because they may enter the body disguised in other foods. Plant pollen, dust, and feathers enter the body through the nose and are inescapable elements of life. Face powder, shaving cream, and chemical dyes, all of which can enter the body through the skin, contain substances that are allergens to many people. It can be extremely difficult for the person sensitive to a substance to avoid contact with that substance.

Another problem allergic people may have is that they may not know they are allergic to a substance until the allergic reaction—often severe—has already set in. Health problems such as asthma (breathing difficulty), hives (itching swellings on the skin), eczema (a painful and itching skin rash), and hay fever are common allergic reactions that affect many people around us. Those of us who do not have allergies are indeed fortunate.

EXERCISE B: Making a Formal Outline. Reread the selection in Exercise A. Then make a formal topic outline of the information similar to the one on page 445.

■ Adding Columns and Summaries

As a study tool, outlining plays an important part in organizing material and in showing how various details relate to major ideas. You may find, however, that the outlines you prepare when taking notes are even more useful if you add columns and summaries.

Taking Notes in Columns. Arranging notes in columns can make notes much easier to review.

Consider arranging some or all of your notes in columns so that you can review more easily.

In the column method of note-taking, major outline headings are set off from the outline of details much as textbook headings are set off from the text or examples. This format makes the notes easy to review because you can cover the column containing the details while examining the column of headings. If you can recall the important details for the first heading, you can move on to the next without moving the covering sheet. On the other hand, if you cannot remember the details, you can easily uncover them and review.

You should allow roughly one third of the page (the left-hand column) for the major headings. The rest of the page (the right-hand side) is then available for the information relating to that heading. As you can see in the following notes taken from the reading on graphology, many of the elements of both modified and formal outlines can be incorporated into a two-column format.

TWO-COLUMN FORMAT:

October 3, 1981—Graphology

Definition	Study of handwriting
	Source of information about people
	1. Health
	2. Character
	3. Personality
	Based on natural occurrences
	1. Individuals' handwritings differ
	2. Changes with changes in life (changes in career, changes in health, aging)
Key Elements	Pressure
	1. Light for shyness
	2. Heavy for powerful personality
	Slant
	1. Upward for ambition
	2. Downward for pride
	Formation of letters—many differences
How Scientific?	Not very
	More like fortune telling
	Fun to compare results with real personality

The two-column method can easily be adapted to a three-column format. The three-column format allows an extra column for additional notes from other texts, audiovisual aids, or other outside sources that you may encounter later.

Writing Summaries.   Once you have outlined your notes, you may find it useful to write a summary.

Use a summary to record main ideas in your own writing.

The following summary could be written from the notes on graphology.

SUMMARY:

> Graphology is the unscientific study of handwriting to gain information about people's characters or personalities. Graphologists look for clues in the pressure and slant of handwriting, as well as in the formation of individual letters.

A two- or three-sentence summary such as this can be very helpful in your final review. As you can see, it incorporates some elements that were not discovered until late in the note-taking (the "unscientific" nature of graphology, for example) and moves them to a key position. Such a summary can be seen as a third step in the note-taking process: (1) listening to or reading information and deciding what to write down; (2) recording the information in a logical, structured pattern; and (3) taking the information you have recorded and summarizing it *in your own words.*

EXERCISE C: Using the Two-Column Note-Taking Format. Read the following selection and take notes in a two-column format similar to the one on page 447. Major headings should appear in the left-hand column. Details should appear in the right-hand column.

Viking ships were used by Scandinavian warriors and sailors who traveled the North Atlantic Ocean and the Baltic and Mediterranean seas around A.D. 1000. These ships were open and carried only one sail. They relied mainly on the power of a crew of thirty-two rowers. The ships seldom had a keel, but they did have an upswept bow and stern, the latter of which was usually decorated with a carved head.

The old Viking ship *Gogstad,* discovered in 1880, is the source for much of our information about Viking ships. This vessel was constructed with overlapping planks and side shields to protect the rowers during battle. Such a ship could well have brought Leif Ericsson to North America a thousand years ago.

EXERCISE D: **Making a Summary.** Using the notes you took in Exercise C, write a two- or three-sentence summary similar to the one on page 448. Make your summary from the notes, not from the entire reading.

■ Adding Annotations

Once you have taken your notes, explanatory notes or markings called *annotations* can make your notes even more useful. Annotations can help highlight important information and show relationships between items of information. Annotations make general reviews easier, and they also provide a short-term review through the very process of going over the material to annotate it.

Use annotations to make important information stand out in your notes.

The annotation symbols in the following chart are commonly used, though you may want to adapt them to suit your own needs and your own style of note-taking.

ANNOTATION SYMBOLS	
◯	Circle main or central ideas.
[ ]	Bracket major supporting details.
———	Underline minor supporting details.
▭	Box important names, dates, and places.

The following annotated notes illustrate one way in which the symbols can be used effectively. You can see how useful the annotations would be in studying for a test. Your review can be limited mainly to the highlighted items.

ANNOTATED NOTES:

November 12, 1981—Annie Oakley

Early Life	Real name—Phoebe Anne Oakley Mozee
	Born in log cabin in Ohio in 1860
	Learned to shoot at age 9 to help feed family
Career	Won shooting match vs. Frank Butler
	Joined Buffalo Bill's Wild West Show in 1885 and stayed 17 years
	Could handle pistol, rifle, and shotgun
	Expert shot
	1. Shot cigarettes from people's mouths
	2. Shot playing cards from 90 feet away
	3. Shot thousands of glass balls thrown into air
Later Life	Paralyzed in railroad accident in 1901
	Remained popular entertainer even after that
Enduring Fame	Nickname—"Little Sure Shot"
	Musical Annie Get Your Gun about her life

A variation of this approach calls for the use of color rather than symbols for identifying different kinds of information. You might, for example, highlight main or central ideas with red underlining, supporting details with green underlining, and so on.

Highlighting information with a light color such as yellow is another useful way to annotate. The use of a yellow marker draws attention to the words that are marked, while making it possible to read the words through the marking. Highlighting too much information, however, defeats the purpose of annotation. If you highlight too much, you will be adding to, rather than cutting down on, what you need to remember for reviews.

Annotations can be used as a fourth method for study and review, following the actual reading, outlining, and summarizing stages. You will soon find that studying using these methods can be more helpful—and certainly much faster—than four readings of the same material.

EXERCISE E: Using Symbol Annotation. Annotate the notes you took in Exercises A and C using the symbols found in the chart on page 449.

APPLICATION: **Evaluating** **Note-Taking** **and** **Outlining** **Skills.**
Evaluate your note-taking and outlining skills regularly by answering the following questions now and every few weeks.

1. Do you use modified outlines to take notes from a lecture?
2. Do you use formal outlines when taking detailed notes from textbooks or reference books?
3. Have you tried taking notes in column form for easier review?
4. Do you make written summaries after outlining?
5. Have you used symbols or color to highlight your notes for review?

Chapter 17

Test-Taking Skills

Taking tests is as inevitable as paying taxes, and to some people it is just as painful an experience. However, this need not be the case. No one can avoid tests, but there are positive steps you can take to keep from panicking.

Whether you are taking a quiz or a final exam in school, a college or vocational school entrance exam, or an aptitude test for job placement, you can probably improve your chances for success by following the suggestions in this chapter. If you have followed logical steps in studying for the test and are familiar with the kinds of questions that commonly come up on such tests, you will go into the testing situation in a more relaxed and confident frame of mind. This positive attitude, along with the study and practice you have been through, should greatly improve your performance on the test.

17.1 Classroom and Standardized Tests

One of the reasons many people worry about taking tests is that the outcome of the test usually influences some desired goal—a good grade, admission to college, or a good job. Knowing how to take classroom and standardized tests effectively can greatly reduce the worry of test-taking. In turn, the less you worry about a test, the easier it will be for you to do well and achieve your goal.

■ Classroom Tests

Although by now you have probably taken one or more standardized tests, the tests you most frequently face are probably classroom tests. Classroom tests come in a variety of forms and at various times during the year or semester. It is good to keep in mind that different kinds of classroom tests are usually weighted differently in terms of how they affect your grade for the course.

Quizzes.   A quiz is usually a brief, short-answer test that evaluates information that should have been mastered within the relatively recent past. It can come either announced or unannounced, and it is seldom weighted as heavily as a more detailed test covering more information. The importance of quiz grades should not be minimized, though, since high grades on several quizzes can often offset a lower grade on a bigger test.

Review recent material frequently to be ready for a quiz.

Some teachers will have quizzes regularly at announced intervals—every Friday, for example. Other teachers prefer the "pop quiz," which is given without warning. To be ready for either kind of quiz, it is important to review regularly material covered since the last quiz or the last big test, whichever is more recent. You should include both textbook and classroom lecture notes in your reviews and keep the following hints in mind.

STUDY METHOD FOR QUIZZES

1. Determine to the extent possible what material the quiz will cover.
2. Read and take detailed notes on textbook material.
3. Mark items in your lecture and textbook notes that you think are likely to be covered in a quiz.
4. If possible, have someone quiz you on information in your notes.

The value of a quiz does not end with the grade you receive. Quizzes can also be a valuable study tool in preparing for more extensive tests. Be sure to correct each quiz promptly, either when your teacher goes over it with the class or on your own. Keep your corrected quizzes in your notebook—either in a special section or with the notes the quiz covered—so that you can find them when it comes time to study for a chapter or unit test.

Chapter and Unit Tests.   Chapter and unit tests are usually given after a particular set of material has been covered or after several weeks of intensive study on a particular topic.

They are important tests that frequently include both short-answer and essay questions.

Because these tests cover a larger body of material than quizzes do, they usually focus mainly on the highlights and major ideas of the material you have studied. Clearly, it would be inefficient to study for this kind of test as you would for a quiz, focusing mostly on details. One of the best ways of preparing for chapter and unit tests is to broaden your focus by using the material that has already been highlighted for you in your textbook.

Use chapter headings and end-of-chapter questions to focus on the highlights of the material as you begin reviewing for a chapter or unit test.

The following suggestions should help you in reviewing for these larger tests.

STUDY METHOD FOR CHAPTER AND UNIT TESTS

1. Rephrase chapter headings and subheadings as questions and try to answer them. If you cannot answer any particular question, find the answer in the text and record it in your notes.
2. Mentally answer all end-of-chapter questions. If you are unable to answer any, find the answer in the text and record it in your notes.
3. Review all corrected quizzes taken since the last major test, looking for any areas in which you are weak.
4. Review both lecture and textbook notes through rereading, symbol marking, and mental and written summaries.
5. Before the day of the test, ask your teacher to explain any material that you are still uncertain about.

When your teacher returns your chapter and unit tests, be sure to go over them promptly. Use your textbook and notes to correct any questions you answered incorrectly or did not complete, including essay questions. If you still do not understand some of the material that was tested, ask your teacher to go over it with you and then promptly make notes covering the explanations. Save your corrected tests as study tools for larger examinations.

Midterm and Final Exams.   Midterm and final exams are the most difficult tests to prepare for because there is so much material to cover. However, most of the material will already have been covered *at least* once in quizzes or chapter and unit tests. In addition, a final will generally concentrate only on the most important facts and ideas covered during the entire semester or year.

> Study for final exams in an organized way, beginning several weeks before the exam. Make use of material highlighted in your text as well as your previous tests and notes.

Many teachers conduct in-class reviews shortly before a midterm or final. In addition, teachers often mention particular information, types of information, or major areas that should be reviewed with special care before the test. If your teacher follows any of these practices, be sure to take thorough and accurate notes during the review session or whenever any other reference to the final exam is made. In addition to such hints from your teachers, the following steps should help you prepare for these major exams.

STUDY METHOD FOR MIDTERM AND FINAL EXAMS

1. Use the table of contents in your text to plan your review. Make note of areas you are strongest and weakest in.
2. Use the table of contents and the chapter headings and subheadings to try to predict the major questions that may appear on the exam.
3. Review old tests and notes, concentrating both on areas in which you are weak and on areas that might be heavily tested.
4. If your textbook has a glossary, use it for a final review. Read the vocabulary words listed there and try to associate each term with the major idea or ideas it relates to.

The biggest mistake most students make is not allowing themselves enough time to prepare for a major exam. It stands to reason that you cannot learn all of the major ideas covered in an entire course by "cramming" one or two nights before the final exam. Begin your study well in advance of the test. (You know you *will* have a final at the end of the course.) After you have conducted a survey of all of the material, organize your quizzes, chapter and unit tests, notes, and outside reports and make a schedule of how much material you can reasonably review in a given number of nights. If you plan your review time efficiently, you will be less likely to panic and overlook important information.

In planning your studying time, set aside some of it to prepare for essay questions. In a final exam, these often make up one third to one half of the total grade, sometimes even more. Use the table of contents to think of essay questions that could be asked about each chapter. Select four or five of the most likely ones from the course and outline your answers to them. While you are outlining, think about how you can relate each question to material from other chapters and what conclusions you can draw from the facts presented. (See Section 28.1 for more suggestions about answering essay questions.)

EXERCISE A: Studying in Pairs for Quizzes and Tests. Pair off with another student to study for a quiz or a test. Together, try to predict the questions that you think the teacher will probably ask. Then quiz one another on these questions.

EXERCISE B: Preparing for Final Exams. Use the table of contents from your science or social studies text to plan a study schedule for a final exam. Decide how much material you think you can review each night, and record on a calendar the specific material to be covered. Keep in mind that all finals usually come within a short period of time and that you will be studying for finals in other courses at the same time.

■ Standardized Tests

A standardized test is a multiple-choice test given to certain students or to an entire grade level. Its purpose is to give a school or a possible employer information about how you rank in comparison with other people taking the test throughout the country. Standardized tests generally fall into one of the categories listed in the following chart.

TYPES OF STANDARDIZED TESTS			
Type	Usual Grade Level	Level of Difficulty	Purpose
Competency	9 or 10	Minimal	To see if you have achieved an acceptable level of competency in reading, language arts, and math

Achievement (for example, the National Merit Scholarship Test, English Composition Test)	any level	Wide range	To show your achievement level in a given subject
Apitude (for example, PSAT, SAT, ACT)	10, 11, 12	Difficult to very difficult	To compare your reading, writing, vocabulary, and math skills with those of other college-bound students
Employment	12	Average	To see how much potential you have for a particular job or career

Taking Standardized Tests. Standardized tests differ from classroom tests in two important ways: (1) You cannot study specific information to prepare for them; and (2) there is no passing or failing grade. In addition, such tests will often deal with some material that you have not covered, and they will seldom allow enough time for you to complete the entire test.

Your attitude toward such tests will often be a major factor in determining how well you will do on them. If you are tense and nervous or extremely tired, your chances of doing well may be greatly diminished.

Recognize that a positive outlook combined with plenty of rest are an important part of preparing to take a standardized test.

Since all types of standardized tests follow basically the same format, learning how to take any type should help you to take them all. The following suggestions should help you both as you prepare for standardized tests and as you take them.

SUGGESTIONS FOR TAKING STANDARDIZED TESTS

1. Ask any questions you may have before the exam begins.
2. Listen carefully to oral instructions.

3. Set aside roughly the same amount of time for each section of the test. Do not spend too much time on one section, but go back if time permits.

4. Skip questions you are having difficulty with. Put a check beside their numbers on the answer sheet and go back to them if time allows.

5. Periodically check to see that the number of the question you are answering lines up with the number of the item you are filling in on the answer sheet. Check also to make sure that you are marking answers clearly.

6. Check to see that your name is on the answer sheet.

Recognizing Kinds of Questions Found on Standardized Tests.

Most standardized tests include sections on vocabulary, reading comprehension, and math. Sections 17.2 and 17.3 treat vocabulary and reading comprehension questions in depth. In addition, standardized tests of verbal skills will often include questions on spelling and written expression. These questions, which are generally in multiple-choice form, may ask you to recognize an error, correct an error, or revise a sentence.

Learn to recognize and answer the kinds of questions you are likely to find on a standardized test.

Standardized tests in *spelling* do not ask you to spell words correctly. Instead, they ask you to identify words and tell whether they are spelled correctly or incorrectly.

EXAMPLE: In each of the following groups of words, one word may be misspelled. Give the number of the word that is incorrectly spelled. If all are correct, give 5 as your answer.

1. (1) doesn't (2) similiar (3) superintendent (4) legible
2. (1) khaki (2) athletic (3) convertible (4) already

Answers: 1. (2); 2. (2)

A variation on the preceding example is the use of complete sentences instead of single words.

EXAMPLE: In each of the following sentences, one word may be misspelled. Give the number of the sentence that includes the incorrectly spelled word. If all words are correct, give 5 as your answer.

(1) Please acknowledge this letter immediately.
(2) Your lisense is about to expire.
(3) We will use parliamentary procedure for all meetings.
(4) Loneliness is often associated with old age.

Answer: (2)

A third method of testing spelling asks you to select the *correct* spelling of a word from the possibilities given.

EXAMPLE: In each of the following groups of words, at least three of the words are spelled incorrectly. Give the number of the word that is correctly spelled. If all are incorrect, give 5 as your answer.

1. (1) vigilance (2) vigillance (3) vigilence (4) vigelance
2. (1) miscelanous (2) misselaneous (3) miscellaneous (4) miscelaneous

Answers: 1. (1); 2. (3)

Test questions such as these are based on studies that show that students' most common spelling errors involve adding a letter, leaving out a letter, or reversing letters. Many students also have trouble including all of the syllables in five- or six-syllable words and distinguishing between homophones. (Homophones are words such as *reed* and *read* that sound alike but have different spellings and meanings.)

To help yourself prepare for spelling questions on standardized tests, you may want to use the following suggestions. The material in Chapter 15 of this text can help you carry out the first two suggestions.

PREPARING FOR STANDARDIZED SPELLING TESTS

1. Know the basic spelling rules.
2. Review lists of the most commonly misspelled words.
3. Pronounce words correctly.
4. Use a dictionary if you are at all uncertain of the spelling or pronunciation of a word.
5. Try to use words that you have trouble spelling frequently in your writing.

The *written expression* portions of standardized tests follow different forms but always include questions about grammar, usage, and punctuation. In most cases these test questions will be similar to the spelling questions; they will ask you to identify either a correct or an incorrect sentence or phrase. One of the most common types of questions asks you to consider one sentence at a time.

EXAMPLE: Each of the following sentences contains an underlined group of words that may be correct or incorrect. Choose the number that shows the correct way of writing that word group.

1. This pamphlet will be of little help to <u>either you or I</u>.
   (1) correct as is (2) either you or me (3) either you nor I (4) either you nor me (5) neither you nor I
2. Not one of the students <u>have ever sang</u> this piece before.
   (1) correct as is (2) have never sung (3) has ever sung (4) has ever sang (5) have ever sung

Answers: 1. (2); 2. (3)

Another method of testing written expression is slightly more challenging. Instead of examining isolated sentences, you are asked to work with a paragraph or several paragraphs. The passage may contain many different types of errors, so you must be alert to all of the possibilities.

EXAMPLE: The following paragraph includes three words and phrases that have been underlined and numbered. Below the reading are three questions numbered to correspond to the items in the passage. For each question choose the answer that represents the best expression for each underlined word or phrase.

The use of solar panels (1) <u>create</u> a new source of energy for our country. The most significant change brought about by the use of solar panels (2) <u>have been</u> the decrease in fuel needed by the homeowner. In some cases (3) <u>homeowners' fuel bills have not only been reduced</u> by 50 percent or more, but their lifestyles have changed as well.

1. (1) correct as is (2) will have created (3) creates (4) has created (5) had created
2. (1) correct as is (2) was (3) will be (4) has been (5) were
3. (1) correct as is (2) homeowners' fuel bills not only have been reduced (3) homeowners' fuel bills have been reduced not only (4) not only homeowners' fuel bills have been reduced (5) not only have the homeowners' fuel bills been reduced

Answers: 1. (4); 2. (4); 3. (5)

A third way of testing written expression is to give a series of sentences written in different ways. You must then select the best of the possibilities.

EXAMPLE: From the following group of sentences, choose the number of the one that is correctly written.

(1) The director was more impressed with the actor's singing ability than with the actor's ability to act.
(2) The director was more impressed with the actor's singing ability than his acting ability impressed him.
(3) The director was more impressed with the actor's singing ability than he was impressed by his acting ability.
(4) The director was impressed with the actor's singing ability, his acting ability didn't impress him.
(5) The director was more impressed with the actor's singing ability than with his acting ability.

Answer: (5)

Still a fourth type of question presents a set of totally different sentences and asks you to select the one that is incorrect.

EXAMPLE: Write the number of the sentence in the following group that contains an error in grammar, punctuation, capitalization, or usage.

(1) Only one among us knows the answer.
(2) "When," Helen asked, "do you expect the package"?
(3) Have you read the poem "Snowbound"?
(4) Either of these choices is acceptable.
(5) Everybody we saw was having a good time.

Answer: (2)

To do well on written expression tests, you must understand the fundamentals of English grammar, usage, and mechanics. In addition, the following chart offers some helpful suggestions for taking such tests.

PREPARING FOR STANDARDIZED WRITTEN EXPRESSION TESTS
1. Read sentences through twice before making any decision.
2. Read only the punctuation actually used in the sentence; do not insert your own.
3. Make your "ear" your first guide to correctness.
4. Check what your ear tells you against the basic rules.

EXERCISE C: Answering Standardized Spelling Questions. Follow the instructions to complete the following questions.

I. In each of the following groups of words, one word may be misspelled. Give the number of the word that is incorrectly spelled. If all are correct, give 5 as your answer.
  1. (1) congenial (2) nuclear (3) shepherd (4) obstacle
  2. (1) crochet (2) aisle (3) ceiling (4) lieutenent
  3. (1) squirrels (2) potatos (3) niece (4) macaroni

II. In each of the following sentences, one word may be misspelled. Give the number of the sentence that includes the incorrectly spelled word. If all of the words are correct, give 5 as your answer.
  (1) We were appalled at his outrageous behavior.
  (2) This medicine is not effective against that disease.
  (3) Both pianos were tuned just prior to the soloists' arrival.
  (4) The manager was disappointed because she had so little leisure time.

III. In each of the following groups of words, at least three of the words are spelled incorrectly. Give the number of the word that is correctly spelled. If all are incorrect, give 5 as your answer.
  1. (1) superceed (2) supersede (3) supercede
     (4) superseed
  2. (1) conceit (2) conseit (3) conciet (4) consiet
  3. (1) greivous (2) greivious (3) grievous (4) grieveous

EXERCISE D: Answering Standardized Written Expression Questions. Follow the instructions to complete the following questions.

I. Each of the following sentences contains an underlined group of words that may be correct or incorrect. Choose the number that shows the correct way of writing that word group.
  1. <u>Driving</u> north on Main Street, the library will be on your right.
     (1) correct as is (2) Having driven (3) When you drive (4) Being driven (5) Having been driven
  2. <u>Neither of us expects</u> a reward.
     (1) correct as is (2) Both of us expects (3) One of us expect (4) Neither of us expect (5) Neither you nor I expects

II. From the following sentences, choose the number of the one that is correctly written.
  (1) I did not want to wait for the Harrison's dog and her.
  (2) I didn't want to wait for the dog or she.

(3) I didn't want to wait for her and the Harrisons' dog.
(4) I did not want to wait for either the dog or she.
(5) I didn't want to wait for she or the dog.

III. Write the number of the sentence in the following group that contains an error in grammar, punctuation, capitalization, or usage.

(1) Each of the boarders has a key to the front door.
(2) The salad contains lettuce, carrots radishes and cucumbers.
(3) The committee has not yet reached its decision.
(4) The letter dated June 14, 1980, contains the details of the contract.
(5) Whom did you wish to see?

APPLICATION: Evaluating Your Test-Taking Skills. After one month of using the test-taking strategies in this section, answer the following questions to evaluate your test-taking skills.

1. Do you frequently review factual information for quizzes?
2. Do you use headings and subheadings to guide your review for chapter and unit tests?
3. Do you correct, save, and review quizzes and chapter and unit tests?
4. Do you take standardized and classroom tests with a positive attitude?
5. During a test do you keep track of time so as not to spend too long on any one part of the test?
6. During a test do you begin with questions you can answer immediately and come back to more difficult ones later on?

Vocabulary Questions 17.2

You will continue to develop your vocabulary throughout your life, but you may find that the vocabulary skills you possess right now are being challenged and measured by standardized tests. You can improve your performance in such tests by becoming familiar with the kinds of questions commonly found on them.

Standardized vocabulary tests call upon your knowledge of a word's definition, but that definition by itself is not always enough. You must be able to look at a word in a number of different ways, finding other words that have similar meanings (synonyms), as well as words that have opposite meanings (antonyms). Standardized tests may also ask you to complete sentences or analogies with the appropriate word. This section will give you practice in handling all of these types of vocabulary questions.

■ Taking Synonym Tests

One of the most common ways of testing vocabulary is through a synonym test. A synonym is a word that has almost the same meaning as another word.

Look for the word with the closest meaning when locating a synonym.

When taking a synonym test, you should always take care to pronounce each word silently to yourself. If you look at a word quickly without pronouncing it, you may mistake it for a word that merely looks similar. Another useful method for locating the proper synonym in a multiple-choice question is to begin by eliminating the incorrect answers.

ELIMINATING INCORRECT ANSWERS ON SYNONYM TESTS

Step 1: Eliminate words that have the opposite meaning.
Step 2: Eliminate words that merely look similar to the given word.
Step 3: Eliminate words that can be associated with the vocabulary word but do not define it.
Step 4: Eliminate words that only define part of the word.

EXAMPLE: Find the word closest in meaning to the given word.

continuous (1) advancing (2) upcoming (3) uninterrupted (4) contiguous (5) broken

If you apply the steps in the chart to the example, you can easily arrive at the answer.

Step 1: *broken* can be eliminated because it has the opposite meaning.
Step 2: *contiguous* can be eliminated because although it looks similar to *continuous*, it is unrelated to it.
Step 3: *advancing* can be eliminated because although it can be associated with *continuous*, it does not define it.
Step 4: *upcoming* can be eliminated because it suggests part of the meaning of *continuous* but not all of it.
Answer: (3) uninterrupted

EXERCISE A: **Locating Synonyms.** Use the steps in the chart on page 464 to help find the word closest in meaning to each of the following words.

1. *complicated* (1) difficult (2) easy (3) compliant (4) puzzling (5) mysterious
2. *fictional* (1) factual (2) imaginary (3) novel (4) fictile (5) readable
3. *glossy* (1) dull (2) glossary (3) glowing (4) shiny (5) radiant
4. *pity* (1) petty (2) sympathy (3) hole (4) pretty (5) sadness
5. *penalty* (1) crime (2) penance (3) reward (4) punishment (5) award
6. *chowder* (1) entree (2) dog food (3) noise (4) soup (5) soap
7. *incipient* (1) receptive (2) insipid (3) earliest (4) concluding (5) deadly
8. *intermittent* (1) whole (2) continuous (3) unreliable (4) periodic (5) deadly
9. *recession* (1) progress (2) inflation (3) finance (4) decline (5) depression
10. *transpose* (1) relax (2) fix (3) remove (4) transport (5) interchange

■ Taking Antonym Tests

Looking for antonyms is not much harder than looking for synonyms. An *antonym* is a word with a meaning opposite to that of a given word. When looking for antonyms, you must constantly keep the word *opposite* in mind to avoid the trap of picking a synonym. You should also avoid choosing words that are only somewhat different in meaning but are not true opposites. True opposites are words such as *in* and *out* or *stop* and *go*, in which one of the possibilities automatically excludes the other.

Look for true opposites when locating antonyms.

EXAMPLE: Find the antonym of the given word.

novice (1) judge (2) beginner (3) novelty (4) expert (5) skier

In an antonym test, you can follow the same basic elimination steps that were suggested for synonyms. The first step in this case, however, would be to eliminate synonyms rather than antonyms.

Step 1: *beginner* can be eliminated because it is a synonym for the word.

Step 2: *novelty* can be eliminated because although it looks like the word, it is unrelated to the word in meaning.

Step 3: *skier* can be eliminated because although it can be associated with the opposite word, it does not define it.

Step 4: *judge* can be eliminated because although it suggests part of the opposite meaning, it is not a true opposite.

Answer: (4) expert

EXERCISE B: Locating Antonyms. Change the first step in the chart on page 466 to eliminating synonyms and then use the steps to help find the antonym of each of the following words.

1. *chubby* (1) fat (2) thin (3) narrow (4) nauseous (5) stocky
2. *prevent* (1) start (2) preview (3) patrol (4) stop (5) continue
3. *drowsy* (1) sleepy (2) droning (3) drawing (4) tired (5) alert
4. *canyon* (1) gorge (2) valley (3) plain (4) mountain (5) chasm
5. *genius* (1) intellectual (2) genuine (3) dunce (4) gifted (5) gentle
6. *hostile* (1) hostel (2) warring (3) amicable (4) angry (5) belligerent
7. *restrictive* (1) late (2) limiting (3) reasonable (4) tight (5) liberating
8. *admissible* (1) allowable (2) related (3) irregular (4) forbidden (5) announced
9. *provisional* (1) temporary (2) permanent (3) impromptu (4) nourishing (5) conditional
10. *proficient* (1) professional (2) adept (3) careful (4) unskilled (5) perfect

■ Taking Sentence Completion Tests

Sentence completion questions are also often used to test vocabulary. They call for many of the same abilities you must use to determine meaning through context, or the meaning of the surrounding words. (See Section 14.2 for more details about the use of context.) The best way of arriving at the correct answer to such questions is to find as many context clues as you can in each sentence.

> Use context clues to locate the correct answer to a sentence completion question.

EXAMPLE: Choose the word that best completes the following sentence.

She wore a mask because she did not want to _____ her true identity.

(1) change   (2) reveal   (3) destroy   (4) conceal
(5) reincarnate

The first two steps in the chart on page 406 of Section 14.2 can easily be adapted to answer this kind of test question.

Step 1: Find other words in the sentence that give clues to the meaning of the missing word.

The words *mask* and *true* suggest hiding the truth.

Step 2: Test the words that come closest to this meaning in the sentence. Word (4) *conceal* means hide but does not make sense in the sentence because of the negative word *not*. When you test its opposite, (2) *reveal*, the meaning of the sentence confirms your choice.

EXERCISE C: Locating the Correct Word in Sentence Completion Questions. Use context clues to choose the word that best completes each of the following sentences.

1. The lemon was so _____ it made my mouth pucker.
   (1) sweet   (2) mild   (3) sour   (4) juicy   (5) volatile
2. He plays the drum, which is a _____ instrument.
   (1) percussion   (2) wind   (3) chamber   (4) brass
   (5) string
3. Her sense of _____ kept everyone laughing.
   (1) balance   (2) pride   (3) beauty   (4) humor
   (5) right and wrong
4. A(n) _____ is a story written by a person about his or her own life.
   (1) autobiography   (2) biography   (3) essay   (4) bibliography   (5) anthology
5. She was an avid _____ so she spent a good deal of time in the _____ .
   (1) skier—lodge   (2) chef—restaurant   (3) equestrian—stable   (4) flier—ionosphere   (5) reader—library

6. The rebels were _____ his home so he had no other choice than to _____ his family.
(1) attacking—defend (2) defending—attack (3) capturing—arrest (4) stoning—stone (5) looting—alleviate

7. To be _____ is to be _____ .
(1) petulant—eager (2) avid—thirsty (3) parsimonious—stingy (4) vacillating—resolute (5) phlegmatic—ardent

8. Such an _____ act of violence was unpardonable.
(1) ominous (2) acute (3) unusual (4) insipid
(5) egregious

9. A _____ is an implied _____ .
(1) guarantee—agreement (2) fissure—crevice
(3) simile—comparison (4) idea—philosophy
(5) metaphor—comparison

10. Trial by jury is the most effective weapon in democracy's _____ to _____ tyranny.
(1) storehouse—preserve (2) arsenal—combat (3) artillery—conclude (4) race—battle (5) machine—erase

■ Taking Analogy Tests

A *word analogy* establishes a relationship between two words and then applies that same relationship to two other words. Word analogies always follow the same formula: A:B::C:D, which can be read "A is to B as C is to D." In word analogy tests, A and B are always given to establish the relationship. Either C or D or both C and D are missing. You must select the word or words from the multiple-choice answers that complete the relationship.

> In solving analogies keep the terms in the order given and look for similar parts of speech.

EXAMPLE: Select the best answer to complete the analogy.

furniture:chair::

(1) food:meat (2) daisy:flower (3) book:pamphlet
(4) olive:green (5) mood:happy

Answer: (1)

Notice that the relationship in the answer follows the same order as the relationship in the original pair. *Meat* is a type of *food*, just as *chair* is a type of *furniture*. Notice also that in this case all four words are nouns. (The parts of speech will not always be identical, but they are an element worth checking.)

The key to solving analogies is found in forming a clear idea of the relationship between the terms. There are many different types of relationships, but the most common ones are summarized in the following chart.

COMMON ANALOGY PATTERNS	
Type of Pattern	**Examples**
Synonyms	A and B are synonyms; so are C and D unhappy:sad::nervous:tense
Antonyms	A and B are antonyms; so are C and D in:out::entrance:exit
Similar categories	A and B are parts of one group; C and D are parts of another oak:maple::rose:tulip
Main categories and subcategories	B is a subcategory of A; D is a subcategory of C tree:oak::flower:rose
Subcategories and main categories	A is a subcategory of B; C is a subcategory of D oak:tree::rose:flower
Whole and part items	B is part of A; D is part of C fork:tine::belt:buckle
Part and whole items	A is part of B; C is part of D tine:fork::buckle:belt
Making categories	A can be made of B; C can be made of D floor:tiles::roof:shingles
Using categories	A uses B; C uses D carpenter:wood::tailor:cloth
Verb relationships	A and B are related verb forms; C and D follow the same relationship is:was::rides:rode
Rhyming words	A rhymes with B; C rhymes with D big:dig::cow:now
Scrambled words	A and B have the same letters; so do C and D tip:pit::pam:map
Homophones	A and B sound alike; so do C and D him:hymn::so:sew

Being able to recognize the patterns listed in the preceding chart should make it easier for you to recognize these and other patterns that may come up on word analogy tests. Keep in mind that both sides of the analogy do not have to come from the same subject area. One side may come from social studies and the other from English literature. Just remember that the relationship of the words, not the subject areas they come from, is the key to analogies.

EXERCISE D: Completing Analogies. Use the chart on page 469 to help select the best answer to complete each of the following analogies. Be prepared to explain the relationship.

1. club:golfer:: . . . .:tennis player
   (1) ball   (2) racket   (3) net   (4) sneakers   (5) court
2. lawyer:attorney::doctor: . . .
   (1) pharmacist   (2) physicist   (3) physician
   (4) surgeon   (5) psychologist
3. dress:buttons:: . . . : . . .
   (1) jacket:pockets   (2) slacks:zipper   (3) skirt:pleats
   (4) sweater:wool   (5) hat:brim
4. frigid:hot::sharp: . . .
   (1) pointed   (2) knife   (3) cut   (4) razor   (5) dull
5. cat:Siamese::dog: . . .
   (1) kennel   (2) canine   (3) Persian   (4) Doberman
   (5) Holstein
6. peach:fruit:: . . . : . . .
   (1) vegetable:corn   (2) tomato:potato
   (3) turnip:vegetable   (4) tomato:vegetable   (5) peas:beans
7. fish:scales:: . . . :feathers
   (1) pillow   (2) bird   (3) chicken   (4) quill   (5) tickle
8. drinks:drank::strikes: . . .
   (1) stricken   (2) struck   (3) stroked   (4) striked
   (5) strokes
9. plagiarism:embezzlement:: . . . : . . .
   (1) punishment:crime   (2) cheating:stealing
   (3) felony:crime   (4) law:order   (5) writing:novel
10. surgeon:scalpel:: . . . .:chisel
    (1) plumber   (2) artist   (3) sculptor   (4) knife
    (5) sculpture

APPLICATION: Evaluating Vocabulary Skills. Make up a twenty-question vocabulary test of your own, containing five questions and multiple-choice answers for each of the following four categories: synonyms, antonyms, sentence completions, and analogies. Exchange tests with another student and answer the questions on his or her test. Exchange papers again and grade your partner's paper. Look at the test you took and correct your incorrect answers.

Reading Comprehension Questions 17.3

Standardized reading tests, whether they are competency tests, achievement tests, or aptitude tests, usually follow one of two basic forms. The most common form presents a passage of one or several paragraphs followed by a series of multiple-choice questions about the reading. The other form requires you to read a paragraph in which one important word is missing. The missing word must be determined through a close examination of the context of the entire paragraph and selected from the multiple-choice possibilities that follow the paragraph.

Both of these methods test your reading comprehension and your knowledge of vocabulary as well as your ability to read rapidly enough to get through most of the reading matter.

■ Basic Reading Comprehension Questions

A passage on a standardized reading test can range in length from a paragraph to an entire page. The content can range from literature to social studies to science, and the multiple-choice questions that follow the passage can be any of six different types: main-idea questions, detail questions, inference questions, definition questions, tone/purpose questions, and form questions.

Learn to identify and answer the six basic types of reading comprehension questions.

Each of the six types of questions will be treated in more detail later in this section. To prepare to work effectively with each type, begin by reading the following passage from a magazine article.

SAMPLE PASSAGE:

Oak Island Mystery

The legend began in 1795. One summer day a Nova Scotia teenager rowed the half mile out to Oak Island and found a depression in the ground under a thick tree limb. Some people say he also found an old block and tackle on the limb.

His curiosity was stirred and the boy got some friends and began to dig. Going down about 30 feet, they found oak platforms every 10 feet but no treasure. They were unable to get more help, and abandoned their search. But word spread that maybe the famous Captain Kidd had buried gold and jewels there.

Over the next 175 years new groups went to the island and continued the quest. What they found turned out to be an inexhaustible source of mystery.

The oak platforms went down at least 100 feet, each one sealed with ship's putty and coconut fiber.

Diggers in 1803 brought up a large stone covered with strange letters. Later, a language professor claimed to have decoded the message to read, *Forty feet below two million pounds are buried.* Then the stone disappeared.

At 93 feet one crew struck something solid. Thinking they had found a treasure chest, the crew made plans to haul up the chest the next morning. But when morning came the whole pit was flooded with salt water.

Later diggers found an underground network of channels that brought sea water from the beaches to the pit. It seemed that whoever had built the pit had gone to immense trouble to protect what was buried there.

Dams were built, but could never completely stop the water. Some small metal links and a tiny piece of sheepskin parchment came up on a drill bit. Evidence indicated that an oak chest and some kind of document were at the 150-foot level.

In the mid-1800's one worker was killed when a steam pump exploded. Another worker plunged to his death when a rope broke. In 1965 a father and son and two other men drowned in a shaft they had sunk to drain the pit.

The legend sprang up that no treasure would be found until the pit had claimed its seventh victim.

Today Oak Island is pocked with hundreds of shafts and holes. The ground near the pit has been dug into so many times that no one can be absolutely sure where the original pit was located. Various groups and individuals have spent fortunes on the island and come up empty. So much time has passed that it is impossible to separate fact from legend. And whatever was put into the pit—if anything ever was—is still unknown.

Ironically, the search might not have lasted so long without the legend of Captain Kidd. People saw him as the greatest pirate of all, one able to find a fabulous treasure and bury it inside a fantastic pit. That idea kept them going.

But the legend of Captain Kidd is mostly myth and no one can really explain how such a huge engineering job could have been done by anyone, let alone a pirate captain and his crew. Some experts even doubt if the pit ever existed. They say that the underground flooding, for example, could have been caused by natural caves and passages under the island.

So Oak Island today is a greater mystery than ever before. For over ten years a group known as Triton Alliance has taken heavy equipment to the island to hold back the water and dig up huge tracts of land down to 200 feet. Once Triton lowered a special TV camera into what it thought was the original pit. It says that a human hand and three chests were shown on the screen, but the pictures were too fuzzy to be conclusive. As far as we know, Triton has found nothing really significant. And Oak Island remains one of the world's great puzzles. —*Read*

While examining more closely each of the six types of questions commonly asked on standardized tests, keep in mind these general principles for eliminating incorrect answers to comprehension questions.

GENERAL STRATEGY FOR ANSWERING QUESTIONS	
Type of Answer	**Reason to Eliminate**
Too narrow	Answer covers too small a portion of the reading.
Too wide	Answer covers a wider area than the reading.
Irrelevant	Answer has nothing to do with the reading or is relevant to the reading but not to a particular question.
Incorrect	Answer distorts or disputes the facts in the reading.
Illogical	Answer is not backed up by the facts in the reading.
Similar form of answer	At a quick glance, the answer looks very similar to the true answer.
Opposite form of answer	Through the placement of the words *not* or *untrue*, the answer is the reverse of the true answer.

Main-Idea Questions. The most important thing to remember when answering a main-idea question is that the statement must be entirely correct and must include as much relevant information as possible.

To answer a main-idea question, look for the answer that covers the majority of the information in the reading.

In asking a main-idea question, the test may direct you to choose the best title, to give the topic of the reading, or to select a sentence that tells what the reading is about. Whatever form the question takes, keep in mind the reasons for eliminating incorrect answers. Applying these reasons, eliminate any answers that you can. In many cases two or three of the five choices may be correct. However, one will always be more complete than the other two.

The following main-idea question is based on the reading about Oak Island. Answer it and then read the answers that follow to see if you have chosen the correct answer and eliminated the others for the appropriate reasons.

EXAMPLE: The Oak Island article is mainly about

(1) undiscovered treasures
(2) how some Nova Scotia teenagers discovered the Oak Island Pit
(3) Oak Island and how it remains one of the world's great mysteries
(4) Captain Kidd and how he buried his treasure on Oak Island
(5) the number of holes and shafts found on Oak Island

Answers: (1) Too wide (2) Too narrow (3) Correct
(4) Incorrect (5) Irrelevant

Detail Questions. Detail questions are the most common type of reading comprehension question. They are also the easiest type to answer because the answers are part of the actual reading. Detail questions ask you to recall or locate specific information.

To answer a detail question, look through the reading for the exact answer to the question.

Detail questions usually ask questions based on one of the 5 W's and H (who, what, where, when, why, and how). Although most ask you to find the one correct answer, a few may ask you to locate the one untrue answer in the group. If this is the case, the word *not* is often in italics to remind you to select the answer that is *not* true.

Use the Oak Island reading to answer the following detail question. Then check the answers to see if you have chosen the correct answer and eliminated the others for appropriate reasons.

EXAMPLE: The message that was found on the Oak Island stone said

(1) dig down to ninety-three, and a treasure there will be
(2) forty feet below two million pounds are buried
(3) two million feet below forty pounds are buried
(4) four feet below two million pounds are buried
(5) none of the above

Answers: (1) Incorrect (2) Correct (3) Opposite form of answer (4) Similar form of answer (5) Incorrect

Inference Questions.   Inference questions are probably the most difficult of all reading comprehension questions. There is no one fact in the passage to go back to, only clues that must be pieced together.

To answer an inference question, look for a number of specific facts that help support your answer.

When answering inference questions, you should try not to read too much into the question. You should also try to back up your answer with specific facts from the reading. Key words that commonly signal an inference question are *think, predict, indicate, feel, probably, imply, suggest, assume, infer,* and *most likely*. Words such as these should alert you to begin looking for clues to back up ideas that are not directly stated in the passage.

Try to answer the following inference question. Then check the answers that follow to see if you have chosen the correct answer and eliminated the others for good reasons.

EXAMPLE: From reading the Oak Island article you can assume that

(1) the digging at Oak Island will not continue
(2) the digging at Oak Island will continue
(3) the legend of Oak Island will never be solved
(4) the government will become involved in the Oak Island mystery
(5) Oak Island will become a recreation area

Answers: (1) Incorrect   (2) Correct   (3) Illogical   (4) Irrelevant   (5) Irrelevant

Definition Questions.   Definition questions are essentially vocabulary questions about difficult or unfamiliar words in the reading. Occasionally a definition question will ask for the meaning of a common word that is used in a special sense in the reading. Be sure to look not for the common meaning but for the more specialized meaning of such a word.

To answer a definition question, look at the words surrounding the unfamiliar word to determine its meaning from the context.

If you have trouble choosing the correct meaning, try mentally reading each possibility in place of the word in the passage. Avoid choosing a look-alike word or a word that sounds impressive without first testing the word in the context.

Try to answer the following definition question based on the Oak Island reading. Then check the answers that follow to see how well you answered the question.

EXAMPLE: The word *inexhaustible* in the third paragraph means

  (1) inexplicable   (2) tiring   (3) ending   (4) endless
  (5) terrible

  Answers: (1) Looks somewhat like the unfamiliar word
           (2) Incorrect   (3) Opposite meaning
           (4) Correct   (5) Illogical

Tone/Purpose Questions.   Tone or purpose questions, which are used less often than the first four types of questions, ask you to determine why or how the writer wrote the passage.

To answer a tone or purpose question, look at the overall style of the passage.

Identifying the type of writing involved in the passage will help you answer this type of question. The following chart lists common types of writing and the purpose of each.

TYPES OF WRITING		
Type	**Description**	**Purpose**
Expository writing	Writing that backs up ideas with explanations	To explain ideas clearly through facts
Persuasive writing	Writing that supports opinions with facts and/or reasons	To convince the reader or urge the reader to action
Descriptive writing	Writing that verbally pictures thoughts	To paint verbal pictures for the reader

Narrative writing	Writing that relates a story	To give an account in story form
Chronicle	Writing that presents a chronological progression of historic events	To sequence factual information
Propaganda	Persuasive writing used to convince or to mislead	To sway the reader to a particular point of view
Humor	Writing that makes something seem funny	To make the reader laugh
Satire	Writing that ridicules a person or situation	To make fun of something in order to inspire correction
Imagery	Writing that produces mental images	To give the reader images through use of words

In addition to looking at the type of writing, you should also look more closely at the writer's tone. Most writing will convey to the reader one or more of the tones listed in the following chart. The tone will be communicated through the writer's choice of words and through the overall impression that the writing gives.

SOME POSSIBLE TONES		
indifference	disappointment	indignation
appreciation	respect	hostility
admiration	approval	doubt
adoration	surprise	suspicion
optimism	anger	rage
pride	regret	pessimism
contempt	restraint	rejection
objectivity	irony	amusement

Try to answer the following tone/purpose question based on the Oak Island reading. Then check to see if you have chosen the correct answer.

EXAMPLE: The purpose of the Oak Island article is to

(1) criticize   (2) amuse   (3) warn   (4) inform
(5) satirize

Answers: (1) Irrelevant   (2) Too narrow
(3) Irrelevant   (4) Correct   (5) Irrelevant

Form Questions.   Form questions usually deal with the type of organizational pattern used by the author. The pattern may follow a certain sequence or order, set up a comparison and contrast, offer a problem and solution, show cause and effect, or merely give a series of examples.

> Look for structural features to determine the form or organizational pattern of a reading passage.

Tone, purpose, and form questions often overlap. A question may, for example, ask what type of publication an article may have been written for, as well as what organizational pattern or literary style has been used. Such questions require solid reading skills, some knowledge of literary style, and logic. They are challenging questions and quickly separate the good reader from the poor one.

Try to answer the following form question. Then check the answers that follow to see if you have chosen the correct answer.

EXAMPLE: "Oak Island Mystery" is organized through

(1) comparison and contrast   (2) a series of examples
(3) a problem and solution   (4) a sequence of events
(5) cause and effect

Answers: (1) Too narrow   (2) Too narrow
(3) Irrelevant   (4) Correct   (5) Too narrow

EXERCISE A: Answering Reading Comprehension Questions.
Read the following selection from a magazine. Then for each question that follows the selection (1) determine what type of question is being asked; (2) find the correct answer; and (3) explain why the other answers are incorrect.

When you read the name *Captain Kidd*, what picture flashes across your mental movie screen? Probably it's the Captain Kidd of legend—the daredevil pirate with fierce eyes gleaming above a long black mustache. This Kidd plundered ships, murdered their crews, and rarely appeared without a cutlass and pistol in either hand.

For 275 years the legend of Captain Kidd has been well pre-served in poems and stories—like Edgar Allan Poe's *The Gold Bug* and Robert Louis Stevenson's *Treasure Island*. And from the legend about the man sprang an even greater legend about his treasure.

No doubt you've heard these tales. But suppose we told you that Captain Kidd was probably not a pirate but a victim? Read on and decide yourself.

William Kidd was born in Scotland about 1645. He moved to America and became a respected shipowner, popular in New York social circles.

Over the years, Kidd earned a reputation as a courageous sea fighter. He fought the French at sea and also served the British government by chasing pirates off the Atlantic Coast. But these were minor expeditions compared to the task that Kidd would soon take on.

In 1695, with British and French ships busily warring against each other, pirates were free to plunder ships along the shores of Africa. Finally England's King William III had to do something.

He and several silent partners, including the soon-to-be governor of New York, purchased a private fighting vessel. Its purpose was to seek pirate and French ships to seize their goods. Any booty captured would be divided between the partners, the ship's captain, and the crew.

By coincidence, Kidd was in London at the time. When first asked to take the job, he refused. After all, he was a 50-year-old family man, hardly the swashbuckling adventurer pictured by artists. But finally he gave in and took command of the ship—to his quick regret.

Shortly after he left London, Kidd's crew was stolen by a British navy recruiting ship. His handpicked men were replaced by a band of cutthroats.

During the next year at sea, Kidd was unable to find even a single pirate or French ship. And no captures meant no pay for Kidd and his greedy crew.

Low on supplies, Kidd had to steal provisions from passing vessels. Though he took only what he needed, rumors of savage acts spread to London.

Then Kidd discovered that one of his men was plotting a mutiny. In a fit of rage, he struck the man's head with a bucket. The man died the next day. (Though this was a violent act, Kidd had not intended to kill.)

Not long after, Kidd did seize two French ships. He gave his crew their share, but this did not prevent nearly 100 from jumping ship. Kidd was obliged to sail home to New York.

No one was more surprised than Kidd to learn he was a wanted man—charged with piracy and murder. Kidd felt he was innocent and he sailed to Gardiner's Island, N.Y., to bury his possessions on the property of a friend. (The government later dug up the treasure.)

Kidd had documents proving that the looted ships were French—and therefore legitimate prizes. But after Kidd's lawyers delivered these papers to the governor of New York, they somehow disappeared. Were the partners trying to get rid of Kidd because of his bad reputation—and also to get more of the loot? We don't know. We *do* know that Kidd was convicted of piracy and premeditated murder—and that the missing documents turned up in London in 1920.

Pirate or not, William Kidd paid the price. On May 23, 1701, he was hanged in London. His corpse was left dangling over the Thames River as a lesson to others. But was his death justified? Was he really a pirate? *What do you say? —Read*

1. Where did Captain Kidd bury his treasure?
   (1) Gardiner's Island   (2) Sullivan Island   (3) Gardenia Island   (4) Treasure Island   (5) Oak Island
2. In the first paragraph the word *plundered* means
   (1) plunged   (2) robbed   (3) rewarded   (4) burned
   (5) none of these
3. The organizational pattern used throughout most of the Captain Kidd article is
   (1) comparison and contrast   (2) cause and effect
   (3) series of examples   (4) sequence of events
   (5) problem and solution
4. A good title for this story would be
   (1) "The Greatest Pirate in History"   (2) "Looking For Treasure"   (3) "Captain Kidd, Truth Versus Legend"
   (4) "Captain Kidd, Respected Shipowner"   (5) "Captain Kidd, Killer"
5. The article on Captain Kidd implies that
   (1) Captain Kidd deserved to be hanged and left dangling over the Thames River   (2) Captain Kidd's partners tried to get rid of him because they wanted to share his loot and go with the French   (3) the real Captain Kidd was not as exciting as the legendary Captain Kidd
   (4) Captain Kidd was too old to be a real pirate
   (5) Captain Kidd was responsible for the buried treasure in the book *Treasure Island*
6. The writer's purpose in this article is to
   (1) amuse   (2) inform   (3) persuade   (4) tell a story
   (5) inspire

■ Cloze Reading Comprehension Questions

The second method of testing reading comprehension, the "cloze" method, is less complicated than the standard method. With the cloze method you simply read a short paragraph or passage with one missing word in order to determine what the missing word should be.

The passage's missing word is always a key word, a word that shows whether or not you have understood the overall meaning of the passage.

Use facts from the entire passage to decide what the missing word in a cloze reading should be.

The following passage is the eleventh paragraph of the Oak Island article. One of the key words of the paragraph has been omitted. Read the paragraph to see if you can determine what the missing word should be.

SAMPLE PASSAGE:

Today Oak Island is pocked with hundreds of shafts and holes. The ground near the pit has been dug into so many times that no one can be absolutely sure where the original pit was located. Various groups and individuals have spent fortunes on the island and come up empty. So much time has passed that it is impossible to separate fact from _____. And whatever was put into the pit—if anything ever was—is still unknown.

Now look at the words in the following example and see if you can fit the proper word into the blank.

EXAMPLE: The missing word in the preceding paragraph is

(1) reality (2) nonfiction (3) obscurity (4) factual
(5) legend

Answer: (1) reality and (2) nonfiction are incorrect because they are too close to the word *fact* in the passage. (3) obscurity, which means "state of being gloomy or covered over in darkness," is completely irrelevant to the paragraph. (4) factual, which has the word *fact* as its root, is also too close to the word *fact*. The correct answer is (5) legend.

EXERCISE B: Answering Cloze Reading Comprehension Questions. Read each of the following passages. Then use the context of the entire passage to help select the correct missing word in each of the passages.

1. At this interesting moment he was called on by the others to regulate the game and determine some disputable point; and his attention was so totally engaged in the business and afterwards by the course of the game as never to

revert to what he had been saying before;—and Emma, though suffering a good deal from _____ , dared not remind him. —Jane Austen

(1) fright (2) anger (3) curiosity (4) surprise (5) fatigue

2. The tremendous variety of colors found in bird feathers is the result of a unique set of evolutionary circumstances. There would have been no reason for the vivid colors and fine patterns many birds have, if birds could not see colors, but unlike mammals (except primates) and reptiles, birds have color vision. The camouflaging patterns that _____ birds don't have to be perceived in color, but the bright colors that communicate things between birds would often be valueless if they couldn't be seen in color. —Roger F. Pasquier

(1) decorate (2) reveal (3) cover (4) conceal (5) paint

APPLICATION: Evaluating Your Reading Comprehension Skills.

Ask yourself the following questions to see how well you are likely to perform on a standardized reading test.

1. Do you try to identify the type of comprehension questions being asked on a reading test?
2. Do you check in the obvious places such as the beginning and end of each reading for clues about the main idea?
3. Are you able to locate specific facts within a passage?
4. Do you use the relationships between facts to make inferences?
5. Can you back up your inferences with specific facts?
6. Do you use context to determine the meaning of unfamiliar words?
7. Do you try to identify the type of writing and the writer's purpose?
8. Do you watch for clues to the writer's organizational pattern?
9. Do you try to eliminate incorrect answers through logic and a knowledge of the various types of incorrect answers?
10. Do you apply what you have learned in English literature class to reading comprehension questions?

Chapter 18

Library and Reference Skills

The modern library has often been described as an information center. In fact, many librarians say that their main function is to bring together people and the information that they need. Always remember this function of librarians when you need help. However, this is not enough—you must also learn to find library material on your own.

When you first look at the library, locating specific items may seem very difficult. There are many different types of material, both print and non-print, including books, pamphlets, magazines, newspapers, records, tapes, and microfilm. You may wonder how, in this welter of sources, you will be able to find the information that you need. What may not be immediately obvious is that all library materials have been collected and arranged so that the people using them will be able to find answers to their questions. In part, this is done by the card catalog; in part, by specialized indexes or tools.

The purpose of this chapter is to remove some of the mystery from the library, to teach you how to find what you need to answer a question, to prepare an assignment, or to research a topic. In the first section, you will learn how to use the basic resources of the library. In the second section, you will learn to use various reference materials. In the final section, you will look at one of the most important reference tools, the dictionary.

The Library 18.1

After reading this section, you should have little difficulty finding books and other materials you want in the library. More specifically, you should be able to plan your research, use the card catalog, find your books, and even cope with the "missing book" problem.

■ Planning Your Research

Although the library is useful for many other things, one of your basic uses of the library in school is likely to be for research. In order to find the information you need for your research, you will need a starting point.

Before you can do research, you must have some basic information about your topic.

Sources of Basic Information.   Ideally, before you come to the library you will have selected a topic and will have a general idea of what the topic covers. In order to do this, you can generally go back to your textbook and your class notes. Sometimes, however, this approach does not work. If it fails, do not panic. There are still ways that the library can help you. If your text cannot supply basic information, the most useful book in the library for you will probably be an encyclopedia. It can provide basic information on most topics and can even help you to select a more specific topic.

In some cases, however, you may not even have been able to pick a topic. Again, the encyclopedia can be very useful. Read a general article covering the material in your course. It may suggest a direction for your research. If that does not work, the library is likely to have books containing suggestions for term papers in various subjects. One such book is *1000 Ideas for Term Papers in American History* by Robert Allen Farmer.

If all else fails, remember to ask the librarian to help you. That is what he or she is there for.

Types of Basic Information.   Once you have chosen a topic, what do you need to know about your topic to find further information about it? What should you be looking for when you consult your textbook or encyclopedia?

The first step is to identify the general subject under which your more specific subject may be listed. This may not be as easy as it seems. If you are doing research about unfamiliar mathematics, find out if it is algebra or geometry. If you are looking for a person, find out with what field the person is associated. If you need information about an author, be sure that you know whether the person is a novelist, a poet, or a playwright. If you are looking for information about solar power, it helps to realize that you are looking for information about energy.

You should also consider alternate names and terms under which you might find your subject listed. Knowing other names and terms will help you in using the library card catalog, because the catalog may use terms that you have not previously associated with your topic.

The time frame and geographical location of your subject are equally important. When and where did Chaucer write? When and where was the cotton gin invented? If you want information about the Duke of York, you must realize that many men throughout history have held that title. Which one do you want?

With this information in hand, you can begin looking for more specific information. If the card catalog does not list your specific topic, you can look under the general subject or under alternate names and terms, using dates and geographic information to help pin down the broader categories. If you still have difficulty, consider the spelling of the names you are looking up. If you are looking for *Jane Addams*, you will not find her if you spell her name *Addoms*.

EXERCISE A: **Finding General Information About a Topic.** Choose a topic for a research paper and use either your textbook or an encyclopedia to find the following items.

1. The name of your subject
2. The general subject or subjects it comes under
3. Alternate names or terms for your subject
4. The time frame of your subject
5. The geographical area involved

■ Using the Card Catalog

In order to use the card catalog properly, you will need to learn what kinds of cards are in it, what kinds of information are on the cards, and how the cards are arranged.

Recognize the many ways in which the card catalog can help you find materials in the library.

Kinds of Catalog Cards. There are several different kinds of catalog cards designed to lead you to your goal.

Title, author, and subject cards can all lead you to a book in the library.

If you know the title of the book, you can go to the card catalog and look for the *title card*. Notice the title *Successful Small Client Accounting Practice* at the top of the following card. The card will be alphabetized under the word *Successful*.

TITLE CARD:

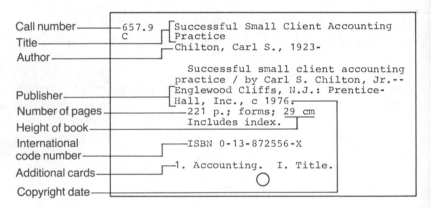

If, however, you know the author, Carl Chilton, but are not sure of the exact title, you would then go to the card catalog and look for the *author card*. It will be alphabetized by the last name of the author. Notice that this card looks just like the previous one except for the absence of the title at the top.

AUTHOR CARD:

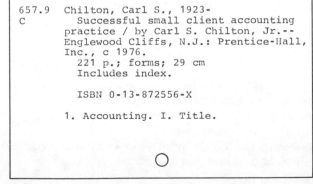

Of course it is also possible that you only know the subject you are looking for. In fact, when you are doing research, this is often the case. Then, you would go to the *subject card.* In looking for the Chilton book, you will find the subject card listed alphabetically under the subject *accounting.* Once again, the card is like the previous cards except that the subject is written across the top of the card.

SUBJECT CARD:

```
657.9    ACCOUNTING
C
         Chilton, Carl S., 1923-
           Successful small client accounting
         practice / by Carl S. Chilton, Jr.--
         Englewood Cliffs, N.J.: Prentice-Hall,
         Inc., c 1976.
           221 p.; forms; 29 cm
           Includes index.

           ISBN 0-13-872556-X

         1. Accounting. I. Title.
```

These three cards are the most basic cards and the ones that are the most important to recognize. They are not, however, the only types of cards found in a card catalog. Another important card that you should know about is called a *cross-reference card.*

Cross-reference cards can be used to find related subjects.

Although you should have your own ideas about alternative names and terms under which a subject may be listed, to a limited extent the card catalog can help you. Most libraries use a standard list of subjects when preparing subject cards. Sometimes the standard word is not the one most commonly used in everyday life, often because the use of the term has changed over time. Therefore, it is assumed that people may not always use the library's term. To help these people, most catalogs contain what are sometimes called *see cards.* Suppose you want to look up information about homebirths. When you look up *homebirth* in the catalog, you may see a card that looks like the following one.

CROSS-REFERENCE CARD:

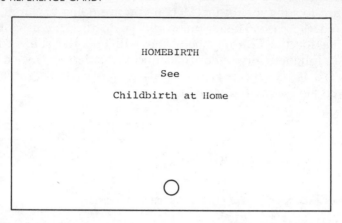

```
                    HOMEBIRTH

                      See

               Childbirth at Home




                       O
```

This card indicates that to find information about homebirths you should look under the subject *childbirth at home*.

Perhaps you know that your topic is about American literature. If you go to the catalog, you will find many books listed under the subject *American literature*. You will also be likely to find a cross-reference card that looks like the following one.

MORE DETAILED CROSS-REFERENCE CARD:

```
                  AMERICAN LITERATURE
                      See also

  American Drama           Letters, American
  American Essays          Newspapers--U.S.
  American Fiction         Periodicals--U.S.
  American Poetry          Sonnets, American
  Authors, American        Wit and Humor, American
  Ballads, American
  Canadian Literature
  College Readers
  German-American Literature


                       O
```

This card tells you that there are books listed in the catalog under all of these related subjects.

Notice that Canadian literature is a closely related subject. Other references, such as American drama and American fiction, are basic parts of the subject.

Another useful card is called an *analytic card.*

Analytic cards can be used to find information about parts of a book.

Perhaps you want to read the play *The Little Foxes* by Lillian Hellman and you find this card in the catalog.

ANALYTIC CARD:

This card indicates that when you look for the play on the shelves, instead of looking for a play called *The Little Foxes* by Lillian Hellman, you must look for a book called *Six Modern American Plays* edited by Allan Halline.

Information Found on the Cards.   Now that you have learned about the different kinds of cards in a library catalog, it is time to look more closely at the cards to see what kind of information you can find on them.

Recognize the type of information found on catalog cards and how it can help you.

The following card happens to be a subject card. As you have already seen, however, subject, title, and author cards for a specific book all contain the same basic information. The only major differences are found in the top line. Thus, you can use any of these three cards to examine the type of information they give.

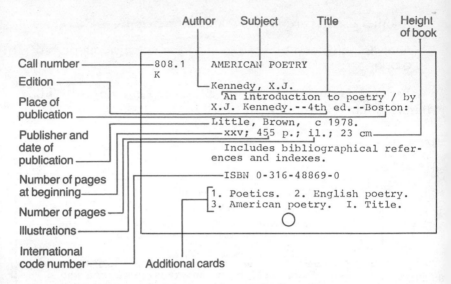

Although it is helpful to know what all of the items on a card mean, some are fairly obvious and others are not very important when you are simply consulting a book. Here, you will consider only the most useful items.

One of the most important items is the number in the upper left-hand corner. This number, called the *call number,* will help you to find the book on the shelf. Notice also that the book is a fourth *edition,* which means that although the book has been around for a while it has been recently updated. In fact, its copyright date is 1978. If it is important for your topic that you have an up-to-date book, be sure to look for the date of the edition.

Another important entry is the one that indicates the length of the book, in this case, 455 pages. Do you need or want a long book? The card also tells you that the book has illustrations, which can often be very helpful. In addition, note that the book includes bibliographical references. These are sources that the author used and which you may wish to consult directly.

Finally, look at the last two lines of the card. The entries there tell you that there are cards in the catalog under each of the listed entries: poetics, English poetry, American poetry, and the title of the book. Why is this important to you? Suppose that you are looking for information in the card catalog and are uncertain of the terminology used in the catalog to apply to your subject. However, you know of at least one book that would help you. Look up the book in the catalog, and then look at the lines at the bottom of the card. You will find a list-

ing of the specific subjects used in the catalog to lead you to
related material.

Arrangement of Cards.   In order to use the card catalog,
you must also know something about basic approaches to catalog arrangement so that you will be able to find the cards you
need. First, you should understand the basic system.

Recognize the type of catalog or catalogs your library uses.

Most small libraries have a single catalog with all of the
cards arranged in continuous alphabetical order. Other libraries have catalogs divided into at least two separate alphabets.
For example, a library may have one catalog for subject cards
and another for authors and titles.

Thus far, only *card* catalogs have been mentioned. You
should, however, realize that there are other types of catalogs.
Some libraries have catalogs in book form. A newer development is called a "COM" catalog. This is a computer-generated
catalog, which can be filed on microfilm or microfiche. However, in all of these cases, the rules for consulting the catalog
will be much the same.

Whatever the basic system, you must also understand the
way in which it is alphabetized. There are two different ways
of alphabetizing: *letter by letter* and *word by word*. In letter-by-
letter alphabetizing, which is found in most dictionaries, the
order of the entries is determined by the progression of letters
in the entire entry, even if the entry contains more than one
word. In word-by-word alphabetizing the order of the entries
is first determined by the progression of letters in the first
word of the entry and then by the progression of letters in the
next word. Thus, in the letter-by-letter system, Newark comes
before New York. In the word-by-word system, New York
comes before Newark. The following chart lists a few more
examples.

Letter by Letter	Word by Word
Newark	New Rochelle
Newfoundland	new times
Newport	New York
New Rochelle	Newark
newspaper	Newfoundland
new times	Newport
New York	newspaper

The important thing to remember is that libraries, unlike dictionaries, generally use word-by-word alphabetizing in the card catalog.

Use word-by-word alphabetizing to find the cards in the catalog.

A few other rules are also helpful in finding cards. The most important one has to do with articles.

Ignore *a, an*, and *the* when they are the first words of the title.

Thus, *The History of the West* would be alphabetized under *h* for *history, not* under *t* for *the*. *A Tree Grows in Brooklyn* would be alphabetized under *t* for *tree*, not under the article *a*.
Another important rule has to do with abbreviations.

Abbreviations and numbers are treated as if they were written out.

Thus, *Mr.* is treated as if it were spelled *mister* and *70* as if it were spelled *seventy*.
Still another useful rule has to do with *Mc* and *Mac*.

Treat *Mc* and *Mac* as if they were both *Mac* and alphabetized accordingly.

Thus, the following are in alphabetical order: MacDonald, mace, McHenry, machine.
A group of subject cards also follows a special rule.

Look for subdivisions of a subject before other longer terms beginning with the name of the subject.

Thus, New York—History would be found before New York Stock Exchange.
A final rule has to do with cards listing books that are written by a person and with cards listing books that are written about the same person.

Look for books by an author before books about an author.

Thus, the author card for Mark Twain's *Huckleberry Finn* would be filed before a subject card listing a biography about Twain.

EXERCISE B: Recognizing Library Cards. Write an author card, a title card, and a subject card using the following book: *When Movies Began to Speak*, by Frank Manchel, published by Prentice-Hall, Inc. in Englewood Cliffs, N.J., in 1969, with 76 pages, illustrations, a height of 24 cm, the ISBN number 0-13-955328-2, and call number 791.43. The subjects for the book are *moving-pictures*, *talking* and *moving-pictures—history*.

EXERCISE C: Using the Information on Cards. Study the following card on adolescent psychology and then list the information requested for each of the numbered items.

1. The call number
2. The author
3. The title
4. The copyright date
5. The publisher
6. The number of pages in the preface and in the book
7. The special features found in the book
8. The other cards that contain the same information

```
155.4     ADOLESCENT PSYCHOLOGY
M
          Medinnus, Gene Roland
            Child and adolescent psychology / by
          Gene R. Medinnus, Ronald C. Johnson.--
          2nd ed.--New York: Wiley, c 1976.
            ix; 553 p.; il.; 24 cm
            Includes bibliographies and indexes.

            ISBN 0-471-59022-3

          1. Child psychology. 2. Adolescent
          psychology. I. Johnson, Ronald Charles,
          joint author.  II. Title.
                        ◯
```

EXERCISE D: Using Word-by-Word Alphabetization. Alphabetize the following sets of cards as they would appear in the card catalog using word-by-word alphabetization.

1. Portland, Port Chester, Portsmouth
2. New London, Newark, *Newsweek*, New Mexico

EXERCISE E: Using Other Filing Rules. Alphabetize the following sets of cards using all of the special filing rules you have learned.

1. *An Empty Room, Antigone, An Art Collection*
2. St. James, *7 Rooms, The Soft Words, Saintly Lives*
3. *Machismo in Spain*, McPherson, McDonald

■ Finding Books

After you have learned to use the card catalog as a guide to the arrangement of the books on the shelves, the next step is to learn how to find the books.

Finding Fiction. Most libraries have separate sections for fiction and nonfiction. Since the arrangement of fiction is easy to learn, it is a good place for you to start.

> Fiction is arranged on the shelves alphabetically by the last name of the author and then by the title of the book.

If you look at the following author card, you will note that there is no call number in the upper left-hand corner. This usually means that the book is fiction. Instead of a call number, the abbreviation *Fic* is used or the letter *F* as a more general kind of location symbol.

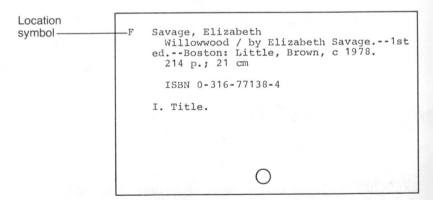

Location symbol

```
F    Savage, Elizabeth
         Willowwood / by Elizabeth Savage.---1st
     ed.--Boston: Little, Brown, c 1978.
         214 p.; 21 cm

         ISBN 0-316-77138-4

     I. Title.
```

As long as you remember that fiction is shelved by the authors' names, you should have no trouble finding the books.

Finding Nonfiction. In the upper left-hand corner of the card for a nonfiction book and on the spine of the corresponding book, you will almost always find a number called the call number. Nonfiction books are arranged on the shelves in call-number order.

Nonfiction is found by using the call numbers of the books.

There are two main systems for classifying nonfiction, the *Dewey Decimal System* and the *Library of Congress System*. The Dewey system is the older one and the one you will find in most of the libraries you use. The Library of Congress system was developed by the Library of Congress and is used primarily in college libraries. Though you do not have to know the details of either system in order to find books on the shelves, it will help if you understand a little about how each one works.

The Dewey Decimal System is a numerical system. It divides all knowledge into ten main classes, which are further divided into 100 divisions. These divisions are subdivided into sections and then refined even further. The following chart shows how the system works.

DEWEY DECIMAL SYSTEM			
Classes	**Divisions**	**Sections**	**Further Categories**
000 Generalities	300 Social sciences	330 Economics	332.1 Banks and banking
100 Philosophy		331 Labor economics	
	310 Statistics		.2 Specialized banking institutions
200 Religion	320 Political science	332 Financial economics	
300 Social sciences		333 Land economics	.3 Credit and loan institutions
400 Language	330 Economics		
	340 Law	334 Cooperatives	.4 Money
500 Pure sciences	350 Public administration	335 Socialism and related systems	.5 Other mediums of exchange
600 Technology	360 Social problems	336 Public finance	.6 Investment and investments
700 The arts			
800 Literature	370 Education	337 International economics	
900 Geography and history	380 Commerce (Trade)		.7 Credit

390 Customs, etiquette, folklore	338 Production 339 Macroeconomics and related topics	.8 Interest and discount .9 Counterfeiting, forgery, alteration

The first column gives you the ten classes. The second column gives you the ten social science divisions as an example of the 100 divisions. The third column gives an example of the subdivisions of one of the social science divisions, in this case economics. Finally, the fourth column gives a further breakdown of one of the economics entries. Thus, in the call number 332.1 the first 3 tells you that the book is classified under the social sciences. The second 3 tells you that the division is economics. The 2 stands for financial economics, and the 1 after the decimal point stands for banks and banking.

This may be helpful, but you still have to find the book. You already know that books are arranged in call-number order, but what does that mean? It means that the basic arrangement of the shelves in a library using the Dewey Decimal System is numerical. The 300's, for example, will be grouped together in numerical order. The following example shows how nine social science books would be ordered on the shelves.

EXAMPLE: 300, 301.4, 301.451, 317.3, 317.47, 336.2, 338, 341.19, 342

The call number also includes a letter, usually the first letter of the last name of the author. The arrangement goes first by number and then by letter. Look at the following example, which shows how these letters are used to arrange books.

EXAMPLE: 300   301   301   317   342   347.3   362
            G   A   D   C   U   A   C

Thus, it is the combination of the Dewey Decimal number and the letter standing for the author's name that shows you how to find a nonfiction book in the library.

You should also know that the Dewey Decimal System is revised periodically and that, therefore, over a period of time the same subjects are assigned different numbers. Therefore, even when you think that you know the number, you should look at the card catalog.

The Library of Congress classification system also uses a combination of letter and numbers, but it begins with letters. The main classes are shown by a single capital letter. Combinations of two letters show the subclasses. Then there is a numerical notation running from 1 to 9999 for the divisions and subdivisions. As in the Dewey Decimal System, there is also a letter to indicate the author.

The following chart shows a part of the system

LIBRARY OF CONGRESS SYSTEM		
9 of the Main Classes	**7 of the Subclasses**	**129 of the Divisions**
A General works	H Social sciences	HB Economic theory
B Philosophy and religion	HA Statistics	1–9 Periodicals
C Sciences of history	HB Economic theory	21 Congresses, exhibitions
D General and Old World history	HC– Economic HD history and conditions	31–55 Collections
E–F American history	HE Transportation and communication	61 Encyclopedias 71 Economics as a science
G Geography, anthropology, folklore, manners and customs, recreation	HF Commerce, including tariff policy	72 Relation to philosophy, religion, ethics
H Social sciences		73 Relation to politics and law
J Political science		74 Relation to other special topics, A–Z
		75– History 129 (including biography)

As you can see from the chart, the number HB 71 consists of H for social sciences, B for economic theory, and 71 for economics as a science.

Finding Other Material.   In addition to the Dewey Decimal System call numbers, other location symbols are occasionally used by libraries, especially for certain materials that are shelved separately.

A card with a symbol that is not purely a Dewey Decimal System number generally indicates material that your library has elected to shelve separately.

One of the most common of these symbols is the letter *R* in front of a call number to show that the book is a reference book. This usually means that it is shelved in a separate place and may not be borrowed from the library.

Biographies may also be removed from the regular Dewey Decimal sequence and shelved together. They may be marked *B, Biog,* or *92* (which is short for 920, the Dewey Decimal System number for biography). In addition, there will be either an initial or a name. The initial *K* might be used under the letter *B* for a biography of John F. Kennedy. In such a system, the biographies are shelved alphabetically by the name of the subject of the biography, *not* by the author.

Some other possibilities for special location symbols are symbols for mysteries, short stories, large print books, and non-print materials. You will generally have to learn the system of your own library to find out what materials are shelved independently.

EXERCISE F: Finding the Books on the Shelves.

1. Arrange the following books of fiction as they would be found on a library shelf.
   a. Richard George Adams—*The Plague Dogs*
   b. Philip Roth—*The Ghost Writer*
   c. Kurt Vonnegut—*Jailbird*
   d. Barbara Hanrahan—*The Peach Grove*
   e. Ann Beattie—*Falling in Place*
2. Arrange the following twelve books of nonfiction as they would be found on a shelf in a library using the Dewey Decimal System.

812,   657.0,   808.1,   808.2,   317.3,   317.47,   629.2,   629.227,
 G   C   K   B   U   A   C   M

973.7,   973,   973.9,   973.91
C   H   K   A

3. Arrange the following books of nonfiction as they would be found on a shelf in a library using the Library of Congress System.

Z 2011.A4,   CR 1,   CN 15,   CN 99,   CT 3700,   PN 6071. A9

4. Pick a foreign country and an author. Look in the card catalog to find two books about each. Write down the call numbers or location symbols of the books you find. Then describe how you would locate the books on the shelves.

■ Coping with the "Missing Book" Problem

Even when you have learned how to find information in the card catalog and how to find a book on the shelf, there may still be times when you will not be able to find the material you need. The books and other materials may not be available on the shelves. Perhaps the problem will be that there are too many people looking for the same material. You may feel ready to give up, but do not, at least not yet.

Use your imagination to find elusive material.

Following are a few suggestions for finding information when the books you want are missing.

Using General and Related Topics.   Try looking under more general and related subjects to find information. If you are looking for information about the French Revolution, try looking up French history, revolutions in general, or eighteenth century European history. If you are trying to find out whether or not the United States' actions in China in the nineteenth century could be considered imperialistic, try books about American foreign policy, American history, imperialism, and Chinese history. Even if the books about imperialism do not mention the United States, look at them, see how they describe imperialism, and read elsewhere about the United States' policy in China.

Learning to Make Connections.   If you have to compare two authors and cannot find anything that has compared them, read books by each author, read books about each author, think about what you have read, and make your own comparisons.

Using Biographies. If you are having problems finding information about nineteenth century Great Britain, try a biography of Queen Victoria. If, on the other hand, you cannot find information on Queen Victoria, try books about English nineteenth century history, European nineteenth century history, or English history over a longer time span.

Using Biographies of Contemporaries. If you need information about Disraeli or Gladstone or Queen Victoria, a biography of any one of them would give some information about the others. You can find the names of people who were close contemporaries of the person in whom you are interested in your initial research.

These suggestions can be expanded. Use your imagination to think of more ways of locating hard-to-find material.

EXERCISE G: Finding Elusive Material. Find information about Mary, Queen of Scots, using the preceding suggestions. Do not use a biography of Queen Mary. List three useful books you have found and tell why you chose them.

APPLICATION: Using What You Have Learned. Complete the following four steps.

1. Choose a topic for a paper and find out as much as you can about your topic in the initial research stage.
2. Go to the card catalog and pick out eight to ten books on the subject. Remember to use cross-reference cards and the lines at the bottoms of the cards if you are having trouble. Remember also the ways to find more information if the direct ways do not work.
3. Go to the shelves and check to see if the books you have found contain the information you need. Choose new books from the catalog if any of the books are missing.
4. Make a list of the books you have found. Where they are not directly related, be prepared to explain why you chose them.

18.2 Reference Materials

Although you may know how to find books in the library, this knowledge is only a beginning. To use the library properly and get the most from it, you should also learn how to use reference materials.

As discussed in Section 18.1, reference books are normally marked with an *R* in front of the call number and are often kept in a separate room or in a separate area. The room or area may then be further divided according to types of materials. These are all things you will need to check out in your own library. What is more important now is that you learn what reference materials are, why you need them, and how they can help you in your search for information.

Reference materials are defined here in a very broad sense. They will even, in some cases, include materials that are not books but are connected in some way with a reference department. There are several ways of categorizing reference books. One is to separate them into two basic types of reference books: fact books and indexes. A fact book contains many different kinds of facts and is not normally meant to be read through but to be consulted for information. An index tells you how to find information in another book or in newspapers and magazines.

Another way of classifying reference books is to describe them as general or specialized. A general reference book includes material about several different subjects. A specialized reference book is devoted to material about a single subject area. In this section you will learn how to use both general reference books and specialized reference books as well as periodicals such as magazines and newspapers. You will also learn how to choose the right reference materials for a particular assignment.

■ General Reference Books

There are probably few books in the library more useful than those described as general reference books. There are several different types of general reference books: dictionaries, encyclopedias, almanacs, atlases, and gazetteers. The dictionary, which is probably the most widely used book in the library, will be discussed in Section 18.3. This section will concentrate on the other major types of general reference books.

Use general reference books to check basic facts.

General reference books will often be your first stop when you are carrying out a research assignment.

Encyclopedias.   General encyclopedias can be invaluable in helping you obtain the background information you need before you start your research. After you have this basic information, you can then go not only to the card catalog but also to the end of the article in the encyclopedia and use the bibliography for suggestions for further sources of information. In addition, an encyclopedia is a good source to consult when you find a gap in your knowledge and need to find one quick piece of information. If you need to know the date Texas became a state, you can find it in an encyclopedia.

A general encyclopedia is usually a multi-volume set with an alphabetical arrangement. One volume, usually the first or last, will generally contain an index, which lists volume and page references for subjects that may not be specifically titled in the encyclopedia or which may have other references in addition to the main article. When you use an encyclopedia as a research source, be sure to use the index. Also use any references to related articles.

The following entry is from the index to the *Encyclopedia Americana*. The first reference is to the main article about the Atlantic Charter. The succeeding references are to other articles that contain additional information. Any of the additional articles may be useful in pinpointing the information you need.

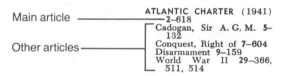

In order to keep the information they present relatively current, many encyclopedias follow a policy of continuous revision. That is, the encyclopedia is not completely revised at any one time. Rather, each time it is issued, some articles are varied to update the subjects most affected by the passage of time, such as medicine or science. In addition, many encyclopedias, especially those that are not revised frequently, publish yearbooks that bring together the events of each new year and add new areas of information. Be sure to use these yearbooks when you are researching current events.

You will probably find many different sets of encyclopedias in your library. Among them may be the *Encyclopedia Americana*, the *Encyclopedia Britannica*, *Collier's Encyclopedia*, and *The World Book Encyclopedia*. They are all very useful, but as you use them you will discover that different encyclopedias are particularly good for certain types of material. The *Encyclopedia Americana,* for example, is an excellent source for information about American cities and towns and has good articles covering centuries as a whole. *World Book* has excellent illustrations and is often the best source for a very concise presentation of the material you need. The latest edition of the *Encyclopaedia Britannica* is unusual in that in addition to the main body called the macropaedia it has a micropaedia, which gives basic information and serves as an index. Compare the following entry about the Atlantic Charter from the micropaedia of the *Britannica* with the index entry you have already seen. As you can see, there is a short description of the Atlantic Charter and then further references to articles in the macropaedia.

Summary article ——

> **Atlantic Charter,** joint declaration issued on Aug. 14, 1941, during World War II, by the British prime minister, Winston Churchill, and Pres. Franklin D. Roosevelt of the still non-belligerent United States, after five days of conferences aboard warships in the North Atlantic.
>
> A propaganda manifesto of common aims, the charter stated that (1) neither nation sought any aggrandizement; (2) they desired no territorial changes without the free assent of the peoples concerned; (3) they respected every people's right to choose its own form of government and wanted sovereign rights and self-government restored to those forcibly deprived of them; (4) they would try to promote equal access for all states to trade and to raw materials; (5) they hoped to promote worldwide collaboration so as to improve labour standards, economic progress, and social security; (6) after the destruction of "Nazi tyranny," they would look for a peace under which all nations could live safely within their boundaries, without fear or want; (7) under such a peace the seas should be free; and (8) pending a general security through renunciation of force, potential aggressors must be disarmed.
>
> The Atlantic Charter was subsequently incorporated by reference in the Declaration of the United Nations (Jan. 1, 1942).

Other articles ——

> · background, participants, and statement **15**:1141a
> · Churchill's role in negotiations **4**:599a
> · negotiation background and provisions **18**:992a
> · Stalin's territorial demands **19**:992b

As you use different encyclopedias, you are likely to find other specialties that will serve to guide you to the most useful set.

Almanacs. Almanacs are perfect examples of the fact book category of reference books. They contain geographic, political, statistical, and historical information, as well as many other kinds of facts. They also contain summaries of the more important events of the year in which they are published. While they are *not* very useful for finding background information about a research topic, they are perfect for finding small items of specific data. If you want, for example, to know the football colors of Yale, you can find the information in an almanac. The best known almanacs are *The World Almanac of Facts* and *The Information Please Almanac.* Since they are not arranged alphabetically, you will have to use the index at the front or back of each book.

Atlases and Gazetteers. There are several different types of atlases. All of them have maps, and most have charts and tables as well as an index of place names at the end of the book.

You can think of the most common type of atlas as a general atlas. In it you will find a number of political maps. These are the maps to which you are probably most accustomed, maps that show the political or governmental boundaries of countries and states, as well as the locations of cities, towns, and waterways. In it you will also find topographic maps that show you the conformation of the land: the prairies, mountains, and so on. Some general atlases also include maps covering special topics, such as types of industry. Among the best-known general atlases are *Goode's World Atlas* and *The World Book Atlas.* An especially useful general atlas covering the geography of the United States is the *National Atlas of the United States.* This reference work includes maps on such varied topics as pollution, climate, topography, history, economics, and population.

Another very important type of atlas is the *historic atlas*, in which maps are arranged to show changes over time. Examples include the *Atlas of American History*, the *West Point Atlas of American Wars*, which specializes in battle maps, and *Shepherd's Historical Atlas*, which covers in depth the time span from ancient Egypt to 1929, with a few maps going to 1975.

Yet a third type of atlas is the *economic atlas*. Examples include *The Oxford Economic Atlas of the World* and *The Oxford Regional Economic Atlas of Western Europe.* Both offer information about such topics as energy, manufacturing, population, and crops.

Closely related to the atlas is the *gazetteer,* which can be used to find geographic information but does not include maps. Gazetteers range from the *Times Atlas-Gazetteer,* which only covers latitude and longitude for places around the world, to *Webster's New Geographical Dictionary,* which gives descriptive and historic material about a much smaller number of places.

EXERCISE A: Using Encyclopedias. Find each of the following items of information in a general encyclopedia or one of its yearbooks. For each item, write the name of the encyclopedia, the volume, the page, and the title of the article in which you found it.

1. The date Wichita, Kansas, was founded
2. A history of the development of language
3. The name of the British Prime Minister in 1980
4. A list of French-speaking countries
5. The birth date of Thomas Harriot

EXERCISE B: Using Almanacs. Find each of the following items of information in an almanac. For each item, write the name, date, and page of the almanac in which you found it.

1. The nickname of the state of Missouri
2. The date of the sinking of the *Titanic*
3. The seven wonders of the world
4. The day of the week on which March 12, 1930 fell
5. The number of Buddhists in North America

EXERCISE C: Using Atlases. Find each of the following items of information in an atlas or gazetteer. For each item, write the name and page of the book in which you found it.

1. The countries bordering France
2. The new countries formed after World War I
3. The latitude and longitude of Hedemora, Sweden
4. The Union advances from Jackson to Vicksburg on May 15–19, 1863
5. The major military bases in the continental United States

■ Specialized Reference Books

In addition to general reference books, there are more specialized reference books that contain information about comparatively narrow fields.

Use specialized reference books to find more in-depth information about a particular field.

Some specialized reference books ˙are variations of more general reference books. These include dictionaries and encyclopedias devoted to special fields. Other specialized reference books follow special patterns to offer in-depth information about various fields. In this section books devoted to the fields of biography, literature, and social studies will be used as examples of these special reference works.

When you read the lists of books in the following pages, you should not feel intimidated by the mass of material. The point is not to memorize a long list of books with details about everything in them. Rather, you should try to gain a working knowledge of what is available and how it can be located. Once you know the general types of books available, you can use the card catalog, the librarian, and the books themselves to refresh your memory about the details.

Specialized Dictionaries.   Like other dictionaries, specialized dictionaries give you definitions of words, usually arranged alphabetically. However, each specialized dictionary gives definitions in an individual field. Thus, they can be used when the words you are looking for are too specialized to be found in a general dictionary. Although there are dictionaries for almost every major field, the ones discussed here are among those most often found in a school library.

One of the most useful kinds of specialized dictionaries is called a *dictionary of synonyms*. When you are writing, you may have difficulty finding exactly the right words to express your thoughts. Sometimes you may need a synonym because you have used a word too often. Other times, you may need a word that is closely related to another word or that is a synonym for one aspect of the meaning of a word. Two very good dictionaries of synonyms are *Funk and Wagnall's Modern Guide to Synonyms* and *Webster's Dictionary of Synonyms*. *Roget's International Thesaurus* also lists synonyms but does not give the detailed definitions found in most dictionaries.

Another useful specialized dictionary is the *Dictionary of American History*, a multi-volume set of books with a separate index. This book is especially good for quickly finding information about any topic related to American history.

Other specialized dictionaries you may find in your library are *Safire's Political Dictionary, James' Mathematical Diction-*

ary, the *McGraw-Hill Dictionary of Art*, the *Harvard Dictionary of Music*, and Steen's *Dictionary of Biology*.

Specialized Encyclopedias. Specialized encyclopedias are another very useful tool. Like general encyclopedias, they are good for background, bibliographies, and quick reference. Unlike general encyclopedias, they will go into more depth because their scope is limited to a specific field. They range from one-volume encyclopedias to multi-volume sets. The organization of material usually follows the format to which you have become accustomed in general encyclopedias.

Like specialized dictionaries, specialized encyclopedias cover many areas. One of the most useful is the *Encyclopedia of the Social Sciences*, which includes information about the entire field. In it you can find information about psychologists such as Sigmund and Anna Freud, about ideologies such as Fascism and Communism, about economists such as Adam Smith and John Kenneth Galbraith, and about political philosophers such as Locke and Rousseau. A similar encyclopedia is the *Encyclopedia of Philosophy*. In this you can find information about ancient philosophers such as Plato and Aristotle as well as information about more modern philosophical movements such as positivism and pragmatism.

Many libraries have religious encyclopedias such as the *Encyclopedia Judaica* and the *New Catholic Encyclopedia*. It is often interesting to compare the way these encyclopedias treat the same person, event, or topic.

Finally, there are a number of excellent science encyclopedias. Two of the best known are *The McGraw-Hill Encyclopedia of Science and Technology* and *The Encyclopedia of Chemical Technology*. The latter is remarkably broad—you can find material about such diverse topics as water pollution, antibiotics, food additives, and shale oil.

Biographical Reference Books. In preparing assignments or writing papers, you may often find that you need certain kinds of biographical information. To find this information, there are a number of biographical reference works you can consult. Some are general; some cover specific fields. Some give a great deal of information; some, very little. Some cover the living; others, the dead.

One of the best general biographical sources is *Current Biography*, a periodical that is published monthly and then bound in annual editions. The work includes an index covering the period 1940 to 1970 and other indexes for each following year. The long articles in each volume include information about well-known people in all fields, as well as illustrations and bibliographies. You will also find a listing of people by their fields. Only people living at the time of publication are included; the only exception is an obituary listing. *Current Biography* is probably the best starting place for current information about prominent people in a wide variety of fields.

A very different biographical reference book is *Who's Who in America*. Here the information is obtained from answers to questionnaires and consists of basic facts, such as occupation, date of birth, schools attended, jobs held, and publications. There are also a number of related publications, such as *Who's Who* (British), *Who's Who in the East*, *Who's Who of American Women*, *Who's Who in Finance and Industry*, and *Who's Who in American Art*. *Who Was Who in America* covers people no longer living. These books tend to be more useful for their inclusiveness than for the quality of their information.

Good sources of material about people no longer living are the *Dictionary of American Biography* and the *Dictionary of National Biography* (British). Both have long articles about the people they include. Two other sources, international in scope, are *Webster's Biographical Dictionary* and *The McGraw-Hill Encyclopedia of World Biography*. They both cover a broad range of people, with fairly short articles about each person.

There are also two excellent biographical *indexes*. The first is *Biography Index*, started in 1940, which indexes material found in selected periodicals as well as in books. The other is *The New York Times Obituary Index*, which indexes obituaries in *The New York Times* from 1858 through 1968. To bring it up to date, you can look under deaths in the regular index to *The New York Times*. It is surprising how often the only information you can find about a person is the information printed when the person dies.

Finally, there are a number of other biographical reference works limited to a single field. *Contemporary Authors* is a good source of information about authors, especially those who are not major authors and, therefore, are harder to research. The articles include information about the authors' lives and works. A good source of information about more famous authors is *Twentieth Century Authors*. An excellent source devoted to scientists is *The Dictionary of Scientific Biographies*, a multivolume set with a separate index. The articles in this book are long and give excellent coverage of the lives and works of the scientists included.

Literary Reference Books. In the area of literature and drama, there are several good reference books. One, *Contemporary Authors*, has already been mentioned.

Reference works in this area can be divided into three types: handbooks or fact books that present information you may need, indexes that make it possible for you to find something that is part of something else (a quote, a play, a short story, or a poem), and indexes that make it possible for you to find critical reviews of literary works.

Among the best fact books are the Oxford and Penguin companion series. In the first series, you will find the *Oxford Companion to American Literature* and the *Oxford Companion to English Literature*, as well as similar volumes about French and Spanish literature. In the second series, you will find the *Penguin Companion to English Literature* and the *Penguin Companion to European Literature*, as well as volumes on classical, oriental, and African literature. Each of these volumes contains brief information about authors, literary works, and literary movements. The books tend to be most useful for checking very basic information.

Indexes will be more useful when you need to find a short story or a poem that has not been published separately or when you need the source of a quotation. *Granger's Index to Poetry* can help you trace an author, subject, title, or first line. *The Short Story Index* can help you find books in which short stories appear. There are also several indexes to plays, among them *The Play Index* and *Ottemiller's Index to Plays in Collections*. Finally, there are several books of quotations. Perhaps the most familiar is *Bartlett's Familiar Quotations*, which is arranged chronologically by author, with author and key word indexes. Other books of quotations, arranged by topic, with author indexes, are the *Home Book of Quotations* and *The Dictionary of Quotations* by Bergen Evans.

Other indexes will help you find a critical review of a specific work. *Book Review Digest*, started in 1905, is an excellent directory of book reviews. Published several times a year and then collected in an annual yearbook, each volume covers books published during a specific year. Books are arranged alphabetically by author, with indexes in each volume. For each book there are short summaries of a number of different book reviews, with references to the periodicals in which the full reviews can be found. A separate publication, *Book Review Index*, is only an index. It simply refers you to the periodical in which the book was reviewed.

Useful publications for in-depth literary criticism, rather than book reviews, are *Twentieth Century Literary Criticism,* covering authors from 1900 to 1960, and *Contemporary Literary Criticism,* containing excerpts of criticism of works by contemporary novelists since 1960. The excerpts are long enough to be informative, although references to the original sources are given as well. In the *Library of Literary Criticism,* you can find volumes covering British and American, modern German, modern French, and modern Slavic literature. Once again, there are summaries and references to original sources, which include both books and periodicals.

Several indexes are more narrowly specialized. Among these are *Dramatic Literary Criticism* and *A Guide to Critical Reviews,* with volumes covering American drama, the musical, and the screenplay. There is also an index to periodicals, the *Humanities Index,* which is a good source for periodical articles containing literary criticism.

A more general index that can be used to find both literary criticism and parts of books is called *The Essay and General Literature Index.* The approach to listing authors is unusual: First the author's own works are listed, followed by general studies written about the author or the author's work. In the following listing for Walter Benjamin, the first thing listed, *Reflections,* is by Benjamin. The next thing listed is an article by R. Alter called "Walter Benjamin: The Aura of the Past," from a book by Alter called *Defenses of the Imagination.*

The Essay and General Literature Index covers such diverse topics as India, population research, technology, literary criticism, and decentralization in government.

Author ─────────────── **Benjamin, Walter**
                              ┌─ Reflections
Author's own work ──────┘   *Contents*
                      The author as producer
                      A Berlin chronicle
                      Brecht's Threepenny novel
                      Critique of violence
                      The destructive character
                      Fate and character
                      Hashish in Marseilles
                      Karl Kraus
                      Marseilles
                      Moscow
                      Naples
                      On language as such and on the language
                          of man
                      On the mimetic faculty
                      Paris, capital of the nineteenth century.
                      Surrealism

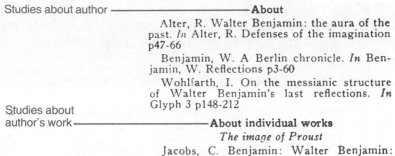

Studies about author ————————————**About**

> Alter, R. Walter Benjamin: the aura of the past. *In* Alter, R. Defenses of the imagination p47-66
>
> Benjamin, W. A Berlin chronicle. *In* Benjamin, W. Reflections p3-60
>
> Wohlfarth, I. On the messianic structure of Walter Benjamin's last reflections. *In* Glyph 3 p148-212

Studies about author's work ————————————**About individual works**

> *The image of Proust*
>
> Jacobs, C. Benjamin: Walter Benjamin: Image of Proust. *In* Jacobs, C. The dissimulating harmony p87-110

Social Studies Reference Books. Social studies is an extremely large field for which an endless number of books are available. The *Encyclopedia of Social Science,* the *Dictionary of American History,* and *Safire's Political Dictionary* have already been mentioned. The following paragraphs will give you a quick introduction to a few other particularly useful books in the field of social studies.

If you need to know about government personnel, you can go to either *The Congressional Directory* or the *United States Government Manual.* If you need more information about the members of Congress, a good source is the *Almanac of American Politics.* This includes information about congressional districts, biographical information, key votes, and ratings by various organizations. It is perhaps the best book available for quickly locating data about the people in Congress.

Upon occasion you may also need information about foreign countries. Two of the best sources for this type of information are the *Stateman's Yearbook* and *Europa Yearbook: A World Survey.* The *Statesman's Yearbook* is published annually as a single volume and gives basic information about all of the countries of the world. It includes short summaries of each country's history, area and population, constitution and government, and economy. *Europa* is a two-volume annual that includes a section about international organizations. It also gives information about the history, government, economy, press, and colleges of each country, and includes names of people as well as historical and statistical information.

For statistics dealing with the United States, there is the *Statistical Abstract of the United States.* Particularly useful are the footnotes that appear after each table to guide you to the original source of the information.

EXERCISE D: Using Specialized Dictionaries. Find each of the following items of information in a specialized dictionary. For each item, give the source consulted and the page.

1. Two synonyms for the word *principal*
2. The historical significance of the Molly Maguires
3. The value of the mathematical symbol *pi*
4. The year in which the composer Mendelssohn died
5. The place where the sculptor Rodin was born

EXERCISE E: Using Specialized Encyclopedias. Find each of the following items of information in a specialized encyclopedia. For each item, give the source consulted, the name of the article, and the page.

1. The theories of the philosopher St. Simon
2. The importance of the philosophy called idealism
3. The way in which the fabric rayon is made
4. The basic meaning of Boyle's law
5. The importance of St. Paul in the development of the Catholic Church

EXERCISE F: Finding Biographical Information. Find each of the following items of information in a biographical reference book. For each item, give the source consulted, the volume, and the page.

1. When and where was Reggie Jackson born?
2. When was Disraeli Prime Minister of England?
3. When did Charlemagne live?
4. What was Elizabeth Cady Stanton noted for?
5. What is Carla Hills noted for?

EXERCISE G: Finding Literary Information. Find each of the following items of information in a literary reference book. For each item, list the source and the page.

1. Who wrote *Tom Jones?*
2. In what books can you find the poem "Trees" by Joyce Kilmer?
3. Who said, "Ask not what your country can do for you, ask what you can do for your country?"
4. Where can you find book reviews of *The Greening of America?*
5. Where can you find criticism of Rawling's *The Yearling?*

EXERCISE H: **Finding Information for Social Studies.** Find each of the following items of information in a social studies reference book. For each item, list the source and the page.

1. Who were the senators from North Dakota in 1978?
2. What kind of government does Albania have?
3. What are some of the newspapers in Greece?
4. When did Nigeria become independent?
5. What was the consumer price index for 1970?

■ Periodicals and Related Material

Periodical is a general term for anything published at intervals during the year. The term is usually used for magazines or journals, but it can also be applied to newspapers. Because of their current nature, periodicals and pamphlets (which may or may not be published on an interval basis) are very useful for some types of information that are otherwise hard to find.

Use magazines, journals, newspapers, and pamphlets for current material about a subject.

Magazines and Journals. The term *magazine* refers to more popular periodicals; the term *journal,* to more scholarly periodicals. There are many periodicals in both categories— some general and others covering almost any specific field that you can name. They are good for current information or for information that was current at the time the periodical was written. They are also good for concise and specialized information. All libraries have at least some magazines and journals. In many libraries some are kept in microfilm form.

How do you find information in magazines and journals? You find information by using indexes. A few indexes have already been mentioned, but there are many others. The one you will probably find most useful is *The Readers' Guide to Periodical Literature,* a guide to the most widely circulated magazines. It is alphabetized by general subject and then by specific subject under the general subject. Each entry gives you the name of the article, the author, the periodical the article comes from, the volume, date, and page. It also tells you whether there are illustrations. In addition, like the card catalog, *The Readers' Guide* gives *see* and *see also* references.

The following example from *The Readers' Guide* shows a partial listing of articles under the heading *Inflation (finance)*. The first items listed are *see also* references to *Index linking (economics)* and *Wage-price policy*. You can look up related articles under these two subject heads. The first entry is for an article entitled "Aftershock of a Price Surge." The *il* means that the article is illustrated; *Bus W* tells you that the magazine in which the article appears is *Business Week* (there is a list of abbreviations in the front of the volume). The listing also tells you that the article goes from page 20 to 22 and is in the March 3, 1980 issue. The lack of an author listing means that it is an unsigned article.

Title of magazine ————————————————————————┐

Illustrated ————————————————————————————┐ │

Subject heading ——————————————┐   │ │

      INFLATION (finance)

         See also

Cross-references ———————— Index linking (economics)

         Wage-price policy

Title of article ———————— Aftershock of a price surge. il Bus W p20-2 Mr 3 '80

         Another U.S. triumph. F. Getlein. Commonweal

Volume: ———┐ ——107:102-3 F 29 '80

page numbers ———— Answer may be either, both, or neither [Consumer Price Index and personal consumption expenditures deflator] Nations Bus 68:92 Mr '80

Author of ———— Are we ready for the pain? M. Stone. U.S. News

article —— 88:92 Mr 17 '80

Date of issue ———— Budgeting for inflation. America 142:237 Mr 22 '80

         Burns: get tougher on U.S. inflation. E. Keerdoja and R. Thomas. por Newsweek 95:

Portrait ———— 14-15 F 11 '80

The Readers' Guide comes out several times a year and is then replaced by a bound volume for the year.

Other magazine and journal indexes include *The Art Index*, the *Education Index*, and the *Business Periodicals Index*. Each of these indexes is more specialized than *The Readers' Guide*; that is, each indexes a much more specialized group of magazines and journals. However, if you learn to use *The Readers' Guide*, you will be able to use any of these other periodical indexes.

Newspapers. *Newspapers*, like other periodicals, are very good for finding current information. However, the information in newspapers tends to be more limited than that found in magazines and journals. It generally covers less information and tends to focus on facts rather than explanations, opinions, and background details.

There are, of course, many newspapers. Your library probably has your local newspaper, and it may have *The New York Times,* which is considered a newspaper of record and has an index that goes back to 1851.

Whatever newspapers your library has, they will not be very useful unless you can find the information you want in them. Several newspapers have indexes; *The New York Times* has one of the most complete. Since the *Times* index is also the one you are most likely to find in your library, you should learn to use this particular index. Like many other indexes, it comes out several times a year and then is replaced by a consolidated index for the year. It is arranged alphabetically by subject, with each of the entries under a subject head giving the name of an article, a digest of the information in it, the date, the page, and the column. The symbols *L, M,* and *S* (long, medium, and short) tell you the length of the article. The index also has *see also* references, often listed by topic and date. The inclusion of the date makes it much easier to find the material. If you practice using this index, you will probably find that although it looks complex you will have no trouble with it.

The following example from the *Times* index shows a partial listing of entries under the subject heading *Energy and Power.* Note that there are several *see also* references. The first regular entry offers a concise summary of what the Carter administration was planning to do on July 1st. No year is given because each volume covers a single year, which is clearly marked on the spine of the book. The *M* indicates that it is a medium-length article. The *JL 1* indicates that it appeared on July 1st. The *1:1* indicates that it appeared on page 1 in the first column.

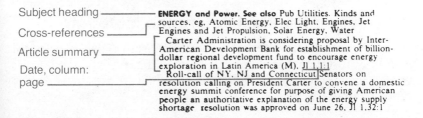

In addition to newspapers, your library may also have *Newsbank. Newsbank* is a service that uses microfiche to reprint articles about urban and public affairs from several different newspapers. *Newsbank* provides an excellent way to compare how various papers describe the same events and to find more information about things that happen in different parts of the country.

Pamphlets.   Pamphlets are small paper-bound texts issued by all sorts of groups: by government, by private agencies, and by companies. Like periodicals, pamphlets are useful because they are current. Unlike magazines, journals, and newspapers, they do not assume that you have any background information. Thus, they give a quick and concise background for the subjects they cover.

Pamphlets are usually arranged in a file, called a vertical file, arranged alphabetically by subject. If you have trouble finding what you need, ask a librarian, because the subject terms used may be unfamiliar to you. Each library is likely to have its own system for deciding which subject headings to use.

EXERCISE I: Using *The Readers' Guide*. Look up solar power in a recent *Readers' Guide*. Make a list of articles you find as well as any related headings. Finally, note the issue of the guide and page or pages you used.

EXERCISE J: Using *The New York Times Index*. Follow the instructions in Exercise I, using *The New York Times Index* instead of *The Readers' Guide*. After you have completed the exercise, compare your new list with the list you made for Exercise I and note any differences in number and type of articles in the two sources.

■ Choosing the Right Reference Materials

Now that you have learned about different types of material and how to find what you need in the library, what is left for you to learn? You now need to learn when to use the different types of material.

Recognize which library materials work best for different assignments.

A good beginning would be to think about when you should use the card catalog and when you might instead begin with an index. The card catalog should obviously be used to find books. An index should be used to find periodicals and parts of books. The part you need may be a short work such as a play or a critical description of either a short or a long work. Many times you may need both the catalog and an index. If, for example, you want criticism of a short story by Edgar Allan Poe, you can start by looking in the card catalog for books about Poe or books about short stories. You can also go to the *Essay and General Literature Index* or some other more specialized index to see if you can find materials containing the story and criticism of the story.

It is also useful to think about whether you need a book, a reference book, a periodical, or a pamphlet. A book will generally give you the most information, and, in some cases, the clearest explanation. A book is also better for information that is not new. For example, you would probably use a book for the history of the blue whale. On the other hand, a book is not likely to be as up to date as other sources. If you need to do a long report about current uses of solar energy, you might start looking in books for background and then go on to newspapers or periodicals to bring your report up to date.

A reference book is good for finding background information and best for finding factual information quickly. If you need to know the population of Germany, use a reference book.

Periodicals are good for finding current information. Remember that this means they are also good for finding information that was current at the time an article was written. If you need to know American reactions to the Munich agreement in 1938, you might go to newspapers and periodicals.

A pamphlet is good for finding current, concise information. It gives you good background information quickly. If, for example, you need enough information for a debate on capital punishment, you might find pamphlets very useful.

EXERCISE K: Choosing the Right Source. For each of the following, decide whether you would use the card catalog, an index, or both, and then give the reason for your choice.

1. Locating a poem
2. Finding criticism about Edith Wharton's *Ethan Frome*
3. Finding information about recent archaeological findings in Greece
4. Finding information about daily life in ancient Rome
5. Finding the play *Death of a Salesman* by Arthur Miller

EXERCISE L: Choosing the Right Material. For each of the following, decide whether you would use a book, reference book, periodical, or pamphlet to locate the information, and then give the reason for your choice.

1. Extensive information about the ancient kingdom of Benin
2. Information about insulin
3. The capital of Kansas
4. American reactions to Pearl Harbor
5. The use of methane as fuel

APPLICATION: Using Library Resources. Follow these steps.

1. Choose a topic for which valuable information can be obtained from books, reference books, periodicals, and possibly pamphlets.
2. Choose eight to ten varied sources for your topic and explain why you chose them.
3. Check to see if these sources are available in your school or public library.
4. If not, find sources that are available.

18.3 The Dictionary

You probably use the dictionary more often than any other reference book. But if you refer to a dictionary merely to check the meaning or spelling of words, you are not getting all you can out of this valuable resource. In addition to meanings and spellings, a dictionary can show you how to break words into syllables and pronounce them correctly. It can also tell you how a word can be used in a sentence. Most dictionaries show the derivations of words as well. A few even tell you when a word first appeared in written English and what it meant at a particular time in history. Many dictionaries also include essential facts about famous people, events, and places and explain the meanings of common abbreviations and foreign words.

Although most of these features and more can be found in a typical dictionary, all dictionaries are not the same. This section will describe some of the different kinds of general dictionaries and what they contain and will explain how to find information in them quickly.

■ Kinds of General Dictionaries

Lexicographers, the people who make dictionaries, always have a particular audience in mind when they prepare a new edition of a dictionary. Thus, if you wanted to buy a dictionary at your local bookstore, you would probably find several shelves of dictionaries representing the work of different lexicographers and publishers. There might be picture-book dictionaries for children just learning to read, dictionaries for students to use in their studies, and dictionaries for adults to use at home or at work. You might even find very large dictionaries intended to help scholars in their research. With such a variety of dictionaries available, it is important that you use one that is right for you.

Use a dictionary that suits your present academic needs.

The dictionary you use at home, in school, or in the library should be neither too easy nor too difficult for you. It should contain all of the words you are likely to encounter in your studies and should explain them to your satisfaction in language you can understand. A picture-book dictionary that you may have had since you were a child will not help you understand all of the words in a Victorian novel or a chemistry text. On the other hand, a scholarly dictionary containing thousands of pages would be both unwieldly and unnecessary for most of your schoolwork. Nevertheless, you should be aware of the two main kinds of dictionaries—abridged and unabridged—and of how they are made so that you know what kind of information you can expect to find in them.

Unabridged Dictionaries. *Unabridged* means "not shortened." The word applies to any dictionary that is not a shortened version of some larger dictionary. It does *not* mean that the dictionary contains all of the words of a language. Unabridged dictionaries generally contain 250,000 to 500,000 words, while it is estimated that the English language contains at least 600,000 words.

To assemble such great dictionaries, lexicographers spend many years researching and writing. Professional readers help lexicographers keep track of new words and changes in the meanings of old words. They glean information from a variety of current fiction, nonfiction, newspapers, and professional and popular magazines. They examine works published not only in the United States but also in other English-speaking countries. The readers record their findings on cards that are gathered and filed alphabetically for later reference. Some lexicographers have begun using computers to organize and store this information since their collections often contain more than three million cards.

As the lexicographers and their staff sift through the card file, they make many decisions. Some new words and meanings, for example, may be intentionally excluded because the lexicographers cannot find enough evidence in the card file to warrant their inclusion in the dictionary. Other words may be excluded because they are considered foreign. As a matter of policy, most lexicographers do not include the new Latin names of plants and animals and the names of rare chemical compounds. Still other words are unintentionally excluded because they entered the language while the dictionary was being assembled. Though many words that are used in English will not be found even in the largest unabridged dictionary, lexicographers do attempt to include all of the words and meanings that their criteria allow.

Two well-known unabridged dictionaries found on special stands in most libraries are *Webster's Third New International Dictionary of the English Language* (published in 1966) and *Random House Dictionary of the English Language, Unabridged Edition* (published in 1967). You should consult these books whenever you need very specific definitions and extremely detailed information about words. On most occasions, however, your regular dictionary will contain all you need to know.

Notice in the following example the detail and thoroughness of an unabridged dictionary's definitions.

UNABRIDGED ENTRY:

her·on \'herən\ *n, pl* **herons** *also* **heron** [ME *heiroun, heroun,* fr. MF *hairon, heron,* of Gmc origin; akin to OE *hrāgra* heron, OHG *heigaro, hreigaro,* ON *hegri;* akin to W *cryg* hoarse, Gk *krike* it creaked, Lith *krȳkšti* to shriek, OHG *scrian* to scream, cry — more at SCREAM] **:** any of various wading birds constituting the family Ardeidae that have a long neck and legs, a long tapering bill with a sharp point and sharp cutting edges, large wings and soft plumage, and the inner edge of the claw of the middle toe pectinate, that exhibit in some species dichromatism and develop in many species special plumes in the breeding season, that frequent chiefly the vicinity of water and feed mostly on aquatic animals which they capture by quick thrusts of the sharp bill, that usu. nest in trees often in communities, and that vary much in size among different species but are not as large as some of the cranes — see GREAT BLUE HERON, GREAT WHITE HERON, LITTLE BLUE HERON; compare EGRET

great blue heron

Another well-known unabridged dictionary is the *Oxford English Dictionary,* commonly known as the O.E.D. Its original twelve volumes took more than fifty years to write and were completed in 1928. The work was finally published in 1933 with a supplement volume. Further supplements began to appear in 1972. The O.E.D. differs from others in that it is *historical.* It organizes a word's meanings by dates and tells you when a word first appeared in written English and how its meanings changed over the years. Each meaning is followed by dates and examples of the word in use. In the following entry for *virus,* compare how the word was used in 1599 with later meanings of the word.

O.E.D. ENTRY:

‖ **Virus** (vəiˑˈrŭs). [L. *virus* slimy liquid, poison, offensive odour or taste. Hence also F., Sp., Pg. *virus.*]

In *Lanfranc's Cirurgie* (c 1400) 77 the word, explained as 'a thin venomy quitter', is merely taken over from the Latin text.

1. Venom, such as is emitted by a poisonous animal. Also *fig.*

1599 *Broughton's Lett.* iv. 14 You..haue..spit out all the *virus* and poyson you could conceiue, in the abuse of his.. person. **1702** MEAD *Poisons* 26 The Story of Cleopatra.. pouring the Virus of an Asp into a Wound made in her Arm by her own Teeth. **1728** CHAMBERS *Cycl.* s.v. *Viper,* By the Microscope, the Virus [of the viper] was found to consist of minute Salts in continual Motion. **1867** DK. ARGYLL *Reign of Law* i. 37 That the deadly virus shall in a few minutes curdle the blood. **1879** R. T. SMITH *Basil Gt.* ix. 111 He it was who hollowed the minute sting of the bee to shed its virus through.

2. *Path.* A morbid principle or poisonous substance produced in the body as the result of some disease, esp. one capable of being introduced into other persons or animals by inoculation or otherwise and of developing the same disease in them.

1728 CHAMBERS *Cycl., Virulent,* a Term apply'd to any thing that yields a *Virus*; that is, a corrosive or contagious Pus. **1771** SMOLLETT *Humph. Cl., To Sir W. Philip* 3 Oct., When he examined the *egesta,* and felt his pulse, he declared that much of the *virus* was discharged. **1799** *Med. Jrnl.* I. 448 Whether opium applied externally, may or may not prove an antidote to the canine virus. **1800** *Ibid.* III. 352 The pustules..contain a perfect Small-pox virus. **1846** S. COOPER *First Lines Surg.* (ed. 5) 165 In consequence of the virus being mixed with the saliva of the rabid animal. **1878** T. BRYANT *Pract. Surg.* I. 79 It should never be forgotten that it is the virus which infects the system. **1899** *Allbutt's Syst. Med.* VIII. 602 Possibly there is some virus acting on the nerve-centres.

attrib. **1860** W. T. Fox in *Trans. Obstetr. Soc.* II. 210 The general symptoms being the result of virus action. *Ibid.* 228 This latter action is alike common to all forms of virus disease.

3. *fig.* A moral or intellectual poison, or poisonous influence.

1778 WARNER in Jesse *Selwyn & Contemp.* (1844) III. 317 Venice is a stink-pot, charged with the very virus of hell! **1807** SOUTHEY *H. K. White* 12 As if there were not enough of the leaven of disquietude in our natures, without inoculating it with this dilutement—this vaccine virus of envy. *a* **1834** COLERIDGE *Shaks. Notes* (1875) 189 The corrosive virus which inoculates pride with a venom not its own. *a* **1884** M. PATTISON *Mem.* (1885) 239 The clerical virus would have lingered in the system.

4. Violent animosity; virulence.

1866 ALGER *Solit. Nat & Man* iv. 360 Two classes of men, however, he did hate with especial relish and virus.

Abridged Dictionaries.   Several companies publish shorter dictionaries especially suited to the needs of the general public and of students in particular. Unless you want special information about a word or need the meaning of a rare word, chances are you will find all you need to know in an abridged dictionary. Often called college or school dictionaries, these books are designed for everyday use at home, in the office, or in the classroom.

SOME ABRIDGED DICTIONARIES FOR EVERYDAY USE	
High School Dictionaries	**College Dictionaries**
Webster's New World Dictionary, Students Edition	Webster's New World Dictionary, Second College Edition
The Scott, Foresman Advanced Dictionary	The Random House College Dictionary
The Macmillan Dictionary	The American Heritage Dictionary

Considerably smaller and less expensive than unabridged dictionaries, abridged dictionaries usually list between 150,000 and 200,000 words; high school dictionaries list somewhat fewer.

In addition to containing fewer words, abridged dictionaries also usually list fewer definitions for a word than unabridged dictionaries do. Compare, for example, the following entry with the one from the unabridged dictionary shown on page 520.

ABRIDGED ENTRY: **her·on** \'her-ən\ *n, pl* **herons** *also* **heron** [ME *heiroun,* fr. MF *hairon,* of Gmc origin; akin to OHG *heigaro* heron, Gk *krizein* to creak, OHG *scrian* to scream] : any of various long-necked wading birds (family Ardeidae) with a long tapering bill, large wings, and soft plumage

EXERCISE A: Comparing Unabridged and Abridged Dictionaries.

Compare an unabridged and an abridged dictionary by completing the following steps.

1. Write the full title and most recent publication date of each dictionary.
2. Write the number of pages contained in each book.
3. Look up the same word in both dictionaries. How does the coverage differ? Be specific.

4. Find five words that are entered in the unabridged dictionary that are not entered in the other. Why, do you suspect, were they left out of the shorter book?

■ What Dictionaries for Students Contain

As a student you should always have a good abridged dictionary within easy reach for quick reference. By consulting your dictionary often and familiarizing yourself with its features, you can increase both your knowledge of words and the precision with which you use them. The rest of this section will describe those features found in most everyday dictionaries. Keep in mind that all dictionaries are not the same. Apply what you learn here to your own dictionary.

Learn to recognize and use the various features of your dictionary.

If you are at all uncomfortable using your dictionary or if you have acquired a new dictionary, the place to begin learning about it is in the book's introduction.

Front Matter.   A good college or high school dictionary contains an introduction that explains how to use it efficiently. In addition to a description of all of the book's features, the introduction will usually give instructions on how to look up a word, how to find words whose spelling you are unsure of, and how to interpret the pronunciation symbols. A complete pronunciation key and a list of all of the abbreviations used throughout the dictionary will also be found in this part of the book.

Back Matter.   Many dictionaries contain helpful charts and lists at the back of the book, such as tables of weights and measures; metric conversion tables; guides to mechanics, manuscript form, and business-letter style; proofreaders' marks; explanations of special signs and symbols; and lists of colleges and universities. Some dictionaries also list foreign terms, biographical names, and geographical names separately at the back of the book rather than alphabetically within the main part of the dictionary.

Main Entries.   In a dictionary each word together with the information about it is called a *main entry*. The word itself is called the *entry word*. All of the entry words are listed in strict letter-by-letter alphabetical order.

EXAMPLE: storied
stork
storm
storm door
stormy
story

An entry word may be a single word, a compound word (two or more words acting as a single word), an abbreviation, a prefix or suffix, or the name of a special event. Many dictionaries also include foreign terms and names of persons and places within the main part of the book.

KINDS OF ENTRY WORDS	
Single Word:	hyp·no·sis
Compound Word:	holding company
Abbreviation:	ICBM
Prefix:	hem·i-
Suffix:	-i·cal
Event:	Hundred Years' War
Foreign Term:	ars lon·ga, vi·ta bre·vis
Person:	Mah·ler
Place:	Yo·sem·i·te National Park

Preferred and Variant Spellings. A dictionary is an authority for the spelling of words. Most English words have only one correct spelling, as shown by the entry word. Some words, however, can be spelled in more than one way. The one most commonly used is called the *preferred spelling*. Less commonly used spellings are called *variant spellings*. If the form you are looking up is a variant spelling, the entry will refer you to another entry, the one that begins with the preferred spelling. Here you will also find the definition of the word.

VARIANT SPELLING: **ka·bob** (kə bäb′) *n. same as* KEBAB

PREFERRED SPELLING: **ke·bab** (kə bäb′) *n.* [Ar. *kabāb*] **1.** [*often pl.*] a dish consisting of small pieces of marinated meat stuck on a skewer, often alternated with pieces of onion, tomato, etc., and broiled or roasted **2.** a piece of such meat

If a main entry lists two spellings of the entry word, the form listed first is usually more commonly used and is thus the preferred spelling.

TWO SPELLINGS: **ka·zat·sky, ka·zat·ski** (kə zät′skē) *n., pl.* -skies [Russ.] a vigorous Russian folk dance performed by a man and characterized by a stop in which from a squatting position, each leg is alternately kicked out: also kazatska (-skä)

Sometimes a rather uncommon variant spelling or form may be listed only at the end of a main entry, as in the preceding example.

Syllabification.   Centered dots, spaces, or slashes in an entry word indicate where words are divided into syllables. If words are already hyphenated, hyphens will take the place of these symbols. The word *short-tempered*, for example, has three syllables: short-tem·pered. Most, but not all, of these divisions can be used for word breaks at the end of a line of writing. (Section 13.6 gives specific rules for breaking words into syllables at the ends of lines of writing.)

Pronunciation.   Pronunciations appear after most entry words, usually in parentheses or between diagonal lines. Pronunciations usually do not accompany entries that are not full words, such as abbreviations, prefixes, and suffixes. Nor are they usually found with entries that are compound words when the individual words that make up the compound word are main entries themselves.

The dictionary indicates how to pronounce words by respelling them in a *phonetic alphabet*. This is a set of letters and special symbols. Each letter or symbol is assigned one sound. Since phonetic alphabets vary somewhat from oneee dictionary to another, it is important to become familiar with the one in the dictionary you use. A *pronunciation key* at the front or back of your dictionary lists and explains all of the pronunciation symbols used throughout the book. Study this carefully. Most dictionaries for students also provide short pronunciation keys at the bottom of every other page to help you pronounce the words.

You should also learn to recognize four particular pronunciation symbols that usually indicate the same kind of vowel sounds in all dictionaries for students. These are the macron (ˉ), the dieresis (¨), the circumflex (ˆ), and the schwa (ə). Knowing these symbols will help you interpret the pronunciations of many words.

FOUR COMMON PRONUNCIATION SYMBOLS		
Symbol	**Sound**	**Example**
macron/ˉ	long vowels (ā, ē, ī, ō, ū)	(dāt) = date (sēt) = seat (flī) = fly (rōm) = roam (fū) = few
dieresis/¨	open *a* (ä)	(tär) = tar
circumflex/ˆ	open *o* (ô)	(sô) = saw
schwa/ə	any unstressed vowel	(bō′ə) = boa (shā′kən) = shaken (van′ə tē) = vanity (kə lekt′) = collect (fō′kəs) = focus

Short vowel sounds are easy to understand in pronunciations. Most dictionaries for students do not mark them.

SHORT VOWELS: (task) = task
(sent) = sent
(fit) = fit
(dot) = dot
(kup) = cup

Dictionaries use different combinations of vowels and symbols to indicate other vowel sounds. Some examples are oi, ou, o͞o, and u̇ or oo.

OTHER VOWEL SOUNDS: (toi) = toy
(kroud) = crowd
(fo͞ol) = fool
(tu̇k) or (took) = took

Consonants seldom pose a problem. Most of them are pronounced as you would expect. Those, such as *g* in *gauge*, that can have either a hard or a soft sound are simply assigned a second letter. *C*, *q*, and *x*, which can be represented by other consonants, are not in the pronunciation key.

EXAMPLES: (gāt) = gate (g = hard *g*)
(jes′chər) = gesture (j = soft *g*)
(kärt) = cart (k = hard *c*)
(sent) = cent (s = soft *c*)
(kwīt) = quite (kw = *q*)
(aks) = ax (ks = *x*)

Finally, three other consonant sounds you should learn to recognize in pronunciations are *th* as in *thin*, *th* as in *then*, and *s* as in *measure*. Most dictionaries represent *s* as in *measure* with zh, and *th* as in *thin* with th. However, the methods used to represent *th* as in *then* vary.

EXAMPLES: (mezh′ər) = measure
             (thin) = thin
             (*th*en) = then
             (t̲h̲en) = then
             (ᴛʜen) = then

In addition to helping you to pronounce the sounds correctly, the dictionary shows you which syllables are stressed. The syllable that gets the most emphasis has a *primary stress*, usually shown by a heavy mark (′) after the syllable. Words of more than one syllable may have a *secondary stress*, shown by a shorter, lighter mark (′) after the syllable. Unstressed syllables have no stress marks. Again, symbols may vary from one dictionary to another. For example, *Webster's New Collegiate Dictionary* places stress marks before the syllables to which they apply and uses a high-set mark (′) for primary stresses and a low-set mark (ˌ) for secondary stresses.

When two or more pronunciations for a word are given, the preferred pronunciation is given first. Here are some entries from different dictionaries, showing their pronunciations. Notice not only the stress marks, but also how additional pronunciations are indicated in abbreviated form.

PRIMARY STRESS ONLY: **just·ly** (just′lē)

PRIMARY AND SECONDARY STRESSES: **jus·ti·fy** (jus′tə fī′)

MORE THAN ONE PRONUNCIATION: **ju·ve·nil·i·a** (jōō′və nil′ē ə, -nil′yə)

Part-of-Speech Labels and Inflected Forms.   The dictionary also tells you how a word can be used in a sentence—whether it functions as a noun, verb, or some other part of speech. This information is given in abbreviated form, usually after the pronunciation of a word but sometimes at the end of the entry. Entries of two or more separate words, such as *chain stitch* or *certified public accountant*, have no part-of-speech labels because they are always nouns. Some dictionaries also omit part-of-speech labels for the names of people and places since these, too, are always nouns. As you can see in the following example, some words can be more than one part of speech.

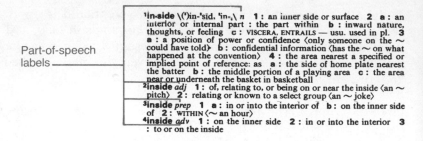

Part-of-speech labels

¹in·side \(')in-'sīd, 'in-,\ *n* **1** : an inner side or surface **2 a** : an interior or internal part : the part within **b** : inward nature, thoughts, or feeling **c** : VISCERA, ENTRAILS — usu. used in pl. **3 a** : a position of power or confidence ⟨only someone on the ∼ could have told⟩ **b** : confidential information ⟨has the ∼ on what happened at the convention⟩ **4** : the area nearest a specified or implied point of reference: as **a** : the side of home plate nearest the batter **b** : the middle portion of a playing area **c** : the area near or underneath the basket in basketball

²inside *adj* **1** : of, relating to, or being on or near the inside ⟨an ∼ pitch⟩ **2** : relating or known to a select group ⟨an ∼ joke⟩

³inside *prep* **1 a** : in or into the interior of **b** : on the inner side of **2** : WITHIN ⟨∼ an hour⟩

⁴inside *adv* **1** : on the inner side **2** : in or into the interior **3** : to or on the inside

When it is necessary, the dictionary shows inflected forms after the part-of-speech label. An inflected form may be the plural form of a noun, the different forms of an adjective or adverb, or the parts of a verb. Notice in the following examples that inflected forms are sometimes abbreviated.

PLURAL FORM OF NOUN: **dis cour te sy** (dis kėr′tə sē), *n.*, *pl.* -sies.

FORMS OF ADJECTIVE: **ti·ny** (tī′nē) *adj.* -ni·er, -ni·est

PARTS OF VERB: **in·fu·ri·ate** (in fyoor′ē āt′) *v. t.*, in·fu·ri·at·ed, in·fu·ri·at·ing.

Etymologies. The origin and history of a word is called its *etymology* or *derivation*. In dictionaries the etymology of an entry word usually appears in brackets soon after the pronunciation or part-of-speech label. In some dictionaries the etymology comes at the end of a main entry.

The historical information in an etymology is organized from the most recent to the least recent. This information is written in a code made up of symbols, abbreviations, and different kinds of type. One kind of type may indicate, for example, a cross-reference to another etymology. As with pronunciation symbols, the codes for etymologies vary from one dictionary to another. You should study the introduction in your dictionary to understand its code.

Knowing a word's etymology can often help you remember its current meaning. In the following example, see how the etymology can help you remember what *obdurate* means.

Etymology

ob·du·rate (äb′door ət, -dyoor-) *adj.* [< L. pp. of *obdurare* < *ob-*, very much + *durare*, to harden] **1.** not easily moved to pity or sympathy; hardhearted **2.** not feeling sorry for what one has done; hardened and unrepenting **3.** not giving in readily; obstinate; stubborn —**ob′du·ra·cy** (-ə sē) *n.* —**ob′du·rate·ly** *adv.*

The etymology indicates that *obdurate* comes from the past participle of the Latin word *obdurare,* which comes from *ob-* meaning "very much" and *durare* meaning "to harden."

Definitions. Many words in English have multiple meanings. These meanings or senses are called *definitions.* All meanings for the same part of speech are grouped together in the dictionary and numbered consecutively. Sometimes a definition will be broken into parts to show different shades of meaning. In these cases the different parts will be arranged by letters: a, b, c, and so on. One college dictionary, for example, lists eighty-six definitions for the word *run;* many of these are broken down further into as many as five parts.

Most dictionaries help clarify the different meanings of an entry word with a phrase or sentence showing the word in use. The following entry for *simple,* for example, lists twenty different definitions (several with more than one part) and gives nine examples of the word in use.

Examples of word in use

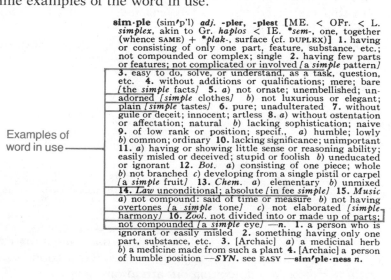

sim·ple (sim′p'l) *adj.* **-pler, -plest** [ME. < OFr. < L. *simplex,* akin to Gr. *haplos* < IE. **sem-*, one, together (whence SAME) + **plak-*, surface (cf. DUPLEX)] **1.** having or consisting of only one part, feature, substance, etc.; not compounded or complex; single **2.** having few parts or features; not complicated or involved *[a simple pattern]* **3.** easy to do, solve, or understand, as a task, question, etc. **4.** without additions or qualifications; mere; bare *[the simple facts]* **5.** *a)* not ornate; unembellished; unadorned *[simple clothes]* *b)* not luxurious or elegant; plain *[simple tastes]* **6.** pure; unadulterated **7.** without guile or deceit; innocent; artless **8.** *a)* without ostentation or affectation; natural *b)* lacking sophistication; naive **9.** of low rank or position; specif., *a)* humble; lowly *b)* common; ordinary **10.** lacking significance; unimportant **11.** *a)* having or showing little sense or reasoning ability; easily misled or deceived; stupid or foolish *b)* uneducated or ignorant **12.** *Bot.* *a)* consisting of one piece; whole *b)* not branched *c)* developing from a single pistil or carpel *[a simple fruit]* **13.** *Chem.* *a)* elementary *b)* unmixed **14.** *Law* unconditional; absolute *[in fee simple]* **15.** *Music* *a)* not compound: said of time or measure *b)* not having overtones *[a simple tone]* *c)* not elaborated *[simple harmony]* **16.** *Zool.* not divided into or made up of parts; not compounded *[a simple eye]* —*n.* **1.** a person who is ignorant or easily misled **2.** something having only one part, substance, etc. **3.** [Archaic] *a)* a medicinal herb *b)* a medicine made from such a plant **4.** [Archaic] a person of humble position —*SYN.* see EASY —**sim′ple·ness** *n.*

When you are checking a word that can have more than one meaning, read each definition carefully to find the one that matches the context of the word in the sentence you are reading or writing. You should be able to substitute the correct definition for the word in the sentence. Which definition of *simple,* for example, can be substituted in the following example?

EXAMPLE: Despite her wealth and regal bearing, she never claimed her ancestors were anything other than *simple* shopkeepers from a rural town in Poland.

As you can see in the following substitution, the ninth definition makes the best sense in this particular context.

SUBSTITUTION: Despite her wealth and regal bearing, she never claimed her ancestors were anything other than *common, ordinary* shopkeepers . . . .

Usage and Field Labels.   Words and meanings that are considered acceptable in formal situations by most speakers and writers of a language are said to be standard usage. Dictionaries indicate informal and nonstandard words and meanings with *usage labels,* such as *Slang, Informal* (or *Colloquial*), *Dialect,* and *British.* The label lets you know that a particular word or meaning may be unsuitable or not understood in certain situations. (See Chapter 11 for more about levels of usage.)

Other words or meanings may be restricted to a particular occupation, activity, or branch of knowledge. Dictionaries indicate this restricted usage with *field labels* such as *Mining, Football,* or *Philosophy.*

Both usage labels and field labels usually appear before the definitions to which they apply.

Usage labels ⎯⎯⎯

Field labels ⎯⎯⎯

pouch (pouch) *n.* [ME. *pouche* < MFr. *poche*, var. of *poque:* see POKE²] **1.** a small bag or sack, as one of leather, plastic, etc., for carrying pipe tobacco in one's pocket ☆**2.** a mailbag; specif., one whose opening can be locked, as for sending diplomatic dispatches **3.** anything shaped like a pouch **4.** [Scot.] a pocket (in clothing) **5.** [Archaic] a purse **6.** *Anat.* any pouchlike cavity or part **7.** *Zool.* *a)* a saclike structure on the abdomen of some animals, as the kangaroo and the opossum, used to carry young; marsupium *b)* a baglike part, as of a pelican's bill or a gopher's cheeks, used to carry food —*vt.* **1.** to put in a pouch **2.** to make into a pouch; make pouchy **3.** to swallow: said of fishes and certain birds —*vi.* to form a pouch or pouchlike cavity

Idioms.   An *idiom* is an expression that has a meaning different from the literal meaning of the words. Expressions such as *steal the show* and *down and out* are idioms.

Idioms are usually found in alphabetical order near the end of a main entry or at the end of the definitions for a particular part of speech. The key word in the expression determines the main entry with which the idiom appears. If the idiom seems to have two or more key words, as in *steal the show,* you should generally look under the noun first *(show).* If there are no nouns in the idiom, as in *down and out,* look under the first key word *(down).*

The following example shows the idioms that one dictionary lists under the entry word *ice.*

ice (īs) *n.* [ME. *is* < OE., akin to G. *eis* (OHG. *īs*), ON. *iss* < IE. base **eis, ein-,* whence Av. *isu-,* icy, OBulg. *inej,* snow flurry] **1.** the glassy, brittle, crystalline form of water made solid by cold; frozen water **2.** a piece, layer, or sheet of this **3.** anything like frozen water in appearance, structure, etc. **4.** coldness in manner or attitude **5.** *a*) a frozen dessert, usually made of water, fruit juice, egg white, and sugar *b*) [Brit.] ice cream **6.** icing; frosting ☆**7.** [Slang] a diamond or diamonds ☆**8.** [Slang] *a*) the illegal profit made in ticket scalping, as through extra payment by ticket brokers to theater management *b*) any money paid in bribes or graft —*vt.* **iced, ic′ing 1.** to change into ice; freeze **2.** to cover with ice; apply ice to **3.** to cool by putting ice on, in, or around **4.** to cover (cake, etc.) with icing **5.** *Ice Hockey* to shoot (the puck) from defensive to offensive territory —*vi.* to freeze (often with *up* or *over*) —**break the ice 1.** to make a start by getting over initial difficulties **2.** to make a start toward getting better acquainted —☆**cut no ice** [Colloq.] to have no influence or effect —☆**on ice** [Slang] **1.** in readiness, reserve, or safekeeping **2.** in abeyance **3.** with success or victory assured —**on thin ice** [Colloq.] in a risky, dangerous situation

Idioms

Derived Words or Run-on Entries.

Words formed by adding a common suffix, such as *-ly* or *-ness,* to an entry word are called *derived words* or *run-on entries.* The suffixes are added to change words from one part of speech to another. Derived words are found at the end of a main entry and are not defined. They simply appear with their part-of-speech labels and, sometimes, with pronunciations. If you are not sure of the meaning of a derived word, look up the meaning of the suffix and combine that with the meaning of the entry word.

in·sep·a·ra·ble \(')in-'sep-(ə-)rə-bəl\ *adj* [ME, fr. L *inseparabilis,* fr. *in-* + *separabilis* separable] : incapable of being separated or disjoined — **in·sep·a·ra·bil·i·ty** \(,)in-,sep-(ə-)rə-'bil-ət-ē\ *n* — **inseparable** *n* — **in·sep·a·ra·ble·ness** \(')in-'sep-(ə-)rə-bəl-nəs\ *n* — **in·sep·a·ra·bly** \-blē\ *adv*

Derived words

Synonymies.

A *synonym* is a word closely related but not identical in meaning to another word. In some dictionaries you will see below the entry a block of words beginning with SYN. Here the differences in meaning among synonyms are explained. Such explanations are called *synonymies. Antonyms,* or words opposite in meaning, are sometimes found here, too.

ef·fort (ef′ərt) *n.* [Fr. < OFr. *esforz* < *esforcier,* to make an effort < VL. **exfortiare* < *ex-,* intens. + **fortiare:* see FORCE] **1.** the using of energy to get something done; exertion of strength or mental power **2.** a try, esp. a hard try; attempt; endeavor **3.** a product or result of working or trying; achievement
SYN.—effort implies a conscious attempt to achieve a particular end *[make some effort to be friendly]*; **exertion** implies an energetic, even violent, use of power, strength, etc., often without reference to any particular end *[she feels faint after any exertion]*; **endeavor** suggests an earnest, sustained attempt to accomplish a particular, usually meritorious, end *[a life spent in the endeavor to do good]*; **pains** suggests a laborious, diligent attempt *[to take pains with one's work] —ANT.* **ease**

Synonymy

Antonym

EXERCISE B: Using Front and Back Matter. Find a college dictionary in a library and use its front and back matter to answer the following questions. Be sure to include the name of the dictionary you use

1. On what page of the front matter does a list appear showing all the abbreviations that are used throughout the dictionary?
2. What are the meanings of these abbreviations: OE., MFr., LL., AmInd or AmerInd, G.?
3. Where is Fordham University and when was it founded?
4. What are the meanings of these symbols: ⊙ (in astronomy), ♃(in biology), ⇔ (in chemistry), ∴ (in mathematics), † (in miscellaneous situations)?

EXERCISE C: Alphabetizing Entry Words. Put the following words in letter-by-letter alphabetical order as you would find them in a dictionary.

1. sound effects
2. soul food
3. sounding board
4. soufflé
5. soundproof
6. soupcon
7. sotto voce
8. sounder
9. soupe du jour
10. soul-searching

EXERCISE D: Determining Preferred Spellings. Use your dictionary to determine whether the following are preferred or variant spellings. If the spelling is preferred, write *preferred* on your paper; if it is a variant spelling of the word, write the preferred spelling.

1. idyl
2. gasolene
3. sideways
4. quintette
5. Tchaikovsky
6. spurrey
7. lachrymal
8. halleluiah
9. labour
10. incase

EXERCISE E: Understanding Pronunciations. Copy from your dictionary the preferred pronunciations for the following words. Be prepared to pronounce them aloud in class.

1. reinterpret
2. aestheticism
3. fleur-de-lis
4. oligarchy
5. engineer
6. ridiculous
7. surprising
8. tortuous
9. expatiate
10. recognition

EXERCISE F: Finding Part-of-Speech Labels. Use your dictionary to determine the part-of-speech labels for each of the following entry words. After each label record the number of definitions listed for that part of speech.

1. scan
2. reflex
3. out
4. break
5. ycllow

EXERCISE G: Interpreting Etymologies. Find the etymologies for the following words in your dictionary. Write a sentence describing the origin and history of each.

1. January
2. uranium
3. nucleus
4. evangelist
5. baccalaureate
6. universe
7. Beelzebub
8. entertain
9. epicure
10. dachshund

EXERCISE H: Applying Definitions to Words in Context. Look up the word *render* in your dictionary. Decide which definition applies in each sentence. Write the appropriate definitions on your paper.

1. A centiliter of the toxin can *render* an elephant helpless.
2. The jury deliberated two days before *rendering* a verdict.
3. *Render* the bacon thoroughly before adding the dry ingredients.
4. Shakespeare's plays have been *rendered* into dozens of foreign languages.
5. The artist deftly *rendered* the scene that lay before her.

EXERCISE I: Finding Usage Labels and Field Labels. Use the usage labels and field labels in your dictionary to answer the following questions.

1. What meaning of *instance* is now obsolete?
2. Where is the hood of an automobile called a *bonnet?*
3. In what country might you encounter the word *billabong?*
4. What does *outlier* mean in geology?
5. What is the botanical meaning of an *escape?*

EXERCISE J: Finding the Meaning of Idioms. Use your dictionary to find the meaning of each of the following idioms. Write the meaning and the entry word under which you find each idiom.

1. get under one's skin
2. walk off with
3. come out in the wash
4. take one's medicine
5. knock for a loop

EXERCISE K: Finding Derived Words. List the following entry words on your paper. After each, write any derived words you find listed under that word in your dictionary.

1. designate
2. comical
3. like-minded
4. imaginary
5. desolate

APPLICATION: Using Your Dictionary Efficiently. Use your dictionary to answer the following questions. Record the time you spend on each question.

1. When did John Keats die? How old was he?
2. What are the Pleiades?
3. What field labels do you find under *jump?*
4. When did the French Revolution begin?
5. What are some synonyms of *deep?*
6. According to its etymology, what did *raccoon* originally mean? From what language did it come?
7. What idioms are listed under *short?*
8. What usage labels are listed for *shear?*
9. How many syllables are in the word *ambidextrous?* Which syllable has a primary stress? Which has a secondary stress?
10. Which is the variant spelling, *meter* or *metre?*

UNIT **VI**

Composition

19
Sentence Length and Structure

20
The Use of Words

21
Clear Thinking in Writing

22
Effective Paragraphs

23
Kinds of Paragraphs

24
Essays

25
Library Papers

26
Papers About Literature

27
Letters and Précis

28
Essay Examinations

19

Sentence Length and Structure

The ability to write complete, well-structured sentences should be one of the major goals of your study of grammar, usage, and mechanics. But your writing should be more than technically correct. It should also please the reader with a varied pattern of sentence lengths as well as an interesting variety of sentence structures.

The purpose of this chapter is to examine the ways of promoting variety in your sentence lengths and structures. By learning to avoid problems such as choppiness or monotonous sentence constructions, you can improve your own patterns. In addition, you can learn from the patterns followed by professional writers to experiment with sentence variety as you write and as you revise.

19.1 Improving Length and Structure

By varying your sentences, you can create a pattern that holds your reader's attention. To create a good pattern, your sentences should not all be short and abrupt. Nor should they tire a reader because they are long-winded and overly complicated. Similarly, sentences that all sound alike will weary a reader. Instead, you can learn to control the rhythm of your sentences. A successful mixture of long and short sentences and different grammatical structures adds rhythm to a series of sentences. In this section you will practice using sentences of different lengths while varying sentence openers and structures. As you revise, you will learn to listen to the rhythm of your sentences and control your sentences to produce a pleasing effect.

■ Different Sentence Lengths

To achieve a suitable variety of sentence lengths, you must first be aware of some obvious pitfalls and learn to avoid them.

Learn to recognize the way in which too many short, choppy sentences or too many long, rambling sentences can weaken your writing style.

A series of short sentences may sound choppy and unsophisticated, as in the following example.

Short, choppy sentences	*The Tempest* is one of William Shakespeare's plays. It can be exciting on stage. The first act opens with a storm. Lightning flashes and thunder roars. Violent waves pound the decks of a sailing vessel.

Long, rambling sentences, on the other hand, can weaken a passage by burdening the reader with too much information all at once.

A long, rambling sentence	*The Tempest*, which is one of William Shakespeare's plays, can be exciting on stage, such as in the first act which opens with a storm during which lightning flashes and thunder roars and violent waves pound the decks of a sailing vessel.

Your purpose should be to find a middle ground, a style consisting of sentences varied in length.

Varied sentences	*The Tempest* by William Shakespeare can be exciting on stage. The first act, for example, opens with a raging storm. Lightning flashes, thunder roars, and violent waves pound the decks of a sailing vessel.

Expanding Short Sentences.   If you find that many of your sentences are too short, you may need to add details or combine ideas. A series of short, choppy sentences may sound awkward and can break up ideas.

Expand short, choppy sentences by adding details or by combining ideas.

One way to lengthen and enliven short, plain sentences is to add details. Modifying words and phrases, appositives, and clauses with additional ideas can add substance to your writing while lengthening short sentences. Examples in the following chart illustrate how many kinds of details can be used to lengthen and develop short sentences.

ADDING DETAILS TO SHORT SENTENCES	
Short Sentence:	**The rat protected her young.**
Adding Adjectives and Adverbs:	The *snarling* rat *boldly* and *instinctively* protected her *helpless* young.
Adding Prepositional Phrases:	*Under the porch* the rat protected her young *with fierce determination.*
Adding Verbal Phrases:	*Defying us to move closer,* the rat protected her young *lying helplessly in the corner.*
Adding Appositive Phrases:	The rat, *normally an inhabitant of the swamp,* built a nest under the porch and protected her young, *a litter of blind, hairless creatures.*
Adding Clauses:	*When we approached the nest under the porch,* the rat protected her young, *which were lying helplessly in the nest.*

Another way to lengthen short, choppy sentences is to combine two or more of them. Two sentences in a series, for example, may contain ideas that are closely related and can be joined in a single, longer sentence.

You might combine sentences by using a compound subject or verb. You might rewrite the idea of one sentence as a modifying or as an appositive phrase and then attach it to the other sentence. Or you might connect sentences to form longer sentences with different structures, creating compound, complex, or compound-complex sentences. As you can see in the following chart, there are many options for combining short sentences.

COMBINING IDEAS TO FORM LONGER SENTENCES	
Short, Choppy Sentences	**Longer, Smoother Sentences**
The speech club sponsored a car wash. The broadcasting club sponsored a car wash.	The *speech* and *broadcasting* *clubs* sponsored car washes. (Compound subject)
The usher closed the doors. He would not let us in.	The usher *closed* the doors *and* *would* not *let* us in. (Compound verb)
Elena waved a stick. She chased the boys.	*Waving a stick,* Elena chased the boys. (Modifying phrase)

The Field Club hosted the C team. The Field Club is Rye's new athletic association.	The Field Club, *Rye's new athletic association*, hosted the C team. (Appositive phrase)
We were late. The show had already started.	We were late, *and* the show had already started. (Compound sentence)
We were all disappointed. We walked farther into town for pizza.	*Because* we were all disappointed, we walked farther into town for pizza. (Complex sentence)
Alan decided to become a doctor. He wrote to five medical schools. They all sent applications.	*When* Alan decided to become a doctor, he wrote to five medical schools, *and* they all sent applications. (Compound-complex sentence)

Simplifying Long Sentences. In contrast to plain, choppy sentences, some sentences can be long and confusing because they contain too much information for a reader to comprehend at a comfortable pace.

Simplify rambling sentences either by separating them into simpler sentences or by moving and regrouping ideas.

Usually, tangled sentences contain too many ideas joined to form long compound, complex, or compound-complex sentences. One way to simplify long, confusing sentences is to separate ideas to form two or more shorter sentences with fewer clauses in each. Notice in the following chart how a long compound-complex sentence has been revised to make a complex, a simple, and a compound-complex sentence. When ideas are separated into different sentences of reasonable lengths, the passage is easier to understand.

SIMPLIFYING BY SEPARATING IDEAS	
A Single, Long Compound-Complex Sentence	**Three Shorter Sentences: Complex, Simple, and Compound-Complex**
If you stand too close to a painting, you can see the ridges where different colors collide, and even lines and	If you stand too close to a painting, you can see the ridges where different colors collide. Even lines and angles

| angles do not appear straight or accurate, but as you move away, colors blend normally and lines develop accuracy and symmetry. | do not appear straight or accurate. But as you move away, colors blend normally and lines develop accuracy and symmetry. |

The problem with an overly lengthy sentence may not be merely one of length. The ideas may also be presented in an awkward order. Thus, another way of simplifying long, rambling sentences is to concentrate on regrouping ideas as you separate them into shorter sentences. In the following chart, you can see how a long compound-complex sentence has been separated and the sentence parts regrouped to form new structures. Notice that the phrase and clause in italics have been moved to the beginning of the first two sentences in the regrouped version.

SIMPLIFYING BY REGROUPING IDEAS	
A Single, Long Compound-Complex Sentence	**A Group of Sentences: One Simple and Two Complex**
Lt. Jo Dunn decided to climb a rope ladder from the gondola to the top of her hot-air balloon *for her stunt* so she moved slowly up the ladder *as spectators watched from more than a thousand feet below,* and her feet dangled frequently in mid-air as she pulled herself hand-over-hand toward the top.	*For her stunt*, Lt. Jo Dunn decided to climb a rope ladder from the gondola of her hot-air balloon. *As spectators watched from more than a thousand feet below,* the lieutenant moved slowly up the ladder. Her feet frequently dangled in mid-air as she pulled herself hand-over-hand toward the top.

EXERCISE A: Adding Details to Short Sentences. Each of the following sentences is too short and plain to be interesting. Rewrite each sentence, adding details so that all five sentences become more informative and lively.

1. The rain fell.
2. The train passed us
3. I looked at the sunrise.
4. The dog smelled bacon.
5. The tugboat helped the ocean liner turn around.

EXERCISE B: Combining Ideas to Form Longer Sentences. Each of the following items contains two or more short sentences that can be combined. Combine the sentences, varying the method you use for each combination.

1. Joan stood outside the door. Another girl was with her.
2. Our play director was late. Several players were late for rehearsal too.
3. All contestants must answer difficult questions. College professors have prepared these questions. The questions cover a wide range of subjects.
4. The fish explored the sunken tire. They swam in and out of it. They looked for a place to hide from predators.
5. William Hicks is Clayburgh's mayor. He will speak at tomorrow's dedication ceremony. His assistant will also speak at the ceremony.

EXERCISE C: Adding Details and Combining Ideas. The following paragraph contains a series of short, choppy sentences. Rewrite the passage, expanding the sentences by adding details and by joining some ideas.

(1) Danny heard the clumping of boots on the upper deck. (2) He knew the pirates would walk in. (3) They would find him. (4) He hid in a barrel. (5) Captain Block and three of his men entered. (6) They dropped a heavy bundle onto a table. (7) Danny could hear this. (8) He strained his ears to overhear their conversation. (9) The pirates spoke in low tones. (10) He heard one mention his name. (11) A chill ran down his spine. (12) Were they still looking for him?

EXERCISE D: Simplifying Long Sentences. The following paragraph contains sentences that are too long and involved. Rewrite the passage, separating some thoughts and regrouping some ideas. Then check for varied lengths and for pleasing rhythms.

(1) A long bus ride down an interstate highway, more than a trip on a train, airplane, or automobile, encourages deep thought, unless you are a person who is addicted to reading, because there are fewer distractions which take your concentration away from the ideas which are unfolding in your mind. (2) Since there are no people walking up and down the aisle, there is no food being served, there is no movie to watch, there are no traffic lights or highway signs to watch for, and, except for certain parts of the country (in the mountains, for example), the scenery along the interstates is usually rather monotonous, you can speculate, daydream, and plan, sometimes imagining what it would be like to work in that diner or to live on that farm, sometimes reliving some happy moment and sometimes thinking about the future, such as about the job you hope to have next summer.

■ Different Sentence Openers and Sentence Structures

Besides focusing on length to achieve strong, appealing sentences, you should pay particular attention to the beginnings and structures of your sentences.

Learn to recognize a series of monotonous sentence openers and a series of sentences that overuse any one sentence structure.

Too many similar sentence openers will create monotony. In the following passage, for instance, all sentences begin with the subject and verb. Even though the sentences differ in length, the sameness among sentence openers creates an awkward, halting effect.

Monotonous passage with sentences all beginning with subjects and verbs

The castaways awoke on an unfamiliar shore. Captain Trilli swore that he had seen lights on the beach as their lifeboat had approached. No evidence of habitation presented itself. Scottie and two of the *Catasauqua's* passengers walked to the tree line and separated. Scottie turned to the east and the others headed west. They looked for any mark of civilization. They returned to Captain Trilli and the other passengers. They had little to report, and hope began to ebb among the members of the group for the first time.

Similarly, repetitious sentence structures are monotonous. In the next passage, a series of complex sentences results in a pattern of awkward starts and stops.

Monotonous passage with all complex sentences

When the castaways awoke, they were on an unfamiliar shore. Although Captain Trilli swore that he had seen lights on the beach as their lifeboat had approached, no evidence of habitation presented itself. When Scottie and two of the *Catasauqua's* passengers walked to the tree line and separated, Scottie turned to the east and the others headed west. After they looked for any mark of civilization, they returned to Captain Trilli and the other passengers. Because they had little to report, hope began to ebb among the members of the group for the first time.

To manage your sentences most effectively, you must alternate your sentence openers as well as the structures of your sentences as in the following passage. Notice that the openers vary and that a simple sentence is followed by a complex sen-

tence, another simple sentence with modifying phrases, and
then a compound-complex sentence.

Passage with varied sentence openers and structures	The castaways awoke on an unfamiliar shore. Although Captain Trilli swore that he had seen lights on the beach as their lifeboat had approached, no evidence of habitation presented itself. Scottie and two of the *Catasauqua's* passengers walked to the tree line and separated, Scottie turning to the east and the others heading west, to look for any mark of civilization. When they returned to Captain Trilli and the other passengers, they had little to report, and for the first time that day, hope began to ebb among the members of the group.

Using Different Sentence Openers.   A great number of possibilities exist for beginning any sentence. Before you begin varying your choices, you must recognize your options.

Choose from among many different sentence openers as you write a series of sentences.

While you may begin many of your sentences with the common, useful subject-verb pattern, you would create a choppy, tiresome pattern if *all* of your sentences began this way. To avoid a monotonous style, try to use the different possible openers in the following chart when they fit your ideas.

WAYS TO BEGIN SENTENCES	
Subject-Verb:	*We* could not hear the speaker's voice.
Adjectives:	*Tired and hungry*, we sat down to rest beside a brook.
Adverb:	*Wearily*, Jan rose to start a campfire.
Prepositional Phrase:	*With a flying leap*, Rex cleared the fence rail and raced away.
Participial Phrase:	*Holding onto her purse*, Maude elbowed her way through the crowd.
Infinitive Phrase:	*To see the stage*, we had to sit on the backs of our seats.
Subject with Appositive Phrase:	The speaker, *a tall, stoop-shouldered man*, spoke in a whisper.
Adverb Clause:	*After the sun had set*, strange lights were visible along the horizon.

One-Word Transition:	*Therefore*, nobody will be permitted to leave class without prior permission.
Transitional Phrase:	*On the other hand*, students with medical excuses will receive special consideration.
Inverted Order:	From the sky came large chunks of ice.

Using Different Sentence Structures. When you vary your sentence lengths and openers, you will often do so by using different sentence structures. Sometimes, however, you can improve your sentences simply by concentrating on varying structure.

Use a variety of simple, compound, complex, and compound-complex sentences to make your writing smooth and interesting.

As you write and revise your sentences, think about using some simple, some compound, some complex, and a few compound-complex sentences. Too many of any one kind of structure can become tiresome, but a variety, used thoughtfully, can highlight your ideas and help to hold the reader's attention.

Notice how the different structures in the following passage avoid sameness and suit the ideas expressed.

(1) Simple
(2) Complex

(3) Complex

(4) Simple
(5) Compound

(1) Some animals have an acute sense of smell. (2) An anteater, for example, has a long funnel-shaped nose, which it uses to smell and locate those delicious red and black ants. (3) (If we humans tried to find ants by smelling them, we would get nowhere.) (4) And even our favorite pets, dogs, are renowned sniffers. (5) Bloodhounds are the traditional trackers by scent, and other breeds, such as German shepherds, help to locate lost people.

Occasionally, checking your sentence structures in a passage by labeling them can help you to develop variety in your writing.

EXERCISE E: Choosing Different Sentence Openers. Most of the following sentences begin in the usual order, subject and verb first. Rewrite each sentence, rearranging the words so that the sentence no longer begins with the subject. Then identify the type of sentence opener (including inverted order) that you have used for each sentence.

1. Mourners marched solemnly along the beach.
2. We could not get the car started until Geoffrey located jumper cables.
3. A protester was seething with anger and waved his fist at the troops.
4. R. F. Travers was a concert pianist who traveled the college circuit and performed for free.
5. No one, however, could determine why the mixture would change color simply by heating it.
6. A thousand acorns tumbled down the attic stairs.
7. You must assemble the right brushes, paints, and canvas to begin painting.
8. Too many lives were lost sadly enough because lifesaving precautions had not been taken.
9. Our food was cold by the time we returned from league practice.
10. A hooded figure standing at the foot of the stairs blocked any chance of escape.

EXERCISE F: Alternating Sentence Structures. Both of the following paragraphs contain too many sentences of similar structure. First, identify the structure of each sentence. Then, rewrite the paragraphs to achieve a variety of sentence structures. Finally, in the margin of your rewritten version, identify the structure of each sentence that you have written.

(1) I was on my own for about an hour, so I walked along the beach. (2) I began my walk near a huge, square-shaped rock, and I stooped periodically to study unusual pebbles and shells in the sand. (3) At that moment they seemed so unique and marvelous, but they might seem drab and dull at other times.

(4) I lost interest soon in the collection of pebbles and shells. (5) They were all along the beach. (6) I moved on. (7) I came to a spot where the sand was almost pure white. (8) Nothing littered the beach. (9) I could not hold myself back finally. (10) I took a running start. (11) I ran splashing into the water. (12) As I swam, I laughed. (13) I laughed at the thought of all this really existing. (14) I laughed that it was all mine for the hour.

APPLICATION 1: Checking Sentences in your Writing. Choose a brief composition that you have written recently. Read the following suggestions for revising your sentences, and then choose *two* of the suggestions to use in revising your work. Follow the suggestions and rewrite your passage.

1. *Read your sentences aloud.* If your voice rises and falls in the same rhythm, then your sentence lengths are probably

too similar. If so, change the lengths of some of your sentences. If your voice halts as you read, or if you run out of breath in the middle of a sentence, you may have further evidence of the need to lengthen some sentences and shorten others.

2. *Ask someone else to read your sentences.* Ask this person to read silently or aloud and then to comment on the sound and flow of your sentences. Then make the changes that seem necessary.

3. *Count the words in your sentences.* If all of your sentences have few words or about the same limited number of words, think of some ways to add details or join ideas to create some longer sentences. If you have a passage of long sentences, shorten some of the sentences.

4. *Label the openers and structures in a passage.* If you are overusing any one opener or structure, rewrite, combine, or separate some sentences.

5. *Use a tape recorder to record your sentences.* Then play it back to listen to the sound of your writing. Make any necessary changes in the length, openers, and structure of your sentences.

6. *Put your work aside for a short period of time to help you "hear" your writing afresh.* Then make any necessary changes in your sentences.

APPLICATION 2: Achieving Sentence Variety. Choose one of the following topics and ideas to write a brief composition (approximately ten sentences). As you write, look critically at your sentence lengths, openers, and structures. When you are finished, use one of the suggestions in Application 1 to help you revise.

An embarrassing incident that happened to you or to someone you know

A description of a farm (ranch, resort, ski lodge, and so on) that you have visited

A historical event, or a local event, that you can relate

Your feelings about moving to a new place (starting a new course, meeting a new friend, joining a new club, and so on)

A famous person you would like to meet

19.2 Exploring New Ideas for Structure

In addition to improving your writing style by concentrating on the length, beginning, and basic structure of your sentences, you can achieve variety by examining your sentences from other angles. You can investigate three different types of sentences that allow you to emphasize ideas in different ways. You can also learn to repeat and break patterns within sentences and within groups of sentences to achieve a desired effect. And, finally, you can see in this section how the work of professional writers can provide models and inspiration for the development of your own writing style.

■ Experimenting with Different Kinds of Sentences

You can emphasize important ideas in a passage by using certain kinds of sentences that meet readers' expectations, attract readers' attention, cause them to read faster, build suspense, or neatly package an idea.

> Consider using different kinds of sentences to achieve special kinds of emphasis for your ideas.

You may already know that the beginning and end of a sentence are the most noticeable, memorable positions for ideas. A reader tends to pay particular attention to these positions. By placing your most important ideas in either of these two positions you can emphasize them. A third way to draw attention to ideas is by using balanced repetition. To some extent, you have probably already been using position and repetition to create certain effects. However, the following paragraphs will help you look at sentences in a new way. By studying three different sentence variations that use position and structure to emphasize ideas, you can learn to adapt position and structure to emphasize the meaning of your own ideas.

Loose Sentences.   One of the most common kinds of sentences in English is the loose or strung-along sentence. A *loose sentence* follows the usual subject-verb-complement order with modifiers and clauses added at the end as the writer thinks of them.

> Use a loose sentence, which places the essential part of the sentence first, to put mild emphasis on the most important words in the sentence.

A loose sentence reveals its important idea first, and then it proceeds to develop and expand upon it. The emphasis is on the first part of the sentence with the important idea readily apparent to the reader. A loose sentence can be simple, compound, complex, or compound-complex, but it always states its important idea first.

EXAMPLES: The winds disturbed the guests in the night by sending beach umbrellas and patio furniture flying and causing shutters to bang loudly again and again.

I recommend that you read the book first and then see the movie because the movie distorts two of the characters and leaves out several key scenes.

Loose sentences are common because they represent a typical way of thinking and because they fulfill the readers' expectations. In loose sentences important words are placed first, as writers naturally think of them and in the order that readers expect to find them. Thus, a loose sentence enables the reader to grasp the meaning quickly from the first part of the sentence and to read rapidly. For these reasons, many of the sentences you write will be loose.

Periodic Sentences.   To emphasize important words even more, you can place them at the end of the sentence. A *periodic sentence* saves the important idea until the end and begins with modifying phrases and clauses. Thus, it is structurally the opposite of a loose sentence.

Use a periodic sentence, which places the essential part of the sentence last, to put an especially strong emphasis on the most important words in the sentence.

A periodic sentence builds suspense by delaying the reader, forcing the reader to read to the end of the sentence to grasp the point. Such a sentence can be particularly effective for emphasis because it holds the reader's attention and finally delivers the main idea as a climax.

In the following periodic sentence, several phrases that add meaning lead to the point of the statement. The main idea is held back until the reader is ready for it.

EXAMPLE: Without warning, without provocation, a soldier turned to the crowd and fired.

Occasionally, a colon or a dash can be placed strategically in a periodic sentence to signal the main idea.

EXAMPLE: An escape from people, closeness to nature, and peace—after she had worked forty years in a noisy, crowded city, she found these rewards in a country house.

Periodic sentences are useful and dramatic but can become heavy-handed and tiresome if overused. Therefore, vary periodic sentences with other kinds and use long, deliberate periodic sentences infrequently, only when such a sentence will suit the importance of a particular idea.

Balanced Sentences. A third way to underscore important ideas is to use a repetitive, balanced structure. A *balanced sentence* contains at least two important contrasting ideas, roughly equal in importance and written in similar grammatical structures.

Use a balanced sentence that joins equal, contrasting ideas to emphasize the contrast.

Each idea in a balanced sentence is given the same weight, and the effect of the sentence is a balance of statements. The important ideas are emphasized equally while the entire sentence draws attention to the ideas it contains.

A balanced sentence usually involves the use of parallelism, generally, the use of two or more structurally similar clauses. The similarity of the parts serves to highlight the contrast between the ideas. A conjunction or a semicolon usually joins the parts of a balanced sentence.

EXAMPLES: Janice was kind and thoughtful, but Terry was neither good nor wise.

Her fame and fortune soared; his declined and then disappeared.

Although the ideas in a balanced sentence do not always have to be presented in strictly parallel clauses, the balanced parts should be closely related in meaning. Like the periodic sentence, the balanced sentence should be used sparingly for emphasis and for variety of rhythm.

EXERCISE A: Writing Sentences to Achieve Emphasis. Identify each of the following sentences as loose, periodic, or balanced. Then write sentences of your own similar to each of the sentences in the exercise.

1. When our work was done, when our bodies were tired, and when our minds were at rest, we collapsed onto our sleeping mats.
2. Jasper loved to dance and sing, but nobody loved Jasper's grace or music.
3. Peace reigned once more in the kingdom so that farmers returned to their fields, merchants reopened their shops, and children played happily, their parents no longer fearful for their safety.
4. The storm besieged the village with steadily falling snow and increasingly loud windy shrieks as the villagers huddled around sputtering fires.
5. After a slow, painful death, the famous millionaire left his mansion, a priceless art collection, a fortune in gold and silver, and a stable of prize horses to his wife.

EXERCISE B: **Adding Emphasis to Your Sentences.** Choose a brief composition that you have recently written. Look for any loose, periodic, or balanced sentences. Then rewrite the passage so that it includes at least one loose, one balanced, and one periodic sentence. Underline the new sentences that you create, and label them *loose, periodic,* or *balanced.*

■ Experimenting with Different Patterns

You can emphasize ideas not only through the positioning and balancing of the important words and ideas in your sentences but also through the use of a series or pattern of similar structures. If you are trying to emphasize similarities or illustrate an idea, a series of similar structures can help the reader understand your intention. If, on the other hand, you want to emphasize a final point, you can establish a pattern with your sentences and then break it. No matter what your specific goal, the nature of your ideas should influence the sound and structure of your sentences. And your sentences should be clear, effective vehicles for your ideas.

Employing Structural Similarities.   Parallelism within sentences and within groups of sentences can signal the reader that ideas are of equal importance or are related in some significant way.

Use similar patterns within sentences and within groups of sentences to underscore ideas.

As you have already seen, parallelism in a balanced sentence can help you emphasize two contrasting ideas. The use of parallel structures for a series of items within a sentence can also draw attention to the ideas, while achieving a uniform listing or building effect. As parts of speech, phrases, or clauses are repeated, a rhythm is created, which carries the reader along. Notice in the following examples how the parallelism achieves special effects.

WITHIN SENTENCES: *Searching the newspapers' advertisements, walking the city blocks, knocking on the doors of one manager's office after another,* they spent hours hunting for an apartment.
(Parallel phrases emphasize the time-consuming process.)

Vote Yes on Student Proposition 3 *because you believe in tutoring, because you support student sponsored programs, because you value the experience,* and *because you care.*
(Parallel clauses list and emphasize the reasons for supporting the proposition.)

Parallelism also works within a group of sentences. It can be used to draw the reader's attention to the underlying relationship between the ideas while establishing a unifying rhythm. In the following passage, three similar sentences give examples of a main idea presented in the first sentence. The first sentence prompts the reader to ask "Why?" and then the parallel sentences after it answer the question. Since the sentences sound alike and follow rapidly one after another, they form a rhythmic unity.

WITHIN A GROUP OF SENTENCES: By no means would the bank lend George another nickel. *His loan payments had been late. He had once defaulted on a note. And his checks now bounced with regularity.*

As shown in the preceding example, a series of similar structures can be effective in accenting ideas and making sound and rhythm enhance meaning. However, such patterns should not be overused or else they will lose their impact.

Employing Structural Differences.   Creating and then breaking a pattern with your sentences can also bring out your ideas, often by highlighting contrasts or by concluding forcefully.

Use a new structure after a series of similar structures to draw attention to a contrast or a final idea.

If you become accustomed to the steady ticking of a clock in a room, you would probably notice immediately if the clock stopped. A similar phenomenon occurs in reading. A reader can become accustomed to the rhythm of your sentences—no matter how short the passage. But when the rhythm of a passage is broken, an interesting thing happens. The reader notices the change and his or her attention increases.

In the following passage, the first two sentences create a "rolling" movement of ideas through the use of conjunctions and modifying phrases. As a result, a comfortable rhythm is established. But the third sentence breaks the rhythm by presenting an important idea in a short, clipped sentence. This contrast, then, focuses the reader's attention on the final idea.

BREAKING A PATTERN: Tears in her eyes, she hugged Skeeter and stroked the fur that never failed to have knots in it. She brushed the fur away from his deep, round eyes, and lowered her forehead to touch his. *Skeeter was home.*

EXERCISE C: Using Structural Similarities Within Sentences.
Choose one of the following topics or make up one of your own to write a sentence in which you will use parallel words, phrases, or clauses to emphasize your idea and create a pattern.

An old cemetery   A scary movie
A difficult task   A bus ride
A pier with ships   A special phone call
An insect   A friend's house

EXERCISE D: Using Structural Similarities Within Groups of Sentences.
Choose one of the following topics and write a brief passage of four or more sentences covering all the items listed and any others you wish to add. Use similar sentence structures to call attention to the relationship among the details.

Reasons why a building was condemned: faulty wiring, crumbling steps, a rusted and broken fire escape, falling roof and ceilings

Safety measures instituted by the school principal: running in hallways forbidden, weekly fire drills, and volunteer student hall monitors and washroom attendants

Reasons why Thorpe's Diner closed: could not keep good waiters and waitresses, had an inexperienced cook, lost business when a new freeway rerouted traffic away from the diner

Things that a potential homeowner should look for to avoid an unsound investment: cracks in the foundation, leaks or sagging timbers in the roof, evidence of fire damage, improperly fitted pipes and other plumbing fixtures

Elements of a suspenseful story: mysterious characters, an unusual or exotic setting, unexplained events or unsolved crimes

EXERCISE E: Using Structural Differences. Choose another topic from Exercise D. Write a passage of four or more sentences in which you set up a pattern and then break it to emphasize a contrast, bring the passage to a strong end, or both.

■ Using Professional Models

Ever since you began to read, you have been exposed to the rhythms and patterns that professional writers use in their sentences. To some extent, you have learned "what sounds good" from both your reading and your listening. You should continue to read with a thought toward discovering new possibilities for your own sentences.

To improve your own sentences, study the sentence structures and patterns used effectively by professional writers.

Whenever you enjoy a piece of writing, examine the kinds of sentences to see what patterns the writer has used. By examining and noting the patterns used, you can get ideas for your own writing.

For example, the opening passage of Charles Dickens' *A Tale of Two Cities* contains a series of parallel structures that emphasize the vivid descriptions and create a rhythm that engages a reader's interest.

Parallel clauses
It was the best of times, it was the worst of times, it was the age of wisdom, it was the age of foolishness, it was the epoch of belief, it was the epoch of

> incredulity, it was the season of Light, it was the season of Darkness, it was the spring of hope, it was the winter of despair, we had everything before us, we had nothing before us, we were all going direct to Heaven, we were all going the other way—in short, the period was so far like the present period, that some of its noisiest authorities insisted on its being received, for good or for evil, in the superlative degree of comparison only. —Charles Dickens

In addition to reading and recognizing memorable professional models, you might collect particularly effective passages that you have read and practice imitating them. Be sure to note the author's name, the title of the work, and the page of the passage if you duplicate the passage. You might also analyze and label the kinds of sentences and use of structures and patterns, as in the following example, to discover what makes the passage work for you.

(1) A loose sentence with some parallelism	(1) The possessions of Christopher Alexander Pellett were these: his name, which he was always careful to retain intact; a suit of ducks, no longer intact, in which he lived and slept; a continuous thirst for
(2) A short sentence	liquor, and a set of red whiskers. (2) Also he had a friend. (3) Now no man can gain friendship, even
(3) A loose sentence	among the gentle islands of Polynesia, except by virtue of some quality attaching to him. (4) Strength,
(4) A periodic sentence	humor, villainy: he must show some trait by which the friend can catch and hold. (5) How, then, explain
(5) A question	the loving devotion lavished upon Christopher Alexander Pellett by Karaki . . . ? (6) This was the mystery
(6) A short sentence	at Fufuti. —John Russel

To write a passage of your own, you might want to use some of the structures and patterns from this model. Notice that the professional model has inspired the following passage and that the new passage reflects the model in its lengths and kinds of sentences.

(1) A loose sentence	(1) Sebastian Dumont III's behavior was disturbing, an unpredictable display of foul temper and dis-
(2) A short sentence	loyalty, which was miserable to experience. (2) Worse, he was violent. (3) Few people can put up
(3) A loose sentence	with constant ill treatment, with indifference, snarls, and destruction of their prize belongings. (4) And
(4) A periodic sentence	then after weeks of ignoring me, snapping at me, and ruining my favorite sandals and Alpine hat, he bit
(5) A question	me. (5) How could I, you might ask, go on living in
(6–7) Short sentences	the same house with Sebastian Dumont III? (6) He was my dog. (7) I loved him.

EXERCISE F: Locating Models of Professional Style. Using the library or collections of books that you might have at home, scan the pages of books that you have read and enjoyed or books that you would like to read. Find three passages whose styles appeal to you. Copy these passages, taking care to write down the author, title of the book, publisher, copyright date, and page of the passage. Then examine the sentence patterns of each model. Be prepared to state whatever makes the pattern unusual, effective, or otherwise noteworthy.

EXERCISE G: Imitating Professional Style. Use one of the models that you found for Exercise F to influence your own writing on any topic that you choose. Employ some of the devices or patterns used by the professional writer. Be prepared to show how your writing has been influenced by the model.

APPLICATION: Experimenting with Sentence Structures. Choose one of the following ideas to write a passage of five to ten sentences. As you write, pay attention to your sentence lengths. Vary your sentence openers and structures. Concentrate on using some other sentence possibilities that you have studied in this section: loose, periodic, and balanced sentences as well as possible patterns for the whole passage. You might also consider using professional models as a guide.

The opening passage of a murder mystery

Your editorial comments (for the school newspaper, for instance) about a school issue, such as vandalism, littering, study halls, grading systems, and so on

A description of a sunset (sunrise, approaching storm, speeding automobile, and so on)

Something frightening that you discovered in the woods, on a camping trip, in your cellar, and so on

The face of someone you love (idolize, respect, and so on)

Chapter 20

The Use of Words

Words are the most basic ingredients of your sentences. If your word choices are poor, your ideas will be weakened, no matter how good they are.

For this reason, this chapter offers several methods for improving your use of words. It includes methods for writing more concisely by eliminating unnecessary or ineffective words from your sentences. It also includes suggestions for using more precise and exciting verbs and modifiers, while maintaining a consistent tone in your writing. In addition, it explores some new possibilities for developing more interesting word choices. Subtle shades of meaning, vivid images, and figurative language can offer you more varied and more powerful ways of transmitting your ideas to your reader.

20.1 Using Words Effectively

To choose the best words for your sentences, you have to keep your audience in mind as you write. Your readers must grasp the ideas right away or they will lose interest in what you are saying. Therefore, you must be concise, eliminating unnecessary words and structures from your writing. In addition, you must choose your words precisely, so that what you say matches what you have in mind. Your words should transmit your ideas directly to your reader.

Besides expressing your ideas, the language you choose communicates your attitudes toward your subject and your audience. You can establish these attitudes clearly and consistently by choosing words that work well together, creating a unified tone from beginning to end. This section will help you write concisely and precisely with a consistent tone.

■ Developing a More Direct Style

Finding the right *number* of words to express your ideas takes practice. Overwriting can be just as confusing to your reader as omitting important ideas.

Learn to recognize when you have used too few words or too many words to convey your ideas.

In the following passage, for instance, the ideas are not fully expressed. The passage is sketchy because details seem to be missing.

Sketchy passage with too few details

Student enrollments are declining, and school trustees plan to save taxpayers' money. One of their plans is to close an elementary school. Some trustees feel that closing a school would reduce taxes and still provide sound education.

Your readers need more information. On the other hand, repetitions, wordiness, and unnecessary constructions can be just as deadly as omission of information, as in this version of the passage.

Wordy passage with empty words and repetitious language

Because of the fact that enrollments of students are declining, school trustees in charge of the schools are examining several possible options that might save money for taxpayers in the future. One of these options, which is the most dramatic of them all, includes one of the elementary schools that would be closed in this case. It is the feeling of some trustees that the money that would be saved from a school closing would result in reduced taxes while at the same time the money would ensure that sound education continued to go on in the remaining schools.

If you can represent all of your ideas and all important details while avoiding wordiness, you can achieve a more direct, more effective style. In this final version of the passage, you should notice that unnecessary words and structures have been eliminated. The message is conveyed fully but concisely.

Well written passage, both concise and complete

Because of declining student enrollments, school trustees are examining several options for saving taxpayers' money. The most dramatic measure includes closing one of the elementary schools. Some trustees feel that money saved from closing a school would reduce taxes while ensuring sound education in the remaining schools.

Eliminating Deadwood.   As you write and check your sentences, you should try to spot any words that contribute little to your ideas. Nonessential words can distract your readers and undermine what you say. With some practice, you can easily learn to locate and eliminate these excess words.

Eliminate all nonessential words from your sentences to make them concise.

The most obviously nonessential words and phrases are called *deadwood*. These words do not contribute to the meaning of a sentence; rather, they pad the sentence with empty language and roundabout constructions. The following chart contains some of the most widely used examples of deadwood.

DEADWOOD		
there is (are)	the thing that	of the opinion that
the area of	to the extent that	what I mean is
by way of	it is a fact that	for the reason that
a great deal (of)	in a manner that	due to
the fact that	is the one who is	while at the same time

Words that hedge and qualify what you say are another form of deadwood. Such words are often used in an attempt to sound noncommittal. But usually they only water down your ideas and sound vague and indefinite, as if you are afraid to commit yourself to your statements.

HEDGING WORDS		
somewhat	it seems (that)	sort of
almost	tends to	kind of
rather	in a way	that might or might not

Although you should avoid qualifying words when they make your writing vague, they may occasionally be necessary to express your ideas precisely. Simply be aware of qualifying words and use them in a way that is not hedging.

As you become familiar with the obvious forms of deadwood, you should also be on the lookout for other words and phrases that pad sentences. Take such words out of your sentences and then compress your ideas into fewer words. You will find sometimes that you will have to rephrase your idea completely in order to eliminate the deadwood. Notice how deadwood has been eliminated in the following sentences and how the ideas can be expressed concisely.

WITH DEADWOOD: Dr. Claver spoke *in a manner that* was confusing.

CONCISE: Dr. Claver spoke in a confusing manner.

WITH DEADWOOD: The builders exerted too much *by way of* pressure on the existing foundation *to the extent that* it collapsed.

CONCISE: Because the builders exerted too much pressure on the existing foundation, it collapsed.

WITH DEADWOOD: Storms *that might or might not* strike the coast could *almost* destroy *a great deal of* property.

CONCISE: If storms strike the coast, they could severely damage property.

Eliminating Redundancy.   Another enemy of conciseness is *redundancy*, the needless repetition of ideas.

Redundant words, phrases, and clauses can overload your sentences.

Saying the same thing twice only adds bulk to a sentence and usually sounds awkward. To locate redundancy in your writing, look for any word or phrase that repeats the meaning of another word, as in the following sentence.

EXAMPLE: Jeremy sat alone by himself.

The phrase *by himself* repeats the meaning of *alone*. It should be eliminated to read more concisely: *Jeremy sat alone.*
Following are more examples of redundant words and phrases.

REDUNDANT: Selma learned to count using the fingers *of her hands*.

CONCISE: Selma learned to count using her fingers.

REDUNDANT: Ghostly halos, bluish green *in color*, outlined the mountains.

CONCISE: Ghostly bluish-green halos outlined the mountains.

REDUNDANT: At this *point in* time, we must choose between frivolity and responsibility.

CONCISE: At this time, we must choose between frivolity and responsibility.

Reducing Wordy Structures.   Other words, besides the obvious forms of deadwood and redundancy, can also pad sentences and weaken their impact. These additional words create long phrases and clauses where shorter expressions might be stronger. Of course, sometimes your ideas will require longer sentences that contain several clauses. However, if you can reduce a longer expression without changing its meaning, you will probably be able to do it by cutting unnecessary words and therefore improving your sentence.

Wherever you can, reduce a phrase or clause to a shorter structure, without changing the meaning.

The words in some phrases are unnecessary. A prepositional phrase such as *in a happy mood* could be reduced to *happy* or *happily*. Notice how reducing this phrase can produce a more concise statement.

WORDY: She was *in a happy mood*.   She sang *in a happy mood*.

CONCISE: She was happy.   She sang happily.

Clauses also may contain excess words. Often, by elminating *who was* or *that is* from a clause, you will have a more concise structure with the same meaning. For example, an adjective clause such as *who was standing in the doorway* could be reduced to *standing in the doorway* and still convey the same idea, as in the following example.

WORDY: We were frightened by a man *who was standing in the doorway.*

CONCISE: We were frightened by a man standing in the doorway.

Look for opportunities to reduce phrases and clauses to shorter structures to make your sentences more concise. Use the following chart as a guide.

REDUCING WORDY STRUCTURES

Wordy phrase: She replied *in a cheerful voice.*
Concise: She replied cheerfully. (Phrase reduced to a single-word modifier)

Wordy phrase: Dr. Larson would send get-well cards *to patients.*
Concise: Dr. Larson would send patients get-well cards. (Phrase reduced to a noun)

Wordy clause: Mrs. Barnett is an eloquent orator and *she is a hardworking administrator.*
Concise: Mrs. Barnett is both an eloquent orator and a hardworking administrator. (Clause reduced to part of a compound complement)

Wordy clause: Explorers entered a cave *that was hidden by vines and bushes.*
Concise: Explorers entered a cave hidden by vines and bushes. (Clause reduced to a participial phrase)

Wordy clause: Mr. Stevenson, *who is the Sheriff of Monroe County,* has been indicted by the state supreme court.
Concise: Mr. Stevenson, the Sheriff of Monroe County, has been indicted by the state supreme court. (Clause reduced to an appositive)

Wordy clause: Horticulturists can prune plants *that are mature.*
Concise: Horticulturists can prune mature plants. (Clause reduced to a single-word modifier)

EXERCISE A: Eliminating Deadwood and Redundancy. Each of the following sentences contains unnecessary words and phrases that obscure the meaning. Eliminate the deadwood, the hedging words, and the redundancy in the sentences, and then rewrite them. In some sentences you will have to change the order of the words or add words.

1. It is a fact that most colleges require application to be made by students early in their junior year if they wish consideration for early acceptance.
2. There was nothing in the expression on his face that seemed to give us any indication of how angry he was.
3. Hester feared that separating the boys apart would cause her to be hurt by a flying fist.

4. At first, Hannibal was somewhat unsure of the extent to which early snows might possibly hamper his march.
5. Untrue lies and unfair assumptions weakened his argument by way of making him sound kind of vicious and uninformed.
6. It seems that when workers are happy in their attitude towards their environment, they are usually somewhat more productive.
7. It was with enormous pride that I walked myself to the front of the auditorium to accept the trophy that was awarded to me.
8. The man who was the chairperson of the committee tapped his water glass, and a great many of the people who were at the dinner stopped talking.
9. There was almost an unearthly heavenly haze lingering in the morning light, but also it was nearly beautiful in the way that it made distant faraway shapes seem to appear to be moving or floating.
10. It is usually possible for satellites to predict weather activity several days or so in advance, but these satellites cannot always make correct predictions accurately all of the time.

EXERCISE B: Shortening Wordy Structures. Each of the following sentences contains at least one phrase or clause that is needlessly long. Eliminate unnecessary words and rewrite each sentence to make it more concise. In some sentences you will have to change the order of words.

1. *Gone with the Wind*, which was written by Margaret Mitchell, became a classic in its own time.
2. The project that was done by Joe received "honorable mention" from members of the faculty.
3. Many settlers who emigrated from Germany and France began farms, and they also built towns in upstate New York.
4. The actress wore rings that were made of 14-karat gold and earrings made of diamonds.
5. Someone who was standing in the rear of the room began to cough in an annoying fashion.
6. Members of the Physics Club built a proton generator, which was to be their presentation as a group at the state science fair.
7. The baseball team boarded the plane silently, and they flew away into the night, which was cloudless.
8. We finally located her number, which was in the phone book and which was listed under the name "Hopkins."
9. In 1954, Colonel MacGuire received the Purple Heart,

which is a medal that is presented for injuries that are suffered in the line of duty.
10. A lamp that was sitting on an end table rose mysteriously, and it floated toward the girl who was standing near the window, which was open.

■ Choosing the Most Vivid Words

In addition to weeding out unnecessary words, you should choose the best words to convey your ideas. Weak verbs, vague modifiers, and other bland words will make what you say sound less interesting, less worthy of your reader's attention.

Learn to recognize and replace colorless, general, inexact words with vigorous, specific, exact words.

The following passage for a school newspaper, for instance, covers the topic adequately but loses some of its impact because of its ineffective words.

| Dull passage with bland, indirect language | Saturday night's junior class talent show was enjoyable to the audience of students and adults. The comedy sketches were laughed at and applauded repeatedly. In particular, Peter Grove's impersonations of Ronald Reagan and Jimmy Carter were enjoyed by members of the audience, as was the "Dance of the Upside-down People," which had been put together by Rita Wilson. |

With stronger action verbs in the active voice, the passage could sound much more direct and alive. A number of other bland words can also be replaced.

| Lively passage with vivid, active language | The audience of students and adults clearly relished Saturday night's junior class talent show. The audience chuckled, guffawed, and clapped constantly during the comedy sketches. In particular, the audience howled over Peter Grove's impersonations of Ronald Reagan and Jimmy Carter. The "Dance of the Upside-down People," choreographed by Rita Wilson, brought hoots and whistles. |

Avoiding Unnecessary Use of Weak Verbs.   An overuse of linking verbs as well as the passive voice can weaken the presentation of your ideas. On the other hand, strong action verbs in the active voice can add vitality to your sentences and can strengthen your presentation.

Wherever possible, use action verbs in the active voice.

A dull sentence can be the victim of a linking verb. If you choose a verb such as *is* or *was* or *seems,* you may be missing a chance to enliven your sentence with specific actions. Of course, linking verbs are useful or appropriate in some sentences, but often your writing style will improve if you consciously look for stronger verbs. In the following chart, you can see how the simple substitution of an action verb for a linking verb can revitalize a sentence.

USING ACTION VERBS TO REPLACE LINKING VERBS
Linking verb: He *was* unsure of an answer.
Action verb: He *struggled* for an answer.
Linking verb: When the river *became* too high, residents *were* upset.
Action verb: When the river *overflowed*, residents panicked.
Linking verb: Alfred *was* awkward with his words.
Action verb: Alfred *stumbled* over his words.

Sometimes the other words in a sentence will help you find a good action verb. If a verb is followed by a noun that can be changed into a verb, you might use the verb form of the noun in a revision of the sentence. Notice in the following chart how some verb/noun constructions can be changed into more direct statements with strong action verbs.

REWRITING VERB/NOUN CONSTRUCTIONS
Verb/noun: This test *is* a *survey* of personal attitudes.
Action: This test *surveys* personal attitudes.
Verb/noun: The committee *gave* a *presentation* of emergency plans.
Action: The committee *presented* emergency plans.
Verb/noun: Election results *caused* severe *disappointment* among liberals.
Action: Election results severely *disappointed* liberals.

Another way to strengthen verbs is to avoid the passive voice whenever you can. Passive verbs usually lengthen sentences and force the reader to wait until the end of the sentence to find the doer of the action. By changing passive voice into active, you can often shorten a sentence and make its message more direct.

The following chart offers examples of passive verbs changed to active. Notice the shorter, clearer sentences.

USING ACTIVE VOICE INSTEAD OF PASSIVE
Passive: At least twenty foul shots *were missed* by our basketball team in the game last night.
Active: Our basketball team *missed* at least twenty foul shots in the game last night.
Passive: Mother's portrait *is being painted* by a famous artist.
Active: A famous artist *is painting* Mother's portrait.
Passive: A passing grade *has been achieved* by only one class member.
Active: Only one class member *has achieved* a passing grade.

Avoiding Unnecessarily Bland Words.   Your ideas will be clearest and most strongly presented if your word choices are the best that you can find. Vague modifiers, overly general words, and overuse of the same word can sap the strength of your ideas and lessen the impact of a whole passage.

Look for specific words to convey your meaning exactly and vividly.

A reader cannot fully appreciate the ideas in your sentences if descriptions are hazy. Vague modifiers—words such as *great, interesting,* and *amazing*—may come quickly to mind while you are writing, but such words only communicate the intensity of your feelings. They are too imprecise to convey exact meaning. Notice that colorless words have been replaced by more precise words in the following chart.

REPLACING VAGUE, COLORLESS WORDS
Vague: The sailor had a *horrible* gash on his face.
Vivid: The sailor had a *red, ragged* gash on his face.
Vague: Her *nice* expression put me immediately at ease.
Vivid: Her *gracious* expression put me immediately at ease.

Besides vague words that can make your writing uninteresting, overly general words can deprive your audience of necessary or helpful information. Generalizations leave details up to the reader to supply, but you cannot expect the reader to read your mind. General verbs such as *said* or *go* are useful, but sometimes they fall short of expressing specific action. Similarly, general nouns can leave the reader uninformed. To communicate clearly, you should supply specific nouns, verbs, and modifiers. Notice how the sentences in the following chart become clearer and more interesting when specific words replace general words.

REPLACING OVERLY GENERAL WORDS
General: He *got* into his sleeping bag and *went* to sleep.
Specific: He *burrowed* into his sleeping bag and *dozed off.*
General: After working at an *institution*, she joined the Governor's *staff.*
Specific: After working at a *home for retarded children*, she joined the Governor's *Committee for Social Research.*
General: *Nobody* knew where John had *gone.*
Specific: *Neither his sister nor his parents* knew where John had *taken the car.*
General: The *group* set up their *instruments* in the *restaurant.*
Specific: The *rock band* set up their *guitars and drums* in the *pizza parlor.*

In addition to avoiding bland and general words, you should avoid the overuse of any particular word. One word repeated a number of times in a sentence or in a passage can stand out unpleasantly in the reader's mind. Sometimes repeating a word several times will have a special effect. Usually, however, you should find appropriate synonyms or rephrase your sentences to avoid relying too much on one word.

In the following chart, you will find a passage weakened by the overuse of a word. The author repeats the word *exciting* instead of looking for other more vivid words that would paint a clearer picture for the reader. Although the word *exciting* might be acceptable if used once in the passage, its repetition is monotonous and dull. Notice how overuse can be corrected by finding more precise replacements.

CORRECTING OVERUSE OF A WORD

Passage with Overuse of a Word

I enjoyed the *excitement* of Robert Louis Stevenson's novel *Treasure Island*. *Exciting* adventures and *exciting* characters made the book spellbinding from beginning to end. For example, in one *exciting* episode, Jim Hawkins, the main character, was captured by pirates.

Passage with Varied and Exact Words

I enjoyed the *excitement* of Robert Louis Stevenson's novel *Treasure Island*. *Dangerous* adventures and characters who frighten and fascinate made the book spellbinding from beginning to end. For example, in one *thrilling* episode, Jim Hawkins, the main character, was captured by pirates.

EXERCISE C: Using Action Verbs in the Active Voice. Each of the following sentences contains one or more weak verbs. Rewrite the sentence by (1) replacing a linking verb with an action verb, (2) rewriting a verb/noun construction, or (3) changing passive voice to active. You will have to rearrange structures and eliminate some words.

1. The death of his old dog was a very sad occasion for him.
2. Student Senate members held a discussion of the topic.
3. Her facial expression alone was an answer to my question.
4. On a crowded subway platform, Don's wallet was stolen by someone.
5. The debating team presented an argument in favor of gasoline rationing.
6. After injections of serum D, most of the white mice were measurably improved.
7. Fred's eyes became brighter and his face became red whenever Ellen spoke to him.
8. The concerto was brilliantly played by Artur Rubinstein.
9. Our school magazine *Door* was awarded a certificate of excellence by the Northampton Literary Guild.
10. Jason gave a hopeless stare to the graphs on his mathematics exam.

EXERCISE D: Using Vivid and Specific Words. Each of the following sentences contains at least one ineffective word. The problems include verb choices that are too common or imprecise, vague modifiers, overly general words, and overuse of a word. Write the words that can be improved on your paper.

Then rewrite each sentence, replacing these words with vivid, more specific words.

1. The loud noises coming from the motor were so noisy that some crew members and passengers expected something terrible.
2. Evelyn saw the person coming closer and thought that he was mysterious.
3. The Dawsons' place in the country had a number of unpleasant qualities.
4. When a voice on the intercom said that a storm was approaching our area, everyone immediately went to the basement.
5. I got the test and looked at the first question.
6. On the street corner was a funny old vendor selling funny things from a little old stand.
7. The insect on the flower had very interesting markings.
8. Uncle Hal's new business did well until his illness.
9. Everyone admired the admirable performance of the athlete.
10. The food served in the restaurant was very unusual.

■ Using an Appropriate Tone

Besides conveying your ideas, your word choices provide definite clues to your thoughts and feelings about your topic, your audience, and your purpose in writing. These attitudes create the *tone* of your writing. Just as listeners respond to a speaker's tone of voice as much as to the content of a speech, so your readers also will sense and react to the tone of your writing as well as to your ideas. But unlike the speaker, who can use voice as well as words, you must rely entirely on your language to create your tone in writing. And therefore you must be especially careful to choose words that will convey your attitudes clearly and accurately.

As you write, you should decide on the tone that is appropriate for your topic, audience, and purpose and choose your words to maintain that tone consistently. Certain kinds of language, however, can weaken and disrupt the tone of your writing. The use of terms the reader may not understand, wornout phrases, misleading words, self-important language, and emotionally loaded language can make your audience less responsive to your ideas. And whatever tone you choose, you should be consistent. Your tone should not switch from the formal language of a research report to the conversational tone of a friendly letter. Finally, whatever your tone, your writing should always be concise, precise, and fresh and should follow the standard rules of English usage.

Avoiding Words That May Not Be Understood. You should select only those expressions that readers will be able to comprehend. Whether you have chosen a formal or an informal tone for your writing, you should be aware that some forms of language such as slang expressions, jargon, and foreign words can confuse your audience.

Do not lose your reader by using slang, jargon, or foreign words.

In most of the writing you do, you should try to avoid slang words and expressions. You cannot be sure that all readers will be familiar with the current meaning of any particular slang expression, particularly since slang becomes dated very quickly. Slang also sounds sloppy and too casual, implying that you have not taken the time to think of more precise or appropriate language. The slang expression in the following sentence, for example, fails to communicate with many readers and also sounds careless.

SLANG: Tires screeching, Jeb's new car *booked* down Highway 59.

REVISED: Tires screeching, Jeb's new car *sped* down Highway 59.

Jargon, which is overly technical language, can also confuse readers and disrupt the tone of your writing. Unless you are writing a highly technical report and need to use terms special to the topic, you should avoid jargon, which besides causing misunderstanding, can also sound self-important. In the following sentence, the technical language clouds the meaning and should be replaced by concrete, more readily understandable language.

JARGON: Engineers sometimes use *gaseous traceable elements* to inspect sewers for leaks.

REVISED: Engineers sometimes use *smoke* to inspect sewers for leaks.

Foreign words, such as *in absentia, de rigueur, inter alia,* and *raison d'être,* can also weaken the tone of your writing. Unless you are sure that a foreign word or expression has a reason for being part of a sentence, you should avoid it. Like jargon, unnecessary foreign words can make your writing sound pretentious, and you always run the risk that your reader will not understand them. In the following sentence, the French expression *nom de plume* is simply unnecessary. As you can see, the English meaning sounds more appropriate.

FOREIGN TERM: Bowing to the prejudices of her society, Mary Ann Evans used the *nom de plume* "George Eliot."

REVISED: Bowing to the prejudices of her society, Mary Ann Evans used the *pen name* "George Eliot."

Avoiding Clichés.   Clichés are commonplace, overused expressions that make your writing sound secondhand. Most clichés started out as fresh ways of saying something, but then they were repeated so frequently that they became stale. For example, the expression *dead as a doornail* might sound vivid if you had never heard it before, but because you have heard it many times, it seems dull.

Eliminate overused expressions that can make your writing sound stale.

Replace clichés with simpler, more concrete language, as in the following sentence.

CLICHÉ: Edward *bit off more than he could chew* and failed most of his courses.

REVISED: Edward *took too many difficult courses* and failed most of them.

You can recognize clichés by their casual, familiar sound: *quiet as a mouse, high as a kite, down in the dumps, a heart of gold, shaking in my boots, dressed to kill, scared as a rabbit,* and so on.

Avoiding Euphemisms.   While clichés represent a misguided attempt to sound fresh and snappy, euphemisms attempt to soften the impact of an idea or even to mislead the reader. For instance, you might say that someone *is no longer with us*, rather than saying that the person *died*. For the sake of others' feelings, you cannot *always* avoid euphemisms, but you should try to eliminate them when they are unnecessary.

Eliminate euphemisms that can make your writing sound insincere.

In the following sentences, clear, more direct language replaces the euphemisms.

EUPHEMISM: The *law enforcement officer* who stopped our car asked to see my driver's license.

REVISED: The *police officer* who stopped our car asked to see my driver's license.

EUPHEMISM: The *maintenance engineer* repaired the hole in our ceiling.

REVISED: The *janitor* repaired the hole in our ceiling.

Other euphemisms include *discomfort* (for *pain*), *pass away* or *pass on* (for *die*), *indisposed* (for *ill*), and *let go* (for *fired*).

Avoiding Self-Important Language. Still another problem with tone is the use of self-important language in an attempt to impress readers with unnecessarily weighty words and long-winded sentences. Self-important language sounds *inflated.* It is usually much less clear than simpler language would be. It may be flowery and over-decorated with useless modifiers. It may be overly formal, with heavy-handed nouns and verbs and many unnecessary qualifying phrases and clauses. It *always* makes the reader feel that the writer is struggling to be impressive.

Replace self-important language with simpler, more direct words.

In the following sentences, self-important language of two different varieties is replaced by simpler and clearer words.

FLOWERY LANGUAGE: The ruddy souls labored with their rudimentary implements to ready the fecund earth to receive the golden kernels.

REVISED: The villagers tilled the fields with hoes and rakes to prepare the ground for planting corn.

OVERLY FORMAL LANGUAGE: To facilitate input by the maximum number of policy-makers, questionnaires were designed and circulated well in advance of the gathering.

REVISED: To encourage discussion, we sent the department heads questionnaires before the meeting.

Avoiding Overly Emotional Language. Overly emotional language can introduce a harsh, irritating tone into your writing and will probably make your readers reject what you say. No matter how strongly you feel about your subject, you should avoid emotional language and replace it with words that sound more rational and fair.

Eliminate overly emotional language to maintain a rational, appealing tone.

You can still make your point strongly without running the risk of offending your reader. In the following example, the writer sounds angry—even irritable. However, such "loaded" language can easily be replaced.

OVERLY EMOTIONAL LANGUAGE: Sure, some students abuse the privilege of unassigned study time. So what? How can anybody criticize all students just because a few rotten apples are not trustworthy?

REVISED: While some irresponsible students may abuse the privilege of unassigned study time, it is unfair to criticize *all* students.

EXERCISE E: Eliminating Problems with Tone. Each of the following sentences includes at least one word or expression that jars the tone of the sentence. Write the ineffective language on your paper and identify it as *slang, jargon,* a *foreign term,* a *cliché,* a *euphemism, self-important language,* or *emotional language.*

1. Bill could not take the physical fitness test on Tuesday because he was indisposed.
2. The idiot who wrote this paper deserves to have his head examined.
3. You have to hang loose and not be uptight if you want to work well with animals.
4. You could have knocked me over with a feather when I heard that Karen had written that essay.
5. The director asked the cameraperson to tighten from a two-shot to a head-shot and then zoom out for a long shot.
6. He has gone before us to a better place.
7. Smoking is verboten in this part of the restaurant.

8. In order for the directive to be accomplished, the administrators must integrate their endeavors with a single, all-encompassing objective.
9. Margie went bananas and Carl hit the ceiling, but I just kept my cool when our song was iced.
10. The country club dance was more fun than a barrel of monkeys.

EXERCISE F: Maintaining a Consistent and Effective Tone. In the following passage written for a local newspaper, the writer does not maintain a consistent tone. Decide what tone would be most appropriate for the passage as a whole. Then look for words and expressions that sound inconsistent with the suitable tone. Eliminate any slang, jargon, foreign terms, clichés, euphemisms, and self-important or emotional language, and substitute more appropriate words. You may have to rewrite much of the passage.

(1) The North Claremont Girls' Basketball Team had an up-and-down season, despite the talents and abilities of team members. (2) Miss Jackie Warren, a gem of a coach, helped most players improve their individual games. (3) However, heavy competition from other schools made some games real bummers.

(4) As a result, North Claremont suffered disgusting losses as well as scored some stunning victories. (5) On the down side, the team lost four more games than it won, two players were indisposed (Maureen Renaldo sprained an ankle and Lisa LaMar broke her arm), and some outrageously unfair referees called "foul" moves and "travelling" against some North Claremont players. (6) On the up side, though, the team played with dedication and persistence, and two players in particular helped the team get it together. (7) Judy Arnold, the team's numero uno player, averaged 13 points a game, 6.8 rebounds, and 44 assists. (8) And Debby Harris averaged 8.5 points a game and achieved an outstanding total of 140 rebounds.

(9) Since only one player is a senior and will be in absentia next year, the team will stay together for at least another season. (10) Players look forward to next year when they plan to wipe out the competition.

APPLICATION 1: Revising Word Choices in Compositions. Choose a passage or composition that you have written recently. Follow the rules presented in this section to eliminate any ineffective word choices and then rewrite the passage.

APPLICATION 2: Improving Sentence Style Through Word Choices. Choose one of the following topics or make up one of your own to write a passage of one hundred to two hundred words. Be concise in the wording of your ideas, be precise in your choices of words, and try for a consistent tone. When you have written a first draft, use the rules in this section to double-check your writing. Make any necessary revisions and then write a final copy of the passage.

An embarrassing experience
The gift that you (or someone else) hopes to receive
The hardest job you ever had to do
An inspiring (or upsetting, thought-provoking, and so on) show
    that you've seen
Someone who made a difference in your life

20.2 Exploring Different Word Choices

In addition to trying to find the right words to suit an idea or mood, you should be aware of some of the many stylistic devices available to you. Certainly, when you are choosing among several alternative words, your final selection should be the word that comes closest to the specific idea or feeling that you wish to express. Often, however, you will want to communicate an idea in a special way to give it particular emphasis. At such times you may want to use more imaginative language to heighten the effect of your ideas.

This section explores some additional possibilities for word choices. It explains how to choose among words with slightly different shades of meaning and how to create figures of speech and use imaginative language to express ideas and feelings. Finally, it presents some passages by professional writers to show how the devices explained in this section have been used successfully.

■ Considering Different Shades of Meaning

Often, when you must choose the right word for a sentence, two or more possibilities will occur to you. In many cases, these words will be *synonyms*. Although synonyms by definition are very close in meaning, they do not always share the same precise meanings, nor do they always bring the same ideas to mind; one word may have a different *connotation* from another.

Every word has a *denotation*, or literal meaning, but it may also have a number of *connotations*, or emotional associations. Connotations can vary from person to person: A camper's set of connotations for the word "fire" may be entirely different from a firefighter's. But there is a certain amount of general agreement regarding differences in connotations. For example, such synonyms as *anger* and *fury* have similar denotations, but most people can sense that their connotations are different: *Fury* suggests an intensity of emotion beyond *anger*. Because of this difference in connotation, you might choose the word *fury* rather than *anger* to convey an idea about very strong—perhaps even violent—feelings.

When choosing among synonyms, pick the word whose connotations seem most appropriate to your ideas.

Choosing the right shade of meaning will strengthen your idea by expressing it more precisely. And it can also heighten the effect of your writing. In the first of the following examples, the word *pleasure* tells the reader that Sam likes to play the piano very much. But if you felt that the word *pleasure* did not express the full extent of Sam's feelings, you might look for another word. Synonyms such as *delight* and *joy* are similar to *pleasure* in meaning, but they carry different connotations. *Delight* implies a sense of fun and excitement, and *joy* suggests a quieter but deeper happiness. Depending on the specific idea you wish to convey, you should choose the synonym with the most appropriate connotation.

EXAMPLES: Playing the piano fills Sam with *pleasure*.

Playing the piano fills Sam with *delight*.

Playing the piano fills Sam with *joy*.

Whenever you doubt that a word suits your idea, think of other synonyms. You might consult a dictionary or a thesaurus to find possibilities, but be sure that you understand the meanings of all the possibilities that you consider.

EXERCISE A: Choosing Connotations. Each of the following sentences contain an underlined word. Write two synonyms for each underlined term on your paper. Then briefly explain how the connotation of each synonym slightly changes the meaning of the sentence.

1. Sergeant Gaynor decided to <u>check</u> the suspect's story, hoping to find an inconsistency in the alibi.
2. With every ounce of her strength, she <u>moved</u> the bureau to the door and prayed that it would prevent the intruder from entering her room.
3. An <u>uncertain</u> look crossed his face as he heard that strange music, a reminder of some time or place in the past that he could not remember.
4. The soldier rose to a shaky attention. Beads of perspiration <u>dropped</u> down his forehead. His hands shook and his knees felt weak.
5. At the foot of Mount Shaker sat a tiny <u>house</u> long since abandoned by a hermit.
6. Applause from the audience brought <u>pleased</u> smiles to the players' faces.
7. Bob was determined to <u>fix</u> his study habits so that he could improve his grades.
8. The kittens made such <u>cute</u> squeaks that I wanted to take all of them home.
9. The ice skater <u>bounded</u> across the rink gracefully.
10. Counsel decided that a <u>request</u> to the governor would be the prisoner's only hope for leniency.

■ Using Comparisons to Make Your Ideas More Vivid

To make an important idea in your writing particularly vivid, you might choose to compare it to something else by using figures of speech such as *similes, metaphors, personification,* and *analogies.*

Similes.   Similes make explicit or direct comparisons between two dissimilar items. In a simile, the words "like" or "as" connect the items being compared. For example, to stress the idea that an old woman is both elegant and fragile, you might write this simile: "His grandmother sat stiffly in the alcove like a tiny antique chair." The simile links two unlike items—an old woman and a chair—on the basis of certain qualities which they share: age, frailty, elegance, stillness, and smallness.

Use similes to link different items imaginatively on the basis of certain shared qualities.

To emphasize some aspect of a particular item, you can compare it to some different item that shares the qualities you want to highlight. The two things linked in a simile should not, however, be normally associated with each other.

In the following sentences, similes emphasize the writer's statement by bringing together two normally dissimilar items.

SIMILES: Her comforting words soothed his troubled spirit like a cool and gentle rain.

With fingers as nimble as hummingbirds, old Mrs. Linden mended the rip in the gown.

Metaphors. Metaphors are different from similes in that they *imply* comparisons between two items, rather than state the comparison explicitly. Whereas a simile states that X is *like* Y, a metaphor is even more imaginative and states that X *is* Y. Of course, the statement is untrue on a *literal* level, but it helps the reader to see and understand the first item with new insight and appreciation.

Use metaphors to heighten the reader's sense of the connections between two different items.

Metaphors are usually stronger statements than similes because they make the literally impossible statement that one thing *is* another. To get some idea of the difference in effect between similes and metaphors, compare one of the preceding similes with the following version.

SIMILE: Her comforting words soothed his troubled spirit like a cool and gentle rain.

METAPHOR: Her comforting words were a cool and gentle rain soothing his troubled spirit.

Because metaphors make such strong identifications, many writers choose to muffle that effect slightly by making the identification of X with Y a little less obvious. Such a device is called a *submerged metaphor*. In the following submerged metaphor, notice that the connection between "her comforting words" and rain is much less evident, and the point is made much more subtly.

SUBMERGED METAPHOR: Her comforting words fell coolly and gently, soothing his troubled spirit.

Personification, a figure of speech similar to a metaphor, attributes human qualities to nonhuman things. It is often used for humorous effects (although it can be used seriously as well). Personification works best if it is not too obvious, as in this example giving a clock the human quality of sternness.

PERSONIFICATION: The clock on the classroom wall sternly ticked off the minutes remaining in the examination period.

Analogies. Analogies are lengthier comparisons than either similes or metaphors, since they compare two sets of circumstances with each other. Constructing an analogy usually requires a few sentences and may involve some narration. Analogies can be thought of as extended similes in which the characteristics of one experience are likened to those of another.

> Use an analogy to illustrate how one condition, or set of circumstances, is similar to another that readers will find familiar.

In the following passage, the writer draws an analogy linking the experience of riding in a sports car with the experience of riding in a roller coaster. Notice that the analogy begins with a simile—a ride in a sports car is *like* a ride in a run-away roller coaster. The comparison is developed and sharpened as the details of each experience are related, establishing an analogy between one set of circumstances and another.

ANALOGY: A ride in Bill's "customized" sports car is like a ride in a run-away roller coaster. First of all, Bill does not observe stop signs and other normal traffic restraints. Consequently, a passenger instantly feels a lack of control, a terrifying helplessness like the sensation of falling into the wild, headlong plunge of a roller coaster. Also, the springs and suspension on Bill's car must be too tight, causing a bumpy ride in which the poor passenger, like the roller coaster rider, must endure endless jounces and jolts.

EXERCISE B: Using Similes and Metaphors. Form ten comparisons using pairs of items, one from each column. Five of your comparisons should be similes, and five should be metaphors. Do not use the same noun more than twice. Each simile and metaphor should be a complete sentence. After each sentence, label the type of comparison you have written.

EXAMPLE: Her <u>eyes</u> were two gleaming <u>diamonds</u>.
            metaphor

eyes	sugar
sand	candle
breeze	lead weights
moon	whisper
sun	marble
trees	palace
shoes	furnace
skin	treasure
house	diamonds
trophy	soldiers

EXERCISE C: Using Analogies. Choose one of the following pairs of ideas or make up one of your own. Write a statement that presents the comparison, and then complete a brief passage, expanding the comparison into an analogy.

An organized person—a smoothly running machine
Reading books—traveling to foreign lands
Taking care of pets—raising children
Walking through a busy crowd—clearing a path in the forest
A good friendship—two musical instruments playing harmoniously

■ Creating Different Moods

Occasionally, in descriptive writing, you will want to create a special mood or feeling about a place, a person, or a series of events by using *sensory impressions* or *symbols*.

Using Sensory Impressions.   You can make what you describe more real to your reader if you appeal to the senses of sight, sound, smell, taste, and feeling.

In a description of a baseball game, for example, the mention of a *hot sun beating down* will recreate such an environment for the reader because the *feel* of a hot sun is a familiar one.

Use carefully chosen sensory impressions to help suggest a mood or feeling.

In the following passage, details such as *frosty winds* and *airborne whirlpools of snow* that *whipped our faces* help the reader feel what it is like to be in the narrator's position. Notice, also, that the sensory impressions help to create a mood of shivery cold.

Description with sensory impressions	Frosty winds blew across the flat landscape for as far as we could see. Airborne whirlpools of snow whipped our faces, blinding us momentarily with absolute whiteness. Then they would pass, and we could see for miles the icy outcroppings of rocks and scattered snow-covered bushes and trees.

Using Symbols.   A particular object or action that you include in your descriptions can become a symbol if it suggests ideas or emotions beyond its obvious literal or surface meaning. A symbol then functions to pull a number of feelings or impressions together into a single, unified idea.

Use symbols to allow persons, places, or objects in your writing to carry and tie together additional, deeper meanings.

Most often, symbols begin as concrete details—objects, persons, or specific actions—within a group of details. A description of a man lost in a desert, for example, might include, besides the sand, the heat, and the sun, the mention of a black vulture circling overhead. These associations lend the vulture a *symbolic* meaning beyond the fact that it is simply another desert creature. Readers will know that vultures detect helplessness and are drawn to the dying. If placed effectively, the reference to the bird might symbolize the man's fate, his inevitable death in the desert.

Symbols are often items about which readers already possess strong feelings. Animals such as snakes and vultures have symbolic value because of their strong associations for most people. A flag might suggest patriotism, an eagle pride, a sunrise hope, and so forth. Because of their general associations, these words evoke feelings beyond themselves, which are shared by reader and writer alike. But you can turn *any* detail into a symbol if you set it up effectively.

In the following passage about a girl's daily visits to her grandmother's home, an old-fashioned stove becomes a symbol for the girl's feelings about the kitchen, her grandmother, and her childhood.

Passage developing a symbol	Running up the path, I could smell the freshly ground coffee and the biscuits puffing up and turning golden in the oven. When I swung open the door, the warm scented air pulled me into the yellow kitchen

toward its glowing center, the cast-iron stove. The old stove bubbled, sizzled, and radiated heat that defrosted my nose and tingling fingers.

"Pam?" Grandma called from the living room.

"Gram, can I have some biscuits?"

Then always until Mom picked me up after work, I would sit there in front of the stove, munching biscuits with butter and honey, working out arithmetic problems, and sharing school news with Grandma.

EXERCISE D: Using Sensory Impressions and Symbols in Your Writing. Choose one of the following items as the subject for a descriptive or narrative passage. You may wish to alter or refocus the topic and select sensory impressions or create symbols other than those suggested. When you have written your passage, underline any sentences that contain sensory impressions or symbols, and be prepared to explain the effects you have tried to create.

1. Describe the interior of a deserted house you have entered. Choose a specific mood that you wish to establish about the place, such as strangeness, decay, or danger. Include appropriate details to stimulate your readers' senses.
2. Write about a young boy being bullied by three or four older boys. The younger boy is angry, but he is also much weaker than the others and would undoubtedly be hurt if the confrontation led to blows. Emphasize the younger boy's situation by including symbols of his vulnerability.
3. Write about a person who has been set free from a hospital, prison, or other institution or condition of confinement. As you relate the person's first steps into the "free" world, develop symbols of his or her new-found independence.
4. Write about a house you used to live in years ago, and include details from the house that have strong associations for you and that symbolize your feelings about the house and your childhood in it.
5. Write about a person cleaning out his or her desk in preparation to leave a job he or she disliked. Describe items in the desk that can serve as symbols of the job and the employee's attitude toward it.

■ Using Professional Models

Now that you can recognize devices such as similes, metaphors, analogies, sensory impressions, and symbols, you will probably notice them more often as you read. Whenever you encounter particularly good uses of language, you should take a moment to study them. You might even copy those that seem special to influence your own writing. Always make a note of the source of your models.

> Develop your writing style by studying professional models and writing down the most striking uses of language, along with the sources in which they appear.

As you come across effective uses of language, stop to examine the passage. Identify the idea or feeling that the writer is aiming for and try to determine the connection between the language used and the mood created. The passage can suggest ways of developing your own style.

If you were reading Marjorie Kinnan Rawlings' *The Yearling*, for instance, you would probably be struck by many powerfully descriptive passages. In one such passage, the writer reveals the traits of a man, Penny Baxter. To illustrate the honesty of this character, the author creates a simile (Penny was as "sound as copper," a standard of currency), and she completes the description with an analogy, comparing the qualities of copper and Penny's character.

Passage with an analogy

> The name [Penny] had been his only one ever since. When he voted he signed himself "Ezra Ezekial Baxter," but when he paid taxes, he was put down as "Penny Baxter," and made no protest. But he was a sound amalgam; sound as copper itself; and with something, too, of copper's softness. He leaned backward in his honesty, so that he was often a temptation to store-keepers and mill-owners and horse-traders. —Marjorie K. Rawlings

In another passage from *The Yearling*, a description of a bear is built from a metaphor. The third sentence presents the comparison, and the succeeding sentences develop the parallel between the bear's threat and the danger posed by an approaching hurricane.

Passage with a metaphor

> Sound filled the swamp. Saplings crashed. The bear was a black hurricane, mowing down obstructions. The dogs barked and bayed. The roaring in Jody's ears was his heart pounding. A bamboo vine tripped him and he sprawled and was on his feet again. . . . A clear space opened at the creek's bank. Jody saw a vast black shapeless form break through. —Marjorie K. Rawlings

Were you to use a similar device, comparing two things that would not ordinarily be associated, you might write a passage like the following. Notice that this original passage begins with a metaphor comparing a student's room to a museum. Notice also that succeeding sentences develop the concept, in this case using even more comparisons.

Metaphor	*My room is my own personal museum*, filled with the artifacts of my life. The walls of my museum are
Metaphor developed	covered with school pennants and travel posters from various places I have visited. A large photograph of the Rockies, for example, stands on the
Simile	bookcase *like a snowy monument*, a reminder of a family vacation in the West years ago. It *cools the*
Sensory impression	*room* with *icy bright* colors. I have pieces of sculpture too: Trophies recalling contests and tournaments sit on my window shelves. One trophy shows the Greek god Atlas holding the earth on his shoulders. It was my first sports award, won at our school fair's weightlifting contest, three years ago. When I walk into my
Symbol	room, I feel as if I am *looking at my memories, organized and made tangible. I feel as if I am looking at my life.*

EXERCISE E: Examining a Professional Model. Read the following passage and look for striking or unusual word choices. List as many such words and phrases as you can, and label each according to the device the writer used: a certain *connotation, simile, metaphor, analogy, sensory impression,* or *symbol.*

(1) A spring as clear as well water bubbled up from nowhere in the sand. (2) It was as though the banks cupped green leafy hands to hold it. (3) There was a whirlpool where the water rose from the earth. (4) Grains of sand boiled in it. (5) Beyond the bank, the parent spring bubbled up at a higher level, cut itself a channel through white limestone and began to run rapidly down-hill to make a creek. (6) The creek joined Lake George, Lake George was a part of the St. John's River, the great river flowed northward and into the sea. (7) It excited Jody to watch the beginning of the ocean. (8) There were other beginnings, true, but this one was his own. (9) He liked to think that no one came here but himself and the wild animals and the thirsty birds. —Marjorie K. Rawlings

EXERCISE F: Locating Models of Professional Style. Using the library or collections of books that you might have at home, scan the pages of books that you have read and enjoyed or of books that you would like to read. Find three passages containing unusual or effective word choices, such as comparisons, sensory impressions, or symbols. Copy the three passages onto your paper, listing the author, title, and page numbers for each. Label the device the writer used in each passage.

EXERCISE G: Using Professional Models. Use any of the models that you found in Exercise F to influence your own writing on any topic that you choose. Employ some of the devices used by the professional writers. Be prepared to show how your writing was influenced by the model.

APPLICATION: Using Different Word Choices in Your Writing. Choose one of the following ideas to write a brief passage of one hundred to two hundred words. Pay special attention to your word choices, selecting the best connotations when several possible choices occur to you, drawing comparisons with similes or metaphors, and creating or enhancing a mood by including sensory impressions or symbols. Also consider using professional models to help guide or inspire your writing.

The opening passages of a ghost story
The time you became lost on a camping trip (shopping expedition, field trip, and so on)
The reactions of passengers on an airliner with mechanical problems
A most unusual substitute coach for your team
A stray dog

Clear Thinking in Writing

When you express ideas and especially when you write full passages, you should pay particular attention to the logical connections between your ideas so that the reader can follow the thoughts easily from sentence to sentence.

This chapter focuses on the specific words you can use to link ideas: transitions, coordinating words, and subordinating words. It also discusses the use of logical patterns, which can make your ideas flow sensibly for a reader. The second section in this chapter explains some of the errors in thinking that you should avoid and suggests studying the patterns of reasoning used by professional writers to improve the logic of your own writing.

Making Clear Connections 21.1

When you explain a concept, describe a scene, or write a letter, the reader needs to understand the relationship that one sentence has with another in order to grasp the ideas of the passage as a whole. Transitions will help to make these relationships clear because such words act as guideposts, telling the reader what to expect next or what order details are following. Coordinating and subordinating words perform similar functions within sentences. They help to show how ideas work together.

As you join ideas, you should also view whole groups of sentences critically. You should check to see that sentences follow a logical order. In addition to improving the flow of your sentences, this section should help you strengthen the underlying logic of your ideas.

■ Using Transitions

Whenever you write a series of sentences, you should make clear the relationship between each idea and the ideas before and after it, often by using transitions.

> **Use transitions to connect thoughts and to clarify relationships among ideas.**

Notice in the following passage that a series of events is written without transitions. The ideas are understandable, but the passage sounds incomplete and choppy.

Passage without transitions

She stepped off the bus knowing she had only moments to reach her sister's house on the outskirts of town. She thought to hail a taxicab, but none were lined up at the taxi stand. She tried calling from a service phone, but the taxi service number was busy. She tried again and again and gave up. She began to run, hoping to spot a cab along the way. A horn blasted alongside her. It was Elmer, her sister's neighbor.

Certain transitions can help clarify the time order in the preceding passage as well as indicate more precisely *how much* time elapses between events. Notice how transitions can make the passage smoother and clearer.

Passage with transitions

She stepped off the bus knowing she had only moments to reach her sister's house on the outskirts of town. *First,* she thought to hail a taxicab, but none were lined up at the taxi stand. *Then,* she tried calling from a service phone, but the taxi service number was busy. She tried again and again but *eventually* gave up. *Finally,* she began to run, hoping to spot a cab along the way. *Moments later,* a horn blasted alongside her. It was Elmer, her sister's neighbor.

Although not every series of sentences needs as many transitions as this one has, a few well-chosen transitions can often make the difference between weak and strong writing. Transitions can help to clarify time relationships, spatial relationships, the addition of new ideas, contrasts between ideas, and the logical results or conclusions of ideas. They can also help to emphasize ideas and introduce examples. When you write a series of sentences, you must decide where you need to put transitions and which ones to use. The following chart shows some common transitions grouped by the relationships they usually clarify.

TRANSITIONS GROUPED BY PURPOSE

Time Relationship		Comparison or Contrast	
first	earlier	however	in contrast
second	before	unlike	nevertheless
third	eventually	yet	in like manner
next	meanwhile	likewise	on the contrary
soon	afterwards	similarly	on the other hand
last	after	instead	
finally	then		
later	at that moment		
during			

Spatial Relationship		Cause and Effect	
outside	before	thus	so because of
inside	ahead	then	on account of
beyond	there	therefore	
here	overhead	as a result	
near	beneath	consequently	
behind	above		

Addition		Emphasis
also	second	indeed
besides	as well	in fact
too	in addition	in other words
moreover	furthermore	
first		

Examples			
for instance	also	that is	as an illustration
for example	in particular	namely	

The following examples show how ideas can be connected logically with transitions. Notice in each case how a transition clarifies a specific relationship among ideas.

TIME: Carpenters hammered loudly on the roof. *Meanwhile,* Dr. Holland slept soundly in the basement.

SPATIAL: A crowd stood patiently on the sidewalk. *Inside,* the early show was about to finish.

ADDITION: The counselor told us not to swim in the lake or hike by ourselves. *Furthermore,* we should not use the archery range or sailboats unless a counselor supervised us.

CONTRAST: Most flying mammals nest in trees or marshlands. Some, *however*, prefer more secure nesting locations such as caves and the hollows of trees, rocks, and even buildings.

RESULT: An unusual cold spell kept temperatures below freezing for more than two days. *As a result*, many oranges froze and spoiled.

EMPHASIS: We did not want to go to the crowded beach. *Indeed*, we hoped never to go there again.

EXAMPLE: Sheila was an avid coin collector. *In particular*, she was interested in early buffalo heads.

EXERCISE A: Adding Transitions.

Each of the following pairs of sentences can be rewritten so that a transition helps the reader understand the development of ideas. Choose a transition to add to each pair of sentences, rewrite the sentences, and then state the relationship clarified by the transition.

EXAMPLE: Iris spent the evening reading. She fell asleep in her chair.

Iris spent the evening reading. *Later*, she feel asleep in her chair.   time relationship

1. Most flowering plants need direct sunlight and sufficient water. Snake plants can develop quite nicely in shady spots or without any direct sunlight.
2. Consumer discount cards will be issued to heads of families of four or more members. A family must earn collectively no more than the median family income to qualify.
3. Documented research papers must contain a title page, references to sources, and a bibliography page. All pages of text should be numbered.
4. By 6:00 p.m. six inches of rain had fallen. Weathermen informed us that the rainfall had broken all records.
5. The student fund could not afford a live band for the spring dance. We rented a jukebox and brought old 45-rpm records.
6. The cows and goats looked dehydrated and weak. The chickens appeared ill.
7. The castaways gathered logs, vines, and tree bark. They laced the logs and vines together and added tree bark to seal the makeshift hull.
8. A power failure has left Culver City nearly crippled. Power company spokesmen have assured the public that partial restorations are being achieved and that full power will return by nightfall.
9. Tornadoes were reported along the western area of the state. Thousands of families have been evacuated from Paton Township.

10. The Emperor's troops camped and trained along the enemy's border. They were ready for a sneak attack.

■ Joining Ideas Through Coordination and Subordination

Another way to connect ideas in your sentences is by showing how one idea is equal in importance to another or how one idea qualifies, supports, or explains another. Again, certain words will clarify for readers these kinds of connections.

Learn to recognize the need for connections between equal and related ideas and unequal but closely related ideas.

Coordination and subordination are two methods of clarifying relationships among ideas. *Coordination* joins equal and related words, phrases, and clauses within a sentence. It is particularly useful in forming compound sentences. *Subordination*, on the other hand, joins unequal but related ideas in phrases and clauses within a sentence. Subordination enables you to form complex sentences.

In addition to making logical connections between ideas, coordination and subordination help to improve the flow of ideas throughout a passage and to achieve logical continuity. The following passage has almost no coordination and subordination. Notice that the relationships among ideas are hard to grasp and that the passage sounds illogical.

Passage without coordination and subordination

> Sailing in open waters leaves room for relaxed maneuvering and even errors in steering. Maneuvering a sailing craft into port demands accuracy. Sailing accidents happen frequently. Inexperienced sailors fail to skirt moored craft in approaching a berth. Many sailors choose to equip their boats with small inboard or outboard motors, relying on the motor power to guide them to dock.

If ideas are connected with the proper coordinating and subordinating words, a passage can be made much more understandable. In the following passage, coordination and subordination pull the ideas together.

Passage connected using

> Sailing in open waters leaves room for relaxed maneuvering and even errors in steering, *but* maneuvering a sailing craft into port demands accuracy.

coordination
and sub-
ordination

Because sailing accidents happen frequently *when* inexperienced sailors fail to skirt moored craft in approaching a berth, many sailors choose to equip their boats with small inboard or outboard motors, relying on the motor power to guide them to dock.

Coordination.   When two ideas of equal importance are joined in one sentence using coordination, the reader is given specific information about the connection between them.

Use conjunctions, conjunctive adverbs, and semicolons to join equal and related ideas.

The following chart lists coordinating words that you can use to join ideas of equal importance. Notice that with some words, a semicolon must be used to connect ideas within a sentence. It can be used with or without a conjunctive adverb. Notice also that many conjunctive adverbs double as transitions.

COORDINATING WORDS	
Coordinating Conjunctions	**Correlative Conjunctions**
and nor but so for yet or	either . . . or neither . . . nor not only . . . but also both . . . and
Conjunctive Adverbs **(And Semicolons)**	
; however, ; consequently, ; indeed, ; for example, ; therefore, ; on the contrary, ; moreover, ; otherwise, ; in addition, ; nevertheless,	

Similar to transitions, these words clarify for the reader logical connections such as addition, contrast, and cause and effect. You should make sure that the words you use to join ideas establish an appropriate relationship between your ideas.

In the following examples, notice that ideas in two separate sentences can be joined with coordinating words to establish specific relationships.

UNCONNECTED: Books must be returned to the storeroom. They should be stacked neatly.

COORDINATION USED TO SHOW ADDITION: Books must be returned to the storeroom, *and* they should be stacked neatly.

UNCONNECTED: Bill cannot perceive color differences. He can take striking black and white photographs.

COORDINATION USED TO SHOW CONTRAST: Bill cannot perceive color differences, *but* he can take striking black and white photographs.

UNCONNECTED: Winds increased during the night. The Coast Guard issued small craft warnings.

COORDINATION USED TO SHOW RESULT: Winds increased during the night; *consequently*, the Coast Guard issued small craft warnings.

The following examples show a semicolon used alone to draw a close logical connection between ideas.

UNCONNECTED: She sat bolt upright in bed. A smell of gasoline filled her room.

WITH COORDINATION: She sat bolt upright in bed; a smell of gasoline filled her room.

UNCONNECTED: He could not eat radishes. She could not eat scallops.

WITH COORDINATION: He could not eat radishes; she could not eat scallops.

Subordination. Ideas that are closely related, but not equally important, can be joined in other ways.

Use subordinating words to show unequal but important relationships between certain ideas.

The following chart lists subordinating words that you can use. Notice that subordinating words help to make logical connections between ideas. They can clarify time relationships, comparisons, and contrasts. They can also indicate how or why ideas relate to one another and add descriptive detail or provide identification.

SUBORDINATING WORDS			
Time Relationships		**Contrasts**	
after	since	though	whereas
whenever	as soon as	although	unlike
before	when		
until	while		
Comparisons		**Cause and Effect**	
as though	as much as	because	whether
as if	as well as	so that	provided that
just as		in order that	
Addition or Identification			
	that	where	
	which	whom	
	who	whose	

Most often, when you use a subordinating word to connect ideas, you will be writing a complex sentence containing an adjective or adverb clause. You will make one idea stand out as the main idea, and you will use a subordinating word to add the clause that modifies the main idea.

The following examples show pairs of sentences joined by subordinating words for clarity.

UNCONNECTED: The conductor tapped the podium. The audience quieted instantly.

SUBORDINATION SHOWING TIME: *When* the conductor tapped the podium, the audience quieted instantly.

UNCONNECTED: He ran through the rose garden. He looked like a man pursued by devils.

SUBORDINATION SHOWING COMPARISON: He ran through the rose garden *as if* he were pursued by devils.

UNCONNECTED: Eleanor felt shy and awkward in her new school. She made new friends quickly.

SUBORDINATION SHOWING CONTRAST: *Although* Eleanor felt shy and awkward in her new school, she made new friends quickly.

UNCONNECTED: Seventy percent of the student body was affected by the flu. Classes were canceled.

SUBORDINATION SHOWING CAUSE AND EFFECT: *Because* seventy percent of the student body was affected by the flu, classes were canceled.

UNCONNECTED: The woman was waiting for a cab. She looked very anxious.

SUBORDINATION SHOWING ADDITION OF DETAIL: The woman, *who* looked very anxious, was waiting for a cab.

Recognizing Problems with Coordination and Subordination. In joining clauses through either coordination or subordination, you should learn to avoid three specific problems. First, you should not use *excessive* coordination or subordination, piling too many clauses into a single sentence. Second, you should make certain that the clauses you want to link through either coordination or subordination belong together, that is, that they are not joined *illogically*. Third, you should not use coordination *inappropriately* to join two clauses when the connection between them is such that subordination would be clearer and more effective.

Avoid excessive, illogical, or otherwise inappropriate use of coordination or subordination when joining clauses in sentences.

Excessive coordination or subordination obscures your meaning by loading too many separate pieces of information into a single sentence. A sentence burdened with too many coordinate or subordinate clauses may be grammatically correct, but it will sound long-winded, awkward, and confusing.

Excessive coordination   I was going to go to the movie, *but* I forgot the address of the theater, *and* I wasn't certain of the time of the feature, *and* so I decided to go to the museum instead, *but* unfortunately, it had already closed for the day by the time I arrived.

Improved coordination   I was going to go to the movie, *but* I forgot the address of the theater, *and* I wasn't certain of the time of the feature. Thus, I decided to go to the museum instead. Unfortunately, however, it had already closed for the day by the time I arrived.

Excessive
subordi-
nation

My sister, *who* lives in New York City, has asked me to call her *as soon as* I know my travel plans *so that* she can make our theater reservations *since* it is difficult to get good seats *unless* you reserve them well in advance.

Improved
subordi-
nation

My sister, *who* lives in New York City, has asked me to call her *as soon as* I know my travel plans *so that* she can make our theater reservations. It is difficult to get good seats *unless* you reserve them well in advance.

In addition to making sure that you have not burdened your sentences with too many coordinate and subordinate clauses, you should also be certain that the clauses you link do indeed belong together.

When you are using coordination to connect two independent clauses, always make sure that there is a strong enough relationship between the clauses to justify the connection. If a single sentence seems to contain several unrelated ideas, rewrite it by breaking it up into two or more complete sentences.

Unrelated
ideas joined
in compound
sentence

David boarded the train on Tuesday evening in Denver, *and* he had spent the entire day at Rocky Mountain National Park, the site of the Continental Divide.

Unrelated
ideas kept
separate

David boarded the train on Tuesday evening in Denver. He had spent the entire day at Rocky Mountain National Park, the site of the Continental Divide.

Similarly, when linking two ideas using subordination, you must make sure that there is a logical relationship between the independent clause and the subordinate clause. You must also decide which subordinating word to use and which clause should logically be the independent clause, which the dependent clause.

INAPPROPRIATE WORD: *Since* I sat down at the table, I lost my appetite.

APPROPRIATE WORDS: *As soon as* I sat down at the table, I lost my appetite.

WRONG CLAUSE SUBORDINATE: *Before* you check the assignment, write your paper.

RIGHT CLAUSE SUBORDINATE: *Before* you write your paper, check the assignment.

A final problem you may face in using coordination and subordination arises when you must make a choice between the two methods. You must be able to recognize when subordination will create a clearer and stronger link between ideas than coordination.

WEAK COORDINATION: Earl played a difficult piece well, *and* he won the competition.

IDEAS STRENGTHENED BY SUBORDINATION: *Because* Earl played a difficult piece well, he won the competition.

EXERCISE B: Adding Coordination. In each of the following pairs of sentences, equal ideas can be joined by adding coordinating words. Rewrite each sentence pair using coordination, and underline the coordinating words you have added.

EXAMPLE: Jenson must build a stone wall around the garden. One of the dogs will trample the flowers.

Either Jenson must build a stone wall around the garden, or one of the dogs will trample the flowers.

1. Settlers in Cumberland Forge planned to irrigate the central valley. They planned to plant their crops in that location.
2. Chester declines to speak in class. He refuses to write even his name on a piece of paper.
3. Texas is larger in land area than California. It is smaller than Alaska.
4. John and his sister voted in the national election for the Republican candidate. Neither of them voted in the primary.
5. English and American speech patterns differ. Neither is considered inferior to the other.
6. Mr. Stapleton followed a suspicious-looking older man into the darkened auditorium. He watched the man climb onto the stage and disappear behind a curtain.
7. You can find a square root simply by entering the number on a calculator and pushing the square root element. You can compute the answer on paper.
8. He was selfish. He brought out selfishness in others.
9. You may decide not to contribute to charity. You should first examine your personal values as well as the needs of the institution asking for your support.
10. Latin is sometimes called a "dead" language. Its value in understanding the English language should not be discounted.

EXERCISE C: Adding Subordination. Each of the following pairs of sentences contains ideas that are related. Combine the sentences using subordinating words to clarify relationships between ideas. Underline all subordinating words that you add.

EXAMPLE: My pen ran out of ink. I finished my outline in pencil.

After my pen ran out of ink, I finished my outline in pencil.

1. Peg was heavier than the rest of us. She could still win in a race.
2. A short in the electrical system caused an alarm to sound. Doors closed automatically in the reactor room.
3. Troop carriers were approaching the beach. The enemy forces were readying their guns behind sand dunes.
4. Turn in your exam. Check your answers for accuracy.
5. Brush fires were moving up from the valley. Homeowners hosed down their roofs and prayed that the traveling conflagration could be halted in time.
6. Chipmunks spend months hoarding nuts and berries in their nests. They can spend the winter months in hibernation.
7. We listened to the foghorn sounding dully in the distance. We wondered whether all of the fishing boats would return safely to harbor.
8. Janet moved to Cleveland in July. She has written home regularly.
9. The color of the solution remained clear. I conclude that barium was not an element in the mixture.
10. You can ride with us to Vermont. You have to promise not to chatter all the time.

EXERCISE D: Correcting Problems with Coordination and Subordination. Each of the following sentences is weakened by one of the following problems: excessive coordination or subordination, illogical coordination or subordination, or coordination where subordination would be more effective. Identify the problem in each sentence, and rewrite the sentence to correct it.

1. Before you put on the suntan lotion, sit out in the sun,
2. Marilyn forgot her history notebook, and so she had to hurry back to her locker, but the building was locked up and she had to go home without her notebook, and, as a result, she was unable to complete her assignment for the next class, but she made up the work.

3. I set the table for six and we had fried chicken for dinner.
4. When the sun rose, we realized that we had covered a great deal of ground during the night, since the terrain was completely different from the view which we had seen when the sun went down on the previous evening as we were driving southwest from St. Louis.
5. Richard bought the record he had picked out, and the snowstorm added to the confusion of the rush hour traffic.
6. I passed my driver's test and my father gave me my own set of keys to our family car.
7. Because I had to ask directions, I lost my way.
8. When Edward heard the door, which led to the cellar and which he had left open, slam shut, he realized with a start that someone else must have entered the house after he came in, since the front door had been latched from the outside when he arrived.
9. George was captain of the football team, and the school scored a number of stunning victories.
10. I bought a watermelon, but it wasn't ripe yet, and so I set it outside in the sun for a few days; however, I must have left it out too long, for it turned to mush and I couldn't eat it, and so I cut it up and gave it to my dog.

■ Establishing and Following Logical Orders

In addition to using transitions, coordination, and subordination to link ideas, you can make your ideas flow more smoothly by arranging them in certain accepted logical orders. If, for example, you are describing a process, it makes sense to mention the steps of that process in the order in which they normally occur. Or, if you are listing four reasons for doing something, your argument will be more effective if you start with the least important point and end with the most important one.

You can organize your ideas within individual sentences and within a series of sentences by drawing on a number of commonly recognized logical orders.

Link your ideas logically within individual sentences and from sentence to sentence by following standard logical orders.

The most frequently used orders are chronological order, order of importance, spatial order, and comparison and contrast order. These orders are illustrated on the next page.

ILLOGICAL ORDER: I pressed the button for the eighteenth floor, entered the building, got into the elevator, and told the guard where I was going.

CHRONOLOGICAL ORDER: I entered the building, told the guard where I was going, got into the elevator, and pressed the button for the eighteenth floor.

ILLOGICAL ORDER: He won the election because all the major newspapers endorsed him, because his opponent was indicted during the campaign for taking bribes, and because he was an attractive family man.

ORDER OF IMPORTANCE: He won the election because he was an attractive family man, because all the major newspapers endorsed him, and because his opponent was indicted during the campaign for taking bribes.

ILLOGICAL ORDER: It was possible to pick out tiny white sails on the horizon against the clear blue sky. We dug our toes into the soft, fine sand. Adults were swimming vigorously in the distance, and children splashed near the shore. Our blanket was surrounded by troops of noisy, happy, sunburnt families.

SPATIAL ORDER NEAR TO FAR: We dug our toes into the soft, fine sand. Our blanket was surrounded by troops of noisy, happy, sunburnt families. Children splashed near the shore and adults were swimming vigorously in the distance. It was possible to pick out tiny white sails on the horizon against the clear blue sky.

ILLOGICAL ORDER: Rowboats are propelled by long, heavy oars, and canoes by shorter, lighter paddles. Canoes and rowboats operate on the same basic principle. Rowboats are larger and heavier than canoes. Both types of boats can be managed by one person.

COMPARISON AND CONTRAST ORDER: Both rowboats and canoes operate on the same basic principle, and both types of boats can be managed by one person. But rowboats are larger and heavier than canoes and are propelled by long, heavy oars, while canoes are directed by short, light paddles.

EXERCISE E: Recognizing and Establishing Logical Order.
Rewrite each of the following items to follow a logical order.
Then identify the type of logical pattern you have used in each
revision.

1. I got out of bed, woke up, and did my daily exercises.
2. The building was in very bad shape: The elevator didn't
   work, the masonry was crumbling, and most of the apart-
   ments had no hot water.
3. I addressed the letter to her at 2900 Platt Road, the United
   States of America, Ann Arbor, the Western Hemisphere,
   the Solar System, North America, the Universe, Michigan,
   Earth.
4. And if elected, I pledge to you that I will make this city the
   great, great metropolis it once was and can become again,
   I will keep your children safe at night, I will clean up the
   streets and sidewalks, and I will throw out the incompe-
   tent people who have been wasting your tax money for the
   last four years.
5. She looked in her mirror and decided that, for once in her
   life, she looked beautiful, striking, even attractive.
6. He walked onto the brightly lighted stage and said his
   first line. He took an hour to put on his makeup for the
   role. He arrived at the theater very early. He stepped into
   his costume carefully, trying not to smear his makeup. He
   stood hidden in the wings, taking deep breaths to calm
   himself.
7. The apartment looked much brighter and larger. I re-
   painted the walls and refinished the hardwood floors. My
   new tenant was willing to pay me $100 a month more rent
   than I had charged the previous resident.
8. Ten-speed bicycles are lighter and more streamlined than
   three-speed bicycles. Both ten-speed and three-speed bicycles have hand brakes and manually operated gear shifts.
   Ten-speed bikes are used primarily for long distance racing, while three-speed bikes hold up better under the wear
   and tear of normal daily use for short and medium distance rides, errands, and so on.
9. He became discouraged over the repeated failure of his experiment. He decided to abandon his career in chemistry
   altogether. He avoided his colleagues. His appearance became more and more careless.
10. I wanted to write a paper about Thomas Jefferson. I finally
    wrote about his strategy in bargaining with Napoleon for
    the Louisiana Territory. I decided to focus on his presi-
    dency. My research led me to become interested in his role
    in the Louisiana Purchase.

APPLICATION: Checking Your Writing for Logical Connections and Order. Choose a brief composition that you have recently written either for class or on your own (for example, a letter). Read it specifically for transitions, the clear use of coordination and subordination, and logical order. Revise it with these qualities in mind and recopy it. Submit both the original version and the improved version to your teacher.

21.2 Exploring Other Issues of Logic

Your sentences should always present ideas that work together logically to carry the reader along and to convey your full meaning. As you continue to practice clear, logical writing, you should learn not only to use logical orders but also to avoid certain gaps in reasoning that can weaken your ideas and mislead readers.

This section discusses some of these potential gaps or errors and methods of correcting them. It also includes some models of professional writing, which show how writers manage to avoid errors in reasoning and thus succeed in developing their ideas fully and logically.

■ Avoiding Errors in Logic

When you develop ideas through a series of sentences, you should try to connect your thoughts with transitions, coordination, subordination, and logical patterns. Every idea should lead clearly to the next. You should also make sure there are no misleading words or incomplete links. To do this, you must learn to recognize certain errors caused by faulty reasoning.

> Recognize errors in logic—contradictions, false assumptions, hasty generalizations, and statements that beg the question— and learn to correct them.

Any of these errors can distort your ideas and confuse a reader.

Contradictions.   A *contradiction* is an assertion or observation that seems contrary to some other statement you have made. As you present information, you may sometimes fail to choose your words carefully and may therefore unwittingly make a statement that contradicts preceding statements.

Recognize a contradiction or inconsistency among your ideas, and add, delete, or alter information to correct the problem.

The contradiction in the following passage results from the writer's failure to clarify certain details. The statement that the actress is "expected to recover at least the partial use of both legs" contradicts the report that she "would not regain the use of her left leg."

Passage
with a
contradiction

Doctors at Mercy General Hospital in San Diego, California, reported that actress Stephanie Simpson, the victim of an automobile accident, would not regain the use of her left leg. Her attending physician, Dr. Joseph Cuervo, stated that Miss Simpson's condition has improved greatly since her admission to the hospital and that she is expected to recover at least partial use of both legs.

The contradiction can be corrected by adding details that clarify the timing of the two apparently contradictory statements.

Passage with
consistent
information

Last week, doctors at Mercy General Hospital in San Diego, California, reported that actress Stephanie Simpson, the victim of an automobile accident, would not regain the use of her left leg. In a subsequent announcement, her attending physician, Dr. Joseph Cuervo, has stated that Miss Simpson's condition has improved greatly since her admission to the hospital and that she is now expected to recover at least partial use of both legs.

False Assumptions. While contradictions are often caused by careless writing, false assumptions are generally caused by careless thinking. A *false assumption* is a gap created by leaving out important information that you have wrongly assumed the reader already knows. Whenever you write, some assumptions about your audience's interests and knowledge are unavoidable. Still, you should not *falsely* assume that your reader possesses more information than is the case. If you fail to provide a vital piece of information, you are making a false assumption about your reader and should correct it by including the material you have overlooked.

Recognize false assumptions, or gaps in information, and improve logical continuity by providing any missing information.

A false assumption can leave a reader guessing how one idea leads to another. The entire point of passage can be lost unless unstated details or ideas are made clear. To do this, you must reread your writing as a reader would see it and imagine that you know little about the topic. If you find a false assumption, you must fill in the gap with connecting thoughts or information.

Notice in the following passage how a false assumption leaves a gap between events. The writer says that the governor proposed a housing bill but does not explain why the legislators defeated it. Such unstated information weakens the passage.

Passage with false assumption	Recently, the governor proposed a housing bill. A majority of the state house naturally voted to defeat the measure against the governor's endorsement.

Notice in the following revised version that important information is added to correct the false assumption.

Passage with necessary information	Recently, the governor proposed a housing bill. *However, members of the legislature found the bill insufficient, since it limited disaster appropriations as well as ceilings on rent hikes.* A majority of the state house naturally voted to defeat the measure against the governor's endorsement.

Hasty Generalizations.   A *hasty generalization* is an incorrect statement that offers sweeping conclusions on the basis of scanty evidence and overlooks exceptions or qualifying factors. Like contradictions and false assumptions, hasty generalizations arise from insufficient information. If you fail to consider all factors related to an idea, you may generalize beyond sound reason.

> Recognize a hasty generalization and delete it or restate the idea precisely to allow for exceptions or qualifying factors.

If you suspect that a statement is a hasty generalization, ask yourself whether it is literally true, without exception. Be wary of words such as *always, never, all,* or *none* because these words leave no room for exceptions and usually distort the truth. If you spot a statement that seems unfair or that glosses over exceptions in a sweeping conclusion, find other words to make the idea more accurate and precise.

In the following passage about baseball players, a hasty generalization about today's selfish "big leaguers" does not allow for exceptions. It makes a blanket statement about players' motivations, which may simply not be fair.

Passage with a hasty generalization	So many of yesterday's ball players—Babe Ruth, Mickey Mantle, Jackie Robinson, and others—earned notice through the baseball records they set and the personal styles they created. They deserved the adulation they received because they gave the public ideals to look up to—talented athletes who pushed themselves to play as well as they could. Today's ball players still draw admiring crowds, but *they don't deserve the admiration. These so-called "big leaguers" are motivated solely by money, those six-figure salaries, rather than by athletic excellence.*

One way to correct a hasty generalization is to omit it entirely from the passage. Another, often superior, way is to re-examine and refocus the idea to make it reasonable. In the passage about ball players, the generalization points at *all* players; the statement could be more acceptable if it were narrowed to *some* players. Also, the reference to the players' motivations is probably unfounded, or at least extremely generalized. The idea could be refocused so that it is accurate and fair, as in the following version.

Passage with a reasonable qualified opinion	So many of yesterday's ball players—Babe Ruth, Mickey Mantle, Jackie Robinson, and others—earned notice through the baseball records they set and the personal styles they created. They deserved the adulation they received because they gave the public ideals to look up to—talented athletes who pushed themselves to play as well as they could. Today's ball players still draw admiring crowds, but *unfortunately some players are noticed more for the salaries they receive than for other relevant contributions they might make to the sports world.*

Begging the Question.   If you write a statement that repeats itself rather than leads to a completely developed idea, you have *begged the question*, or ducked the issue by going around in circles. This type of error is also called *circular reasoning*.

> Recognize the problem of begging the question, or circular reasoning, and rewrite the statement to provide a completely developed idea.

Begging the question will actually sound ridiculous if you read your statement carefully and hear the meaninglessness of what you have said. If you write "He is proud because he is pleased with himself" you have said practically nothing. You might just as well have written "He is proud because he is proud."

The next statement also begs the question.

BEGGING THE QUESTION: I liked the lecture because it was enjoyable.

In effect, the statement repeats the writer's liking for the lecture and leads nowhere. Instead, the reasoning should progress to another substantial idea. Notice how the following revision corrects the problem.

REASONING IMPROVED: I liked the lecture because Professor Edwards used slides and tape recordings to illustrate his safari.

EXERCISE A: Identifying Errors in Logic. Each of the following items contains an error in reasoning. In each case, identify the error in logic as one of the following: *contradiction, false assumption, hasty generalization,* or *begging the question.*

1. It is said that walking under a ladder will bring a person bad luck. We were not surprised when Leon sprained his ankle.
2. Pierre LaRoche was one of the greatest chefs of France because he was a good cook.
3. A recent study showed that America has more television sets and automobiles per person than any other country on earth. This study proves that Americans are more content than any other people in the world.
4. A successful reporter must go out and dig for stories. After working hard on several stories for the past two months, Harold Johnson lost his job with the paper.
5. The school administration vetoed our proposals because they were opposed to them.
6. Roger Maris set a record by hitting 61 home runs in 1964. No one will ever surpass this.
7. A professional tennis player needs to be in remarkable physical condition. Paul Schwinn never exercises and he wins most of his tennis matches.
8. People always buy designer-name clothes because they are socially insecure. Some sociologists point to a buyer's need to belong as one form of pressure to conform to popular styles. Some others point to the impact of saturation advertising.

9. Jules Verne became known as one of the most imaginative novelists of all time because he wrote creatively.
10. Cyclamates were banned years ago by the Food and Drug Administration. More recently, saccharine was declared a dangerous substance. Despite the agency's method of testing materials with experimental animals, saccharine is still used in commercial products.

EXERCISE B: Correcting Errors in Logic. Write a revision of each of the ten statements in Exercise A, correcting the particular error in reasoning. You may have to use your imagination to add information or details to items that contain gaps in logic.

■ Using Professional Models

By learning to recognize typical errors in reasoning, you can improve the logic and organization of your writing. In addition, the works of professional writers can show you how to develop an idea or line of reasoning smoothly, without gaps or errors. A skilled writer knows how to present all necessary information and how to support points with understandable evidence, so that the reader can follow the progression of ideas easily.

Study the work of professional writers to learn how to use logical reasoning in your own writing.

In your reading, you can benefit from studying particularly effective passages that rely on logical approaches to develop complex ideas. Notice how the following two passages, written by professionals, discuss rather difficult concepts straightforwardly, clearly, and logically.

In the first of the following passages, a writer explains scientist Albert Einstein's theory of time relativity, a difficult idea to grasp. The writer makes no false assumption about the reader's knowledge of the subject. Instead, he provides the information necessary for the reader to follow his explanation.

Main idea	Einstein held that events at different places occurring at the same moment for one observer do not occur at the same moment for another observer moving relatively to the first. For example, two events
Example	judged as taking place at the same time by an ob-

Restatement
of main idea

Application
(specific
example from
real life)

server on the ground are not simultaneous for an observer in a train or an airplane. Time is relative to the position and speed of the observer, and is not absolute. Applying this theory to the universe, we see that an event on a distant star, say an explosion, witnessed by an earth dweller, did not occur on the star at the same time as it was seen on earth. On the contrary, though light moves at 186,000 miles a second, an occurrence on a remote star may have taken place years before news of it reached the world. The star seen today is actually the star as it appeared long ago. Conceivably, it may have even ceased to exist. —Adapted from Robert B. Downs

In the next passage, the writer begins by presenting a qualified generalization and then backs up his claim with examples, which readers can recognize in their own experience, and with statistical evidence about the prevalence of second jobs among employed Americans.

Qualified
generali-
zation

Evidence in
support of
generali-
zation

It is questionable whether American citizens are prepared yet to cope even with the semileisure of a four-day week. They hate to be idle even more than most people. Their three-week vacations are generally periods of frenzied activity. When they find themselves favored with a short work week, many get themselves a second job. More than four million of them have joined the ranks of "moonlighters" or double-job holders. —Vance Packard

If you locate and save good examples of logical reasoning and clear patterns, you can build an idea file, which will serve as an inspiration for your own writing.

EXERCISE C: Finding Professional Models. Using books and magazines that you find in the library or at home, look for passages that reflect clear, logical presentations of ideas. You might start with scientific journals or books about anthropology or social issues. Look particularly at works by such writers as Margaret Mead, George Orwell, Rachel Carson, and William F. Buckley. Find two passages that you decide are good examples of logical presentations. Copy these and write down the title, author, and page number of each model. Then, explain how the writer has logically presented his or her ideas to carry the reader along smoothly.

APPLICATION: Using a Logical Pattern in Your Writing. Choose one of the following topics or one of your own for a passage of one hundred to two hundred words. As you identify a main point for the passage, present it in a single sentence and then add information or evidence in some logical pattern. (To guide your writing, you can use any of the professional models you have found and studied.) When you have written a first draft of the passage, check it for clear connections between ideas. Look for any contradictions, false assumptions, hasty generaliza- tions, or statements that beg the question. Make revisions, checking the pattern of reasoning you have followed, and re- copy the passage in final form.

A poll or statistic that disturbs you or that you disagree with

Reasons that you think your education has prepared you for the future

Talents necessary to excel in a particular sport or hobby

Your reactions to a news story about some public figure

An interesting scientific theory or an experiment that you have performed

22

Effective Paragraphs

A paragraph is a series of related sentences that present a unit of thought. Marked by the indentation of the first word in the first sentence, paragraphs aid writers in developing and organizing their ideas and help readers in both reading and understanding those ideas.

This chapter discusses the features of effective paragraphs, some practical steps in writing paragraphs, and some methods of revising paragraphs.

22.1 Recognizing Key Features of Paragraphs

A standard paragraph is a well-developed unit of thought. The paragraph explains or elaborates on a main idea, usually presented in one sentence called the topic sentence. The rest of the sentences in the paragraph discuss the main idea in the topic sentence, adding specific information. To be effective, a standard paragraph should also be unified and coherent: All of the ideas and information in the paragraph should be related, and everything should be logically organized and clearly and smoothly connected.

This section will help you learn to recognize these basic features, as well as those of some special kinds of paragraphs that differ somewhat from standard paragraphs.

■ The Topic Sentence

In a standard paragraph, the topic sentence states the topic of the paragraph and reveals the writer's purpose.

The topic sentence expresses the main idea of the paragraph and defines the scope of the paragraph.

The topic sentence can be located at the beginning, in the middle, or at the end of the paragraph. A topic sentence at the beginning of a paragraph prepares the reader for the information that follows. A topic sentence in the middle of a paragraph usually follows introductory or transitional sentences and then leads the reader into the supporting information that follows. And a topic sentence at the end of a paragraph usually summarizes or ties together the supporting information presented earlier in the paragraph.

A high percentage of the standard paragraphs that you will read and that you will write will begin with their topic sentences. In the following paragraph, the first sentence states the main idea that the rest of the information in the paragraph develops and clarifies.

TOPIC
SENTENCE

One of the great seventeenth-century contributors to science and the use of the lens was Galileo Galilei (1564–1642). While he was in Venice in 1609, Galileo heard about an instrument, rumored to have been invented the year before, which made objects in the distance appear larger and nearer. The principle of this new instrument interested him, so he immediately set to work making such a device himself. The result was his telescope. Galileo fitted into one end of a metal pipe a convex lens, called the objective, and at the other end of the tube he fixed a concave lens, called the eyepiece. The eyepiece intercepted the converging light rays, which proceeded from the objective, before they reached the point of focus. As they passed through the concave eyepiece, the light rays again changed direction. They no longer converged, but diverged, and passed on to the eye of the viewer. Galileo improved the telescope until his third attempt magnified observed objects thirty-three times. Here was a combination of lenses—mere bits of ground and polished glass—assembled in such a way that it was possible for the human eye to see far beyond its natural limitations. The principle of Galileo's telescope is still used today in opera glasses.
—Anne Huether

Supporting
information

In the next paragraph, the first four sentences give information that guides the reader in understanding the topic sentence. The topic sentence then acts as a bridge between the introductory statements and the specific supporting information that follows it.

Along island beaches, the water changes color as it becomes deeper. In the shallows it is a milky green. In deeper waters over the coral heads and reefs, the color is clear greenish-blue. The color line changes from green-blue to deep blue where the drop-off into deep water begins. *The drop-off marked by this color change is the best place for a good swimmer to see Hawaii's underwater scenery.* Here are deep lava-rimmed valleys paved with white sand. Here are lava rock arches and tunnels and caves where big fish, lobsters, and big eels live. Looking through a face mask into water sixty feet deep, a diver can see that the coral and sand bottom appears a pale, bleached blue. In the deep water, big fish hover in schools like herds of cattle browsing by. A great sea turtle paddles along. A manta ray swims below with the same graceful swoops as a bird in flight. Its big side flaps move like wings. Its pop eyes watch the diver watching it. —Adapted from Ruth M. Tabrah

Introductory statements

TOPIC SENTENCE

Supporting information

Sometimes the main idea of the paragraph is stated in the last sentence, as in the following paragraph. Notice that this topic sentence at the end summarizes the thought of the entire paragraph.

Supporting information

TOPIC SENTENCE

The word toy may come from the Dutch *tuig*—tools, things, or stuff—or, as once suggested, from the Danish *toeve*, meaning to stay, to tarry. The variety of toys is almost limitless. They may be large or miniature, lifelike or caricatures. Some are static, such as dolls' houses and furniture, to be admired and cherished rather than used; others are dynamic, mechanical toys that you can put into action. *From autos to dolls, diamonds to games, toys are anything that enables us to tarry during the fast whip of ordinary life.* —Athelstan Spilhaus

EXERCISE A: Locating Topic Sentences. Read each of the following paragraphs to find the topic sentence. Then copy the topic sentence of each paragraph onto your paper.

(1) One of the most fascinating features of cells is their potential immortality. In 1912 the late Alexis Carrel of the Rockefeller Institute snipped out a piece of chicken heart. Periodically it was fed nourishing broth, and from time to time excess tissue was trimmed away. The cells remained alive for thirty-four years—and were permitted to die only when the experiment had fulfilled its usefulness. —*Our Human Body*

(2) We were so impressed by the comforts and quiet organization of the Mollers' home that we were subdued and on our best behavior. But the biggest change was in Mother. Ensconced

again in the bedroom in which she had grown up, she seemed to shed her responsibilities and become again "one of the Moller girls." Automatically, she found herself depending on her father to make the important decisions, and on her mother to advise her on social engagements and the proper clothes to wear. She seemed to have forgotten all about motion study, her career, and the household back East. Her principal worries seemed to be whether her parents had slept well, how they were feeling, whether they were sitting in drafts. —Frank B. Gilbreth, Jr. and Ernestine Gilbreth Carey

(3) Anyone who has ever had a toothache knows how uncomfortable the experience can be, especially if a quick trip to a dentist does not appear possible. Unfortunately, but frequently, toothaches occur late at night or on Sundays when dentists are unavailable. For these reasons, sufferers should be familiar with a variety of steps that can be taken to ease dental pain. Of course, one should start by taking two aspirin, a procedure that should be repeated every three to four hours. Some oil of cloves, which is pleasant tasting, should then be applied to the painful area, since this acts as a mild anesthetic. Since dental pain is often aggravated by cold, it makes sense not only to avoid cold food and drinks, but even to apply a hot water bottle or a heating pad to the affected region. Finally, rinsing periodically with warm salt water may relieve some discomfort; salt water acts as an anti-inflammatory agent within the mouth and reduces painful swelling of the gums.

(4) During the Great Depression that began in 1929, companies laid off men, and families cut down their grocery buying. This cutback in spending caused farm prices to sink further. As jobless families drew savings out of banks, many of the banks had to close their doors. Those who had not yet withdrawn their money lost it forever. Each closed factory was a blow to all businessmen who sold it raw material and parts. Each family without a breadwinner bought less of everything, from toys to telephone service. They gradually became unable to pay their property taxes, so that local governments had less to spend on relief, money, or goods given to those who needed financial help. Eventually, all Americans, except a lucky few, suffered from the crash. —Adapted from Bernard A. Weisberger

■ Supporting Information

In addition to a topic sentence, a paragraph should contain enough specific information to make the main idea understandable, meaningful, or convincing to the reader.

Supporting information should develop a topic sentence with adequate examples, details, facts, reasons, incidents, or any combination of these.

At least five different kinds of support are possible in the development of a paragraph. The following chart lists and describes these kinds.

KINDS OF SUPPORT
Examples: are particular instances of a general idea or principle. In a paragraph about the best shows on Broadway, for instance, examples might include three or four particular shows.
Details: are small items or pieces of information that make up something larger. Details often make up descriptions. A paragraph describing a person, for example, might include details of the person's appearance and behavior.
Facts: are specific pieces of information that can be verified as being true and accurate. A paragraph about an election might include the names, backgrounds, and policies of the major candidates.
Reasons: are explanations, justifications, or causes. They often answer the question *Why?* about the main idea. If a topic sentence presents an opinion about the legal driving age, for instance, the supporting information might offer reasons that the age should be lowered.
Incidents: are minor events or happenings. One or more incidents can be used to illustrate a main idea. A paragraph about the dangers of roller skating might relate an incident describing some of these dangers.

Well-developed standard paragraphs contain enough supporting information to meet the reader's expectations formed by the topic sentence and to make the paragraph seem complete. Notice the varied and thorough supporting information in the following paragraphs.

In the first of the following paragraphs, the supporting information consists mainly of examples that illustrate the topic sentence.

TOPIC
SENTENCE

In the 1880's and '90's the bicycle became the adventurer's magic carpet. Young people went in for racing—"scorching," it was called. Handlebars were turned down and the serious scorcher rode almost flat on the bike, like a jockey leaning forward along the neck of a race horse. Sober elders disapproved of scorchers, but often went in for touring themselves. Bicycle parties would set out to explore unknown

Supporting
information:

Examples
with facts
and details

> country fifty miles from home for a week at a time, and anyone who had ridden one hundred miles in eighteen hours could join the Century Road Club of America and sport a gold bar for every hundred miles. Americans had "gone somewhere" before— west across the country as pioneers. Now "going somewhere" was becoming fun. —Elizabeth Janeway

The next paragraph uses details to describe for the reader "the handsome burial mask of Tutankhamen."

TOPIC
SENTENCE

Supporting
information:
Details

> *The handsome burial mask of Tutankhamen, one of the last rulers of the Eighteenth Dynasty, is a life-size masterpiece by an artist who worked in the royal court of Thebes.* Directly covering the head of the young Pharaoh, the mask is made of solid gold. It represents Tutankhamen at eighteen, his age of death. On the hood part of the mask are the royal emblems of protection: the heads of the vulture goddess Nekheb of El Kab and the cobra of Buto. The stripes on the hood, eyebrows, and eye linings are blue-glass inlays. The eyes of the mask are composed of white calcite and very dark obsidian. The richly decorated collar, which covers the chest and ends at the shoulders with two falcons, is inlaid with segments of semiprecious stones, quartz backed with red pigment, and green feldspar engraved to simulate beads, and pendants made of glass. —Anne Huether

Sometimes a paragraph can be developed mainly with facts, as in the following example.

TOPIC
SENTENCE

Supporting
information:
Facts

> But the United States' difficulties with avalanches pale in comparison with those of other countries. *In Europe, avalanches have been wreaking havoc for millennia.* They are thought to have played an important part in decimating Hannibal's army during its epic crossing of the Alps in 218 B.C. Napoleon's army was likewise plagued in the Great St. Bernard Pass on its way to the Battle of Marengo in 1800. And the beginning months of 1689, 1720, 1889, and 1951 are notorious in Alpine history for avalanche destruction. In 1720, at Obergestein in Switzerland's Rhône Valley, an avalanche from a slide track called the Galen killed eighty-eight people. But, in recent times, the winter of 1950–51 was the worst: 279 people died. —James Balog

A paragraph developed with reasons is easy to imagine. Many topic sentences that present opinions, for example, will naturally be backed up with reasons supporting that opinion.

A paragraph can also be developed with an incident. In the following paragraph, the writer uses facts and an incident told with specific details to provide evidence for the statement that polar bears and people do not get along.

TOPIC SENTENCE	*Polar bears and people don't mix well at all.* Now that mineral exploration and exploitation have brought more people to the Arctic, the potential for bear attacks has increased accordingly. The root of
Supporting information: Facts	the problem is Nanook's extreme inquisitiveness and awesome power. A polar bear in quest of food can overcome virtually anything that gets in its way. For example, a Manitoba biologist recently built a beau-
Incident with details	tiful camp on the west coast of Hudson Bay as headquarters for his long-range goose studies. To make his large, well-equipped hut bear-proof, he surrounded it with an eight-foot mesh fence, plus electrified barbed wire. In the fall, the bears came and broke through the fences and reduced the hut to splinters. Inside, everything breakable had been smashed, and amidst the rubble lay the refrigerator, broken and battered. In addition, the bears had pounded big dents into the metal bathtub, apparently as their parting gesture. —Fred Bruemmer

EXERCISE B: **Recognizing Kinds of Support.** Reread the paragraphs in Exercise A and examine the supporting information. List the pieces of support used in each paragraph on your paper. Then, identify the support in each paragraph as mainly examples, details, facts, reasons, incidents, or any combination of types.

■ Unity

Another quality of well-written paragraphs is unity, which means including only pertinent information that relates directly to the topic sentence or to another piece of supporting information.

In a unified paragraph, all the sentences and pieces of information are related to the main idea and to each other.

A paragraph without unity can confuse a reader with unnecessary ideas and unrelated information. Either giving too much attention to one piece of supporting information and not enough to the others or shifting topics momentarily can cause disunity in paragraphs. When one or more sentences stray from the focus of the paragraph, leading the reader too far from the main idea, the unity of the paragraph is broken.

The following paragraph is not unified because it introduces two ideas that are not related to the topic sentence.

TOPIC SENTENCE	Why has Chinese food become so popular among Americans today? For one reason, a complete Chinese meal is often less expensive than the fare in the Italian restaurant next door, the American steakhouse across the street, or that fancy French restaurant across town. *Prices of just about everything have risen astronomically.* While being economical, most Chinese dishes are also quite healthful, containing such nutritious standbys as soy, bean curd, rice, and many other vegetables. *We all know that many Americans worry about their weight.* Most enticing perhaps is the wide variety of edibles provided by any Chinese restaurant. From different soups such as egg drop and won ton to the foo yongs, the sweet and sours, and the gai pans, any diner can find a choice that he or she will like; in fact, so many possibilities make choosing difficult so that many Americans become repeat customers.
Supporting information without unity	

Because the sentences on prices and weight do not help develop any of the writer's reasons, they do not belong in the paragraph. If you reread the paragraph omitting the unrelated information, you will find that the paragraph is clearer.

EXERCISE C: Maintaining Unity. The following paragraph contains sentences that stray too far from the main idea. Locate these sentences and write them on your paper. Then reread the paragraph without these sentences to check for unity.

(1) The haiku is a simple yet beautiful form of poetry that has gained popularity in this country in recent years. (2) Developed in sixteenth-century Japan, the haiku has three lines, the first and third lines having five syllables each, and the second line containing seven syllables. (3) Other traditional types of poetry have different requirements: Sonnets, for instance, require twelve or sixteen lines. (4) Like all types of poetry, the haiku's purpose is to evoke emotion. (5) Connoisseurs of any kind of art appreciate works that evoke feeling. (6) The haiku traditionally achieves this by means of images drawn from nature and frequently from descriptions of common people involved in everyday activities. (7) Children at play are common themes as well. (8) The greatest works of some famous painters are simple de-

scriptions of common people at work, play, or rest. (9) Anything, really, can be the subject of haiku, and because the form is so simple, almost anyone can write one.

■ Coherence

Coherence is another quality of well-written paragraphs. In a coherent paragraph, the topic sentence and all supporting ideas must follow a logical order while transitions and other connecting devices clarify the relationships among the ideas.

Orders That Aid Coherence.   The supporting information in a paragraph should be arranged in a logical order so that the reader can easily follow the ideas.

> Pieces of supporting information should follow a logical order. Among the most useful orders are order of importance, chronological order, spatial order, comparison and contrast order, and developmental order.

A number of orders or plans can be used to organize paragraphs. *Order of importance* arranges major pieces of supporting information from least important (or interesting, expensive, and so on) to most important (or interesting, expensive, and so on). *Chronological order* presents major pieces of supporting information in a time sequence. *Spatial order* arranges support by position: from near to far, outside to inside, ceiling to floor, and so on. *Comparison and contrast order* groups similarities and differences by presenting one item completely and then comparing and contrasting a second with the first or by comparing and contrasting two or more items point by point. *Developmental order* is not as structured as the preceding orders. It simply arranges information in the most logical way for the particular topic sentence and group of support.

The order you use should suit the main idea of the paragraph and should keep the ideas moving in a clear direction. No matter which logical order you choose, supporting information should build on the information that precedes it or refer directly to the topic sentence.

In the following paragraph, supporting information follows both chronological and spatial order. Notice that both orders suit the topic—the appearance of a.tsunami, or tidal wave, approaching the shore. Words such as *when, on the land,* and *on the seaward side* help to clarify the relationships among the pieces of information.

TOPIC
SENTENCE

Support
organized in
chronological
and spatial
order

When the tsunami reaches shallower water, it undergoes a profound change. The drag from the bottom slows down the onrushing set of waves, bunching the individual crests closer together. Unable to expend their huge supply of energy in horizontal speed, the waves build upwards, sometimes cresting into breakers more than 100 feet high. It is the massive waves, bursting upon the seashore as terrifying walls of water, that cause death and destruction. Awestruck spectators *on the land* see a monstrous mass of water surging inexorably towards them. Observers *on the seaward side* of tsunamis see the huge waves suddenly rising from the ocean ahead of them to plunder low-lying coastal areas. —Peter Gwynne

In the following paragraph about trumpets and cornets, the support is arranged through a series of comparisons and contrasts. First, the paragraph focuses on the similarities among some parts of the instruments and then on the differences among other parts. Notice that words such as *both, yet, on the other hand, final,* and *unlike* help to point out likenesses and differences between the instruments.

TOPIC
SENTENCE

Support
organized in
comparison
and contrast
order

The trumpet and the cornet are often confused with one another. *Both* are small brass horns with three valves, a metal mouthpiece, and a flared opening through which the sound produced by the horn player escapes. *Both* produce a rather high-pitched metallic tone associated particularly with parades and other martial events. *Yet* the cornet has a slightly shorter body and is more conical than the trumpet, and the cornet is considered the more versatile of the two. The trumpet's tone, *on the other hand,* is more brilliant, and the trumpet is more difficult to play properly. The *final* distinction between the two horns is one of function: *Unlike* the trumpet, the more recently developed cornet is rarely heard in the concert hall because its tone is subtler.

Another common order for supporting information is *developmental order*. Developmental order includes any logical order other than the highly structured order of importance, chronological, spatial, and comparison and contrast orders. The only requirement for using developmental order is that the pieces of supporting information follow smoothly and logically from the topic sentence and from each other. Notice that the following paragraph uses developmental order and ends with its topic sentence. Although the paragraph is well-organized, the pieces of support could possibly be arranged in a number of different ways because this particular topic sentence does not dictate a rigid order.

Support organized in developmental order	The duckbill platypus is a land mammal that lays leathery eggs as a reptile does. It has a flat, rubbery bill, no teeth, and webbed feet like a duck. It suckles its young with milk but has no nipples. It lives and feeds in rivers and lakes but sleeps in burrows in the bank. It is crepuscular, that is, active mainly at dawn and dusk. *And* the male has venom glands and can strike like a snake with its hind leg spurs. In Australia, the platypus has sometimes been called a "bits-and-pieces animal"—a fitting nickname.
TOPIC SENTENCE	

—Janet L. Hopson

Transitions.   In addition to logical orders, transitions can make the flow of ideas smooth. Transitions connect ideas and point out the direction of ideas in the paragraph. A few well-placed transitions can often strengthen a paragraph.

> Well-chosen transitions can help to clarify the relationships among ideas in a paragraph.

Transitions can indicate the order of ideas and guide the reader. Certain transitions are more appropriate for one kind of order than another, as the following chart shows.

SOME POSSIBLE ORDERS WITH USEFUL TRANSITIONS			
Order	**Transitions**		
Order of Importance:	first	next	moreover
	second	for one reason	even greater
	third	finally	greatest
	most	final	also
Chronological:	first	later	formerly
	next	final	after
	meanwhile	finally	afterward
	at last	last	before
	soon	then	moments later
Spatial:	outside	inside	beyond
	behind	overhead	beneath
	in front	in the distance	to the left (right)
	near	under	

Comparison and Contrast:	besides	in addition	just as . . . so
	similarly	in contrast	also
	like	whereas	but
	too	however	on the contrary
	also	both	on the other hand
	yet	final	
Developmental:	and	finally	along with
	also	indeed	thus
	furthermore	for example	therefore
	in fact	for instance	consequently
	accordingly	next	as a result

In the example paragraphs on the preceding pages, the words in italics are transitions. Notice *when, on the land,* and *on the seaward side* in the first paragraph, *both, yet, on the other hand, final,* and *unlike* in the second paragraph and *and* in the third paragraph.

Other Words That Aid Coherence. A continuity of ideas can also be achieved through repetition of a main word, the use of synonyms for main words, and the use of consistent pronouns. In a paragraph about exhibits in a museum, for instance, the writer may need to repeat the word *exhibits* several times to remind the reader of the topic and focus of the paragraph. Sometimes the writer might also use synonyms for the main word. In the same paragraph about exhibits, for example, the writer might use the synonym *displays* at one point rather than repeat the word *exhibit* one time too many.

Using consistent pronouns can also contribute to coherence. Sometimes, instead of using main words or synonyms, use appropriate pronouns, which can add smoothness and variety.

> Repeating main words, such as important nouns and verbs, using synonyms for main words, and using consistent pronouns can enhance coherence by adding subtle connections and smoothness.

In the following paragraph, the writer focuses the reader's attention on the topic by repeating the main words *hot water* and by using the synonyms *steam* and *steaming puddles*. The writer also achieves smoothness and variety by using the pronouns *some* and *it.*

TOPIC
SENTENCE

Paragraph
connected by
repeating
main words
and using
synonyms
and clear
pronouns

In Beppu, Japan, *hot water* is the keystone of tourism, but *it* also plays an important part in the daily lives of the city's residents. *Steam* is trapped in cement blockhouses at every accessible vent and forced into a tangle of pipes leading to homes and businesses. *Some* of *it* goes into houses and restaurants for cooking vegetables and rice; *some* is funneled to factories, where *it* drives heavy machinery. Children boil eggs in *steaming puddles* on the road, and mothers scrub clothes in *water* brought from the nearest communal faucet. The *hot water* is also used for agricultural research, physical therapy and, of course, recreational bathing. —Constance Brown

Parallelism and Concluding Sentences. Other ways to connect ideas within paragraphs and to add smoothness include using parallelism and writing a concluding sentence. By using the same grammatical structure for a series of words, phrases, or clauses, you can indicate to the reader that ideas are related and equal in importance. For example, very similar sentences can be used to present four related facts that support a main idea. A concluding sentence, on the other hand, can add polish and connections by bringing the paragraph to a satisfactory end.

Parallelism and concluding sentences can contribute to the coherence of a paragraph by tying ideas together.

Parallelism uses similarities and repetition as a signal to the reader that ideas belong together and are of equal rank. In the following paragraph, the writer employs loosely parallel sentences to pile up examples of the main idea. Almost all of the sentences in the middle of the paragraph follow a subject-active verb-prepositional phrase or complement pattern. Notice that the writer indicates the end of this detailing of tourists with the transition *even* and a longer sentence. Because the paragraph employs parallelism, it resembles a well-developed catalog which conveys to the reader the great number and variety of tourists who visited ancient Pompeii. As you can see, the pattern would not fit all or most paragraphs, but it can be very effective when appropriate.

TOPIC
SENTENCE

Paragraph
connected by
parallelism

Pompeii's ancient tourists were of every class and social condition. The rich owners of luxurious villas, which dotted the surrounding countryside like so many domed and pillared villages, visited friends and shopped for luxuries produced in the city's busy workshops. Merchants arrived with their wares. Itinerant artisans executed commissions in mosaic, sculpture, stucco, or paint for wealthy clients. Lovers followed their hearts. Traveling troupes of actors played local engagements. Soldiers, temporarily detached from their units, passed through. The pious offered sacrifices at urban temples. Citizens of neighboring communities attended games in the amphitheater. Even slaves from the countryside came to Pompeii to run errands for their masters, who were either prosperous farmers or the owners of aristocratic villas. —James Packer

Like parallelism, concluding sentences do not belong in every paragraph. Sometimes, however, a concluding sentence can summarize the information in a paragraph, remind the reader of the topic sentence, or simply mark the completion of the thought of the paragraph. When a concluding sentence has a strong impact or when it ends with particular flair, it is called a *clincher.*

Look again at the following paragraph about the trumpet and cornet that you read earlier. A concluding sentence could improve this paragraph by referring to the main idea and by adding a statement that wraps up the supporting details.

TOPIC
SENTENCE

Supporting
information

Concluding
sentence

The trumpet and the cornet are often confused with one another. Both are small brass horns with three valves, a metal mouthpiece, and a flared opening through which the sound produced by the horn player escapes. Both produce a rather high-pitched metallic tone associated particularly with parades and other martial events. Yet the cornet has a slightly shorter body and is more conical, and the cornet is considered the more versatile of the two. The trumpet's tone, on the other hand, is more brilliant, and the trumpet is more difficult to play properly. The final distinction between the two horns is one of function: Unlike the trumpet, the more recently developed cornet is rarely heard in the concert hall because its tone is subtler. *While at first or second glance, a beginner may see only the surface similarities between the two instruments, the trained musician knows their difference as well as he or she might "know" two different people with two different personalities.*

EXERCISE D: Achieving Coherence in Paragraphs.

Each of the following two groups of sentences is a jumbled paragraph. One sentence in each group is a topic sentence. The other sentences contain supporting information, and in each group there may be a concluding sentence. Identify the topic sentence. Then logically reorder the sentences. Finally, write the complete, organized paragraph on your paper.

1

a. On the right or north side of the plaza is the similar-looking Avery Fisher Hall, which houses the New York Philharmonic.
b. One of the most imposing and beautiful landmarks to be found in Manhattan is New York's Lincoln Center for the Performing Arts.
c. In the middle, is the Metropolitan Opera House, perhaps the most beautiful of all.
d. Aesthetically as well as practically, the center is one of New York's greatest assets.
e. Entering the center from Columbus Avenue, a visitor first encounters a large, square plaza with a fountain in the center and an enormous marble building on each of three sides.
f. To the left, or in a southerly direction, is the New York State Theater, home of the New York City Ballet and the City Opera Company.

2

a. By 5:45 A.M., when power was restored, the dying fires and sleeping bodies huddled around fireplaces all over town resembled pioneer encampments.
b. Nothing relieves the monotony of daily routine like an unexpected incident or adventure.
c. The "Great Blackout," as it was called locally, was such an event.
d. When lightning struck a main power line at 6:32 P.M., all power stopped abruptly.
e. The adventure began when the storm blasted through the area and the lights flickered.
f. The Great Blackout was an incident to remember, a step into the past.
g. Most homes reverted to nineteenth-century means of heat and light: candles, oil lamps, and hearthfires.

EXERCISE E: Recognizing Devices That Aid Coherence. Using the paragraphs you reordered in Exercise D, complete the following activities for each paragraph.

1. Identify the order of arrangement of ideas in the paragraph, and list any transitions that help clarify the order.
2. List any main words that are repeated throughout the paragraph. Also list any synonyms of the main words and any pronouns that replace main words throughout the paragraph.

3. If the paragraph uses parallelism, identify where and how it is used. If the paragraph has a concluding sentence, copy the sentence. Otherwise, write *none*.

■ Special Kinds of Paragraphs

Among the most important features of standard paragraphs are topic sentences, adequate supporting information, unity, and coherence. Some paragraphs differ from standard paragraphs with regard to a few of these features. These paragraphs may have implied rather than stated topic sentences, for example, or may consist of only one or a few sentences. Such paragraphs are usually found in longer works such as newspaper or magazine articles and chapters of books. These special kinds of paragraphs usually work with other paragraphs to develop some central or overall idea.

A paragraph may differ in topic sentence, length, and development from a standard paragraph, but it should be unified and logically organized.

A paragraph may be of a special kind because it is serving a particular function in a longer piece of writing. It might be an introductory or concluding paragraph or a transitional paragraph between two standard paragraphs. It might simply continue the development of the main idea found in an earlier paragraph. Or it might imply, rather than state, the topic sentence, in which case the reader would have to infer the main idea from the supporting information. No matter how these special kinds of paragraphs vary from the standard paragraph, they should seem logical and clear to the reader.

In the following series of paragraphs, notice that the first paragraph is standard: It contains a topic sentence (*Signs of growth were everywhere*) and adequate supporting information that provides facts and examples. The second paragraph is not standard because it does not contain a topic sentence; instead, it continues to develop the main idea of the first paragraph. It is unified and coherent, however. The information it contains is pertinent to the topic, and the details are arranged logically, in spatial order. The third paragraph is standard with a long topic sentence. The last paragraph, a brief one, is not standard. Instead, it presents a single sentence that functions as a concluding idea, one that might not fit easily within the preceding paragraph yet should be mentioned.

Standard (main idea and supporting information)	Signs of growth were everywhere. The metropolis is the fourth fastest growing in the nation, its population swollen to 1.7 million, more than twice that of twenty-five years ago. A dozen new skyscrapers gleamed downtown, and beside them rose the steel girders of more to come. The barnacle-like encrustation of warehouses along Interstate 70 pushed eastward, toward Kansas City.
Not standard (supporting ideas arranged spatially to develop paragraph 1)	To the west, housing developments had been notched into the foothills of the Front Range, while to the southeast and south spread a vast suburban sea. The metropolis's borders were marked, for the moment, by bulldozers scraping former ranchland, and by the tracery of street curbing set in the raw earth, outlining the shapes of the communities soon to rise there.
Standard (main idea and supporting information)	From a distance the city seemed to sit on land as flat as a table top, the mountains to the west no more awesome than the great flat plain that rolls eastward as far as the eye can see. It is that great, dry plain that gives the city an aura of remoteness, of isolation. It is the mountains that lend it an aura of promise. It was thus when Denver was founded 120 years ago by a handful of gold prospectors and land speculators. It remains so today.
Not standard (single sentence as a concluding idea)	The promise varies: For some it is a fortune to be made, or profits; for others, a better opportunity, or the good life in the sun; and for others yet, simply a chance, or even a refuge. —John J. Putman

EXERCISE F: Analyzing Special Kinds of Paragraphs. Most of the paragraphs in the following items are not standard. Read each item carefully and identify the nonstandard paragraphs. Then explain how they differ from standard paragraphs and tell what special functions they are likely to have.

(1) Hope Ryden was born in St. Paul and grew up in Illinois, but every summer her family retreated to a cabin in the woods of northern Wisconsin. There were few other children for miles around the Rydens' cabin, so she became accustomed to spending hours in the forest alone, watching animals. She recalls a time when she was about nine years old, meeting one of the last wolves in that part of the country: "I was walking in the woods when all of a sudden, there it was. We looked at each other a long moment. That wild animal struck a deep note in me." —Patricia Curtis

(2) There is the creak of the beam swinging from side to side as the boat shifts in the water. The wind hits the wet canvas

with a *thwack*, and the sail beats loudly like a sheet on a clothesline. There is the low strumming of the boat as it glides through the waves. And, all around, there is the cry of gulls and the lapping, whooshing, sucking sound of the sea.

(3) *Little Women* is a novel that has been wept over and loved by millions of Americans, but apparently its author, Louisa May Alcott, was never one of them.

After initially resisting the suggestion of her editor that she write a book for children, Miss Alcott reluctantly set down a somewhat idealized history of her own family, whom generations of readers have come to know as the March family of *Little Women*. She included numerous moralistic passages, which she herself believed to be saccharine and preachy, but which were expected in young people's fiction at that time. The book's popularity astounded Miss Alcott, and she found herself called upon to devote the rest of her literary career to churning out more and more children's stories, the unwilling captive of her own success.

(4) It is not particularly difficult to make lasagna if you don't mind spending a messy half hour layering one semiliquid substance on top of another. First, the long flat noodles must be boiled and the sauce, a mixture of browned, seasoned meat and tomato paste, must be prepared. Once you have done this, line up your various cheeses before you like a series of fingerpaint pots. Cover the bottom of a long baking dish with the sauce and pave it with your first layer of noodles. Plaster this over with a layer of ricotta cheese, covering this in turn with a layer of shredded mozzarella cheese, then another layer of sauce, and finally a sprinkling of parmesan cheese.

Repeat this sequence until you have filled the baking dish almost to the brim, ending with a layer of noodles covered with sauce so that they don't dry out. Meanwhile, heat the oven to about 425 degrees Fahrenheit. Gingerly set the loaded baking dish in the oven, and spend the next half hour cleaning the kitchen, which may look as if it has just served as the arena for a food fight among a crew of plasterers.

APPLICATION: Evaluating a Paragraph. Choose a paragraph from a magazine or a paragraph that you have recently written. Evaluate the paragraph using the following instructions.

1. Copy the topic sentence of the paragraph onto your paper.
2. List the kind(s) of support used to develop the topic sentence: examples, details, facts, reasons, or incidents.
3. Examine the paragraph for unity. Write *unified* if the paragraph sticks to one main topic. If the paragraph lacks unity, identify the unrelated ideas.

4. Write the logical order used to arrange supporting information.
5. List all transitions as well as any repetitions of main words, synonyms, or pronouns.
6. If the paragraph uses parallelism or has a concluding sentence, write these features on your paper.
7. If the paragraph is not a standard paragraph, briefly explain how it differs from a standard paragraph.
8. Rewrite the paragraph to improve or add any of the features you have just examined.

22.2 Planning and Writing Paragraphs

This section explains steps that you can follow in writing standard paragraphs. First, you will *plan* to write by thinking out your paragraph, discovering ideas, and organizing them. Then, you will *write*, giving special attention to the connections between ideas and the smoothness of your paragraph. When you have completed these steps, you can use the steps for revising and polishing your writing found in Section 22.3.

■ Writing the Topic Sentence

To compose a well-written standard paragraph, you should begin by pondering and exploring possible topics and by shaping a likely topic into a main idea. Consideration of your audience and purpose should go into this thinking process. Your ideas for a paragraph should grow in your mind and on paper by a process of probing and analyzing. Eventually you may determine your own special way to zero in on a topic and an aspect of that topic appropriate for a paragraph, but for now the following steps should help you get started.

Discovering a Paragraph Topic. When you are writing a single paragraph, you can simplify your task by choosing a topic that you—with your knowledge and interests—can write about in one paragraph. You should begin by listing possible topics that appeal to you and then dividing them into smaller, more manageable topics. An appropriate paragraph topic is one that can be treated in some depth and in an interesting way in one paragraph.

> Explore possible topics, divide general topics into smaller topics, and choose one suitable for a paragraph.

Sometimes, when you begin to plan, you may have a general idea; other times, you may have an assignment with suggested topics; and still other times, you may be starting with no definite ideas. In any of these cases, letting your mind generate and explore ideas and jotting down these ideas, examining them, and limiting them will lead you to a possible topic. If you decide to write about a historical figure, for example, you can see that this is only a general category for which you will have to supply more specific topics. You might search for a topic by listing topics and by breaking down the one you are particularly interested in into smaller topics, as in the following chart.

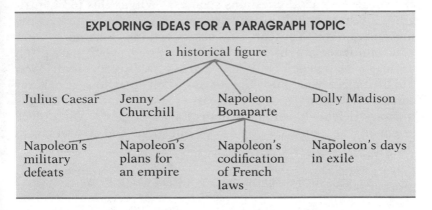

EXPLORING IDEAS FOR A PARAGRAPH TOPIC

a historical figure

Julius Caesar · Jenny Churchill · Napoleon Bonaparte · Dolly Madison

Napoleon's military defeats · Napoleon's plans for an empire · Napoleon's codification of French laws · Napoleon's days in exile

Once you have listed these topics, you might decide that Napoleon's military defeats would be your best choice.

Shaping a Main Idea to Fit Your Audience and Purpose. Your next planning step involves studying your topic, identifying what you plan to say, and deciding whom you wish to address. Your basic goal will be to limit your paragraph topic further and sharpen it to a main idea about your topic. To do this focusing, you should decide what aspects of your topic are most interesting and important to you. What do you want to cover in the paragraph? Determining your audience can also help you figure out what you want to say. Will your audience be other students who have studied the topic, students unfamiliar with the topic, children, experts, or a general audience?

At this point, you may also want to consider your purpose. If you decide beforehand that you will inform, explain, persuade, describe, or entertain in your paragraph, this decision can influence your choice of main idea. In other cases, your purpose may develop out of your main idea.

When you have a main idea, you can express it as a topic sentence.

Shape your paragraph topic into a main idea and then into a topic sentence by considering your audience and purpose.

One workable method for figuring out a main idea is to ask yourself questions to stimulate your thinking about your paragraph topic. Through these questions you can discover exactly what aspect of your topic you are most prepared to write about and most interested in. At this point, knowing who your audience is can help you pose thoughtful questions. You may ask yourself general questions such as, "Why is this topic intriguing? What should others know about it? What interests me most about it?" You can also ask questions concerning what your audience might want to know about your paragraph topic. If Napoleon's military defeats were your topic, you might expect your audience to ask such questions as "What caused Napoleon's military defeats?" and "What effect did his military defeats have on his plans for an empire?" On a piece of paper you should jot down your questions and answers as in the following chart.

QUESTIONS LEADING TO POSSIBLE MAIN IDEAS	
Paragraph Topic: Napoleon's military defeats	
Questions	**Possible Main Ideas**
Why am I interested in this topic?	—Napoleon was a great general and conqueror whose military defeats were a sad end to a brilliant career
What caused Napoleon's military defeats?	—many long years of war, growing strength of the powers against Napoleon, unfavorable weather
What effect did Napoleon's military defeats have on his plans for an empire?	—led directly to his downfall, destroyed his plans for an empire

From your list of possible main ideas, you should choose the one that appeals to you most and the one for which you have the most information. When you select your main idea, check it against your intended audience and purpose. All of the main ideas in the preceding chart would be appropriate for an audience of students unfamiliar with the topic. The first main idea would suit a persuasive purpose because it offers an opinion. The second main idea about the cause of defeat would also suit a persuasive purpose. The last main idea could be written to inform or explain. You might choose the last main idea because you want to focus on the effect of the defeats on Napoleon's life.

When you have a main idea, you should write several sentences that present it clearly. You should experiment with different wordings until you find the one that captures your idea most precisely. Think about your audience and purpose as you try to express your main idea in the best words. However, also keep in mind that your sentence may still need polishing after you have planned the rest of your paragraph.

Using the third main idea in the chart, you might write versions of your topic sentence such as those in the following chart.

POSSIBLE TOPIC SENTENCES
Main Idea: Napoleon's military defeats led directly to his downfall.
1. A series of military defeats led to the downfall of Napoleon.
2. Losing several major military campaigns led to Napoleon's downfall.
3. A series of major military defeats led to Napoleon's final abdication and exile.
4. A series of military defeats led to Napoleon's downfall.

Any of these topic sentences could be used for your paragraph. They differ only slightly in wording and in the amount of information given. You might choose the fourth version as your topic sentence for its directness and particular focus.

EXERCISE A: Choosing a Topic. Choose one of the following ideas as a general topic for a paragraph. Then list as many smaller related topics as you can think of. If necessary, choose one of the smaller topics and narrow it still further until you have a topic narrow enough for a thorough treatment in a single paragraph.

A sport
Symptoms of a disease
A natural disaster
A television show or movie
Astronomy or astrology
Habits of an animal
How something operates

Theme (central idea) of a
movie, play, poem
A mathematical concept
(such as pi, ratio, infinity,
or computing square
roots)

EXERCISE B: Shaping a Paragraph Topic into a Topic Sentence. Use the paragraph topic you narrowed in Exercise A and complete the following steps.

1. Briefly describe the audience to whom you intend to write (for example: students in your class, the faculty of your school, students in another part of the country, and so on).
2. Study your paragraph topic and think about your audience. Then ask yourself at least three questions about your paragraph topic that could lead to the discovery of possible main ideas. Jot down your questions and answers on your paper.
3. Look at your list of answers (possible main ideas) and decide what purpose each would suit.
4. Then choose the main idea you will use for your paragraph and make sure that it does fit the audience you have chosen and the purpose you intend to have.
5. Write at least three versions of your topic sentence.
6. Finally, select the topic sentence that seems the most clear and interesting to you. Circle it on your paper.

■ Developing Support for a Topic Sentence

The second major step in the planning process involves discovering, remembering, and gathering supporting information that illustrates and explains the main idea in your topic sentence. A person reading your topic sentence will naturally have certain expectations about the content of your paragraph. You should try to anticipate and meet these expectations by including in your paragraph supporting information that answers possible questions a reader might have. When you have gathered supporting information that will answer these questions, select from it the best information to ensure that your paragraph will be unified and complete.

Brainstorming for Specific Information.   Gathering supporting information should be a creative process in which you think of all the related facts and examples you know about your main idea. As you continue to think about your main idea, you may come up with examples, details, and reasons that had not occurred to you before. If you are listing facts, you may discover other related pieces of information that you have learned from your reading and studying. Your goal should be to list an abundance of support for your main idea.

Brainstorm for examples, details, facts, reasons, and incidents that will explain and develop your main idea.

Your main idea, as you have expressed it in your topic sentence, can stimulate your thoughts about support. You may want to write your topic sentence on a piece of paper and then free-associate from your main idea, jotting down every idea, example, detail, fact, or reason that comes to mind. If you digress too far from your main idea, read your topic sentence again.

Another method you might try involves asking yourself questions, particularly questions that a reader might ask about your topic sentence. Again, you would write your topic sentence on a piece of paper. After reading your topic sentence and thinking about your audience, you would list questions about your main idea on your paper and answer the questions with specific supporting information. Your questions should cover terms that might need to be defined or parts of your main idea that might need explanation. During this searching process, you should list all the supporting ideas that occur to you. Later you can weed out those that do not closely pertain to your main idea.

If you were to ask yourself questions using the topic sentence on Napoleon's military defeats for an audience of students unfamiliar with the topic, you might produce a list similar to the following.

QUESTIONING TO FIND SUPPORT FOR A TOPIC SENTENCE

Topic Sentence: A series of military defeats led to Napoleon's downfall.

What were the military defeats?

—campaign against the Russians in 1812

—battle against the armies of Austria, Prussia, and Russia at Leipzig in October 1813

—battle against Great Britain, led by the Duke of Wellington, and Prussia, led by Major Gebhard von Blücher, at Waterloo in 1815

How did these defeats lead to Napoleon's downfall?

—throughout his earlier career Napoleon had been a brilliant strategist, detecting and using his enemies' weaknesses

—Russia—formerly an ally of France—made peace and opened up trade with Great Britain

—Napoleon wanted to punish Russia—assembled an army of 600,000 and marched into Russia

—Russians retreated toward Moscow—burned and destroyed everything behind them

—Russia—always fairly safe from invaders because of size, rugged terrain, and harsh weather

—Napoleon reached Moscow—found people and army gone and city burning

—Russia wouldn't accept a truce

—Napoleon had to return across Russia in freezing cold of winter—army died from hunger, illness, some killed by attacking Russians

—only 100,000 men left

—defeat weakened Napoleon's power and credibility; enemies gained confidence

—Napoleon raised another army with difficulty

—won a few battles but at Battle of Leipzig enemies proved too strong

—defeats prompted his allies to desert him and countries he had subdued to rebel

—French senate wanted a Bourbon king—Napoleon abdicated and was exiled to Elba in 1814

—Napoleon escaped, raised another army, couldn't match the strength of Wellington and Blücher at Waterloo

If you use either the free-associating or questioning method, you will probably gather more information than you can use in one paragraph. However, not all the information you listed may be relevant to your main idea. Having more ideas than you need will enable you to select the best information.

Evaluating Support for Unity and Completeness. At this point in the planning process, you should do some analyzing and sorting. In a sense, you are checking and revising when you examine your support to see if it will contribute to a reader's understanding of your main idea. You should look for pieces of support that are unrelated, unimportant, or unnecessary and also for any important facts or examples you may have overlooked. Finally, you should reexamine your topic sentence to determine if it fits the body of support you have collected.

Eliminate pieces of support that add nothing to the main idea or the rest of the support. Jot down any necessary pieces of support to fill in gaps. Revise your topic sentence if necessary to fit your supporting information.

As you read over your list of supporting information, consider each piece of support. Ask yourself, "Would the reader need this information to understand my main idea? Does this information strengthen or clarify any other pieces of information?" and "Do I have too much or too little support for a well-developed paragraph?" If you have too many facts, examples, or reasons, select those that are the strongest and most colorful. If you have too little supporting information, ask yourself a few more questions. You can continue to use your list of support by crossing out or adding information on the same paper.

If you examine the following chart, which shows the evaluation step for the support on Napoleon, you can see that one new fact has been added and that five pieces of extra or unrelated supporting information have been crossed out.

EVALUATING A LIST OF SUPPORTING INFORMATION
Topic Sentence: A series of military defeats led to Napoleon's downfall.

What were the military defeats?

—campaign against the Russians in 1812	—battle against Great Britain, led by the Duke of Wellington, and Prussia, led by Major Gebhard von Blücher, at Waterloo in 1815
—battle against the armies of Austria, Prussia, and Russia at Leipzig in October 1813	

How did these defeats lead to Napoleon's downfall?

—~~throughout his earlier career Napoleon had been a brilliant strategist, detecting and using his enemies' weaknesses~~	—Napoleon had to return across Russia in freezing cold of winter—army died from hunger, illness, some killed by attacking Russians
—~~Russia—formerly an ally of France—made peace and opened up trade with Great Britain~~	—only 100,000 men left
	—defeat weakened Napoleon's power and credibility; enemies gained confidence
—~~Napoleon wanted to punish Russia—~~ assembled an army of 600,000 and marched into Russia	—Napoleon raised another army with difficulty
—Russians retreated toward	—won a few battles but at Battle of Leipzig enemies proved too strong

Moscow—burned and destroyed everything behind them

~~Russia—always fairly safe from invaders because of size, rugged terrain, and harsh weather~~

—Napoleon reached Moscow—found people and army gone and city burning

—Russia wouldn't accept a truce

~~defeats prompted his allies to desert him and countries he had subdued to rebel~~

—French senate wanted a Bourbon king—Napoleon abdicated and was exiled to Elba in 1814

—Napoleon escaped, raised another army, couldn't match the strength of Wellington and Blücher at Waterloo

—exiled to island of St. Helena—died there in 1821

In addition to evaluating your support, check to see if the topic sentence you wrote earlier accurately covers all the supporting information. If the topic sentence does not cover all important ideas, you may need to broaden it by adding a few words or a phrase. Or if the topic sentence seems too general for the support, you may need to limit and focus it more.

The topic sentence on Napoleon's military defeats, for example, could possibly be made more accurate and precise. Notice that the supporting information consists of three major military defeats between the years 1812 and 1815, at the end of Napoleon's career. To reflect this limit and specific focus, the topic sentence could be sharpened.

REVISED TOPIC SENTENCE: Three major military defeats between 1812 and 1815 led to Napoleon's downfall.

Even if you revise your topic sentence at this stage, you should continue to recheck both your topic sentence and your support as you plan and write.

EXERCISE C: Gathering Supporting Information for a Topic Sentence. Use your topic sentence from Exercise B to carry out the following steps.

1. At the top of a blank piece of paper write your topic sentence.
2. Use either free-associating or questioning to gather a list of supporting examples, details, facts, reasons, or incidents that illustrate or explain your main idea. Write down all the ideas that occur to you. If you are asking and answering questions, write down the questions as well as the sup-

porting information. Do not sort your information at this point.

EXERCISE D: Checking Supporting Information. Examine the list of ideas that you wrote in Exercise C. Try to envision the completed paragraph to decide which ideas are best suited to the paragraph. Keep the best information, but draw lines through any ideas that are inappropriate. Add any new ideas that occur to you. Then reexamine your topic sentence and revise it if it should be more precise or general to fit your supporting information.

■ Organizing the Paragraph

When you know approximately what you will say in your paragraph, you are ready to think about organizing your ideas. A crucial step in the writing process, organizing can be done a number of ways.

Once you have a topic sentence and a solid list of supporting information, you should examine these raw materials of your paragraph to see what order emerges.

Organize your supporting information in the most logical order.

Organizing your paragraph can make the writing go more quickly. It can also help you to focus on finding a way to present your information clearly and sensibly to fulfill your audience's expectations.

As part of the organizing step, you should decide if your topic sentence will work best at the beginning of the paragraph (to introduce and point toward the support), at the end (to wrap up and summarize the support), or in the middle (after a few introductory sentences). The topic sentence on Napoleon, for example, could go at either the beginning or end of the paragraph. You might decide to put it first to guide the reader's understanding of the supporting information. If it were placed at the end of the paragraph, you might need to reword it to sound like a topic sentence that concludes the preceding information: *Napoleon's eventual downfall, then, resulted largely from three major military defeats.*

To organize your paragraph further, you should look for an underlying logical order in your supporting information. Your main idea and support may suggest, if not already follow, a specific order, such as order of importance, chronological order, spatial order, or comparison and contrast order. If, for example, you were writing about the reasons for joining a political party, you might decide which reasons are most convincing and group these by order of importance. If none of these orders fits, determine what particular developmental order your topic sentence suggests, and then arrange your supporting information by categories, for instance, or any other order the topic sentence suggests.

From the list of support about Napoleon's military defeats, you can see the time element involved. In fact, the supporting information is almost in a chronological order already. The paragraph should present each battle with all the listed facts and details about the battle. You may choose to organize by numbering your pieces of support logically or by jotting down a modified outline similar to the following. The outline can later serve as a guide as you draft your paragraph.

Notice that the outline has three major pieces of supporting information with other pieces of information arranged logically underneath them.

(Topic Sentence)   Three major military defeats between 1812 and 1815 led to Napoleon's downfall.

Campaign Against the Russians in 1812

1. Pursued the Russians, who retreated toward Moscow leaving the countryside burnt behind them
2. Found the people and army gone and Moscow burning
3. Returned across Russia in the winter after Russians refused a truce
4. Lost about 500,000 men out of 600,000—from hunger, illness, cold, and the Russians
5. Weakened by great loss which encouraged enemy

Battle of Nations at Leipzig in October 1813

1. Raised another army with difficulty
2. Was overcome by forces of enemies; deserted by Austria, France's ally, which fought against Napoleon with Prussia and Russia
3. Defeated and then exiled in 1814 by French senate who wanted a Bourbon king

Battle of Waterloo in 1815

1. Escaped and raised another army
2. Defeated by combined strength of Britain's Duke of Wellington and Prussia's Major Gebhard von Blücher
3. Was exiled to St. Helena, died there in 1821

EXERCISE E: Ordering Support Logically. Use your list of supporting information from Exercises C and D to carry out the following steps.

1. Consider the best place in the paragraph to put your topic sentence.
2. Study your topic sentence and your list of supporting information to see which order best suits your main idea and information. Then choose an order and write it on your paper.
3. Organize your supporting information according to the order you have chosen. If you use a modified outline, write your topic sentence as a complete sentence at the top and then list support in phrases under appropriate headings.

■ Writing the Paragraph

If you have done a thorough job of thinking, planning, and organizing, the actual writing of your paragraph should go smoothly and quickly. Because you will not have to focus entirely on *what* you are saying, you can think about *how* you are expressing your ideas. You should concentrate on writing clearly and on connecting your ideas logically. Your order of ideas or modified outline should guide you as you put ideas into complete sentences and add transitions and other devices for coherence.

As you draft your paragraph from your rough outline, try to write clear, varied sentences and to connect your ideas with transitions, repetition of main words, synonyms, consistent pronouns, and possibly parallelism and a concluding sentence.

When you draft your paragraph, follow the organization you have chosen but keep an open mind toward making any necessary adjustments. You might see the value of rearranging some ideas, adding to them, or even eliminating something that no longer seems appropriate.

As you write, also think about the flow of your sentences and the connections between your ideas. Add transitions, repeat main words, use synonyms for main words, and make sure any pronouns that replace main words are consistent. Concentrate on guiding the reader and helping the reader follow your ideas.

In the paragraph about Napoleon's military defeats, for instance, transitions should help the reader follow the events in chronological order. In the following completed paragraph, notice the transitions *first, after, a year later, second, shortly thereafter, after,* and *final*. You would probably want to repeat the main words *major, defeat, Napoleon,* and *forces* as well as use synonyms such as *loss, overwhelm, overcome, troops,* and *army* to avoid monotony and to add smoothness.

TOPIC
SENTENCE

Three major military defeats between 1812 and 1815 led to Napoleon's downfall. The *first* defeat came in 1812 when Napoleon's troops pursued the Russians to Moscow only to find the countryside and Moscow itself evacuated and burning. Refused a truce by Russia, Napoleon's army returned across the wintry land, struggling against cold, hunger, illness, and assaults by the Russians. The loss of 500,000 men out of 600,000 weakened Napoleon's power and image and gave energy and confidence to his enemies. *After* such a loss, Napoleon raised another army with difficulty. *A year later* in October 1813, the armies of Prussia, Russia, and France's former ally, Austria, overcame Napoleon's forces in the Battle of Nations at Leipzig. This *second* major defeat and the restoration of a Bourbon king to the French throne sent Napoleon into exile in 1814. Although he escaped and gathered another army, he could not regain his former power. *Shortly thereafter* in 1815, the British under the Duke of Wellington and the Prussians under Major Gebhard von Blücher overwhelmed Napoleon at the Battle of Waterloo. *After* this *final* defeat, Napoleon was exiled to the island of St. Helena, where he died in 1821.

Once you have a complete draft of your paragraph, you should reread it several times, preferably aloud, to check for clarity of ideas, logical connections, and the flow of your sentences. When you have corrected any weaknesses or errors, you can prepare a final copy.

EXERCISE F: Writing the Paragraph. Use your organization from Exercise E to guide your writing of the first draft of your paragraph. As you compose sentences, add any transitions, repetition of main words, synonyms, and pronouns for main words that you think necessary or helpful. Consider using parallelism and a concluding sentence. As you write, recheck the paragraph for smoothness, logical flow of ideas, and sentence variety.

APPLICATION: Planning and Writing a Paragraph. Choose one of the following topics or make up one of your own. (Remember that some topics may need to be narrowed more than others.) Then carry out the following steps. You can refer back to the preceding pages for ideas and guidance, if necessary.

A dangerous occupation or activity

Helpful community services

Training for a sport or athletic event

Problems facing today's consumers

Budgeting time or money

Weather

National flags

Superstitions

Home furnishings

Politics

1. Narrow and focus your topic.
2. Find a main idea by asking yourself questions and thinking about your audience and purpose.
3. Write at least two versions of your topic sentence.
4. Use free-associating or questioning to brainstorm for supporting information.
5. Check supporting information for unity, and recheck your topic sentence, making any adjustments necessary.
6. Examine your support and choose a logical order. Then organize your support on your list or in a modified outline.
7. Use your organization or outline to write a first draft, adding transitions, any helpful repetitions of the main words, synonyms, pronouns, and possibly parallelism and a concluding sentence.
8. Reread your paragraph silently and aloud. Correct any errors, combine or separate sentences for variety, add any needed transitions, and clarify any awkward passages.
9. Write a good final copy.

Revising and Rewriting Paragraphs 22.3

Revision is an important part of the writing process. It is a chance to make improvements in your writing.

This section discusses revising the major features of paragraphs: topic sentences and supporting information. In addition, it explains how to check paragraphs for unity and coherence and how to make stylistic improvements in your writing.

You should use the following questions as a general guide to revising your paragraphs. They will help you read your paragraphs objectively and find any weak areas.

CHECKLIST FOR REVISING PARAGRAPHS

1. Does the topic sentence accurately express the main idea developed in the paragraph?
2. Does the supporting information include enough examples, facts, reasons, and so on to explain and develop the topic sentence?
3. Does the supporting information contain any inappropriate material—any repetition, unsubstantiated opinions, vague statements, or generalizations?
4. Does the supporting information include any extraneous material?
5. Is the supporting information presented in the most logical order?
6. Have you included transitions to help your reader follow your ideas?
7. Have you repeated main words and used synonyms, pronouns, and parallel constructions to help tie ideas together?
8. Do you need a concluding sentence?
9. Can the writing style be made more smooth or interesting? Are the sentences varied in structure? Do any points need to be given more emphasis?
10. Have you corrected all errors in grammar, punctuation, and spelling?

The following section will help you become familiar with ways in which you can carry out the points in this checklist. It will show you the importance of critically examining, rethinking, and revising your writing.

■ Revising Topic Sentences

Because the topic sentence identifies the main idea for the reader, it must be accurate; that is, it must cover exactly the range of ideas in the paragraph—no more, no less.

Learn to recognize a topic sentence that is too general or too narrow for the paragraph.

If the topic sentence is *too general*, it will either contain too many ideas, or it will fail to give a precise picture of the paragraph's topic or purpose. If the topic sentence is *too narrow*, it will leave out some important ideas covered in the support.

Topic Sentences That Are Too General.   If your topic sentence seems to cover more ideas than your supporting information, it does not suit the paragraph.

Revise an overly general topic sentence by narrowing its focus to suit the supporting information or by eliminating a portion of the sentence that is not developed by the support.

Sometimes the topic sentence will be too vague. If it presents an idea in general words but is supported by specific information, the topic sentence must be refocused. For instance, the supporting information in a paragraph about swimming might explain that certain swimming strokes are more difficult to learn than others. However, if the topic sentence of the paragraph stated that "Everyone can learn to swim," it would not reflect the contrasts among swimming strokes. It would fail to direct the reader's attention to the main thrust of the support. This overly general topic sentence should be refocused so that it includes the contrasts and thereby points more accurately toward the support: "Although everyone can learn to swim, certain swimming strokes are more difficult for a beginner to master than others."

Another type of overly general topic sentence contains *more* ideas than are covered in the support. In a paragraph about Edgar Allan Poe's horror stories, the topic sentence would be too broad if it stated, "Readers should find a wealth of ghastly details in Edgar Allan Poe's stories and poems." If the paragraph does not discuss the poems, they should not be mentioned in the topic sentence. The extra idea can be eliminated and the topic sentence rewritten this way: "Readers should find a wealth of ghastly details in Edgar Allan Poe's short stories."

Topic Sentences That Are Too Narrow.   If your topic sentence fails to cover all of the information presented in the paragraph, it falls short of expressing the main idea.

Revise a topic sentence that is too narrow by expanding its focus to include all important ideas in the support.

If the support develops several important ideas, the topic sentence must cover all of them. If you wrote a paragraph about a hotel, and you gave examples of both poor service and shabby decor, your topic sentence would be too narrow if it stated, "Vacationers have found service at the Hotel Ponte to be sadly lacking." This topic sentence omits the idea of decor, which is covered in the support.

To correct a narrow topic sentence, you must add at least one idea, or otherwise broaden it to cover more information. Revising the sentence about the hotel, you might write this: "Vacationers have found both the service and decor at the Hotel Ponte to be sadly lacking."

EXERCISE A: Rewriting Topic Sentences. Locate the topic sentence in each of the following paragraphs and decide if it is too general or too narrow. Then write a revised topic sentence that suits the supporting ideas. If a topic sentence fits the support, simply write *accurate* on your paper.

(1) The study of ancient languages can prove beneficial in a number of ways. Many of our English words have their roots in Latin, for one thing, and therefore studying the language of the Romans can serve to strengthen one's vocabulary. Second, the study of Latin invariably increases a student's knowledge of Roman civilization and culture. Finally, an understanding of Latin syntax and grammar provides a firm foundation for the study of any of the five "Romance" languages—French, Spanish, Italian, Portuguese, and Romanian—which are Latin's modern-day descendants.

(2) People who are overweight may need professional help to solve the problem. Because being overweight is usually the result of overeating, the person who needs to reduce can often find a workable diet that will bring satisfactory results. Being overweight may also be caused by lack of exercise. Again, the person who needs to reduce can find an exercise program—or just a change of daily habits—that will "burn off" excess pounds. Sometimes, however, being overweight can be caused by a malfunction of the thyroid gland. In this case, an overweight person should seek help from a doctor, who may suggest medical treatment as well as special programs of eating and exercise to combat the problem.

(3) Each winter millions of Americans are made uncomfortable by either a head cold or flu symptoms. The common head cold is easy enough to recognize, being characterized by nasal stuffiness, sore throat and headaches, and sometimes a cough or an earache. Cold sufferers may also run low-grade fevers. Although scientists are fairly certain that the common cold is *not* caused by exposure to cold weather, they are at a loss for a positive cure; penicillin and vitamins don't seem to have definite effects on cold symptoms. Sufferers, therefore, have limited means to combat colds besides bed rest and aspirin, but fortunately most head colds are brief, disappearing usually within seven days.

(4) If you can forsake the joys of beaches and baseball parks, you might find that a summer job offers certain rewards. Aside from the obvious monetary benefits, you have the opportunity to meet some new and interesting people. You will almost invariably return to school with fascinating and frequently hilarious character sketches of those with whom you have worked. Finally, you may have a chance to learn new skills.

(5) New storefronts along Main Street have greatly improved the appearance of the town's business and shopping center. With a grant from the Urban League, storeowners have ripped away the old, crumbling steps, arches, and window sills that once faced the street, and they have replaced these with modern raised platforms, sleek plate-glass display windows, and, in some cases, ornamental entranceways with soft lighting, giving the area a well-lighted but cozy appearance at nighttime. Across from the stores, the strip of park that lines the east side of Main Street has been totally refurbished. Funds from the Urban League and private donations bought new park benches and parallel rows of antique-looking lampposts. In addition, the grassy areas have been replanted, and by springtime, shoppers should notice forsythia and azalea bushes in bloom.

■ Revising Supporting Information

You should also examine your supporting information to determine if it is thorough and accurate.

Learn to recognize supporting information that is inadequate or inappropriate.

If the support fails to cover the entire main idea as expressed in the topic sentence, or to develop it clearly, you should add examples, reasons, details, or other information. If the support contains overly general, repetitious, or nonessential ideas, or presents statements of opinion rather than fact, you should eliminate these weak phrases, clauses, or sentences.

Inadequate Support. Supporting information is inadequate when it does not provide enough specific material to develop the main idea. If a topic sentence indicates that several points are going to be discussed, the supporting information must include specific material on each of those aspects of the main idea.

Strengthen inadequate supporting information by adding specific facts, details, examples, and other material to develop your main idea.

The following paragraph contains a satisfactory topic sentence, but the supporting information is thin. Only two examples are offered in explanation of the main idea, and those examples are not clearly defined. The paragraph is therefore underdeveloped.

TOPIC
SENTENCE

Too few
examples

Too little
explanation

> In his novel *Cat's Cradle*, Kurt Vonnegut creates a philosophy/religion—complete with its own special vocabulary—that defines ordinary life from a most unusual point of view. This philosophy/religion, called Bokonon, explains that every person on earth is part of a *karass*. According to Bokonon, "If you find your life tangled up with somebody else's life for no very logical reasons, that person may be a member of your karass." A *duprass*, on the other hand, consists of only two people. A totally devoted lifelong partnership, for example, is a duprass.

Two different methods can be helpful in expanding an underdeveloped paragraph. First, you can reexamine the topic sentence, list additional examples, reasons, and other kinds of support that might develop it more concretely, and then incorporate this additional information into your paragraph. Second, you might try to elaborate on some of the supporting information that your original paragraph presents. Perhaps some of the ideas are too sketchy and require additional explanation or detail. Often, supporting information is underdeveloped because a writer has taken shortcuts in expressing the ideas. A reader may need only a few additional words to understand the ideas more fully.

The preceding paragraph should contain at least one more example of Bokonon's unusual definitions of ordinary life. In addition, the definitions of *karass* and *duprass* should be more precise and complete to give readers a better understanding of the two concepts. The following revision of the paragraph corrects these problems.

TOPIC
SENTENCE

Three
examples
fully
explained

> In his novel *Cat's Cradle*, Kurt Vonnegut creates a philosophy/religion—complete with its own special vocabulary—that defines ordinary life from a most unusual point of view. This philosophy/religion, called Bokonon, explains that every person is part of a *karass*, a group of people whose lives cross. According to Bokonon, "If you find your life tangled up with somebody else's life for no very logical reasons, that person may be a member of your karass." A *karass* can consist of any number of people, but the smallest karass is called a *duprass*, which consists of only two

people. According to Bokonon, "A true duprass can't be invaded, not even by children born of such a union." A totally devoted lifelong partnership, then, is a duprass. But perhaps the most illuminating of Bokonon's definitions is the *granfalloon,* a group of people who become partners or cohorts through a perfectly meaningless association. Says Bokonon: "[Some] examples of granfalloons are the Communist Party, . . . the International Order of Odd Fellows—and any nation, anytime, anywhere."

Inappropriate Support.   Sometimes the problem may not be the *amount* of supporting information in a paragraph but rather the *quality* of that information.

Eliminate vague statements, generalizations, weak opinions, repetition, and other inappropriate material and, wherever possible, replace them with specific supporting information.

Vague statements, generalizations, unfounded opinions, and ideas that simply restate the topic sentence without developing it do not truly support the main idea and should be omitted from a paragraph.

The following paragraph contains a satisfactory topic sentence and some solid support. But it is padded with vague statements, generalizations, and other inappropriate material.

TOPIC
SENTENCE

Support filled
with vague
statements,
generaliza-
tions, and
unsupported
opinions

I find the atmosphere in fast-food restaurants not conducive to pleasant dining. The decor is always made of the same synthetic materials and thus contributes to my discomfort. The lights are unpleasant, and these restaurants are always crowded. Often while eating in such a place, I find myself being serenaded not only by "canned" music but also by the cries and whoops of the many preschool children who are allowed to run wild down aisles and among tables. All young children are inconsiderate, and they should be taught better manners. As a fast-food customer, I must serve myself and find a table without assistance, and I must eat by hand from greasy paper and styrofoam. And what about the "decorations" on my table? Why, the greasy paper and styrofoam left by the last people who sat there comprise the ornaments. Litter is everybody's problem, yet none of the people who frequent fast-food restaurants care enough to pick up after themselves.

The support in the preceding paragraph consists mainly of a number of vague statements that need to be made more specific, blanket generalizations that need to be qualified, and opinions that need to be supported with fact and reason. Note, for example, that the words *always, all,* and *none* turn what could be valid criticisms into inaccurate statements. (There are usually exceptions to any rule.) The paragraph may be improved by eliminating inappropriate statements and by adding reasonable support.

TOPIC SENTENCE Clear statements, qualified generaliza- tions, and reasons for opinions	The atmosphere in most fast-food restaurants is not conducive to pleasant dining. The decor usually consists of plastic, formica, and fiberglass—materials that unsuccessfully imitate the wood, stone, metal, tile, and marble of older, more established restaurants and therefore contribute to a sense of the interchangeability and impermanence of fast-food restaurants. The lighting is usually fluorescent, greenish, and harsh, and these restaurants are often quite crowded. While eating in many fast-food restaurants, the customer must listen to the same "canned," preprogrammed music that one hears in elevators, shopping malls, and supermarkets, another reminder of the lack of individuality of fast-food restaurants. Furthermore, because of the informality of these places, young children are frequently noisier than they would be in conventional restaurants. And because fast-food restaurants are informal and can give only minimal attention to customer service, customers must carry their own paper and styrofoam containers to and from their tables, which are often littered by the remains of a previous meal.

EXERCISE B: Revising Support. Read the following paragraphs and examine the topic sentence in each carefully to understand the main idea and purpose of the writer. Then decide if a paragraph needs additional support to be complete and thorough. Also, determine whether a paragraph contains such inappropriate support as vague statements, blanket generalizations, or weak opinions. Once you have identified the weaknesses, revise each paragraph accordingly. Use your judgment to revise or eliminate inappropriate support, and use your imagination to add relevant new material.

(1) Daytime serials, or "soap operas," are characterized by a number of common features, which even the most casual viewer can recognize. Each daily installment lasts only thirty to sixty minutes, a large proportion of which is devoted to reviewing the events of the recent past. Most of them also involve a limited, self-contained cast of characters whose relationships evolve over time and have been known to swing wildly from one emotional extreme to another.

(2) Baseball is a slower-moving, more leisurely game than football. Football is far the better game. All baseball contests consist of an endless series of games of catch between pitcher and catcher. These are punctuated by a few, rare, sporadic bursts of activity that involve only one or two players on some remote portion of the field. In football, by contrast, all players are drawn into every play, and the action is more frequent and concentrated than it is in baseball. Everyone enjoys watching football games and finds the slower pace of baseball boring.

■ Revising Paragraphs for Unity

A second look at your writing may reveal that some of your support is not only inappropriate but also totally unrelated to your main idea as it is developed in your paragraph.

Learn to recognize and correct disunity in a paragraph.

Extraneous information creates disunity in your paragraph and should be eliminated or moved to another paragraph.

Eliminating Extraneous Material.   Any ideas in a paragraph that do not develop your main idea directly or contribute to other supporting information are probably extraneous and should be omitted from the paragraph.

Improve unity in a paragraph by eliminating information that does not pertain to the main idea as stated in the topic sentence or to other pieces of supporting information.

As you test for unity in a paragraph, use your topic sentence as your first guide. Look carefully at any piece of supporting information that cannot be related directly to the main idea. Then check that piece of information with the rest of the supporting material in the paragraph. If the item you are examining does not build upon or help explain other supporting information in the paragraph, you should probably eliminate the point altogether.

The following paragraph about athletic facilities at a school contains two sentences that stray from the main topic. As you read the paragraph, notice that the sixth sentence takes off from the point about poor security in the lockers to mention that theft is a school-wide problem. The eighth sentence speaks about the rights of female athletes, whereas the rest of the paragraph concentrates entirely on the deterioration of specific athletic facilities. Although the two sentences *are* related to other supporting information, their relationship is not one of further explanation but rather one of new information. Thus both sentences should be removed.

TOPIC
SENTENCE

Extraneous
idea

Extraneous
idea

(1) Athletic facilities at Midwood High have deteriorated, and, in some areas, they require immediate attention to avoid serious accidents and losses. (2) The condition of the gymnasium is quite poor. (3) Loose boards on the playing court as well as loose railings along the stands invite injury to both players and other students and to spectators in general. (4) The locker and shower areas are also hazardous to students and are the sources of daily problems. (5) Some locker doors are broken, and many do not lock, a situation that has encouraged thefts of students' supplies. (6) Of course this problem exists throughout the rest of the school as well. (7) And within the shower stalls, some tiles have worked loose and some shower knobs are broken or missing. (8) Sadly, what is an unfortunate situation for boys at Midwood is equally bad for the girls, even though girls are almost invariably denied equal rights in athletics. (9) The playing field, certainly, has become unattractive. (10) It is bare of grass and no longer level because of wind and rain erosion. (11) In addition, some areas of the field are pitted and gullied from water run-off.

The sixth and eighth sentences should be eliminated to preserve unity because they contain ideas that do not belong in the paragraph. That theft may be a school-wide problem is not relevant to the deterioration of the athletic facilities. And the idea that poor facilities are "equally bad" for girls as well as boys is obvious, while the comment about equal rights for girls in athletics strays entirely from the main idea.

Building From Disunity.   When you are revising for unity, you should identify and eliminate all extraneous ideas in the paragraphs you write. If you are writing about a larger topic, however, you may find that ideas discarded from one paragraph are useful in another.

Consider moving an extraneous idea from one paragraph to a more appropriate place.

Especially if you are writing a report or a series of paragraphs on a topic, you may find that ideas extraneous to one paragraph will provide useful support elsewhere or might even inspire you to write an additional paragraph.

The paragraph about the Midwood athletic facilities might be part of a larger paper discussing school-wide athletics. In that case, the idea about equal rights for female athletes at Midwood High, which was not directly relevant to the paragraph on athletic facilities, would certainly have a place in some other paragraph.

EXERCISE C: Eliminating Disunity from a Paragraph. The following paragraph is not unified. It contains one or more sentences that stray from the topic. Identify these sentences and rewrite the paragraph to preserve its unity.

(1) The new automatic money-dispensing machines, which many banks have installed in recent years, have greatly simplified the withdrawal of cash from checking accounts. (2) Many banks have also set up cashiers at drive-in windows. (3) To withdraw money from a checking account by means of a cash machine, you simply insert what looks like a credit card into a slot. (4) The card is encoded with a number that is not printed on it and that only you and the bank know. (5) You punch in your secret number, punch in the amount of money you want to withdraw, and let the machine do the rest. (6) America is truly becoming a credit card society. (7) After about ten seconds, a drawer pops open containing envelopes with crisp, new bills inside. (8) With the new cash-dispensing machines, bank customers can withdraw money at any time of the day or night.

EXERCISE D: Developing a New Paragraph from an Extraneous Idea. Take any sentence that you eliminated from Exercise C and use it as either the main or a supporting idea in a new paragraph that you create.

■ Revising for Coherence

As you revise your paragraph for coherence, make sure that all of the ideas and pieces of information are clearly, smoothly, and logically connected.

Learn to recognize and eliminate problems with coherence.

If you find any breaks in the flow of thought, improve the coherence of your paragraph by rearranging your ideas, or by adding transitional devices.

Improving Logical Order.   As you recheck your paragraph, look closely at the order followed by your supporting ideas to see if it is clearly established and if all ideas are logically connected.

Improve problems in coherence by finding a more logical arrangement for your supporting information.

If you have used no special order in organizing your paragraph, you might find that you could arrange your ideas into a definite and understandable pattern—such as chronological order, spatial order, or order of importance. Even if you have followed a particular order, you might still want to shift certain ideas around so that the order is more apparent to your reader.

For example, look again at the paragraph about Midwood High's athletic facilities on page 648. The support follows a general developmental order. However, it is apparent from the support that some facilities are more dangerous than others. The supporting information could thus be rearranged and strengthened by the use of order of importance. The writer could begin with the least hazardous problem and end with the most hazardous problem. In the following revision, notice that the ninth sentence in the original paragraph becomes the first supporting sentence of the revised paragraph because it mentions the playing field, the least dangerous facility.

TOPIC SENTENCE	Athletic facilities at Midwood High have deteriorated, and, in some areas, they require immediate attention to avoid serious accidents and losses. The
Least dangerous	playing field, certainly, has become unattractive. It is bare of grass and no longer level because of wind and rain erosion. In addition, some areas of the field are pitted and gullied from water run-off. The locker and shower areas are also hazardous to students and are the sources of daily problems. Some locker doors are broken, and many do not lock, a situation that has encouraged thefts of students' supplies. And within the
Most dangerous	shower stalls, some tiles have worked loose and some shower knobs are broken or missing. Most hazardous, perhaps, to the greatest number of people is the condition of the gymnasium itself. Loose boards on the playing court as well as loose railings along the stands invite injury to both players and other students and to spectators in general.

Adding Transitions and Bridge Ideas.   To improve coherence, you might also consider adding transitional words and phrases to your paragraph. In the preceding paragraph, transitions such as *in addition, and,* and *most* help to add ideas and to establish the order of their importance clearly.

However, a transitional word or phrase may not always be enough to connect ideas clearly and logically for your reader. You may, in some cases, notice that you have left an actual gap in the development of your ideas or you may feel that your reader will need an additional idea to be fully prepared for the information that follows. You may therefore need to introduce a new idea to establish the link you want. A *bridge idea* is an explanation, fact, or concept that connects one piece of information with another. It can take the form of a phrase, a clause, a whole sentence, or even, occasionally, several sentences. As you revise, consider adding bridge ideas wherever you feel that your reader needs help to move from one point to another.

Use transitions to connect thoughts in your paragraph, and where a transition alone cannot make a clear connection between your thoughts; consider adding a bridge idea.

In the paragraph about Midwood's athletic facilities, one more idea could be useful: a bridge idea between the first example (the playing field) and the second (the locker and shower areas). The reader might need to understand that while the playing field might not be especially hazardous, the examples that follow deserve increasing attention. In the following revision, the bridge idea not only connects the first example to the others, it also helps clarify the order by pointing toward the most dangerous examples. Both the bridge idea and the transitional words have been italicized.

TOPIC SENTENCE	Athletic facilities at Midwood High have deteriorated, and, in some areas, they require immediate attention to avoid serious accidents and losses. The playing field, certainly, has become unattractive. It is bare of grass and no longer level because of wind and
Transition Bridge idea	rain erosion. *In addition*, some areas of the field are pitted and gullied from water run-off. *While this problem is mainly one of aesthetics, other facilities have deteriorated to points where they are truly unsafe.*
Transition	The locker and shower areas, *for instance*, are actually hazardous to students and are the sources of daily problems. Some locker doors are broken, and many do not lock, a situation that has encouraged
Transition	thefts of students' supplies. *And* within the shower stalls, some tiles have worked loose and some shower
Transition	knobs are broken or missing. *Most hazardous*, perhaps, to the greatest number of people is the condi-

tion of the gymnasium itself. Loose boards on the playing court as well as loose railings along the stands invite injury to both players and other students and to spectators in general.

Other Devices for Improving Coherence.   There are a number of other techniques at your disposal for increasing the coherence of your paragraphs.

Consider using the repetition of main words, as well as synonyms, pronouns, and parallel constructions, to improve coherence in your paragraphs.

The repetition of main words helps to connect the sentences in which they appear. Similarly, the use of synonyms establishes links between ideas, and the substitution of pronouns for nouns helps the flow of ideas from one sentence to another. It is important, however, to use these devices correctly and carefully. The obvious and excessive repetition of words and the labored use of synonyms and pronouns can make a paragraph sound awkward and lumbering. For example, the following sentences could be improved by a more selective use of repetition and synonyms and a more careful, consistent use of pronouns.

Awkward use of repetition, synonyms, and pronouns
In buying a *dress, one* should make sure that the *garment* is well made. *You* should look at the hem of the *dress* to see if it is closely stitched. *One* should also check to see whether the facings around the neck and arms of the *gown* are tacked down, particularly if the *dress* is expensive.

The following revision uses these devices more selectively and consistently.

Improved use of repetition, synonyms, and pronouns
In buying a *dress, you* should make sure that *it* is well made. Look at the hem of the *garment* to see if it is closely stitched. *You* should also check to see whether the facings around the neck and arms are tacked down, particularly if the *dress* is expensive.

Another effective way of establishing connections between ideas in a paragraph is by using parallel constructions. Ideas that are expressed in parallel sentences, clauses, or phrases will naturally appear to be associated with one another, even if you have not made any obvious connections through transitional words or phrases. In the following sentences, the use of parallel structure alone directs the reader to associate the actions taking place with each other and with the overall fact that twilight is gathering.

| Parallelism to connect ideas | Twilight is gathering. The stores are closing; the bells are ringing; the children are skating. |

The following paragraph could be made more coherent through the repetition of certain words and the selective use of synonyms, pronouns, and parallel constructions.

| Awkward and unconnected passage | Part of the pleasure *one* experiences in eating a *lobster* comes from the sense that *you* have accomplished a complicated and difficult task. First, *one* must select *one's* dinner while the *creature* is still alive in the lobster tank. The *shellfish* is then boiled. Then, *you* must take your *lobster* apart and extract the meat that is inside the hard *shell*. The operation involves tapping the *carapace* against *one's* plate. Also, nutcrackers can be used to crack the *shell*, and *one* can poke the meat out of the corners with picks. At the end of the meal, *you* sit with a large pile of hollow coral *shells* on the plate. *You* are tired and full. But certainly *one* is content, having completed a difficult job. |

Note how the following revision has been made more coherent and less awkward through the careful repetition of main words and the use of synonyms and consistent pronouns. Notice also the subtle use of parallelism in the two clauses that begin with *you must* and the three phrases that describe how a lobster must be eaten.

| Revised, well-connected passage | Part of the pleasure *you* experience in eating a *lobster* comes from the sense that *you* have accomplished a complicated and difficult task. First, *you* must select your *dinner* while it is still alive in the lobster tank. Next, the lobster is boiled. Then, when your bright orange steamed *lobster* is served to you, you must extract your *dinner* from its hard *shell*. This operation involves tapping various parts of the *lobster* against your plate, squeezing it with nutcrackers, and poking at it with picks and other utensils. At the end of the meal, *you* sit with a pile of hollow coral *shells* on your plate. You are tired, full, and content, having completed a difficult job. |

EXERCISE E: Improving Coherence by Rearranging Supporting Information and Adding Transitions. The following paragraph contains an appropriate topic sentence and ample support, but

the supporting information could be arranged more logically, and the flow of ideas could be improved through the addition of transitions. Rewrite the paragraph to improve its coherence. Consider adding a bridge idea if you think it will help the reader to understand the writer's ideas more fully.

(1) During England's Victorian era, the calling card was an important social requirement. (2) A gentleman or a lady would present a card to a servant when arriving at someone's home. (3) The calling card was proof of refinement and good breeding. (4) Failure to present a card would have been considered extremely poor taste. (5) Often a Victorian gentleman would ask a woman to dinner or to the theater by leaving his card. (6) If she wished to accept or decline the invitation, she could do so by writing a note on her own card.

EXERCISE F: Using Other Devices to Improve Coherence. The following paragraph includes a number of ineffective uses of repeated words, synonyms, and pronouns. Identify the awkward, incorrect, or otherwise ineffective uses of repetition, synonyms, and pronouns, and rewrite the paragraph to correct them.

(1) Half the battle in singing well is learning to breathe properly. (2) Many beginning vocalists do not realize the vital importance of correct respiration in one's singing. (3) Most young songsters breathe too shallowly, from the chest, whereas you should support your notes by aspirating from the diaphragm. (4) This sort of breathing does not come easily to young vocalists, and one must work very hard in order to acquire the discipline you need to change something as fundamental as your breathing habits.

■ Revising for Style

When you revise, you should also examine the style of your paragraph to increase the impact, sharpen the focus, or otherwise improve the level of writing.

Once you have completed your other revisions, polish your paragraph stylistically by changing the structure of your sentences wherever you can improve them.

Revising should involve evaluating the structure of the individual sentences you have written to add liveliness and to emphasize your ideas. Sections 19.1 and 19.2 on pages 536–555 offer several methods for increasing variety in your sentence structure. You can experiment with mixing simple, compound, complex, and compound-complex sentences in the same paragraph to create certain rhythms. In addition, you should keep in mind the various effects of loose, periodic, and balanced sentences. Finally, you should consider the use of a series of similar structures and should take advantage of all of these possibilities in revising your paragraph for style.

You might also consider writing a concluding sentence. Its position in the paragraph gives it special emphasis. It could sum up what the rest of the paragraph has developed; it could "clinch" your main idea and make it memorable for the reader. The concluding sentence may also be an especially good spot in which to place a dramatic change in sentence structure.

The following paragraph represents a polished version of the paragraph on page 651, discussing the deterioration of athletic facilities at Midwood High. Notice that the revisions, by changing sentence structure slightly, have increased the emphasis of certain portions of the paragraph, building more definitely from the sense of aesthetic deterioration to the idea that the athletic facilities have become hazardous. Notice also that the addition of a concluding sentence, longer than the sentences that immediately precede it, and balanced in structure, helps to underline the message of the paragraph.

Sentence tightened	Athletic facilities at Midwood High have deteriorated to the point that they require immediate attention to avoid serious accidents and losses. The playing field has become unattractive: Eroded by wind and rain, it has become grassless and uneven, and some areas have been pitted and gullied by water run-off. But, while this problem is mainly one of aesthetics, other facilities have become truly unsafe to use. The locker and shower areas, for instance, present a hazard to students: Some locker doors are broken, many do not lock (thereby encouraging theft), and, within the shower stalls, tiles have worked loose and knobs are broken or missing. But perhaps the greatest hazard to the greatest number of people is posed by the condition of the gymnasium itself. Loose boards on the playing court expose student athletes to injury. Loose railings along the stands threaten the safety of students and of spectators in general. In short, the athletic facilities at Midwood High not only make it difficult for athletes to perform at their peak but also constitute a safety hazard for all who are forced to use them.
Simple sentences combined	
Parallel ideas joined in compound sentence	
Ideas given more emphasis in separate sentences	
Concluding sentence	

EXERCISE G: **Revising Your Paragraphs for Style.** Choose a paragraph that you have recently written and use at least one of the preceding methods to improve the style. Make any alterations right on the paper, and then write a revised copy of the paragraph.

APPLICATION: **Writing, Revising, and Rewriting.** Choose one of the following topics or make up one of your own. (Remember that some topics may need to be narrowed more than others.) Then carry out the following steps.

A human characteristic
of a particular animal

The telephone: a
modern-day crutch

Student checking
(savings) accounts

Exercise (athletic
training) routines

Hunting (fishing, sailing,
and so on)

A special social function you
attended

Airplanes

Mythical (real?) monsters

How *not* to get lost

How to spoil a friendship

1. Narrow and focus your topic.
2. Write your topic sentence.
3. Brainstorm for supporting information.
4. Check supporting information for unity, and revise your topic sentence, if necessary.
5. Choose a logical order and prepare a rough or modified outline.
6. Use the outline to write a first draft, adding transitions and any helpful repetition of main words.
7. Reread and reexamine the paragraph. Use the checklist on page 640 to make any necessary corrections.
8. Write a final copy of the paragraph.

Chapter 23

Kinds of Paragraphs

Every paragraph is written to serve a particular purpose. The reader of the paragraph must have a clear sense of *why* the writer is communicating. This chapter discusses paragraphs written for different purposes: *expository* paragraphs, which explain and define; *persuasive* paragraphs, which seek to change the reader's mind; *descriptive* paragraphs, which attempt to paint a picture for the reader; and *narrative* paragraphs, which relate a series of events to the reader.

Occasionally, these purposes overlap. For example, an expository paragraph might include some description. In certain cases, a persuasive paragraph might include some explanation or narration. Understanding the distinctive features of each kind of paragraph, however, can help you to write most effectively whatever the writing situation.

Expository and Persuasive Paragraphs   23.1

Many of the paragraphs you write will be either expository or persuasive. The purpose of expository writing is to explain something to the reader by providing facts and examples. Expository writing attempts to increase the reader's knowledge. Persuasive writing, on the other hand, attempts to convince the reader to accept new ideas, to change his or her opinion, or to take action. Persuasive writing attempts to influence the reader's beliefs and behavior. While expository paragraphs present factual information objectively, persuasive paragraphs express and defend the writer's personal opinions and interpretations.

This section discusses some of the special considerations you should have in mind when you write expository and persuasive paragraphs.

■ Writing Expository Paragraphs

Expository writing can be used to do a number of different things. It can be used to answer an examination question, to direct someone to your house, or to tell a friend about a project on which you are working or a place that you have just visited. An expository paragraph can explain what something is or how it operates; it can tell the reader how to do something, such as make a kite, or it can define some concept or term to increase the reader's understanding. Because much of the writing you are likely to do will involve expository paragraphs, you should become familiar with the main features of expository writing.

An Explanatory Purpose and an Informative Tone. Everything in an expository paragraph is directed towards explaining something—a concept, a process, an event, the meaning of a term—to a reader. To achieve this explanatory purpose, an expository paragraph should establish and maintain an informative tone.

The main features of an expository paragraph are an explanatory purpose and an informative tone.

In order to serve its purpose and maintain its tone, an expository paragraph should contain factual statements and verifiable examples, not opinions. As you read the following statements of fact and opinion, note that the statement of fact can be checked in public records whereas the statement of opinion is a personal judgment that is arguable.

STATEMENT OF FACT: According to local police, incidents of vandalism this year outnumber incidents of any other type of criminal activity in our community.

STATEMENT OF OPINION: The increasing number of incidents of vandalism in our community indicates that many young people have little respect for the property of others.

An expository paragraph should have a factual topic sentence and objective supporting information. The topic sentence should present a main idea that is a statement of fact and the rest of the paragraph should develop and explain that factual statement with objective, specific examples, details, facts, and incidents. Often an expository paragraph will include verifiable information from experts and from reliable sources of facts, such as almanacs, encyclopedias, scientific experiments and data, historical records, and case studies. The entire paragraph should expand the reader's knowledge of the topic by supplying particular, relevant information. For example, a paragraph on mountain climbing might focus on the skills and equipment necessary for the climber. A paragraph about changes in recorded weather patterns from 1900 to the present might make a general statement and then include documented facts about temperature, rainfall, snowfall, and other weather conditions.

An informative tone should help the paragraph fulfill its explanatory purpose. The writer should focus on instructing and informing the reader, and this focus, combined with the writer's awareness of the reader's knowledge, should guide the writer's choice of language and supporting information. If the topic is unfamiliar to the reader, the writer should choose straightforward information and understandable words to explain the information clearly. If, on the other hand, the reader is knowledgeable on the topic, the writer must choose more detailed or difficult information and more technical terms so that the paragraph will be informative for that particular audience. In all expository paragraphs, direct, specific language contributes to creating an informative tone.

The following expository paragraph focuses on the objective presentation of information to a general audience. Notice that it states a fact and then clarifies it with examples and explanations, while maintaining an informative tone.

Expository paragraph with an explanatory purpose and an informative tone	Davy Crockett became a myth even in his own lifetime. He was made the hero of a hundred popular tales repeated by word of mouth and circulated in newspapers and almanacs. After his death in 1836, his adventures and character were boldly appropriated by the popular fancy. His heroic stand at the Alamo was richly described and laments arose in the western wilderness. Then Crockett reappeared in popular stories as though he had never died, assuming an even bolder legendary stature than before. In one of the almanacs the story of his life began by picturing him as a baby giant planted in a rock bed as soon as he was born and watered with wild buffalo's milk. Another story declared that as a boy he tied together the tails of two buffaloes and carried home five tiger cubs in his cap. In still another story, he wrung the tail off a comet and announced that he could "travel so all lightnin' fast that I've been known to strike fire agin the wind." Once he escaped

up Niagara Falls on an alligator. "Now I tell you
what," people would say of some strange happening,
"it's nothing to Crockett."
—Adapted from Constance Rourke

In addition to its primary explanatory purpose and its underlying informative tone, an expository paragraph may sometimes have a secondary purpose and tone. For instance, the explanation in an expository paragraph can define a concept,
instruct a reader in a process, or even entertain the reader. The
informative tone can range from the serious and formal to the
lighthearted and casual. Notice that the following paragraph,
through its humorous examples, seeks to entertain as well as
to offer information.

Expository paragraph that entertains and has a casual tone	To goad callers into leaving a message, some owners of answering machines have elevated "Hello" into an art form. One pianist croons into his machine: "Feelings. Please don't hurt my feelings. Leave your name and number, and I'll get back to you." And a screenwriter greets his callers with the following announcement: "Don't be tricky. This machine will recognize your dial tone and get you right back. So you might as well leave a message."

—*Consumer Reports*

Pointers for Writing Expository Paragraphs. When you write
an expository paragraph, you should narrow your topic, brainstorm, arrange your supporting information, draft your paragraph, and revise with an emphasis on conveying information
to a particular audience to increase that audience's knowledge.

Focus on explaining the topic and informing the reader when
you choose the content and language for an expository
paragraph.

The following guidelines will help you write expository paragraphs that fulfill their purpose and meet the reader's
expectations.

SUGGESTIONS FOR WRITING EXPOSITORY PARAGRAPHS

1. Use your knowledge and interests to choose a topic that *you* can
   explain, as well as one that lends itself to a factual treatment.
2. Determine any secondary purpose and tone.
3. Determine your audience's knowledge of the topic.

4. Develop a main idea about the topic and write a factual topic sentence.

5. Gather the supporting information that you need to explain your main idea thoroughly to your audience.

6. Organize your paragraph for clarity.

7. Concentrate on explaining (and on carrying out any other secondary purpose) as you write.

8. Revise your paragraph for clarity (including both unity and coherence) and examine your word choices to make sure that your tone is objective and informative as well as consistent. (See the checklist for revising on page 640 for additional help.)

EXERCISE A: Recognizing the Features of Expository Paragraphs. Read each of the following expository paragraphs. Identify the factual topic sentence in each. Then, list the supporting examples and facts. Finally, identify any secondary purpose or tone.

(1) A term that has been applied to describe what has happened to many metropolitan areas of the U.S. since World War II is "doughnut complex." In many places the hole in the doughnut is a decaying central city and the ring is a prosperous and growing suburban and exurban region. In a few major municipalities such as New York the hole is a core area of the city that is being revitalized and the ring is a surrounding part of the city that is becoming increasingly blighted; the entire central-city doughnut is surrounded by the usual prosperous suburban area.—George Sternlieb and James W. Hughes

(2) To clean fish, experts recommend that you use a sharp knife or a fish scaler and work with a steady, confident touch. Beginning this sometimes slimy process, you should place the fish on heavy paper or a cutting board. Hold the fish firmly on the cutting surface and begin scraping off the scales. Work from the tail toward the head, holding the knife or scaler at an angle so as not to slice the skin of the fish. Some professionals suggest rinsing the fish immediately after scaling. When the scaling is done, slit the underside of the fish, remove the insides, or entrails, and rinse the fish again under cold running water.

EXERCISE B: Planning, Writing, and Revising Expository Paragraphs. List five general topics on which you could write interesting and accurate expository paragraphs. Then choose one and use the suggestions in the chart above as well as your knowledge of paragraph writing to write an expository paragraph. Refer to the checklist for revising on page 640 when you revise your paragraph.

■ Writing Persuasive Paragraphs

Persuasive writing can be found in editorials, speeches, reviews of books and movies, and advertisements. Whenever you write to express an opinion or interpretation or to defend a course of action, you are using persuasion. To write convincing persuasive paragraphs, you should know about the main features of persuasive writing.

A Persuasive Purpose and Tone.   Ideas and word choices in a persuasive paragraph should work together to win the reader's consideration or acceptance of the writer's opinion. To convince the reader of something, the language of a persuasive paragraph must appeal to the reader's interest and reason.

The main features of a persuasive paragraph are a persuasive purpose and a reasonable, convincing tone.

To serve a persuasive purpose, the topic sentence should be a statement of opinion. It must be controversial—that is, arguable and not factual. It should also be relevant to other people and supportable with facts and logical arguments. The following examples illustrate the difference between appropriate and inappropriate topic sentences for persuasive paragraphs.

STATEMENT OF OPINION: American presidential campaigns last too long.

STATEMENT OF FACT: American presidential campaigns last longer than their European counterparts.

SIGNIFICANT OPINION: Too much sugar in one's diet can cause health problems.

INSIGNIFICANT OPINION: I like sugar.

SUPPORTABLE OPINION: Usually Strindberg's plays are darker and more violent than those of Ibsen.

UNSUPPORTABLE OPINION: Ibsen would have been incapable of writing plays in the style of Strindberg's plays.

The entire persuasive paragraph should attempt to "sell" the writer's opinion, to influence the reader's thinking. The supporting information should consist of interesting, specific evidence to make the opinion seem reasonable and worth considering. Fitting examples, strong facts, well thought out reasons, logical arguments, and relevant incidents can help convince the reader.

In order to be effective, a persuasive paragraph must also achieve a reasonable, convincing tone that presents the writer's opinion and yet shows respect for the reader's views. The language should be direct and forceful but not offensive. Reasonable language can win the reader's agreement, whereas emotionally loaded words may offend the reader. Specific, concrete words, interesting comparisons, and clear explanations can be persuasive because of their ability to engage the reader's interest.

The following persuasive paragraph expresses and supports the opinion that land developers are destroying the countryside. The specific language underlines the writer's beliefs without bullying the reader, and the use of supportive arguments and the observations of another critic add to the persuasive tone of the paragraph.

Persuasive paragraph with a persuasive purpose and a reasonable tone

> Already bulldozers, like droves of army ants, are chewing up the loveliest pastoral settings outside such cities as Boston, Philadelphia, and San Francisco. William H. Whyte, Jr., in the book, *The Exploding Metropolis*, estimates that bulldozers are flattening three thousand acres every day as "urban sprawl" spreads. Great metropolitan areas once widely separated are starting to bump up against each other. Metropolitan Dallas is bumping into metropolitan Fort Worth; Cleveland is on the verge of bumping into Akron; Hartford and Springfield have almost merged as areas; and even those two great colossi, metropolitan New York and metropolitan Philadelphia, are at the point of colliding—and swallowing up the breadth of the sovereign state of New Jersey between them. —Vance Packard

Although a persuasive paragraph should always have a persuasive purpose and a convincing tone, the intensity of the purpose and tone may vary. For instance, your purpose in writing a persuasive paragraph may simply be to prompt someone to consider something from a new angle. Or you may actually want to change your reader's opinions, or even to stir your audience to do something immediately, such as vote or join a club. Similarly, you can write persuasively within a whole range of tones. You can be casual and friendly, simply offering your interpretation of a play, book, or sports event. On the other hand, you can be urgent and compelling, emphasizing the need for immediate action.

The following paragraph by E. B. White attempts to shape the reader's ideas about New York, but the purpose, while it is persuasive, is not pressing, and the tone is light and even humorous.

Persuasive paragraph that entertains and has a humorous tone	It is a miracle that New York works at all. The whole thing is implausible. Every time the residents brush their teeth, millions of gallons of water must be drawn from the Catskills and the hills of Westchester. The subterranean system of telephone cables, power lines, steam pipes, gas mains and sewer pipes is reason enough to abandon the island to the gods and the weevils. Every time an incision is made in the pavement, the noisy surgeons expose ganglia that are tangled beyond belief. By rights New York should have destroyed itself long ago, from panic or fire or rioting or failure of some vital supply line in its circulatory system or from some deep labyrinthine short circuit. Long ago the city should have experienced an insoluble traffic snarl at some impossible bottleneck. . . . It should have been touched in the head by the August heat and gone off its rocker. —E. B. White

Pointers for Writing Persuasive Paragraphs. While you follow the usual paragraph-writing steps in preparing a persuasive paragraph, you should concentrate on a deliberate slant or approach. You should assume that your audience disagrees with you and should think about convincing these unsympathetic or apathetic readers to accept your ideas.

> Focus on defending your opinion and on winning the reader's agreement when you choose the content and language for your persuasive paragraph.

When you are preparing a persuasive paragraph, one of the most important tasks is to gather accurate, specific, convincing evidence for the opinion in your topic sentence. The more controversial your opinion is, the more you will need strong supporting evidence and the more you should think about the opposing arguments. When you gather evidence for an especially controversial opinion, you should always try to answer the arguments that might be brought up against your own position. For example, if you were supporting the opinion that the method of choosing vice-presidential candidates should be changed, you might build a defense by listing arguments for and against your opinion and then additional counter-arguments that directly answer the arguments against your opinion. The following chart demonstrates how you can build a persuasive defense using this method.

BUILDING YOUR DEFENSE		
Topic Sentence:	**The nomination of vice-presidential candidates by the major parties should be made more democratic and systematic.**	
Evidence For	**Evidence Against**	**Additional Evidence For**
—The potential responsibilities of the vice-president are too important to permit the choice to be left entirely up to the presidential nominee	—Actually the vice-president's job, given its undemanding nature, could be filled by anyone	—Regardless of what the vice-president actually does from day to day, four of our last seven presidents had been vice-presidents
—Often presidential candidates are too exhausted from the ordeal of winning the nomination to give much attention to the choice of vice-president	—Presidential campaigns are already too long and elaborate—no need to complicate the process even further by adding a race for vice-president	—The process of choosing a vice-president need not be as complicated as the presidential nominating process
—Petty political considerations are usually the sole determining factor in selecting the running mate of the presidential nominee	—The presidential candidate should be allowed to choose a running mate who is compatible, rather than be forced to accept the choice of the nominating convention or popular primary	—The presidential candidate could submit a list of acceptable vice-presidential candidates to the convention or during the primaries

Building a defense for a highly controversial opinion can also help you arrange your arguments in the paragraph. If the opposition does have some convincing arguments you can actually strengthen your own position by acknowledging one or more of these good points. This strategy, called *conceding a point*, indicates that you are fair-minded and well-informed. You may even want to construct your paragraph by answering a number of the opposition's arguments with your own stronger ones in a con-pro-con-pro arrangement, ending with your strongest, most forceful argument.

The following more complete guidelines will help you prepare all kinds of persuasive paragraphs including those that treat highly debatable opinions.

SUGGESTIONS FOR WRITING PERSUASIVE PARAGRAPHS

1. Use your knowledge and convictions to choose an opinion that you can support, as well as one that is truly arguable.

2. Determine the intensity of your purpose and tone (how controversial the opinion is and how persuasive you must be).

3. Determine your audience's probable response to your opinion (unconcern, mild disagreement, or strong disagreement).

4. Focus your opinion in a topic sentence that is direct, significant, and supportable.

5. Gather specific examples, facts, details, reasons, and incidents to support your opinion. For a highly controversial opinion, consider the opposition and list evidence for and against your view.

6. Organize your supporting information logically by order of importance or interest. For highly controversial topics, consider the possibility of conceding one or more points to the opposition and the possibility of organizing your defense around the opposition's arguments.

7. Write your paragraph concentrating on concrete, specific, and reasonable but compelling language and smooth, logical connections.

8. Revise for persuasiveness, and examine your words to make sure that the tone is fair, forceful, and consistent. (See the checklist for revising on page 640 for additional help.)

EXERCISE C: **Recognizing the Features of Persuasive Paragraphs.** Read each of the following persuasive paragraphs. Identify the statement of opinion that is the topic sentence in each. Then, list the supporting evidence. Finally, identify the intensity of purpose and tone as mild or highly committed.

(1) Bent on changing our habits to suit the wishes of product manufacturers, advertisements always try to tell us how to spend our money. Television commercials, for example, in their mock concern for our attractiveness, warn us to use certain deodorants and toothpastes to avoid social embarrassment. Pushy announcers in radio ads tell us to run to a certain automobile dealership before its dwindling supply is depleted by the last lucky customer. Even trains and buses display "instructive" ads that tell us where to do our banking and what brand of gum to chew. If we took all advertisements seriously, we would seldom have to think for ourselves and would probably go flat broke.

(2) *M*A*S*H* is a marvelously unstable comedy, a tough, funny, and sophisticated burlesque of military attitudes that is at the same time a tale of chivalry. . . . The picture has so much spirit that you keep laughing—and without discomfort, because all of the targets *should* be laughed at. The laughter is at the horrors and absurdities of war. . . . The title letters stand for Mobile Army Surgical Hospital: The heroes, played by Donald Sutherland and Elliott Gould, are combat surgeons patching up casualties a few miles from the front during the Korean War. They do their surgery in style, with humor; they're hip Galahads, saving lives while ragging the military bureaucracy. . . . The heroes win at everything. . . . They're so good at what they do that even the military brass admires them. They're winners in the war with the Army. —Pauline Kael

EXERCISE D: Planning, Writing, and Revising Persuasive Paragraphs. List five general topics about which you could formulate opinions suitable for a persuasive paragraph. Choose one of these topics and then use the suggestions in the chart on page 666 to write a persuasive paragraph. If your opinion lends itself to debate, consider the opposing arguments and use a chart to build your defense. Refer to the checklist for revising on page 640 when you polish your paragraph.

APPLICATION: Writing and Evaluating Expository and Persuasive Paragraphs. Choose one of the following general topics to become the basis of two paragraphs, one expository and one persuasive. Follow the suggestions in this section to write, first, an expository paragraph and, then, a persuasive paragraph on the topic.

After completing the first drafts of your paragraphs, exchange papers with another student. Analyze the other student's paragraphs, identifying any secondary purposes or tones and suggesting improvements using another color of ink. Then revise your own paragraphs taking into account the other student's suggestions as well as the points in the checklist in Section 22.3. Revise and recopy both your paragraphs and submit them to your teacher along with the first drafts.

A popular style of clothing
Foreign cars
Fire
Finding your way around an unfamiliar city
A concept such as loyalty, honesty, or prejudice
A machine

The way your student government is run
A current television show (or movie, book, or record album)
A political figure
Cartoons

23.2 Descriptive and Narrative Paragraphs

Both descriptive and narrative writing attempt, with language, to depict real experience. *Description* focuses on the qualities of a person, place, object, or event—what the senses observe, what the memory recalls, of a particular item. *Narration*, on the other hand, relates what happened in a series of events. It is mainly concerned with capturing action. Both forms of writing appeal to the senses, emotions, and imagination of the reader through the use of concrete, colorful, and vivid language.

This section discusses the basic features of descriptive and narrative writing and can help you gain experience and skill in writing these imaginative paragraphs.

■ Writing Descriptive Paragraphs

Descriptive paragraphs focus on a single dominant impression and draw upon particularly vivid language to describe and elaborate on that impression for the reader.

A Descriptive Purpose and Descriptive Language. The basic purpose of descriptive writing is to transmit the writer's dominant impression of an experience, person, place, or object through sensory details that allow the reader to see, hear, smell, taste, touch, and imagine the topic.

> The main features of a descriptive paragraph are a descriptive purpose focused on a dominant impression and descriptive language that appeals to the senses, imagination, and emotions of the reader.

To serve a descriptive purpose, a paragraph should convey a single dominant impression. This dominant impression can be the strongest, most noticeable quality of the topic, such as the mysteriousness of a person, the darkness of a room, or the fragility of an object. It can also be a *mood:* a feeling that the topic produces in the observer and reader. For example, the wind howling around an empty schoolyard might suggest a mournful mood; a bird feeder crowded with chirping birds might evoke a cheerful mood. The dominant impression will often be explicitly stated in a topic sentence at the beginning, at the middle, or at the end of the paragraph. But it should also be woven throughout the language and details of the entire paragraph.

A descriptive paragraph should also contain strong, specific details that allow the reader to feel as if he or she were actually seeing or experiencing the thing described. Features such as color, size, texture, shape, and condition should be expressed clearly and sharply in action verbs, precise nouns, and colorful adjectives. Notice in the following examples the difference between weak description that offers only a sketchy image and strong description that captures a specific scene.

WEAK DESCRIPTION: It was a windy day.

STRONG DESCRIPTION: The aspens trembled in the warm breeze.

WEAK DESCRIPTION: He looked exhausted.

STRONG DESCRIPTION: Shuffling into the room, he created little dust clouds with every step. A crumpled baseball cap dangled from one hand. A rip in his threadbare jeans exposed a raw, pebbly knee, and his shirt hung out of his pants, loose and mud-splattered. His face was red and stretched, his eyes glazed.

Descriptive language also includes sensory impressions and figures of speech. Sensory impressions are actually specific details that appeal to the senses, calling up sights, sounds, tastes, temperatures, textures, and feelings that a reader can experience through his or her own memory and imagination. Figures of speech, or imaginative comparisons that link the familiar with the unfamiliar in a striking way, can also touch the reader's memories and emotions. An appropriate simile, metaphor, personification, or analogy can help the reader see the thing described in a new and revealing light. (For a detailed explanation of sensory impressions and figures of speech, see Section 20.2.)

A descriptive paragraph also needs to present its topic in a meaningful, organized way. For example, a writer cannot simply give the reader a random catalog of everything in a room and expect the reader to *see* the room as the writer sees it. Instead the writer should arrange the specific details spatially— for example, from top to bottom or near to far—so the reader can grasp the relationship of one detail to another.

When your language and details work together to create a dominant impression, you can produce a psychological effect on your reader. In the following passage from *The Great Gatsby*, by F. Scott Fitzgerald, figurative language and specific detail combine to make the reader visualize and experience a particular airy room. The dominant impression, established in the first sentence and interwoven throughout, is one of drifting, hovering, floating, and the mood is detached and dreamy.

Descriptive paragraph creating an impression of drifting airiness

A breeze blew through the room, blew curtains in at one end and out the other like pale flags, twisting them up toward the frosted wedding-cake of the ceiling, and then rippled over the wine-colored rug, making a shadow on it as wind does on the sea. The only completely stationary object in the room was an enormous couch on which two young women were buoyed up as though upon an anchored balloon. They were both in white, and their dresses were rippling and fluttering as if they had just been blown back in after a short flight around the house. Then there was a boom as Tom Buchanan shut the rear windows and the caught wind died out about the room, and the curtains and the rugs and the two young women ballooned slowly to the floor.
—F. Scott Fitzgerald

Descriptive language can be used to create a variety of impressions or moods and can serve a variety of purposes. For example, the Fitzgerald passage might have emphasized the heat and boredom of the people in the scene, evoking a mood of depression rather than one of dreaminess. The piling up of sensory details—particularly those with a strong emotional impact (for example, certain sounds, certain types of weather, certain colors)—can all contribute to the dominant impression of a paragraph.

Notice how the feverish activity of a dance as described by Edith Wharton in the following passage from *Ethan Frome* establishes a mood of exhilaration and anticipation.

Descriptive paragraph creating a mood of exhilaration

Frome's heart was beating fast. He had been straining for a glimpse of the dark head under the cherry-colored scarf, and it vexed him that another eye should have been quicker than his. The leader of the reel danced well, and his partner caught his fire. As she passed down the line, her light figure swinging from hand to hand in circles of increasing swiftness, the scarf flew off her head and stood out behind her shoulders, and Frome, at each turn, caught sight of her laughing panting lips, the cloud of dark hair about her forehead, and the dark eyes which seemed the only fixed points in a maze of flying lines.
—Edith Wharton

In addition to the artistic functions shown in the preceding paragraphs, descriptive passages may have secondary purposes or may be put to other uses in longer works that are essentially expository or persuasive in purpose. For example, descriptive skills are often used in technical and scientific writing, such as that found in encyclopedia articles.

The following passage by Andrea O. Dean about the home of the Mexican architect Luis Barragán shows the use of description in expository writing. The writer has given a very detailed account of both the style and the structure of the house.

Descriptive paragraph that explains with technical description	The house still serves him as both refuge and work-place. To the street it presents only a blank wall punctured by small openings and a large window high above the street. Inside, it is divided into three levels with a spacious, double-height living room, articulated by low partitions that allow space and diffused light to flow from room to room. Barragán's famous, surreal-looking stairway of cantilevered pine boards without railings seems to float upward to a door that is always closed. Near the stair is a simple, sturdy desk. An enormous window extends at one end of the living room from floor to ceiling, opening on an overgrown, walled garden framed by the window's cruciform mullions. This garden is the house's center and heart. In every room, Ambasz writes, "roughly plastered walls and volcanic rock floor tiles are contrasted with polished wood floors, velvety carpets and homespuns." —Andrea O. Dean

Pointers for Writing Descriptive Paragraphs. When you write a descriptive paragraph, you should concentrate on painting a picture or creating a mood for the reader by focusing on a single dominant impression and communicating that impression through precise and vivid language.

Focus on enabling your reader to see, hear, and otherwise experience what you are describing.

The following guidelines will help you write strong descriptive paragraphs.

SUGGESTIONS FOR WRITING DESCRIPTIVE PARAGRAPHS

1. Choose a topic—one *particular* person, place, object, or experience—that you know well and that you can describe with specific, interesting words.

2. Decide on the dominant impression of your topic, and draft a topic sentence that states this impression.

3. Determine any secondary purpose, such as entertaining or instructing your reader.

4. By observing your topic directly or imagining it, list as many details and sensory impressions as you can, and think of particularly vivid words and imaginative comparisons that will help communicate your dominant impression to a reader.

5. Organize your support to make the reader familiar with your topic.

6. Concentrate on involving the reader's senses, emotions, and imagination as you write.

7. Revise your paragraph for vividness, for the consistency of its mood, and for the strength and unity of its dominant impression. (See the checklist for revising on page 640 for further revising suggestions.)

EXERCISE A: Recognizing the Features of Descriptive Paragraphs. Read each of the following descriptive paragraphs. Identify the stated or implied dominant impression. Then, list the specific details, sensory impressions, and figures of speech used in each. Finally, identify any secondary purpose.

(1) The running styles were as different as the physical characteristics. Dick Crompton, a small Texas scatback, ran with sharp exhalations when he had the ball, *ah-ah-ah*, like piston strokes—a habit he had picked up in high school which he felt gave power to his run. He could be heard across the width of the field. . . . Jake Greer also had a distinctive run—moving his spindly body in leaps like a high jumper moving from the crossbar, high, bouncy steps, and then he stretched out fast, and when he got to the defending back he feinted with his small high-boned head, sometimes with a tiny bit of toothpick working in it. . . .
—George Plimpton

(2) Between the girls and the others the distance widened; it began to seem that they would be left alone. They looked around them with the same eyes. The shorn uplands seemed to float on the distance, which extended dazzling to tiny blue grassy hills. There was no end to the afternoon, whose light went on ripening now [that] they had scythed the corn. Light filled the silence which, now [that] Papa and the others were out of hearing, was complete. Only screens of trees intersected and knolls made islands in the vast fields. The mansion and the home farm had sunk below them in the expanse of woods, so that hardly a ripple showed where the girls dwelled. The shadow of the same rook circling passed over Sarah, then over Henrietta, who in their turn cast one shadow across the stubble.
—Elizabeth Bowen

EXERCISE B: Planning, Writing, and Revising Descriptive Paragraphs. List five topics you could use for a descriptive paragraph and then choose one. Use the suggestions in the chart on page 671 to complete a descriptive paragraph. Refer to the checklist for revising on page 640 when you revise.

■ Writing Narrative Paragraphs

Although narrative paragraphs may be written for many different reasons and may appear in such different kinds of writing as letters, novels, reviews, and scholarly articles, the basic purpose of narrative writing is to tell a story in graphic language, which engages the reader's imagination in the happenings.

A Narrative Purpose and Graphic Language.   The fundamental purpose of narrative writing is to relate an experience, to tell a series of events, usually to entertain. More than the other types of paragraphs, narrative paragraphs attempt to convey the flow of physical and mental action through time. To achieve this purpose, narrative writing uses graphic language, which captures both action and sensory impressions, to help the reader witness the events.

> The main features of a narrative paragraph are a narrative purpose focused on telling a series of related events and graphic language that recreates action and captures sensory details.

To serve its narrative purposes, a narrative paragraph may be a self-contained story, or it may be part of a longer story. In most cases, especially when the paragraph is self-contained, it will have its own beginning, middle and end; it will give the reader the sense that time is passing, that something has happened, that one event has led to another.

The topic sentence of a narrative paragraph can vary in its form and function. It can appear at the beginning of the paragraph and present a general truth, which the story will illustrate, or it may appear at the end to offer an interpretation of the story. In still other paragraphs, it may simply set the scene and start the action of the narrative.

To serve a narrative purpose, a paragraph that tells a story must have a storyteller or a *narrator*, often described as the *point of view*. Although the narrative point of view must be consistent throughout, the writer can use one of several points of view, or narrators, to tell the story. A *first person* or *"I" narrator* tells the story from his or her vantage point as a participant in the action. The "I" narrator can describe the action as he or she sees it, and can also relate his or her thoughts, feelings, and reactions to what is going on. For other stories, a writer might prefer the distance of a *third person objective narrator* who relates the story as an outside observer without using the word "I." This narrator can report the physical action of the story but does not have access to the thoughts and feelings of the characters. On the other hand, a writer can choose a *third person partially omniscient narrator* who tells the story, again without using the word "I," through the eyes of one character, relating the thoughts of that character, but not of anyone else in the story. Finally, a writer can choose a *third person generally omniscient narrator* who has access to the thoughts of several or all of the characters. In most narrative paragraphs, the writer will choose a first person, a third person objective observer, or a third person partially omniscient narrator.

The supporting information in a narrative paragraph consists of the events, both mental and physical, of the story. The point of view determines the amount of mental action that can be included in the story. For example, a third person objective narrator cannot reveal the mental activity of any of the characters. Instead, a paragraph with such a narrator would concentrate on observable physical action. A first person and a third person partially omniscient narrator, on the other hand, would be confined not only to the mental activity of one character but also to those *physical* actions that one character can see.

The mental and physical events of the narrative paragraph should be arranged in chronological order. Even if the paragraph occurs within a larger narrative, the narrative paragraph will have its own starting and ending points. Occasionally, a writer may begin with the ending point in order to show the events that led up to it. But even in this case, the writer should maintain a sense of the normal flow of time from one point to another.

The language of narration should be graphic; it should attempt to bring the narrated experience to life for the reader. Such language should include the precision and sensory detail of descriptive writing, but it must also show the actions of the story. Besides exact and vivid nouns and modifiers, the graphic language of a narrative should use strong action verbs, which will draw the reader on to the next event in the story. Transitions and other connecting words can also help move the story along, linking one event to the next, and recreating the continuity of experience.

The following narrative paragraph from Ernest Hemingway's *A Farewell to Arms* allows the reader to share the moment-to-moment experience of a man struggling against drowning. The topic sentence suggests the scene and launches the action. Notice how the use of the first person narrator, strong action verbs, and numerous connecting devices increase the reader's involvement in the action.

Narrative paragraph with a first person narrator

> I watched the shore come close, then swing away, then come closer again. The timber swung slowly so that the bank was behind me and I knew we were in an eddy. I could see the brush, but even with my momentum and swimming as hard as I could, the current was taking me away. I thought then I would drown because of my boots, but I thrashed and fought through the water, and when I looked up, the bank was coming toward me, and I kept thrashing and swimming in a heavy-footed panic until I reached it. I hung to the willow branch and did not have strength to pull myself up but I knew I would not drown now. —Ernest Hemingway

Narrative writing can be nonfictional as well as fictional and can tell a story in order to serve a variety of secondary purposes—for example, to inform, to amuse, to criticize in order to inspire change, or to convince the reader. Narrative writing, like descriptive writing, can create a variety of moods as well. For example, the following paragraph by Doris Lessing contrasts strongly with the Hemingway paragraph in secondary purpose and mood. Whereas the reader was caught up in the desperation of the Hemingway scene, Lessing's passage distances the reader from the characters and scene by the use of a third person objective narrator who does not enter into the minds of the characters. In addition, there is a satiric edge to the writing, as the two old men are made to appear ridiculous—almost like characters in a cartoon.

Narrative paragraph with a third person objective narrator

> The two elderly gentlemen emerged onto the hotel terrace at the same moment. They stopped, and checked movements that suggested they wished to retreat. Their first involuntary glances had been startled, even troubled. Now they allowed their eyes to exchange a long, formal glare of hate, before turning deliberately away from each other. They surveyed

the terrace. A problem! Only one of the tables still remained in sunlight. They stiffly marched toward it, pulled out chairs, seated themselves. At once they opened newspapers and lifted them up like screens.
—Doris Lessing

Pointers for Writing Narrative Paragraphs.   When you write a narrative paragraph, you should concentrate on making the story seem real to the reader through your particular narrator's account of events.

Focus on guiding your reader through the physical and mental events of your story by means of your narrator and on translating the experience into the language of description and action.

When you write a narrative paragraph, you must remember several things. The following chart breaks down the process of writing narrative paragraphs into a number of tasks.

SUGGESTIONS FOR WRITING NARRATIVE PARAGRAPHS

1. Choose an experience—either real or imagined—that you can tell in a series of events and translate into clear and graphic language.

2. Decide on the point of view from which you will tell your story. Experiment with several different narrators to see which approach seems most comfortable to you and to the story that you want to tell. Once you have chosen your narrator, do not switch to another point of view.

3. Determine any secondary purpose, such as amusing or instructing your reader, and any mood that your passage will convey.

4. Decide the kind of topic sentence you will use and write one that either conveys the general truth your story illustrates or that sets the scene and launches the action of the story.

5. List the major physical and mental events of the experience you want to relate, making sure that they are consistent with your point of view. List appropriate details and sensory impressions.

6. Select and organize the events in your story according to chronological order.

7. As you write, concentrate on the action of the story as presented from a consistent point of view. Keep the reader reading by helping him or her to visualize the action through your graphic language.

8. Revise your paragraph for consistency of point of view and for clarity and vividness of action. Reread your story, looking for spots that could confuse readers or lose their attention. (See the checklist for revising on page 640 for further suggestions.)

EXERCISE C: Recognizing the Features of Narrative Paragraphs. Read each of the following narrative paragraphs. Identify the topic sentence or main idea in each and state whether it presents a general truth or simply sets the scene. Then, identify the point of view used in the paragraph. Next, list the events in chronological order and give examples of graphic language. Finally, identify any secondary purpose or mood.

(1) Anna pretended not to notice the father with his son. A small yipping dog, a golden dog, bounded near them. Anna turned shyly back to her reading: She did not want to have to speak to these neighbors. She saw the man's shadow falling over her legs, then over the pages of her book, and she had the idea that he wanted to see what she was reading. The dog nuzzled her; the man called him away. She watched them walk down the beach. She was relieved that the man had not spoken to her.
—Joyce Carol Oates

(2) Upstairs, close to our heads, my grandfather, in a voice frail but still melodious, began to sing. "There is a happy land, far, far away, where saints in glory stand, bright, bright as day." We listened; and his voice broke into coughing, a terrible rending cough growing in fury, struggling to escape, and loud with fear he called my mother's name. She didn't stir. His voice grew enormous, a bully's voice, as he repeated, "Lillian! Lillian!" and I saw my mother's shape quiver with the force coming down the stairs into her; she was like a dam; and then the power, as my grandfather fell momentarily silent, flowed toward me in the darkness, and I felt intensely angry, and hated that mass of suffering, even while I realized that I was too weak to withstand it.
—John Updike

EXERCISE D: Planning, Writing, and Revising Narrative Paragraphs. List five experiences or "stories" you could relate in narrative paragraphs. Then choose one and follow the suggestions in the chart on page 676 to write your paragraph. Refer to the checklist for revising on page 640 when you polish your paragraph.

APPLICATION: Writing and Evaluating Descriptive and Narrative Paragraphs. Choose a person, place, or object that has played a significant part in your life or choose one of the following ideas for a two-paragraph composition. You can describe your topic in the first paragraph and then tell a story about that person, place, or object in the second paragraph. Or you can combine description and narration in both of your paragraphs. Then, exchange papers with another student and evaluate the quality of the description and narration in his or her paragraphs. Write a brief critique commenting on how well the writer has made the topic come alive for the reader. Finally, revise your own paragraphs according to the other student's comments and checklist for revising on page 640 and recopy them.

A storm, earthquake, or blizzard—a horrifying experience
A place you love—a memorable experience
A food someone detests—the first time that person tried it
An object from your childhood—an experience losing or finding this object
A person who made problems for you or someone else—trying to avoid or outwit that person

Chapter 24

Essays

An essay is a *group* of paragraphs that are closely associated and work together to present and elaborate on a main point. In this chapter first you will learn to recognize the main features of an essay, and then you will practice writing essays of your own. Finally, you will concentrate on writing different types of essays for special purposes.

The Importance of Form, Unity, and Coherence

24.1

Before you can think about writing an essay, you should have a clear idea of what one is. As you will see, an essay is a carefully structured composition containing an introductory paragraph, separate paragraphs that develop the essay's main point, and a concluding paragraph. You will also see that many of the features you have learned to recognize in good paragraphs are found in good essays as well. Essays should be unified, the ideas they contain should follow some logical, coherent order, and the ideas should be clearly connected for the reader. Recognizing the features of an essay will help to prepare you for this kind of writing.

■ The Key Features of an Essay

An essay has three parts: a beginning, called the introduction; a middle, called the body; and an ending, called the conclusion. Its other key features include a title and a thesis statement, which is the controlling or unifying idea of the entire essay. A thesis statement is to an essay what a topic sentence is to a paragraph.

Each of these features has important functions. The title of an essay generally reveals the topic and seeks to engage the reader's interest. The introduction, the first or first few paragraphs of an essay, sets the tone, involves the reader in the topic, and leads into and includes the thesis statement. By appearing early in the essay, the thesis statement informs the reader of the point, scope, and purpose of the essay. Just as supporting information follows a topic sentence in a paragraph, so a number of body paragraphs containing supporting information develop the main point of an essay. These paragraphs contain relevant examples, details, facts, and reasons. Finally, a conclusion, often in a final paragraph, completes the essay by reminding the reader of the main point and offering parting remarks on the topic. The following diagram shows these features as they might appear in an essay of six paragraphs.

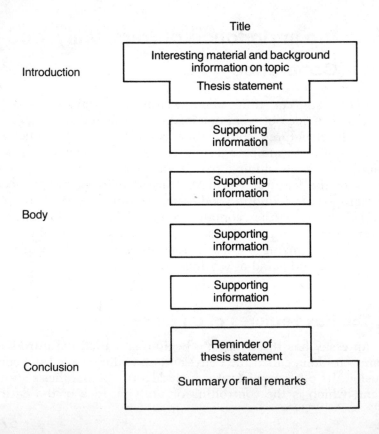

By learning more about the functions of each of these features, you can prepare yourself to write good essays.

The Title.   Since a reader sees the title of an essay first, it should be engaging and informative.

A title of an essay can identify the topic, arouse the reader's curiosity, or suggest the main point and tone of the essay.

The title of an essay should suit the topic, main point, and tone of the essay and should serve as an advertisement for the essay. Either straightforward and clear or clever and provocative, a title should indicate something about the topic of the essay and possibly about the writer's main point. A title should also reflect the tone of the essay; a serious, scholarly title, for example, will lead a reader to expect a formal, scholarly paper. A title should be original and not too long. Most of all, a title should attract the reader's attention and spark the reader's interest so that he or she will read on.

The following chart shows some topics for essays along with corresponding titles. Most of the titles provide both a preview of the essay's topic and a means of arousing the reader's curiosity.

SAMPLE TITLES FOR ESSAYS	
Topic	**Title**
Ancient methods of measuring time	Clocks Without Hands
The joys of skiing	Flying Down the Mountain
Long distance train travel	Amtraking
How to grow African violets	The Care and Feeding of African Violets
Astronomy	Lost in the Stars

Introduction with Thesis Statement.   The first paragraph (or first few paragraphs in a long essay) forms the introduction.

The introduction should catch the reader's attention and establish the writer's purpose and tone. It should also lead up to and include the thesis statement, which states the main point of the essay.

The introductory paragraph should lead the reader, step by step, into the essay. It will usually begin with some general remarks identifying the topic, providing background information, and stimulating the reader's interest. In this way, it prepares the reader for the ideas that follow and perhaps suggests why the topic is significant or interesting. The language of the introduction sets the tone of the essay. It establishes the writer's attitude toward both subject and audience—showing whether the writer's attitude is formal or informal, serious or casual, scholarly or friendly. The introduction closes in on the topic, gradually leading the reader from a broader to a narrower view of the topic. Usually the thesis statement, a well-focused sentence or two, comes at the end of the introduction. By then the reader is ready for the writer's main point, which the rest of the essay defends or explores.

The thesis statement is the heart of the essay, its controlling idea. It can state a fact if the essay is expository, express an opinion if the essay is persuasive, state a general impression if the essay is descriptive, or offer a general truth if the essay narrates a personal experience. Besides expressing the main point, the thesis statement may indicate the subtopics that will develop this point. Sometimes these subtopics will be stated explicitly in the thesis statement, and sometimes they will be implied. But, one way or another, the thesis statement controls the shape and direction of the rest of the essay, and for this reason, it must be carefully focused and clearly written.

The following chart offers some sample thesis statements, several of which include stated subtopics.

SAMPLE THESIS STATEMENTS	
Thesis Statement	**Stated Subtopics**
The life of the frog is divided into two separate and distinct phases, the first one of which is spent by the animal underwater, and the second, primarily on land.	(1) Phase spent underwater (2) Phase spent on land
People interested in tracing their family genealogies can draw on several sources of information: statements of living relatives, family documents, and public records.	(1) Statements of relatives (2) Family documents (3) Public records

Learning to fly an airplane has been the most thrilling experience of my life.	None
The United States space program climaxed in the first moon landing in 1969.	None

The following paragraph is the introduction to an essay about frogs. The first few sentences prepare the reader for a discussion of the life cycle of frogs. Then the final sentence presents the main point with two subtopics: the two separate phases of the frog's maturation. Also notice that the language, such words as "scientists note," establishes an objective tone and an explanatory purpose.

Introduction	Although the frog is a common animal in many
Opening ideas	parts of the country, scientists note its rather uncommon life cycle. The word "amphibian," generally used to characterize frogs, literally means "having
Thesis statement with two subtopics	two lives," although, of course, the frog only lives once. But that one life is divided into two separate and distinct phases, the first one of which is spent underwater, and the second, primarily on land.

The Body Paragraphs. The central portion of the essay, consisting of two or more body paragraphs, develops the thesis statement with relevant examples, details, facts, or reasons. Often, each body paragraph will focus on one subtopic as presented in the thesis statement. At the same time, however, each of these paragraphs usually has its own topic sentence, and each one is unified and coherent.

> The body of an essay should contain two or more paragraphs that explain or develop all relevant aspects of the essay's main point with strong supporting information.

The number of body paragraphs will vary according to the thesis statement, the number of subtopics, and the amount of supporting information the writer has. Sometimes, the number of body paragraphs in the essay will match the number of subtopics in the thesis statement. In the essay about the life cycle of frogs, for example, the thesis statement presents two subtopics. The body of the essay could have two paragraphs, one devoted to each stage of the frog's growth. Each paragraph could then explain a phase of the life cycle with supporting examples and details. Other times, two or more paragraphs may develop each individual subtopic. No matter how many paragraphs the body of an essay contains, however, it should completely develop the thesis statement with specific information.

The Conclusion.   The conclusion, usually one final paragraph, brings the essay to a close while reminding readers of the main point. It can also include any other final remarks that will help unify the essay or help the reader understand and appreciate the essay.

An essay's conclusion should refer to the main point and bring the essay to a satisfying close.

The concluding paragraph should wrap up all the ideas in the essay without being unnecessarily repetitive. It should leave the reader feeling content with the coverage of the topic and main point. The conclusion might bring up a final example or observation that demonstrates the main point, it might suggest the topic's significance for the reader, or it might elaborate on a few ideas from the introduction in a striking way. The final sentence of the conclusion is particularly effective when it acts as a clincher, presenting an especially forceful, eloquent, or witty statement.

Complete Essay Showing the Key Features.   The following complete version of the essay on the life cycle of the frog demonstrates the features and structure of the standard essay. As you read it, notice that it is somewhat conversational in its tone and informative in its purpose.

Title	The Double Life of the Frog
Introduction	Although the frog is a common animal in many parts of the country, scientists note its rather uncommon life cycle. The word "amphibian," generally used to characterize frogs, literally means "having
Thesis statement with two subtopics	two lives," although, of course, the frog only lives once. But that one life is divided into two separate, distinct phases, the first one of which is spent underwater, and the second, primarily on land.
First body paragraph (develops first subtopic)	During the initial stage of a frog's life, it is not really a frog at all, but rather a tadpole or pollywog. When such a tadpole hatches from an underwater jelly-like mass of eggs, it very much resembles a fish in outward appearance, with a vertical tail and with gills on the sides of its little head. The tadpole also possesses a fishlike two-chambered heart. As it grows,

the tadpole spends day and night swimming about underwater, obtaining oxygen from the water through its gills, feeding on minute vegetable matter, and evading predators such as big fish. During this stage, however, fundamental changes in the tadpole's physiology are taking place; it is beginning to resemble a land creature. Lungs develop, and, most dramatically, legs begin to grow.

Second body paragraph (develops second subtopic)

Sixty to ninety days after birth, the former tadpole emerges from its watery home as an animal very similar to the adult frog so familiar to most Americans. Although it still possesses a tail, the immature frog no longer relies on its tadpole gills, but rather breathes through its pair of lungs. Its circulatory system has become more complex as well. The emerging frog now has a heart with three chambers and it has by now grown four legs. Even after its tail has been resorbed, a frog can still swim very well, but it is no longer capable of breathing underwater and must come to the surface for air. Thus, it is more at home on land than under the water. Although the frog must keep its skin moist in order to breathe efficiently, the only one of its activities that requires a return to the water is mating, which begins a new life cycle.

Reminder of thesis statement

Conclusion

The metamorphosis of any amphibian is a fascinating process, most dramatically displayed in the life cycle of the frog. Few other animals lead a comparable "double life," changing from sea creature to land creature overnight. Perhaps it is not surprising that the frog, almost magical in reality, should become the frequent disguise for princes in fairy tales.

EXERCISE A: Identifying the Features of an Essay.

The following essay on the novel *The Caine Mutiny* was written by a student. Read it carefully, and then answer the questions that follow it.

In Defense of Mutiny

In the novel *The Caine Mutiny* by Herman Wouk, Captain Queeg demonstrated his incapability for leadership from the moment he assumed command of the *U.S.S. Caine* until he was relieved of his responsibilities by his Executive Officer. There are several reasons why I believe Captain Queeg was mentally unfit to command the *Caine*. First, he gave orders that were absurd and unreasonable. Second, he failed to give any suitable commands or to exhibit any bravery during harsh adversity. And third, he failed to show any concern for what was occurring on his ship.

During his command, Queeg gave orders to his crew that were absurd, even ridiculous. When he first took command of the *Caine*, he gave orders that confused the engine room operators to the point that the ship ran aground. On another occasion, when the *Caine* was leading a string of lighter craft toward an enemy island, Queeg ordered the *Caine* to go at an unreasonably fast speed, which the lighter vessels could not manage. When they complained of excessive speed, Queeg responded that his ship would throw a dye marker when it reached the spot. Obviously, this solution was inadequate because the other boats could not navigate for themselves, and they had been depending on the *Caine* to lead them all the way to the island. Another example of Queeg's irrational commands was his rearrangement of sleeping hours. Without regard for the various duty shifts, Queeg abruptly ordered that officers be given an automatic unsatisfactory fitness rating if they were sleeping after eight o'clock in the morning or before eight at night. This sleeping order was clearly unreasonable because there were officers who came off the mid-watch, and they could not get any sleep before the morning.

During his command, Captain Queeg also failed to give any suitable orders or to exhibit any bravery during adverse situations. On the day of the *Caine's* first military engagement under Queeg, the crew saw that their captain froze in the face of danger. As the *Caine* moved away from the island of the battle, the Officer of the Deck kept yelling desperately to request permission to fire. Queeg just stood at an open window with a strange smile on his face. The crew found that Queeg was never on the side of the bridge exposed to the battle. Instead, he would hide in the wheelhouse during the fighting, emerging at certain intervals to give some illogical order, and then walking quickly back into the wheelhouse. Queeg's inability to act during periods of crisis became most obvious when the *Caine* was caught in a typhoon. As the storm worsened, Queeg began to look sick and just stood still, dumfounded. Instead of responding to the warnings of danger given by his Executive Officer, Queeg just threw him a frightened glance and then automatically obeyed his subordinate's commands, as a puppy obeys its master.

But perhaps even worse than Queeg's incompetence and cowardice was his habitual isolation and failure to demonstrate any concern for what was occurring on the *Caine*. For instance, during a battle, when a long line of attack boats was spotted heading towards the ship. Queeg was found perched happily out of sight of the transports, smoking and chatting casually with the signalman. At the OOD's warning, he simply giggled and continued his conversation. At another point, the radioman relayed a vital message to the OOD, who in turn tried to deliver it to Captain Queeg. He found the Captain eating ice cream with one hand and fitting pieces into a jigsaw puzzle with the other. Queeg glanced at the relayed order and then asked for another plate of ice cream and another cup of coffee. Obviously, this type of behavior was inappropriate, not to mention abnormal, for a ship's captain. On long voyages, Queeg became more touchy and reclusive. For much of the time that Queeg commanded the *Caine*, he remained in his cabin sitting, sleeping, eating, playing with jigsaw puzzles. He was a hermit, seeking to be alone, though occasionally calling people into his cabin to serve him, day or night.

Captain Queeg was obviously ill-suited to command a war vessel, since he became unreasonable and even cowardly under pressure and isolated himself from his responsibilities. Because his personality was unbalanced and because his actions were often unpredictable, particularly at moments critical to other lives, Queeg deserved to lose the respect of his crew, and, finally, to lose the command of his ship. —Jim Tooker

1. What is the title of the essay? Why is it a good title for the essay?
2. How long is the introduction?
3. Is the introduction an effective preparation for the rest of the essay? If so, why? If not, why not?
4. What is the writer's purpose from the beginning to the end of the essay?
5. What audience did the writer seem to have in mind? What tone does the writer establish?
6. What is the thesis statement? What, if any, subtopics does it explicitly mention?
7. How many body paragraphs does the essay have? What is the topic sentence of each body paragraph?
8. List the supporting information presented in each of the body paragraphs. How does this information develop the main point of the essay?
9. How long is the conclusion?
10. How does the conclusion remind the reader of the thesis statement? Does the conclusion satisfactorily complete the essay?

■ Unity and Coherence

Unity and coherence should be characteristics of any good piece of writing, whether it be a paragraph, an essay, or an even longer work. In fact, unity and coherence become more and more important the longer a piece of writing is because a more complicated work demands more of the reader. Unity and coherence help hold the reader's attention and enable the reader to follow the writer's thoughts. In essays, unity and coherence are necessary both within individual paragraphs and throughout the larger structure of the essay itself. (For more information about unity and coherence in paragraphs, see Section 22.1.) The next few pages will focus on unity and coherence as structural features of the essay as a whole.

Unity.   All of the ideas and information in a unified essay belong together and are essential to the development of the main point. The various parts of the essay—the introduction, thesis statement, body paragraphs, and conclusion—all focus on that point, and all are necessary for a thorough treatment of the topic. Furthermore, each individual paragraph within the essay is also unified.

> An essay is unified if each paragraph is unified and if all the paragraphs support and relate to the thesis statement and to each other.

Probably the most important factor in an essay's unity is the clarity of the thesis statement. If the thesis statement is carefully focused and clearly written, it indicates the scope of the essay and establishes the boundary line between relevant and irrelevant information. Similarly, the subtopics—whether stated or implied—should be logical outgrowths of the main point as presented in the thesis statement. If the subtopics clearly represent significant aspects of the main point and are clearly related to each other as well, the essay will most likely be unified. For example, the following thesis statement could have a number of relevant subtopics: *The United Nations is a highly structured organization, made up of several subordinate bodies, each of which has specific powers and duties.* Natural subtopics would be the activities of several or all of the United Nations' subordinate bodies: the Security Council, the General Assembly, UNESCO, and so on. However, the architecture of the United Nations' buildings or one particular Security Council debate would not make suitable subtopics and would not result in a unified essay because these ideas do not pertain to this particular thesis statement.

The introduction as a whole also helps to unify the essay by setting the tone for the essay. For an essay to be unified, it must maintain a consistent level of language and project a consistent attitude toward the subject and reader. If it begins with formal language and a scholarly tone and then shifts into more casual language and a conversational tone, it will sound confused and the essay will be disjointed.

Taken together, the introduction and conclusion also contribute to the essay's unity by establishing and then returning to the essay's main point. A conclusion can give the reader the sense that the essay is unified by echoing ideas or important words used in the introduction. By the end of the essay, such words mean a great deal more to the reader than they did in the introduction, since they have been discussed throughout the essay.

Coherence.   A coherent essay moves smoothly and logically from thought to thought.

An essay is coherent if the ideas within each paragraph and within the essay as a whole are presented in logical order and together form a smoothly connected pattern.

The coherence of an essay, like that of a paragraph, depends on two things: a clear, appropriate ordering of ideas and the use of various transitional devices to link ideas and sentences. A number of possible orders can be used to organize ideas within individual paragraphs and within the body as a whole: order of importance, chronological order, spatial order, comparison and contrast order, or developmental order. (For a detailed explanation of orders and coherence, see Section 22.1, page 616.) In addition, if subtopics are given in the thesis statement, they should be treated in the body of the essay in the same order.

The logical arrangement of ideas in an essay is determined by the topic, the thesis statement, and the supporting information. The following chart offers examples of possible orders for some sets of subtopics.

POSSIBLE ORDERS FOR SOME SUBTOPICS	
Subtopics	**Possible Order**
Three reasons for voting for Assemblywoman Barnett	Order of importance
Stages in refinishing old furniture	Chronological order
The various parts of the Parthenon	Spatial order
The principal differences between speed skates and figure skates	Comparison and contrast order
Four principal features of Jacobean drama	Developmental order

To be coherent, each paragraph in the body of an essay should either focus on a new subtopic or continue to develop the previous subtopic. In addition, the ideas within each paragraph should be logically arranged.

Besides being logically organized, a coherent essay flows smoothly from one thought to the next because its ideas are connected by transitions, repetitions of main words, synonyms, and pronouns. Transitions such as *for example, on the other hand, also,* and *for this reason,* among many others, indicate the relationship of one idea to another. They can be used to lead into a new subtopic or to tell the reader that a new paragraph is expanding the ideas in a preceding paragraph. The repetition of main words, synonyms, and pronouns can also help tie ideas together within paragraphs and relate ideas from one paragraph to the next. Occasionally, concluding sentences at the end of body paragraphs or parallelism within body paragraphs can also enhance the relatedness of ideas.

The following diagram schematically illustrates the interconnections between the paragraphs and parts of an essay, showing places where transitions and other devices can help establish the relationship of ideas.

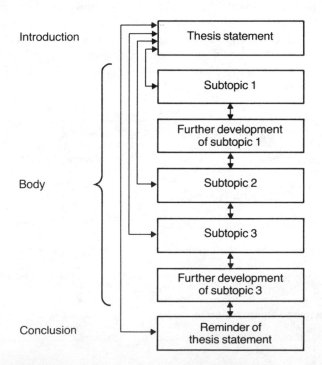

Essay Showing Unity and Coherence.   In the following essay on the structure of the United Nations, notice how the body paragraphs concentrate on the main point while discussing the different activities of the various arms and agencies. Notice also how the main words and synonyms for those words (which are circled), the transitions (which are in bold type), and the consistent pronouns, connect the parts of the essay. The essay moves in developmental order from the most prominent UN bodies to those that are less well-known, in order to emphasize the degree to which the United Nations is highly structured, as well as to illustrate the great range of its activities.

Title	The United Nations: A Sum of Many Parts
Introduction	The United Nations is an international organization formed after the Second World War to replace
Thesis statement	the League of Nations as a world peace-keeping body. Highly structured, the United Nations was organized by its Charter into six principal bodies each with specific powers and responsibilities: the General Assembly, the Security Council, and four other important but lesser-known bodies.
Subtopic 1: the General Assembly	The most widely publicized body of the United Nations is the General Assembly. It is the only body in the organization in which all member states are represented. The Assembly meets at least once annually, and its principal function is to provide a forum for the discussion of worldwide economic, political, and social issues. The General Assembly includes among its various responsibilities the admission of new member states to the United Nations and the approval of the organization's budget. It is also empowered to pass various advisory resolutions.
Subtopic 2: the Security Council	The Security Council is **also** mentioned often in world affairs. It has only eleven member states, five of them (the United States, China, France, Great Britain, and the U.S.S.R.) permanent and the others elected for two-year terms by the General Assembly. The Security Council is the United Nations body that is held primarily responsible for the maintenance of peace throughout the world. To accomplish this end, it can institute economic sanctions against particular countries, call for the formation of military peace-keeping forces, and even involve itself in a country's

domestic problems if they pose a potential threat to international peace.

Subtopic 3: lesser-known bodies

The lesser-known bodies of the United Nations are responsible for a variety of tasks from administrative matters to international judgments. The Secretariat, **for instance,** handles all of the administrative duties of the United Nations. This body is headed by the Secretary General, who serves a five-year term. **Another** body, the International Court of Justice, is located at The Hague in the Netherlands and serves as the United Nations' major judicial body. Composed of fifteen judges chosen by the General Assembly and Security Council, it attempts to resolve disputes between consenting member states. The United Nations Economic and Social Council, generally known as UNESCO, meets at least twice a year and is made up of eighteen nations elected for three-year terms by the General Assembly. It is primarily charged with investigating and reporting on major international economic and social questions. UNESCO **also** oversees the activities of several special United Nations agencies, such as the Population Commission and the Commission on Human Rights. **And finally,** the Trusteeship Council, perhaps the least familiar to the general public of all United Nations bodies, oversees territories that are not yet self-governing, in the hope that the inhabitants of these areas will peacefully and effectively achieve self-rule.

Conclusion with reminder of the thesis statement

Thus, the United Nations is a complex organization, comprised of a number of individual bodies, each of which has its own specified functions and areas of concern. The founders of the United Nations seemed to have realized that the task of handling world affairs would be a many-faceted responsibility that could be undertaken only by a highly structured institution.

EXERCISE B: Recognizing Unity and Coherence in an Essay.
Reread the student essay "In Defense of Mutiny" on page 685, this time studying it for unity and coherence. Then answer the following questions.

1. What is the single, clear point made in the thesis statement?
2. How are the subtopics related to the thesis statement?
3. How are the subtopics related to each other?
4. Is the tone of the essay consistent throughout? What words and phrases help to establish and maintain the tone?
5. How would you rate the general unity of this essay?
6. In what order are the subtopics arranged?
7. Is this order appropriate and effective? If so, why?
8. What words or phrases act as transitions in the essay?
9. What repeated main words and synonyms contribute to the coherence of the essay?
10. Examine one paragraph from the essay for coherence. How is the paragraph organized? What transitions, repeated main words, and synonyms unify the paragraph? Are pronouns clear and consistent throughout the paragraph?

APPLICATION: Analyzing an Essay. Look in anthologies of nonfiction, in magazines, or in special sections of newspapers for a unified, coherent essay. Use the questions in Exercises A and B to analyze the essay and evaluate its unity and coherence.

Planning, Writing, and Revising Essays 24.2

Because an essay is a sustained piece of communication, it requires more complex planning than a single paragraph does, although many of the thought processes are similar. A good essay is the result of several different steps of thinking and writing. This section will present some useful steps for finding an appropriate essay topic and formulating a thesis statement, for developing support for that thesis statement, for organizing the essay, and for drafting and polishing it. Knowing these steps will make it easier for you to do your best work whenever you write an essay.

■ Planning an Essay

Some of the most important steps in writing an essay are the first ones—the planning stages. You must find something you want to write about, explore that topic, and discover several possible approaches to it. As you isolate one of these, you will decide what you want to say about the topic, who your audience will be, and what your purpose in writing will be. You should take time to make these decisions so that you will be able to write more smoothly and easily later on.

Finding an Appropriate Essay Topic.   An appropriate essay topic is one that appeals to you, one that you know something about, and one that is manageable in an essay. Generally, the broader your topic is, the less depth your essay can have.

> Choose a topic appropriate to your interests and knowledge, and reduce it to a more specific topic that you can cover thoroughly in an essay.

A topic for an essay can come from an assignment, from your own ideas and interests, or from books and other materials you have read. If you can choose the topic, you should explore your interests. After brainstorming, you might jot down subjects that appeal to you. Your brainstorming should involve mentally reviewing things you have read, experiences you have had, and skills you have developed. When you have thought of some promising topics, break them down into more specific topics, if necessary. Brainstorming could produce a list of topics like the following.

BRAINSTORMING FOR AN ESSAY TOPIC

Nostalgia
—current fascination with earlier styles
—personal childhood memories
—why people like to reminisce

Flying
—how to fly an airplane
—free-falling
—early flying machines
—fear of flying—why?

Television
—breakdown of people's viewing habits
—still a "vast wasteland"?
—life without it

The orchestra
—best or favorite orchestras
—role of the conductor
—one orchestra's change over time

Choosing a college

Mysteries versus science fiction

Baseball
—still the American pastime?
—how different from fifty, seventy-five years ago?
—all-time, all-star dream team

Recent developments in solar energy

How to spend a day at the Grand Canyon

Notice that some of these topics, for example, *Choosing a college* and *How to spend a day at the Grand Canyon*, are already fairly specific, while others such as *Nostalgia, Baseball,* and *The orchestra* must be broken down further into more specific, manageable topics. After examining this list, you might decide that you would like to write about the *Role of the orchestra conductor.*

Focusing on Your Main Point, Audience, and Purpose. When you have found and narrowed a topic for your essay, you must decide on a specific idea about it that you want to demonstrate, explain, or defend. This step will help you narrow your topic even further and lead you toward a thesis statement. As you find a focus for your topic in this thesis statement, you should decide not only what you want to say, but who your audience is and what effect you want your essay to have on that audience.

Shape an essay topic into a thesis statement by determining your audience, purpose, and main point and by expressing this main point in a concise sentence.

Considering different audiences and purposes for your essay can help you generate different ideas *about* your topic. For example, an essay about the role of the orchestra conductor could be written for an audience of experts, who are familiar with the basics of orchestra conducting. Or the essay could be written for an audience of beginners, who know little about orchestras and conducting. Once you have decided on your audience, you might think further to determine your purpose and main point. You could ask yourself questions relevant to the topic, and each answer could supply you with a possible main point. If you were writing about orchestra conducting for an audience of beginners, you might ask questions like those in the following chart.

QUESTIONS LEADING TO POSSIBLE MAIN POINTS	
Question	**Main Point**
What are some of the responsibilities of the conductor?	—conductor unifies the tempo, controls the volume of various sections and performers, makes instrumental choices left unclear by the composer of a piece of music

What single idea do I most want my audience to remember?	—conductor should be more appreciated—is central in the art of performing symphonic music
Why is the conductor so important?	—conductor is sole coordinator and main interpreter of the entire orchestra

Each of these possible main points deals with the role of the conductor, but each suggests a different purpose and treatment. The first point defines several of the conductor's specific responsibilities; its principal purpose is to explain. The second and third points are both aimed at persuading the audience of the conductor's significance. The third point also spells out the major responsibilities of the conductor, while the second point focuses on the need to recognize the general importance of the conductor in the performance of music.

You could formulate your thesis statement by making one of these main points into a complete sentence, experimenting with different wordings and emphases. You should write several versions of a thesis statement in order to give yourself a few choices and to help you focus your point even further. The formation of your thesis statement can also contribute to the molding of the entire essay, since some potential thesis statements may contain topics that can help you organize the rest of the essay.

The following chart suggests several sample thesis statements that express the third of the main points.

POSSIBLE THESIS STATEMENTS

Main Point: Conductor is sole coordinator and main interpreter of the entire orchestra

1. The conductor of a symphony orchestra bears the ultimate responsibility for the performance of the orchestra as a whole and for the interpretation of the piece of music performed.
2. Vital to the orchestra, the conductor coordinates the various independent actions of the performers and interprets the work of each composer whose music is performed by the orchestra.
3. The two essential functions of the conductor of a symphony orchestra are to interpret the piece of music being performed and to turn that performance, made up of contributions of numerous artists, into a unified whole.

4. Any symphony conductor will tell you that conducting involves ensuring that the musicians are playing the same piece and playing it together.
5. The conductor guides the orchestra through rehearsals and the performance, shaping the sound that the audience hears.
6. Controlling the tempo and volume of the orchestra, choosing and discarding shadings offered by various musicians, the conductor is both captain and navigator of his ship, making his crew pull together and setting the course of their voyage.

These six versions of the third main point in the chart of questions are quite similar in meaning, and yet each phrases that meaning in a decidedly different way. The fourth and sixth versions are the most unusual, each suggesting a very definite tone: the fourth, casual and understated, and the sixth, formal, elaborate, and metaphoric. The first three versions are more similar to each other, although they differ in the emphasis they put on the uniqueness of the conductor's contribution. The third focuses particularly on defining the role of the conductor in terms of the two principal functions. The fifth statement, perhaps the most general, concentrates on the conductor's shaping of a piece from beginning to end, from rehearsal to performance. After considering the various shadings and strengths of each of these thesis statements, you might choose the second for its combination of specificity and forcefulness. It also contains two subtopics: the coordination of the orchestra and the interpretation of the work of music.

EXERCISE A: Selecting and Refining Topics for Essays. Choose one of the following general topics (or think of one of your own) and break it down into three or four more limited topics. Then circle the topic that you would like to use for an essay.

Old age	Cooking
A personality trait	Extracurricular activity
Painting or sculpture	Ancient history or customs
Sports	Television or radio
Childhood memories	Theater or film

EXERCISE B: Preparing a Thesis Statement. Using the topic you chose in Exercise A, follow these instructions.

1. Decide on your audience and describe it.
2. Write at least three questions about the topic to help you decide what you want to communicate to your audience.

Then answer each question to make a list of possible main points.

3. Decide which purpose each main point suggests. Then decide on the purpose you want your essay to have. Choose the main point you want to develop, and make sure that it suits your audience as well as your purpose.

4. Write at least three versions of your thesis statement based on this main point.

5. Choose the thesis statement you like best, the one that you find most interesting and usable.

■ Developing Support for a Thesis Statement

You are now ready to gather support for your thesis statement in another, more focused brainstorming session. The process of shaping your thesis statement will probably already have given you some ideas about supporting information. You should begin with these specific ideas and pieces of information and then examine your thesis statement and review your knowledge of your topic for more examples, details, facts, and reasons to support your main point.

Using your thesis statement as a guide, brainstorm for examples, details, facts, and reasons to develop, clarify, or defend your main point.

This step represents the principal exploration of your topic as focused by your thesis statement. You should generate as much information and as many ideas as you can so that, later on, you will be able to select only the strongest, clearest support.

One method you can use to develop supporting material is to free-associate by writing your thesis statement on a piece of paper and jotting down whatever related ideas occur to you. Another useful method involves asking yourself questions and thinking of answers that will help you find and remember specific, relevant supporting information. Asking yourself questions about your main point can lead you to examples, details, facts, and reasons that a reader will expect to find in the essay. You should write down all the information you have that is related to your thesis statement, knowing that later you can sift through it, evaluate it, and arrange it.

If you were to use the questioning method to find support for the thesis statement about the role of the orchestra conductor, you might write a list of questions and answers similar to the following.

BRAINSTORMING FOR SUPPORTING INFORMATION

Thesis Statement: **Vital to the orchestra, the conductor coordinates the various independent actions of all of the performers and interprets the work of each composer whose music is performed by the orchestra.**

How does the conductor coordinate the different performances?

—directs other musicians
—only figure visible to all musicians
—signals when to begin, end, begin again ("downbeat," "cut-off")
—sets time and rhythm for orchestra as a whole
—makes sure orchestra works as whole
—provides "sign language" for musicians to follow
—balances soloists with orchestra

—signals changes in volume
—signals changes in speed
—takes charge of rehearsals to polish performance
—cues entrances of different instruments
—selects, evaluates individual performances
—orchestra made up of many musicians—sometimes more than one hundred people
—only single focus for whole orchestra throughout the entire piece

How does the conductor act as the interpreter of music?

—critics identify orchestra with conductor
—composer can't indicate and fix every aspect of performance and score
—even terms composers use to suggest tempo and volume are open to interpretation—no absolutes
 – e.g., each must decide what "mezzoforte" means in a particular score
—decisions performing artist would make in solo performance become province of conductor when many

artists are involved
—can shape emphasis of certain passages: play up some, play down others
—"liberal" conductors have altered instrument choices of composers—have altered intended size of orchestra and number of instruments
 – Sir Thomas Beecham added trombones, cymbals, triangle to "Hallelujah Chorus"
—same piece can sound very different under different conductors

EXERCISE C: Brainstorming for Supporting Information. Use the thesis statement you wrote for Exercise B and follow these instructions.

1. Write two or more questions about your thesis statement that your audience would be likely to ask.
2. Answer each question with as much supporting information as you can think of: all the examples, details, reasons, incidents, and facts that come to mind.

■ Organizing Your Essay for Unity and Coherence

At this point you will have finished the groundwork for your essay. You will have everything you need in front of you to write it. Now you must begin the job of sorting, refining, and pulling the supporting information together. You must select the most effective method of organizing your supporting information, eliminate those pieces of support that are weak or extraneous, and replace weak support with strong support. As a final organizational step, you should make a blueprint or rough outline of the essay.

> Organize and sort supporting information according to logical subtopics of your thesis statement. Add more support if necessary, and develop a plan or rough outline to guide your writing.

Your ideas will be meaningful to a reader only if they are clearly organized; therefore, you should now examine the list of supporting ideas and information that you produced in the brainstorming stage. You must develop an overall plan for the body of the essay, based on subtopics, or natural divisions of your main point. Decide, first, how your pieces of supporting information can be grouped to form two or more subtopics. You may have already found subtopics in writing your thesis statement. For example, the thesis statement about the role of the orchestra conductor contains two stated subtopics—*the conductor's coordination of the work of the musicians* and *his or her interpretation of the piece of music to be performed*. If your thesis statement does not contain stated subtopics, the questions you asked when you brainstormed for supporting information may help you determine the subtopics for the body of your essay. You might also find that your supporting information itself can easily be divided into groups or might suggest natural categories, steps, outgrowths, or divisions of your main point.

Once you have decided on your subtopics, the subtopics and the supporting information under each can be organized according to one of a number of logical orders: order of importance, chronological order, spatial order, comparison and contrast order, or developmental order. (For more information on orders for coherence, see Section 22.1, page 616.) Subtopics should follow an overall order, and the information under each subtopic should also be logically arranged. You might want to organize your supporting information right on your original list.

In the essay on the role of the orchestra conductor, you might decide that the conductor's *artistic* contribution to the performance is most important, and, therefore, that the subtopic that concerns the conductor's role in interpreting a piece of music should be emphasized. In this case, you could arrange the subtopics by order of importance with the conductor's role as coordinator of musicians first and the conductor's role as primary interpreter for the orchestra last.

Having arranged your subtopics, you should examine each piece of information that will develop the subtopics. You should consider each piece of support to decide if and where it belongs in the essay, in order to weed out any information that might destroy the unity of the essay. As you read over your list, look for repetitious, unrelated, and vague ideas. Then replace them with stronger, more useful information related to your subtopics. You may even have to revise your thesis statement at this point so that it fits your subtopics and the supporting information that you have selected. You should also number or rewrite the information you have chosen to show the order you will follow under each subtopic.

At this stage, you may find it useful to make a rough outline or plan for the body of your essay that shows the organizing you have done. The form of outline you choose should depend on your teacher's preference and your own working style. You may use your revised list of support as a rough plan. You may prepare a modified outline with subtopics as headings and supporting information listed in logical order under each heading, or you may find that you can better judge the logic and development of your ideas by making a more formal topic outline.

For the essay on the role of the conductor, you might write a topic outline like the following. Notice that the subtopics follow an order of importance, the information under the first subtopic follows developmental order, and the information under the second subtopic builds from the most basic to the most extreme instances of the conductor's interpretation of a given piece of music.

Thesis Statement: Vital to the orchestra, the conductor coordinates the various independent actions of all of the performers and interprets the work of each composer whose music is performed by the orchestra.

I. Conductor as coordinator of musicians
  A. Keeps orchestra playing together
    1. Signals start with "downbeat"
    2. Signals end with "cutoff"
    3. Keeps time in between
  B. More specialized communications ("sign language")
    1. Indicates change in volume
    2. Indicates change in tempo
    3. Cues individual entrances
II. Conductor as interpreter of music
  A. Interprets score
    1. Decides for orchestra exact meaning of composer's directions
      a. For tempo
      b. For volume
    2. Decides relative emphasis given to parts of score
      a. Particular passages to be highlighted
      b. Linking or isolating movements of symphony
  B. Some instances of greater independence
    1. Altering choice of instruments
    2. Altering size of orchestra (example: Sir Thomas Beecham adding trombones, cymbals, triangle to "Hallelujah Chorus")

EXERCISE D: Ordering Supporting Information. Use the list of supporting ideas and information you developed in Exercise C to organize the body of your essay following these instructions.

1. Think about your thesis statement and the material you have developed to support it, and list two or more subtopics that emerge from your thesis statement and support.
2. Arrange these subtopics in the most logical, effective order.
3. Arrange information under each subtopic and evaluate each piece of support, eliminating the repetitious, insignificant, or extraneous pieces and including only those details, reasons, and examples that are relevant to your thesis statement and subtopics. Add support if necessary to fill in gaps.
4. Evaluate your thesis statement, and revise it if necessary to reflect your ordered and unified subtopics and support.
5. Finally, prepare a modified outline or topic outline for the body of your essay to show the organization you have chosen.

■ Writing the Essay

You are now ready to draft your essay, using your outline to produce a unified, coherent piece of writing. You should probably consider possible titles, sketch out ideas for the introduction, and think of ideas for the conclusion before you actually begin writing. As you draft the essay, transform the ideas in your outline into complete sentences by adding transitional words and phrases. Try to maintain a consistent tone and a continuous flow in your writing from sentence to sentence and from paragraph to paragraph.

Rough out ideas for your introduction and consider jotting down a few ideas for your title and conclusion before starting to draft. Then write a complete, coherent version of the essay.

Because the introduction comes first in the essay, you should plan it before you actually begin to write, if you have not done so earlier. You should experiment with ideas for your introduction and think about ways to involve the reader. You might find ideas on your list of support that could introduce your topic and that are not being used in the body. As you plan and write the introduction, think about catching the reader's attention, establishing an appropriate tone, and leading smoothly into your thesis statement.

Although you can think about a title and a conclusion at any time during the writing step, planning ideas at this point can be helpful. Considering different titles can help you choose a style for your essay. You should look for a short, direct title that will interest the reader and suggest the main point of the essay. Also, having a few ideas reserved for your conclusion might motivate you throughout the writing of the essay.

The actual writing of your essay should go quickly and smoothly if you write from your outline and think about presenting your ideas in a logical sequence. You should try to give the reader a firm sense of the order of ideas within each paragraph and from paragraph to paragraph. You should also think about connecting ideas with transitions, repetitions of main words, synonyms, clear pronouns, and possibly an occasional concluding sentence or use of parallelism to emphasize ideas. In addition, you should try to find the most exact, vivid words and the most interesting, varied sentences to express your ideas. If new ideas that sharpen your main point and further your purpose occur to you when you are writing, include them in your essay.

EXERCISE E: Planning an Introduction, Title, and Conclusion. Using your outline and original list of supporting information, sketch out a few ideas for an introduction—particularly approaches that will draw your reader into your topic. Experiment with two or three possible titles for your essay, and list two or three ideas for your conclusion. Draft an introduction that ends with your thesis statement.

EXERCISE F: Completing a First Draft. Using your introduction as your starting point and your outline as your guide, draft your essay. Write in complete sentences, using transitions to connect and clarify ideas. Try to achieve a lively, interesting style and a consistent tone.

■ Revising the Essay

The final step in writing an essay—revision—gives you the opportunity to correct and polish what you have written. You should look for ways to improve your overall presentation of ideas, as well as your language and style.

Checking Content and Organization.   Before you write the final copy of your essay, you should always check your first draft to make any necessary improvements in the presentation of ideas.

> Check your essay to make any necessary improvements in content and organization before you write your finished copy.

In rereading your essay, you should check particularly for unity and coherence. Reconsider each idea, even the minor details, to make sure that each is helpful and relevant. Also look closely at the arrangement of the ideas to see if you can improve the order or if that order needs to be reinforced with more transitions.

Checking Language and Style.   Two effective methods you can use to improve and refine the language and style of your essay are (1) to examine it as if you were a reader seeing it for the first time or (2) to read the essay silently and then aloud. While using either method, you should pay particular attention both to the tone you establish through your word choices and to your sentence structures. Your words should sound as if they belong together, and the length and structure of your sentences should vary.

Check your draft for consistency of tone, suitable words, and variety of sentence lengths and structures.

As you read through your essay, you should decide if all your words project your intended tone. Are some more formal than they should be? Are some too casual? You might even read the essay aloud to someone else for an objective opinion. However you perform this evaluating step, you should remember your purpose and intended audience as you check your word choices for an overall unified tone.

Your sentences, also, should receive some attention at this point. You should reread your essay, this time listening to the sound of a series of sentences. You should listen especially for choppy sentences, monotonous sentences, and tangled sentences. You may want both to change a few sentences to achieve a smoother, more fluid and appealing style and to vary your sentence openers.

Using a Checklist to Review the Final Product.   A checklist can be used throughout the revising step to isolate problems in your essay. Use a checklist also to review the final product. The following checklist should help you review your entire essay before you recopy it.

CHECKLIST FOR REVISION OF YOUR ESSAY

1. Is the title appropriate for the style and content of the essay? Does it attract the reader's attention and suggest the main point of the essay?
2. Does the introduction lead up to the thesis statement by providing necessary background information and establishing your purpose? Does it capture the reader's interest?
3. Does the thesis statement clearly present one main point, with or without stated subtopics?
4. Do the body paragraphs develop significant subtopics of the thesis statement? Does each body paragraph contain a topic sentence?
5. Does each body paragraph contain enough supporting examples, details, facts, reasons, or incidents?
6. Are the subtopics arranged in logical order: order of importance, chronological order, spatial order, comparison and contrast order, or developmental order?

7. Are the ideas under each subtopic arranged in a logical order? Are ideas clearly linked by transitional devices?

8. Does the conclusion remind readers of the main point without being repetitious? Does it bring the essay to a satisfying end?

9. Do the word choices convey the tone you intend? Are your words and the tone consistent throughout the essay?

10. Are the sentences varied in their length and structure?

11. Are there any errors in grammar, usage, punctuation, or spelling? If you are uncertain about any of these areas, check a reliable source, such as a dictionary or the earlier units of this book.

If you were to complete the essay on the role of the orchestra conductor, it would probably resemble the following finished essay. The marginal comments point out the essay's structure, and some of the transitions have been italicized. Notice the repetition of main words and synonyms throughout the essay to guide the reader: *responsible, coordinating, performing, performance, concert, signals, communicates,* and *interpret.*

Title	The Mastermind of the Orchestra
Introduction	Some people believe that a symphony conductor serves no significant purpose but simply stands upon a podium, madly waving a baton, while the orchestra does the real and important work. This opinion is not valid. Vital to the orchestra, the conductor coordinates the various independent actions of all of the performers and determines the interpretation of each work that it performs.
Thesis statement with two subtopics	
Topic sentence	*Fundamentally,* a conductor is a director, responsible for coordinating the activities of often more than one hundred musicians, not only during a concert *but* also at the many rehearsals that usually precede a performance. The conductor is the only figure visible to the entire orchestra. Standing in a prominent place, the conductor provides a single focus for all the musicians. The conductor indicates the start of a piece with a "downbeat," ends it with a "cutoff," and acts as a timekeeper in between, indicating the beat for the orchestra. Through "sign language," a conductor *also* communicates to the players changes in dynamics (volume) and tempo (speed), and he or she often signals musicians when to begin playing by providing them with special "cues," such as nodding the head or pointing the baton. Thus, the conductor
Subtopic 1: coordinating many individual performances	

makes the orchestra work together as one; without the conductor, confusion and discord might reign.

Topic sentence

Second, and *artistically most important*, a symphony orchestra conductor must interpret each written piece, or "score," of music. Since it would be impossible for a composer to indicate on paper exactly how fast or loud a piece should be played, directions such as "mezzo-forte" (Italian for "medium-loud") and "lento" ("slowly") are provided, and the interpretation is left up to the individual conductor. The conductor may feel that a certain woodwind passage, *for instance*, should be emphasized, or that the third movement of a symphony should lead directly into the fourth without the traditional pause.

Subtopic 2A: interpreting the piece for the orchestra

Topic sentence

Sometimes conductors have taken *even greater responsibility* for the presentation of a piece of music. Some "liberal" conductors have altered a composer's choice of instruments or have changed the originally intended size of the orchestra. *For instance*, Sir Thomas Beecham, the British conductor, added trombones, cymbals, and even a triangle to the instruments that Handel's "Hallelujah Chorus" traditionally requires. Although many conductors do not go this far, all are required to interpret the musical score, a responsibility that determines the overall impression created by the orchestra.

Subtopic 2B: interpreting the piece— more creative interpretations

Conclusion with reminder of main point

A conductor's job is complex, and his or her contributions to music, many. After all, coordinating many different performers to produce one interpretation of music is a demanding responsibility and is of primary importance to the orchestra. In a sense, the conductor is the orchestra's brain, its mastermind.

Clincher

EXERCISE G: Checking and Revising Your Essay. Check for content, organization, language, and style. Then use the checklist on page 705 for a final review. Make any necessary alterations and corrections on your first draft. When you are satisfied, write a final copy of the essay, proofread it carefully, and submit it to your teacher.

APPLICATION: Planning, Writing, and Revising an Essay. Choose another topic for an essay from the following list or think of a topic of your own. Follow the steps for thinking, brainstorming, organizing, writing, and revising discussed in this section to prepare a second essay. When you reach the revising step, exchange essays with another student in the class. Use the checklist on page 705 to evaluate the other person's essay. Write your answers to each question about the essay on a separate piece of paper and then add any other suggestions for improvement. Return essays and revise your own, using the helpful comments you have received. Then recopy the essay in final form.

Machinery (inventions, computers, and so on)	Art
	The law (crime, punishment, courts)
Animal behavior	
Money	Customs of the United States
Food(s)	
Families (relatives, family life, and so on)	Politics
	Clothing

24.3 Writing Essays with Different Purposes

When you write an essay, you always write to accomplish some purpose. You may write to increase your reader's understanding by transmitting information, to change your reader's point of view about something, to communicate facts, or to communicate opinions or feelings. Sometimes you may even tell a personal experience in detail, action by action, to illustrate a general truth. In any case, you should always have some objective in mind, which will affect both the form and the content of your essay.

This section will focus on expository and persuasive essays, the two kinds of essays that will probably represent the major portion of your writing, both in and out of school. Expository writing is meant to inform the reader of something; persuasive writing is intended to influence the reader's opinion. In this section, you will learn to recognize the basic features of each kind of essay, and you will practice applying the writing steps you have already learned to the particular purposes of expository and persuasive essays.

■ Writing Expository Essays

Whenever you write an essay to report information, to explain how something works, to define some term or concept, or to give instructions, you are writing an *expository* essay. This kind of essay is usually objective and straightforward, containing concrete factual information. The next few pages will help you become familiar with the special features of the expository essay.

An Explanatory Purpose and an Informative Tone. As you may have learned already from studying the section on expository paragraphs in Section 23.1, the special features that distinguish expository writing are an explanatory purpose and an informative tone. Above all, expository writing is intended to communicate information, to expand the reader's store of knowledge. It is *not* meant to express an opinion, or to change the reader's mind about something.

> Expository essays explain a concept, event, or process. They present factual, objective material and have an instructional, informative tone.

An expository essay should follow the three-part structure of any standard essay, but its thesis statement should be distinctively explanatory. It should present a factual statement, which the body of the essay will clarify, elaborate on, and explain with objective, observable evidence. As you read the following statements, notice the difference between a statement of fact and a statement of opinion. A fact can be observed or verified in a public record. An opinion, on the other hand, represents one person's viewpoint and is open to disagreement.

STATEMENT OF FACT: The percentage of eligible voters who cast ballots in the 1976 presidential election was lower than ever before.

STATEMENT OF OPINION: In recent elections, the apathy of the American voter has reached alarming proportions.

The following chart presents three thesis statements appropriate for an expository essay. Notice that each one expresses a main point that is factual and that can be developed with objective information. The last one also includes stated subtopics.

SAMPLE THESIS STATEMENTS FOR EXPOSITORY ESSAYS		
Thesis Statements	**Purpose**	**Stated Subtopics**
According to biologists, crocodiles are better equipped for survival than alligators.	To report	None

Plants obtain their nourishment from the sun through a remarkable process known as photosynthesis.	To explain	None
The popular notion of freedom includes both the absence of restraints and the quality of autonomy.	To define	(1) Absence of restraints (2) Autonomy

Supporting information in an expository essay should serve the explanatory purpose by providing enough specific examples and details to give the reader the understanding promised by the thesis statement. Such information can be drawn from your own experience, from your reading, and from the statements of experts. This material should be logically organized under subtopics that will develop the most important aspects of the main point.

The tone of an expository essay should be informative; that is, it should convey the sense that the writer is presenting new knowledge to the reader. The presentation of information and choice of language should take the reader's level of knowledge or experience into account. Just as opinions are out of place in an expository essay, so are careless choices of words. You should try to project objective, unemotional attitudes toward the subject and reader through carefully chosen words and the presentation of verifiable factual information. For example, in the preceding thesis statement about crocodiles and alligators, the phrase "According to biologists" establishes an informative, objective tone. Some of the expository essays you will write may be formal and serious, while others may be conversational and light, but all should maintain this informative tone.

Pointers for Writing Expository Essays.   When you write an expository essay, you should follow the planning, brainstorming, organizing, drafting, and revising steps that are useful in preparing any essay. You should give special attention, however, to your particular purpose, audience, and tone.

Focus on your explanatory purpose, particular audience, and informative tone as you prepare an expository essay.

Your explanatory purpose should guide you as you choose and focus a topic. Consider topics you know well and ones that lend themselves to objective, factual presentations. Decide whether you will report, explain, instruct, or define.

When you narrow your topic to a main point, you should make sure that your thesis statement expresses a fact and not an opinion. If you have said something that needs to be defended, rather than explained, then you have expressed an opinion and will need to rethink your main point. Your thesis statement should make your specific expository purpose clear. For example, notice how the following thesis statement suggests that the essay will explain the stages of a process: *Plants obtain their nourishment from the sun in a remarkable process known as photosynthesis.*

Having a clear idea of your purpose and intended audience will help you brainstorm for supporting information. If you are writing for a less experienced or less knowledgeable reader, you will have to provide helpful background information and explanations. On the other hand, if you have a more knowledgeable reader, you can explore your subject in greater depth.

The purpose indicated in your thesis statement will also aid you in organizing your supporting information. For example, an essay developing the thesis statement about the survival of alligators and crocodiles could present its information in a comparison and contrast order, and an essay explaining the process of photosynthesis could follow a chronological order.

As you write your essay, think about explaining your topic to the members of your audience, almost as if you were talking to them. Try to draw the reader into the topic by making the introduction interesting and informative. In the body of the essay, move logically through the steps of a process or the supporting ideas for a concept by providing all of the information the reader will need. By using transitional devices, you can unify the essay and enable the reader to follow your explanation.

When you have completed your first draft, revise your essay for clarity and consistency of tone, using the checklist for revision given in Section 24.2, page 705.

EXERCISE A: Recognizing the Features of Expository Essays. Read the following expository essay, written by a student, and then answer the questions that follow it.

The Superior Crocodile

The alligator and the crocodile are two animals that are commonly confused with each other. The sole survivors of the great group of reptiles, Archosauria, which included the dinosaurs, these animal families are unique in our time. Certainly, alliga-

tors and crocodiles look alike. And even though these two animals do not share the same biological family, few observers
could note any obvious differences in their mannerisms. Yet
their differences, however subtle, play a large role in the survival of these animals. Although alligators and crocodiles resemble one another in most aspects, such as basic appearance and
habits, biologists note the superior ability of the crocodile to
survive.

Right from birth, crocodiles are better equipped to face
threats from the environment. Both alligators and crocodiles are
hatched from eggs and guarded by their mothers. But crocodile
eggs number ten to sixty more per nest and incubate for a period of one to two months longer than alligator eggs. Because
they spend more time in the egg, crocodiles are four inches
longer than alligators at birth. The baby crocodiles stay close to
their mother for the first few days of life, whereas baby alligators, by instinct, do not. As a result, baby crocodiles are less vulnerable to predators than baby alligators are, and the greater
number of eggs ensures that more crocodiles will survive.

Their different habits also favor crocodiles. Native to
warmer parts of Africa, Asia, Australia, and some island groups,
crocodiles are better adapted to adverse living conditions than
alligators are. Crocodiles will walk some distance in search of
water, if necessary, whereas alligators never stray from the
banks of their rivers. Crocodiles can also be found in brackish
water, which alligators find unacceptable, and will swim out to
sea, while alligators almost never leave their river basins. In
their natural habitat, crocodiles form colonies to protect themselves against predators. Alligators, on the other hand, go their
own separate ways and are therefore more vulnerable. Both species are cannibalistic, but when basking in sunlight, crocodiles
divide into groups of equal-sized animals, and smaller crocodiles thus are kept well away from larger ones. Alligators are
cannibalistic to an even greater degree than crocodiles, yet they
do not form any collective defenses. As a result, large alligators
prey easily on the young. In the past, this natural predatory instinct has helped to keep the alligator population under control,
but, as environmental dangers increase, the alligator population
may shrink to dangerous levels, and perhaps even approach
extinction.

Even the destructive habits of humans have favored crocodiles. In recent times our species has become virtually an enemy
of the alligator. The search for alligator skin for shoes and hand-
bags has caused a drastic decrease in the population, as well as
in the overall size of the animals. Land drainage by American
developers has also affected the alligator population in this
country, while in China, alligators have fallen prey to other
forms of commercial exploitation.

Therefore, experts predict that crocodiles will most likely
continue as a species whereas alligators may not. Although alligators and crocodiles are amazingly similar, the small differences between them can ultimately prove quite significant.

These variations have favored the crocodile by enhancing its chances for survival. In a few centuries, people may no longer mistake alligators for crocodiles. By then, the alligator might not be around to confuse the issue. —Aari Ludvigsen

1. What does the title contribute to the essay?
2. How does the introduction prepare the reader for an expository essay?
3. What is the thesis statement?
4. What are the subtopics developed in the body?
5. In what order are these subtopics arranged? Can you think of any alternative order(s)?
6. What are three specific pieces of supporting information presented in the body paragraphs?
7. What are five instances in which transitions, repetitions of main words, or synonyms help to tie the ideas in the essay together?
8. How is the concluding paragraph related to the thesis statement? What words and ideas link the introduction and conclusion?
9. How does the last sentence help to "clinch" the ideas of the essay?
10. To what extent does the essay fulfill its explanatory purpose? What words contribute to the informative tone of the essay?

EXERCISE B: Planning, Writing, and Revising an Expository Essay. Choose any of the following topics for an expository essay. Narrow your topic to a main point and decide on your purpose and audience. Gather supporting information and then organize your essay. Write a complete version of your essay and think of a suitable title. When you revise, check especially for strong transitions, unified supporting information that thoroughly explains your main point, and an objective, informative tone that conveys your purpose to share information with the reader.

Some little known historical event

Home remedies for ailments

The concept of "Manifest Destiny"

Hypochondria

Unusual ways you can learn a foreign language

How to prepare an exotic food

The workings of the telephone

Sibling rivalry

Symptoms of a particular illness

What happens during lunar and solar eclipses

■ Writing Persuasive Essays

Some of your most vigorous and enjoyable writing may be persuasive. A persuasive essay seeks to win readers over to your way of thinking on some social, political, or intellectual issue.

Persuasive writing is usually very forceful and subjective, but it also contains reasoning and factual information to defend opinions. The following pages highlight the special features of persuasion to help you write effective persuasive essays.

A Persuasive Purpose and a Reasonable Tone.   The persuasive essay is distinguished from other kinds of essays by its special persuasive purpose and tone. Unlike other essays, the persuasive essay enlists every word to influence the audience. It may seek to make readers see something in a different way, or it may try to persuade them to do something. But whatever the specific goal of the writer, the persuasive essay attempts to convince the reader to accept an opinion. While the tone of the essay may vary according to the topic and the urgency of the writer's feelings, it should always be reasonable and compelling.

> Persuasive essays attempt to convince the audience to accept the writer's opinion by presenting reasons and facts reasonably and forcefully.

The thesis statement of a persuasive essay should reveal the persuasive purpose and reasonable tone. It should state the opinion that the entire essay seeks to defend. Whereas an expository essay is based on a factual statement, a persuasive essay is based on a controversial statement. Notice the difference in these two kinds of statements in the following examples. The first statement is debatable and indicates that the writer has formed an opinion after considering evidence. The second statement simply makes an observation with which no one could argue. Consequently, it is not suitable as a main point of a persuasive essay.

CONTROVERSIAL STATEMENT: UFO sightings and other reports point overwhelmingly to the fact that life exists beyond our planet.

FACTUAL STATEMENT: Some scientists believe that life exists beyond our planet.

The following chart presents several thesis statements that would be appropriate for persuasive essays. Each one expresses an opinion that can be defended. The last thesis statement includes stated subtopics.

SAMPLE THESIS STATEMENTS FOR PERSUASIVE ESSAYS	
Thesis Statements	**Stated Subtopics**
The film *Bringing Up Baby* is the best example of the popular and delightfully peculiar comedies of the 1930's.	None
City dwellers concerned about their health should consider installing a home water purifying system.	None
Because of Senator Hugh Morris's great experience, his record in Congress, and his concern for individuals in his state, voters will serve themselves and their fellow citizens best by electing Hugh Morris to a third term in the Senate.	(1) Experience (2) Congressional record (3) Concern for individuals

Supporting information in a persuasive essay should serve the persuasive purpose by providing convincing evidence for the opinion in the thesis statement. The evidence can take the form of logical reasons or examples, facts, and details. Under no circumstances, however, should support in a persuasive essay consist only of unsubstantiated opinions. Instead, support should be solid, authoritative, rational, and believable and should appeal even to the reader who does not care about the question or who actively disagrees with you.

In its introduction and conclusion as well as in its thesis statement and body, a persuasive essay should have a persuasive but reasonable tone. You should try to be forceful but respectful of opposing viewpoints. Through your choice of language and supporting information, you should show the reader that you are well informed and that you have considered different sides of the issue. You should always avoid emotional language and name-calling that might antagonize the reader.

Within these broad guidelines, the tone of persuasive essays may vary widely. You might want to use a lighthearted or humorous approach to your subject, or you might feel that your ideas require serious attention. You might be writing in defense of an unpopular idea and therefore might anticipate strong opposition; on the other hand, you might simply be interested in expressing an original interpretation of a subject, which your audience might never have considered. In each case, you should adjust the tone to suit the audience and the intensity of your persuasive purpose.

Pointers for Writing Persuasive Essays.   Throughout the planning, brainstorming, organizing, writing, and revising of a persuasive essay, you should never lose sight of your goal to persuade the reader. During the process of writing a persuasive essay, you should always have a strong awareness of your audience.

> When writing a persuasive essay, anticipate your audience's thoughts and focus on convincing that audience with reason and evidence.

You should begin planning a persuasive essay by choosing a topic you are interested in, know a great deal about, and have opinions about. You should then focus the topic by deciding exactly what you think about it and what you want your readers to think by the time they have finished reading the essay. Determining a specific, supportable opinion will help you write the essay. For example, trying to persuade a reader that Senator X is the finest person in the Senate is not a very useful goal because the opinion is too general. On the other hand, trying to persuade a reader that Senator X is the most experienced candidate with the most impressive record *is* a manageable topic and a suitable opinion because it can be supported factually and argued intelligently. You should choose an opinion that you can defend amply and convincingly. When you write the opinion as a thesis statement, you should state it clearly and directly for your audience.

The support you develop for your thesis statement should suit the intensity of your purpose and your audience. For instance, different kinds and amounts of support are needed to awaken a reader's interest, to win a reader's consideration of an unusual idea, to change a reader's opinion, or to spur a reader to action. Similarly, in choosing supporting information, you should take into account whether the audience is likely to be sympathetic, apathetic, or strongly opposed. Whatever your particular aim and whoever your intended audience, you should gather many specific reasons, examples, details, and facts from your own experiences and your research.

When you are writing on highly controversial topics, one very effective way of developing supporting information is to list the principal arguments for your side, then to marshal the strongest arguments you can find *against* your viewpoint, and then answer those opposing arguments with other counter-arguments for your side. Such a list might even help you organize your essay by revealing which of your own arguments is strongest and which of your opponents' points will be the most difficult to answer. The following chart suggests how you might build an argument persuading readers to vote for a particular candidate.

BUILDING STRONG ARGUMENTS FOR A PERSUASIVE ESSAY		
Thesis Statement:	**Senator Hugh Morris, the best candidate in the race, should be elected to a third term in the U.S. Senate.**	
Evidence For	**Evidence Against**	**Counter-Arguments For**
—Senator Morris has more experience in government than any of his opponents	—it's time we had a new face in the Senate	—novelty and inexperience are not qualifications for high office; why waste years of experience?
—Senator Morris has consistently voted for projects that have benefited the citizens of this state	—Senator Morris is a big spender who has shown little fiscal responsibility in twelve years	—Senator Morris has not voted indiscriminately for government spending—he has voted against projects that were not worthwhile
—Senator Morris has, in his record and statements, demonstrated concern for the poor and disadvantaged	—are the poor always benefited by handouts and more government bureaucracy?	—Senator Morris has supported several self-help programs and has often voted to curb bureaucracy

You might use a list like this to help you organize your essay around the arguments of your opposition. This approach can be particularly effective if you are trying to convince your reader to endorse a controversial point. Also, you can often improve your defense if you answer opposing arguments and acknowledge the validity of some of these arguments. This practice is known as *conceding a point*. It suggests that you are informed and fair-minded enough to recognize that the opposition has *some* right on its side. If you do concede a point, however, you should always end with your own arguments and present your own evidence forcefully to show that it is stronger than the opposite view.

In general, you will probably find order of importance most useful in organizing persuasive writing. Such an organization places your best argument last in a strategic position where it will clinch your defense. A variation of this approach would be to begin with the most obvious and predictable arguments for your side and build to the least obvious ones. This strategy takes advantage of the potentially powerful impact of the unexpected on your reader.

When writing your essay, you should begin by trying to capture the reader's interest rather than antagonizing the reader. You should then lead gradually toward the thesis statement. You should also try to maintain a reasonable and consistent tone in the body of the essay, avoiding emotional language or loaded words. Imagine that you are speaking directly to the reader and that you have to hold the reader's attention. Transitional devices should underscore the logic of your ideas and guide the reader from argument to argument. In the conclusion, you should rephrase your main point and end confidently. Finally, you should give your essay an appealing, fitting title.

When you revise, you can touch up your essay to make it even more persuasive. You should use a checklist similar to the one on page 705. As you read over your essay, try to examine your supporting evidence objectively. Will a reader find the essay interesting and convincing? Are your arguments and ideas sound? Make sure that your word choices suit your audience's level of knowledge and that everything you say is directed towards winning understanding and agreement from the audience.

EXERCISE C: Recognizing the Features of Persuasive Essays. Read the following persuasive essay on the topic of the decline of motion pictures, and then answer the questions that follow it.

Where Have All the Great Films Gone?

Movie buffs single out different periods as the "Golden Age of Films." For some, Hollywood has never equaled the great movies of the silent era. Others prefer the brilliant escapist comedies and romances of the 1930's, while still others favor the exciting adventure films of the 1940's. But few people pick a period in the last thirty years—and for good reason. Clearly, both the quantity and the quality of movies have declined since the late 1940's because of the escalation in the costs of film production and because of the breakdown of the studio distribution system.

There can be no doubt about the decline in the quantity and quality of the films produced by Hollywood. This statement does *not* deny that some excellent films are produced each year— films such as the two *Godfathers, Nashville, Annie Hall*—which might rival anything from a so-called "Golden Age." But the problem is that far fewer movies are released every year. A studio might make only a fifth—or a tenth—of the number of films it would have produced thirty years ago. For that reason alone, the chances for the production of a large number of excellent films are understandably small.

But why are so few films being produced? Certainly inflation has driven up production costs, so that fewer movies are being made for more money. But inflation has hit all businesses without lowering production levels so drastically. And in the case of movies, ticket prices have risen with production costs, since there is no such thing as price competition among first-run movie theaters. Highly popular films—such as *Jaws* and *Star Wars*—have made more money than movie producers could have dreamed was possible thirty years ago.

But, despite the obvious success of a few "blockbusters" and another few "sleepers" (like *Animal House* or *Breaking Away*), most producers are faced with staggering risks when they undertake a film project. The source of this risk is more complicated than inflation alone. The movie studios no longer control the distribution of their films. As the result of a Supreme Court decision, they no longer own chains of movie theaters and can no longer guarantee a certain number of rentals and showings for a particular movie. Consequently, any given film can easily, as the jargon goes, "sink into the market without a trace."

Thus, producers—who are naturally more concerned, as they have always been, with making money than with making art— are fearful of investing in any project that does not promise to be financially worthwhile. More than ever, the successful films are turned into formulas and are copied until the public becomes tired of the model. While the number of releases has sharply declined, the proportion of copies has inevitably risen. The result is a pattern that does little to raise the general quality of the films coming out of Hollywood.

One might point out that the decline of the studios has freed the independent artist from the tyranny of the movie moguls—

that movies are not being mechanically churned out by the studio factory system nowadays, but rather are being made only by people who believe in them. But the independent filmmaker, like everyone else in the business, is faced with monumental difficulties in raising money for a project. Unless certain guarantees are offered—a successful director, a popular star—the independent producer's project can be frozen forever by the timidity of financial backers, just as, forty years ago, it might never have come to the attention of one of the big studios.

This decline in good films is especially unfortunate, given the great expansion of interest in and knowledge about films among Americans in the postwar period. Probably now more people than ever before want to make movies and have the background and the familiarity with film techniques to make them well. But such talent and skill seldom find their way into the first-run theater or the neighborhood shopping center, where patrons are more often than not faced with the choice of being either bored or insulted. And yet people keep on going to the movies, and filmmakers keep on making fewer movies. And so more and more people are seeing fewer and fewer—and worse and worse—films each year.

1. How is the title appropriate or inappropriate?
2. How does the introduction prepare the reader for a persuasive essay?
3. What is the thesis statement? What are the subtopics?
4. What major arguments are offered in favor of the thesis statement?
5. In what order are the body paragraphs organized? What alternative order could have been used?
6. Where does the writer mention opposing arguments? Which points, if any, are conceded?
7. What additional arguments for *or* against the main point can you think of?
8. What transitions, repetitions of main words, and synonyms are used to tie ideas together?
9. What words help to establish a reasonable, persuasive tone? Do you as a reader feel sympathetic or antagonistic towards the writer? Why, or why not?
10. How does the final paragraph help to "clinch" the writer's argument?

EXERCISE D: Planning, Writing, and Revising a Persuasive Essay. Choose one of the following topics, or think of one of your own, and write a persuasive essay, following the planning, writing, and revising steps you have learned. Keep in mind your persuasive purpose as your write, and try to maintain a reasonable, persuasive tone that will appeal to your audience.

The relative worth of a particular book
The superiority of one magazine to another in the same
    category
The worth (or the lack thereof) of environmental regulation
The most interesting spectator sport
The wisdom of stricter laws for owning pets in cities
The school regulation that everyone would be better off
    without
The historical figure whom you would most like to see alive
    today
The worst (or best) program on television
The most useful (or least useful) course you have had so far
Decreasing dependency on nuclear power

APPLICATION: Focusing on a Purpose in Writing an Essay. The
following ten topics could suit either an expository or a persuasive essay, depending on the perspective you choose.
Choose a topic and decide on your purpose. Then write the appropriate essay, keeping in mind the features that have been
discussed in this section. Have someone in your class evaluate
your rough draft and comment, in two to three sentences, on
its effectiveness in achieving its purpose. Then revise your essay using any insightful comments you have received and recopy it in final form.

The earliest photographs
Different kinds of sharks
TV violence—How much is
    too much?
A book or film review
African cultures
American and foreign
    products
Revising the school
    curriculum
Current status symbols
Concerns of students in the
    1980's
How to grow something

25

Library Papers

If you are able to write good paragraphs and essays, you should find writing library papers relatively easy. Many of the characteristics of library papers, such as structure and style, resemble those of essays, and many of the planning and writing steps are the same. The major difference is the research which must accompany the planning and be reflected in the content of the library paper.

This chapter will first examine the important features of a library paper. It will explain the documentation of research—that is, the footnotes that show where you have obtained direct quotations and special ideas and the bibliography that lists all the sources you consulted in planning and writing the paper. The second section will examine a number of steps that can be used in planning, writing, and revising a library paper. The major objective of the chapter is to help you write successful library papers.

25.1 Special Characteristics of Library Papers

Many of the features of essays are also found in library papers. In particular, they have very similar structures. A library paper differs from an essay, however, in that it will always show your familiarity with the ideas of other writers. Often, it will include specific facts and interesting, relevant quotations that you have gathered from your research in books, magazine articles, and other works about the paper's topic. As you will see, this basic difference will affect all parts of a library paper.

■ The Use and Citation of Sources

In writing a library paper you will have any one of a number of purposes in mind: to explain, to report, to define, to instruct, or perhaps to persuade others to agree with you or to take some specific action. If you are familiar with the purposes of essays, you will recognize that the purposes of a library paper are similar. What differentiates the purposes of the library paper from the purposes of an essay, however, is that you will have to do research to write your library paper. You will back up your own ideas, explanations, or arguments with the words and ideas of experts in different fields. Your choice and use of material can thus help fulfill your basic purpose. At the same time, your research will serve an additional purpose of the library paper: the condensation of the ideas of many different people into one short paper.

To carry out this secondary purpose, you must know something about the documentation and correct use of sources, as well as the preparation of a bibliography.

Documentation of Sources.   A library paper will contain ideas and often quotations taken from books, magazines, or newspapers. Two different methods can be used to document, or give credit to, these sources within the paper.

> To document information taken from research sources, a library paper must contain either informal citations given in parentheses within the text of the paper or footnotes written at the bottom of the pages of the paper or at the end of the paper.

The simplest way to document a piece of information you have used in your paper is through an *informal citation,* which includes the author's name, the title of the book or article, the magazine and date for an article, and the number of the page on which the information can be found. These citations are enclosed in parentheses and placed in the text immediately after the information to which they refer.

In the following passage, you can see how two quotes from the same book have used in a report about *Romeo and Juliet.* Notice the informal citation that follows the first quote; it contains the full name of the author, the title of the book, and the page number. Notice, also, that when the same work is quoted again, the citation is abbreviated. Only the last name of the author, the title of the book, and the page number are given.

Passage with
informal
citations

William Shakespeare probably based the story of Romeo and Juliet on more than imagination; he is likely to have been inspired by myths and other ancient tales that were popular in his day. One such ancient tale is the story of Pyramus and Thisbe, lovers noted for their beauty and youth: "he the most beautiful youth and she the loveliest maiden of all the East" (Edith Hamilton, *Mythology*, p. 100). In the version of the story told by Ovid, a Roman poet, the two lovers were at first kept apart by a feud between their families. In a series of events similar to those in *Romeo and Juliet*, these two lovers "longed to marry, but their parents forbade them. Love, however, cannot be forbidden. The more that flame is covered up, the hotter it burns. Also love can always find a way. It was impossible that these two whose hearts were on fire should be kept apart" (Hamilton, *Mythology*, p. 100).

To cite sources formally, put footnotes at the foot of any page on which borrowed information appears. Place a small number above the line after the borrowed material. Place the same number at the bottom of the page with author's name, title of the work, publishing information, and page number.

In the following version of the passage about Romeo and Juliet, the footnote method of citing sources is used. Notice again that the first footnote gives all the details about the book, but the second footnote—because it is a second reference to the same work—lists a shortened version of the details.

Passage with
footnotes

William Shakespeare probably based the story of Romeo and Juliet on more than imagination; he is likely to have been inspired by myths and other ancient tales that were popular in his day. One such ancient tale is the story of Pyramus and Thisbe, lovers noted for their beauty and youth: "he the most beautiful youth and she the loveliest maiden of all the East."[1] In the version of the story told by Ovid, a Roman poet, the two lovers were at first kept apart by a feud between their families. In a series of events similar to those in *Romeo and Juliet*, these two lovers "longed to marry, but their parents forbade them. Love, however, cannot be forbidden. The more that flame is covered up, the hotter it burns. Also love can always find a way. It was impossible that these two whose hearts were on fire should be kept apart."[2]

---

[1]Edith Hamilton, *Mythology* (Boston: Little, Brown, 1942), p. 100.

[2]Hamilton, *Mythology*, p. 100.

A modified version of the footnote method calls for a single page of footnotes, numbered according to the footnote numbers in the text and placed after the last page of the report, immediately preceding the bibliography.

Whether you use informal citations, footnotes, or a single footnote page, the following chart can be used to find an appropriate method of citing a variety of different types of sources.

FORMS FOR THE CITATION OF SOURCES		
Kind of Source	**Informal Citation**	**Footnote**
Book	(Edith Hamilton, Mythology, p. 100)	[1]Edith Hamilton, Mythology (Boston: Little, Brown, 1942), p. 100.
Book (with two authors)	(Will Durant and Ariel Durant, The Age of Voltaire, p. 151)	[1]Will Durant and Ariel Durant, The Age of Voltaire (New York: Simon and Schuster, 1965), p. 151.
Magazine article (signed)	(R. Steven Fuller, "Winterkeeping in Yellowstone," National Geographic, December 1978, p. 832)	[1]R. Steven Fuller, "Winterkeeping in Yellowstone," National Geographic, December 1978, p. 832.
Magazine article (unsigned)	("An Exile Laid to Rest," Time, August 11, 1980, p. 34)	[1]"An Exile Laid to Rest," Time, August 11, 1980, p. 34.
Encyclopedia article (signed)	(Grolier Universal Encyclopedia, 1965 ed., "Henry Wadsworth Longfellow," by Allardyce Nicoll)	[1]Grolier Universal Encyclopedia, 1965 ed., "Henry Wadsworth Longfellow," by Allardyce Nicoll.
Encyclopedia article (unsigned)	(The Encyclopedia Americana, 1976 ed., "Egypt")	[1]The Encyclopedia Americana, 1976 ed., "Egypt."

Newspaper article (signed)	(Earleen Tatro, "Forgotten Pharaoh May Live Beneath His Ruined Pyramid," The New York Times, June 22, 1980, p. A20)	¹Earleen Tatro, "Forgotten Pharaoh May Live Beneath His Ruined Pyramid," The New York Times, June 22, 1980, p. A20.
Newspaper article (unsigned)	("Error in Cloning by Top Scientist Halts Lab Tests," The New York Times, August 8, 1980, p. A12)	¹"Error in Cloning by Top Scientist Halts Lab Tests," The New York Times, August 8, 1980, p. A12.
Collected or selected works of a single author	(Thorstein Veblen, The Portable Veblen, ed. Max Lerner, p. 184)	¹Thorstein Veblen, The Portable Veblen, ed. Max Lerner (New York: Viking, 1948), p. 184.
Collected or selected works of several authors	(Sylvan Barnet, Morton Berman, and William Burto, eds., Eight Great Tragedies, p. 32)	¹Sylvan Barnet, Morton Berman, and William Burto, eds., Eight Great Tragedies (New York: New American Library, 1957), p. 32.
Translated work	(Anton Chekhov, Ward Six and Other Stories, trans. Ann Dunnigan, p. 113)	¹Anton Chekhov, Ward Six and Other Stories, trans. Ann Dunnigan (New York: New American Library, 1965), p. 113.
Work in several volumes	(Carl Sandburg, Abraham Lincoln, vol. 1, p. 100)	¹Carl Sandburg, Abraham Lincoln, vol. 1 (New York: Harcourt, Brace, 1926), p. 100.

Correct Use of Sources.　Besides citing sources by providing appropriate information in informal citations or footnotes, you should use material found in sources correctly. You should know when an idea is special to a certain source and a footnote is needed and when the material is so commonly known that a footnote is not needed. Using another writer's words or special ideas as your own *without* documenting the source is a form of theft called *plagiarism*.

> In a library paper, avoid plagiarism by clearly identifying any words, special ideas, or little-known facts that have been found in specific sources.

Plagiarism can result from the incorrect use of someone else's words, of someone else's ideas, or of little-known facts. Using another person's words without placing them in quotation marks and crediting the source is plagiarism. Similarly, either taking ideas and expressing them in your own words or using facts that are not well known without citing the particular source from which these ideas or facts come is incorrect and dishonest. However, if an idea or fact is well known, if it is used in numerous books, then it is not necessary to provide a footnote or informal citation.

You can avoid plagiarism by keeping track of the direct quotations, ideas, and facts that you gather from your research and by preparing accurate citations.

The following examples present two passages. The first is from a book entitled *The Bermuda Triangle*—one source that might be used for research on mysteries surrounding the Bermuda Triangle. The second passage is from an unacceptable library paper that uses this source incorrectly. The word-for-word plagiarism in the second passage is underlined.

Passage from a book

There is a section of the western Atlantic off the southeast coast of the United States, forming what has been termed a triangle, extending from Bermuda in the north to southern Florida, and then east to a point through the Bahamas past Puerto Rico to about 40° west longitude and then back again to Bermuda. This area occupies a disturbing and almost unbelievable place in the world's catalog of unexplained mysteries. This is usually referred to as the Bermuda Triangle, where more than 100 planes and ships have literally vanished into thin air, most of them since 1945, and where more than 1,000 lives have been lost in the past twenty-six years, without a single body or even a piece of wreckage from the vanishing planes or ships having been found. Disappearances continue to occur with apparently increasing frequency, in spite of the fact that the seaways and airways are today more travelled, searches are more thorough, and records are more carefully kept.
—Charles Berlitz

Passage
from an
unacceptable
library paper

Plagiarism

Mysterious disappearances of ships and aircraft in the area known as the Bermuda Triangle have long puzzled people. In fact, no other sizeable portion of the globe remains as much a source of wonder and fear. More than 100 planes and ships have literally vanished into thin air, most of them since 1945, and more than 1,000 lives have been lost in the past twenty-six years, without a single body or even a piece of wreckage from the vanishing planes or ships having been found.

The preceding passage can be cited as an example of plagiarism not only because quotation marks have not been placed around the direct quotation but also because the source of a number of the ideas has not been acknowledged. The passage also contains an example of poor choice of quotation. The information quoted directly could more appropriately be rephrased in the writer's own words, with proper citation. Notice in the following version how the writer has incorporated and rephrased the information and given credit where it is due.

Passage from
an acceptable
library paper

Facts and
ideas used
correctly

Source
credited

Mysterious disappearances of ships and aircraft in the area known as the Bermuda Triangle have long puzzled people. The statistics that have been collected concerning these disappearances are startling and disturbing especially because the disappearances seem unnatural. For example, in the last few decades over 100 planes and ships have vanished and over 1,000 people have died in that area, leaving no traces (Charles Berlitz, *The Bermuda Triangle*, pp. 11-12).

In addition to citing whatever sources you decide to use, you should make sure that your readers will understand the ideas and terms in the borrowed material. You may need to write an explanation to introduce the quotation or to rephrase the idea in your own words, as in the preceding example, while still crediting the source.

Preparation of a Bibliography. Still another part of using sources well in a library paper involves compiling a list of all the sources you consulted when you did your research for the paper. This list, which goes at the end of the paper, is called a *bibliography*.

To show the amount of research you have done, a library paper must contain a bibliography listing all sources consulted during the research and other planning steps.

The bibliography shows the extent of your research. By identifying the sources, you make it possible for the reader to weigh the overall strength of your work and to consult directly any sources of special interest.

Even if you used a particular source only to gain an overview of the topic and did not cite it within the paper, you must list it in your bibliography. You must also give complete information about each source: the author, title, place of publication, name of the publisher, and date of publication. You do not need to include page numbers for books since significant pages have already been given in the citations. Page numbers should, however, be given for magazine and newspaper articles.

For most bibliography entries, you must write the author's name, last name first, and then the title of the work. If a source has no particular author, you can begin the entry with the title of the book or article. All bibliography entries must be listed in alphabetical order.

The following chart shows a number of sample entries for a bibliography. Notice that different types of sources are listed differently just as they were in the citations and footnotes.

FORMS FOR BIBLIOGRAPHIES	
Kind of Source	**Bibliographic Entry**
Book	Hamilton, Edith. <u>Mythology</u>. Boston: Little, Brown, 1942.
Book (with two authors)	Durant, Will and Durant, Ariel. <u>The Age of Voltaire</u>. New York: Simon and Schuster, 1965.
Magazine article (signed)	Fuller, R. Steven. "Winterkeeping in Yellowstone." <u>National Geographic</u>, December 1978, pp. 829–857.
Magazine article (unsigned)	"An Exile Laid to Rest." <u>Time</u>, August 11, 1980, p. 34.
Encyclopedia article (signed)	<u>Grolier Universal Encyclopedia</u>, 1965 ed. "Henry Wadsworth Longfellow," by Allardyce Nicoll.
Encyclopedia article (unsigned)	<u>The Encyclopedia Americana</u>, 1976 ed. "Egypt."
Newspaper article (signed)	Tatro, Earleen. "Forgotten Pharaoh May Live Beneath His Ruined Pyramid." <u>The New York Times</u>, June 22, 1980, p. A20.

Newspaper article (unsigned)	"Error in Cloning by Top Scientist Halts Lab Tests." The New York Times, August 8, 1980, p. A12.
Collected or selected works of a single author	Veblen, Thorstein. The Portable Veblen. Edited by Max Lerner. New York: Viking, 1948.
Collected or selected works of several authors	Barnet, Sylvan, Berman, Morton, and Burto, William, eds. Eight Great Tragedies. New York: New American Library, 1957.
Translated work	Chekhov, Anton. Ward Six and Other Stories. Translated by Ann Dunnigan. New York: New American Library, 1965.
Work in several volumes	Sandburg, Carl. Abraham Lincoln, vol. 1. New York: Harcourt, Brace, 1926.

EXERCISE A: Preparing Citations. Choose one of the following topics or think of one of your own. Then find *four* different kinds of sources on your topic in the library (for example, a book, a magazine, an encyclopedia, and a newspaper). For each source, prepare both an informal citation and a footnote.

The evolution of a popular dance
Methods of training circus animals
Life on a farm or ranch
Social unrest in South Africa
The Hindu belief in reincarnation

Mysteries surrounding Egypt's pyramids
Benefits of life insurance policies
Causes of anxiety
Processing fertilizer
The first trade routes to the Far East

EXERCISE B: Knowing When to Cite Sources. If you were writing a research paper about the early days of radio you might use the information from the following source in your paper. Write a paragraph in which you include your own ideas and *three* pieces of information from this passage. The parenthetical credit for each item should be (Frank Buxton and Bill Owen, *The Big Broadcast*, pp. 91–92).

The Dr. IQ quiz show, sponsored by Mars Incorporated, makers of Snickers, Milky Way, Three Musketeers, Forever Yours, and Mars bars, was broadcast from different cities where it played in a local theater. At the start of the program, Dr. IQ would introduce several announcers who were stationed in various parts of the theater with hand-held microphones. The announcers would select contestants in the audience, and frequently you would hear, "I have a lady in the balcony, Doctor." Then Dr. IQ would say, "I have ten silver dollars for that lady if she can tell me. . . ." (The amount of money varied with the difficulty of the question.) Winning contestants were paid in silver dollars, and losers received a box of the sponsor's candy bars and "two tickets to next week's production here at Loew's Victoria!" Dr. IQ frequently told losing contestants, "Oh, I'm so sorry but I think you'll find the answer is . . . ."—Frank Buxton and Bill Owen

EXERCISE C: Preparing a Sample Bibliography. Using the sources for which you prepared informal citations and footnotes in Exercise A or four other varied sources on one topic, list your sources in a bibliography, using correct bibliography form.

■ Structure and Features of a Library Paper

In overall structure, a library paper resembles an essay because it contains an introduction, a body, and a conclusion. In addition, it will typically include additional features not necessarily found in an essay.

> A library paper must have a title, an introduction with a thesis statement, a body, and a conclusion as well as citation of sources throughout and a bibliography.

A short library paper may be five or six paragraphs long, approximately the size of an essay. Other library papers may consist of many more paragraphs, depending on the amount of information necessary to cover the topic. The amount of information taken from sources can have a major effect on length.

The title and introduction will generally serve two basic functions: They can capture the interest of your readers and they can present the purpose of the paper. The *introduction* will generally contain only one paragraph, leading to a thesis statement, which is usually the last sentence of the introduction. Sometimes, you will have enough introductory or opening remarks to warrant two or more paragraphs. In this event, the thesis statement will generally appear at the end of the final introductory paragraph. The following diagram illustrates introductions of one and two paragraphs.

One–Paragraph Introduction   **Two–Paragraph Introduction**

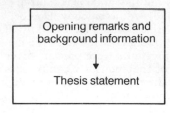

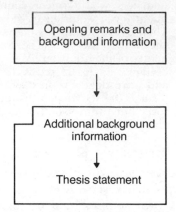

Although your introduction may contain credited ideas from research sources, the thesis statement itself must always present your own idea.

The *body* of the library paper should develop the thesis statement with supporting examples, facts, details, and other information, much of it taken from research sources. The library paper can contain any number of paragraphs, with the information in them arranged logically, just as in essays.

In a longer library paper, which contains many body paragraphs, you may find it useful to group body paragraphs in subsections under headings of their own. If two or three body paragraphs develop one subtopic of the thesis statement and two or three other body paragraphs develop another subtopic, subtopic headings for each group of body paragraphs can help guide a reader through the ideas you are presenting.

The last paragraph of the library paper is a *conclusion*, which summarizes the main point, the subtopics, and the evidence presented in the body. Although a conclusion usually contains only one paragraph, it will occasionally contain two.

In addition to these structural parts, a library paper must include consistent documentation of sources throughout and a complete bibliography at the end, which lists all the sources you have consulted in the preparation of the paper.

NOTE ABOUT OTHER FEATURES: Most library papers will also have a title page, a separate page at the beginning of the paper that gives the title of the paper, your name, the date, and the class for which you are submitting the paper. You may also be asked to include a formal outline of your paper.

The following library paper uses the three-part structure and includes the other features explained in this section.

Lincoln's Universal Appeal

In November of 1858, several newspapers and private persons nominated Abraham Lincoln to head the Republican presidential ticket for 1860. In a conversation with his friend Jesse Fell, Lincoln expressed his doubts on the subject ". . . what's the use of talking of me for the Presidency, whilst we have such men as Seward, Chase, and others. . . ? Everybody knows them. Nobody, scarcely, outside of Illinois, knows me." But to this, Fell replied, "What the Republican Party wants, to insure success in 1860, is a man of popular origin, of acknowledged ability, committed against slavery aggressions, who has no record to defend, and no radicalism of an offensive character. . . . You have sprung from the humble walks of life . . . and if we can only get these facts sufficiently before the people . . . you can be made a formidable, if not a successful, candidate for the Presidency."[1] Fell's analysis was correct. Lincoln's humble origin and manner and fine upstanding character, aided by his ability to deliver an honest, convincing speech, gave him the universal appeal that was the deciding factor in his election victory.

Lincoln's common beginnings led to his casual, down-to-earth attitude, which distinguished him later in life. He was born in a small town and spent the majority of his life with little money. When he reached a position of political prestige and wealth, he never became snobbish or wasteful of money, living by the ethics that he had gained earlier in life. He never considered himself too rich or too good to speak to lower-class people. According to Sandburg, many Americans of the era knew well Lincoln's humble manner: As he traveled, Lincoln could always find time to talk simply and frankly with the "common man"; he was known to answer the door in his shirt and slippers rather than allowing a servant to do it; and during his campaign, Lincoln was never wasteful of money given him by supporters. The only time political money was spent in any abundance was when the Republican Party gave celebrations for him, and Lincoln always asked that these expenditures be kept to a minimum.[2]

During his whole life, Lincoln was known for his honesty and modesty. Never promising any political favors in exchange for a vote, he refused to allow any of his supporters to do the same, saying, "I authorize no bargains and will be bound by none."[3] He never boasted or bragged of his fitness for office or demeaned other candidates to build his own image. He let the party choose him as its man for President by never mentioning his intention to try for the office in any of his speeches prior to his nomination.[4] Answering letters personally, he exhibited a freshness not often found among other politicians, who often took more pompous, lofty attitudes. On returning from campaign trips, Lincoln answered his accumulated mail as quickly as possible, often writing as many as ten letters at once. After Lincoln was nominated, he made very few speeches and seldom released statements. Once he addressed his followers with: "You will kindly let me be silent."[5] He clearly wanted the voters to choose their candidate without propaganda from him.

Much of Lincoln's initial recognition was gained through his speaking talent. Lincoln began practicing as a young boy, speaking to farmers, and this was probably the beginning of his familiar offhand style.[6] Lincoln filled his speeches with anecdotes and analogies which conveyed his simplicity and honesty to people in a language they could understand and respect, one without superiority or pretentious airs. He was equally well received by crowds of farmers and of the upper class. Many people just heard of Lincoln through the popularity of his speeches during the debates between him and Stephen Douglas. Both the simplicity and the powerful ideas in Lincoln's speeches caused them to be published and republished in papers across the country.[7] This national exposure allowed the public to become aware of Abraham Lincoln long before his election to the White House.

Abraham Lincoln had a very general appeal. People readily recognized the depth and sincerity of his spiritual convictions. He carried with him a book of daily scripture, which he read to affirm his faith in God, and many quotes in his speeches and many of his ideals reflected his spiritual leaning.[8] He lived a life of simplicity and truthfulness, yet he was honorable and venerable among other great men. In 1860, before Lincoln's election, Melton Hay addressed Lincoln on behalf of the local Republican Club on his rise from "obscurity to distinction." He said, "Our history is prolific in examples of what may be achieved by ability, perseverance, and integrity . . . but in the long list of those who have thus from humblest beginnings won their way worthily to proud distinction there is not one who can take precedence of the name of Abraham Lincoln."[9] Hay recognized Lincoln as a man who was able to use rather than shun his common past as a way to handle greatness. Lincoln's ability to preserve a humble, down-to-earth quality while speaking and acting in the best of faith made him a candidate that Americans found it easy to vote for in November of 1860.

---

[1]Carl Sandburg, <u>Abraham Lincoln</u>, vol. 1 (New York: Harcourt, Brace, 1926), pp. 243–244.

[2]Sandburg, <u>Abraham Lincoln</u>, vol. 1, p. 188.

[3]Sandburg, <u>Abraham Lincoln</u>, vol. 1, p. 285.

[4]Stephen B. Oates, <u>With Malice Toward None: The Life of Abraham Lincoln</u> (New York: Harper and Row, 1977), pp. 161–162.

[5]Sandburg, <u>Abraham Lincoln</u>, vol. 1, p. 293.

[6]Oates, <u>With Malice Toward None: The Life of Abraham Lincoln</u>, p. 12.

[7]Oates, <u>With Malice Toward None: The Life of Abraham Lincoln</u>, pp. 161–162.

[8]Carl Sandburg, ed., <u>Lincoln's Devotional</u> (Great Neck, N. Y.: Channel Press, 1957), pp. i–vi.

⁹Benjamin P. Thomas, Abraham Lincoln (New York: Knopf, 1952), p. 205.

Bibliography

Kelly, Regina Z. Lincoln and Douglas: The Years of Decision. New York: Random, 1954.

Lincoln, Abraham. Collected Works of Abraham Lincoln, vols. III and IV. Edited by Roy P. Basler. New Brunswick, N.J.: Rutgers University Press, 1953.

Oates, Stephen B. With Malice Toward None: The Life of Abraham Lincoln. New York: Harper and Row, 1977.

Sandburg, Carl. Abraham Lincoln, vol. 1. New York: Harcourt, Brace, 1926.

Sandburg, Carl, ed. Lincoln's Devotional. Great Neck, N.Y.: Channel Press, 1957.

Thomas, Benjamin P. Abraham Lincoln. New York: Knopf, 1952.

EXERCISE D: Recognizing the Structure of a Library Paper.

Answer the following questions about the library paper on Lincoln.

1. How does the title capture the reader's interest?
2. What does the reader learn in the paper's introduction?
3. What is the thesis statement of the paper? What subtopics does it include?
4. How many body paragraphs does the paper have? What is the topic sentence of each body paragraph?
5. How does the supporting information in the body follow the subtopics presented in the thesis statement?
6. How does the conclusion bring the paper to a close?

APPLICATION: Analyzing the Features of a Library Paper.

Answer the following questions about the use of sources in the library paper on Lincoln.

1. Which of the two systems for citing sources is used in the paper?
2. How many different sources does the writer cite?
3. What kind of information is used in each case: quotations, ideas, or little-known facts?
4. From how many different types of sources has the writer used information: books, encyclopedias, magazines, and so on?
5. How many sources are listed in the bibliography? Of these, which are *not* cited in the paper itself?
6. What additional sources from your school or public library might you have consulted if you had written a paper on this topic? List *three* sources as bibliography entries.

25.2 From Idea to Final Paper

To write a library paper, you can follow steps similar to the steps you follow in essay writing. The main difference is the research you must do for the library paper. You should begin your research early in the planning stage by exploring books, magazines, and other sources. Later, your research sources will play a central role as you organize, outline, and write your paper.

In this section you will follow certain useful steps in planning, writing, and revising a library paper. As you do this, you will also be locating sources, taking information from them, incorporating and documenting ideas, writing footnotes, and preparing a bibliography.

■ Finding a Suitable Topic

You should choose a topic for a library paper after considering your own interests and the scope of the topic and after determining the number of available sources on the topic.

Selecting and Refining a Topic.   Your first ideas for a paper are likely to be general ones. Your teacher may have suggested some possible topics, or you may have some ideas of your own. As you consider different topics, you should look for sources of information about each of the possibilities. Then you should choose one topic, break it down into smaller topics, and select one that is manageable in a library paper.

> Choose a topic that is interesting and relevant to your studies, is covered adequately in available sources, and is narrow enough for one paper.

For courses such as science and social studies, you should choose a general topic that relates to something you have studied during the year. If you have read about labor movements in American history, for instance, you might begin with this general topic and then choose a key labor organizer as your specific topic or trace the establishment and growth of a particular labor union, such as the garment workers' union. Choosing a topic related to your studies will enrich your understanding of the subject and may also provide you with useful information for class tests.

Whatever topic you choose to write about, you should also consider your interest in it. Choosing a topic that appeals to you will improve your chances of writing a good paper.

In addition, choose a topic for which you can find ample books, magazine articles, and other sources. Not only will these sources help you narrow the general topic to a more specific one, but they will also give you many of the ideas and much of the information that you will include in your paper.

Once you have chosen a general topic that is researchable, you need to determine what specific aspect of it you want to write about. The sources you have located on your general topic can help you find a specific topic. For example, the subheadings under a topic in *The Readers' Guide to Periodical Literature*, the divisions under your subject listing in the card catalog, and the tables of contents of some of your potential sources can suggest possible smaller topics.

If you were to choose a general topic such as *Human rights*, you might break this category down into smaller topics and then possibly narrow down one of these smaller topics even further. Gradually, you could zero in on a topic that would suit your needs and the length of the paper you have in mind. You might make a list like the following.

NARROWING A GENERAL TOPIC	
General Topic:	Human rights
Smaller Topics:	Abolition
	The Universal Declaration of Human Rights
	Equal employment
	Women's rights
	Susan B. Anthony
	Angelina Grimké
More Specific Topics	Angelina Grimké's work with the Quakers
	The writings of Angelina Grimké
	Angelina Grimké's fight for rights of slaves and women

From a list like the preceding one, you might choose one of the specific topics because it looks interesting and manageable.

Preparing Bibliography Cards. Once you have a specific topic for your paper, you should list, preferably on note cards, all the sources related to your topic that you plan to consult.

The complete publishing information about each of your sources will also be useful later as you write your paper.

For every source that you plan to read and take notes on, record all information necessary for bibliography entries.

The following chart suggests an efficient method for preparing bibliography cards that will be easy to use later.

MAKING BIBLIOGRAPHY CARDS
1. Use one note card or one piece of paper for each source.
2. For a book, write down the author, the title, the city of publication, the publisher, and the date of publication at the top of each card.
3. For a magazine article, write down the author, the title of the article and the title of the magazine, the publication date, and the page numbers at the top of each card.
4. For newspaper articles and sources with several authors or an anonymous author, write down the information shown in the chart on page 729 in Section 25.1 at the top of each card.
5. For all sources found in the library, record the call number or location symbol to help you locate the sources.
6. Note which sources contain illustrations, maps, charts, or tables that you might find useful.

You should have more sources listed on bibliography cards than the assignment requires or than you will probably use. For all library papers you prepare, you should have at least five sources listed on cards.

EXERCISE A: Finding and Narrowing a Topic. Choose a general topic for a library paper, either one that your teacher suggests or one that you think of on your own. Then check the sources available on the topic by going to the card catalog and *The Readers' Guide to Periodical Literature* as well as any other appropriate indexes. You might have a second and third choice in mind in case your first choice proves difficult to research. Browse through a few of your sources for ideas about how to narrow your general topic down into more specific topics. Then jot down your general topic and the possible smaller topics and choose the specific topic that interests you most and that is discussed in five or more different sources.

EXERCISE B: **Preparing a Working Bibliography.** On note cards, write down all the information you will need for writing bibliography entries and for locating the sources that you plan to consult on your topic. You should have at least five bibliography cards.

■ Researching and Organizing the Library Paper

When you have a narrowed topic and a list of sources on that topic, you can begin planning your research, gathering information, and preparing your library paper.

Planning Your Research.   Before you begin reading and taking notes on the sources on your topic, you should think about the information you will be investigating.

Prepare some key questions and a rough version of your thesis statement to guide your research.

If your topic were *Angelina Grimké's fight for the rights of slaves and women*, you might list questions such as those in the following chart.

SAMPLE QUESTIONS TO DIRECT RESEARCH
1. What experiences in Angelina Grimké's early life developed her interest in human rights?
2. How did Angelina Grimké's Quaker beliefs influence her fight for human rights?
3. What did she do to fight against slavery?
4. What did she do to fight for the rights of women?
5. For what specific achievements or contributions is Angelina Grimké remembered?

In addition to formulating questions that you will try to answer as you do your research, you should express a possible main point for your paper in a single sentence. This rough version of your thesis statement should be based on the facts or opinions you have about the topic and should indicate the purpose you plan to achieve in the paper.

A preliminary thesis statement as well as a few significant questions will simplify and speed up your research. Having a main point in mind will help you concentrate on specific information as you skim many sources. For example, writing about the life and contributions of Angelina Grimké is likely to be too broad an idea for a library paper, but focusing on a particular observation or main point will channel your research. For a paper on Angelina Grimké's fight for human rights, you might use the information you already know about Angelina Grimké's life to state the following opinion as your main point.

PRELIMINARY THESIS STATEMENT: Angelina Grimké distinguished herself as a forerunner in the fight against oppression of American slaves and women.

Keep in mind that your preliminary thesis statement is likely to be rough because it is a first attempt. As you gather information and as your paper takes shape, you may want to polish or alter your thesis statement to reflect your new knowledge.

Taking Notes on Your Sources.   You are now ready to begin systematic reading and note-taking on your topic, using your questions and thesis statement to guide you.

While reading your sources, take accurate notes in the form of modified outlines, summaries, and quotations. Record information and the page numbers on which the information appears.

One effective method of taking notes is to record information on well-labeled note cards. The following chart explains this method.

TAKING NOTES
1. Use a different card for each source. If one source covers many major ideas of interest to you, use a different card for each new major idea.
2. In the upper left-hand corner of each card, write down the information you will need for informal citations or footnotes. See the chart on citations in Section 25.1 for exact information.
3. In the upper right-hand corner of each card, write a subject heading that tells you what information the card covers. Usually you will have a number of different subject headings and many cards with each one.
4. Always write down a page number for each fact, idea, or quotation that you record.

You should begin the note-taking process by locating the sources listed on your bibliography cards. From these sources, select the ones most likely to contain thorough information related to your main point and questions. You may want to consult a few sources just to get an overview of your topic, but you should begin note-taking using your most helpful sources. Skim the material first and then reread the most useful parts, taking notes at the same time. If the same information appears in several sources, just record it once.

You should use the form of notes that best suits the information in the source. When you find useful ideas and facts, you may want to rephrase them in your own words and record them in modified outlines. When you find particularly well-stated ideas that you might want to quote, you should copy the information word-for-word and enclose it in quotation marks. If information is pertinent to your topic but quite general, you may want to summarize it in your own words. For all the information you record in your notes, you should indicate the pages in the source where you found the information.

In the following note card from a source about Angelina Grimké, you can see how some information about her early childhood has been recorded. Publishing information is given in the upper left-hand corner. The basic topic is stated in the upper right-hand corner, and details are given with page numbers in a modified outline form.

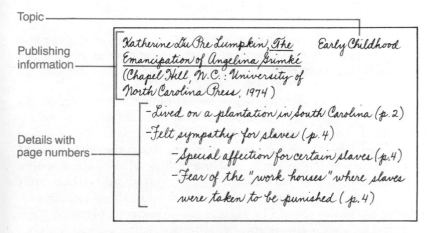

While you take notes, you may discover that your sources do not contain information that answers all the questions you formulated. In that case, you may have to locate and consult additional sources on your topic.

Revising Your Thesis Statement.   When you have thoroughly researched your topic, you should consider revising your thesis statement to reflect the insights and information in your notes.

Revise your thesis statement so that it states your main point precisely.

Your revised thesis statement should clarify your purpose, suit the audience you have in mind, and fit the information you plan to use in the paper. Your word choices in the thesis statement should be appropriate for the level of understanding of your readers. You may also want your thesis statement to present subtopics to prepare the reader for your discussion of the main point in the body of the paper. A revised thesis statement for the paper on Angelina Grimké might resemble the following.

REVISED THESIS STATEMENT: Before slavery became a national issue and before the women's rights movements gained attention, Angelina Grimké recognized the social and political conditions that oppressed slaves and women and fought to change these conditions.

Writing an Outline.   At this point, you will have all the raw materials of your library paper. You are thus ready to plan the introduction, body, and conclusion of your paper.

Arrange your own ideas and the information in your notes in a topic or sentence outline that sketches out the development of your thesis statement.

To write your outline, begin by listing introductory remarks and background information that you consider helpful and interesting. These items may be your own ideas or information that you have found in your sources. Your thesis statement should be written at the end of the outline of the introduction.

To outline the body of the paper, you should group your note cards according to subtopics of your thesis statement. These subtopics should be logical divisions, categories, or steps related to your main point, organized in some logical fashion. At this point you should also sort your note cards and look for an order for the information to follow under each subtopic. At the same time, you should reexamine the information on your note cards in order to eliminate any extraneous or insignificant ideas. If you are planning to use any charts, diagrams, or other graphics in the paper, you should include them in this portion of the outline along with your supporting information.

Finally, you should outline the conclusion, including your own ideas and any information you might want to mention from your research.

The following is a skeleton topic outline for the paper about Angelina Grimké. Notice that the body is divided into two subtopics.

I. Introduction
    A.
    B. } Introductory ideas and background information
    C. Thesis statement: Angelina Grimkés early partic-
       ipation in the fight for the rights of American
       slaves and women
II. Subtopic 1: Angelina Grimké and slavery
    A.
    B. Information—facts, details—about her early life on a
    C. plantation and her work with abolitionists
    D.
III. Subtopic 2: Angelina Grimké and women's rights
    A.
    B. Information—facts, details—about her writings, speeches,
    C. and other efforts to gain equality for women
    D.
IV. Conclusion
    A.
    B. } Closing remarks and restatement of the ideas in the
    C. thesis statement

EXERCISE C: Researching Your Library Paper. Use the topic you selected and worked with in Exercises A and B, and follow these instructions.

1. Think of five questions about your topic that you will answer when you consult your sources.
2. Draft a preliminary thesis statement.
3. Locate all the sources listed on your bibliography cards, and choose the most useful ones to read and take notes on first.
4. First, skim the sources and find the most relevant information. Then reread the important parts, recording information accurately. Use modified outlines, summaries, and word-for-word quotations, and follow the method for taking notes suggested in the chart on page 740. Remember to

include all necessary information on each card, especially the page numbers for each piece of information.

EXERCISE D: Polishing Your Thesis Statement. Revise the thesis statement you wrote in Exercise C so that it suits the information you have gathered and expresses your main point clearly. Make sure that it also fits your audience and purpose.

EXERCISE E: Organizing Your Library Paper. Use the information you gathered in your notes in Exercise C and your revised thesis statement to outline the introduction, body, and conclusion of your paper. If your thesis statement does not include stated subtopics, think of subtopics now and organize them in a logical way. Then group your note cards according to subtopics and organize the note cards in some logical order under each subtopic. Reexamine your note cards and set aside any that do not relate directly to your main point and subtopics. Finally, prepare a topic outline following the model on page 743.

■ Writing and Revising the Paper

With your outline completed, you can begin a first draft of the paper. Remember that a first draft is only a rough version; you may still have adjustments and refinements to make. For this reason, revising is also an important step. Your final paper should go through careful proofreading, revising, and rewriting stages.

Writing a First Draft.   When you feel that you have a good working outline, you are ready to write a first draft.

Refer to your outline and your note cards when you write a first draft.

As you write, you should use every other line of your paper—double-space if you type—so that you can later make alterations, corrections, and revisions right on the paper.

Compose your sentences following the arrangements of ideas in your outline, adding any new ideas as they occur to you and any transitions that will make logical connections between ideas. When you include quoted information, be sure to place these words in quotation marks. You should also remember to use either informal citations or footnotes to indicate both quotations and other ideas from your sources. Formats for citations and footnotes are found in Section 25.1.

Checking and Revising. When you have finished your first draft, you need to recheck it, both to find mechanical errors and to make content improvements.

Check your first draft with a view toward improving and refining it, using a checklist to inspect all parts of the paper.

Before you write a final copy of the paper, use the following checklist. Make any corrections and revisions directly on the paper. Do not be afraid to rewrite whole portions of the paper if you can see a better order for details or ways to express ideas more concisely and precisely.

CHECKING YOUR LIBRARY PAPER

1. Do the opening statements in your introduction provide enough background information or other ideas for the reader to understand the thesis statement and the body paragraphs that follow?

2. Does the thesis statement clearly present the main point of the paper as well as your purpose in writing it?

3. Do the paragraphs in the body present a well organized development of the thesis statement and its stated or unstated subtopics?

4. Does each body paragraph contain a topic sentence?

5. Are the details and other pieces of information in each paragraph arranged in a logical order?

6. Do transitions help to clarify orders and connect ideas logically?

7. Are direct quotations marked with quotation marks and cited in informal citations or footnotes?

8. Are all other borrowed ideas and facts cited in a consistent manner?

9. Does the conclusion contain a reference to the thesis statement and the subtopics?

10. Are sentences throughout the paper varied in length and structure? Is the language suitable for your audience and purpose?

11. Are there any spelling mistakes, usage problems, or mechanical errors?

Writing the Final Copy, a Title Page, and a Bibliography.
Once you have proofread and rechecked your first draft and
made revisions using the checklist, you are ready for the last
stage.

> Write a corrected, revised final copy of the paper, adding a ti-
> tle, a title page, and a bibliography.

Your final copy should be carefully handwritten or typewritten, using double-spacing if you type. You should leave
margins around your material on all four sides of your paper.
In addition, you should probably include your name on every
page of your paper, along with any other headings your
teacher may suggest.

At this point you should also decide on the title of your paper if you have not already done so. The title will go on a title
page, a separate page at the beginning of the paper. The title
should be centered on the page, followed by your name, the title of the course for which you are submitting the paper, and
the date of submission. Again, your teacher may request a special format that differs somewhat from this basic format.

As a final step, you should add a bibliography at the end of
the paper. Here you must list all sources that you used in the
planning and writing of the paper. Even if you do not cite a
source within the body of the paper, you must still list that
source in the bibliography if you have learned anything at all
from it.

In the sample library paper that follows, you will see a bibliography that you can use as a model. Note also the annotations at the sides that show how the paper is organized.

Angelina Emily Grimké: Equality for All

Introductory
remarks
reveal a
persuasive
purpose

Two-
paragraph
introduction
gives back-
ground details
leading up to
purpose and
thesis
statement

Angelina Emily Grimké was born and raised on a
plantation in South Carolina. Although she lived
with slavery throughout her childhood, she never felt
comfortable with it. Her earliest experiences made
her aware of oppression, and her sensitivity and
strong values instilled in her the compassion that,
later in her life, would direct her to help others.

Despite periods of regression, the United States
has come a long way in the past hundred years in
guaranteeing the rights of all citizens. During this
time, many men and women have championed the
causes of equal rights for all races and creeds as well
as equal rights for women. Not only must Angelina
Grimké be counted as a champion of human rights,
but she must also be recognized as a forerunner in
the equal rights movement. Long before slavery be-

Thesis
statement
includes two
subtopics

came a national issue in the 1850's and '60's and
long before women's rights movements gained attention at the turn of the century, Angelina Grimké recognized the social and political conditions that oppressed all slaves and women and fought to change
them.

Optional
heading is
chosen to
introduce
first subtopic

Angelina Grimké and Slavery

Even as a child of eight, Angelina was repulsed by
violence toward slaves. As an adult, Angelina re-
called her childhood fear of the "work house," the
place on her parents' plantation where slaves were
taken to be punished.[1] Even at such an early age, Angelina was horrified by the injustice of the slaves'
suffering. At the age of thirteen, Angelina recorded in
her journal incidents in which she felt that slaves on
her parents' plantation were treated cruelly.[2]

Raised
numbers
show that the
source will
be given in a
footnote

Not until she was in her twenties, however, could
Angelina Grimké act upon her insights into and attitudes about slavery. By this time, she had explored
her religious beliefs and had converted from the Ep-
iscopalian faith to the Presbyterian. She then became

Transitions
and other
words reveal
chronological
order for this
section

devoted to the Society of Friends. In this association,
her Quaker sisters helped convince her to take a
stand against slavery.[3] Despite her feelings about
slavery, Angelina's family and many of her closest
friends were proponents of slavery—many of them
dependent upon slave labor—and Angelina had to
separate her personal loyalties from the moral position that she was soon to take. Finally, in 1828, Angelina returned home with a promise to herself and
to her Quaker friends to convince the slaveholders
that the practice of slavery was sinful.[4]

At home, Angelina encountered opposition to her
plan and rejection by those she loved. Perhaps her
most painful ordeal was the treatment she received
from her mother. Calling her daughter a hypocrite,
Mary Grimké pointed out that Angelina herself had
once owned a slave named Kitty. Angelina explained
the circumstances in this way: "I had determined
never to own a slave; but, finding that my mother
could not manage Kitty, I undertook to do so, if I
could have her without any interference from anyone. This could not be unless I consented to own her.
Soon after, one of my mother's servants quarrelled
with her and beat her. I determined she should not
be subject to such abuse, and I went out to find her
a place in some Christian family."[5]

Disappointed by her unsuccessful efforts to combat slavery, Angelina turned to writing and, through
this medium, gained recognition. After she wrote her
Appeal to the Christian Women of the South, the

American Anti-Slavery Society invited her and her sister Sarah to speak at small parlor gatherings of women in New York. The first meeting drew such a sizeable audience that the next speech had to held in a church. Angelina's words and sentiments were heard by increasing numbers of people.[6] Soon, the Grimké sisters were being attacked in newspaper editorials for both their views and their aggressiveness and, as a result, their popularity increased. While her views about slavery were drawing attention, Angelina also began to focus her attention on women's rights, and throughout her adult life she fought for both causes.[7]

Angelina Grimké and Women's Rights

By the time Angelina Grimké joined the Quakers, and prior to her efforts to convince slaveholders of the sins of human "ownership," she had come to believe that just as slaves deserved equality, so did women. From her experiences with other religions, she came to recognize attitudes toward women's roles in society as "spiritually dead," "bigoted," and "narrow."[8] Among the Quakers, she found greater freedom and equality among men and women. She admired the Quakers' "principles of liberality," and soon she became a leader, organizing a "female prayer meeting."[9]

Later, when Angelina began to write and speak, her hosts were most often women's groups. Her speeches against slavery were related to the issue of rights denied to women. However, her advocacy of women's rights evoked mixed reactions from her abolitionist peers. Many of Angelina's friends and supporters implored her to abandon the women's rights question lest it interfere with the support she had won for abolition. But Angelina addressed the problem by replying, "We cannot push Abolitionism forward with all our might until we take up the stumbling block out of the road. You may depend upon it, tho' to meet this question may appear turning out of our road, that it is not. IT IS NOT: we must meet it and meet it now."[10]

Even after she officially retired from public speaking, Angelina continued to be active in women's rights, particularly on the issue of women's suffrage. On May 14, 1863, she came out of retirement to speak at the New York meeting of the Loyal Women of the Nation.[11] Later, she and her sister led forty women of Hyde Park, Massachusetts, through a blinding snowstorm to deposit ballots in a ballot box made by women who were demonstrating for their right to vote.[12]

Optional heading is chosen to introduce second subtopic

Transitions again show chronological order

Conclusion
restates ideas
in thesis
statement

Angelina Grimké was more than a woman with a dual cause. As she fought to improve social conditions for both blacks and women, she brought to the task a deep personal knowledge of human dignity and individual needs, an instinctive understanding of human rights that developed from her early childhood. In that regard, Angelina never changed—she had always been mindful of human needs—and during her lifetime she sharpened her beliefs and courageously pursued equality for all people. In her actions as well as in her writings, Angelina Grimké revealed the love that was her motivation: "Hoping, though against hope, that thou mayest one day know how precious is the reward of those who can love our oppressed brethren and sisters in this day of their calamity, and who rejoice to stand side by side with them, in the glorious conflict between Slavery and Freedom, Prejudice and Love unfeigned, I remain thine in the bonds of universal love."[13]

---

[1]Katherine DuPre Lumpkin, The Emancipation of Angelina Grimké (Chapel Hill, N.C.: University of North Carolina Press, 1974), p. 4.

[2]Lumpkin, The Emancipation of Angelina Grimké, pp. 6–7.

[3]Lumpkin, The Emancipation of Angelina Grimké, p. 25.

[4]Lumpkin, The Emancipation of Angelina Grimké, p. 25.

[5]Catherine H. Birney, The Grimké Sisters: Sarah and Angelina Grimké: The First American Women Advocates of Abolition and Women's Rights (New York: Scholarly Press, 1970), p. 41.

[6]Carol Hymowitz and Michaele Weissman, A History of Women in America (New York: Bantam Books, 1978), p. 81.

[7]Hymowitz and Weissman, A History of Women in America, p. 86.

[8]Lumpkin, The Emancipation of Angelina Grimké, p. 25.

[9]Lumpkin, The Emancipation of Angelina Grimké, p. 25.

[10]G. H. Barner and D. L. Dumond, eds., Letters of Theodore D. Weld, Angelina Grimké Weld and Sarah Grimké (New York: Appleton-Century-Crofts, 1970), pp. 429–430.

[11]Eleanor Flexner, Century of Struggle: The Women's Rights Movement in the U.S. (Cambridge, Mass.: Harvard University Press, 1975), p. 110.

[12]Flexner, Century of Struggle: The Women's Rights Movement in the U.S., pp. 110–111.

[13]Angelina E. Grimké, Letters to Catherine E. Beecher (New York: Arno Press, 1969), p. 41.

BIBLIOGRAPHY

Barnes, G. H. and Dumond, D. L., eds. Letters of Theodore D. Weld, Angelina Grimké Weld, and Sarah Grimké, vols. 1 and 2. New York: Appleton-Century-Crofts, 1970.

Birney, Catherine H. The Grimké Sisters: Sarah and Angelina Grimké: The First American Women Advocates of Abolition and Women's Rights. New York: Scholarly Press, 1970.

Flexner, Eleanor. Century of Struggle: The Woman's Rights Movement in the U.S. Cambridge, Mass.: Harvard University Press, 1975.

Grimké, Angelina E. Letters to Catherine E. Beecher. New York: Arno Press, 1969.

Hymowitz, Carol and Weissman, Michaele. A History of Women in America. New York: Bantam Books, 1978.

Lumpkin, Katherine DuPre. The Emancipation of Angelina Grimké. Chapel Hill, N. C.: University of North Carolina Press, 1974.

EXERCISE F: Writing a First Draft. Use the outline you developed in Exercise E and your notes to write a first draft of your paper. As you write the draft, write only on every other line of paper and leave margins around your copy. Use one method, informal citations or footnotes, to cite the information you have borrowed from your sources. If you wish, include headings for the subtopics of your paper.

EXERCISE G: Revising and Writing a Final Copy. Reread the first draft you wrote in Exercise F. Use the checklist on page 745 to check your paper. Make all corrections, alterations, and revisions right on the paper. Then write a good final copy, adding a title, title page, and a bibliography.

APPLICATION: Planning, Writing, and Revising a Library Paper. Choose another subject for a paper, a topic that your teacher assigns or one that you think of on your own. Follow the planning, writing, and revising steps provided in this section.

Chapter 26

Papers About Literature

While you are in school you will often be required to write about literature you have read either in class or on your own. Writing about short stories, novels, poems, plays, and nonfiction works calls for a number of skills: your ability to read and comprehend literature, your ability to analyze and draw conclusions about what you read, and your ability to write clearly to share your knowledge and interpretations.

This chapter discusses one kind of composition you can write to present your reactions to works of literature: the literary review. The first section discusses the content and structure of literary reviews, and the second section explains some helpful steps you can follow to write them.

The Literary Review 26.1

A literary review is a written reaction to a work of literature—a short story, a novel, a poem, a play, a biography, or another work of nonfiction. Literary reviews appear in newspapers and magazines and are used to inform readers about new works of literature and to persuade them to read or not to read these new works. The literary reviews you will write can simply explain a work, but most often they will delve deeper into the work to interpret and evaluate. A literary review should indicate that you, the reviewer, have read and thoroughly understood the work. Your review can also help readers to decide if they want to read the work or else help them to appreciate it more if they have already read it.

The content and structure of most literary reviews follow a few general guidelines. A literary review has a general topic, which is usually one work of literature, and several subtopics, which consist of aspects of the work that the reviewer thinks are interesting or important. A literary review contains a series of paragraphs that identify the work, discuss significant aspects of it, and evaluate it. The review has a beginning, a middle, and an end, although its structure is usually less defined than that of an essay or a library paper. Each part of the review must have unity and coherence. When you have become familiar with some typical review topics and when you have studied the forms your reviews can take, you will be ready to write your own literary reviews.

■ Key Features of a Literary Review

A literary review has three key features. (1) It has a work of literature as its topic. (2) It offers explanations, interpretations, and evaluations of that work. (3) It draws most of its ideas and supporting information directly from the work that is being discussed.

Topics for Literary Reviews.   A literary review should give the reader an overview of a work and an in-depth look at some of the elements of that work, such as the theme or the characters. Thus the general topic of a review is the overall work, and the subtopics are the elements of the work that you choose to explain or interpret in some detail.

> A literary review can focus on several specific elements that you find significant in a work, such as theme, characters, conflict, plot, setting, point of view, imagery, symbols, and tone, and on your reactions and evaluations.

In order to select the elements of the work that you will discuss and to evaluate the work for the reader, you must first analyze the work and make sure that you understand it. You should consider the author's intentions in writing the work, the author's techniques, your reactions to the work, and the significance of the work for you and for other readers. You can come to understand a work by examining its elements. Although theme, characters, plot, and the other elements are all interrelated, analyzing these elements separately can help you to evaluate and appreciate the whole work. Identifying and thinking about each of the major elements in the work you choose will also help you select the elements you want to concentrate on in your review.

The following chart gives definitions of the elements, which you can apply to the literary work you are planning to review.

ELEMENTS FOR ANALYSIS AND DISCUSSION IN A LITERARY REVIEW	
Element	**Definition**
Theme	A general truth or central idea implied or dramatized by all the elements in the work. One theme might focus on the idea that human beings are often isolated by their selfishness. Another might present the idea that people grow in wisdom and character through suffering. A work can have more than one theme.
Characters	The people in a story, poem, or play. Readers get to know characters through their actions, dialogue, effects on other characters, and sometimes through direct statements by the narrator. Characters act out the author's themes.
Conflict	A central struggle between opposing people or forces. Conflict can be external—between characters, between a character and society, or between a character and God or Fate. Conflict can also be internal—within a single character. Conflict may arise, for example, between what a character knows she should do and what she wants to do.
Plot	The planned ordering of events so that the action of the work develops from character and conflict. The plot usually builds toward a climax, which resolves the conflict.
Setting	The time, place (physical location), and general background of the work.
Point of view	The voice or consciousness telling the story, generally called the narrator. A *first person narrator* uses "I" and participates in the story, recounting the events as he or she observes or experiences them. A *third person objective narrator* tells the story from outside, reporting only observable actions. A *third person partially omniscient narrator* is also outside the story but tells the story through the eyes and mind of one character, whom the reader comes to understand best. A *third person omniscient narrator* is outside the story but can see into the minds of many or all of the characters.

Imagery	Words that create word pictures that appeal to the senses; the use of sensory impressions and figures of speech (such as similes, metaphors, and personification) to appeal to the senses, emotions, and imaginations of readers.
Symbols	Concrete objects, characters, places, or events that have deeper, more universal meanings beyond their obvious, literal representations.
Tone	The author's attitude toward the subject and the audience.

Once you have identified the theme or themes, characters, conflict, plot, setting, point of view, imagery, symbols, and tone of the work you are studying, you can choose two or more of these elements to explore in depth. For example, if you were planning to write about Mark Twain's humorous sketch "The Great French Duel," you might jot down a description of some of these elements as possible subtopics for your literary review. Your list of elements to develop in your review might resemble the following.

SAMPLE SUBTOPICS FOR A LITERARY REVIEW OF ONE WORK	
Element	**Possible Subtopic for a Review**
Theme	How the story dramatizes two themes: one about how people often go to great lengths to look good for society and one about how people often hide their cowardice behind senseless ceremonies.
Characters	How Twain reveals M. Gambetta's cowardice disguised by his pompous manner.
Conflict	The false, exaggerated pride of two French politicians versus the narrator's common sense.
Setting	How the fog and the crowd gathered for the duel dramatize the theme of the sketch.
Point of view	The first person narrator's participation in setting up and fighting the duel.
Tone	How Twain makes fun of the custom of dueling.

Although your review may touch on all of these points, it might develop only two or three. The general topic of your review would be the whole sketch. Subtopics of your review might be comments on the story's conflicts, point of view, and tone. In discussing conflicts, you might write about the narrator's opposition to the duel. In discussing point of view, you might write about the amusing view of the duel that the narrator gives, and in discussing tone, you might write about how Twain achieves his humorous, mocking tone through the words he chooses.

Purposes for Literary Reviews.   A literary review can be (1) essentially expository throughout; (2) expository, concluding with an evaluation that expresses your opinion of the work; or (3) essentially persuasive throughout. Most of the reviews you will read and write will be persuasive throughout. Except for a factual summary of the work, they will most likely present interpretations, criticisms, and evaluations of specific elements and of the work as a whole.

> A literary review can focus on informing the reader about a work or on explaining the work and then evaluating it. Usually it will focus mainly on interpreting and evaluating the work for the reader.

A literary review that is expository throughout simply attempts to explain the work to the reader. You might write this kind of review if you were reporting on the contents and style of a book for students who had not read it. Or you might write an expository review to show that you had read and understood the work. When your purpose is simply to explain the work, you should discuss the elements of the work factually. You should objectively report what is in the work and explain the techniques the writer used, while letting readers draw their own conclusions. A review of this kind would call for examples, facts, and details from the work and would require that you select and organize your explanations since you could not cover every aspect in detail.

A literary review can also be explanatory and yet end with an evaluation. You might write this kind of review if you were both informing other students about the content of a work and trying to influence them to read or not to read it. The first part of such a review might explain some of the elements and the final part might present your conclusions, interpretations, and evaluations. For instance, you might end your explanations by telling why you enjoyed reading the book or why the book is a significant commentary on modern life.

Most of the reviews you write will be persuasive although they will depend on thorough explanations of the work to back up your interpretations and conclusions. If you wanted to convince other readers to accept your interpretation of a work and to persuade them to read the work, you would write this kind of review. You might also be asked to write such a review to show your critical thinking skills by interpreting the meaning of a work or evaluating the writer's success in, for instance, creating a character. In this kind of persuasive review, you would most likely include an objective summary of the contents of the work. Your discussion of your chosen subtopics, however, would present your opinions about the meaning and effectiveness of the elements in the work. The review might end with an overall evaluation and recommendation.

Kinds of Support for Literary Reviews.   Whatever elements in a work you choose to write about and whatever purpose your review has, it should be based on specific supporting information from the work itself.

> Support for a literary review can include (1) short summaries, (2) specific examples, details, and facts from the work, and (3) direct quotations from the work.

Including specific information from the work that you are reviewing shows that you have read and understood it, helps to focus your discussion, and makes your explanations and interpretations more meaningful to the reader. You do not have to use all three kinds of support in every review, but you should always include enough specific information to make your review complete and convincing.

Short summaries can inform the reader of important ideas or events in a work. If your review deals with plot, for instance, a short summary of the plot can make your review more understandable to the reader. If you include a summary in your review, write it in your own words and simply give the facts without inserting your own opinions.

Another kind of support—examples, details, and facts from the work—can back up your explanations and interpretations. For example, if you state that a character is believable, you should specify which of the character's actions and thoughts led you to form this opinion. If you are stating that the plot of a story is unsatisfying because the author has left too many questions unanswered, give examples of these omissions. This specific, concrete evidence makes your review more interesting and contributes to your reader's desire to read or not read the work.

The direct quotation is a third kind of support that enables the reader to become familiar with the work. Direct quotations can support your general statements and opinions. If you are arguing that a poem uses particularly powerful images, include a few in your review to substantiate your claim. If a character's distinctive personality is revealed through speech, giving a sample of this character's speech will illustrate your point. If you use direct quotations in your review, keep them short and always place them in quotation marks. You may also want to cite the page on which you found them.

EXERCISE A: Finding Topics for Literary Reviews. Choose a short story, novel, play, poem, or book of nonfiction that you have recently read. If none is appropriate, read one specifically for this assignment. The work should be interesting and thought-provoking. Use the chart on page 753 to help identify the major literary elements of your work. (For nonfiction books, you can substitute central idea and main ideas for theme.) When you have listed particular elements from your work, such as the point of view used, one or more main characters, the kind of imagery used, and so on, indicate *three* elements that you think readers would want to know about.

EXERCISE B: Deciding on a Purpose for a Literary Review. Using the work of literature you chose and the elements you indicated in Exercise A, determine a purpose for your literary review. Think about your audience and your reason for writing. On your paper, identify your audience as other students who have read the work, other students who have not read the work but are considering doing so, or some other audience. Write down your reason for writing the review: to inform others of the content and organizaion of the work, to interest others in reading the work, and so on. Then write down whether your review will be expository, expository with a persuasive ending, or persuasive and interpretive throughout.

EXERCISE C: Identifying Support for a Literary Review. Using the work you chose in Exercise A, complete the following instructions.

1. Write a short summary of the work. In a short paragraph, tell what the work is about. Make your summary objective, factual, and accurate.

2. For each of the elements you selected in Exercise A, list *two* specific examples, details, or facts that a reader might find interesting and that would further the explanatory or persuasive purpose you chose in Exercise B.
3. Finally, find *two* quotations from the work that could support one or more of the elements you chose. Write down each quotation accurately, enclose it in quotation marks, and indicate the page (or line for a poem) on which it is found. Briefly explain why you would include each quotation in your review.

■ Structure of a Literary Review

Although the structure of a literary review is more flexible than that of a standard essay or library paper, the review must be a unified, smoothly connected piece of writing. A literary review consists of a series of well-developed paragraphs, each exploring some element of the work of literature and each related to the others by the common general topic. Introductory remarks should engage the reader's interest and lay a foundation for the discussion that will comprise the middle of the review. A final paragraph should summarize the ideas presented in the review and can also evaluate the effectiveness or value of the work and offer recommendations to people who might want to read it.

A literary review should have a beginning, a middle, and an end and have unity and coherence throughout. It should consist of a series of paragraphs identifying the work and author, highlighting a few elements of the work, and often evaluating the work.

The structure of a literary review will vary depending on whether you are reviewing a book of poetry or one poem, a recent novel or a classic, a play or a short story. How familiar your audience is with the work will also shape your review. However, most literary reviews will have some or all of the structural features explained in the following chart.

PARTS OF A LITERARY REVIEW
1. *A title*: The title may simply state the title and author of the work being reviewed. A more imaginative title, however, might

suggest the topic of the review while hinting at the reviewer's purpose and approach to the work.

2. *Introductory remarks*: These should interest the reader in the work, identify the author and work, specify the kind of work it is (a detective novel, a comedy in three acts, a narrative poem, and so on), and state the author's probable intentions in writing the work.

3. *A summary of the contents*: A summary or description of the work should include enough information for the reader to get a feel for the work and to be able to understand the review. The summary may be combined with the introductory remarks or, occasionally, may be spread throughout the review. It should usually be brief.

4. *A discussion of the striking elements*: An in-depth look at two or three of the elements should make up the middle paragraphs of the review. These paragraphs should focus on some significant aspects of the work that can be discussed with specific supporting information from the work. These subtopics should be something the reader would want to know about.

5. *Final statements*: The final paragraph should pull together the ideas in the review by summarizing them in a few words. Often, the review will end with an evaluation that judges the success of the work (How good is it for what it attempts to do?) and the significance of the work (Should the work have been written? What does it add to life?). A few concluding remarks may either recommend that the work be read or try to dissuade readers from reading it.

The following diagram illustrates the structure of a literary review written about Mark Twain's "The Great French Duel." Notice that the five-paragraph review is interpretive and persuasive throughout. Notice, also, that the review has a title, "A Duel to Remember," which suggests the reviewer's opinion of the sketch.

A DUEL TO REMEMBER	
Introductory remarks and summary	"The Great French Duel"—humorous sketch by Mark Twain from his book *A Tramp Abroad*, published in 1880; Twain's intention is to make fun of the French custom and method of dueling.
Discussion of conflict	Of the two related conflicts in the story—M. Gambetta versus M. Fourtou and the narrator versus the French code of dueling—the second is Twain's main concern. (Supporting information)

Discussion of point of view	Twain makes his first person narrator` participate in the duel and expose it as an absurd joke. (Supporting information)
Discussion of tone	Twain puts words with double meanings into the narrator's mouth: Seeming to state facts and give praise, he humorously ridicules French customs. (Supporting information)
Final statements	The conflicts, point of view, and tone make this sketch an effective satire. Readers will get a laugh out of these self-important characters and their ridiculous duel.

EXERCISE D: Analyzing a Literary Review. Following is a poem by Emily Dickinson entitled "A Narrow Fellow in the Grass" and a literary review written about the poem. Read the poem and the review, and then follow the instructions given after the review.

A Narrow Fellow in the Grass

A narrow Fellow in the Grass
Occasionally rides—
You may have met Him—did you not
His notice sudden is—

The Grass divides as with a Comb—
A spotted shaft is seen—
And then it closes at your feet
And opens further on—

He likes a Boggy Acre
A Floor too cool for Corn—
Yet when a Boy, and Barefoot—
I more than once at Noon

Have passed, I thought, a Whip lash
Unbraiding in the Sun
When stooping to secure it
It wrinkled, and was gone—

Several of Nature's People
I know, and they know me—
I feel for them a transport
Of cordiality—

But never met this Fellow
Attended, or alone
Without a tighter breathing
And Zero at the Bone—

—Emily Dickinson

A Close Encounter

Emily Dickinson's poem "A Narrow Fellow in the Grass" surprises and pleases the reader with its vividness and intensity. This poem, composed of six stanzas of four lines each, is about encountering a snake in a field. Through the poem the poet is conveying a feeling and sharing an emotional experience: Meeting a snake in the grass is a startling, chilling event.

Dickinson makes the narrator's feelings toward the snake, as well as the snake's physical being, sharp and clear to the reader through her use of exact images and crisp language. The personification "A narrow Fellow" and the image of "a spotted shaft" suggest the length, shape, color, and slithery quality of a snake. The poet captures the reptilian coldness and wetness of a snake by associating it with muddy swamps: "He likes a Boggy Acre/ A Floor too cool for Corn." The imagery also depicts the snake in motion and the effect this motion has on an observer. The snake "rides" in the grass, suggesting its gliding movement. And the image, "It wrinkled, and was gone," helps the reader see the undulation of the snake and sense its unnerving disappearance. The movement of the snake is further clarified by the simile that compares its progress through the blades of tall grass to the way a comb parts hair; the reader can visualize the grass separating and coming together again as the snake slides by partly unseen. The appearance of the snake in action is most dramatically captured by a metaphor in which the snake is "a Whip lash/ Unbraiding in the Sun."

All these images contribute to and express the tone of the poem, which is a fascinating blend of pleasure and fear. Dickinson writes the poem using a speaker or narrator who is a man, probably a farmer or other country dweller. On the one hand, the speaker delights in the outdoors and its creatures. He addresses the reader in a familiar, friendly way, assuming that the reader is also a lover of nature. The speaker personifies the animals as "Nature's People" and says that he has a warm, friendly feeling toward these creatures. In contrast, the particular images describing the snake and the speaker's reactions to it convey fear and discomfort. The first stanza suggests this attitude when it mentions the alarming abruptness of the snake's appearance: "His notice sudden is." All the images give the impression that the speaker finds the snake startling, clammy, elusive, unfriendly, and slightly mysterious. And in the sixth stanza, the speaker fully expresses his distress and unpleasant physical reactions to the snake with these words: "tighter breathing" and "Zero at the Bone." These two phrases alone capture the gasp and chill associated with sudden fright.

This tone of cheerful familiarity and tingling fear created by the precise, compact, well-chosen images works in the poem to convey a vivid experience and a strong feeling. "A Narrow Fellow in the Grass" merits reading and rereading. It lingers in the reader's mind and inspires a closer observation of nature. After reading this poem, the reader feels eager to sample more of Emily Dickinson's nature poems.

1. On your paper, write down the topic of this review and the elements examined.
2. Identify the purpose of the review. Specify the audience you think the writer had in mind and the writer's probable reason for writing.
3. List the different kinds of support used in the review and give at least *one* example of each.
4. Using the diagram on page 759 as a guide, draw a diagram of this review, briefly indicating the parts of the review, such as the introductory remarks, summary, and so on.
5. Give *two* examples of ways the writer has made the review unified and coherent.
6. How effective is the review in fulfilling its purpose?

APPLICATION: Finding and Analyzing a Literary Review. Find a professional literary review by looking through magazines such as *The New Yorker, Newsweek, Horn Book, Time*, or the Sunday edition of newspapers. Read the literary review carefully, and then use the instructions in Exercise D to analyze it.

26.2 Writing the Literary Review

Writing a literary review involves analyzing a work of literature to reach a thorough understanding of it and expressing your thoughts about the work in an interesting way. Preparing a literary review should prompt you to examine your reactions to the work and to discover insights about the author's intentions and techniques. Your completed review should pique readers' curiosity to read this work, inform them of the limitations of the work, or increase their understanding and appreciation of it.

This section offers some steps to follow to analyze literary works and to write reviews that accurately reflect the work in a unified, coherent, and enjoyable way.

■ Reacting to a Work of Literature

Before you can write well about a work of literature, you will have to examine it carefully and explore your reactions to it. You cannot discuss every detail of a work in one review. Therefore, you should select elements to discuss that you think are the most thought-provoking, the most important, or the most interesting to other readers. Another essential step in your planning is to consider your audience and your reason for writing the review.

Examining the Elements in a Literary Work.   Every work of literature has several elements to examine, such as theme, characters, setting, imagery, and tone. These elements will be woven together, but by examining them singly, you can discover how they combine to create the meaning and effect of the work as a whole. You should also remember that not all kinds of works will include all the elements. For instance, a poem may not have a plot or characters. When you examine your work, then, you should figure out which elements it contains, describe them in order to understand them, and think about their significance in the work. This process of examination should involve jotting down your reactions to the elements and asking yourself questions about the author's craft and ideas.

Begin your analysis by identifying the elements in the work, by asking yourself questions, and by taking notes.

If a work is well written, the way in which the author has combined the elements may not be immediately apparent. You may have to probe, reread parts of the work, and take notes on your reactions. You should ask yourself questions about the elements to further your understanding and to help find the parts of the work you want to write about in your review. The following chart lists some of the questions you might ask yourself.

IDENTIFYING ELEMENTS TO UNDERSTAND AND DISCUSS IN YOUR REVIEW

1. Did you like the work? What did it make you feel or think?
2. What is the author trying to say? What is the major theme or central idea?
3. Who are the main characters in the work?
   —Do the characters change in the course of the work?
   —Which methods of revealing character (actions, dialogue, thoughts, and so on) has the author used most?
   —Does the author seem to criticize the characters or sympathize with the characters?
   —Can you identify with the characters?

4. What characters or forces oppose the main characters, creating a conflict?
   —What scenes or events display this conflict?
   —What is the crisis or climax?
   —How is the conflict resolved?

5. What aspects of the plot make it particularly interesting or exciting?

6. What is the setting?
   —Is the setting strongly felt or is it simply a backdrop?
   —Does the setting change?

7. What point of view has the author used?
   —How important is the point of view to the work?
   —Would another point of view work as well?

8. How does the imagery contribute to the effect and meaning of the work?
   —Is the imagery sparse or abundant?
   —Are there any patterns of imagery such as night sounds and smells, bird imagery, and so on?

9. Do any objects, characters, or places act as symbols, having meanings beyond their surface meanings?

10. Does the work have a dominant tone?

You may not be able to ask and answer all these questions, especially if the work you choose is long. Instead, you might think about four or five of these questions as well as your own reactions to the work. For example, if you read Edith Wharton's novel *Ethan Frome*, you might jot down answers to the questions about your own reactions, the theme, the main characters, the conflicts, the setting, the point of view, and the symbols. Depending on which elements interest you the most, you might decide to focus on one of the main characters, the setting, and the point of view in your review. These three elements would then become your subtopics.

Determining Audience and Purpose.   Once you have analyzed some of the major elements in the work and have chosen a few to concentrate on in your review, you should decide for what audience you are writing and for what specific reason. These decisions will help you determine your purpose.

Identify your audience and determine the purpose for your review.

When you begin planning your review, you should have a specific audience and reason for writing in mind. These can guide you in focusing on your purpose throughout the review and in choosing the most appropriate ideas and details from the work.

If you are writing for an audience that is *unfamiliar* with the work, you have three choices for your reason for writing and your purpose. First, you can simply attempt to explain some of the main elements or the organization of the work without offering opinions. Basically, this review would say, "This is what this work is about." Second, you can explain some of the main elements of the work but conclude your review with an evaluation and a recommendation in which you offer your opinions. This kind of review might say, "This is what this work is about, and I think you would enjoy reading it." Your third choice is to interpret the work. You would offer your opinions, support them, and conclude with an evaluation and a recommendation. A review that is essentially persuasive might say, "The author uses these elements particularly well in the work, and you will find the work exciting and rewarding to read."

If you are writing for an audience *familiar* with the work, your reason for writing will most often be persuasive—to convince other readers to accept your interpretation and evaluation of the work. Your readers may not know the work as well as you do or may disagree with you about its meaning or worth. Your task would then be to present your interpretations, well supported with examples, details, and facts from the work. Persuasive writing in a review will necessarily involve a considerable amount of explaining, and the more controversial your interpretations are, the more evidence and explanations you will have to include from the work.

If you had just read *Ethan Frome* on your own, you might decide to write your review for the members of your class who had not read the book. You might decide to share your opinions that the author's techniques are successful and that the book is well worth reading. Your discussion of three elements—a main character, setting, and point of view—would then have a persuasive slant.

EXERCISE A: Responding to a Work and Its Elements. Choose a literary work—a poem, short story, novel, or some other work—that you have recently read. If none is appropriate, choose one to read for this assignment. Examine the elements in the work using some of the questions in the chart on page

763 and at least *two* of your own questions. Jot down answers to the questions as well as your reactions to specific parts and features of the work. Then choose *three* elements that seem most significant or interesting to discuss in your review.

EXERCISE B: Choosing an Audience and Purpose. Decide who your audience will be and why you are writing. Write down these decisions on your paper, and write down whether your review will be expository, expository with an evaluation at the end, or persuasive.

■ Developing Support for a Literary Review

Now you are ready to gather the ideas and information that will form the substance of your review. To do this creative thinking step, you will have to consult your notes, do some more analyzing of the elements you have chosen to focus on, and jot down your own reactions to the work in the form of evaluations and recommendations.

Reexamine the work, your notes, and your thoughts to find ideas, examples, details, facts, and possibly quotations from the work to develop the parts of your review.

As you learned in Section 26.1, a literary review should have a number of parts: a title, introductory remarks, a summary of the work, a discussion of several elements of the work, and final statements. Thinking about these parts, your audience, and your purpose can help you find material for your review. For this task you should have your notes and the work before you, and you should be prepared to do some brainstorming and additional analysis. The steps in the following chart can help you find the ideas and information you need for your review.

STEPS FOR DEVELOPING SUPPORT FOR A LITERARY REVIEW
1. On a piece of paper, identify your work, the author, and the nature of the work. (Has the author written a historical novel, a comic novel, a tragic novel, an autobiography, a lyric poem?)
2. Briefly summarize the contents of the work. Remember that your audience should determine how detailed your summary will be.

3. Focus on each of the elements you have chosen, one at a time. Ask yourself questions about each element and brainstorm for answers. You may have to return to your notes or take further notes at this point to find something interesting and accurate to say about each element. Jot down as many relevant examples, details, facts, and quotations from the work as you can. You can sift through and evaluate these pieces of information later.

4. For an expository review, jot down ideas for the final paragraph, a summary of the review. Remember that you will probably have to revise these ideas after you have actually written the review. For a review ending with an evaluation, jot down summary ideas and also ask yourself some questions, such as "How good is this work for what it attempts to do? What insights into life does it provide? Is it worth reading?" Then write down answers that express your opinions and recommendations.

If you were writing a persuasive review of *Ethan Frome* for an audience who had not read the novel and if you were planning to discuss three subtopics—a character (Ethan Frome), the setting, and the point of view—your support might resemble that listed in the following chart. Notice that the list contains more ideas and information than can probably go into one review, but the best ideas can be selected from this thorough list. Notice, also, that the questions and answers developed in brainstorming about the elements suit a persuasive purpose. Finally, notice that direct quotations are enclosed in quotation marks.

SUPPORT FOR A LITERARY REVIEW ON ETHAN FROME
Topic: Ethan Frome
Identification of work and author —the tragic novel *Ethan Frome* by Edith Wharton (1911)
Summary of work —a farmer, Ethan Frome, contends with the harsh climate of New England, poverty, and an unhappy marriage —Mattie, young relative of Ethan's wife, Zeena, comes to visit to help sickly Zeena with the household chores —Ethan imagines what life would be like married to Mattie —Ethan's personality and the conditions of his life work together to shatter his dreams

Why is Ethan a believable, memorable character?

—he has life-like strengths, weaknesses, and contradictions
—is sensitive to natural beauty:
stars, rocks, trees, sunsets
—is silent, stern, inarticulate
—is capable of great feeling
and tenderness
—is interested in world outside
Starkfield

—slaves at his sawmill and on
his barren land
—patiently endures his empty
life
—does not pursue feeble
chance to escape because of
his honesty, pride, and kind
heart

What is unusual or important about the setting?

—setting becomes a character
in the story
—plays a part in all the actions
—influences all the characters
—is Starkfield, Massachusetts,
in late 1800's
—is a lonely, cold place to live
—has long winters: "six
months' seige"
—climate called "the enemy"

—influences Ethan's
decision to marry Zeena
—throws the narrator and
Ethan together in a blizzard
—keeps Ethan's farm poor
because of long winters and
barren soil
—setting contributes to Ethan's
defeat
—neighbor explains "Guess
he's been in Starkfield too
many winters."

How does the point of view affect the book and influence the reader?

—point of view creates suspense and intensity
—two different narrators
—beginning and end of
novel told by first-person
narrator
—middle (flashback) told by
third-person partially
omniscient narrator
—first-person narrator stirs up
reader's curiosity
—notices Ethan at post office
—notices unusual qualities:
"Even then he was the
most striking figure in

Starkfield, though he was
but the ruin of a man."
—wonders about him: Why
didn't Ethan leave
Starkfield? What was the
smash-up? Why won't
people talk about Ethan?

—third-person partially
omniscient narrator enables
reader to see into the mind of
young Ethan
—learn about his youth
—learn about his feelings for
Mattie and Zeena

Summary, evaluation, recommendation   (How good is this work for
what it attempts to do? Why should someone read the book?)

—good story-telling techniques
—story comes alive and moves the
reader

—realistic, touching portrait of
human feelings and suffering
—well worth reading but
very intense and sad

EXERCISE C: Gathering Supporting Material for a Literary Review. Using the elements you chose in Exercise A and the audience and purpose you identified in Exercise B, follow the steps for developing support given in the chart on page 766. At this point, just try to get your ideas down on paper. You can evaluate and sort them later.

■ Organizing a Literary Review

Once you have gathered ideas and information for your review, your next task is to organize your subtopics.

Organize your review by ordering your subtopics and by evaluating and ordering the supporting information under each subtopic.

Since the different parts of a literary review provide a basic organization, begin now to organize the subtopics you have chosen and the information you have gathered about each subtopic. At this point you should examine your list of support to decide whether your subtopics should follow the order they are in or whether another order would be more logical. Often you will use developmental order, although order of importance and chronological order are also possibilities. You should also consider how you will move from the discussion of one subtopic to the next. What logical connections and transitions can you use?

Next you should examine the information listed under each subtopic. Are there any pieces of support that are unrelated, repetitious, or vague? Sometimes using one quotation might be better than using two. You may also think of new relevant ideas to improve the discussion of a subtopic. Then consider whether your supporting information under each subtopic should follow order of importance, chronological order, spatial order, comparison and contrast order, or developmental order. Sometimes, if a subtopic is especially interesting or significant, you may want to devote two or more paragraphs to it. After making these decisions, you should order the information for each paragraph.

You may place the subtopics and the supporting information for your review in order right on your list of support by numbering or circling the pieces of information. Another alternative is to relist the information in a modified outline on another piece of paper.

In writing about *Ethan Frome*, you might decide that the review would be smoother and more interesting if you re-ordered the subtopics so that you discuss setting first, point of view second, and the character of Ethan Frome third. After looking at your list of supporting information, you might also decide that your discussion of point of view would take two paragraphs, one on each of the narrators. You might then cross out a few pieces of supporting information that seem unnecessary and decide that the information will follow developmental order under each subtopic.

EXERCISE D: Selecting and Arranging Your Supporting Information. Examine the list of support you worked on in Exercise C and follow these instructions.

1. Decide what order your subtopics will follow.
2. Examine the information that is grouped under each subtopic, weed out extraneous, repetitious, or weak support, and add any relevant new ideas that occur to you. Then decide on an order for the information under each subtopic.
3. Formally organize the subtopics and the information under them, either on your list of support or in a modified outline.

■ Writing the Review

To complete the process of writing a literary review, you should write a first draft of the entire review and then revise and recopy it.

Preparing a First Draft. Writing the review involves connecting all the parts you have developed into a unified, coherent piece of writing with a beginning, a middle, and an end. At this point, you may find it helpful to refer to the chart in Section 26.1, page 758, describing the parts of a literary review.

Concentrate on your audience, purpose, and the literary work as you write the review from your list of support, from your notes, and possibly from an outline.

When you draft your review, you should flesh out the ideas from your list of support in smooth, complete, varied sentences. You should first write an introductory sentence or two that will interest your audience. After identifying the work and author and summarizing the work, you should proceed into the discussion of the significant elements you have chosen. While you are drafting, include new ideas or alterations that occur to you and that strengthen your purpose and subtopics. Whenever you include direct quotations, be sure to enclose them in quotation marks and possibly cite the page (or line for a poem). Use transitions to move from one subtopic to the next and to make your ideas flow under each subtopic.

Your final statements should wrap up the review with a summary of its ideas and probably with an evaluation and a recommendation of the work. Try to make your closing remarks concise, memorable judgments of the work. Finally, write a title for the review that reflects an important idea about the work.

Revising and Rewriting. Revising is your opportunity to improve and to polish your review for clarity and style.

Revise your review by reexamining and refining it, using a checklist to guide you.

The key to successful revising is to read your review critically as a reader would. After reading each question in the following checklist, return to your review and consider its content, organization, and style.

CHECKLIST FOR REVISING A LITERARY REVIEW

1. Does the title suit the ideas and focus of the review?
2. Do the introductory remarks spark the reader's interest and identify the work?
3. Does the summary of the work provide enough background information for the reader to be able to understand and appreciate the review?
4. Are the elements you discuss interesting to the reader and well-developed with specific material from the work?
5. Do all explanations and interpretations present the work accurately and clearly?
6. Are the subtopics and the information under them logically arranged and smoothly connected with transitions and other linking devices?
7. Do the final statements summarize the ideas in the review in a satisfying way? Are evaluations and recommendations decisive and memorable?
8. Does the review have a pleasing style: vivid word choices and varied sentence lengths and structures?
9. Can you find errors in grammar, usage, spelling, mechanics, or the presentation of direct quotations?

You can make revisions and corrections right on your first draft. Preparing a neat final copy is your last step.

If you had written the persuasive literary review of *Ethan Frome* discussed in this section, it might resemble the following. Notice that the review includes all the appropriate parts as well as a summary. It also includes examples, details, facts, and direct quotations to support the interpretations. The few direct quotations give some of the flavor of the work. Notice, also, that transitions link the discussion of the different elements.

Title	The Painful Pleasure of <u>Ethan Frome</u>
Introductory remarks	The novel <u>Ethan Frome</u>, written by Edith Wharton in 1911, is a tragic, haunting story of love, suffering, and defeat. It recounts the struggles of a farmer,
Summary of the plot	Ethan Frome, against the sad circumstances of his life: the harsh climate of New England, poverty, and an unhappy marriage. When Mattie Silver, a young relative of Zeena, his sickly wife, comes to live with the Fromes to help Zeena with household chores, Ethan imagines what his life would be like if he were married to Mattie. But Ethan's honesty and kind heart and the conditions of his life conspire to shatter his dreams and waste his life and the lives of those around him.
Subtopic 1: discussion of setting as a character	One element that the reader soon notices is the setting of this story, which functions as a character, ever-present and powerful in its negative influence on the human characters. The story takes place in Starkfield, Massachusetts, in the late 1800's, when many New England villages were bleak, lonely, uneventful places to live. The narrator describes the winter as a "six months' siege" every year, implying that the climate is an aggressive enemy. When Ethan's mother dies in the middle of a dreary winter, this enemy impels him to marry Zeena, his mother's nurse, so that he won't be alone. This enemy lurks in the shadows and chills the farmhouse during most of the scenes in the novel when Ethan and Mattie realize their love for each other. Furthermore, it is the severe weather combined with the rocky, barren soil that keeps Ethan in debt and bound to his farm. This enemy traps, controls, and helps to defeat him. One neighbor describes Ethan's losing battle against this character: "Guess he's been in Starkfield too many winters."
Subtopic 2A: discussion of point of view:	In addition to having an effective setting, which gives the story a forlorn mood, this novel has a point of view that creates suspense and intensity. The be-

ginning and end of the novel are told by a first person narrator, who arouses the reader's curiosity about Ethan. This narrator is an outsider who stays in Starkfield one winter and notices Ethan Frome at the post office: "Even then he was the most striking figure in Starkfield, though he was but the ruin of a man." The reader catches this narrator's contagious curiosity about Ethan and wants to know the answers to many questions: Why didn't Ethan leave this empty town when he was a young man? Why does Ethan look aged when he is only fifty-two? What was the "smash-up" that gave him a red gash on the forehead and a severe limp? Why won't the townspeople talk about Ethan? When the narrator finds his answers—"It was that night that I found the clue to Ethan Frome . . ."—the time and point of view of the novel shift.

Most of the novel consists of this flashback told by a partially omniscient narrator, who draws the reader into the story by playing out Ethan's life. The flashback takes the reader back twenty-four years to when Ethan was a young man. This more intimate narrator intensifies the story. He sees inside Ethan's mind and reveals his thoughts about his youth, his developing feelings for Mattie, and his conflicts with Zeena.

Because the reader sees the outer Ethan from a stranger's point of view and the inner Ethan as he sees himself and life, Ethan becomes a real person with life-like strengths, weaknesses, and contradictions. The young Ethan is silent, stern, and inarticulate, but he is also capable of great feeling and tenderness, which he shows when he helps Mattie with the chores she doesn't know how to do and comforts her after Zeena's scoldings. He is a tireless worker, grinding out a living from his poor sawmill and bare land, but he is also sensitive to the beauty of the constellations and the local granite formations, a sensitivity that he shares with Mattie. Ironically, he is too proud, too honest, too patient, and too kindhearted to pursue his feeble chances to leave Starkfield and start a new life: His personality and life are against him. The reader sympathizes with this character and aches for the young, vigorous Ethan buried forever within "the ruin of a man."

In <u>Ethan Frome</u>, good story-telling techniques bring to life a heart-rending drama of dreams and feelings thwarted by antagonistic surroundings, personal relationships, and the characters themselves. The reader glimpses New England's past and watches its frosty climate exert its coldness and loneliness on

---

the first-person narrator

Subtopic 2B: discussion of point of view: the third-person partially omniscient narrator

Subtopic 3: the character of Ethan Frome

Final statements

Summary of the review

Evaluation and recommendation	the characters. Spurred on by unanswered questions, the reader demands to know what has turned Ethan Frome to stone. The novel rewards the reader with an engrossing look into one man's heart—a painfully intense glance into the chasm between what might have been and what was.

EXERCISE E: Drafting a Literary Review. Use the review you worked out and organized in the earlier exercises, to write a complete draft, focusing on your audience, purpose, and the work. Pay special attention to engaging the reader's interest, to fulfilling your purpose, and to presenting your ideas clearly. Use transitions and other devices to achieve coherence, and place any direct quotations in quotation marks.

EXERCISE F: Polishing a Literary Review. Reread your first draft with an eye toward making corrections and refinements. Read it aloud or have someone else read it and comment on how well you achieve your purpose. Use the checklist on page 771 to guide you to problem areas that need improvement. When you are satisfied with your revisions, write a good final copy of the review.

APPLICATION: Reviewing Other Kinds of Literature. If you reviewed a novel or short story before, try reviewing a poem, biography, essay, or play, and find someone else in the class who is interested in reviewing the same literary work. Discuss the work with this other student, using the questions on page 763 and some of your own. Then individually plan and write your reviews following the steps presented in this section. Find someone in the class not familiar with the work to evaluate your review using the checklist for revision on page 771. When you examine another student's review, briefly identify its strengths and weaknesses. Finally, revise your own review, taking into account the comments you have received, and re-copy it.

Chapter 27

Letters and Précis

Throughout your life, you will probably have to write many letters and short informative reports. You may have social obligations that require correspondence with friends and relatives, or you may need to write letters for business reasons, to order merchandise, or to apply for a job. For a class or for your own purposes, you may have to write short compositions, called *précis*, that condense the information in an article or chapter you have read.

In this chapter, you will study the structures and styles of personal and business letters, along with models of different types of letters that you may need to write. You will also examine the features of the précis and steps in writing précis so that you can adapt your writing skills to preparing these specialized summaries.

Writing Personal and Business Letters 27.1

You have probably already written several different types of letters. As you continue in school and enter college or begin a career, you will continue to write letters for a variety of purposes. Basically, your letters will almost always fall into either of two categories: personal or business. You should have a clear idea of the different requirements of personal and business letters as well as their different purposes.

■ Writing Personal Letters

In addition to the personal information that you would naturally include in any personal letter, you must include several other things that readers expect to find. Personal letters should always follow a certain structure. A heading, for example, should be included to provide your return address and the date on which you are writing. Personal letters should also be written in an acceptable style. Finally, they should be prepared properly for mailing. In the following pages, you will find guidelines for structure, style, and mailing.

Basic Structure of the Letter.   To write a good personal letter, you must know the different parts of the letter and how to arrange them on plain paper or personal stationery.

> Follow the basic five-part structure of a personal letter by including a heading, a salutation, a body, a closing, and a signature.

The *heading* of a personal letter should include your street address, town or city, state, and zip code. The last line of your heading should be the date on which you are writing. The heading of a personal letter is placed in the upper right-hand portion of the paper.

The *salutation*, made up of the words you use to greet the receiver of the letter, should be placed below the heading on the left side of the letter. The salutation will generally begin with the word "Dear," although other, less formal greetings are acceptable in certain circumstances. The salutation of a personal letter is always followed by a comma.

FORMAL SALUTATIONS:	Dear Peg,	Dear Miss Murray,
	Dear Uncle Jim,	Dear Mrs. Campbell,
LESS FORMAL SALUTATIONS:	Hi Teddy,	Hello good Friend
	Greetings Sy,	Hey Buddy,

In the *body* of a personal letter, which should begin two or three lines below the salutation, you can include as many sentences and paragraphs as you like. The body should contain the ideas, feelings, and other personal information meant for your reader.

The *closing*, made up of the words you use to signal the end of the letter, should be placed two or three lines below the body, on the right side of the letter. The first word of the closing is always capitalized and the closing is always followed by a comma. Your choice of words should suit the tone of the letter or your relationship with the receiver.

CLOSINGS: Sincerely yours,   Very truly yours,

Yours truly,   Love,

Your *signature* should be placed a line or two beneath the closing. You should generally use the name by which the receiver normally addresses you. When writing to a friend, you will probably choose to sign your first name or a nickname. When writing to someone older or to someone whom you do not know well, you will generally sign your full name. Sign your name in ink, even if you have typed the letter.

NOTE ABOUT INVITATIONS: On letters of invitation, you may also include an *R.S.V.P.*, which tells the receiver to respond, stating whether he or she will accept or decline the invitation. Usually, an R.S.V.P. (which stands for the French words *répondez s'il vous plaît*, or *respond please*) is placed in the lower left-hand corner of an invitation.

Possible Letter Styles.   As you write a personal letter, you can arrange the different parts in either of two styles.

Choose either indented or semiblock style for your personal letter.

Indented style, shown in the model at the left, calls for an indentation of the lines of the heading, closing, and signature. *Semiblock style*, shown in the model at the right, calls for all lines of the heading, closing, and signature to begin at the same point.

Indented Style   **Semiblock Style**

Heading	
Salutation	
Body	
Closing	
Signature	

Procedures for Mailing.   After completing your letter, you must prepare it for mailing.

Fold your letter correctly and prepare an envelope.

Folding a letter can be accomplished in one of two ways. If the letter is written on a small piece of paper, you can probably fold it in half and slip it into an envelope. Standard-sized paper ($8\frac{1}{2} \times 11$ inches, or 21.6×27.9 cm) can be folded into thirds by folding the lower third of the letter up to cover the central third and then by folding these two thirds up to cover the remaining third. Folding can be completed in two steps.

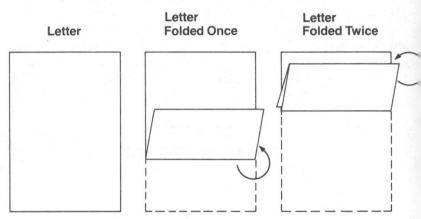

Letter

Letter Folded Once

Letter Folded Twice

The *envelope* of a personal letter should be written in the same style, indented or semiblock, as the letter itself.

Indented Style

Semiblock Style

Regardless of the style you use, you should also follow a few other general guidelines as you write the envelope. Type the envelope if you have typed the letter; handwrite it if the letter is handwritten. Make sure your return address includes your name, address, and zip code. Avoid using such titles as Mr., Miss, or Ms. in your own name. As you write the name and address of the person receiving the letter, include all necessary mailing information: apartment number, route number, and zip code. Avoid any unclear abbreviations, and check for mistakes in spelling and punctuation.

NOTE ABOUT SMALL ENVELOPES: On small envelopes, you may write your return address on the reverse side. But you should check with your post office to see if the envelope is large enough for mailing.

Types of Personal Letters. To write letters that are appropriate for different social situations, you should be aware of the different types of personal letters, each of which has a special purpose.

Know the characteristics of different types of personal letters: friendly letters, invitations, letters of acceptance and regret, and other kinds of social notes.

A *friendly letter* is one written to a friend, acquaintance, or family member. Often, such a letter will be very informal. In this kind of letter, you may want to refer to and perhaps continue the correspondence of an earlier letter or phone call. You may also want to tell about events that have happened to you since your last contact with the receiver. Throughout, you should take care to emphasize things or people that the receiver knows about, is interested in, or might especially enjoy hearing about.

It often helps to imagine that you are about to meet, face-to-face, the person to whom you are writing. In such a case, what would you want to tell the person? What might the person say in return? Thinking about such a meeting can help generate ideas for your letter.

As you write a friendly letter, you should also follow the rules of spelling, usage, and mechanics, and you should use your paragraph- and essay-writing skills, as in the following example.

Box 412
Tarr Hall
Stillwater, North Carolina 02354
September 30, 1980

Dear Laura,

Please pardon my delay in writing, but settling into my dorm room at Brett Academy and looking for a job in Stillwater have taken all of my free time. But — at last — my room is organized, my roommate and I seem compatible, and I have found part-time work as a disc jockey (a record-changer, really) at a roadside hamburger place that allows dancing.

It's a good feeling to have all these small requirements of daily living, not to mention schoolwork, in reasonable order. So I wanted to share with you my satisfaction and bring you up to date since I saw you in August.

I received a card from Esther last week, and she reports that you were elected class vice-president. How great! Please write to tell me more about it. I'll look forward to Thanksgiving vacation when we will all see one another again. Until then, stay well.

Love,
Greg

You may also need to write *invitations*, which are simply brief social notes written to invite someone to an event that you are organizing. In such a letter, you should offer specific details about the time, date, and place, as well as what kind of event it will be. You should also mention what to wear if the receiver is likely to have any question about it. When sending such a letter, you should allow sufficient time for the receiver to decide whether to attend and to respond. If you desire a specific "yes" or "no" from the receiver, you can include an R.S.V.P. The following is a sample invitation.

2726 Ellendale Place
Los Angeles, California 90007
May 10, 1981

Dear, Gina,

After receiving the good news that I will graduate on May 27, 1981, I and some of my classmates decided to plan a graduation celebration. We are inviting relatives and close friends to a buffet dinner, with dancing afterwards.

The party will begin at 6:00 p.m. at my home on graduation day. Dress is informal. I hope, Gina, that you can attend. It would be great to see you again.

Sincerely,
Clint Potter

R.S.V.P.

A *letter of acceptance or regret* is a social note sent in response to an invitation. To write one, you should begin with your answer, positive or negative, and, if your answer is negative, you should offer a reason for being unable to attend. If you accept, you should repeat the date, time, and place to avoid any misunderstanding. Whatever your response, you should express your appreciation for having been invited. Notice in the following letter of acceptance that the writer has carefully followed all of these requirements while giving the letter a very personal tone.

1170 Huntington Drive
South Pasadena, California 91030
May 15, 1981

Dear Clint,

    You can count on me on May 27. Thanks for inviting me. It has been too many months since we've seen each other, and I would enjoy catching up on news and meeting your friends.

    I am looking forward to seeing you and will be there at 6:00 p.m.

                    Sincerely,
                    Gina Beechetti

Other kinds of social notes include thank-you letters for gifts and entertainment, letters of congratulations, and letters of condolence. To write any such letters, you can follow the general guidelines for writing personal letters, while allowing the body of the letter to express your purpose: to say thank-you, to express congratulations, or to extend condolences. Like other social notes, they should generally be brief, direct, and timely.

EXERCISE A: Practicing with Structure and Style. Using two separate pieces of paper, sketch two skeleton letters with lines instead of words for the body. For one letter, use indented style, and, for the other, use semiblock. Fill in the five parts of each letter by using your own address for the heading and someone else's name for the salutation.

EXERCISE B: Preparing Envelopes for Personal Letters. Prepare envelopes for the skeleton letters in Exercise A. Make sure that each envelope matches the style of its letter. Fold each letter properly and place it into its envelope.

EXERCISE C: Writing Different Types of Personal Letters. Choose one of the following ideas for writing a personal letter. Include all five parts of the letter, using your own name and address for the heading as well as someone else's name for the salutation. Keep in mind the type of personal letter that you are writing. When you are finished, prepare an envelope for your letter.

1. Write a friendly letter to a classmate, relative your own age, or a distant friend to bring him or her up to date on your activities.
2. Write a letter of invitation to someone whom you would like to see at a barbecue you are planning. Include any details that the receiver would find helpful and interesting.
3. Imagine that you have received an invitation to some event and respond either positively or negatively. Be sure that your letter refers to the nature of the event.
4. Send a letter of congratulations to someone you know who has received some kind of honor or award. Make up the details.
5. Suppose that your neighbor has been hurt in a car accident. Send a letter of sympathy to him or her.

■ Writing Business Letters

Business letters have structures similar to those of personal letters. Like personal letters, they can also be written in different styles and to serve different purposes.

Basic Structure of the Letter.   To write a business letter, you must know the different parts of the letter and how to arrange them on plain paper or business stationery.

Follow a six-part structure for a business letter by including a heading, an inside address, a salutation, a body, a closing, and a signature.

The *heading* of a business letter should include your complete address and the date on which you are writing. The heading is placed about one inch (2.54 cm) from the top of the paper. Depending on the style you use, you will place the heading either on the right-hand side of the paper or along the left margin.

The *inside address* is made up of the name and the complete address of the person or business to whom you are writing. If a title is included it should follow the name. The inside address is placed about two or three spaces beneath the heading.

INSIDE ADDRESSES: Mr. Earl Burrows, President
The Loyal Order of Muskrat
Route 17
Sandisfield, Massachusetts 01255

Tompkins Heating Service
1300 Palmer Parkway
Ithaca, New York 14850

The *salutation* of a business letter, which greets the receiver, is placed about two lines beneath the inside address. A business salutation is usually formal. If you are writing to a business, rather than to a specific person, you can use one of the general greetings shown in the following examples. In any event, the salutation should be followed by a colon.

SALUTATIONS: Dear Sir: Dear Dr. Ormsby:

Dear Sir or Madam: Gentlemen:

The *body* of the letter should include all information necessary to conduct the business you have in mind. It may include a request, an order, a complaint, or any other ideas that serve your purpose in writing. While the body of the letter can be any length, business letters are usually brief and to the point.

The *closing* signals the end of the letter. The closing begins with a capital letter and ends with a comma, as in the following examples.

CLOSINGS: Very truly yours,   Cordially,

Sincerely,   Respectfully yours,

Your *signature* should include your full name: first and last name as well as middle initial, if any. If your letter is typed, you should also type your full name beneath your signature. Your signature is placed beneath the closing, with the typed version of your name directly beneath your signature.

NOTE ABOUT TITLES WITH SIGNATURES: Women sometimes indicate how they prefer to be addressed in return correspondence (Miss, Mrs., Ms., Dr., and so on) by placing the abbreviation in parentheses before the typed name.

Possible Letter Styles. As you write the different parts of a business letter, you can use one of three business styles.

Choose either block style, modified block style, or semiblock style for your business letter.

If you choose *block style*, you must begin all parts of the letter at the left margin. No lines are indented, not even the first line of a paragraph. Because there is no indentation for paragraphs, you must leave space to indicate that one paragraph has ended and another has begun.

Block Style

If you choose *modified block style*, you must place the heading on the right-hand side of the letter. The closing and signature are also placed on the right-hand side, while the other parts—inside address, salutation, and body paragraphs—begin at the left margin. Again, since paragraphs are not indented, space must be left between them.

Modified Block Style

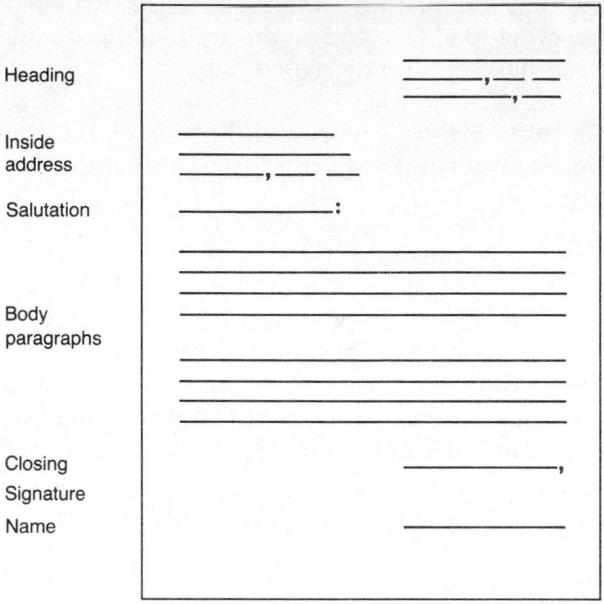

If you choose *semiblock style*, you will follow modified block style with one exception: You will indent the first line of each paragraph in the body.

Semiblock Style

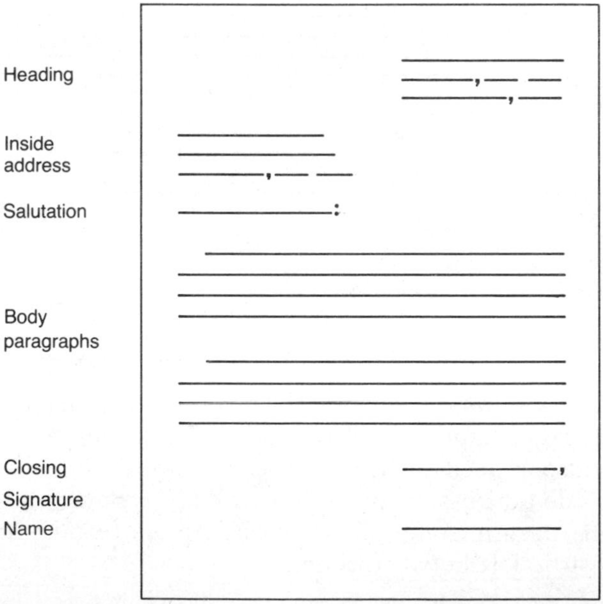

If you need to write a *second page* for your business letter, you should place the name of the receiver of the letter, the page number of the letter, and the date at the top of the paper.

NOTE ABOUT OTHER STYLISTIC DETAILS: Business letters are usually typed on standard-sized white paper (8½ × 11 inches, or 21.6 × 27.9 cm). Margins of at least one inch (2.54 cm) are left on all sides and double or triple spacing is used between paragraphs and other parts of the letter.

Procedures for Mailing.   Once you have written a business letter, you should follow proper procedures for mailing it.

Fold your letter correctly and prepare an envelope following regulation business style.

The *envelope* for your business letter should be standard business size to match your stationery. Place your own name (without title) and address in the upper left-hand corner of the envelope and the name and address of the receiver in the center. The mailing address should match the inside address on the letter. Always prepare the envelope this way.

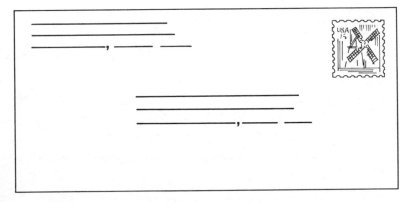

Types of Business Letters.   As you write to suit your different needs, you should be aware of different types of business letters.

Know the characteristics of different types of business letters: request and order letters, letters of application, and letters of complaint and opinion.

In *request and order letters*, you will be asking for information or ordering merchandise. These letters contain the basic structural parts, but the body should also contain a number of special details. In the body, you must begin by stating your specific request for information or merchandise. If you need special information, you should provide a reason for your need. If you are placing an order, you should be brief and to the point, specifying precisely the items that you require as well as any other identifying information such as order numbers. If the order requires payment, state the amount of your order and state the method of payment you are using, such as a check or money order. The following is an example.

```
                              210 P Street N.W.
                              Washington, D.C. 20037
                              February 1, 1981

Order Department
Resnick's, Inc.
1100 Bay Turnpike
Gaithersburg, Maryland 20760

Dear Sir:

    From your Christmas 1980 catalogue, I would

like to order the following items:

        1 pair      Ranger Painter's Pants
                    Size:  30
                    Order Number: 09640     $19.95

        1 set       Ranger Handkerchiefs
                    Color: Red
                    Order Number: 02311     $ 9.95

                                            $29.90

    I have enclosed my personal check for $29.90,

understanding that postage and handling are includ-

ed in the list prices.

                         Sincerely,

                         Warren Wright
                         Warren Wright
```

When you are looking for employment, you may need to write a *letter of application*. Again, you should include all parts of the basic business letter as well as certain special details. In the body, you should begin by identifying the position you are applying for. You should also enclose a résumé if you have one or include the information generally found in a résumé in the body: your experience, your schooling, and references if you think them appropriate. In either the résumé or the letter you should also include any other relevant details about your qualifications. Finally, make sure that your address and phone number are part of the letter (and résumé if you are enclosing one). A letter without a résumé is shown below.

41 Stoneleigh Place
Dobbs Ferry, New York 10522
May 2, 1981

Golden Bridge Inn
Route 6
Wellfleet, Massachusetts 02663

Dear Sir:

I will be spending this summer on Cape Cod with my family and am seeking summer employment as a waitress or counterperson. Knowing that you hire students for the summer season, I would like to be considered for any openings that you have.

I am seventeen years old and a senior at Dobbs Ferry High School. I have worked for eight months as a counterperson at the Green Hill Diner, Dobbs Ferry, New York. My former employer is available to offer a reference:

Mrs. Susan Down, Manager
Green Hill Diner
14 Saw Mill River Road
Dobbs Ferry, New York 10522

I can be reached at my home in the event of an opening. My phone number in Dobbs Ferry is (914) 555-4423.

Sincerely,

Elaine S. Klein

Elaine S. Klein

Other types of business letters include *letters of complaint and opinion*. In a letter of complaint, you are seeking to solve some business problem. You may have received faulty merchandise, or a company may have failed to send you items that you had ordered, or perhaps you were overcharged. Whatever the complaint, you must present it clearly and objectively at the beginning of the letter, and you should include any information that will help the receiver to understand your problem.

In a letter of opinion, you will generally be writing to express your view of something. Perhaps you will state your views to the editor of a newspaper or to the president of a radio or television station. Again, you must begin with a main idea, state your view clearly, and then support your position. In such a letter, you may wish to use some of the techniques of persuasion discussed in the sections covering persuasive paragraphs and essays. Whether your letter offers praise or criticism, you should be as polite as possible while trying to persuade your reader to consider your view.

EXERCISE D: Practicing with Structure and Style. Using two pieces of paper, sketch two skeleton letters with lines instead of words for the body. Use one style for the first letter and another style for the second. Label each letter with the style you are following. Fill in the six parts of each letter by using your own address for the heading and two different addresses for actual businesses in your town or city for the inside address and salutation.

EXERCISE E: Preparing Envelopes for Business Letters. Prepare an envelope for one of the skeleton letters in Exercise D. Make sure that you follow proper business form. Fold the letter properly and place it in the envelope.

EXERCISE F: Writing Different Types of Business Letters. Choose one of the following ideas for writing a business letter. Include all six parts of the letter, and use your own name and address in the appropriate places. When you are finished, prepare an envelope for your letter.

1. Write to a company such as a department store, requesting some merchandise. Be sure to give enough information so that your order can be filled promptly. Choose either something practical or something very special that you dream of someday owning.

2. Write to a foreign embassy, requesting information about their country. Be as specific as possible about the information you would like to receive and provide a reason for your desire to have this information.
3. Apply for a summer job. Include all the information you think a prospective employer would need in order to consider you for the job. (Try putting yourself in the place of the employer and thinking about what you as an employer would be looking for in a summer employee.)
4. Write a letter of complaint concerning a record that you have never received from a music club that you have recently joined.
5. Think about a television program that you watched recently and write to someone responsible—the manager of the station or the film company that made the program—to express your views.

APPLICATION: Writing Your Own Personal or Business Letter. Use this exercise as an opportunity to write a letter that you have been planning to write to a friend or that you need to write for school or for business purposes. Before you write the letter, identify the *type* of personal or business letter it will be, review the guidelines for this type of letter, and then begin writing. When you have written the letter, prepare an envelope.

Writing Précis 27.

The term *précis* means "a summary, abstract, or abridgement." A précis is a shortened version of the main ideas and major points of an article, chapter, or some other piece of writing, written in your own words.

You can use a précis for a variety of purposes. It can be used during research to help you remember exactly what an article contains. It can help you judge how well you have understood a piece of writing. And it can give you practice in writing accurately and coherently. For example, a teacher may assign a technical article or a chapter in a textbook for you to read and may evaluate your understanding of it by asking you to write a précis.

This section will help you recognize the basic features of a précis and will give you practice in planning, writing, and revising this specialized kind of composition.

■ The Key Features of a Précis

A précis is a condensation of another piece of writing. It is a summary that accurately indicates the basic content and intent of the original work while omitting the less important details. A précis should also preserve the original article's order of ideas. In a précis you should not offer an analysis or critique by stating your own reactions or opinions. You, the précis writer, should simply read the material, condense it, and present it in your own words and in smooth, varied sentences that are easy for a reader to understand.

> A précis should be a condensation or summary that accurately represents the ideas and intent of the original, closely follows the order of the original, uses different words from the original, and contains smooth, varied sentences.

In the following example, a magazine article has been reduced to a précis. The main ideas and major pieces of support are compressed and reworded, and the précis is faithful to the ideas and organization of the article.

ARTICLE:

Once every 17 years, little holes appear in lawns and backyards, hillsides and woodlands. Out will pop millions of dark little bugs. They will scamper up almost any upright object—trees, poles, buildings—and soon strike up a joyous racket.

They are periodical cicadas, the world's longest-lived insects. Despite a locust-like appearance, they neither bite nor sting nor devastate vegetation. Entomologists currently count 19 separate "broods," which appear at various times in different parts of the country, some once every 13 years. But all follow roughly the same miraculous life cycle. Growing through five skin-shedding molts and sucking nourishing juices from roots, they emerge with uncanny precision, triggered by some still mysterious internal clock.

In the open, they shed their dry, yellowish skins for the last time. Soon the males strike up their cacophony of ticking, buzzing, and shrill whirring sounds. It is all music to the females, who slit open tree bark after they have been impregnated and store their fertilized eggs there. A few weeks later, both parents die. But cicada life goes on as the eggs hatch. The newborn nymphs drop to the ground, burrow, and the age-old cycle starts anew.

Baffled scientists are still unsure why the cicadas behave as they do, but suspect that it may all be a defense against predators like birds. As entomologist Chris Simon of the State University of New York at Stony Brook writes in *Natural History*, when the cicadas finally emerge, it is in the shadows of dusk. They also gain protection from their monstrous numbers—as many as 1.5 million per acre. Finally, since they appear only once every 13 or 17 years, nature may have endowed them with an unlikely mathematical defense. These are prime numbers, divisible only by themselves, and so parasites would have to live at least as long—a half or a quarter would be improbable—to partake in a 17-year feast. —*Time*

PRÉCIS:

Every seventeen years cicadas, which resemble locusts, emerge noisily from the insect world's longest hibernation.

Entomologists have identified nineteen types of cicadas, which burst forth after long intervals at different times around the country, but all cicadas seem to have about the same life cycle. During hibernation, they all molt five times and appear after precise periods. Once above ground, they molt again and begin their noise-making and mating. Soon after laying and securing their eggs in tree bark, the adults die. When the eggs hatch and fall, newborn cicadas burrow into the ground and begin another cycle.

Cicadas have bewildered scientists, who now think that the evening emergence, the vast numbers, and the lengthy hibernation cycles may protect these insects from natural enemies.

Examining the key features of a précis will prepare you to write your own.

Condensation.   To condense means to express in fewer words or to retain main ideas while eliminating finer points. The length of a précis can be anywhere from less than one tenth the length of the original to a little less than one half the length of the original, depending on the length of the original and the desired length of the précis. For instance, a précis of a 4,000-word story or article could be 100 words, 400 words, or 1,000 words, depending on the amount of detail the writer wanted to include. The précis about the cicadas, for example, is a little over one third the length of the original article. Notice that minor details such as descriptions of the cicadas' appearance and eating habits have been eliminated. Most of the précis you write will probably be a quarter to a third of the length of the original article.

You can achieve the desired length by selecting the main ideas and important details and excluding the lesser details. You can select the main ideas by distinguishing the essential information from the inessential. A précis may combine ideas from several sentences, several paragraphs, or even several sections into one sentence.

Accurate Representation of Ideas and Intent.   A précis should also remain faithful to the ideas and purpose of the original. It should capture the main ideas and major details of the original and present them accurately. It should stick to the original's content with no additions, changes, or opinions included. The writer of a précis should be factual and objective and should not criticize or draw conclusions. In addition, a précis should reflect the purpose of the original, whether it be to explain, define, instruct, persuade, describe, tell a story, or entertain, and it should be true to the tone of the original.

Following an Order.   One way that a précis can capture the content, intent, and tone of the original work is by closely following the original's order of ideas. If the original follows a particular logical pattern, such as order of importance, chronological order, or developmental order, the précis should preserve this order as faithfully as possible. If the original emphasizes one idea by devoting more space to it than to others, the précis should indicate that emphasis. Similarly, if the original has sections, perhaps a distinct introduction, body, and conclusion, the précis should observe this order of ideas even though it is a much shorter piece of writing. A précis might reduce five paragraphs to one or two paragraphs, but the order of the content of each paragraph should be recognizable in the précis. For instance, in the précis about the cicadas, the ideas of the second and third paragraphs of the original were combined in the original order into the second paragraph of the précis.

Rewording.   The wording of the précis should also reflect the content and purpose of the article. But except for the main words needed to identify the topic and important ideas, the précis writer should use different words from those in the original. Rewording has two advantages: It compels the writer to understand the original article and it helps the writer to find more concise wordings to condense the article. While the writer must find new ways to express the ideas in the original, he or she must also choose words that are comparable to the original words in terms of formality and shade of meaning.

A Pleasing Style.   Still another key feature of a good précis is a pleasing style; that is, although the précis is an abbreviated reworking of another piece of writing, it should still be a smooth, coherent, stylistically interesting composition in its own right. The sentences should be varied in length and structure. Each sentence and paragraph should read smoothly and clearly. Thus, the précis should be more than a rough list of the ideas in the original. While it probably will not have the texture or flair of the original because it lacks the colorful specific details and uses different wording, it should have variety and all the other characteristics of good writing.

EXERCISE A: Recognizing the Key Elements of a Précis. Read the following article. Then read the précis of the article. As you answer the questions that follow, you may need to refer to both original and précis for comparison.

ARTICLE:

They call Newbury Street Boston's Fifth Avenue. A stately old gentleman of a street, it is not as breathtaking as a Parisian boulevard, nor as teeming with excitement as an avenue in New York, but it is crusty, rich and dignified in the best proper-Bostonian manner. Newbury Street begins at the Ritz and, as one resident lovingly notes, goes downhill from there—downhill past eight alphabetically named blocks to be exact, from the Ritz-Carlton Hotel on the Arlington Street border of Boston's immaculate Public Garden, all the way to the cozy Avenue Victor Hugo bookstore at Massachusetts Avenue.

The entire street lies southwest of Beacon Hill and downtown Boston, right in the middle of an area known as Back Bay. In old Federal Boston, the Back Bay was nothing more than a salt-water mudbank of the Charles River. But in the mid-1800's, the marsh was drained and filled, and the European authors, architects, and artists who first settled the new waterfront property left their mark in richly styled Victorian town houses, striking churches, and lavish public buildings.

The story of Newbury Street is the story of Boston. When you first walk the city's cobblestone streets, listening to the furious clang/dong of distant cathedral bells or watching pigeon-colored skies roll in from steel-blue seas to wrap the whole city in a chilling mist, it seems as though Boston is mercilessly entrenched in its own timeless traditions. But woven into the starched white fabric of old Boston is a bright new enthusiasm. On Newbury Street, and indeed, all around it, Boston dances with the finest blue-blooded vitality in America. —Karen MacNeil

PRÉCIS:

Boston's Newbury Street, along which many well-known landmarks are located, reflects the dignity and significance of the city. Created from mudflats in the mid-1800's, the Newbury Street area became the residence of fashionable European intellectuals. The stylish buildings in which they lived stand as a reminder of them. The cobblestones, church bells, and misty air evoke Boston's past; however, Newbury Street, like all of Boston today, also displays the liveliness of modern times.

1. Compare the lengths of the article and the précis. Is the length of the précis appropriate? Why?
2. Has the writer of the précis included all the main ideas and important details from the original article? What others, if any, would you have included?
3. To what extent does the précis accurately represent the ideas and intent of the original?
4. How closely does the précis follow the order of ideas in the original?
5. What main words from the article has the précis writer necessarily repeated? What other words are used as substitutes for the original words?
6. How varied and smooth are the sentences in the précis? How would you polish them further?

■ Planning, Writing, and Revising a Précis

Planning and writing a précis requires both reading and writing skills. Your goal should be to produce an accurate condensation of the original in considerably less space. You should probably read the article, chapter, story, or passage through several times, each time paying more attention to important points and eventually taking notes. Then you should write the précis, following the original's order of ideas and varying and connecting your sentences. Finally, you should check your précis against the original and revise and condense it further if necessary.

Planning a Précis.   Planning a précis involves first careful reading and then thoughtful note taking.

> As you plan a précis, you should read for an overall understanding and then reread, taking notes on main ideas and major details in your own words.

Your preparatory reading for a précis should consist of several steps in itself. You should first read the article or chapter through to get an understanding of the main idea and the author's intent and tone. Then you might reread the article concentrating on the main ideas and major details and observing the organization of the material. If you come across any words or points you do not understand, you should try to figure them out by checking the content closely and consulting the dictionary or another reference book, if necessary. When you have a good grasp of the overall material as well as a feel for the parts and structure, you are ready to take notes.

At this point, you should decide approximately how long you intend your précis to be in proportion to the original. You might count or estimate the number of words in the original and set an approximate word limit for your précis. Determining length before you take notes will help you know how much information you must leave out of your notes. For a very short précis, you should select only the main ideas. For a précis one-quarter to one-third the length of the original, you can include major details besides the main ideas.

When you take notes you should digest and synthesize the material; that is, you should condense by selecting only the most important information and reword that information as you jot it down. If the original has a number of paragraphs or sections, identify and write down the main ideas for each section. Then under the main ideas, jot down the major pieces of support. As you take notes, decide exactly what pieces of information are needed to show accurately the content of the original. Sometimes the original will contain many specific details that you will have to summarize with a few general facts. Other times you will have to overlook minor points, such as technical terms, entirely. When you take notes, recognize which words from the original are main words that you should use and which words can be replaced with words of your own.

Once you have written brief notes that follow the order of ideas in the original and that are in your own words, check your notes for accuracy against the original. Ask yourself, "Have I represented this information as it is in the original? Have I written down only what is in the original and not any of my own ideas and opinions?" When you have evaluated your notes, you are ready to write the précis.

Writing a Précis.   As you write from your notes, you should think both about the work you are summarizing and the piece of writing you are creating.

As you write the précis, group and phrase your ideas into well structured sentences that both condense and capture the essential content, purpose, tone, and organization of the original.

Writing the actual précis involves putting the main ideas and major details you have selected from the original into complete, meaningful sentences and paragraphs. You should aim for the length you tentatively set before taking notes. As you group the ideas into sentences, you should be conscious of the original's purpose, tone, and organization. You may have to experiment with the phrasing and structure of your sentences. For example, in reducing the ideas from one paragraph to one sentence, you may have to try several versions to get a concise, accurate sentence. Also, you must resist the tendency to add words in order to express the ideas clearly. If your précis is becoming too long, you may have to eliminate or generalize some more ideas or simply find a shorter way to say the same thing. You should also try to use different structures for your sentences and make them flow together to produce a unified, coherent piece of writing.

Revising a Précis.   The revising stage gives you a chance to condense further, to check for accuracy, and to polish for style.

> As you revise the précis, look for ways to improve the brevity, the accuracy, and the quality of the writing.

In addition, you should compare the précis to the original to make sure that it is faithful to the ideas, intent, tone, and order. If possible, place your précis alongside the original and follow the main ideas in each to make sure that you have covered all the important pieces of information. You should also check to see that you have observed the order of ideas in the original. Revise any ideas that do not fairly represent the original, and eliminate any facts or opinions of your own that you may have inadvertently added. Also change any words or phrases that seem to repeat the original too closely or to misrepresent the tone or meaning of the original. Once you have written the précis, you should check the length of it by counting the words. Determine whether the précis is the length you intended and in appropriate proportion to the original or whether you will have to do further condensing. If you have to condense further, look for any pieces of information you can omit and try to think of more concise wordings.

You should also read your précis aloud, silently, or both to hear the rhythm and emphasis of your sentences. You may have to combine or connect sentences with transitions to smooth out choppy or awkward sections. Or you may have to simplify and regroup ideas to correct long, confusing sentences.

To help you identify and correct any weaknesses in your précis you can use the following checklist.

CHECKLIST FOR REVISING A PRÉCIS
1. Does the précis reduce the original to a much shorter piece of writing?
2. Does the précis present the main ideas and any other major details from the original?
3. Have you objectively presented the ideas in the original without adding any opinions or outside pieces of information?
4. Does the précis reflect the purpose and tone of the original?
5. Does the précis follow the basic organization of the original?
6. Are most of the words and phrases in the précis different from the original yet true to the original in terms of formality and shade of meaning?
7. Can the précis stand on its own as a unified, coherent piece of writing?
8. Is the précis free of grammatical and mechanical errors and spelling mistakes?

EXERCISE B: Preparing to Write a Précis. Read the following passage several times. Decide how long your précis should be. Then take notes in your own words, choosing only the main ideas and major details and omitting lesser details. Maintain the order and emphasis of the original passage.

That the buffalo somehow managed to stagger out of the last century into our own is a bit of a miracle; or, if not, then, it was nothing less than colossal good luck. No one will ever know how many of them were out there when the first paleskin scouts poked west toward the shining mountains for beaver. The prevailing guess is 60 million. And there may have been more than that in pre-Columbian times, before hunters acquired the horse, and before the buffalo's range drew inward to the Plains from Oregon's Blue Mountains and the Appalachian highlands in the East.

About ten years, roughly in the 1870s—less than a human generation—is all it took to tumble the millions into hundreds, thanks to the railroads, the long-range Sharps rifles, and an inordinate national appetite for robes and hides. By 1903, the zoologist William T. Hornaday could feel some confidence about the accuracy of numbers; that year he counted 969 buffalo remaining in the United States. With somewhat less confidence in their latest figure, census takers nowadays put the purebred North American buffalo population at 80,000. By all counts, the numbers have nowhere to go but up.

No doubt the buffalo would have gone the way of the passenger pigeon but for the foresight of such men as Hornaday, cofounder of the American Bison Society, and the rancher Charles

Goodnight of Texas, whose domesticated herd helped reseed the wild one at Yellowstone Park after poachers nearly wiped it out in the 1890s. Nevertheless, the animal itself deserves some measure of credit for its comeback, for it is a large, gregarious, take-no-guff kind of creature, and it adapts easily to a variety of climates and habitats. The average weight of an adult bull, for example, is 2,000 pounds. Nothing in North America with warm blood and wild heritage grows so large. Its forequarters are massive, yet in an open-ended race it can sometimes outrun a horse. Prudently, it will escape danger if it can, but if cornered will fight fiercely. Its stolidity and its strong herding instinct served the buffalo well against skulking wolves on the open plains. Against human predators with rifles, hanging tough almost brought the species to extinction. —John G. Mitchell

EXERCISE C: Drafting a Précis. Write the précis you prepared for in Exercise B. Pay attention to the length, to the accuracy of the ideas, and to the smoothness and style of your sentences.

EXERCISE D: Polishing a Précis. Revise the précis you wrote in Exercise C by counting the words, comparing it to the original article, and using the checklist on page 799 to locate and correct any weaknesses. When you have made any necessary revisions, write a good final copy.

APPLICATION: Practicing Précis-Writing Skills. Work with another student or a group of students to write a précis of the same chapter, article, story, or passage. Follow the steps in this section. Then, before you revise, exchange précis with someone else and answer the questions in the checklist on page 799. Compare précis to help each other write the most accurate, readable précis. When you have made corrections and revisions on your own précis, copy it in final form and hand it in along with your evaluator's comments.

Chapter 28

Essay Examinations

Throughout your academic and professional life, you will be asked to write paragraphs and essays to answer questions on examinations. Usually you will be given a limited time in which to plan and write your answer. This chapter explains how to adjust the writing processes with which you are familiar to meet the requirements and restrictions of writing short compositions on examinations.

Writing Answers to Essay Exam Questions

28.1

To complete essay exams successfully, you should develop several important skills: the ability to budget your time effectively, to identify the different requirements of essay questions, to develop and organize your answers, and to write and check them within the specified time limits. This section will give you practice in these skills.

■ Budgeting Your Time

On any essay exam, you must work within a time limit. Often, your limit will be the duration of a class or some other period of time set by examiners. Because essay writing, especially in answer to an exam question, requires several steps, you must allot time for each step. And if the exam requires two or more essays, you must budget time to prepare and write each answer.

Budget your time before you begin an examination by considering the number and difficulty of essay questions as well as the other types of questions on the exam.

At the beginning of the examination, you should look quickly through the exam to see how many and what kinds of questions you must answer. You should then sketch out a schedule, deciding how much time you should spend on each question. Remember to allot more time for the questions that appear more difficult. If you have an hour, for instance, to answer ten multiple choice questions and two more difficult essay questions, you might use the following schedule.

SAMPLE SCHEDULE FOR A ONE-HOUR EXAM		
Activity	**Time**	**Breakdown**
10 multiple choice questions	10 minutes	1 min. per question
First essay	25 minutes	6 min.: Plan and outline 15 min.: Write 4 min.: Check and revise
Second essay	25 minutes	6 min.: Plan and outline 15 min.: Write 4 min.: Check and revise

Scheduling your time in this way should enable you to spend adequate time on each question. You can also help yourself by deciding approximately when you should finish each answer or section of the exam in order to complete the whole exam on time. Then from time to time you can check the clock to see whether you are on schedule.

EXERCISE A: Planning Your Time. For each of the following five items, make a schedule showing how you would divide your time. As you plan time for essay writing, keep in mind the steps: planning and outlining, writing, and checking.

1. Thirty minutes for one essay
2. Forty-five minutes for two equally difficult essay questions
3. Forty-five minutes for twenty multiple choice questions and one essay
4. One hour for ten multiple choice questions, ten true or false questions, and two essays

5. One hour for ten multiple choice questions, one short essay question, and two more difficult essay questions

■ Identifying What the Essay Question Is Asking

To answer an essay question on an examination, you must first determine exactly what the question is asking you. What kind of information and ideas are expected?

Identify the major requirement of the essay question and find clues that point to the types of support that you will need.

Different essay questions call for different responses. In order to write well and quickly on the essay exam, you must be able to figure out rapidly the kind of answer each question calls for.

Essay questions follow certain patterns, often indicated by certain word clues. If you can learn to recognize these word clues and the kind of information they call for, you can generally proceed directly to developing an appropriate answer. The following chart explains some common kinds of questions along with the words that identify them and the support you should include in your answer.

WORD CLUES TO KINDS OF ESSAY EXAM QUESTIONS		
Kind of Question	Words That Offer Clues	Support and Development Needed
Compare	*compare, similarities, resemblances, likenesses*	Look for and stress similarities with specific examples.
Contrast	*contrast, differ, differences*	Look for and stress differences with specific examples.
Definition	*define, explain*	Explain what something means or is. Give examples.
Description	*describe*	Give the main features with specific details and examples.
Diagram	*diagram, draw, chart*	Provide a drawing or chart in your answer. Label it and include explanations.

Discussion	*discuss, explain*	Make a general statement that shows you understand the concept in the question. Then support your main idea with examples, facts, and details.
Explanation	*explain, why, what, how*	Offer examples, details, and facts that illustrate how something happens, what it is, or why it is so.
Illustration	*illustrate, show*	Provide concrete examples and explain each one to demonstrate the truth or significance of the main idea.
Interpretation	*significance, meaning of quotations or events, influence, analyze*	State a main idea about meaning. Give examples, facts, and reasons to explain and back up your interpretation.
Opinion	*what do you think, defend your idea, state your opinion*	State your opinion clearly. Support and develop it with examples, facts, and reasons.
Prediction	*If . . . . then* *What . . . . if*	Predict and state a logical outcome based on your knowledge. Offer information and arguments to support your position.

EXERCISE B: Interpreting Essay Questions. Read each of the following essay questions carefully. Then examine each one, looking for word clues. Write down the type of question each is and briefly indicate the type of support and development needed to answer the question. Try to work rapidly and limit yourself to *three* minutes for each question.

1. What is the significance of Huck's statement at the end of *Huckleberry Finn* that he is going to "light out for the Territory"?
2. How does the process of carbon-14 dating work?
3. Which character in Shakespeare's play *Julius Caesar* do you find more admirable—Brutus or Mark Antony? Why?
4. Contrast the two principal methods of making steel.

■ Preparing and Outlining an Answer

Once you understand the kind of response required by an essay question, you can develop and organize your answer. Following a few suggestions and steps can help you make the best use of your time.

Stating a Main Idea or Point and Listing Support. Sometimes your answer should be a paragraph with a main idea expressed in a topic sentence and developed with supporting material to show your knowledge of the subject. Other times your answer should be a short essay. It should consist of a main point expressed in a thesis statement; at least one paragraph, usually two or more, developing the thesis statement; and some concluding statement, often a short final paragraph.

> Decide on a main idea or point, express it in one sentence, and jot down relevant ideas and pieces of information.

Because the planning of your answer is a crucial step that can save you time overall, you should budget about a quarter of your time for thinking, recalling information, and outlining.

To develop a main idea or point you should try to answer the essay question in a single sentence. Reducing your answer to one sentence causes you to focus your ideas and limit your answer to the most important point. You may find it helpful to restate portions of the original question in your sentence along with your own idea. Notice the way the following essay questions have been turned into thesis statements appropriate for an essay-length answer.

DEVELOPING A THESIS STATEMENT FOR AN ESSAY-LENGTH ANSWER	
Question	**Thesis Statement (Answer)**
What would happen if all the planets in the solar system were aligned on one side of the earth away from the sun?	Some scientists think that planetary alignment away from the earth and sun would cause tidal imbalances and other climatic disruptions on the earth.
In *Gone with the Wind*, Scarlett O'Hara declares, "Tomorrow is another day." What does this statement reveal about her character?	Scarlett O'Hara's comment about the future reveals that she is both stubbornly hopeful and unrealistic about herself.

Explain how the British government functions.	The British government is a parliamentary democracy; in name, the monarch is the head of state, but the real power to govern rests with the Parliament.

When you have a topic sentence or a thesis statement that presents your main idea or point, you should supply the kind of supporting material that the question calls for. On your test or on a separate piece of paper provided by your teacher, list as many relevant facts, examples, details, or reasons as you can think of. Try to recall material you have read and studied and to state your own ideas. Try to channel your thoughts to explore the point at hand, but write down your ideas freely as they come to you.

Organizing Your Answer.   Once you have gathered at least three or four major pieces of supporting information, you are ready to arrange your ideas.

Sort and organize your supporting information in a modified outline.

To organize your answer, look back at the question, and examine your topic sentence or thesis statement and your list of supporting information. Then quickly group your ideas in a logical order. Any of the logical orders—order of importance, chronological order, spatial order, comparison and contrast order, and developmental order—can help you arrange your supporting information in a meaningful way. Arranging your ideas will make your answer more coherent, more authoritative, and easier to write. While you are organizing your ideas, you should also weed out any pieces of information or ideas that do not pertain closely to your main idea or point and the rest of your support. Add any other significant ideas that occur to you. Then jot down a modified outline for your essay including your topic sentence or thesis statement and your ordered list of support.

In a modified outline for a paragraph-length answer, simply list the information in the most suitable order. For an essay-length answer, sketch out the body of your essay and roughly plan the number of paragraphs you will have. You might also put down a few ideas for your conclusion.

SAMPLE MODIFIED OUTLINES

Paragraph Answer

<u>Topic Sentence</u>: Britain is a parliamentary democracy in which the party that controls the Parliament runs the government.

—people vote every six years for representatives in the House of Commons
—party winning a majority of seats "forms a government"
—its head becomes Prime Minister
—executive branch (Prime Minister and Cabinet) and legislative branch are not separate

—Prime Minister and Parliament are more likely to cooperate with each other than American President and Congress
—British voters vote more for the party than the individual
—system ensures that winning party's policies will be put into practice

<u>Concluding Idea</u>: British system of government attempts to make the government responsive to the will of the people.

Essay Answer

<u>Thesis Statement</u>: The British government is a parliamentary democracy; in name, the monarch is the head of state, but the real power to govern rests with the Parliament.

<u>Parliament</u>
—Parliament consists of House of Commons and House of Lords
—Commons are elected
—Lords are hereditary or appointed (less powerful)
—Head of majority party in Commons becomes Prime Minister, head of government

<u>Connection Between Executive and Parliament</u>
—executive and legislative branches are not separate
—Prime Minister and Cabinet come from majority party in Commons

—elections are held every six years
—party heads are chosen before elections

<u>Relations Between Executive and Parliament</u>
—Prime Minister's connection with majority party ensures that Parliament will usually support his or her policies
  —system furthers cooperation more than the American relationship between the President and Congress
—British voters vote more for the party than for the individual
—system ensures that winning party's policies will be put into practice

<u>Conclusion</u>: British parliamentary democracy attempts to make government responsive to the will of the people, while the monarch lends overall stability to the government.

EXERCISE C: **Planning an Answer to an Essay Question.** Find an essay question that relates to one of your classes by looking at study questions at the ends of chapters, questions in study guides, or questions on old tests. Choose a question that you have not answered before. Give yourself five to ten minutes to prepare an essay-length answer following these steps.

1. Determine what information the question is asking for.
2. Write your answer to the question in one sentence, which can serve as your thesis statement.
3. On a piece of paper gather and list supporting information under your thesis statement.
4. Jot down a modified outline for your essay, including your thesis statement, your supporting information in a logical order, and a few ideas for your conclusion.

■ Writing and Checking Your Answer

You should allow about two thirds of your time to write your answer, and you should schedule a few minutes at the end of the test time to proofread and check what you have written.

Follow your outline and fill in details as you write your answer. Then proofread and make final corrections and revisions.

A few suggestions can help you produce the best answer under time pressure. Use your outline to guide you from thought to thought and to help you flesh out each idea and piece of information in a complete sentence. You may want to add details and specific information to the items on your outline. If new ideas occur to you or you remember some worthwhile information that belongs in the answer, add it, but do not stray far from the order of your outline. Transitions can be particularly helpful in linking your ideas to each other and to the thesis statement. When you are under pressure, transitions can also help you to maintain your focused flow of thoughts. Remember that you may have to write quickly to keep on the time schedule you have set for yourself. But no matter how fast you write, try to make your writing readable. You might try to maintain wide margins on either side of the page or skip spaces between lines to allow room for changes and corrections.

Before you proceed to the next test question or before you turn in your exam paper, be sure to reread your answer carefully. Check to make sure that you have not left out important ideas or words or made careless mistakes that might detract from your answer. You should ask yourself questions similar to those in the following checklist.

CHECKING YOUR ANSWER

1. Does the paragraph or essay have a topic sentence or thesis statement that presents your basic answer to the question?
2. Have you answered the question fully with the kinds of supporting examples, facts, details, and reasons called for in the question?
3. Does the answer need any more specific information?
4. Is the answer organized logically?
5. Do transitions connect the ideas?
6. Does the answer end clearly?
7. Have you corrected any errors in grammar, mechanics, or spelling?
8. Is the paper readable?

The following model is an essay-length answer to the question on page 806 about the British government. Notice that it follows standard essay form. It begins with a short introductory paragraph containing a revised thesis statement that answers the question directly. Three body paragraphs present supporting examples and details, and the conclusion ends the answer with a reminder of the main point. Note the use of transitions throughout to tie ideas together.

Essay
answer
to an
exam
question

The British government is a parliamentary democracy with a monarch as its head of state; this means that, while the king or queen is the ruler of the nation in name, the real power to govern rests with the legislature, or Parliament.

The British Parliament consists of two houses. The House of Commons is the principal legislative body, and its members are elected by the British people. The House of Lords is composed of titled persons who have inherited their positions or have been appointed to them. It has much less power than the House of Commons because it is not a representative body. The actual head of the government, who functions somewhat like our President, is the Prime Minister, who is the head of the party holding a majority of seats in the House of Commons.

The most important feature of the parliamentary system as it works in Britain is that the executive and legislative branches of the government are not separate, as they are in the United States. The Prime Minister and other Cabinet Ministers—the British executive branch—always come from the party controlling the Parliament. Elections are held at least every six years—and often more frequently—in which British voters choose their representatives in the House of Commons. The party that wins a majority of seats in the election is invited to "form a government." Each political party has already chosen its head, and this official assumes the role of Prime Minister when the results of the Parliamentary election are known.

Because the Prime Minister leads the party controlling the Parliament and is closely identified with that party, his or her policies are usually supported and carried out by the resolutions passed by Parliament. This feature of the parliamentary democracy contrasts sharply with the American system, in which the Congress and the Presidency are completely separate and might be controlled by different parties with conflicting policies. The British people do not vote for a particular person to run the government, as Americans elect their President. Rather, the British vote for the policies of a particular party, and their parliamentary system ensures that those policies will be put into practice if that party carries the election.

Thus, the British system of parliamentary democracy represents an attempt to make the government as responsive as possible to the will of the people. And while the monarch lends permanence and stability to the government, the Parliament and Prime Minister can change from election to election, reflecting major shifts in the voters' opinions whenever they occur.

EXERCISE D: Writing and Checking Your Answer. Using your outline from Exercise C as a guide, give yourself about thirty-five to forty minutes to write an essay-length answer. Use the checklist on page 809 to review your answer. Do the correcting and revising that you think your essay needs right on your paper in the margins and between the lines.

APPLICATION: Planning, Writing, and Checking an Answer to an Exam Question. Take a question from a recent exam or a question that your teacher supplies. Or make up a question that you would like to answer about something that you have been studying recently in one of your classes. Pretend that you are taking the exam and complete the following steps to write an essay-length answer.

1. Think about the amount of time you need to spend on an answer. Decide on an amount of time for planning and organizing, for writing, and for checking the answer, and try to observe this time schedule.
2. Identify the major requirement of the question and decide on the kinds of support you will need to write a thorough answer.
3. Then write a thesis statement stating your basic answer to the question.
4. List all the supporting examples, details, facts, reasons, and ideas you can think of to develop your thesis statement.
5. Organize your answer logically by numbering your items of information or by jotting down a modified outline.
6. Follow and flesh out your outline as you write the essay. Use transitions to guide your thinking and to make your answer easy to follow.
7. Use the checklist on page 809 to review and revise your essay. Revise your essay in the margins of your paper.
8. Check to see if you have kept to your time schedule throughout. If you have not, explain briefly where you need to improve.

Manuscript Preparation

The most important part of any writing you do is, of course, the ideas that it contains. The composition unit offers many suggestions for developing, organizing, and expressing your ideas in clear and interesting language. However, when you hand in a paper there are also certain technical things that you should provide. The following pages give suggestions for basic manuscript preparation, for dealing with mechanical and other technical aspects of writing, for giving credit to your sources, and for understanding and using correction symbols.

Basic Preparation

Whether handwritten or typed, your manuscript should follow certain basic rules. The following chart shows the suggested procedures for each style.

PREPARING A MANUSCRIPT	
Handwritten	**Typed**
1. Use white 8½ × 11 inch (21.5 × 28 cm) lined paper, but never pages ripped from a spiral binder.	1. Use white 8½ × 11 inch (21.5 × 28 cm) paper.
2. Use black or blue ink only.	2. Use a clear black ribbon.
3. Leave a margin of 1 inch (2.54 cm) on the right, using the paper's own rules as your margin on other sides.	3. Leave a margin of at least 1 inch (2.54 cm) on all sides.
4. Indent each paragraph.	4. Double-space all lines and indent each paragraph.
5. Use only one side of each paper.	5. Use only one side of each paper.
6. Recopy if necessary to make your final copy neat.	6. Retype if necessary to make your final copy neat.

You must also identify your manuscript, following either an elaborate or simple style. For long and important papers, such as library papers, you will probably want an elaborate style. Set up a title page as shown on page 814. The next page and all the other pages should carry only your name and the page number, beginning with page one.

With Title Page

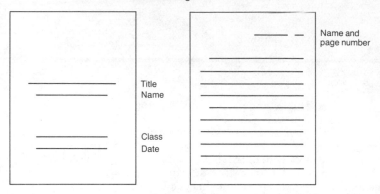

For shorter papers, use the simple style. Basic identification appears on the first page, while the second page carries your name and the page number, beginning with page two.

Without Title Page

Dealing with Mechanics

The following chart offers basic guidelines for using punctuation marks and other mechanical items that seem to cause most manuscript problems.

CHECKING MECHANICS		
Item	Basic Guidelines	Further Reference
Capitalization	Use common sense in capitalizing proper nouns, proper adjectives, and first words.	Section 12.1, pages 294–314

Abbreviation	Avoid most abbreviations in formal writing. Feel free, however, to use abbreviations such as Mr. and Mrs., a.m. and p.m., and well-known abbreviations for organizations such as NATO and VISTA.	Section 12.2, pages 314–332
Commas	Take care not to overuse commas. Also check to make sure you are not dividing compound verbs with commas.	Section 13.2, pages 338–354
Hyphens	Check compound words in the dictionary. Hyphenate at the end of the line only when absolutely necessary and only at a syllable break.	Section 13.6, pages 383–387
Apostrophes	Avoid using apostrophes incorrectly in personal pronouns such as *its* and *theirs*.	Section 13.7, pages 388–395

Handling Other Technical Matters

Other technical matters should also be checked to make your paper more readable and more persuasive.

CHECKING OTHER ITEMS		
Item	**Basic Guidelines**	**Further Reference**
Spelling	Keep a dictionary at your side and check it whenever you are in doubt.	Section 15.2, pages 426–434
Usage	Take special care to make sure your subjects and verbs agree.	Section 8.1, pages 205–220, for subject-verb agreement; Section 10.2, pages 254–277, for a list of eighty common usage problems
Sentence Faults	Check for fragments, run-ons, problems with modifiers, and faulty parallelism or coordination.	Chapter 5, pages 128–146
Numbers	Spell out most numbers that can be written in one or two words and all numbers at the beginning of a sentence. Use numerals, however, for lengthy numbers, for dates, and for addresses.	Section 12.2, pages 324–328

Giving Credit to Sources

Whenever you are quoting the words or using the ideas of another writer, make sure you have given credit to that person. The chart in Section 25.1 on pages 725–726 shows the different forms for these kinds of citations.

Using Correction Symbols

You may find the following symbols very useful when you are proofreading your own manuscript. Your teacher may also choose to use these or similar marks when grading your papers.

	USING CORRECTION SYMBOLS	
Symbol	**Meaning**	**Example**
⌐	delete	The colors is red.
⌢	close up	The color is reebd.
∧	insert	The color ∧ red.
#	add space	The coloris red.
∿	transpose	The colro is red.
¶	new paragraph	¶ The color is red.
no ¶	no paragraph	no¶ The color is red.
cap	capitalize	the color is red.
lc	use small letter	The Color is red.
sp	spelling	The colar is red.
us	usage	The colors is red.
frag	fragment	The red color and the blue.
RO	run-on	The color is red the house is blue.
mod	problem modifier	Newly painted, I saw the house.
awk	awkward	The color is, I think, kind of red.

Index

Bold numbers show pages on which basic definitions and rules can be found.

A, an, 35–36, 254
A, an, the, 35–36
Abbreviations, **314**–332, 397
  acronym, **329**–330
  commonly used, 330–332
  of geographical locations, **321**–**322**, 323
  for Latin phrases, **324**
  for measurements, **325**–326
  of names of organizations, **328**, **329**, 330
  of names of people, **315**
  for numbers, **326**
  period in, **336**
  of states, **322**–323
  of time references, **319**, **320**–321
  of titles of people, **315**, **316**, **317**–318
Abstract noun, 19
Accept, except, 254
Acceptance, letter of, **779**, 781
Accuse, allege, 254–255
Acronym, **329**–330
Action verb, **29**, **564**
Active voice, **186**, **188**–189
Adapt, adopt, 255
Addition, transitions of, 587
Addition or identification, subordination in, 592
Address, direct, 21
Adjectival phrase, **86**
Adjective, 34–**35**, 78
  and adverb, 236–249
  or adverb, 41
  article, 35–36
  comma with, **341**–**342**
  comparison of, **236**–**238**, **239**, **240**–241
  compound, 36, 80
  noun as, 36–37
  as part of speech, 18, 53
  predicate, **74**–75
  pronoun as, 36, 37–38
  proper, 36, **305**, **306**–307
  verb as, 36, 38
Adjective clause, **102**–106
  with relative adverb, **104**–105
  with relative pronoun, **104**, 121–122
Adopt, adapt, 255

Adverb, 34–35, **39**–41, 78
  or adjective, 41
  with adjective, 40
  with adverb, 40
  comparison of, **236**–**238**, **239**, **240**–241
  conjunctive, 48–49
  that expresses time, **175**
  noun as, 40–41
  as part of speech, 18, 53
  as part of verb, 40
  with verb, 40
Adverb clause, **106**–107, 123–124
  elliptical, 107
Adverbial phrase, 86–**87**
Advice, advise, 255
Affect, effect, 255
Aggravate, 255
Agreement, 205–235, 290–291
  pronoun and antecedent, 220–235
  subject and verb, 205–220
Ain't, 255
Allege, accuse, 254–255
Allot, a lot, alot, 256
All ready, already, 256
All right, alright, 256
All together, altogether, 256
Almanacs, 504
A lot, alot, allot, 256
Alphabetizing, rules for, 491–**492**
Already, all ready, 256
Alright, all right, 256
Altogether, all together, 256
Among, between, 256
Amounts, **389**
  agreement, **217**–218
An, a, 35–36, 254
Analogy, **578**
  test, **468**–471
Analysis of a literary work, **763**
Analytic card, **489**
And, 140–**143**, **212**, **221**
Annotation, **449**–450
Antecedent, pronoun, **22**, 220–235, **228**
  agreement, **220**–235
  implied or vague, **229**–230
Antonym, 531
  test, **465**–466
Anxious, 257

Any one, anyone, every one, everyone,
  257
Anyway, anywhere, everywhere,
  nowhere, somewhere, 257
Apostrophe, 388–391
  forming contractions, **392**–394
  with plurals, **394**–395
  with possessive nouns, **388**–**389**,
   390
  with possessive pronouns, 391–392
Application, letter of, **787**, 789
Appositive, **88**, 194, 196
  formal, 358–**359**
  nonessential, **377**
Appositive phrase, 85, 88, **89**–91, 116
Article, 35
As, 257
As, as if, like, 264
As if, like, as, 264
As to, 257
At, 257
At about, 258
Atlases, 504
Atlases and gazetteers, 504–505
Audience, 627, **628**–629
  for an essay, **695**–696
  for a literary review, 764–765
Author card, **586**
Auxiliary verbs, **33**–34, **184**–185
Awful, awfully, 258
A while, awhile, 258

Balanced sentence, **549**
Barely, 252
Basic verb form, 153, 164–165
Be, verb, forms of, 30
Beat, win, 258
Because, 258–259
Being as, being that, 259
Beside, besides, 259
Between, among, 256
Bibliography, **278**
Bibliography card, 737–**738**
Biographical reference books,
  507–508
Block style, 785
Body, **776**, **783**, 784
  of an essay, **683**
  of a library paper, **731**, 732
Books, finding, 494–499
  general reference, **501**–505
  specialized reference, 505, **506**–511
Brackets, 376, 381, **382**
Brainstorming, 630, **631**
  for an essay topic, **694**–695
  for supporting information,
   698–699
Bridge idea, **650**, **651**–652

Bring, take, 259
Burst, bust, busted, 259
Business letter, 783–791
  capitalization in, **311**–313
  structure of, 783–785
  types of, 787–790
Bust, busted, burst, 259
But, 140–141, 252

Can, may, 259
Can't help but, 260
Capitalization, **294**–314, 397
  of awards, 302
  of brands, 302, **305**
  of celestial bodies, 300
  of crafts, 302
  of directions, 299
  of events, **300**–301
  of geographical names, **298**–300
  of government bodies, **301**
  of groups, **301**
  of hyphenated adjective, **306**
  of languages, **301**–302
  in letters, **311**–313
  of nationalities, **301**
  of organizations, **301**
  of persons' names, **298**
  of place names, **298**–300
  of political parties, **301**
  of prefixes, **306**
  of proper adjectives, **305**–307
  of proper nouns, **297**–304
  of races, **301**
  of religious references, **301**–302
  of times, **300**–301
  of titles of people, **307**, **308**
  of titles of works, **307**, **309**
Capitalization of first word
  after a colon, **296**
  of an interjection, **296**
  of a line of poetry, **296**
  of a question fragment, **296**
  of a quotation, **295**
  of a sentence, **295**
Card catalog, **485**–494, **489**, **491**
Case, **190**–204
Cause and effect
  subordination in, 592
  transitions of, 587
Checklists
  for essay revising, 705–706
  for paragraph revising, **640**
  for study skills, **437**
Chronological order, **616**–618
  in an essay, 689
Citation of sources, **723**–726, 727,
  728–730
Clarity, punctuation for, **351**–352,
  385–386

Classroom participation, improving, 441
Classroom test, 452–456
Clause, **101**–111, 114–127, 148
  adjective, **102**–106
  adverb, **106**–107, 123–124
  agreement, **208**
  fragment, **128**, 130
  independent, **101**–102
  noun, **108**–109, 124–126
  subordinate, 101, **102**
Cliché, **570**
Clipped words, 260
Closing, 349–**350**, **776**, **783**, 784
"Cloze" reading comprehension test, 480–**481**
Coherence
  concluding sentence, **620**–621
  essay, 687, **689**–690, 700
  paragraph, **616**–623
  paragraph revision for, **649**, **650**, **651**, **652**–653
  with parallelism, **620**–621
  repetition for, **619**–620
  using synonyms, **619**–620
Collective noun, 20
  agreement, **215**
Colon, 357, 361
  with formal appositive, **359**
  before a list, **357**–358
  with quotation, **358**, **366**
  with summary sentence, **358**
Comma
  with addresses, **349**
  with adjective, **341**–342
  for clarity, **351**–352
  with dates, **348**–349
  in direct quotation, **350**–351
  in elliptical sentence, **350**
  with geographical names, **349**
  with independent clause, **338**–340
  with introductory material, **343**–344
  with nonessential expression, **346**–347
  with numbers, **350**
  with parenthetical expression, **345**
  with quotation marks, **365**
  with salutations and closings, 349–**350**
  in a series, **340**–341
  with titles, **349**
Comma splice, 131
Common noun, 21
Comparative degree, **236**, **238**–239, 244–246, **245**
Comparison
  and absolute modifier, **248**–249
  balanced, **246**

clear, 244, **245**, 292
degrees of, **236**–244, 291–292
double, 242–**243**
irregular, **240**–242
other and *else* in, **247**–248
regular, **238**, **239**
subordination in, 592
Comparison and contrast order, **616**, 617, 619
  in an essay, 689
  transitions of, 587
Comparison of ideas, 576–579
Complaint, letter of, **787**, 790
Complement, 68–75, **69**, 82–84
Complete predicate, 55, **56**
Complete subject, 55, **56**
Complex sentence, **112**–113, 121
Composition
  essay, 679–721
  essay examination, 801–811
  letter, 775–791
  library papers, 722–750
  papers about literature, 751–774
  paragraph, 608–656, 657–678
  précis, 791–800
  sentence length and structure, 536
  word use, 556–584
  writing, 585–607
Compound adjective, 36, 80
Compound adverb, 80
Compound-complex sentence, **112**–113, 126–127
Compound modifier, hyphen with, **385**
Compound noun, 20, **389**
Compound object, **195**
Compound preposition, 43
Compound sentence, **111**–113, 120
Compound subject, **60**, 79, 193
  and verb agreement, **211**–212
Compound verb, 60–**61**, 79–80
Compound word, hyphen with, **384**
Conclusion
  of an essay, **684**
  of a library paper, **731**, 732
Concrete noun, 19
Conjugation, verb, **164**–167, 288
  basic form in, 164–165
  emphatic form in, 167
  infinitive form in, 165
  principal parts of, 164
  progressive form in, 165–166
Conjunction, 43, **46**
  conjunctive adverb, 46, 48–49
  coordinating, 46–47, 140–141, **338**–340, **590**
  correlative, 46, 47, **590**
  as part of speech, 18, 54
  subordinating, 46, 48

Conjunctive adverb, 46, 48–49
  related ideas with, **590**
  and semicolon, **355**–356
Connections
  clear, 585–600
  with coordination, **589**, **590**–591,
    593–597
  with subordination, **589**, **591**–597,
    593
  with transitions, **586**–589
Connotation, 574–**575**
Context, using, **404**–406
·Context clue
  in English classes, 409
  in general reading, 407–409
  in sentence completion test,
    466–**467**
  in textbook reading, 406–407
  types of, 405
Contraction, 392–393
  with dialogue, 394
  with numbers, 393
  with *o, d, l,* 393–394
  with poetry, 393
  with verbs, 393
Contrast, subordination in, 592
Coordinating conjunction, 46–47
  comma with, **338**–340
  related ideas and, **590**
Coordination, 142, **143**
  connections with, **589**, **590**–591,
    593–597
  faulty, 142, 143–146, **144**
Correlative conjunction, 46, 47
  related ideas and, **590**
Critical present, **168**, 169
Cross-reference card, **487**–488

Dangling modifier, **136**–137
Dash, **376**, **377**, **378**
  for change of thought, **376**
  for interrupting ideas, **376**–377
  for nonessential appositive, **377**
  for nonessential modifier, **377**–378
  with parenthetical expression, **378**
  with summary statement, **377**
Dates
  abbreviations of, **320**–321
  punctuation of, **348**–349, **379**
Deadwood, **558**
Declarative sentence, **63**, **65**
  punctuation of, **333**
Definite article, 36
Definition, dictionary, 529–530
Degrees of comparison, **236**–244,
  291–292
Demonstrative adjective, 37
Demonstrative pronoun, **24**
Denotation, 575
Derived word, 531

Descriptive paragraph, **668**–672
  writing, 671–672
Details
  in developing support, **611**, 612,
    631
  in expanding sentences, **537**, 538
Developmental order, **616**–619
  in an essay, 689
Dewey Decimal System, 495–496
Diagraming
  basic parts of a sentence, 78–84
  sentence with phrases or clauses,
    114–127
Dialect, 278, **282**
Dialogue, punctuation in, **367**–368,
    394
Dictionary, 518–531
  abridged, 522
  features of, **523**–531
  general, **519**
  specialized, 506–507
  unabridged, 519–521
Different from, different than, 260
Direct address, 21
Direct object, **69**–70, 82
Direct quotation, 361–**362**
  punctuation of, **350**–351, **362**, **363**,
    364–366, 367
Doesn't, don't, 260
Done, 260
Don't, doesn't, 260
Double comparison, 242–**243**
Double negative, **250**–251
Drafting
  essay, **703**–704
  essay examination, **808**
  library paper, **744**–745
  literary review, **770**–771
  paragraph, **637**–639
  précis, **797**–798
  sentence, 536–555
Due to, 260
Due to the fact that, 261

Each other, one another, 261
Effect, affect, 255
ei and *ie* rule, **426**
Ellipsis marks, omission indicated
  by, **369**
Elliptical clause, pronoun in,
  202–204
Elliptical sentence, 58, **350**
Emigrate, immigrate, 261
Emphasis
  inverted sentence for, **65**–66
  superlative degree for, 245
  transitions of, 587
Emphatic form of a verb, 153
  conjugation of, 167

Encyclopaedia Britannica, 503
Encyclopedia, 502–503
  specialized, 507
Encyclopedia Americana, 502
End mark, 333–337
English, 278–286
  nonstandard, 278, 282–284
  standard, 278, 279–282
Enthused, enthusiastic, 261
Entry words, kinds of, 524
Envelope, **778**–779, **787**
-er, in comparative degree, **238**–239
Essay, 679–721
  coherence, 687, **689**–693
  drafting, 703–704
  features of, 679–**681**, 682–**683**,
    684–685
  kinds of, 708–721
  prewriting, 703–704
  revision, 704–707
  unity, 687–**688**, 689, 691–693
Essay and General Literature Index,
    510–511
Essay examination, 801–811
  answering, 808–810
  budgeting time for, 801, **802**–803
  drafting, **808**
  identifying the question, **803**–804
  outlining the answer, **806**–807
  prewriting, 801–807
  revising, 808–810
  thesis statement for, **805**–806
  writing answers to, 801–811
Essential expression
  adjective clause, **103**
  participial phrase, 93–94
-est, in superlative degree, **238**–239
Etc., 261
Etymology, 528–529
Euphemism, 570–**571**
Every one, everyone, any one, anyone,
    257
Everywhere, anyway, anywhere,
    nowhere, somewhere, 257
Exam, midterm and final, 454–**455**,
    456
Examination, essay, 801–811.
  See also Test
Except, accept, 254
Exclamation mark
  as end mark, **335**
  with quotation, **366**
Exclamatory sentence, **63**–64, **67**
  punctuation of, **335**
Exercises, review
  grammar, 147–150
  mechanics, 395–398
  usage, 286–292
Expletive, 65, 81
Expository essay, 708, **709**–710,
    711–713

Expository paragraph, 657, **658**–660,
    661
  writing, **660**

Farther, further, 262
Faulty coordination, 142, 143–146
  correcting, **144**–145
Faulty parallelism, 137, **139**–142
  in comparisons, 141
  correcting, 140–141
  in series, 139–141
Fewer, less, 262
Fiction, finding, **494**
Field label in a dictionary, 530
First person point of view, 674
Flash cards, 402
Foreign words
  punctuation of, **372**
Formal English, 278, 279–**280**
Former, latter, 262
Fraction, hyphen with, **383**
Fragment, **57**–58, 128–**131**
  clause, 129–130
  phrase, 130
  series, 130
Friendly letter, **779**
Further, farther, 262
Fused sentence, 131
Future perfect progressive, 166,
    172–173
Future perfect tense, 153, 165, **172**
Future progressive, 166, **172**
Future tense, 153, 164, **172**

Gender and pronoun agreement,
    220–221, **222**–223
Generic masculine pronoun, **223**
Gerund, **96**–98, 118
Gerund phrase, **97**–98, 118
Get, got, gotten, 262
Good, lovely, nice, 262
Good, well, 241
Got, gotten, get, 262
Grammar
  parts of speech, analyzing, **52**–54
  parts of speech, basic, 18–**51**
  phrases and clauses, 85–127
  review exercises, 147–150
  sentence faults, 128–146
  sentence parts and patterns, 55–84

Hardly, 252
Hard-to-find subject, 64–68, **65**, **66**,
    67, 80–82
Heading, **776**, **783**–784
Healthful, healthy, 262–263
Hedging word, **558**
Helping (auxiliary) verb, **33**–34,
    184–185

Historical present, use of, **168**, 169
Hyphen, 383, 387
    for clarity, **385**–386
    for compound words, **384**–**385**
    for dividing words, **386**–**387**
    for numbers, **383**–384
    for word parts, **384**
Hyphenated proper adjective, 306

Idiom, 530–531
ie and *ei* rule, **426**
Immigrate, emigrate, 261
Imperative mood, 182
Imperative sentence, **63**, **67**, 80
    punctuation of, **333**, **335**
In, into, 263
Indefinite adjective, 37–38
Indefinite article, 36
Indefinite pronoun, **26**
    agreement, **216**–217, 224, **225**
    possessive of, **391**
Indented style, **777**
Independent clause, **101**
    pronoun in, 24–25
    punctuation of, **338**–340, **354**–**355**,
        357–358
Indicative mood, 182–183
Indirect object, **70**–72, 82–83
Indirect quotation, **362**
Individual ownership, **390**
Infinitive, **98**–101, 119
    as modifier, 100
    as noun, 99–100
    forms of, 99, 165
    time sequence with, **179**–181
Infinitive phrase, **100**–101, 119
Inflected forms in a dictionary,
        527–528
Informal English, 278, **280**–281
Inside address, **783**, 784
Intensive pronoun, **23**–24
Interjection, 43, 50–**51**
    first word of an, **296**
    as part of speech, 18, 54
    punctuation of, **335**
Interrogative adjective, 37
Interrogative pronoun, **25**
Interrogative sentence, **63**, **66**, 81
    punctuation for, **334**–335
Into, in, 263
Intransitive verb, **32**
Introduction of a library paper,
        731–732
Inverted sentence, **65**–66
    agreement, **214**
Invitation, **777**, **779**, 780
Irregardless, 263
Irregular verb, **156**–160
Its, it's, 263

Jargon, **569**

Kind of, sort of, 263

Language
    descriptive, **668**, **671**
    graphic, **673**
    levels of, 278–286
    nonstandard, 278, 282–284
    overly emotional, **572**
    self-important, **571**–572
    standard, 278, 279–282
Latter, former, 262
Lay, lie, 264
Learn, teach, 263
Leave, let, 263–264
Less, fewer, 262
Let, leave, 263–264
Letter, written
    business, 783–791
    capitalization in, **311**–313
    personal, 775–783
    punctuation in, 349–**350**
Letter of alphabet, **372**, **380**, **394**
Library, using the, 483–500
Library and reference skills, 483–534
Library of Congress System, **495**, 497
Library paper, 722–750
    checking, **745**
    drafting, **744**–745
    features of, 722, **723**–727, **728**–730,
        731–735
    prewriting, **736**–738, **739**, **740**–742,
        743
    revision of, 744, **745**
    structure of, **731**–735
Lie, lay, 264
Like, as, as if, 264
Linking verb, 29, **30**–31
    agreement, **215**
Listening skills, 436, **438**–440
Literary reference books, 509–511
Literary review, 751–774, **755**
    drafting, **770**–771
    features of, **752**–758
    organizing, **769**–770
    prewriting for, 762, **763**, **764**–766,
        767–**769**, 770
    revision of, **771**–774
    structure of, **758**–762
Literature, papers about, 751–774
Logic, errors in, **600**, **601**, **602**,
        603–604
Logical order
    in an essay, **689**–690
    in ideas, **597**–598
    in paragraph, **616**–621, **635**–636
    revision for, **650**
Loose, lose, 264

Loose sentence, **547**
Lose, loose, 264
Lovely, good, nice, 262

Magazines and journals, **513**–514
Main entry in a dictionary, **523**–524
May, can, 259
May be, maybe, 261 265
Measurements, **325**–326
  agreement, **217**–218
Mechanics
  capitalization and abbreviation,
    294–332
  punctuation, 333–395
  review exercises, 395–398
Metaphor, **577**
Misplaced modifier, **134**–135
"Missing book" problem, **499**–500
Modified block style, **785**
Modified outline, **443, 806**–807
Modifier
  absolute, **248**
  dangling, **136**–137
  that expresses time, **175**
  misplaced, **134**–135
Mood, verb, 182–185, 288
  imperative, 182
  indicative, 182
  subjunctive, 182, **183**–185
More, in comparative degree,
  238–239
Most, in superlative degree, **238**–239

Names
  abbreviations for, **315, 328, 329**
  capitalization of, **298**
Narrative paragraph, 668, **673**–676
  suggestions for, **676**
Narrator or point of view, 673
Negative prefixes, 253
Negative words, 250–252
Newspapers, 514–515
New York Times Index, 515
Nice, good, lovely, 262
Nominative absolute, **94**–95
Nominative case, **190**, 191–**193**
Nonessential expression
  adjective clause, **103**
  appositive, **377**
  modifier, **378**
  participial phrase, 93–94
  punctuation of, **346**–347, **377, 378**
Nonfiction, finding, 494, **495**–498
Nonrestrictive expression. *See*
  Nonessential expression
Nonstandard English, 278, 282–284
Nor, 211, 212, **221, 222**
Notebook, spelling, **420**
Note-taking

  in columns, **447**–448
  for the library paper, **740**–741
  skills, 442–443
Noun, **18**–21
  abstract, 19
  as adjective, 36–37
  as adverb, 40–41
  collective, 20, **215**
  common, 21
  compound, 20–21, **389**
  concrete, 19
  of direct address, 21
  number, singular and plural,
    206–207
  as part of speech, 18, 53
  plural, 20, **427**–428
  plural-looking, subject and verb
    agreement in, **215**–216
  possessive, **388, 389**
  proper, 21
  singular, 20
Noun clause, **108**–109, 124–126
  introductory words in, 109
*Nowhere, somewhere, anywhere,
    anyway, everywhere,* 257
Number
  of noun, 206–207
  and pronoun agreement, 220, **221**
  of pronoun, 207
  and subject agreement, **207**–220
  of verb, 206–207
Numbers
  apostrophes with plurals, **394**
  commas with, **350**
  contractions with, 393
  hyphens with, **383**
  in a series in parentheses, **380**
  underlining, **372**
  writing, **326**

Object
  direct, **69**–70, 82
  indirect, **70**–72, 82–83
Objective case, **190,** 191–192,
    195–197
Objective complement, **72**–73, 83
Objective pronoun, **195**–196
Object of the preposition, 44
Of, 265
OK, O.K., okay, 265
One another, each other, 261
Opinion, letter of, 787, 790
Or, **211, 212, 221, 222**
Order
  in an essay, **689**–690
  of ideas, **597**–598
  in the literary review, **769**–770
  in a paragraph, **616**–621, 635–636,
    650
  with useful transitions, **618**–619

Order letter, **787**, 788
Order of importance, **616**, 618
  in an essay, 689
Ought, 265
Outlining, 443, **444**–446
  essay, **702**
  essay examination, **806**–807
  library paper, **742**–743
  modified, **443**, **806**–807
  paragraph, 636
  periods in, **336**
Outside of, 265
Overly technical language, 283–**284**
Oxford English Dictionary, 521

Pamphlets, 516
Paragraph
  coherence, **616**–623, **649**, **650**, **651**,
    652–653
  drafting, **637**–639
  effective, 608–656
  features of, 608–626
  kinds of, **657**–678
  order, **616**–621
  organization, **635**–636
  planning and writing, 626–639
  prewriting, 626–637
  revising, 639–656
  special kinds of, **623**–625
  supporting information in, **611**–614
  topic, choosing a, **626**
  topic sentence for, 608, **609**–611
  unity, **614**–616, **647**, **648**–649
Parallelism, **138**–139, **550**–551
  coherence with, **620**–621
  in comparisons, 141
  faulty, 137–138, **139**
  revision for, **652**–653
Parentheses, 376, **379**, **380**, **381**
  for asides, **379**
  for dates, **379**
  for letters, **380**
  for numbers, **380**
  with other punctuation, **380**–381
  in showing uncertainty, **337**
Parenthetical expression
  case with, 200–201
  punctuation for, **345**, **378**
Participial phrase, **93**–94
Participle, **92**–93, 117
  time sequence with, **179**–181
Parts of sentence, 55–57, 78–84
Parts of speech, 18–51, 147
  identifying, **52**–54
  labels in a dictionary, 527–528
Passive voice, **186**–189, **564**–565
Past emphatic, **170**–171
Past participle, 92, 154
Past perfect progressive, 166,
  170–171

Past perfect tense, 153, 165, **170**, 171
Past progressive, 165–166, **170**, 171
Past tense, 153, 154, 164, **170**
Pattern, sentence, **75**–77, 147, **550**
Perfect participle, 92
Period
  in abbreviations, **336**
  as end mark, **333**–334
  in outline, **336**
  with quotation marks, **365**
Periodicals, **513**–516
Periodic sentence, **548**
Personal letter, 775–783
  capitalization in, **311**–313
  kinds of, **779**
  structure of, **776**–777
Personal pronoun, **22**–23
  agreement, **220**
  and antecedent agreement,
    221–222, **231**–232, **233**–234
  case of, 191–**193**
  in elliptical clause, **202**–204
  and gender, 221, **222**–223
  and generic masculine pronoun,
    223
  and indefinite pronoun agreement,
    224, **225**
  and number, 205, **206**–207
  and person, **220**, **222**–223
  possessive of, **391**–392
Persuasive essay, **714**–716, 717–721
Persuasive paragraph, 657, **662**–666,
  664
  writing, **664**
Phonetic alphabet, 525
Phrase, **85**–101, 147–148
  agreement, **208**
  appositive, **85**–91
  fragment, **128**, 129–130
  prepositional, 44, **85**–91
  verbal, 91–**92**
Plagiarism, 726, **727**–728
Plenty, 265
Plural
  compound or hyphenated, 428
  forming with apostrophes, **394**–395
  not ending in -*s*, 266
  noun, 20, **427**–428
  number, **206**
  spelling changes to form, **427**–428
  verb form, 164–167
Poetry, punctuation in, **296**, 393
Point of view or narrator, 673
Positive degree, **236**
Possessive adjective, 39
Possessive case, **190**, 191–192, 196
Possessive noun, **388**, 389
Precede, proceed, 266
Précis, 791–800
  drafting of, **797**–798
  features of, **792**–796

prewriting, **796**–797
Predicate
    complete, **56**–57
    simple, **58**–59
    See also Verb
Predicate adjective, **74**–75
Predicate nominative, 73–75, **74**, 193
Preferred spelling, 524
Prefixes, 411–414
    adding, **428**–429
    hyphen with, **384**
    negative, 253
    with proper adjective, **306**
Preposition, **43**–44
    or adverb, 45
    object of, 44
    as part of speech, 18, 53
Prepositional phrase, 44, 85–91,
    114–116
Present, 153, 154, 164, **168**–169
Present emphatic, **168**, 169
Present participle, 92, 154
Present perfect progressive, 166, **170**,
    171
Present perfect tense, 153, 165, **170**,
    171
Present progressive, 165, **168**, 170
Prewriting
    essay, 693, **694**, **695**–697, **698**–**700**,
        701–702
    essay examination, 801, **802**–**803**,
        804, **805**–**806**, 807
    library paper, **736**–738, **739**,
        740–**742**, 743
    literary review, 762, **763**, **764**–**766**,
        767–**769**, 770
    paragraph, 626–637
    précis, **796**–797
Principal, principle, 266
Principal parts of a verb, 154
Principle, principal, 266
Proceed, 266
Professional models
    for logical reasoning, **605**–606
    for sentence length and structure,
        553–554
    for writing style, 581, **582**–583
Progressive form of a verb, 153,
    165–166
Pronoun, **22**–28
    as adjective, 36, 37–38
    agreement, **228**–231
    and antecedent agreement,
        220–235
    case, **190**–204
    demonstrative, **24**
    in elliptical clause, 202–204
    gender, 220–223
    generic masculine, 223
    indefinite, **26**, 29–30, 46, **216**, 254,
        262, **416**

    intensive, **23**
    interrogative, **25**
    number, singular and plural,
        206–207
    as part of speech, 18, 53
    personal, **22**–23, 191–**193**, **220**, 224,
        225, **231**–232, **233**–234
    person of, 22–23, 220, 222–223
    possessives of, **391**–392
    problems with, 198–204
    reference, **228**, **229**–230, **231**–232,
        233–234, 290
    reflexive, **23**–24, **227**
    relative, **24**–25, 104, 121, 208–**209**
    usage, 190–204
Pronunciation, 525
Pronunciation key, 525–527
Pronunciation symbol, 526
Proper adjective, 36, **305**, **306**–307
Proper noun, 21, **297**–304
Punctuation
    apostrophe, **388**–395
    brackets, 376, 381–**382**
    colon, **357**–361
    comma, 340–351, 365
    dash, **376**–378
    ellipsis, **369**–370
    end mark, 333–337
    hyphen, **383**–387
    parentheses, 376, 379–381
    quotation marks, 361–**362**,
        363–370, 373
    semicolon, 354–357
    underlining, 361, 371–373

Question
    fragment, **296**
    punctuation of, **334**–335
Question mark
    as end mark, **334**–335
    with quotation marks, **366**
    to show uncertainty, **337**
Questions
    to direct research, **739**
    to find support, 631–632
    leading to main ideas, 628
    reading comprehension, **471**–473,
        474, **475**, **476**, 478–480
Quizzes, study method for, **453**
Quotation
    brackets within, **382**
    capitalization for, **295**
    colon to introduce, **358**
    direct, **362**
    fragment, **364**
    indirect, **362**
    omission indicated by ellipsis,
        369–370
    punctuation for, **361**–370, 368
    within a quotation, **370**

Quotation marks, 361–370
  with dialogue, **367**–368
  with direct quotations, **362**
  with long quotations, 367, **368**
  with other punctuation, 363–364,
    365, **366**–367
  with titles, **373**

Raise, rise, 266
*Readers' Guide to Periodical
  Literature,* 514
Reading comprehension test,
  471–480
Real, 266–267
Redundancy, **559**–560
Reference materials, 500–513
  choosing, **516**–517
Reflexive pronoun, **23**–24, **227**
Regret, letter of, **779**, 781
Regular verb, **156**
Relative adverb, 104–105, 122
Relative pronoun, **24**–25, 104, 121
  and antecedent agreement, **227**
  in subject and verb agreement,
    208–**209**
Repetition
  coherence with, **619**–620
  revision with, **652**–653
Request letter, **787**, 788
Research, planning, **484**–485
  for the library paper, **739**
Restrictive expression. *See* Essential
  expression
Review exercises
  grammar, 147–150
  mechanics, 395–398
  usage, 286–292
Revising
  essay, **704**, **705**–707
  essay examination, **808**–810
  library paper, **745**, **746**–750
  literary review, **771**–774
  paragraph, 639–656, **640**
  for paragraph coherence, **649**, **650**,
    651, **652**–653
  for paragraph unity, **647**, **648**–649
  précis, **798**–799
  sentence, 556–583
  for style, 654–655
  supporting information, **643**–645,
    646
Rise, raise, 266
Roots, 414–416
R.S.V.P., 777
Run-on entries, 531
Run-on sentence, **131**–134
  correcting, 132

Salutation, 349–**350**, **776**, **783**, 784
Says, 267

Scarcely, 252
Semiblock style, **777**, **785**, 786
Semicolon, 354–357
  to avoid confusion, **356**
  with independent clause, **354**–355,
    356
  with quotation marks, **366**
Sensory impressions, 579–580
Sentence
  basic parts of, 55–57, **56**
  capitalization of, **295**
  drafting, 536–555
  faults, 128–150
  kinds of, 62–64
  negative, 250–254
  openers, **542**, 543–544
  punctuation of, **333**, **338**–340
  revising, 556–583
  simplifying, **539**–540
Sentence combining, **537**–539
  with adjective and adverb, 538
  with appositive phrase, 538
  with clause, 538
  with prepositional phrase, 538
  using coordination, **589**, **590**–591,
    593–597
  using subordination, **589**, **591**–597,
    593
  with verbal phrase, 538
Sentence faults, 128–146
Sentence functions, 62–64
Sentence models, **553**–554
Sentence pattern, **75**–77, 147, **550**
  without complement, 76
  with linking verb, 76–77
  with transitive verb, 76
Sentence structure
  classifying, 111–114
  differences in, **552**
  improving, 536, **537**, **542**–543, **544**
  new ideas for, **547**, **548**, **549**
  similarities of, **550**–551
Series
  fragment, **128**, 130
  punctuation in, **340**–341, **356**
Set, sit, 267
Shall, will, 267
Signature, **776**, 777, **783**, 784–785
Simile, **576**–577
Simple predicate, **58**, 59
  See also Verb
Simple sentence, **111** 113
Simple subject, 58
Singular noun, 20
Singular number, **206**
Singular verb form, 164–167
Sit, set, 267
Slang, 278, **283**, 569
Slow, slowly, 267
So, 267
Social note, **779**, 782

Social studies reference books, 511
Somewhere, anyway, anywhere, everywhere, nowhere, 257
Sort of, kind of, 263
Spatial order, **616**, 617, 618
  in an essay, 689
  transitions of, 587
Speaking skills, 436, **440**–441
Spelling
  demons, 422–424
  forming plurals, **427**–428
  improvement, 420–434
  problem areas of, **424**–426
  techniques for improving, 420–426
Spelling rules, 426–434
Spelling tests, standardized, 459
Standard English, 278, 279–282
Study skills
  basic, 436–451
  checklist for, **437**
  evaluating, 436, **437**–438
  library, 483–500
  reference skills, 500–534
  test-taking, 452–482
Style
  direct, **557**–563
  letter, **777**, **785**–786
  revising for, **654**–655
Subject and verb, 55
  and agreement, **207**, **208**, **209**–**211**, **212**
Subjects, 55–57
  complete, **56**–57
  compound, **60**, 79, 193, 211
  confusing, 214–218
  in declarative sentence, **65**
  for emphasis, **65**–66
  in exclamatory sentence, **67**
  hard-to-find, 64–68, **65**, 80–82
  identifying, 59–60
  in imperative sentence, 66–67
  in interrogative sentence, **66**
  in sentences beginning with *here*, 65
  in sentences beginning with *there*, 65
  simple, **58**–59, 78
  understood, 67
Subjunctive mood, 182, **183**–185
  auxiliary verb for, **184**–185
  with a *that* clause, 183–184
  verb tense in, 175–179
Subordinate clause, **102**
  case in, 200–201
  pronoun in, 25
Subordinating conjunction, 46, 48
Subordination, connections through, **589**, **591**–597, **593**
Suffixes, 416–418
  adding, **429**–431
  confusing, **431**–434

Summary, writing a, **448**–449
Superlative degree, **236**, **238**–**239**, 244–246, **245**
Support
  developing, **698**–699
  evaluating, **632**, **633**–634
  kinds of, **611**–612, **631**
  questions to find, 631–632
Supporting information
  developing, 630, **631**, **632**, **633**–634
  in a literary review, **756**–757, **766**–768
  in a paragraph, **611**–614
  revising, **643**–**645**, 646
Syllabification, 525
Symbol, **580**–581
Synonym, 531, 574–**575**
  coherence using, **619**–620
  revising with, **652**–653
  test, **464**–465
Synonymies, 531

Take, bring, 259
Teach, learn, 263
Tense, verb, **152**–182, 288
  expressing time through, 168–182
  sequence, 175, 176–181, 288
Test
  analogy, **468**–471
  antonym, **465**–466
  chapter and unit, 453, **454**
  classroom, 452–456
  reading comprehension, 471–480
  sentence completion, 466–467
  standardized, 456–463, **457**, **458**
  synonym, **464**–465
  See also Essay examination
Test-taking skills, 452–482
Than, then, 268
That, which, who, 268
That there, this here, them there, 268
Their, there, they're, 268
Them, them there, these here, this here, that there, 268
Then, than, 268
There, their, they're, 268
These here, this here, that there, them, them there, 268
Thesis statement
  choosing a, **695**, 696–697
  for an essay, **681**–683
  for a library paper, **742**
They're, their, there, 268
Third person point of view
  generally omniscient narrator, 674
  objective narrator, 674
  partially omniscient narrator, 674
This here, that there, them, them there, these here, 268

Time and tense
future, **172**–173
with modifiers, **175**
past, **170**–172
present, 168–170
sequence of, 175, **176**–181
Time references
abbreviations of, **319**, **320**, 321
apostrophe with, **389**
Time relationships
subordination in, 592
transitions of, 587
Title
abbreviations of, **315**, **316**, **317**–318
agreement, **217**
of books, **309**, **371**
capitalization of, **307**–311
of essay, **681**
of library paper, **731**
after a name, **349**
punctuation of, **273**, **371**–373
unmarked, **373**
Title card, **486**
Title page of a library paper, 732
To, too, two, 268–269
Tone of writing, **476**–477
appropriate, 568–574
for paragraphs, **658**, **662**
Too, to, two, 268–269
Topic, choosing a
for an essay, 695–696
for a library paper, **736**
for a literary review, **752**–755
for a paragraph, 628
Topic sentence
in a paragraph, 608, **609**–611
prewriting, **626**
revising, **640**, **641**–643
Transitions, 48, **586**–589, **618**–619
in a paragraph, **650**–**651**, 652
and the semicolon, **355**–356
Transitive verb, **32**
Two, to, too, 268–269

Underlining, 361, **371**, **372**, **373**
foreign words, **372**
letters, **372**
names, **372**
numbers, **372**
for stress, **373**
titles of works, **371**
words, **372**
Understatement, 253
Unique, 269
Unity
in an essay, 687, **688**–689, **700**
evaluating, 632
paragraph, 614–616
revising for, **647**, **648**–649

Usage
adjective and adverb, 236–249
agreement, 205–235
levels of language, 278–286
problems, 250–277, 292
pronoun, 190–204
review exercises in, 286–292
verb, 152–189
Usage label in a dictionary, 530

Variant spelling, 524–525
Verb, **29**–34, 59, 78
action, **29**–30, **564**
as adjective, 36, 38
compound, **61**
conjugating, **164**–167
helping, **33**–34
identifying, 59–60
intransitive, **32**–33
linking, **30**–31
mood, 182–185
number, singular and plural,
206–207
as part of speech, 18, 53
phrase, **33**–34
as predicate, 59
principal parts of, **154**–156
and subject, 55–62
and subject agreement, **207**, **208**,
209–**211**, **212**
tense, **152**–182, 287
transitive, **32**–33
usage, 152–189
voice, 185, **186**–187
weak, 563–**564**
Verbal phrase, 91, **92**, 116–120
Vertical file, 516
Vocabulary building, 400–419
techniques for, 400, **401**–404
Vocabulary notebook, **401**
Vocabulary questions, 463–471
Voice, verb, 185, **186**–189, 288,
564–565

Ways, 269
Well, good, 241–242
When, where, 269
Which, who, that, 268
Who, cases of, **198**–201, 268
Whoever, cases of, **198**–201
Whose, 199–201
Whosever, 199–201
Will, shall, 267
Win, beat, 258
-wise, 269
Word choices, 574–584
Word meanings, 574–576

Words
bland, general, **565**–566
coordinating, 390
foreign, **569**–570
hedging, **558**
hyphens in, **386**, **387**
negative, 251–252
overused, 566–567
problem, **120**
subordinating, 592
underlining, **372**, **373**
use of, 556–584
vivid, **563**

Word structure, 404, **411**–419
Word study, three-column format, **401**
Wordy structure, reducing, **560**–561
Writing, clear thinking in, 585–607
Writing, types of, **476**–477
Written expression test, 461

You, understood as subject, **67**

Acknowledgments

The authors and editors have made every effort to trace the ownership of all copyrighted selections found in this book and to make full acknowledgment of their use. The dictionary of record for this book is *Webster's New World Dictionary*, Second College Edition, copyright © 1980 by Simon & Schuster, Inc. The basis for the selection of vocabulary words appropriate for this grade level is *The Living Word Vocabulary: The Words We Know* by Edgar Dale and Joseph O'Rourke, copyright © 1976.

Citations follow, arranged by unit and page for easy reference.

Usage: Pages 280 Barbara W. Tuchman, *The Proud Tower* (New York: The Macmillan Company, Copyright © 1962, 1963, 1965, 1966). **281** Russell Baker, "Just Plain Nice," *The New York Times* (May 4, 1980), Copyright © 1980 by The New York Times Company. Reprinted by permission. **284** Renee Weisberg, "A Comparison of Good and Poor Readers' Ability to Comprehend Explicit and Implicit Information in Short Stories Based on Two Modes of Presentation," *Research in the Teaching of English*, Vol. 13, No. 4 (December 1979). The National Council of Teachers of English.

Study Skills: Pages 471–473 *Read*, adapted from "The Oak Island Mystery" (January 30, 1980). Special permission granted by *Read* Magazine published by Xerox Education Publications © 1980 Xerox Corp. **478–480** *Read*, "The Pirate Who Never Was?" (January 30, 1980). Special permission granted by *Read* Magazine, published by Xerox Education Publications © 1980 Xerox Corp. **502** *Encyclopedia Americana*, Vol. 30. Reprinted with permission of *The Encyclopedia Americana*, copyright 1980, The Americana Corporation. **503** Reprinted with permission from *Encyclopaedia Britannica*, 15th edition, © 1976 by Encyclopaedia Britannica, Inc. **510–511** *Essay and General Literature Index* Copyright © 1978, 1979 by the H.W. Wilson Company. Material reproduced by permission of the publisher. **514** *Readers' Guide to Periodical Literature* Copyright © 1980 by the H.W. Wilson Company. Material reproduced by permission of the publisher. **515** From *The New York Times Index* © 1979 by The New York Times Company. Reprinted by permission. **520** By permission. From *Webster's Third New International Dictionary* © 1976 by G. & C. Merriam Co., Publishers of the Merriam-Webster Dictionaries. **521** *Oxford English Dictionary* (Oxford, England: Oxford University Press). **522, 528** (first item), **531** (second item) By permission. From *Webster's New Collegiate Dictionary* © 1980 by G. & C. Merriam Co., Publishers of the Merriam-Webster Dictionaries. **524, 525, 527, 529, 530, 531** (first, third items) With permission. From *Webster's New World Dictionary*, Second College Edition. Copyright © 1980 by Simon & Schuster. **528** (second item) From THORNDIKE-BARNHART ADVANCED DICTIONARY by E. L. Thorndike and Clarence L. Barnhart. Copyright © 1973 by Scott, Foresman, and Company. Reprinted by permission. **528** (third, fifth items) With permission. From *Webster's New World Dictionary*, Students Edition. Copyright © 1981 by Simon & Schuster. **528** (fourth item) From the *Macmillan School Dictionary*. Copyright © 1981 Macmillan Publishing Co., Inc.

Composition: Pages 554 John Russel, "The Price of the Head," from *Stories They Wouldn't Let Me Do on TV*, by Alfred Hitchcock (New York: Simon & Schuster, 1957). **582, 583** Marjorie K. Rawlings, *The Yearling*. Copyright 1938 by Marjorie Kinnan Rawlings. Copyright renewed. Reprinted with the permission of Charles Scribner's Sons. **605–606** From BOOKS THAT CHANGED THE WORLD, by Robert B. Downs. Copyright © 1956 by Robert B. Downs. Reprinted by arrangement with The New American Library, New York, New York. **606** Vance Packard, *The Waste Makers* (New York: David McKay Company, 1960). **609, 613** From pp. 92–93 in GLASS AND MAN by Anne Huether (J.B. Lippincott). Copyright © 1963 by Anne Heuther. Reprinted by permission of Harper & Row, Publishers, Inc. **610** Ruth M. Tabrah, *Hawaii Nei* (Chicago, Illinois: Follett Publishing Company, 1967). **610** Athelstan Spilhaus, "A Collector Finds Toys Are Not Meant Only for Children," *Smithsonian* (December 1980), p. 158. **610** *Our Human Body: Its Wonders and Its Care*, The Reader's Digest Association, 1962, pp. 32–33. **610–611** Excerpt from page 87 in CHEAPER BY THE DOZEN, by Frank B. Gilbreth, Jr. and Ernestine Gilbreth Carey. (Thomas Y. Crowell) Copyright 1948 by Frank B. Gilbreth, Jr. and Ernestine Gilbreth Carey. Reprinted by permission of Harper & Row, Publishers, Inc. **611** Adapted from Bernard A. Weisberger, *The Impact of Our Past* (New York: American Heritage Publishing Co., 1972). **612–613** Elizabeth Janeway, *The Early Days of Automobiles* (New York: Random House, 1956). **613** James Balog, "Second-Guessing Mother Nature in the High Snows," *Smithson-*

ian (December 1980), p. 63. **614** Fred Bruemmer, "Never Trust Nanook," Copyright 1979 by the National Wildlife Federation. Reprinted from the July–August issue of INTERNATIONAL WILDLIFE Magazine. **617** Peter Gwynne, "Here Comes the Wave!" Copyright 1978 by the National Wildlife Federation. Reprinted from the September–October issue of INTERNATIONAL WILDLIFE Magazine. **618** Janet L. Hopson, "A Queer Mammal of Ducklike Bill and Reptilian Walk," *Smithsonian* (January 1981), p. 63. **620** Constance Brown, "Some Like It Hot," Copyright 1978 by the National Wildlife Federation. Reprinted from the September–October issue of INTERNATIONAL WILDLIFE Magazine. **620–621** James Packer, "Lively Last Days and Nights," With permission from *Natural History*, April 1979. Copyright the American Museum of Natural History, 1979. **624** John T Putman, "Denver, Colorado's Rocky Mountain High." *National Geographic* (March 1979), pp. 383–384. **624** Patricia Curtis, "Wide, Wild World of Hope Ryden, Bedroll Naturalist," *Smithsonian* (November 1980), p. 122. **659–660** Constance Rourke, adapted from *American Humor*. By permission of Harcourt Brace Jovanovich, New York. **660** *Consumer Reports*, "Telephone Answering Machines" Copyright 1979 by Consumers Union of United States, Inc., Mount Vernon, N.Y. 10550. Excerpted by permission from CONSUMER REPORTS, June 1979. **661** George Sternlieb and James W. Hughes, "The Changing Demography of the Central City," *Scientific American* (August 1980), p. 48. By permission, W.H. Freeman and Company for Scientific American, Inc. **664** Abridged from "Here Is New York" in ESSAYS OF E.B. WHITE by E.B. White. Copyright 1949 by E.B. White. Reprinted by permission of Harper & Row, Publishers, Inc. **667** From "Blessed Profanity" by Pauline Kael. Copyright © 1970 by Pauline Kael. First appeared in *The New Yorker*, January 24, 1970. By permission of Little, Brown and Company in association with the Atlantic Monthly Press. **671** Andrea O. Dean, "Luis Barragan, Austere Architect of Silent Spaces," *Smithsonian* (November 1980), p. 160. **672** George Plimpton. Abridged from p. 62 in PAPER LION by George Plimpton. Copyright © 1964, 1965, 1966 by George Plimpton. Reprinted by permission of Harper & Row Publishers, Inc. **672** Elizabeth Bowen, "The Happy Autumn Fields," *Reading Modern Fiction*, Winifred Lynsky, ed. (New York: Charles Scribner's Sons, 1962), p. 31. **675** Ernest Hemingway, *A Farewell to Arms* (New York: Charles Scribner's Sons, 1929). **675–676** Specified excerpt from p. 54 in THE HABIT OF LOVING by Doris Lessing (Thomas Y. Crowell) Copyright © 1957 by Doris Lessing. Reprinted by permission of Harper & Row, Publishers, Inc. **677** Joyce Carol Oates. Reprinted from MARRIAGES AND INFIDELITIES by Joyce Carol Oates by permission of the publisher, Vanguard Press, Inc. Copyright © 1968, 1969, 1970, 1971, 1972 by Joyce Carol Oates. **677** John Updike, *Pigeon Feathers and Other Stories* (Crest Books, 1962) Reprinted by permission of Alfred A. Knopf, Inc. New York. **727** Excerpt from THE BERMUDA TRIANGLE by Charles Berlitz. Copyright © 1974 by Charles Berlitz. Reprinted by permission of Doubleday & Company, Inc. **730–731** Frank Buxton and Bill Owen, *The Big Broadcast* (New York: Viking Press, 1972). **760** "A Narrow Fellow in the Grass" by Emily Dickinson. Reprinted by permission of the publishers and the Trustees of Amherst College from THE POEMS OF EMILY DICKINSON, edited by Thomas H. Johnson, Cambridge, Mass.: The Belknap Press of Harvard University Press, Copyright 1951, © 1955, 1979 by the President and Fellows of Harvard College. **792–793** "Wedding Whirs," *Time* Magazine (May 28, 1979) Reprinted by permission from TIME, the Weekly Newsmagazine; Copyright Time, Inc. 1979. **795** "Newbury Street" by Karen MacNeil. Reprinted by permission of *Travel and Leisure*, March 1980, Vol. II, No. 3, p. E30/6. **799–800** John G. Mitchell, "Saved Just in Time, the Buffalo Graze Again on Our Plains," *Smithsonian* (May 1981), pp. 72–73.